ONE NATION

UNINSURED

Why the U.S. Has
No National Health Insurance

JILL QUADAGNO

OXFORD
UNIVERSITY PRESS

OXFORD
UNIVERSITY PRESS

Oxford University Press, Inc., publishes works that
further Oxford University's objective of excellence
in research, scholarship, and education.

Oxford   New York
Auckland   Cape Town   Dar es Salaam   Hong Kong   Karachi
Kuala Lumpur   Madrid   Melbourne   Mexico City   Nairobi
New Delhi   Shanghai   Taipei   Toronto

With offices in
Argentina   Austria   Brazil   Chile   Czech Republic   France   Greece
Guatemala   Hungary   Italy   Japan   Poland   Portugal   Singapore
South Korea   Switzerland   Thailand   Turkey   Ukraine   Vietnam

Copyright ©2005 by Oxford University Press

First published by Oxford University Press, Inc., 2005
198 Madison Avenue, New York, NY 10016
www.oup.com

First issued as an Oxford University Press paperback, 2006
ISBN-13: 978-0-19-531203-4
ISBN-10: 0-19-531203-1

Oxford is a registered trademark of Oxford University Press

The Library of Congress has cataloged the hardcover edition as follows:
Quadagno, Jill S.
One nation, uninsured : why the U.S. has no national health insurance /
by Jill Quadagno.
p. ; cm.
Includes bibliographical references.
ISBN-13: 978-0-19-516039-0   ISBN-10: 0-19-516039-8
1. National health insurance—United States—History—20th century.
2. Medically uninsured persons—United States—History—20th century.
3. Insurance, health—Government policy—United States—History—20th century.
4. Right to health care—United States—History—20th century.
5. Health services accessibility—United States—History—20th century.
6. Health care reform—United States—History—20th century.
7. Medical policy—United States—History—20th century.
[DNLM: 1. National Health Insurance, United States
2. Universal Coverage
3. Health Policy
4. Medically Uninsured
5. Politics
6. United States
W 275 AA1 Q14 2005]
I. Title
RA412.2.Q33 2005   362.1'0425—dc22   2004022644

9 8 7 6 5 4 3 2 1

Printed in the United States of America
on acid-free paper

Praise for *One Nation, Uninsured*

"A strongly argued account that provides useful ammunition for anyone seeking to effect change in a medical system that willfully excludes so many who need it."

—*Kirkus Reviews*

"Briskly written . . . an excellent primer for anybody interested in picking up the reform banner today. . . . Fresh, engaging."

—Jonathan Cohn, Washington Post Book World

"An important book. Jill Quadagno provides an impressive array of historical evidence to advance original arguments for why the United States lacks a comprehensive health care system and why health insurance should be viewed as a social right. This book is must reading for those concerned about health care reform in the United States."

—William Julius Wilson, author of *When Work Disappears*

"A solid and not-too-wonkish guide to health-care reform today."

—*Booklist*

"Jill Quadagno has produced the most comprehensive and up-to-date account of the power and effectiveness of interest groups in defeating a century of national health insurance reform campaigns. An impressive combination of theory and historical research, *One Nation, Uninsured* sets the parameters for the next round of debate over why the U.S. remains the only country without universal health insurance and how it might still expand access while reigning in costs."

—Lawrence R. Jacobs, University of Minnesota

"Readable and engaging. . . . Some of the most interesting portions come from Quadagno's own archival searches and her interviews with people who lived the history that she describes. . . . Quadagno's sustained focus on interest-group politics seems right on target."

—*New England Journal of Medicine*

"A chilling historical account of how powerful groups with self-serving financial interests have successfully blocked attempts to enact national health insurance for seven decades, leaving tens of millions of our citizens without adequate health care coverage and often without even minimal care. Anyone eager to seek reform of our badly fragmented health care system must study its lessons and its blueprint for action; a task that will require nearly unprecedented political skills and monumental organizational prowess."

—Jerome P. Kassirer, M.D., author of *On The Take: How Medicine's Complicity With Big Business Can Endanger Your Health*

"Quadagno, a distinguished sociologist with a long-standing interest in policy, explores a century of government attempts to create universal health care and the powerful forces that have defeated those attempts. . . . Her sociological insights illuminate a path to reform."

—Judy Goldstein Botello, *The San Diego Union-Tribune*

For Laura

Contents

Preface

In 1994 I had the most interesting experience of my career. A Guggenheim Fellowship would pay my salary during my sabbatical from teaching while I worked in the Capitol on a committee of my choosing. Eventually I would write a book. I had taught about policy for fourteen years. Now it was my chance to observe the policy-making process up close. By sheer luck, a new government commission, the President's Bipartisan Commission on Entitlement and Tax Reform, which would be chaired by Senator Bob Kerrey, was just in the process of selecting staff. A call to a friend and I had an interview with the staff director. During the interview I learned that the commissioners' task would be to evaluate options for cutting Social Security, Medicare, Medicaid, and the hundreds of other smaller federal entitlement programs. Despite my ambivalence about the mission, I knew that I would learn a lot. Two months later I was headed to Washington to begin my job.

As the Entitlement Commission proceeded with its hatchet work, President Clinton was pursuing his own ambitious plan for a new (and most certainly costly) program for universal health care. How, I wondered, could President Clinton possibly succeed when Congress seemed determined to cut social spending? By the time the Entitlement Commission folded in December, the Democrats had lost control of Congress, the congressional staffers in the House who had been too swamped to respond to my queries in the summer were calling to ask if my university had any job openings, and health care reform was dead. As I pondered that heady but disheartening experience, I decided I needed to learn more about why a proposal that had seemed sure to succeed just a few months earlier had suffered so ignominious a fate. And so my journey began. For the next four years, I shuffled through reams of documents in the National Archives, the Library of Congress, and various presidential libraries, read many oral histories, and interviewed some of the warriors who had been involved in the struggle. Along the way I discovered that health care policy was not the arcane topic it might seem but rather was a prism that reflected the grand historical events of the twentieth century—the Red scare of the 1910s, the trade union movement in the 1930s, McCarthyism in the 1940s, the civil rights movement in the 1950s, Lyndon Johnson's Great Society in the 1960s, the impeachment of President Nixon in the 1970s, the mobilization of senior citizens in the 1980s, and the downing of the Black Hawks in Somalia in the 1990s.

My task was greatly facilitated by many colleagues who have provided helpful comments on various chapters and papers derived from the project. Thanks go to Ted Marmor, Jim Morone, Larry Jacobs, Debra Street, Larry Isaac, Pat Martin, Joane Nagel, Taeku Lee, Julian Zelizer, John Myles, Mary Ruggie, Donald Light, Edward Berkowitz, Jacob Hacker, John Manley, Karen Kruse Thomas, and David Mechanic. I benefited greatly from the insights of the group of scholars who collaborated on a retrospective assessment of Paul Starr's book *The Social Transformation of American Medicine*. Among those whose suggestions were particularly helpful were Judy Feder, Larry Casolino, Bernice Pescosolido, Sydney Halpern, Jennifer Klein, and the project editors, Mark Schlesinger, Keith Wailoo, and especially Tim Jost, who was on call at all hours of the day or night with a speedy response to my many questions regarding legal issues. Others whom I consulted on specific policy issues include Marilyn Moon and Josh Weiner.

As always, I am in the debt of archivists. I appreciate the help I received from Kristen Wilhelm, Patricia Anderson, and Marjorie Charlianti at the National Archives; John Nemmers, project librarian at the Claude Pepper Library; and Albert Nason at the Jimmy Carter Library. Over the course of the project, my graduate research assistants, Michael Stewart, Lori Parham, Steve MacDonald, Jennifer Reid Keene, and Brandy Harris, did Internet searches for historical records, helped me track obscure sources, and performed various and sundry tasks that made my job easier. I was also fortunate to receive an Investigator Award in Health Policy Research from the Robert Wood Johnson Foundation, which provided the funding for me to pursue my research and travel to collections. David Colby and Jim Knickman at the foundation encouraged me to pursue the project, and I greatly appreciate their support. I should add, however, that the views expressed in this book are my own and do not imply endorsement by the Robert Wood Johnson Foundation.

I would especially like to thank Rashi Fein, who invited me for a pleasant dinner at his home, spent hours allowing me to interview him, then mailed me his extensive files covering two decades of his work as technical director of the Committee for National Health Insurance. Others who merit special mention are Mort Lebow, the former public information officer for the Office of Equal Heath Opportunity; Mal Schechter, the former Washington editor of the journal *Hospital Practice*; Robert Ball, former commissioner of the Social Security Administration; and Carlton Spitzer, who served as director of the Office of Public Information in the Department of Health, Education, and Welfare from 1965 to 1968. The fine editorial skills of Alison Anderson, managing editor of the University of Pennsylvania Press, greatly improved the manuscript.

At Oxford University Press I was blessed with a wonderful editor, Dedi Felman, whose enthusiasm for my book kept me on track for the past four years. I eagerly looked forward to her "yay" when she was satisfied with a chapter, and knew I wasn't finished when she said "needs work." She read every chapter at least twice and some chapters three or four times. My husband patiently tolerated my late nights on the computer, and as always I am grateful to share my career with someone who understands the academic life. What would I have done these past four years without Pat, Luann, Sheryl, Lerena, and Peg? They shared their own health care struggles with me and lured me out to the tennis courts when I needed a break. But that's what friends are for. I'm fortunate to have the best.

One Nation, Uninsured

Introduction

One rainy Sunday afternoon a few years ago, I went to see *The Rainmaker*, the film based on John Grisham's legal thriller about a young lawyer who sues a large insurance company, Great Benefit, on behalf of his client, Donny Ray Black. Donny Ray dies of leukemia because Great Benefit refuses to pay for a bone marrow transplant that might save his life. When the jury awards Donny Ray's parents $50 million in punitive damages as retribution for Great Benefit's greed and arrogance, the audience in the theater cheered wildly. The film's story of an insurance company refusing to pay for necessary medical treatment clearly resonated with the experiences of many in attendance.

Perhaps some of the people in the audience had read about David Goodrich, the 41-year-old district attorney who died of stomach cancer after Aetna, his insurance company, refused to approve the cancer treatment recommended by his doctor.[1] Or perhaps they had had an experience like that of my sister, Linda, who lost her job as vice president for marketing when First Interstate Bank merged with Wells Fargo. Although her family could purchase the health insurance that First Interstate had provided, the cost would be nearly $12,000 a year. Linda decided to shop around for a less expensive policy and quickly discovered the hard truth of the health insurance marketplace. Several insurers could provide cheaper coverage for my sister and her two children, but no one wanted to insure her husband. Stan had—in insurance industry jargon—the dreaded "preexisting condition" that made him uninsurable.

When I spoke with others about my sister's dilemma, nearly everyone had similar stories to recount. My friend Connie Laughlin's husband, Michael, died suddenly of a heart attack at the age of 56. After

Michael's death, Connie found herself struggling not only with the grief of widowhood but also with the frustration of trying to find an affordable health insurance policy. As she told me one day:

> Well, I had had abnormal pap smears for about three years. Because that was on my record, the insurance that would be in my range, everything came back denied. You know, I said, I am the same person that I was six months ago before Michael died. I kept calling other insurance companies, and I went to a lot of them. They would write me insurance but they were always going to exclude these gynecological things. Well, that's a woman's entire health.[2]

Connie finally purchased a major medical policy costing $7,000 a year. Her policy would cover any large health expenses she might incur—after she had paid the $3,000 deductible. But if her abnormal pap smear turned into cervical cancer, her health insurance would pay none of the costs. How was it, I wondered, that people with seemingly secure lives could so rapidly reverse course through no fault of their own? Why should people who experience normal life events—a layoff, the death of a spouse, a serious illness—face the prospect of losing their insurance, being denied care, or having their insurer refuse to pay for the health problems they are most likely to have?

The right to health care is recognized in international law and guaranteed in the constitutions of many nations.[3] With the exception of the United States, all Western industrialized countries, regardless of how they raise funds, organize care, and determine eligibility, guarantee every citizen comprehensive coverage for essential health care services. To the extent that care is rationed, it is done on the basis of clinical need, not ability to pay.[4] Most countries allow, and some encourage, private insurance as a supplement or a means of upgrading to a higher class of service and/or a fuller array of services. In Canada private insurance covers items not included in the government program, such as prescription drugs or amenities including private hospital rooms.[5] In Great Britain private insurance is also used for extra services or quicker access for operations that have long waiting lists, such as cataract removals, hernias, and hip replacements.[6] In Denmark, too, private insurance covers various supplementary services.[7] In every case, however, the practices of insurance companies are heavily regulated to prevent them from engaging in the more pernicious forms of medical under-writing that are commonly employed in the United States.

Medical underwriting is the practice health plans use to segment people and employee groups into different risk pools according to their health profile. It is governed by what Donald Light calls the law of inverse coverage: the more coverage you need, the less you will receive and the more you will pay.[8] Thus people who have allergies, high blood pressure, depression, or arthritis will be charged higher premiums than healthy people; people with "preexisting conditions" such as cataracts, asthma, or migraine headaches may be offered a policy with an exclusion clause that does not cover those conditions; and people with serious illnesses such as AIDS, leukemia, or emphysema will likely be denied coverage altogether. Insurers may also avoid entire occupations or industries considered high risks, including beauty shops, bars, law practices, roofing companies, and restaurants.

The complexity of the health insurance marketplace, the high cost of coverage, and medical underwriting leave many people at risk of being uninsured. In 2003 45 million Americans, more than one out of every six people, had no health insurance.[9] That number, as large as it is, tells an incomplete and potentially misleading story, because many more people are uninsured for some period over any two-year time span. In 2002 and 2003 nearly 82 million people—one out of every three Americans—went without health insurance for all or part of the two years.[10] Most were average people in working families. Nearly eight out of ten were working, and another 6 percent were looking for work. Only 15 percent were not in the labor force, in most cases because they were disabled, chronically ill, or family caregivers.[11]

Many uninsured people are in the same boat as Diane MacPherson. Diane lost her job at a relocation management company and with it her health coverage for herself, her four-year-old daughter, and her husband, Bob, a construction worker whose job doesn't offer health benefits. Even though Bob made $75,000 that year, with Diane out of work, the family could not afford the $931 monthly premiums it would have cost to cover their family. Instead Bob and Diane decided to insure only their daughter at $271 a month. When Diane's unemployment benefits ran out, they had to drop even their daughter's health insurance.[12]

Some uninsured people work at jobs where health benefits are not offered. Such jobs are more likely to be with small companies rather than large firms. (You are certain to have excellent health benefits if you work for a Fortune 500 firm but likely have poorer coverage or none at all if you work for Mom and Pop's Pizza.) In other instances, uninsured people are offered health benefits from their employers but decline the offer because they can't afford to pay their share of the premiums. That is the case with Diane Schroeder, a 51-year-old woman from Coralville, Iowa, who cleans buses for a living. Because of her poor health—she suffers from migraines, arthritis, and an anxiety disorder—Diane only works part time. She takes home $400 a month.[13] Although the transit company where she works would pay half of her health insurance premium, she cannot afford her share, $122 a month. In 2003 employers contributed 73 percent of the cost of family health benefits with employees paying the remainder, at an average cost of $2,412. While $2,412 sounds like a good deal (and indeed it is), it represents 25 percent of the income for someone working full time at minimum wage ($5.15 an hour in 2004).[14] Few low-wage workers can afford to spend one-quarter of their income on health benefits when they have rent to pay, groceries to buy, and car payments to make.

Being uninsured reduces access to medical care and imperils health and well-being. Take Jesus Vivas. A native of Mexico, Jesus moved to Texas in 1994 and found a job earning $55 a day painting houses. His life was going well until he fell off a ladder. Although he was bent over in pain, his arm swollen, his boss sent him home, not wanting to pay his medical expenses. Jesus' family drove him to the emergency room of the local hospital, where doctors put a splint on his wrist, gave him pain medication, and referred him to a physician's office. When he arrived, the doctor refused to see him because he had no insurance.[15] Three weeks later he showed up at a public clinic, where doctors found that his left wrist was fractured, an injury that the emergency room doctors had missed.

The uninsured, such as Jesus, are often denied care that is available to people with insurance. Many uninsured people do not have a regular family doctor and thus do not receive preventive health services such as cholesterol-lowing drugs or screening for potentially fatal diseases such as cancer, diabetes, or heart disease. As a result, their health problems are often diagnosed at more advanced stages, resulting in higher mortality rates.[16] Frequently the care they do receive is in an emergency room where there is no primary care and no follow-up care.

Uninsured children are less likely to have a pediatrician who provides regular care or to receive basic immunizations, and they are more likely to be hospitalized for an illness that could have been treated without a hospitalization.[17]

Being uninsured can place severe financial strains on families. Nearly half of all individual bankruptcy filings are due to medical bills.[18] DeFannie Davis, an uninsured mother who is the sole caregiver for her disabled husband, describes the pall being uninsured casts over her life: "Being uninsured means living with fear every day. I fear getting sick and not being able to work, I fear an injury that will leave me with bills I am unable to pay, and I fear getting a regular check-up that results in finding something that needs further treatment."[19]

The uninsured raise the costs of health care for everyone. The expense of their care is borne by taxpayers through various government programs or through cost shifting by physicians and hospitals to privately insured patients.[20] Cost shifting, in turn, forces insurance companies to either reduce covered services or raise premiums, co-payments, and deductibles for people with insurance. As premiums rise, fewer employers offer coverage, so more people wind up being uninsured.[21] Thus a never-ending cycle is perpetuated.

In other countries, national health insurance has proved to be a major tool for restraining costs and controlling inflation, while in the United States planning the rational distribution of health care resources has been impossible. The result is duplication of services; unnecessary procedures, tests, and drugs; inefficient use of technologies; and rampant inflation that motivates employers to outsource jobs overseas.[22] Why is the United States the only nation that fails to guarantee coverage of medical services, that rations care by income, race, and health, and that allows for-profit private insurance companies to serve as gatekeepers to the health care system? As the prominent historian David Rothman remarks:

> Americans do not think of themselves as callous and cruel, yet, in their readiness to forgo and withhold this most elemental social service, they have been so. This question arises: How did the middle class, its elected representatives, and its doctors accommodate themselves to such neglect?[23]

How indeed? I believe I have an answer to Rothman's question. Current arrangements for financing care have been hammered out through contentious struggles between social reformers, physicians, employers, insurance companies, and trade unions over the proper relationship between government and the private sector. Across an entire century, each attempt to enact national health insurance has been met with a fierce attack by powerful stakeholders who have mobilized their considerable resources to keep the financing of health care a private affair. Whenever government action has seemed imminent, they have lobbied legislators, influenced elections by giving huge campaign contributions to sympathetic candidates, and organized "grassroots" protests, conspiring with other like-minded groups to defeat reform efforts. The only instance where this was not the case was with Medicare and Medicaid, programs that fund care for the residual population groups—the aged and the very poor—that private insurers have no desire to cover.[24]

This book offers an account of how those stakeholders have kept universal health insurance in the United States at bay, allowing for reforms only when it served their self-interest. It looks at how physicians and then insurers and employers were able to mobilize powerful allies to defeat national health insurance and institutionalize market-based alternatives. I argue that until we view health insurance as a social right, not a consumer product, we will never receive the coverage we need.

The Politics of Health Policy

From the Progressive Era to the 1960s, physicians were the most vocal opponents of government-financed health care. Their goal was to erect a barrier against any third-party payer, especially the government, that might intrude in the sacred doctor-patient relationship.[25] Doctors understood that if third parties assumed responsibility for financing care, these parties would need to establish some way to control their financial liability, which would invariably mean regulating physicians' fees. In the practice of medicine, physicians had the authority not only to name diseases and offer prognoses but also to make judgments that extended beyond determinations of illness. They were asked to decide whether people were disabled or fit enough to work, to pronounce death, and even to judge whether the deceased had been mentally competent when they wrote their wills.[26] Why shouldn't they also decide who would pay for medical care and how those payments would be organized?

Physicians pursued their political endeavors through the American Medical Association (AMA), a powerful professional association with an organizational structure perfectly suited to political action. At the bottom of the AMA hierarchy were the county medical societies. Membership in a county society automatically conferred membership in the state medical society, which, in turn, was part of a confederation governed at the national level by the House of Delegates.[27] This federated structure made it possible for the AMA to be converted from a professional association into a hard-driving political machine at the local, state, and national levels in each skirmish against government-financed care.

In the 1910s state medical societies worked to defeat a plan for compulsory health insurance.[28] Dr. James Rooney, president of the Medical Society of New York, rallied physicians against the proposal, declaring: "If the profession is to save itself [from health insurance] it must organize as it has never organized before."[29] During the Great Depression, the AMA waged a ferocious campaign to prevent federal officials from including national health insurance in the Social Security Act of 1935.[30] The AMA president, Dr. Morris Fishbein, condemned even a modest proposal for "voluntary" private insurance, claiming it smacked of socialism and communism and might incite revolution.[31] When a plan for national health insurance was revived in the late 1930s, the AMA reluctantly endorsed Blue Cross/Blue Shield plans that the hospitals and doctors had created themselves as a way to head off a government program. Physicians' worst fears were realized in 1946 when President Harry Truman made national health insurance the key domestic issue of his Fair Deal. The *Journal of the American Medical Association* lambasted this threat to liberty: "[If this] Old World scourge is allowed to spread to our New World, [it will] jeopardize the health of our people and gravely endanger our freedom."[32] Following a bitter campaign, Truman was forced to concede defeat.

How did physicians, merely a professional group, defeat the will of social reformers, powerful politicians, and even presidents for more than half a century? Sociologist Paul Starr argues that the key to physicians' political influence was "the absence of [any] countervailing power," but the historical evidence suggests that the opposite is the case.[33] It was not the absence of a countervailing power that allowed physicians to assert their parochial concerns into the policy making process but rather the fact that their objectives coincided with those of other groups with greater clout and deeper pockets. Once these interests diverged, the fragility of physicians' power base was revealed.

In the Progressive Era, physicians won their campaign against compulsory health insurance because they colluded with employer groups, insurance companies, and trade unions.[34] Their allies included the Insurance Economics Society, an organization of large insurance companies, which financed their campaign; the National Civic Federation, a group of employers dedicated to civic improvement; and the American Federation of Labor (AFL), whose president, Samuel Gompers, denounced compulsory health insurance as "a menace to the rights, welfare and liberty of American workers."[35] When President Truman launched his plan in the 1940s, physicians appealed to the business community, winning over organizations such as the National Association of Manufacturers and the U.S. Chamber of Commerce. The Chamber charged that Truman's plan would lead to the "widespread destruction of our voluntary institutions," create a new army of government employees who would wield "dangerous political power," and "jeopardize our traditional liberties."[36] In Congress physicians also had the support of conservative Republicans such as Ohio senator Robert Taft, a presidential hopeful who had campaigned on a promise to roll back the New Deal, and of southern Democrats such as South Carolina senator Strom Thurmond, who feared any program that might give federal officials the right to intervene in local racial practices. From 1938 until 1964 this conservative coalition endured, thwarting all efforts to enact national health insurance.

Physicians' power base first began to erode in the 1950s, when the trade unions abandoned their preference for collectively bargained benefits and won a campaign for disability benefits in 1956, negotiating behind the scenes with members of Congress who depended on trade union support for reelection. The labor victory demonstrated organized medicine's vulnerability when faced with an opponent with equal resources and organizational strength and greater political savvy. The trade unions next turned to health insurance for the aged. The AMA was as vehemently opposed to Medicare as it had been to national health insurance and disability insurance. When Medicare was under consideration in the 1960s, a Virginia physician sent a letter to Representative

Aime Forand (D-RI), the sponsor of the legislation, declaring that he "should be castrated and his progeny die in embryo."[37] Although it took more than a decade, Medicare was finally enacted in 1965, following a Democratic sweep of the House and Senate and an AFL-CIO campaign that mobilized trade union members and retirees in every key congressional district.

Although Medicare was a victory for reformers, it was also a victory for providers. Medicare would not intervene in the health care system but merely serve as a neutral conduit through which all federal funds would pass.[38] Hospitals would be reimbursed on a cost-plus-2-percent basis, physicians would be paid their "usual and customary" fees with no upper limit, and the provider-friendly private insurance industry would monitor charges and pay claims. Given these arrangements, health care inflation was inevitable. Before Medicare, hospital daily charges had increased between 6 and 9 percent per year. In 1965 they jumped nearly 17 percent. The fees of general practitioners rose 25 percent, those of internists 40 percent. By 1966 there were predictions that overall health care inflation might top 25 percent.[39] According to one critic, Connecticut senator Abraham Ribicoff, public funds and third-party payments had spawned "the civilian equivalent of the defense establishment. . . . Both [had] an apparently insatiable appetite for money and an enormously well developed talent for avoiding public accountability and controls."[40]

As health care costs skyrocketed, the major purchasers of care—the federal government and employers—began asking what they were receiving for their money and whether medical services were worth the costs. Answering these questions required close scrutiny of core aspects of medical practice, jeopardizing physicians' essential prerogatives: the ability to restrict competition, limit regulation, and define standards.[41] The first challenge to physicians' professional sovereignty came from the federal government. Before Medicare made a single payment, federal officials forced hospitals to create utilization review boards, set quality standards for hospitals and nursing homes, and dealt a death blow to racial segregation by withholding funds from hospitals that refused to integrate.

These initial forays into the providers' domain were followed by attempts, first by President Richard Nixon and then by President Jimmy

Carter, to control hospital costs. Carter's first plan, to set a yearly cap on hospital cost increases, sparked a flurry of lobbying activity by the American Hospital Association and the Federation of American Hospitals. Conceding defeat, the following year Carter tried to enact a weaker measure but failed to win congressional support. Carter's beleaguered secretary of health and human services, Joseph Califano, wearily concluded that health care reform was impossible with "a Congress whose members depend on private contributions for election campaigns . . . and who will always worry about offending hospital trustees and influential state and local medical societies."[42] Despite Carter's failure, in 1983 Medicare's open-ended method of reimbursing hospitals was replaced with a prospective payment system that set a fixed amount for each hospital stay, depending on the patient's diagnosis and regardless of the cost of treatment. The prospective system was tacked onto a Social Security reform bill at the last minute and generated little attention at the time. It was followed a few years later by a fee schedule for physicians' services.

The second challenge to physicians' autonomy came from large corporations such as Chrysler and Bethlehem Steel and business associations such as the Chamber of Commerce and the National Association of Manufacturers. With their powerful lobbyists, ample economic resources, connections with insurance companies, and captive patient-employees, these organizations seemed well positioned to confront the medical profession.[43] Leading corporate employers lobbied for greater regulation of providers and a larger voice for business in health policy decisions and helped win the prospective payment system and physician fee schedules for Medicare, which they hoped would exert a constraining influence on private sector payments. But when they tried to exert their clout as large purchasers to negotiate lower fees and premium charges in their company health plans, the providers refused to cooperate.[44] Then corporations turned to managed care, unleashing a powerful adversary whose sole objective was to tame the health care system. Managed care firms delved deeply into the most minute details of physicians' practices. They reviewed tests and procedures, evaluated charges, analyzed patient records to see if unnecessary procedures were being performed, and then held physicians financially accountable for the costs of their medical decisions.[45] Thus, ironically, the private health insurance system that physicians had helped to construct became a mechanism for undermining their sovereign rule.

As physicians' antipathy to national health insurance dwindled, tempered by the benefits of guaranteed payment and splits among various specialty groups, health insurers moved to the forefront of public debates. In the 1980s the Health Insurance Association of America, an organization that represented most of the small and medium-sized insurance companies in the country, joined with the National Federation of Independent Business to crush a proposal for home care benefits for the disabled. Insurers saw home care as a threat to the fledgling private long-term care insurance market, while small-business owners feared the tax hike that would be needed to pay for the benefit. When President Bill Clinton proposed a plan to guarantee universal health care coverage in 1993, the same coalition of insurers, corporations, and small-business groups mobilized against him. The coalition funded a public relations campaign against the Clinton plan, hired lobbying firms, and stepped up their campaign contributions, with the largest contributions going to members of the committees that had jurisdiction over health reform.[46] Besieged by the opposition, the Clinton plan met the same fate as had its predecessors.

The defeat of national health insurance in the United States can only be understood in the context of the shifting power structure within the health care system, signified by the erosion of physicians' cultural authority, the corporate purchasers' revolt, and the ascendance of managed care. The changing composition of the antireform coalition, dominated first by physicians and then by insurers and business groups, has obscured the persistence of stakeholder mobilization as the primary obstacle to national health insurance. Given the ever-shifting scope of these debates, it is not surprising that many Americans find the health care issue too confusing to understand or resolve.

Other social scientists attribute the lack of national health insurance to such factors as enduring antigovernment sentiment, a weak labor movement, the racial politics of the South, the distinctive character of American political institutions, or the way early policy choices crowded out subsequent policy options. I would argue not that these explanations are incorrect but rather that they are incomplete in a crucial way. They take as the object of analysis the programs and policies surroundin health care system and largely ignore medical care and the political battles fought over its control as the object of study and primary forces in their own right.

Political Theories of the Welfare State

Antistatist Values –ideology

According to one common argument, the chief impediment to national health insurance has been an antistatist political culture. Because Americans honor private property, hold individual rights sacred, and distrust state authority, reformers have found it difficult to make a convincing case for government financing of health care.[47] Americans' ambivalence toward government and their bias toward private solutions to public problems stands in the way. We can no more trust the state to make decisions about our health care than we can about what make of car to drive, what color shirt to wear, or which brand of dental floss to use, or so the thinking of many goes.[48]

Antistatism has been described as the underlying force in the various failed attempts to guarantee universal coverage across the entire twentieth century. In the Progressive Era, the compulsory state health insurance plan was supposedly defeated by the public's antipathy toward a larger government role in health care.[49] Medicare's peculiar public-private formula, with its numerous concessions to providers and insurers, was a way to assuage public concern about government intervention.[50] Distrust of government undermined public confidence in Clinton's health plan, allowing his opponents to claim that federal bureaucrats would destroy the doctor-patient relationship and take away people's right to choose their own doctors.[51]

Certainly, antistatist themes have been used in political debates to undermine public confidence in national health insurance. Less certain is whether values were a principal causal force. If antistatism has been an enduring feature of American politics, then why have some programs been enacted that contradict this core value? After all, Medicare involved as significant a federal presence in the health care system as national health insurance would. What is also uncertain is how antistatist values get translated into policy decisions. In most accounts, values are simply presumed to have some kind of unexplained effect on the policy-making process. How do antistatist values shape the decisions that elected officials make?[52]

Weak Labor – *labor*

A second argument attributes the failure of national health insurance in the United States to the absence of a working-class movement and labor-based political party such as the Labour Party in Great Britain.[53] In many European countries working-class parties have organized on behalf of public pension programs such as Social Security that provide older workers with a dignified exit from the labor force and a dependable source of retirement income. They have also fought for unemployment insurance to provide workers with a buffer against downturns in the economy. In the United States, by contrast, the trade unions pursued a different path. They never formed a separate political party and in some instances actively opposed government social programs. As noted previously, early in the twentieth century the AFL denounced state health insurance proposals, claiming that they would subordinate workers to the state and undermine workers' efforts to resolve their own problems.[54] The Social Security Act of 1935, the single most important piece of social welfare legislation of the twentieth century, was enacted without strong labor backing.[55] In other instances, however, state federations and local union chapters challenged their national leaders on these issues. In the 1910s some AFL chapters endorsed the compulsory health insurance bill. In the 1920s the United Mine Workers worked for state old-age pensions, then supported a federal old-age pension plan.[56] The question, then, is why the trade unions have supported some legislative measures but not others and what allowed them, in some instances, to mobilize politically absent a labor party.

Racial Politics of the South – *Race*

A third explanation attributes the failure of national health insurance to the racial politics of the South.[57] For the first two-thirds of the twentieth century, southern politicians opposed any government intrusion into the health care system because they feared federal intervention in local racial practices. They used their control of key congressional committees to bottle up legislation entirely or to demand that new social programs be locally administered. At their insistence, agricultural and domestic workers (two-thirds of all black workers) were excluded from the Social Security and unemployment insurance programs of the Social Security Act, and local welfare authorities were allowed to determine who would receive benefits from the means-tested programs for the poor (Aid to Dependent Children and old-age assistance).[58]

Health care financing would seem to be distantly removed from the racial politics of the South. Yet the southern health care system, like other southern institutions, was racially segregated. Most hospitals maintained "white" and "colored" floors, labeled equipment by race, and denied staff privileges to black physicians. National health insurance posed the threat that federal funding of health care services would lead to federal demands to integrate health care facilities and tear down racial barriers.

The racial politics of the South had a stifling effect on health policy debates from the 1930s to the 1960s. What is less clear is how racial politics influenced debates over health care reform in the post-civil-rights era, when the conservative coalition no longer exerted a negative, controlling influence on federal policy.

State Structures and Policy Legacies - stakeholders

According to a fourth argument, the structure of the American state has continually frustrated efforts to enact national health insurance.[59] In the United States, political power is diffused to a degree unmatched in any other country. At the national level, authority is divided among three branches of government—the executive branch, Congress, and the courts, each with its own independent authority, responsibilities, and bases of support—and among the sovereign states, which have the right to nullify federal legislation. At the legislative level, authority is further split between the House and the Senate as well as numerous committees and subcommittees.[60] This decentralized structure impedes policy innovation by increasing the number of veto points (i.e., the courts, the legislative process, the states) where even small numbers of opponents can block policy initiatives. It allows special interests to exercise a unique influence on policy outcomes through lobbying of individual legislators to support their preferred policies, opposing those that obstruct their agendas and helping to determine the issues that legislators interpret as important in the first place.[61]

This "state structure" argument is often used in comparative studies to explain cross-national variations in policy outcomes. Thus, for example, some would argue that national health insurance failed in the United States but succeeded in Canada because the Canadian parliamentary political system is more centralized and less diffuse than the American political system.[62] However, this argument falls flat when applied to variations across time in policy decisions within the United States. Why did Medicare succeed when confronted with the same institutional arrangements as national health insurance? A variable (social welfare benefits) cannot be explained by a constant (decentralized institutions). Few would disagree that the American political system with its checks and balances is designed to slow down the policy-making process and prevent decisions from being made abruptly. But that argument explains little about how the complex configuration of public and private health benefits came to be. Although a state structure argument may predict the prospects for reform, it cannot explain why one policy succeeds while another fails, nor can it account for the form of policies that are enacted.[63]

Critics of the state structure approach counter that it is more important to understand how early policy choices influence subsequent policy options by giving rise to widespread public expectations and vast networks of vested interests.[64] Initial policy decisions narrow the menu of future options by forming self-reinforcing paths that become increasingly difficult to alter. Thus Social Security succeeded while national health insurance failed. Social Security was enacted before a private pension system developed. By contrast, the private health insurance system was solidly entrenched by the time reformers began to press for a government solution, crowding out the public alternative.[65] But to say that national health insurance failed because it was crowded out by private health benefits begs the question of why national health insurance was not on the political agenda in the first place.

Each of these forces—antistatist values, weak labor, racial politics, policy legacies—may account for the defeat of national health insurance in a given instance. None provides an overarching framework that can explain the outcome of health care reform debates across the grand panorama of twentieth-century history. That is the task that I undertake in the chapters that follow. By clarifying the persistent threads in the campaign against universal health care, my hope is that the organizational steps for easing the crisis and facilitating the adoption of national health insurance may become clearer as well.

Chapter 1 describes how, from the Progressive Era to the 1950s, physicians mobilized against proposals for government health insurance. Chapter 2 investigates why the trade unions helped promote the nascent private health insurance system but also led the drive for disability insurance and Medicare. Chapter 3 shows how the racial politics of the South were played out within the health care system and how the enactment of Medicare provided federal officials with the resources to impose racial integration on southern hospitals. Chapter 4 explains how Medicare and Medicaid created uncontrollable inflation in the health care system, triggering a purchaser's revolt. Chapter 5 describes the decade-long struggle of federal officials to introduce cost containment measures and discusses the effect this struggle had on the prospect of national health insurance. Chapter 6 explains how the failure of federal cost containment aroused corporate purchasers to experiment with their own tactics for controlling costs, giving way to managed care in the 1990s and triggering internecine warfare between physicians and insurers. Chapter 7 shows how a coalition of insurance companies, small businesses, and managed-care firms crushed a proposal for home care for the disabled in the 1980s, then launched an attack on President Clinton's plan for universal health care in the 1990s. Finally, Chapter 8 evaluates alternative explanations of the American case in light of the historical evidence presented and analyzes prospects for health care reform in the twenty-first century. I argue that the reason we don't have the health care system we need is not because the solution is too difficult to grasp or because of the legacies of antistatism, racial politics, or something inherent in the American political system. The reason we don't have the system we need is because we have failed to grasp how much we have ceded our health care to private interests. Once we understand, to return to the chapter's opening, how Donny Ray's death could be in our hands, not Great Benefit's, we will be more than halfway to the health care reform that is so desperately needed.

one

Doctors' Politics and the Red Menace

In 1911 Eugene V. Debs, the presidential candidate of the Socialist Party, declared that the "class of privilege and pelf has had the world by the throat and the working class beneath its iron-shod hoofs long enough." Deep-seated discontent had "seized upon the masses"; capitalism was "rushing blindly to its impending doom."[1] In the 1912 election Debs won over 900,000 votes, 6 percent of the presidential total. Scores of Socialist Party candidates were elected as well, including 1,200 municipal officials, 79 mayors in 24 states, and 2 members of Congress.[2] As the public took note of this turn of events, alarm about the spread of socialism was heightened by the bloody Russian Revolution of 1917. Consternation increased when Russian communists made peace with Germany in the closing months of World War I.

Postwar unemployment sparked a rash of over 3,300 labor strikes that involved over 4 million workers in 1919, sending a ripple of fear across the nation. In May bombs were sent through the mail to prominent business leaders and politicians, inflaming anxieties that anarchists were bent on destroying the American way of life. When Russian communists established the Comintern to promote world revolution, Americans found a convenient scapegoat for their troubles.[3] A police strike in Boston and a steelworkers' strike in Pittsburgh were thought to be Bolshevik-inspired. Any departure from conventional thought was seen as part of a diabolical communist plot. The Red scare reached a climax in 1920 when the attorney general staged raids on pool halls, bowling alleys, and restaurants—anyplace suspected communist sympathizers might congregate. Four thousand people were jailed, and 550 of these were deported. The raids paralyzed the Socialist Party, which had split into factions with one group rejecting Soviet communism and the other breaking away to form the American Communist Party.

Despite the weakening of the radical movement, the socialist threat hovered over the political landscape for the next half century, providing a rallying cry for conservatives against any plan for government intervention in the private sector. The Red scare's lasting legacy was a suspicion of socialist sympathies attached to any group looking to alleviate social problems through government action.

The Campaign for Compulsory Health Insurance in the Progressive Era

Socialism stood in contrast to Progressivism, the spirit of reform that swept the nation between the 1890s and the end of the First World War. Progressivism was inspired by the same problems that gave rise to socialism—harsh working conditions, unemployment, urban poverty, and labor unrest—but the remedies were reformist rather than revolutionary. The vanguard of the progressive movement was the new middle class, young educated professionals who believed that they could use their expertise to improve society. These progressives, as they were called, formed hundreds of voluntary organizations such as the National Child Labor Committee, the National Consumers League, and the Women's Trade Union League to "root out corruption in government, make cities more liveable and improve industrial working conditions."[4] Whereas socialists believed that the existing government was a tool of capitalists, progressives were convinced that public power could be used to protect the common welfare. They sponsored state laws for minimum wages, an eight-hour workday, old-age pensions, insurance against industrial accidents, and limits on the working hours of women and children.

The American Association for Labor Legislation (AALL) was one of the many reform organizations created during the Progressive Era. Founded by academics and upper-middle-class social reformers, AALL members disavowed socialism and sought to use scientific methods to identify the needs of wage earners and curtail the worst abuses of the capitalist system.[5] One prominent AALL member was social worker Jane Addams, who had founded Hull House in the slums of Chicago to connect college-educated and wealthy young people with "the starvation struggle."[6] Another member was AFL president Samuel Gompers. A cigar maker by trade, Gompers was a squat but powerful man with "a huge torso, short legs, magnetic hazel eyes and a pipe organ voice."[7] He believed that the way to improve workers' condition was to use whatever means were available under the law. That meant organizing to increase wages and improve working conditions through strikes and boycotts that put direct economic pressure on employers but not through partisan politics. Gompers never attempted to deliver the labor vote to any politician and explicitly rejected the idea that workers should form a separate political party. Business leaders such as Frederick Hoffman, a Prudential insurance executive who was a renowned medical statistician and pioneer in public health research, also joined.

Beginning in 1914 the AALL took on three major campaigns aimed at improving workers' health. The first, to eliminate poisonous materials in the workplace, resulted in federal legislation banning the use of phosphorus in match factories. The second, to provide compensation for workplace injuries, succeeded in getting 33 states to adopt workmen's compensation laws. Elated by these victories, AALL leaders felt optimistic about securing support for their next goal: compulsory health insurance. The idea of providing insurance against the risk of medical expenses was largely unknown at that time. No government programs existed, and commercial insurance companies had not yet ventured into the business of insuring health, which was considered an uninsurable moral hazard.

In 1914 the AALL Social Insurance Committee began drafting a model bill that would provide workers with free medical services and hospital care, sick pay, and a modest death benefit. Hoping to win physicians' support, the AALL intentionally left out any specific provisions regarding how physicians would be paid.[8] Those details would be decided after medical opinion on the issue had been gathered.

By 1917 the AALL bill had been introduced in 14 state legislatures, but the only states in which it was seriously considered were New York and California. The battle in California was short-lived. When the California social insurance commission recommended a state health insurance plan along the lines of the AALL bill, physicians formed the League for the Conservation of Public Health to coordinate the opposition. Their ally was the Insurance Economic Society, an organization of insurance companies led by the major insurers, Prudential and Metropolitan.[9] Commercial insurers feared that a government program would undermine the private market for life insurance and funeral benefits and eventually lead to a government takeover of all industry products. The Insurance Economic Society financed the campaign against the AALL bill, and in 1918 the referendum was defeated by a large margin.[10]

When the AALL bill was first introduced in New York, reformers were optimistic about its prospects. It had the support of some socialists who believed that compulsory health insurance did not contradict their own goals. While they were waiting for the revolution, workers needed immediate reforms. Compulsory health insurance represented the first step toward socialism.[11] New York Medical Society officers also hailed the AALL bill as "the next step in social legislation" and worked with AALL leaders to draft provisions that would be acceptable to physicians. But they hadn't reckoned with physicians from upstate New York's cities and rural areas, who decried the bill as "un-American," not democratic. Their leader, Dr. James Rooney, traveled around the state, encouraging the county medical societies to denounce compulsory health insurance as striking at the "fundamental law of our land: life, liberty and the pursuit of happiness" and representing the first step toward "state socialism."[12] County doctors deposed the physician who had chaired the state committee that endorsed the AALL bill, and they elected new representatives to the national House of Delegates. Even though the AALL tried to mollify physicians by agreeing that they could set their own fees and head the health insurance commission that would be created to run the program, the doctors' wrath only increased in intensity.

Despite physicians' opposition, the New York Senate passed the AALL bill, arousing employers and insurance companies to action. Employers' organizations created a health insurance committee to gather statistics that could be used to discredit AALL estimates of illness rates among workers and began investigating the feasibility of employer-sponsored health plans as an alternative to a government program.[13] Frederick Hoffman, himself an AALL member, turned against his colleagues and became Prudential's unofficial lobbyist against compulsory health insurance. He lectured extensively around the country and took several trips to Europe, financed by Prudential, to investigate the evils of the German social insurance system. Another insurers' association, the Insurance Federation of New York, lamented that the AALL bill was just the entering wedge that "would mean the end of all Insurance Companies and Agents."[14] Some insurance companies began to reconsider the possibility of offering a health insurance product. Equitable added disability benefits to its life insurance policies in 1917, Metropolitan sold its first individual health policy in 1921, and Prudential began selling group health insurance in 1925.[15]

The labor movement was deeply divided on the issue of compulsory health insurance. On one side was the national AFL, led by Gompers, who teamed up with the National Civic Federation, an organization of business leaders, to work against the plan in the state legislature.[16] On the other side were some AFL affiliates, such as the United Mine Workers and the International Ladies' Garment Workers' Union, who broke with Gompers and championed the AALL bill. The AALL could not overcome the combined force of the opposition, and the bill died in committee in 1919, ending the Progressive Era campaign for compulsory health insurance. But the AALL plan coalesced physician opinion on government-financed health care, initiated the themes that would dominate all subsequent debates about health care reform, and gave physicians a false sense of the extent of their political power. As historian Beatrix Hoffman noted, the defeat of the AALL plan "contributed to the making of a limited welfare state, a distinctive health care system and a political culture and configuration of interest-group power that would resist universal health coverage for the rest of the century."[17]

Compulsory Health Insurance in the New Deal

Compulsory health insurance was revived in 1929 when a group of social reformers, physicians, and academics formed the Committee on the Costs of Medical Care. For five years the committee studied the problem of paying for health care and finally issued a 27-volume report, which was endorsed by the majority of its members. Among their numerous recommendations, the two that generated the most opposition among physicians were that medical care could be more effectively provided through groups rather than solo practices and that the costs of care could best be met through some sort of voluntary group prepayment arrangement. Isidore (Ig) Falk, the quiet, competent, and politically liberal professor who had served as associate director of the committee, recalled, "These . . . were the two on which the battles really centered."[18] The physician members issued a blistering minority report, condemning any departure from individual, fee-for-service medicine and denouncing voluntary insurance as communistic.[19] AMA president Dr. Morris Fishbein denounced the majority report, and shortly thereafter the House of Delegates unanimously endorsed the minority report. Given the intransigence of the AMA, Falk became convinced that voluntary insurance had no chance. For the rest of his career, he became the foremost advocate of a compulsory government program:

> I saw potentials for voluntary insurance rather optimistically at that time. I did not swing back to the compulsory insurance approach until the AMA made this colossal blunder of taking a firm position against voluntary insurance. . . . When the AMA pulled the rug from under all of us . . . I changed.[20]

The stock market crash of 1929 sent the economy into a tailspin, ushering in an economic crisis of unprecedented magnitude. As the Depression deepened, hospital occupancy rates dropped steeply, because most people had no way to pay for medical care.[21] Some hospitals, seeking a way to develop a stable source of revenue, set up prepayment "service" plans where members would pay a monthly fee and then be eligible for free hospital services if they needed care. These plans initially covered just hospital employees but were then extended to other groups such as teachers and firefighters. Although the AMA thundered against them, the American Hospital Association (AHA) helped hospitals establish these group plans and succeeded in rescuing many floundering community hospitals. Prepayment plans became the precursor to what would become Blue Cross.[22]

As the social devastation of the depression revealed the inadequacies of state relief programs for the aged, the unemployed, and the poor, it became apparent that some federal response was required. In 1934 President Roosevelt created an advisory Committee on Economic Security to determine the best way to safeguard people "against misfortunes which cannot wholly be eliminated."[23] The committee considered including national health insurance in its model bill for economic aid in a preliminary report, alarming the AMA. Fearful that a legislative proposal might follow, the AMA called a special meeting of the House of Delegates, which adopted a resolution that "all features of medical service . . . should be under the control of the profession."[24] In a small concession to moderates, the House of Delegates accepted the concept of voluntary insurance as long as it was controlled by county medical societies. Then the siege began. AMA members bombarded members of Congress with letters, postcards, and phone calls decrying compulsory health insurance. As the executive director of the Committee on Economic Security, Edwin Witte, recalled, we were "at once subjected to misrepresentation and vilification" by the AMA.[25] Even the president's personal physician, Dr. Ross McIntyre, lobbied the First Lady, Eleanor Roosevelt, warning "that national health insurance would be very bad for the country."[26] According to one federal official, national health insurance was dropped at the last minute: "It was really very much nip and tuck whether or not the recommendations for the Social Security Act would not include some provision for health insurance."[27] Perhaps President Roosevelt could have one of his "fireside chats and carry it along." But the president felt he had "bitten off about as much as he could chew."[28] Worried about jeopardizing his entire Social Security bill, Roosevelt decided to put national health insurance on hold. As a result, the Social Security Act of 1935, the largest expansion of federal authority into the social welfare system in American history, created new programs for the unemployed, the aged, widows, single mothers, and poor children but did not include national health insurance.[29]

With the threat of a public program temporarily abated, Blue Cross solidified its status as the major hospital insurance carrier. In 1938 all Blue Cross local member plans were organized into corporations. Each local plan was required to join the national Blue Cross Association and to establish an agreement with at least 75 percent of the hospitals in its area.[30] In return, member organizations had the advantages of national advertising, the exclusive right to provide benefits in a given service area, and a mechanism for transferring subscribers who moved from one area to another. The AHA then lobbied to exempt these corporations from state laws that regulated commercial insurance companies and from state taxation; by 1945 these laws were operating in 35 states.[31] The Internal Revenue Service, following the precedent accepted by the states, exempted Blue Cross plans from federal income taxes as well.

These arrangements allowed Blue Cross plans to grow unimpeded by competition from commercial insurance companies.[32] Blue Cross thus stabilized the flow of income to hospitals and gave the AHA a virtual monopoly over health care financing in most communities.

Blue Cross plans were able to achieve these tax advantages because they differed from commercial insurance in two key ways. First, they were "community-rated," meaning that everyone who belonged to the group paid the same rate and received the same benefits, regardless of age or health status. By contrast, commercial insurance plans were "experience-rated," with rates determined by the perceived risk factors of the group or individual.[33] A second difference was that Blue Cross offered service benefits that provided subscribers with free hospital care when needed, while commercial insurers offered indemnity plans that reimbursed patients a fixed amount for expenses incurred during a hospital stay. For these reasons, Blue Cross could serve the community in ways commercial insurance could not. Despite their fundamental differences, neither Blue Cross nor commercial insurers imposed any controls on hospital charges. Thus the fledgling health insurance industry evolved as a passive vehicle for the transmission of funds from patients to providers and exerted no oversight.

Blue Cross was given a boost by the trade unions. For decades some unions had maintained old-age pension and health funds for their members and retirees, but the Depression had revealed the insufficiencies of these funds. Many unions were unable to pay promised pension benefits or meet members' medical bills. Beginning in the late 1930s, some unions began negotiating their own group plans with hospitals. After Blue Cross was formed, the unions worked to formalize agreements to cover their members' health expenses. From the unions' perspective, Blue Cross was preferable to commercial insurance, because it was nonprofit, it was community-rated, and it offered full benefits with no deductibles or co-payments.[34]

Even though Blue Cross was provider-controlled, the medical societies often opposed these efforts. Walter Reuther, the United Auto Workers (UAW) vice president at that time, recalled:

> We then went to the medical society in Flint where we got one lone doctor to agree to participate in Blue Cross. The medical society launched a propaganda campaign that charged that this was

socialism. We pointed out that the government was not involved at all—that this was a non-governmental, voluntary group through which we could share the cost through an insurance approach. Two weeks later, our one doctor asked for his contract back. He said, "My wife and I are both being ostracized socially, and they're threatening to take away my hospital privileges."[35]

Medical societies opposed Blue Cross because some plans sought to include medical care in their service benefits. Because medical care was a standard part of many commercial insurance plans, Blue Cross had a difficult time competing with these more comprehensive benefits. But the Depression had also had a negative impact on physicians' ability to practice medicine. In many communities doctors didn't know from month to month whether they could keep their practices open or how they would pay their rent, their secretaries, their nurses, or even their electric bills.[36] In 1939 California physicians developed a medical care benefit plan as part of a successful effort to derail a state health insurance program. Medical societies in other states followed suit. In 22 states medical societies lobbied for legislation to restrict the creation of competing commercial health plans, those not controlled by physicians, and ostracized physicians who joined such plans. According to one state legislator, "No measure opposed by the medical societies had a chance of passage."[37] In 1943 the AMA created a commission to coordinate these statewide physicians' plans on a national basis, giving birth to Blue Shield, a national organization of medical care plans designed and controlled by doctors.[38]

National Health Insurance in the Postwar Era

The Social Security Act had introduced new programs to ameliorate the uncertainty that accompanied old age or downswings in the economy. It also created a new federal agency, the Social Security Board, to run these programs. In 1938 the Social Security Board organized a conference on the health needs of the nation. In response, the AMA called an emergency meeting of the House of Delegates. Conceding that federal aid for the medically indigent might be necessary, AMA officers insisted that the needs of the rest of the population could best be met by the nascent private health insurance system. National health insurance was not an acceptable option. Nor was a measure proposed by Senator Robert Wagner (D-N.Y.) to provide federal funds for state health programs. President Roosevelt remained silent on the Wagner bill, and it died in committee.

In 1943 Senator Claude Pepper (D-Fla.) introduced a resolution to establish the Committee on Wartime Health and Education. Pepper, a farm boy from the red clay country of eastern Alabama who never saw a paved road until he went to college, entered public life because he believed that government could be a force to enhance the greater good. He liked to describe himself as Roosevelt's ideological soul mate, a New Dealer before there was a New Deal.[39] When Pepper's committee was convened, the AMA opened a Washington office to keep closer tabs on political events.[40] The Pepper committee surveyed the health needs of the nation and was disturbed to learn that thousands of young men and women had been rejected for military service because of poor health. The committee evaluated existing private health insurance plans and concluded that national health insurance was the only effective way to ensure access to health care. Being the first congressional committee ever to endorse national health insurance made the announcement a news-worthy event. As Senator Pepper recalled, "What we were doing more than anything else was developing, stimulating, cultivating public opinion to a degree of acceptability."[41] The release of the committee's report generated a flood of newspaper articles on national health insurance, and a poll found that 82 percent of the public agreed that something should be done to help people pay for medical care.[42] That year a national health insurance bill was introduced in Congress (Wagner-Murray-Dingell), but it suffered the same fate as the Wagner bill that preceded it. Speaking to a member of the Senate, President Roosevelt admitted, "We can't go up against the State Medical Societies; we just can't do it."[43]

The entry of the United States into World War II derailed any further plans for domestic welfare legislation. The nation could scarcely afford national health insurance in the midst of war. In the 1944 election Roosevelt won an unprecedented fourth term as president. He promised to unveil a proposal for national health insurance in the spring, but he never had a chance to fulfill that promise. On April 12, 1945, the president died of a massive stroke, and his vice president, Harry Truman, took over the reins of government.[44] Unlike the patrician Roosevelt,

Truman came from humble origins. A Missouri native, he had plowed corn, clerked in a bank, run a failed haberdashery business, and entered politics when Mike Prendergast, boss of the Democratic Party machine in Kansas City, asked him to run for county judge. Despite his start in ward politics, Truman became known for his honesty and personal integrity, a reputation that helped propel him to a Senate seat in 1934.[45] When Roosevelt decided to replace his vice president, Henry Wallace, with a more moderate running mate in 1944, he selected Truman. Truman had compiled an impressive record uncovering waste and corruption in wartime production and would solidify Roosevelt's support in the Midwest.

Now, having served as vice president for less than four months, Truman faced the daunting task of calming the fears of a bereaved nation and converting an economy mobilized for war to peacetime purposes.[46] On September 6, 1945, President Truman delivered a message to Congress outlining his Fair Deal, an ambitious plan to expand Social Security benefits, raise the minimum wage, build public housing, clear slums, and improve health care. Health care was his special concern. As a county judge, Truman had "been troubled by seeing so many sick people unable to get the care they need, turned away from hospitals because they had no money."[47] He had witnessed doctors refusing to treat his poor clients and "built up a very strong feeling about their negative attitudes at the time."[48] His Fair Deal was to fund hospital construction, provide grants to states for public health, and create a national health insurance program.[49] On the same day that Truman made his speech, bills were introduced in the Senate (S. 1606) and in the House (H.R. 4730), but no action was taken during the following year. In the 1946 congressional election, Truman's grandiose plan provided a rallying theme for Republicans, who blasted big government, big labor, big regulation, and the New Deal, which they claimed had created a welfare state inspired by communist ideals and principles.[50] Thirty-nine of the 69 most liberal Democrats in Congress lost their seats, and Republicans trumpeted their win, their largest midterm victory since 1894, as a mandate to toss out the communists and "fellow travelers."

The charge that the New Deal was communist-inspired was given credence by the ambience of the postwar era, as tensions between the United States and the Soviet Union over communist aggression in Central and Eastern Europe escalated into a protracted cold war.[51] On March

11, 1945, federal agents raided the offices of *Amerasia*, a left-wing schol-
arly journal, and found thousands of classified State Department documents. They arrested the journal's publisher and editor, a journalist, a
naval reserve officer, and two State Department employees. An FBI investigation into the incident revealed that government employees had
been passing secret documents to the Communist Party.[52] Following
the release of the FBI report, Republicans charged that communists had
infiltrated the State Department, and they demanded that federal employees be screened to weed out security risks. To alleviate concerns
that the American Communist Party was preparing the way for a military conquest, Truman appointed a temporary loyalty board that would
review federal job applicants, a measure he made permanent the following March. Congress also passed a provision permitting the secretary of state to fire without a hearing any foreign-service employee who
appeared to be a security risk. The House Appropriations Committee
then began examining files of State Department employees to identify
suspects and uncovered several employees who were affiliated with
communist organizations.[53]

Beyond Soviet espionage, public alarm over communism was heightened by revelations of the House Un-American Activities Committee,
known as HUAC. HUAC was created in the 1930s to investigate American fascism and Nazism. It took on renewed energy in 1938 under the
chairmanship of Representative Martin Dies (D-Tex.), one of a sizable
group of conservative Democrats from the rural South and West who
"resented the domination of the Democratic party by the New Deal
coalition of urban liberals, organized labor, Jews, blacks, Catholics and
Eastern European ethnics."[54] Dies, hoping to weaken the coalition by
tainting the entire enterprise as communist, used HUAC investigations
to tarnish liberal Democrats and undermine public support for New
Deal legislation.

When Republicans gained control of the House in 1946, HUAC
launched a widely publicized investigation of communist infiltration
of the movie industry. Screenwriters, actors, and producers were called
to testify about their political beliefs and organizational affiliations.
Although the hearings failed to show that Hollywood communists had
inserted anti-American propaganda into films, they were a huge success in inflaming public fears.[55]

Mostly the bailiwick of extremists and bigots, HUAC's newest member in the 80th Congress was freshman Republican Richard Nixon (R-Calif.), the only member to advance in politics. Nixon gained prominence for the role he played in HUAC's investigations of communists in government. The target of one investigation was Alger Hiss, a Harvard Law School graduate who had left a prestigious law firm to work for a New Deal agency, rising to become a high-ranking State Department official. HUAC charged Hiss with being a member of the Communist Party and passing secret documents to a communist agent. While Hiss was convicted only of perjury, the case convinced the public that communists had actually infiltrated the government, and Nixon was credited with nailing the most notorious spy in the State Department's history.[56] As fear of communist subversion gripped the entire country, state and local governments, the judiciary, universities, and labor unions all sought to purge themselves of real or imagined subversives.

Although Truman had no chance of gaining legislative support for any of his programs in the Republican-controlled 80th Congress, nonetheless in 1947 he reaffirmed his commitment to national health insurance.[57] To get the ball rolling, he appointed Oscar Ewing to head the Federal Security Agency (the precursor of the Department of Health, Education, and Welfare). Ewing, the son of a midwestern farmer turned businessman, had attended Indiana University, where he had served as president of both his junior and senior classes. After graduation, he went to Harvard Law School, where he was elected to the *Harvard Law Review*. He became a captain in the army during World War I, then was offered a position with the prestigious law firm of Hughes, Schurman, and Dwight when the war ended. Although Ewing had no special qualifications to head the Federal Security Agency, he had many influential connections. His law firm's senior partner, Charles Evans Hughes, had served as secretary of state from 1921 to 1925 and became chief justice of the Supreme Court in 1930. One of his fraternity brothers, Paul McNutt, had been elected governor of Indiana in 1932, and aspired to be a candidate for president in 1938.

When Ewing's nomination was submitted to the Senate for confirmation, a Dr. Robins, the Democratic national committeeman from Arkansas and a high-level AMA official, wrote asking his position on national health insurance. Robins suggested that the AMA might oppose Ewing's nomination if he gave the wrong answer. Ewing answered truthfully that he didn't know enough at that time to say where he stood, and the AMA allowed him to be confirmed.

Truman then ordered Ewing to mobilize "all the resources within the Federal Security Agency for vigorous and united action toward achieving public understanding of the need for a National Health Program."[58] Ewing's first step was to convene the National Health Assembly to help educate the country, "so that [he] would have the people of the country with [him]."[59] In February 1948 the assembly held a conference in Washington, D.C. More than 800 representatives from farm, business, labor, civic, and professional organizations participated. The assembly agreed on two objectives: that medical care should be financed by contributory health insurance and that everyone should have adequate medical care without regard to race, color, or creed. Notably, it did not endorse national health insurance as a way to achieve these objectives.[60]

The following September, Ewing released his own analysis, *The Nation's Health: A Report to the President*. Ewing noted that great disparities existed in services across the country. Sixty percent of Blue Cross enrollees lived in the six most affluent industrial states. In Rhode Island and Delaware, for example, more than 50 percent of the population was covered by Blue Cross, compared to only 2.2 percent in South Carolina. In Mississippi and Arkansas, Blue Cross was virtually nonexistent. With only 3 percent of the population having "anything approximating comprehensive insurance protection," it seemed clear that the private sector could not meet these needs. The only solution was to mobilize "the group purchasing power of the people" through national health insurance. National health insurance would "help build a more effective organization for providing the best in prevention, diagnosis and treatment, largely solve the individual's problem of paying for medical care . . . and create a stable and assured financial basis for health services."[61]

Ewing's emphasis on inequality in access to care posed a direct challenge to the South, where racial discrimination permeated the health care system.[62] Truman had taken the strongest stance on civil rights issues of any president to date. He had issued an executive order banning racial discrimination in the armed forces and had created the President's Committee on Civil Rights. In so doing he had asserted that it was the duty of the federal government "to act to preserve liberty when state or local authorities abridge or fail to uphold these guarantees."[63] If federal officials attempted to increase access to care through national health insurance, might they not then also confront the inequality in access posed by racial segregation?

Ewing's report also made him the enemy of Republicans, who viewed him as a partisan, liberal ideologue.[64] After all, the National Health Assembly had not endorsed national health insurance. So why was he "spending untold millions in tax money to spread its erroneous 'facts' and false conclusions—forming a government lobby to sell Compulsory Health Insurance to the people of America"? Ewing's report demonstrated the "insidious infiltration of left-wing Democrats into high places." Ewing had become a dangerous man. He had sold the president on the idea of the National Health Assembly and now had "the funds, field organization, and personal staff in Washington to put over his scheme of State Socialism."[65]

To halt Ewing, Republicans launched an aggressive probe into administration efforts to promote national health insurance. They set out to prove that members of the executive branch had ventured into the realm of legislative salesmanship and that tax dollars had been spent to influence public opinion on this communist-inspired measure. On May 28, 1947, Republican members of the obscure House Committee on Expenditures in the Executive Department formed a nominally bipartisan subcommittee of Republicans and southern Democrats to investigate workshops organized by the Social Security Board, the AFL, and the Congress of Industrial Organizations (CIO), the union of industrial workers. The workshops, they charged, were devised "to build up an artificial federally stimulated public demand . . . for enactment of legislation for compulsory health insurance."[66] Federal bureaucrats on the Social Security Board were trying

> to impose a nation-wide scheme of socialized medicine upon the United States. Wherever some form of dictatorship prevails in government, there we also find some manifestation of socialized medicine. The brand name of dictatorship makes no difference— Communism, Fascism, Nazism, Socialism—all are alike in that they enforce a system of State Medicine.

Great Britain's Labour Party had just created the National Health Service, an event that was widely publicized.[67] If the United States pursued the same course, "the medical profession and all our hospitals can be taken over by the federal government and forged into a new and gigantic health bureaucracy . . . it would only be a matter of time until Washington likewise moved into the field of education, religion, the press, the radio. Freedom soon would be in total eclipse."[68]

Subcommittee members also used the investigation to demonstrate that national health insurance was an insidious communist plot: "American communism holds this program as a cardinal point in its objectives; in some instances, known Communists and fellow travelers are at work diligently with federal funds in furtherance of the Moscow party line."[69] One of these "fellow travelers" was Ernst Boas, chairman of the Physicians' Forum, an organization of a thousand maverick physicians who supported national health insurance. Boas reportedly had been identified by HUAC as a member of eight communist-front organizations. Another was Jacob Fisher, a young Social Security Board staffer, who ostensibly was an associate of "various Communist-front and fellow traveler organizations" that were involved in "avowedly sponsoring the Moscow Party Line in the United States."[70] Hazel Huffman, an investigator for the subcommittee, went to see Maureen Mulliner, acting commissioner of the Social Security Board, regarding Fisher's alleged infractions. Mulliner asked what the charges against Fisher were: "Were they that he is a Communist?" Huffman replied that she wouldn't say that, but rather that he was "communistic."[71] Fisher's crime? He had published a report on socialized medicine in New Zealand in the *Social Security Bulletin*. The Social Security Board immediately called off a scheduled trip by Fisher and ordered an FBI investigation into the matter. Fisher was later cleared of any communist affiliation.

When the hearings ended, the subcommittee voted to turn the evidence over to the FBI for prosecution, but since no crime had been uncovered, no action was taken.[72] The hearings had accomplished their objective. National health insurance had been discredited as part of a communist plot to spread socialized medicine, threaten liberty, and undermine the democratic way of life. National health insurance proponents had been smeared as agents of this plot, either communists themselves or "fellow travelers." As Falk recalled,

> There were some members of Congress who tried to make a big shindig out of an attempt to show that we were behind these workshops and the inclusion of some very leftish people in them. We

were not responsible. . . . That was a phony performance from beginning to end. . . . It was a smear business, that's all.[73]

Republicans also called hearings to promote alternative health insurance proposals. Ohio senator Robert Taft, a dour, unbending man devoid of personal charm, was the leader of the conservative wing of the Republican Party. A complex man who aspired to capture his party's presidential nomination in the 1948 elections, Taft was dead set against government intervention on most issues, yet he was willing to support a federal housing program and federal funding for hospital construction. As a result of the Republican gains in 1946, Taft now chaired the Senate Labor and Public Welfare Committee, which he used as a forum to convince the public of the dangers of national health insurance and to promote his alternative plan for federal aid to the states for medical care for the poor. During committee hearings, Taft called 29 friendly witnesses but only a single opposition witness, a representative of the International Workers Order, a well-known communist organization. The hearings became an inquisition into "socialized medicine."[74] Witnesses testified that Taft's proposal would allow states to develop their own programs "under minimum federal safeguards," while the Truman plan would "socialize the practice of medicine in the United States" and "abolish free enterprise in the medical field."[75] Taft also used the threat of national health insurance to court physicians, his natural political allies. In an address to the Wayne County Medical Society, Taft warned his audience that the Truman plan would be the first step toward a British-type national health service.[76]

In the months preceding the 1948 presidential election, Truman's popularity hit an all-time low, and polls predicted his certain defeat. His own party was splintered into warring factions, with one contingent supporting former vice president Henry Wallace and his Progressive Party candidacy and another faction supporting Senator Strom Thurmond (D-S.C.) and his States' Rights Party. Thurmond had formed the States' Rights Party after southern delegates walked out of the 1948 Democratic National Convention when a civil rights plank was included in the party platform. Black voters rewarded Truman's support for civil rights by providing the swing votes in key northern states.[77] Truman lost four southern states but won the presidency, and the Democrats regained control of both houses of Congress.

During the election Truman had campaigned for national health insurance. Public interest was at its peak. Now was the time to act. As AFL official Nelson Cruikshank explained, "The high tide of the pressure was in '48 right after the dramatic victory of Truman."[78] Three months after his inauguration, a new national health insurance bill (S. 1679) was introduced. The bill included a ban on racial discrimination in health care but made a concession to the South. Southern states would be allowed to provide "separate facilities for persons of different race or color" as long as they were of "equal" quality to white facilities.[79]

That provision did not reassure southern Democrats, who in the 1948 Democratic victory had regained the control of the key congressional committees through which all social welfare legislation had to pass.[80] If national health insurance succeeded, it would be without the support of the South. Instead, Alabama senator Lister Hill introduced his own bill for federal assistance to the states to subsidize Blue Cross coverage for low-income people.[81] The program would be administered by state health departments, which in most instances were "deeply influenced by the state medical societies."[82]

(Truman versus the Medical Lobby) *This is an example*
socialism v capitalism *for Theme #1*

As the Truman administration geared up to promote national health insurance, the AMA launched the National Education Campaign to prevent its implementation and to encourage the spread of private health insurance. Oscar Ewing, the Federal Security Administration chief, was the first target.

At the start of the National Education Campaign, the AMA assessed each member $25, then hired the public relations firm of Whitaker and Baxter. A husband-and-wife team, Clem Whitaker and Leone Baxter had worked for the California Medical Association to help kill a state health insurance bill promoted by Governor Earl Warren. In the California battle, they had sponsored radio broadcasts criticizing the Warren proposal, developed a newspaper distribution network that provided local papers with free editorials, and gathered dirt on health experts who supported Warren's plan.[83]

Whitaker and Baxter now applied the tactics they had honed in California to the national political scene. A massive amount of campaign literature was produced. Posters, pamphlets, leaflets, form resolutions, speeches, cartoons, and publicity materials for state medical societies all had one goal: "to keep public opinion hostile to national health insurance."[84] As Whitaker explained to a reporter:

> All you have to do is give it a bad name, and have a Devil. America's opposed to socialism so we're going to name national health insurance "socialized medicine." And we've got to have a devil. We first thought of making President Truman the devil, but he's too popular. But this man Ewing is a perfect Devil and we're going to give him the works.[85]

Addressing the AMA convention in Atlanta in 1949, Whitaker sought to motivate his audience with a call for action:

> This fight that American medicine is waging is a fundamental struggle against government domination. . . . The trend toward State-ism in America has become unmistakable . . . it is only a short step from the "Welfare State" to the "Total State," which taxes the wage earner into government enslavement, which stamps out incentive and soon crushes individual liberty.[86]

AMA national headquarters told state medical societies to organize every county society "into a hard-driving campaign organization" with battle orders going out by "letter, telegraph and telephone." State organizations were given form speeches to "get laymen for medicine in this fight." They were instructed to approach local newspapers to get the "real facts" before the editors. Every newspaper in the country should be called on, "preferably by a doctor who knows the editor and has his confidence." The book *The Road Ahead*, describing how Great Britain's national health service was leading toward socialism, was widely disseminated.[87] A special assistant was hired to coordinate publicity with the AMA's Department of Press Relations. Doctors received copies of the pamphlet *The Voluntary Way Is the American Way* to place in their reception rooms and colored posters with the caption "The Doctor: Keep Politics Out of This Picture" to display in their offices. Auxiliaries of physicians' wives organized the National Women's Campaign to distribute literature, win endorsements from women's clubs, and help build a national speakers bureau for community events.

Every venue promoted the message that national health insurance was part of a communist plot to destroy freedom. Editorials in the *Journal of the American Medical Association*, articles, and pamphlets all decried the threat to liberty. National health insurance would "regiment doctors and patients alike under a vast bureaucracy," doubling or tripling the cost of medical care.[88] The administration of such a "colossal plan from Washington" would create hundreds of new federal employees to operate the system, handle paperwork, check on physicians, and investigate "real or imaginary infringements" of federal, state, and local regulations. It would also require hundreds of regulations.[89] Patients would surrender liberty and receive in return "low-grade assembly line medicine."[90] There would be long lines in doctor's offices, and the close doctor-patient relationship would be destroyed.[91]

Any physician who deviated from the AMA line chanced being expelled from membership and thus risked losing hospital appointments and referrals. Dr. Caldwell Esselstyn ran the Rip Van Winkle Clinic in rural Hudson, New York. One of the small group of physicians who publicly supported national health insurance, he fully understood the potential costs:

> If anybody, like a surgeon whose ability to support his family depends entirely on the referrals that he gets from the other physicians in the county medical society, this lifeblood can be shut off very effectively by physicians who . . . will find a reason never to refer a patient to you, simply because you don't follow the party line. And this goes for your social life in the community where you're really ostracized by the other people in your medical profession, and it also goes for the way your kids are handled in school. . . . For somebody who depends on referrals, the economic sanctions that can be lowered by organized medicine are tremendous.[92]

The AMA also initiated an "all-out drive to provide the American people with voluntary health insurance coverage."[93] Doctors were advised to "encourage patients to get good, sound voluntary insurance for their own protection and the protection of their families."[94] A group of physicians headed by the director of the Michigan Medical Service Plan recommended that every state adopt a voluntary, nonprofit health insurance program organized like Blue Cross.[95] The group asked the AMA to finance the necessary organizational work in the states: "If the voluntary machinery can be put in motion simultaneously in all states and the plan can be given publicity in the press, in magazines, on the air and by speakers before civic and other groups, . . . [national health insurance] will be effectively blocked." Private insurance already covered more than 55 million people, either through commercial insurance plans or through "the great Blue Cross Hospital System." It was "one of the most rapid and spectacular economic developments in our time."[96] In just the past two years, more than 15 million additional people had been covered.[97]

To enlist the support of other organizations, the AMA invited local Chamber of Commerce chapters, real estate boards, Farm Bureaus, American Legion chapters, women's clubs, Parent-Teacher Associations, and insurance companies to meet with its leaders "with a view to gaining their support and having additional outlets for informative materials. . . . These organizations could offer strong opposition to the nationalization of medicine and could aid in promoting voluntary insurance."[98] Blue Cross, the Insurance Economic Society, and the Chamber of Commerce all took a public position opposing national health insurance and endorsing private insurance. Edward O'Connor, managing director of the Insurance Economics Society, testified that private insurers were "writing a large volume of disability, hospital and medical care insurance." A federal program that intervened in the private market would be "un-American."[99] Insurance industry executive Ray Murphy explained:

> In contrast to the Federal compulsory plan, voluntary insurance plans are diverse in origin and sponsorship. They are dynamic, experimental, and progressive. The proposed Federal Government model is monopolistic as well as compulsory. The principle of competitive selection between plans is discarded and voluntary choice is abolished.[100]

(The U.S. Chamber of Commerce released its own pamphlet, *You and Socialized Medicine*, charging that "top administrators of the Federal Security Agency have a plan for socialized medicine in America."[101])To those who see in the "compulsory insurance program of the Democrat planners another step toward further state socialism and the totalitarian welfare state prevailing in foreign lands, there is an alternative in keeping with the freedom-loving policies of a free nation"—voluntary health insurance for the majority of Americans coupled with federal aid to the states for medical care for the poor.[102] Chamber publications told employers they should explore the possibilities of group insurance plans to help their employees pay their health care costs.[103] After all, "in 1947 the American people [had] spent $10 billion for liquor, $4 billion for tobacco and over $2 billion more for cosmetic items."[104] If they cut down on unnecessary purchases, they could easily pay for their own health care.

The pharmaceutical and drug manufacturers were initially neutral, but Ig Falk, an excellent technician but a poor judge of politics, made a tactical error by insisting on including a provision that would allow the government to set drug prices. That stirred up the entire pharmaceutical industry against the bill.[105]

The American Hospital Association was less hostile to the Truman plan, but hospital administrators could ill afford to buck the AMA. As Dr. Michael Davis, a liberal physician who worked for national health insurance, explained:

> The hospital administrators are both the bosses and the servants of the medical staff of the hospital . . . their medical staffs derive their income from the private practice of medicine. . . . Well, a hospital administrator who gets the antagonism of his medical staff because he's an advocate of socialized medicine, will generally speaking, not carry the job in that hospital very long. The board of trustees, who has the ultimate control, will get rid of him if he's unpopular with the medical staff.[106]

The AMA campaign brought national health insurance to a standstill. As Ewing admitted:

> Our proposed legislation was getting nowhere with the Congress. Many of our representatives and Senators whom we thought would go along with us, wouldn't. . . . You would talk to a Congressman or Senator and so often he would say, "You have no idea what political influence a doctor has in his local community, and I don't want to get them stirred up against me."[107]

In 1945 75 percent of Americans supported national health insurance; by 1949 only 21 percent favored President Truman's plan.[108] A frustrated Truman wrote to his old friend Ben Turoff, "I can't understand

By the end of the 1940s the public was increasingly critical of the AMA for abusing physicians' moral authority as healers. Library of Congress, Prints and Photographs Divisions, © *St. Louis Post Dispatch*, 1962

the rabid approach of the American Medical Association—they have distorted and misrepresented the whole program so that it will be necessary for me to go out and tell the people just exactly what we are asking for."[109]

During the campaign the AMA drew heavily upon physicians' cultural authority as experts on health issues. By the end of the decade, the abuse of this authority for such blatantly selfish ends made the public increasingly critical of the AMA, perceiving it as a negative organization that was against everything. The AMA had opposed aid to medical schools on the grounds that federal aid would lead to federal control.[110] The AMA had also helped kill disability insurance and had blocked measures to provide school health programs and medical care to veterans' dependents. People were especially outraged when the AMA paid the Reverend Dan Gilbert $3,000 to mail Protestant clergymen a letter calling national health insurance "this monster of anti-Christ."[111] As one critic complained:

> A lot of us laymen are fed to the teeth with the AMA's methods.
> With its persistently negative approach to everything. With its
> unvarying misrepresentation of the efforts other countries are
> making to solve the problem. With its "crusade" and its "battle"
> and its vilification of the government, the public, and its own
> members who speak out.[112]

Some dissident physicians began to criticize the AMA openly. Dr. Esselstyn called the AMA "an inbred group of people who become wrapped up in medical politics and who really become pretty near-sighted."[113] Dr. Bernard Meyer testified before the Senate that "character assassination, intimidation, fear of reprisal, etc. discourage a frank repudiation of many society-sponsored policies." At the annual meeting of the New York Medical Society, 38 percent of physicians attending voted for the candidates who supported national health insurance.[114] Hospital administrators also began to have concerns about their public image as close associates of physicians. One administrator wrote, "Some doctors and their friends do question whether it is right to use the county medical society . . . for political purposes and whether the sacred patient-physician relationship should be subverted to political ends."[115]

Democratic supporters of national health insurance tried to capitalize on public suspicion of the AMA. Representative John Dingell (D-Mich.)

blasted the AMA lobby, calling its anti-health-insurance campaign "one of the most cold-blooded lobbying operations in American history." Oscar Ewing awarded the doctors' lobby first prize among business lobbies for spending $353,990 during the first nine months of 1948.[116] Seeking to take advantage of this split, Senator Pepper invited AHA officers to come to Washington to discuss the issues. Although many hospital administrators said privately that a compromise might be possible, their close ties to physicians prevented them from publicly repudiating the AMA. The hospitals were "not unsympathetic to national health insurance," but they had been "blackmailed into supporting the position of the AMA. . . . [If] the medical profession was opposed to a thing, they felt that it was smart for them to be opposed."[117]

When Republicans held a rally to define their campaign themes for the 1950 congressional elections, they focused on cultivating physicians' fears of national health insurance. Physicians were warned that if Democrats picked up seats in the House and Senate, they would capture the 82nd Congress and "socialize our medical profession and imprison it under the iron rule of a Federal bureaucracy."[118] These arguments were given credence by a series of events that seemed to demonstrate that the communists were indeed intent on taking over the world. In November 1949 the Soviet Union established a communist government in occupied Germany. Then in the final months of the year the nationalist government in China collapsed and the entire Chinese mainland came under the control of communists.[119] A few months later, at a Lincoln's birthday dinner in Wheeling, West Virginia, Joseph McCarthy, an undistinguished first-term senator from Wisconsin, claimed to have a list of 205 Communist Party members working in the State Department.[120]

In the 1950 election physicians provided crucial support for Republicans and targeted for defeat Democrats who had supported national health insurance. In Pennsylvania's 26th District a "Healing Arts" committee organized against the Democratic candidate who had endorsed Truman's plan in 1948. Physicians mailed nearly 200,000 personal letters to their patients, explaining that there were "evil forces creeping into this country" and asking them to vote for Republican candidates.[121] They even posted notices in waiting rooms asking, "Will you please do me a favor by going to the polls on September 13, 1949 and voting for John P. Saylor? If you need transportation on that day, please notify me at once."[122] AMA women's auxiliaries conducted house-to-house calls and ran telephone banks. On Election Day spot radio announcements were made every hour on the hour. In Wisconsin doctors started a Physicians for Freedom campaign to defeat Representative Andrew Biemiller (D-Wis.), a House sponsor of national health insurance. Utah doctors worked against Biemiller's Senate Cosponsor, Elbert Thomas (D-Utah).[123]

In Florida, physicians mobilized to defeat Claude Pepper. A prominent urologist wrote his colleagues asking for money and endorsing Pepper's opponent, George Smathers. He wrote, "We physicians in Florida have a terrific fight on our hands to defeat Senator Claude Pepper, the outstanding advocate of 'socialized medicine' and the 'welfare state' in America. . . . In eliminating Pepper from Congress, the first great battle against Socialism in America will have been won."[124] Another doctor was so agitated that he donated a month's income to the race.[125] When Smathers visited any county, he just called a prominent doctor, "and that doctor would have all the prominent doctors of the city and their wives and several of the most important businessmen there."[126] As Pepper recalled:

> The doctors in Florida agreed that the first three minutes of every consultation with every patient would be devoted to attacking socialized medicine and Claude Pepper. They were so bitter that their wives took to the streets and highways. They tried to paint me as a monster of some sort.[127]

Physicians also ran half-page ads of a photo showing Senator Pepper with the African American singer Paul Robeson, who was a member of the Communist Party. In the primary, six liberal Democratic senators were defeated, including Pepper. In Pepper's view, the single most influential factor in his defeat was the doctors' opposition.[128] But he also had a powerful enemy in Edward Ball, a wealthy businessman who despised Pepper for his support of minimum-wage and tax legislation. Ball organized a group of Florida businessmen who raised millions of dollars to defeat Pepper. They collected every photo of Pepper with African Americans, monitored his "every statement on civil rights" and on the need for the United States to be more tolerant of the Soviet Union, and charged that northern labor bosses were "paying ten to twenty dollars to blacks to register" and vote for him. Pepper later admitted, "I never knew what hit me."[129]

In 1950 Ewing attempted to develop a scaled-down plan that would just cover hospital bills, convinced that the AMA would not object if physicians' services were excluded. In Falk's view, that was a naive tactic that would not succeed:

> The AMA said, "Oh, that's just the camel's nose, and it's a hell of a big nose, getting under the tent. Sure if you get hospital benefits, how long will it be before you tack on medical benefits?" And whenever anybody asked that question, we said: "no comment." Because that was the intent.[130]

Truman did not run for reelection in 1952, and the Republican Party chose General Dwight D. Eisenhower, the former World War II supreme Allied commander, as its candidate. Eisenhower liked to describe himself as a middle-of-the-roader, liberal on social issues but fiscally conservative. He had little sympathy for either Senator Joseph McCarthy's Red-baiting tactics or the conservative old-guard wing of his own party. In the months leading up to the election, the AMA and the insurance industry continued their campaign against national health insurance proponents. *Medical Economics*, a drug trade publication sent to all doctors, declared:

> A number of professions and industries are ready to band together in a massive election-year campaign against all forms of state socialism. Their target will be the national candidates who lean towards schemes like compulsory health insurance. Their techniques will be those exploited so successfully by the medical profession last year.[131]

Eisenhower, who firmly believed that social needs could best be met by the private sector, denounced national health insurance during the campaign as a "vast and unfair government system" that would foreclose future opportunities for private insurers to show they could deal with the problem.[132] He won the election, becoming the first Republican president after two decades of Democratic rule, and his victory was widely interpreted as a referendum against national health insurance. During the eight subsequent years of Republican administration, national health insurance disappeared from the political agenda. For Truman it was his most "bitter disappointment," the defeat that troubled him most "in a personal way."[133]

A Subsidy for Insurers

Throughout his term President Eisenhower remained a foe of national health insurance. In 1954 he consolidated three departments into a new Department of Health, Education, and Welfare (HEW) and charged HEW to devise a private solution to counter mounting pressure in Congress for a program to ease the burden of individual medical costs.[134] Alan Pond, a special assistant at HEW, recalled: "There was a general feeling that unless there was substantial stimulation of the private insurance business . . . there would not be the kind of universal coverage which would be necessary if some form of federal insurance wasn't to come into being."[135] The objective was clear: "promote the private sector in the health insurance business, be sure it keeps moving."

Private insurance had rapidly expanded from covering just 22 percent of Americans in 1946 to over 50 percent by 1952, but its dramatic growth also starkly illuminated its flaws.[136] Although commercial insurance companies had become experienced at marketing group policies and estimating actuarially sound group premiums, they had quickly learned that it was unprofitable to insure high-risk individuals. No insurance company wanted to cover disabled people or people with chronic health problems such as diabetes, arthritis, or heart disease, and they especially did not want to cover the elderly, who might both be disabled and have numerous chronic conditions. The burden of covering these individuals fell to Blue Cross, with its community-rated plans and communitywide mission.

So far the commercial insurers had moved "timidly and slowly in the field of health insurance."[137] The dilemma was how to devise a workable plan that they would not oppose.[138] According to Pond:

> In the Republican party the executives of corporations large and small have played an important role. This was particularly true of the health insurance business. Many of the executives in the health insurance business were very active Republicans. They were convinced . . . that there was no need for a tax supported health insurance scheme for any part of the population except for the very poor.[139]

A Blue Cross administrator from Philadelphia, panicky about increasing demands on Blue Cross to insure the sick and the elderly, concocted a "reinsurance" scheme. Under reinsurance, private companies would cover basic health expenses and the government would pick up the catastrophic costs. If insurers had protection against catastrophic losses, they would be able to experiment with new forms of coverage for these groups.[140]

Eisenhower seized upon reinsurance as a way to derail national health insurance and encourage the development of private plans. Fearing that "the top brass" had not been involved "in any concerted way," he invited the presidents of the 15 largest insurance companies to a White House luncheon to discuss his reinsurance plan and persuade them that he had no interest in becoming involved in private insurance or in regulating the industry. He explained that reinsurance could "accelerate the development of private health insurance . . . and encourage companies to be venturesome and to step forward in untried areas." It was "a hundred per cent endorsement of the principle of private insurance."[141] But the executives were unconvinced. The reinsurance formula required the government to calculate insurers' losses. That meant federal scrutiny of company records, which involved "getting our noses into their accounts." Worse, reinsurance might establish a precedent for federal regulation of the industry, thus undermining the sacred principle of the insurance industry: keep regulation at the state level.[142] Although Eisenhower made a nationally televised plea for the reinsurance proposal and appeared personally before the National Association of Insurance Commissioners to assure them that he had no desire to regulate their products, his efforts were to no avail.

The AMA, ever watchful of government intervention, immediately denounced reinsurance as socialism and lobbied against it in Congress. According to another HEW official, the AMA took the "simplistic and doctrinaire position" that it would be the first step toward a compulsory government program. "As to how it would possibly affect a doctor in and of itself, they couldn't really answer and that wasn't their pitch." Instead they reiterated insurers' arguments that the plan was unworkable, "a hopeless morass."[143] HEW officials tried to persuade the president of the AMA, "a wiry little doctor of stern and unmoving features," that he was wrong on the merits, but "he was unmoved."[144] After meeting with some AMA representatives, they came away feeling the doctors were "not very bright and not particularly helpful and certainly not very forward-looking."[145] Within the Eisenhower administration, the general attitude toward the AMA was one of contempt:

> The AMA presidents all were people who had come up through their hierarchy of committeeships and officerships and who were in a sense captives of the staff. They couldn't really have an independent thought . . . by the process by which they were selected there was almost a weeding out of leadership rather than the contrary.[146]

The reinsurance bill was defeated in the Senate by one vote. Following the defeat, Eisenhower bitterly complained that the AMA hierarchy was "just plain stupid . . . a little group of reactionary men dead set against any change."[147]

Conclusion

For the first half of the twentieth century, physicians drew upon their cultural authority as healers to revive the Red scare of the 1910s and define proposals for national health insurance as socialist-inspired. The most respected and highly paid professional group in the country, physicians were able to insert their parochial interests into the political process to preserve their control over the mechanisms for financing health care through the organizational clout of the AMA. As doctors abused their healing power for self-serving ends, political leaders and ordinary citizens came to believe that they had overstepped professional boundaries. Instead of being viewed as worthy of veneration, they were increasingly perceived as an interest group like any other, self-protective, insular, and negative. Thus they achieved their political objectives but paid a heavy price.

Ironically, what allowed physicians to win these battles was the fact that they had powerful allies among employers and insurers in the private sector and among conservative Republicans and southern Democrats in Congress. As long as physicians' interests coincided with these other stakeholders, they could be assured of success. That coalition began to disintegrate in the 1950s. As the private health insurance system expanded rapidly with large corporations becoming the main financiers of health insurance for the able-bodied, full-time members of the labor force, an unfilled need remained. Who would insure the remainder, the vulnerable individuals that private insurance companies refused to cover—poor single mothers and their children, elderly men and women, people with disabilities? Surprisingly, the labor movement reversed course and led the way for disability benefits and health insurance for the aged, trumping physicians' dominance in health policy debates.

two

Organized Labor's Health Benefits

On April 1, 1946, John L. Lewis, the fiery president of the United Mine Workers, called his miners out of the coal pits. A powerful figure with his massive head, black hair, and bushy eyebrows, Lewis refused to settle the strike until the mine owners met his demand for a desperately needed health and welfare fund.[1] The coal miners, with their black sputum, sunken chests, and emaciated torsos, were in the poorest condition of all the workers. Miners had the highest rates of tuberculosis, pneumonia, and black lung disease.[2] Over the course of the 35 years from 1910 to 1945, more than 2 million men had been mangled in the mines, and 68,842 had been killed.[3] As Lewis pleaded:

> When a man is killed or taken away, or his back is broken or his flesh is burned from his bones, we have no replacements in the mines. . . . Why not remove from their minds the horror that tomorrow they may be killed by the fall of a hanging rock or by the terrible ravages of a burning mine explosion that tears through the galleries of the mines?[4]

Health and welfare benefits would guarantee that injured miners would receive medical care and provide them and their families with a source of income if they were injured or killed.

As the strike wore on, it began to exact its toll on the economy. The railroads laid off 51,000 workers, Ford Motor Company began to shut down operations, and New Jersey declared a state of emergency.[5] With a national crisis looming, Lewis declared a two-week truce but then resumed the strike when the truce date came and went with no settlement. Finally, on May 29, the 59-day strike was settled when mine owners agreed to contribute 10 cents for each ton of coal to set up a health and welfare fund. The fund would provide free medical care for miners and their families, hospital care with free choice of a physician, cash benefits for disabled miners, and survivors' benefits for their widows.[6] Moreover, the fund would not be solely controlled by the owners but would be run by a trusteeship that included a union representative.[7]

The United Mine Workers set a precedent that other unions quickly followed. From 1940 to 1966 the number of people with insurance against the costs of medical care increased from 6 million to more than 75 million, with most of the growth occurring through trade union action.[8] As Beth Stevens noted, "The political pressure exerted by the American labor movement was . . . a demand for a private alternative to state-run welfare programs."[9] Why did the American trade unions pursue private benefits instead of a federal program? One answer is that organized labor was averse to political action, preferring to improve the lot of the working class through collective bargaining agreements. As George Meany, secretary-treasurer of the AFL in the late 1940s, explained, "We certainly don't look to the political structure for our wages and working conditions: we get them our way."[10] Another answer is simple political expediency. Although the AFL supported Truman's plan, when national health insurance appeared to be a lost cause, the unions focused on issues where they had a greater chance of success. But neither pessimism nor a preference for collective bargaining alone can explain why the trade unions fought for private health insurance. The answer lies in the labor-management struggles of the postwar era, when the trade unions, confronted by hostile business and conservative forces that sought to sharply curb their broader ambitions, came to view collectively bargained health benefits as the best weapon for recruiting and retaining members.

The Development of Private Health Benefits

The Second World War ended the debilitating depression that had gripped the nation in the 1930s. Deflation, economic sluggishness, and unemployment vanished in the boom created by wartime industrial expansion. The armed forces drew more than 15 million men and women out of the civilian labor force, creating a serious labor shortage.[11] Tightening labor markets meant higher wages but also inflation, overwork, and work speedups. Although workers were earning higher wages, their gains were eroded by rising prices. Simmering discontent among workers erupted in a wave of strikes that threatened wartime production. Congress repeatedly attempted to quell the strikes with a series of bills restricting unions and outlawing strikes. Once the United States officially entered the war in November 1941, the unions made a no-strike pledge for the war's duration, fearing they would appear unpatriotic if their action threatened production. In return for their cooperation, President Roosevelt created the National War Labor Board to mediate settlements in labor disputes and set policy regarding the scope of collective bargaining.[12]

Two wartime rulings accelerated the growth of private health plans. The first was the Revenue Act of 1942, which to prevent wartime profiteering levied an excess-profits tax on corporate earnings. The tax of 80 to 90 percent applied to any corporate profits that were higher than prewar levels. However, employer contributions to group pension and health insurance plans were excluded from the calculation of profits, because they were considered a tax-deductible business expense. This ruling gave corporations an incentive to reduce excess profits by depositing them in trust funds for fringe benefits.[13]

The second important ruling was a 1943 decision by the National War Labor Board that employer contributions to employee benefit plans would not be counted as wages. The trade unions had been unable to demand higher wages because they were bound by their no-strike pledge. The board's decision gave them the opportunity to negotiate health and pension benefits in their collective bargaining agreements as a substitute for wage increases.[14] Some commercial insurers also recognized the potential of the National War Labor Board ruling and began aggressively marketing group health insurance policies directly to employers.[15] Employers viewed fringe benefits as a way to build a company identity among their employees, separate from the unions' growth.[16]

Together these rulings opened the floodgates to health insurance and pension programs. In nonunionized firms employers purchased generous health insurance packages from commercial insurers, hoping to ward off unionization. In unionized firms employers began offering health benefits, without union input, to convince workers they had no need to join the union. The major business groups encouraged these activities. The Chamber of Commerce urged employers to move quickly to install voluntary health insurance plans. The National Association of Manufacturers (NAM) agreed that "management should not surrender its initiative in this matter to the union."[17] Once the plans were installed, the field of battle shifted to new turf: which party would control these funds? Could employers run the plans unilaterally or would the union participate in decisions about terms and conditions?

The trade unions emerged out of the war in a position of strength. By 1946 nearly one-third of American workers belonged to unions, a proportion equal to that in many European countries.[18] But when President Truman turned to the trade unions in his fight for national health insurance, he received at best lukewarm support. Lewis had initially promised Truman the backing of the United Mine Workers on this issue, but once the miners had won their own health benefits, he withdrew his support.[19] The United Auto Workers had never been an unwavering advocate of national health insurance. When UAW official Clayton Fountain spoke at a workshop organized by the Social Security Board to promote national health insurance, he decried "the dangers of the bureaucratic movement" and declared that "under such a plan one would be considerably kicked about."[20] A few months later, the UAW negotiated its own health care plan with General Motors, the first in the mass production industries. The CIO had been actively involved in writing the Wagner-Murray-Dingell bill for national health insurance in 1942. But once the Republicans won control of Congress in the 1946 elections, the CIO passed an official resolution calling for "Security Through Bargaining." The union would now work to secure health benefits in collective bargaining contracts.[21]

The newly elected Republicans of the 80th Congress, eager to reverse the pro-labor New Deal policies, introduced 65 bills pertaining to unions or collective bargaining. These efforts culminated in the Taft-Hartley Act in 1947. Taft-Hartley rescinded many of the rights unions had won during the 1930s. It prohibited secondary boycotts, permitted states to ban the closed shop (which had made it easier for unions to carve out bargaining units by forcing all covered employees to be union members), and imposed severe penalties for staging unauthorized strikes. A separate clause banned communist members.[22] In the wake of Taft-Hartley, the CIO expelled 11 communist-controlled unions, triggering internecine warfare among the large industrial unions and dramatically narrowing the scope of political debate within the labor movement.[23]

Although Taft-Hartley outlawed independent, union-run welfare funds through a provision that employers had to share equally in the administration of any pension or health plan, it had left unresolved the issue of whether employers had to bargain over fringe benefits.[24] In 1948 the National Labor Relations Board ruled that fringe benefits *were* subject to collective bargaining, a decision that was upheld by the Supreme Court. Then in 1949 the Wage Stabilization Board, whose job was to keep inflation from wage increases under control, determined that fringe benefits were not inflationary. With many options for increasing membership closed off, union leaders made bargaining for fringe benefits a top priority. Collectively bargained benefits obtained on union terms were viewed by labor leaders as the "virtual equivalent of a closed shop."[25] Fringe benefits became organized labor's key strategy for recruiting and retaining members. Over half of strikes in 1949 and 70 percent in 1950 were over this issue.[26]

Between 1946 and 1957 the number of workers covered by negotiated health insurance plans rose from 1 million to 12 million, plus an additional 20 million dependents. Close to 95 percent of industrial workers represented by the CIO were covered, compared to only 20 percent of skilled craft workers affiliated with the AFL.[27] As for national health insurance, most industrial unionists now "gave [it] only lip service." Private health insurance "had taken the heat off."[28]

The expansion of private health benefits divided the working class into those who had health insurance and those who did not, and it transformed the way organized labor mobilized politically. Instead of requiring leaders who could inspire the troops to stand by the barricades, the labor movement needed leaders who could master complex financial instruments.[29] The next battle would be won by policy experts with calculators, not charismatic militants who could issue a call to arms.

Winning Disability Insurance

In 1955 the trade unions shifted strategy. Since 1938 the union movement had been embroiled in internecine warfare over goals and the means to achieve them. The CIO hoped to build on wartime economic measures to craft a corporatist state with unions, employers, and government jointly negotiating broad economic policy. The AFL opposed any corporatist arrangement and demanded a return to free collective bargaining unfettered by federal regulations.[30] In 1952 new leaders who were unburdened by the feuds of the past took the helm of the two organizations. George Meany, a burly Irishman from the Bronx who had begun his career as a business agent for the plumbers' union, was elected AFL president, and Walter Reuther, the redheaded son of German immigrants, was elected president of the CIO. Within 48 hours of his election Reuther called Meany to plan a reunion of the two unions, and in 1955 the warring factions of the labor movement merged into a single organization.[31] They had been fighting each other for nearly two decades. Now it was time to set an agenda to demonstrate what a unified labor movement could achieve.

There were two gaping holes in the welfare state: disability insurance and health insurance for the retired. These were issues where the trade unions could take the lead. The AFL-CIO created a new Social Security Committee and appointed Nelson Cruikshank to serve as director. Cruikshank, a former minister, was known for his ironic sense of humor and his pragmatic approach to union concerns. He was always able to temper his "fervor for social action with a tolerance for the morally ambiguous ways in which Washington worked."[32] The assistant director was Katherine Ellickson, a Vassar graduate who had taught high school in New York city for two years and then became interested in labor issues. She was one of the first employees of the CIO in 1935 and then worked for the Social Security Board until 1940. After taking two years off to have her two children, she returned to the CIO in 1942 and helped prepare the Wagner-Murray-Dingell bill for national health insurance, even though the chances of success were low:

> I don't think we ever thought we had any chance of getting it through in the near future. I think this is something that we were for, just as we were for other things . . . but this didn't mean that we thought we were really going to get it.[33]

Also on board as head of the legislative department was former Congressman Andrew Biemiller (D-Wis.), the labor activist who had lost the 1950 election for supporting national health insurance.

The AFL-CIO decided to tackle the disability issue first. Disability benefits were a union concern because disabled workers had no government benefits until they became eligible for Social Security at age 65. That placed the burden of their support on the unions. Some unions negotiated benefits for disabled members in their collective bargaining agreements but in return had to make concessions on wage increases for working members. Thus the incentive to shift this cost to the government was intense.

In 1956 the AFL-CIO made the fight for disability insurance "a kind of wedding ceremony."[34] Cruikshank and Ellickson wrote a bill to expand Social Security to include disabled workers and immediately won support in the House of Representatives. The bill got hung up in the Senate Finance Committee, however, when the AMA protested "the potential involvement of the federal government in relationships with physicians and determinations of disability."[35] Even though disability benefits involved no medical care, the AMA feared any measure that would allow the government to extend its reach. When the Advisory Council on Social Security had recommended disability benefits in its 1947 report, the AMA had fought it "tooth and nail" in the press and in the halls of Congress.[36] Hoping to appease the AMA, Cruikshank promised that federal officials would set no fee schedules for physicians' examinations of applicants but would accept whatever the state rehabilitation agencies established as the going rate.[37] That failed to dampen AMA opposition. According to Ig Falk, they thought, "Oh, this is just a camel getting his nose under the tent and therefore they opposed it . . . because the next thing you'd have a broader disability program and the next thing you'll be giving medical care to the disabled."[38]

The deadlock in the Finance Committee meant that there would be a fight on the Senate floor. In a "flash of genius," reformers agreed to allow state agencies to administer the program, the formula favored by southerners, and to limit disability insurance to workers age 50 or older, as a concession to the insurance industry.[39] That provision appeased commercial insurers, who had initially opposed disability insurance for fear it would be the first step toward socializing the entire industry. As Edward O'Connor, managing director of the Insurance Economic Society, warned physicians, "If we should be regimented first with compulsory disability compensation, government compulsory medical care will follow. . . . What the Government shall subsidize, it shall control."[40]

Once benefits were limited to older workers, insurers agreed not to lobby against the bill.

To break the deadlock, Cruikshank and Biemiller approached Senator Walter George (D-Ga.), the Finance Committee chairman, who was planning to retire when his term ended. George, one of the southern politicians Roosevelt had tried to purge in the 1938 election, had been saved when the local craft unions held a mass rally on his behalf. That gave the unions special access to him. Cruikshank convinced him that "the disability bill would be the George bill, his valedictory. . . . This would be his last bill." He knew that George's "prestige was so great that . . . if we got him to support us, . . . we could get a majority of the Senate that would support it." Once Senator George agreed to vote for the measure, "immediately, when he attached his name to it, there were six Senators, all from the South."[41] Southern Democrats who had sided with Republicans against national health insurance voted for disability insurance because it would be locally administered and would thus pose no threat to racial practices. The day the vote was scheduled, President Eisenhower sent Vice President Nixon to preside over the Senate in case of a tie vote. The measure carried by a vote of 47 to 45. One more nay vote and Nixon would have been able to break the tie.[42] Conceding defeat, Eisenhower signed the bill into law.

The AMA had depended on southern Democrats to vote against any measure that would affect the medical system but were caught off guard by the disability bill. In the 1956 election campaign the AMA attempted to retaliate against politicians who had voted for disability insurance and defeated incumbent Senator Earl Clements (D-Ky.).[43] The experience conveyed a powerful message, however, by demonstrating that the AMA could be defeated when confronted with a rival with equal organizational capacity and greater political skill. The key to success was to pick off AMA allies with concessions that responded to their concerns.

Insuring Retirees

Health insurance for the aged was next on the AFL-CIO agenda. The idea of government-financed health care for this group had first been broached eight years earlier by Oscar Ewing, Truman's point man for national health insurance, who had been "casting around for something that we might save out of the defeat."[44] One night when Ewing was having cocktails at the home of his longtime friend William Randolph Hearst, the wealthy and influential newspaper publisher, Hearst suggested narrowing the focus to just the elderly. A few weeks later Ewing met with Louis Pink, head of New York's Blue Cross program, and listened to his thoughts about that idea. Pink complained that Blue Cross was rapidly losing business to commercial insurers who experience-rated their premiums to attract young, healthy customers, leaving the Blue Cross plans with the older, sicker individuals. Some plans were forced to raise their rates. Others abandoned community rating, where all policyholders would pay the same rate (regardless of health risk), and started basing premiums on health risk.[45] In Pink's view, here was a situation where government intervention would be legitimate:

> There is one phase of this whole problem where I think the government might be very helpful. It's the over-65 group. We really have no actuarial experience or data upon which we could formulate a program covering them. We can't prophesy what our losses would be, what we ought to charge, what the premiums should be.[46]

Ewing discussed the matter with Social Security Administration officials but initially received a cool reception. They still hoped for a universal health plan and felt this would be "a betrayal of their cause."[47] Ewing finally won over Ig Falk and then approached President Truman, who concurred that the narrower approach should be considered. A bill for federal hospital benefits for the aged was introduced in the Ways and Means Committee in 1952, but it died in committee with the AMA watching warily from the sidelines: "there was no need or chance to express a view but those bills were carefully studied."[48]

In 1956 the AFL-CIO, flush with victory over disability insurance, decided it was time to revive health benefits for the elderly. Throughout the 1950s the trade unions had negotiated better health benefits for current workers in each collective bargaining agreement, but generally these plans excluded retired workers. Worn-out workers had pensions for their leisure years but no health insurance. The situation worsened after 1958 during a fierce contract struggle when the United Auto Workers union was "cajoled" into signing the "never, never letter," promising never again to "demand negotiations for those on retirement."[49] That promise lasted only until 1961, when the UAW wrested an agreement from American Motors to pay half of retirees' Blue Cross/Blue Shield premiums. Then in 1964 the UAW negotiated fully paid premiums for retirees.[50] Winning health benefits for retirees solved one problem but often created another by forcing the unions to give up wage increases. This problem was exacerbated by the practice of experience rating.[51] As Cruikshank complained, "You get an experience rated thing and you get a program loaded with the costs of retirees and it always meant you had to give up something else, you see, if you added this expense."[52] The dilemma of balancing the concerns of active workers against the needs of retirees gave the trade unions a vested interest in turning the financing of health insurance for the aged over to the government. If the government absorbed this cost, then the unions would be able to negotiate higher wages and better benefits for current workers.

During strategy sessions, Cruikshank and Ellickson focused on three issues: how to avoid alienating the hospitals and Blue Cross, what kind of provision might attract nurses, and how to minimize physician opposition. To placate hospital administrators, they conceived a strategy of policy by stealth. Instead of imposing rigid hospital regulations at the start, standards would be brought in incrementally. Initially, "the government would only intervene in hospitals for licensing." Scrutiny would gradually be increased, and "after two or three years" higher federal standards would be imposed.[53]

Cruikshank and Ellickson discussed having Blue Cross and the commercial insurance companies administer the program as a way to gain their cooperation. But they were wary of including insurers because of their experience with the state workmen's compensation programs. These programs, which were administered by private insurance companies, provided income and health benefits for sick and injured workers. In workmen's compensation, insurers "simply met bills that were presented to them without any real consideration of whether the expenditure was necessary or not." Their passivity made it difficult to enforce quality standards or control costs. Further, they had learned that if insurers had a vested interest in a benefit, they "got interested in opposing improvements in legislation." A different concern arose regarding Blue Cross and Blue Shield: "would they be representing the hospitals or the federal government and could they very well represent both?"[54]

To avoid antagonizing the AMA, Cruikshank and Ellickson initially planned to exclude medical services entirely, but the steelworkers' union demanded that surgical care be included.[55] Even though that was not "necessarily the best thing from the point of view of politics," it would help sell the program to the rank and file. How could a cost that was covered under collectively bargained plans not be included in a federal program? As Ellickson explained, "Because surgical charges were so high . . . if you didn't cover that, a lot of workers might feel, Well, this isn't much of a program."[56] Even though a provision was included specifying that the government would exert no supervision over the practice of medicine or the manner in which medical services were provided, the AMA was not reassured.[57] However, there were some physicians who would meet with the AFL-CIO "from time to time." Members of the Group Health Association provided helpful advice too.[58]

In 1956 Cruikshank convinced Ways and Means Committee member Representative Emmanuel Cellars (R-N.Y.) to introduce his model bill, but Cellars' bill for health insurance for retirees died in committee. It was revised in 1957, this time with physicians' services excluded entirely. Cruikshank then approached the two highest-ranking Democrats on Ways and Means, both southerners, to sponsor the revised bill, but they refused.[59] Finally, Representative Aime Forand (D-R.I.), a little-known congressman from Rhode Island, agreed to consider it. Forand "dropped the bill in the hopper," surprising Cruikshank, who thought he wasn't going to do it.[60] Forand's role in promoting the bill was minimal at first: "He didn't really carry the ball in the committee. He introduced the legislation. He had his name on it."[61] But later he became its foremost advocate in Congress. In 1958 Ways and Means held the first hearings on the Forand bill, but no vote was taken. When the committee finally voted in 1960, the tally was 17 nay, 8 yea, with seven southern Democrats siding with conservative Republicans.[62]

For the next five years, health insurance for the aged dominated the AFL-CIO Social Security department.[63] Lisbeth Bamberger Schorr, who had been on the front lines negotiating UAW health plans in the 1940s, recalled: "The AFL-CIO became a sort of headquarters . . . for the people who were trying to get something done about health insurance for the aged. . . . I remember the scene . . . when we were assembling, cutting and pasting a bill." They supplied the technical staff, drafted speeches for Medicare supporters in Congress, and sponsored lunches and meetings. They prepared a "truth sheet" refuting Republican allegations about socialized medicine. They also invited supporters on the House Ways and Means Committee to discuss testimony that might come up during hearings and briefed them on areas where opponents might probe. "Our activities there were directed at two things—one, making a good record, and secondly, at trying to get the committee members to understand what the substantive issues were."[64]

The first presidential candidate to recognize the political potential of the senior vote was John F. Kennedy, the handsome, youthful, politically ambitious junior senator from Massachusetts. Polls showed that medical care for the aged was a leading concern of the public, second only to preventing inflation.[65] As one of his campaign supporters, Madison, Wisconsin, mayor Ian Nestingen later explained, "Of all the issues on which he campaigned . . . the one that constantly provoked the most interest or had the most queries raised of a spontaneous nature was the Forand bill. I don't think there's any question the President noticed this public interest and apparent support."[66] Convinced this issue could help him win his party's nomination, Kennedy endorsed the Forand bill, then asked Cruikshank to draft a measure he could introduce in the Senate.[67] Kennedy also created the Senate Committee on Aging and formed the Senior Citizens for Kennedy organization to cultivate older voters.

As momentum for federal action built, the AMA issued a "legislative alert." More lobbyists were hired, new task forces were created, and a field division was established to involve the state and local medical societies and educate physicians. Educating physicians was especially critical because they could "relate to their representatives in Congress" and build a legislative action program within the states. By 1960 the AMA had 950 people working on political issues, with 75 percent of their time devoted to health legislation.[68]

AMA leaders understood that a fallback position was needed and hatched a plan with Blue Cross wherein the government would subsidize private insurance premiums for the low-income elderly to purchase private health benefits.[69] As Walter McNerney, president of the Blue Cross Association, explained: "Our initial preference was that we would take a risk. We would quote a rate and the government would help the aged pay that rate. It wouldn't be a subsidy to Blue Cross. It would be a payment to the aged."[70]

Although the AMA subsidy plan won the support of Richard Nixon, who was running for president, the Republican Party instead supported a plan to expand existing public assistance for health care.[71] After a lengthy and bitter debate, these activities culminated in the Kerr-Mills Act of 1960, a program of federal grants to the states for health care for the aged poor.[72] Kerr-Mills satisfied southern Democrats because it would provide states with funds without permitting federal officials to intervene in the racially segregated health care system. It also mollified the AMA because payments would be made through state health agencies, which physicians largely controlled. As Social Security Administration actuary Robert Myers explained:

> The Kerr-Mills bill . . . was developed really as a counter-fire against the social insurance approach. . . . Mr. Mills and Senator Kerr didn't want the social insurance approach because of their fear that this would burgeon on out . . . and destroy a lot of private insurance and eventually develop into national health insurance or even socialized medicine.[73]

What the AMA failed to recognize was that Kerr-Mills also established the principle that the federal government had financial responsibility for medical care for the aged.[74]

Yet Kerr-Mills did not have the intended effect of dampening demand for a social insurance program for the aged, because it provided health insurance for only a minuscule portion of the elderly population. When the Senate Committee on Aging investigated the Kerr-Mills Act in 1963, committee members discovered that nationwide only 148,000 older people—fewer than 1 percent—had received any help under Kerr-Mills. Only 28 states had implemented the program by 1963, and only 4 provided the full range of care.[75] Many states that had established programs lacked sufficient state funds to finance them.[76] Even when a program was operating, doctors and hospitals refused to participate because payments were below the prevailing rate.[77] In most states, restrictive means tests excluded many of the aged who needed assistance. Twelve states had "family responsibility" provisions that effectively imposed a means test on the relatives of the aged, deterring many poor, elderly people from applying for support. In Pennsylvania, for example, the elderly had to provide detailed information on their children's finances to qualify for Kerr-Mills benefits.[78] In New York, many older people withdrew their applications on learning that their children would be involved. One man said, "Please kill my application. I don't want my son questioned."[79] Nine states also had "recovery" clauses, providing that beneficiaries' homes would be sold after their deaths to reimburse the state for the cost of care. This was a particularly repellant practice to the elderly, whose self-respect depended on owning their own homes free and clear.

When it appeared that a federal health insurance program for the aged was making headway, the commercial insurance companies decided it was time to get involved politically:

> The insurance industry was a force to be concerned with, particularly with regard to individual congressmen and Senators. They tended to do what they did behind the scenes. More of the insurance company opposition was directed toward that part of the iceberg that didn't show up in public. They did support candidates and oppose candidates based upon their views. They got out a lot of information against the program.[80]

Insurers were able to mobilize political support at the state and local level: "The insurance companies do have tremendous political influence because so many local political machines got involved with insurance. A good many state legislators are said to be insurance agents or are lawyers for insurance companies."[81] In 1958 260 commercial insurance companies joined together to form the Health Insurance Association of America to counter the efforts of the AFL-CIO. According to Ellickson, the insurance companies "provided the technical attacks of costs, the cost estimates . . . And the insurance people would talk against it at the meetings where we were talking for it." Then, "when the legislative issues were hot, they developed these plans that were launched as alternatives." Continental Casualty created Golden 65, the first hospital insurance program for the aged, in 1957. Prudential negotiated a group policy with the American Association of Retired Persons (AARP) in 1958. Mutual of Omaha developed a Senior Security program that same year, and Continental Casualty followed in 1962. Despite the proliferation of commercial plans, most policies covered only a portion of hospital costs and no medical care, leaving old people with many expenses to absorb. For example, Continental Casualty and Mutual of Omaha provided only $10 a day for hospital charges for room and board, less than half the average cost.[82] Furthermore, commercial plans were quite expensive, costing $500 to $600 a year for an elderly couple when the median annual income of people 65 and older was only $2,875. For this reason, fewer than half the people in this group purchased these policies.[83] Commercial insurers also skimmed off the younger, healthier elderly, forcing Blue Cross to raise premiums and add deductibles. As premiums and charges rose, many older people were priced out of the market entirely.[84]

By the 1960 election, the various factions had coalesced into two camps. In one camp were Republicans, southern Democrats, the AMA, and the Health Insurance Association of America. In the other camp were Kennedy, northern Democrats, the AFL-CIO, and senior citizens. During the campaign, the Democratic Party platform included what the press was now calling Medicare, and Kennedy embraced the issue as his own. After Kennedy defeated Nixon in a close contest, the AFL-CIO decided the hour was at hand.

The first task was to educate the unions' own rank and file as well as the general public about the issues. Trade union representatives participated in radio and TV programs, gave speeches, and organized educational conferences.[85] Cruikshank explained their strategy:

> If it was a political campaign, you tried to get it set up right in your platform. You tried to get people who were running for office committed. You tried to get editorials. You tried to get debate. You tried to get time on the radio. There was never any point at which you were not constantly feeling out the opportunity to make a case either to the public or to the people who were going to vote.[86]

Despite efforts to shed the association with socialized medicine, the threat of socialism hovered over the campaign. Clinton Anderson (D-N.M.), the leading Medicare supporter in the Senate, received many letters from constituents such as Martha Botts, who complained,

> I have no doubt that you are most sincere in feeling that Medicare will not lead to socialized medicine, but I still can't help feeling that any insurance that is forced upon me can't help but lead to something else I don't want. What a horrible waste all our wars for Democracy were if we go back to autocratic rule or throw it away on socialism.[87]

Ned Flightner wrote, "Just witnessed your appearance on the Today Show and I must say you sounded more like a Socialist than a Democrat."[88] Mrs. J. L. Flinchum pleaded with Senator Anderson, "You fail to represent me when you advocate government controls for any health care bill. Let Americans remain free Americans."[89] Senator Anderson was forced to defend Medicare, stating

> I have been interested to see how many people have the incorrect impression that the financing of health or hospital care for the aged through the Social Security system would lead to socialized medicine. We are trying harder than the American Medical Association to keep away from socializing American medicine.[90]

Since the Physicians' Forum "had been pretty much discredited and red-baited a great deal" during the Truman era, the AFL-CIO created a new organization, the Physicians' Committee, whose members were not tainted by communist associations. Its leader was Dr. Esselstyn, the physician-reformer who had run the Rip Van Winkle Clinic and who had worked on behalf of the Truman plan in the 1940s. Dr. Esselstyn had witnessed firsthand in his clinic the negative consequences of welfare medicine. He had seen elderly patients who delayed seeking medical care for fear of involving their children in the welfare system. As he recalled:

> I can think of a call one time we got from my next door neighbor. They said that mother was hemorrhaging from a rupture. When I got there—it was in the middle of winter—here was Grandma in the middle of the kitchen. It was a single room house with outdoor toilet facilities, and here was Grandma in the middle of a pool of blood. It turned out that she had an umbilical hernia, that's one that's around the navel, which hung out maybe 18 inches, and about a week before, she hadn't gotten dressed as well as she might have, and she was cooking pancakes for her family, and she leaned over the griddle, and her protruding hernia burned on the griddle. Here it was ten days later.[91]

Dr. Esselstyn had great empathy for hardworking farmers who toward the end of their lives were unable to pay for medical care but who feared going through "the kind of Inquisition they have to go through" to qualify for Kerr-Mills.[92] Esselstyn viewed the Physicians' Committee as a forum for doctors who opposed the AMA to speak out.[93] As Dr. Esselstyn explained:

> When we reached the Forand stage, there were no physicians speaking for the bill except the Physicians' Forum and . . . they might have been the kiss of death as much as anything else. . . . It was a question of the organizations which some of the members had belonged to at some time or another, which were under question. The days of McCarthy were over and dying, but it was in that general frame of reference. We thought we had troubles enough of our own without borrowing trouble.[94]

Many physicians who joined the Physicians' Committee were attached to medical schools or, like Esselstyn, to public health clinics, which gave them the freedom to express their opinions without fear of reprisal. Their goal was to show "that there were some perfectly common sense people with their feet on the ground who were not necessarily involved at that time in banning the bomb or other things of a far out nature."[95] The AFL-CIO remained in the background but furnished the Physicians' Committee with financing and advice on the legislative in and outs on Capitol Hill. As one staff member explained, "Esselstyn used our telephone when he came to Washington. And when he needed a statement mimeographed, we did that and we proofread copy on it."[96] Although many prestigious doctors signed on, including pediatrician Dr. Benjamin Spock, noted heart surgeon Dr. Michael DeBakey, and two Nobel prize winners, they could not penetrate the AMA, whose official stance was to ignore them.[97] When Esselstyn attempted to run an ad in the *AMA News*, the ad was rejected on the grounds that "the wording was misleading."[98]

The AFL-CIO also created a new organization, the National Council of Senior Citizens, to emphasize the support of the elderly. As Cruikshank noted: "What would the whole program have looked like if you hadn't had a Senior Citizen movement? Here is a bill designed for people age 65 and [what] if there hadn't been any Senior Citizen movement?"[99] At first, most council members were retired trade unionists from the clothing industries—first-generation immigrants, mainly Jewish, socialist in orientation but vehemently anticommunist, who in their day had fought fiercely for the right to unionize.[100] The council also recruited members from the retiree departments of the steelworkers' and autoworkers' unions, providing an instant network in key electoral states such as Florida, Michigan, and Ohio. Over 20,000 retired railroad workers subscribed to the union newspaper, *The Voice*, giving the council an immediate audience with that group. The railroaders' strengths were often in states where other senior organizations were weak, such as Tennessee, Nebraska, and Georgia.

The National Council of Senior Citizens was headed by Blue Carstenson, a former HEW staffer known as a salesman and a showman but not as a particularly effective organizer. Former colleagues considered him divisive, someone who would "make alliances and then run around and try to manipulate one group against another."[101] Carstenson attempted to purge members with ties to communist organizations, ostensibly to protect the council from charges that it was "socialistic." When the United Electrical Workers retirees in Philadelphia asked to join, Carstenson explained, "We thought they were probably Communist-controlled. These were the ones at GE who were thrown out of the AFL-CIO. They're still trying to get in." Carstenson did a background check on one member who had refused to testify before HUAC in the 1940s. Although HUAC "had nothing to validate that he was a Communist, that he probably had been back in the '30s but that he was [not] connected at that time . . . we always kept an eye on him."[102] Despite his failings, Carstenson was effective in creating public empathy for senior citizens and drawing attention to their grassroots movement:

> We had to make it a cause and we made it a cause. . . . We charged the atmosphere like a campaign. We tried to create this. . . . We were always jammed in there and there was a hustle and bustle atmosphere. And when reporters came over they were always impressed by telephones ringing and the wild confusion and this little bitty outfit here that was tackling the whole AMA in a little apartment on Capitol Hill. . . . This was news. It used to make every reporter chuckle or smile.[103]

In 1962 Carstenson organized petition drives and letter-writing campaigns among National Council of Senior Citizens clubs. Thousands of senior citizens bombarded their representatives with letters like this one from a retired railroad worker:

I am an old rail who retired in Jan. 1942, we have two retired clubs in San Antonio, Texas and I don't believe any of us understand just what the Medicare Bill would do for the retired people, could you send me something on the Medicare . . . something that would help our cause if we could get one of our daily papers to run it. They give the doctors' side of why they oppose the Medicare bill. Why not give our side of why it's needed.[104]

Whenever congressional hearings were held, council members were on the scene. As AMA lobbyist Joseph Stetler ruefully noted, "They effectively organized testimony at the time of hearings. They had those groups of golden age clubs that would come here and testify. It was effective, I'm sure."[105]

During the 1940s, the AMA had set the terms of the debate and made national health insurance proponents the enemy; now the National

The National Council of Senior Citizens was effective in lobbying on behalf of Medicare. Library of Congress, Prints and Photographs Divisions, LC-USZ62-122433

Council of Senior Citizens turned the tables. Their campaign literature explained that the aged were a deserving group who desperately needed health insurance. Many were in poor health, a high proportion lived in poverty, and few were adequately insured. Commercial insurance would never meet their needs. As Carstenson related:

> In every piece of material and we did this religiously, we spelled out one, two, three, four, what was in Medicare. We put out literally millions and millions and millions of pieces of literature . . . there's been no other bill in history where the details have been as widely disseminated. . . . We did a hard sell, a real hard sell. . . . You can let the AMA interpret it or we can interpret it.[106]

A council pamphlet entitled *Operative Negative* sought "to discredit the AMA on the basis of their record."[107] Other council materials described the AMA as "being against everything."[108] An AFL-CIO briefing paper charged that the AMA was as "opposed as ever to effective action." It was conducting a "cynical campaign with a massive onslaught of distortion, misrepresentation and beguiling promises of something better."[109]

By 1962, when public support for Medicare had reached 69 percent, President Kennedy began a major push to get a bill passed. Even some Republicans favored government action.[110] Yet the House Ways and Means Committee was chaired by fiscal conservative Wilbur Mills (D-Ark.), the cosponsor of Kerr-Mills. Mills' first congressional campaign in Arkansas had been financed by a group of doctors, and his opposition proved to be an insurmountable obstacle.[111] Unable to get a bill out of committee, President Kennedy took Medicare to the Senate floor, attaching a Medicare rider to a welfare bill that had already passed in the House. The measure was defeated 52 to 48, with the majority of Republicans and 21 southern Democrats voting against it. The following year Kennedy sent a new Medicare proposal (King-Anderson) to Congress. Behind the scenes insurers lobbied against it, testifying at Senate hearings that there was no need for a government program, because private insurance among older people had increased from only 2 percent in 1952 to 60 percent by 1963 and continued to grow rapidly.[112] But when Ways and Means voted this time, the results were closer: 13 against, 12 for.[113]

The efforts of reformers neutralized the AMA, which during these years used every propaganda tactic it had employed during the Truman era.[114] The AMA ran newspaper ads and radio and TV spots declaring that Medicare was socialized medicine and a threat to freedom. Doctors were provided with speeches, pamphlets, radio tapes and scripts, and guidelines for using the material. Their wives held afternoon parties for friends and neighbors at which they discussed the evils of Medicare and listened to a recorded talk by Ronald Reagan. "One of the traditional methods of imposing statism on a people has been by way of medicine," Reagan told his listeners.[115] When states held governors' conferences on aging, "the AMA began to organize very effective flying squadrons to come and try to lobby against Medicare."[116] Representative Forand recalled mail he received from a physician who "used his prescription blanks and prescribed tranquilizer pills."[117] The AMA also created a political action committee, AMPAC, to keep from tarnishing its professional image. AMPAC would identify the personal physicians of members of Congress and get their physicians to lobby against Medicare. Then "they went even further and began to hunt down the physicians of people of influence in other organizations."[118]

To refute the argument that the aged had a compelling problem that could only be solved by a government program, the AMA released its own statistics. The aged were not "universally frail and feeble, constantly ill, and doddering from one visit to the doctor to the next." Rather, the vast majority were in good health; only 4 percent of people 65 or older were confined because of chronic illness. Nor were the aged especially needy. After tax obligations and family size were taken into account, aged households had only slightly less income than younger families and fewer financial obligations.[119] Most could afford to pay for their own health care. Why, asked AMA President Ed Annis, should wage earners be forced to pay higher payroll taxes for hospital care for everyone over 65, even those who were wealthy or already had insurance?[120]

When President Kennedy spoke on behalf of Medicare to a crowd of cheering senior citizens in Madison Square Garden, Annis responded the following day. Speaking to an empty arena, still not cleaned up from the previous day's rally, Annis responded point by point to each of Kennedy's comments. AMA lobbyist Joseph Stetler recalled: "We had about four television sets and we broke into teams of two . . . and critically analyzed what he did . . . that night the script was written for Ed

Annis to use the next day. We stayed up all night working on it."[121] Annis then showed a film prepared by a professional writer and television producer. Kennedy's speech was widely viewed as a failure and Annis's response as highly effective. Annis had less success when he attempted to speak to a group of senior citizens in Florida: "They sure scared Dr. Annis. He physically was very concerned at that point because they were very angry, as only Miami senior citizens can get."[122]

Despite this one public relations victory, AMA arguments against Medicare failed to resonate with the public for several reasons. One was that the AFL-CIO had been successful in convincing the public that a real need existed. According to Oscar Ewing, "What brought that public education about was the organization of the Senior Citizens Council . . . their political weight was able to way outbalance the political weight of the doctors. You had 19 million people over 65, and you had 185,000 doctors."[123] Another was that private health insurance now covered 68 percent of the population, making the idea of covering the uninsured both comprehensible and acceptable. As Ellickson explained, "The idea of federal health insurance for those who couldn't afford it or for those who somehow were excluded from private or voluntary health insurance was a perfectly natural . . . thing to do."[124]

How the AMA Was Defeated

On November 22, 1963, President Kennedy was gunned down by an assassin as he rode in an open convertible in a motorcade in Dallas, Texas. His vice president, Lyndon Baines Johnson, still in a state of shock and bewilderment, was sworn in as president that afternoon.[125] In the ensuing chaos, all political decisions were placed on hold.

At his first meeting with Kennedy aides, Johnson asked them to draw together the threads of the fallen president's domestic program. A consummate politician both bluntly honest and calculatingly devious, Johnson could persuade his legislative foes to support his agenda and "outmaneuver them when persuasion failed."[126] With an election just 11 months away, President Johnson chose to mount an attack on poverty, targeting the hard-core poor, those who had no chance to benefit from economic growth. Having grown up in Texas, where he had witnessed the damaging effect of poverty and bigotry, he turned Kennedy's modest proposal for programs to help the Appalachian poor into an ambitious war against poverty. His Great Society would increase funding for education, child health, nutrition, job training, and community action. The capstone would be health insurance for the elderly.

Hearings held by the Senate Subcommittee on the Health of the Elderly in April of 1964 provided a stark illustration of the limits of private health insurance.[127] In just the past year, private insurance rates had increased by as much as 43 percent. Committee members had received thousands of letters from older people all over the country protesting the hikes with "no end in sight."[128] Bankers Life and Casualty admitted that of 76,764 policies issued during 1961 in its plan for those over 65, only 41,130 were still in force in 1963. Some policyholders had died, but more had dropped their coverage because they were unable to pay the premiums. Costs were not the only problem. Insurers threatened that people who filed claims would be dropped unless they agreed to waive future benefits or accept substandard coverage. Furthermore, some companies had provided misleading data to Congress to create the impression that no further action was needed. Tactics included inflating the number of policyholders by including weekly indemnity policies, which paid only a minimal flat amount unrelated to hospital charges or services, or counting someone who held three policies as three separate policyholders.[129]

When the Democrats held their 1964 presidential convention in Atlantic City, members of the National Council of Senior Citizens arrived by the busload. In an impressive show of solidarity, 14,000 senior citizens marched ten blocks down the boardwalk to the convention hotel. That fall the Senate approved a Medicare amendment to a House-passed bill on Social Security benefit increases, thanks to the defection of two southern Democrats, but the measure died in conference committee.[130] Oscar Ewing, now retired, advised the National Council of Senior Citizens, "You'd better make darn sure that your key spokesmen in Congress get back," because the AMA "was too darn powerful."[131] Following Ewing's advice, the council worked to ensure that no Medicare supporters were defeated at the polls, zeroing in on the Ways and Means Committee to pack it with Medicare supporters:

> We knew that we had to defend every single pro-Medicare Senator and Congressman and that we had to try to pick off the key

opponents. . . . If any of these went down, we were in trouble. . . . Also if members of the Ways and Means Committee who [supported] Medicare went down to defeat, these, too, would be signs of the struggle.[132]

When Senator George Smathers (D-Fl.) came out against Medicare, the AFL-CIO decided to "educate" him by holding hearings in Florida. Cruikshank explained:

We really went to work—the National Council of Senior Citizens and our unions . . . to really make these demonstrations . . . in Fort Lauderdale they had to change the hall three different times. Smathers came and looked out over a sea of several thousand old people. And while they were orderly and all, there were banners all over the place for Medicare.[133]

In the 1964 election, Barry Goldwater, a conservative Arizona senator who opposed Medicare, headed the Republican ticket. He won the staunch support of the AMA, whose own "almost psychotic fear of government" meshed with Goldwater's frontier philosophy that the best government is the one that governs least.[134] Johnson won the election by 61 percent, the largest margin ever received by a president. The Democrats swept both the Senate and the House by wide margins, with northern Democrats gaining a majority without the South for the first time since the New Deal. No incumbent, Republican or Democrat, who supported Medicare lost.[135] The AMA had put everything into the fight against former HEW secretary Abraham Ribicoff, who was running for the Senate. Ribicoff turned to the National Council of Senior Citizens for support. He ran on a pro-Medicare ticket, printing a million mock Medicare cards with his photo on the back. Senior citizen clubs passed out the cards in large quantities, and Ribicoff was victorious.[136]

In his State of the Union address, President Johnson made Medicare a priority. As it became apparent that some measure would be enacted, the key interest groups began jockeying to ensure that they had a voice in the final legislation. The negotiations were conducted by Robert Ball, a politically skilled tactician who had come up through the ranks in the Social Security Administration and was widely respected for his expertise and dedication. Even those who opposed Ball's desire to expand the Social Security program admired his commitment. As Robert Myers, the actuary of the Social Security Administration, conceded, "Never let it be said that Bob Ball isn't quite intelligent and savvy in the ways of the world."[137] As early as 1961, Ball had had secret telephone conversations with Harry Becker, a Blue Cross official, to try to recruit him as an ally.[138] Ball and AFL-CIO officials also met with AHA representatives, who "would never come in here as the American Hospital Association, but they would come in as individuals who were very knowledgeable in this field and start off by saying, 'Of course, we're against this legislation, but if it's going to pass, it ought to do this.'"[139] The hospitals were carrying a considerable part of the financial burden of care for the aged either through outright charity or by accepting low state welfare payments.[140] From one-third to one-half of their aged patients could not pay their bills.[141] Although AHA representatives "were extremely proper and discreet in their discussions with us, never indicating their own viewpoints . . . we were pretty sure that they were not unsympathetic."[142] In 1962 the AHA adopted a resolution supporting Medicare on the condition that Blue Cross be given responsibility for administering the program, a move that was considered a severe defection by the AMA.[143]

Commercial insurance companies had become resigned to the need for a government program. The aged had proved to be unprofitable clients, forcing insurers to load their costs onto paying customers. Although the commercial insurers never said so publicly, another reformer recalled that privately they had "a great deal of misgiving" about their efforts to insure the elderly. Some of the more farsighted insurance company executives recognized that they were engaged in a self-defeating cause.[144] As early as 1961 the president of the Health Insurance Association of America had begun to discuss how insurers could offer supplemental policies to fill the gaps that would invariably be a part of any government program.[145] Some member companies broke ranks and openly supported Medicare.[146]

A week after the election, Ways and Means Committee chairman Mills indicated that Medicare would be considered as soon as the new Congress convened. The election had threatened his control of his committee. Now he declared he would work out a plan for moving Medicare forward. On January 4, 1965, Medicare bills were introduced in the House and Senate. In a last-ditch effort, the AMA proposed Eldercare, a slightly modified version of Kerr-Mills that would increase federal support to help defray the health insurance costs of the elderly poor.[147] To promote Eldercare the AMA coupled a nationwide newspaper ad campaign with spot announcements on 346 television and 722 radio stations and distributed 10 million pamphlets attacking Medicare. This effort was a total flop.[148] By playing hardball, the AMA not only had lost public respect but also had alienated even their congressional supporters. Elizabeth Wickenden, who was the Washington representative of the Public Health Association, witnessed this gradual erosion:

> While I was working with the Congress . . . there was a total change of attitude toward the medical profession. . . . Part of the psychology of a physician is that he is used to being a very strong authoritarian figure to his patients and a father figure to them . . . he can be authoritarian and still have a conviction that he's doing it for their own good and he can't understand anybody who deliberately goes against him in the doctor-patient relationship. Now in the early period of this battle, it seems to me that the AMA was approaching the Congressmen very much in the same spirit. . . . But over the years . . . this was no longer effective. . . . It was more of a discrediting of the medical profession. It was really a puncturing of this aura of omniscience.[149]

When Ways and Means refused to give Eldercare a public hearing or allow a debate on the House floor, the AMA complained about a brush-off. The House Counsel responded contemptuously that the AMA had testified at length in the 88th, 87th, 86th, and 85th Congresses: "It can hardly be said, therefore, that the American Medical Association has not had an opportunity to present its views on the subject."[150]

A third proposal on the table was Bettercare, a plan for a federal subsidy for the purchase of private health insurance. Bettercare was written by Aetna lobbyists and sponsored by Representative John Byrnes (R-Wis.), the ranking Republican on the Ways and Means Committee.[151] In an effort to prevent deadlock, Mills decided to combine the three approaches—the AFL-CIO hospital insurance plan, the AMA's Eldercare, and Aetna's Bettercare—in one bill, his "three-layer cake." According to Robert Ball, everyone in the room was "flabbergasted."[152] The first layer, Medicare Part A, would pay for hospital care, for skilled nursing care for a limited period, and for some home health care for people recovering from an illness. Part A would not pay for any long-term nursing home care for people with chronic illnesses, a deficiency that would prove to be a big problem in years to come. The second layer was Part B, an optional program that would pay for physicians' services. The third layer was a slightly expanded version of Kerr-Mills termed Medicaid, a program of health insurance for people who were "categorically" eligible for the federal/state cash assistance programs, old-age assistance, and Aid to Families with Dependent Children, the plan favored by the AMA and some conservatives.[153]

Medicare left many health care costs uncovered. Beneficiaries would still have to pay premiums for Part B coverage, co-payments for many services, and the costs for eyeglasses, prescription drugs, and long-term care. Thus the private insurance industry would be relieved of the large, unpredictable costs of serving an elderly clientele but would retain a predictable market for supplemental "medigap" policies.

As a compromise with Blue Cross officials who demanded to administer Medicare (and bolstered that demand by repeated threats of a hospital boycott), federal officials agreed to appoint "fiscal intermediaries" to handle claims, determine payment amounts, and reimburse providers.[154] "You can't stand to talk to a government official? Okay, have somebody else talk for you. . . . If you want a buffer, fine."[155] Although Blue Cross hoped for sole responsibility for administering Medicare, arguing that it "didn't need the false check and balance of a competitive element," at the last minute the commercial insurance companies were also allowed to bid.[156]

AFL-CIO officials were disappointed by many of the features in Mills' proposal, feeling that he had sold out far short of what really could be accomplished.[157] They opposed the last-minute addition of Part B, which they feared would create rampant inflation, and suggested adding some price controls, to no avail.[158] They had also "fought like the dickens against letting the insurance companies into this program," concerned that they would do nothing to keep costs under control.[159] But under the Johnson administration, the labor movement's role had become largely ceremonial. Although administration officials consulted with labor officials, it was largely to keep "the labor boys happy without anything of real substance happening as a result."[160] One AFL-CIO staff member explained: "It was disappointing to be working on this for years and years in every detail and then within a matter of an hour have the entire picture changed totally and be presented with this and not really have had a part in it."[161]

The National Council of Senior Citizens held a rally on Capitol Hill at which more than 100 elected officials endorsed Medicare. On April 8 the Medicare bill passed the House, with 40 southern Democrats opposed. On June 30 it passed in the Senate Finance Committee, 12 to 5. All four southern Democrats and two Republicans who had never before voted for Medicare voted yes.[162] On July 6 it won approval in the full Senate, with southern Democrats and Republicans evenly split. Florida senator George Smathers voted in favor. So did powerful Virginia senator Harry Byrd, who was bullied into it by President Johnson. Medicare was enacted on July 30, 1965, the largest expansion of the welfare state in the second half of the twentieth century.[163]

Politically, Medicare filled the remaining gap that negotiated plans could not cover, removing all pressure for national health insurance. Immediately, as the burden of the older, otherwise uninsured population was removed, Blue Cross began lowering its rates across the country. As Nelson Cruikshank admits:

> What we were really doing was making voluntary insurance viable for almost all of the working population in the country. Now without Medicare, had this burden existed as a threat or had they attempted to meet it, their system would have broken down, which in either case would inevitably have brought on national health insurance.[164]

Soon after Medicare became law, Cruikshank traveled to Independence, Missouri, to visit the Truman Library. Harry Truman warmly welcomed him, holding out his hand and saying, "Hello Cruikshank. Are you still fighting the AMA? Don't give the sons of bitches an inch."[165]

The enactment of Medicare was a turning point for the medical profession. It resulted in the loss of key allies, including the AHA, the Blue Cross Association, and the insurance industry. It also undermined physicians' cultural authority, as the AMA developed a "reputation for intolerance" with the public and politicians.[166] Unlike the insurance industry, whose role was played out behind the scenes, leaving no "residue of anti–insurance company feeling," the AMA's activities were highly visible.[167] AMA general counsel Joseph Stetler ruefully acknowledged, "It doesn't deserve the bad reputation it has and the extensive lack of popularity that it enjoys from the public and even from some elements of the profession and certainly from the government. . . . They were very unpopular with a lot of people and ultimately with a lot of members of Congress and politicians."[168]

Conclusion

During the 1940s, the American trade unions followed a different course than their European counterparts. Instead of working on behalf of national health insurance, they focused their energies on the right to bargain for fringe benefits in their employment contracts. As a result, there was no labor-sponsored, grassroots initiative to counter the AMA or the commercial and nonprofit insurers, for whom collectively bargained health benefits had opened a large new market of viable employee group insurance pools. Why, then, did the trade unions take the lead in promoting disability insurance and Medicare? That answer is that these programs not only could demonstrate what a unified labor movement could accomplish but also could solve the problem of insuring disabled and retired members, whose high costs raised the stakes when trade unions tried to negotiate wage increases and other benefits for working members.

The AFL-CIO won Medicare by mobilizing its extensive union network of state federations and local chapters, organizing a grassroots senior citizens' movement, and supporting Democratic Party members who served on key congressional committees. Although union leaders were subsequently pushed to the sidelines during Lyndon Johnson's Great Society, there is little doubt that the trade unions paved the way for the final Medicare vote.

The 20-year period between the end of World War II and the enactment of Medicare in 1965 solidified the private health insurance system in several ways. The spread of private health insurance in collective bargaining agreements effectively removed organized labor from the broader struggle for national health insurance and gave the trade unions a vested interest in the private welfare state. Medicare further reinforced private health insurance by providing coverage for a costly group and removing from political debates over national health insurance a constituency considered worthy and deserving.

three

Provider Sovereignty and
Civil Rights

As the battle for health insurance for older Americans was waged in Washington, another social revolution of greater magnitude surged up from the South.[1] Beginning with the bus boycotts of the 1950s, civil rights activists engaged in an escalating wave of protests, mass marches, lunch counter sit-ins, and freedom rides. Courageously facing arrests, brutal beatings, and even murder, they demanded an end to segregated schools, restaurants, stores, and public facilities, and insisted on equal opportunity for good jobs.

The legal basis of racial segregation derived from *Plessy v. Ferguson*, the 1896 Supreme Court ruling that "separate but equal" facilities were constitutional. Writing the majority opinion, Justice Henry Brown rationalized:

> Legislation is powerless to eradicate racial instincts or to abolish distinctions based on physical differences, and the attempt to do so can only result in accentuating the difficulties of the present situation. . . . If one race be inferior to the other socially, then the Constitution of the United States cannot put them on the same plane.[2]

At the state level, the "separate but equal" principle was protected by harsh racial codes mandating racial segregation; at the national level, southern congressmen insisted on the primacy of states' rights and used their control over key congressional committees to block any measures that might allow federal authorities to intervene in local racial practices.[3]

Racial discrimination was as rampant in the health care system as in other southern institutions. Some southern hospitals refused to admit any black patients. Others maintained separate "white" and "colored" entrances, water coolers, and bathrooms and reserved certain wards and rooms for black patients only. Segregation also extended to hospital personnel practices, as black physicians were excluded from local medical societies and denied hospital staff privileges.

The sole health care measure of Truman's Fair Deal to be enacted was the Hill-Burton Hospital Survey and Construction Act of 1946. Hill-Burton was a response to a vigorous lobbying campaign by the American Hospital Association for aid for hospital construction, a need that had been deferred by more than a decade of depression and war. To win the votes of southern congressmen, Alabama senator Lister Hill inserted a statute that allowed hospitals to practice racial segregation but still receive federal funds. The statute was justified on the grounds that hospitals were *private* entities whose operations could be regulated only by the states, not by federal authorities. As Hill testified on the Senate floor:

> Who shall practice in the hospitals, and the other matters pertaining to the conduct of hospitals, we have sought in the bill to leave to the authority and determination of the States, and not have the federal government, through this bill, invade the realm of the operation and maintenance of the hospitals.[4]

Senator Hill's statute also appeased physicians and hospital administrators, who might otherwise have rejected the hospital construction program for fear it would "open the door to federal influence."[5] As Ig Falk explained, the Truman administration accepted segregation as "the price we had to pay for getting this legislation through."[6] Despite the concession, AMA officers were chagrined when Congress designated the Public Health Service, one of the numerous agencies within the Department of Health, Education, and Welfare, to administer Hill-Burton. In their paranoid view of the world, the Public Health Service was an agency controlled by left-wingers and Negro sympathizers, a view that could hardly be further from the truth.[7] To placate physicians, Surgeon General Thomas Parran promised that the federal role would be "largely that of guidance," with day-to-day administrative decisions left to local Public Health Service offices.[8]

Hill-Burton did require hospitals to sign a nondiscrimination assurance, agreeing to provide care to people who were unable to pay and to offer care to all persons regardless of race, creed, or color. However,

Section 622 allowed Hill-Burton funds to be used to construct separate facilities for different "population groups" as long as these facilities were of "equal quality." It also allowed racial segregation within a hospital as long as no patient was denied admission if beds allotted to the "other population group" were available. Furthermore, hospitals could deny staff privileges based on race, because these were issues of "internal" hospital policy outside the jurisdiction of the federal government.[9] As long as hospitals were legally defined as private organizations, the federal government would have no authority to intervene in "internal" hospital affairs. That prohibition included administration, personnel, maintenance, and hospital operations.[10]

Hill-Burton and Racial Segregation

Hill-Burton was especially aimed at poor and rural communities that lacked access to health care.[11] Between 1947 and 1974, the Hill-Burton program spread hospital-based care to the rural South. Half of all southern hospitals were constructed in the program's first decade. Some Hill-Burton hospitals admitted black patients but maintained racially segregated wards, even separate nurseries for newborns.[12] Others were entirely segregated, built either solely for whites or solely for blacks. For example, Alabama used Hill-Burton funds to construct racially segregated or separate facilities in all but 2 of its 67 counties.[13] North Carolina built 2 all-white hospitals, 2 all-black hospitals, and 54 hospitals that were segregated by ward.[14] While a few hospitals, such as those in Ahoskie and Greenville, North Carolina, granted admitting rights to black physicians from the beginning, most white hospitals regularly denied staff privileges to black physicians.[15]

In 1954 the Supreme Court overturned the doctrine of "separate but equal," ruling in *Brown v. Board of Education* that segregation deprived minorities of the equal protection of the laws as guaranteed by the Fourteenth Amendment: "Does segregation of children in public schools solely on the basis of race, even though the physical facilities and other 'tangible' factors may be equal, deprive the children of the minority group of equal education opportunities? We believe it does."[16]

The *Brown* decision raised the question whether the "separate but equal" provisions of the Hill-Burton program were constitutional. The

Court had indicated that its decision applied to areas other than education, including public housing, public golf courses, and public auditoriums. Could federal funds be used to finance hospital construction projects of doubtful constitutionality? Within the Public Health Service, attorneys debated how the *Brown* decision would affect agency policy. They concluded that the Public Health Service could continue funding segregated hospitals as long as the separate facilities were "of like quality."[17] But Public Health Service officials refused to evaluate whether segregated hospitals were actually providing a similar quality of care to all patients. As one official explained, "We are not intending to suggest at this time that we are required to be concerned with relative quality of segregated services."[18] Public Health Service attorneys also decided that the federal government had no jurisdiction over internal hospital policies such as admission practices or room assignments, which fell under the category of hospital "operation."[19] Until it was "definitely established that segregation on the basis of race in public hospitals is unconstitutional, the Surgeon General is certainly under no statutory mandate to anticipate the outcome of court tests of that issue." Hospital administrators who inquired were informed that "the propriety of separate hospital facilities for separate racial groups is not directly affected by court decisions to date."[20] The school desegregation decision did not relieve the Public Health Service of its responsibility to carry out the Hill-Burton statute as written, even if that meant allowing segregated facilities to continue current practices.[21]

The Civil Rights Challenge to "Separate but Equal"

In the wake of *Brown v. Board of Education*, civil rights advocates organized protests and demonstrations against hospitals and picketed the headquarters of white medical societies that refused to admit black physicians. Since most hospitals made membership in the local medical society a prerequisite for staff privileges, this form of discrimination exacted a double penalty. Not only did it mean that black physicians couldn't admit patients to the local hospital, it also meant that they were cut off from patient referral networks. When the NAACP joined with the National Medical Association, an organization of black physicians, to request admitting rights at Hill-Burton hospitals, some hospitals, embarrassed by the demonstrations, agreed to revise their policies. Greenville's new Pitt County Memorial Hospital, a 120-bed Hill-Burton facility with a 30-bed Negro wing, offered admitting privileges to two black doctors.[22] But many hospitals remained adamantly committed to preserving segregation.[23]

In the face of this resistance, civil rights advocates directed a stream of complaints at the Public Health Service, Congress, and White House officials. The complaints originated from regions where the movement had extensive grassroots mobilization and well-organized networks of activists.[24] For example, Catherine Patterson, from the Gadsden Freedom Movement, objected that the new Baptist Memorial Hospital in Gadsden, Alabama, had separate "white" and "colored" entrances and reserved just 25 beds for Negro adults.[25] Horace Reed, president of the Volusia County, Florida, branch of the NAACP, complained that Halifax Hospital maintained racially separate wards, that "even the most insignificant equipment [was] labeled 'Negro' and 'white,' and that Negro employees were required to occupy a segregated area in the cafeteria."[26] In James A. Walker Memorial Hospital in Wilmington, North Carolina, black patients were segregated in "old sections" of the hospital in a ward that had two toilets for 25 black patients: "The ward was in a building separated from the main hospital so that to reach the operating room, the delivery room, or x-ray facilities, patients were exposed to the elements as they were wheeled across ninety feet of an open yard to the main hospital."[27] In Charlotte, North Carolina, there was "a tacit agreement between the hospital, city police and ambulance operators that black patients be sent to the inferior all-Negro Good Samaritan Hospital."[28] One outrageous incident highlighted the injustice of segregated care. It began when Hughie David, a 34-year-old black man, complained of a severe headache. His white physician, Dr. Richard James, sent him to the emergency room at Charlotte Memorial, the white hospital. When Dr. James examined his patient, he concluded that Mr. David needed immediate hospitalization for a subarachnoid hemorrhage. But since all the "Negro" beds was taken, Mr. David was sent to Good Samaritan Hospital, where there was no neurosurgeon on staff and no facilities where an angiogram could be performed. Mr. David died the following morning for lack of treatment.

In 1963 the civil rights leader Martin Luther King Jr. was arrested for defying a court order to desist from organizing nonviolent protests and sit-ins in Birmingham, Alabama, the most segregated city in the country. During his incarceration, King wrote his famous "Letter from Birmingham Jail," explaining why African Americans had lost patience with southerners' resistance to integration. Following his release from jail, a series of demonstrations by black children was met with brute force by the mayor of Birmingham. As the public witnessed peaceful demonstrators on national television being beaten by police, attacked by dogs, and blasted with high-pressure fire hoses, public opinion turned against white southerners. When Alabama governor George Wallace defiantly blocked the doorway of the University of Alabama as two black students attempted to register, declaring, "Segregation now, segregation tomorrow, segregation forever," President Kennedy determined that new federal legislation was needed.[29]

Hospitals presented a powerful barrier to civil rights objectives because they were still legally defined as private organizations and thus insulated from the legal prohibitions that applied to public entities, including the equal protection provision of the Fourteenth Amendment.[30] Ending segregation required challenging hospitals' immunity from federal oversight. In 1956 the NAACP filed the first of a dozen lawsuits against hospitals, asking the courts to declare the "separate but equal" provision of the Hill-Burton program unconstitutional and to force hospitals to integrate patient care facilities and student training and grant staff privileges to black physicians.

Some suits were dismissed. Others resulted in incremental change as hospitals made minor concessions to ward off more drastic measures. A 1959 suit against the city of Lakeland, Florida, charged that Lakeland General Hospital had received Hill-Burton funds to construct an addition to an existing hospital that had a wing reserved for black patients.[31] When the new wing became overcrowded, the hospital administrator moved all Negro patients to the old building.[32] Although the district court dismissed the case for lack of evidence, the hospital renovated the old building and began admitting patients of both races. The psychiatric and nursery facilities in the new building were also opened to both white and black patients.[33] A 1962 suit against Grady Hospital in Atlanta charged the hospital with racial discrimination in staffing practices, patient admissions, and nursing school admissions.[34] The plaintiffs asked the Court to declare the "separate but equal" provision of the Hill-Burton Act unconstitutional and to issue an injunction against the continued operation of facilities on a segregated basis. In response to the suit, the hospital opened a psychiatric ward for black patients, improved the black maternity ward, and made plans to open a black orthopedic ward. The Fulton County Medical Society admitted to active membership two black physicians who were recent additions to Grady's visiting staff.[35] Another suit, against Lynchburg General Hospital, alleged that even though the hospital had a private board, its practices fell within the scope of civil rights statutes because it was "almost a wholly tax supported institution with tax money coming from the city of Lynchburg and the state of Virginia."[36] In response, the Lynchburg hospital's board moved to transfer the hospital's assets into a private corporation.[37]

Until 1963, court decisions continued to uphold the principle that the equal protection clause of the Fourteenth Amendment did not apply to private institutions. These claims were finally overturned in the case of *Simkins v. Moses H. Cone Memorial Hospital*. The Simkins case was initiated by Dr. George Simkins Jr., a black dentist who had spearheaded a drive to integrate Greensboro, North Carolina's public golf course. When Moses Cone Hospital denied admission to his patient, a man with an abscessed third molar, Simkins called a lawyer who had worked on other integration cases. On further digging, they learned that Moses Cone had received $1,269,950 in federal Hill-Burton funds. Simkins and the NAACP filed a lawsuit against Moses Cone and the other segregated Greensboro hospital, Wesley Long, charging unequal treatment under the law.

For the first time the Department of Justice intervened on behalf of the plaintiffs, arguing that the government had an obligation to protect citizens from unconstitutional action made possible by operation of a federal statute. In 1962 the U.S. District Court, Fourth Circuit, dismissed the complaint on the grounds that the hospital was private in character and therefore beyond the reach of the Fourteenth Amendment. Participation in the Hill-Burton program "in no way transformed hospitals into public agencies subject to federal constitutional inhibitions against discrimination." Simkins appealed the decision, and on March 2, 1963, the Fourth Circuit Court of Appeals ruled that the statute that provided the legal basis for the "separate but equal" clause of Hill-Burton was unconstitutional.[38] Because the hospital received federal funds, it was not a private entity but an "arm of the state" and thus subject to the Fourteenth Amendment. The *Simkins* decision prohibited internal segregation in any facility on the basis of race, creed, or color, banned hospitals and other health care facilities from denying staff privileges on the basis of race, and asserted that all benefits associated with staff privileges had to be available without discrimination.[39] It thus not only challenged the constitutional basis of the practices and procedures that had guided Public Health Service funding decisions for 17 years but also directly contradicted the key premise that had protected hospitals and physicians' sovereign control of the health care system.

The Public Health Service first responded to the *Simkins* ruling by issuing new Hill-Burton regulations that expanded the definition of nondiscrimination. Under the new definition any institution applying for Hill-Burton funds had to prove that it did not discriminate in admissions, room assignments, or staff privileges. The problem was that the Public Health Service had little authority to force hospitals to comply, because the regulations only applied to *pending* applications.[40] Although projects approved on the "separate but equal" basis were unconstitutional, HEW could take action only against a hospital that sought further federal assistance.[41] Hospitals that had violated their nondiscrimination assurances in the past could not be asked to repay federal funds that had been improperly used.[42] The Public Health Service also did not respond forcefully because staff in its local offices had deeply embedded ties to local political structures and were satisfied to leave the resolution of conflicts to local officials.[43]

A June 1964 HEW survey found that all 11 Deep South states still had statutes—enforced through fines or imprisonment—mandating segregation by race.[44] Even though these statutes often violated hospitals' nondiscrimination assurances, Public Health Service officials decided they could not intervene unless a court ruled "the applicable portion of the statute invalid or inoperative." If no court decision existed, the Public Health Service would rely on the opinion of the state attorney general. While these statutes likely would eventually be judged unconstitutional, the Public Health Service could "have little effect on an applicant who may be subject to local enforcement efforts."[45]

By 1964 HEW's cautious approach had created pressures from without and within. As civil rights had moved to the forefront of the national political agenda, members of Congress became openly contemptuous of Public Health Service policies. Senator Harrison Williams (D-N.J.) complained to a Public Health Service official:

Your description is . . . of an agency following a narrow interpretation of the letter of the law and wholly ignoring the intent of the law. By stating that Hill-Burton does not specifically outlaw segregation once the patient has been admitted into the hospital, you are, in effect, adopting the principle of separate but equal facilities. Considering that the United States Supreme Court, in a unanimous decision, declared this doctrine unconstitutional, I find it hard to accept your position. I cannot think that a Federal agency must continue to operate, some eight years after the Court's decision, in a manner that perpetuates this principle.[46]

Within the Department of Health, Education, and Welfare, new staff members appointed by the Kennedy administration also pushed for change. Lisle Carter, HEW deputy assistant secretary, angrily asked whether segregated facilities could ever be nondiscriminatory.[47] HEW assistant secretary James Quigley argued that it was imperative that the Public Health Service reconsider its position in regard to the Hill-Burton program: "whatever justification there may have been for the original interpretation at the time it was made in the late 1940s, which permitted internal segregation, no such justification exists in 1963." Quigley feared that "if we do not act in this area quickly and effectively, we are going to have pickets outside our door one of these mornings."[48]

The first bill prohibiting any institution that practiced segregation from receiving federal funding had been proposed in the House in 1957 by Representative Adam Clayton Powell (D-N.Y.), a black civil rights activist.[49] The measure was defeated by a vote of 123 to 70, as were bills introduced in succeeding years. The *Simkins* ruling lent the legitimacy of the courts (and by implication the Constitution) to the issue. When Congress enacted the Civil Rights Act of 1964, the watershed racial legislation of the century, the Powell amendment became Title VI. Title VI stated that "no person in the United States shall, on the grounds of race, color or national origin, be excluded from participation in, be denied the benefits of, or be subject to discrimination under any program receiving federal assistance."[50] No longer would racial discrimination by any private organization that received federal funds be tolerated.

Title VI applied to more than 400 federal programs administered by 33 agencies. Next to the courts, HEW became the foremost government agent for changing the nation's racial patterns. HEW had the largest Title VI enforcement office in the federal government. It was responsible for coordinating all compliance investigations in all its programs. Each regional agency in turn was responsible for carrying out day-to-day enforcement activities.[51] This arrangement meant that regional managers and field staff who for decades had complied with local practices that promoted racial segregation now became Title VI compliance investigators.

HEW's task was complicated by loopholes inserted into Title VI by southern congressmen.[52] One provision prohibited federal officials from applying sanctions until they demonstrated that compliance could not be secured voluntarily. Others specified that any regulations adopted had to be approved by the president, that funds could not be terminated to a recipient who ignored the regulations unless the proper congressional committee gave consent, and that the termination applied only to the program that was not in compliance. Title VI also excluded employment practices, which were covered by other titles of the Civil Rights Act and thus administered by other federal agencies.[53]

Within HEW the Public Health Service was given responsibility for desegregating 20,000 hospitals, 2,000 nursing homes, and over 1,000 home health agencies through a newly created Office of Equal Health Opportunities (OEHO). OEHO was headed by Robert Nash, a career civil service employee, who viewed Title VI as an opportunity to use the threat of withholding funds to demand compliance.[54] The problem was that OEHO had only 31 full-time office staff and a field staff of 72. Although Nash could investigate complaints and try to speed up integration, he had no real leverage.[55] A year after the Civil Rights Act was enacted, virtually no progress had been made in hospital desegregation.

Implementing Medicare

The leverage to enforce Title VI came from a different quarter—the implementation of Medicare. During debates in Congress over Medicare, reformers in the Social Security Administration (SSA) had purposely avoided any mention of civil rights. Robert Ball, who was now

SSA commissioner and an expert long-range strategist, recalled, "We didn't want it brought up legislatively. It would have been a big barrier to passage in the Senate, particularly if it had been clear that this was going to be applied. I think everyone knew it, but they didn't want to have to go on record about it."[56] The SSA had just begun planning the process of certifying hospitals and nursing homes for Medicare eligibility on the basis of quality, and now Medicare was swept into the Title VI compliance efforts. To become eligible for federal funds, hospitals applying for Medicare certification also had to prove they were not discriminating.

In fall 1965, representatives from the SSA met with Public Health Service officials to plan the compliance effort. They agreed that the SSA would contribute staff and help formulate rules and procedures to determine whether hospitals would be eligible for Medicare funds. The Public Health Service would take responsibility for large city hospitals and university hospitals, while the SSA would evaluate smaller hospitals, nursing homes, and home health agencies.[57] The SSA regional offices would then review all the compliance reports to see if they were complete and acceptable. About 6,900 small hospitals were immediately cleared on civil rights compliance, leaving 5,500 requiring further follow-up. A hastily assembled staff of nearly 1,000 people, 500 from the SSA and 500 from the Public Health Service, plus medical students on summer internships and outside consultants, was given a three-week crash training program in civil rights and sent south to inspect hospitals and decide if they were complying with the law.

In many respects, the SSA was the ideal government agency to implement Title VI. It had field and regional offices already operating to administer Social Security as well as a large staff of managers and field representatives. It had just issued 19 million Medicare cards, opened 100 district offices, and hired thousands of people to implement Medicare. The SSA was also the only federal agency that was relatively free from both national and local political pressures, because benefits were not provided through local relief authorities but went directly to beneficiaries.[58] The SSA also had a policy legacy that was compatible with civil rights objectives. Its historical agenda was to protect the vulnerable; its clients were the elderly, the widowed, and the disabled. As Robert Ball explained:

> From the very foundation of the social security program, our ob-
> jective has been to provide courteous, efficient service and equal
> treatment under the law to all claimants. Our training activities
> have always stressed this. Our legislative proposals . . . have al-
> ways been prepared with this in mind. . . . The whole process of
> certifying the eligibility of providers of services, including their
> compliance with Title VI of the Civil Rights Act, is merely an ex-
> tension of these principles to a new group of beneficiaries.[59]

The same could not be said of the Public Health Service. Its state agencies, which had been involved in the certification of segregated hospitals
for Hill-Burton for decades, now had to confront these same hospitals
and demand they change their practices. Said one Public Health Service
physician involved in the effort, "I am not sure they were 100 percent
enthusiastic about the task. They lived in those communities."[60]

Yet SSA officials had struggled for Medicare for more than a decade.
Ending racial segregation while trying to implement a new program
that had been resisted by physicians every step of the way seemed a
daunting task to Robert Ball:

> It seems to me that one of the greatest threats to the successful
> administration of this pioneering program of health insurance is
> the fear that hospitals and the medical profession have of federal
> interference. If our first contact with them, even before the first
> agreement is signed or the first benefit is paid, is for the Social
> Security Administration to inspect the hospitals for Title VI com-
> pliance, we will be putting an unnecessary barrier in the way of
> getting . . . off to a good start. . . . I do not believe that we can be
> asked to do more than what is inherent in the social security re-
> sponsibility without serious risk.[61]

Using Medicare certification to determine Title VI compliance might
damage delicate public relations surrounding the new program. As Ball
explained:

> The first hard news coming out of implementation of the hospital
> insurance program would be controversy over whether certain
> providers of service [discriminate]. . . . Not only would these con-
> troversies be aired in the public press long before benefits [were

paid], they would be aired at the very time we are making every effort to quiet the fears of doctors and others about the Federal Government's involvement in the areas of hospital and medical insurance.[62]

To counter these fears, early in 1966 the SSA embarked on an aggressive public information campaign. Booklets explaining Title VI requirements were distributed to hospitals, nursing homes, and home health agencies. Talks were presented to labor groups, the insurance industry, religious groups, fraternal organizations, senior citizens' groups, and organizations of hospitals and physicians. The help of the AHA and the AMA was enlisted to prepare hospitals to comply with Title VI.[63] Carlton Spitzer, director of the HEW Office of Public Information, set up interviews with hospital administrators to explain SSA's objectives and allay their concerns, often encountering resistance and suspicion. He also attempted to meet with local newspaper editors to get them to run op-ed pieces on the integration effort. Many refused even to see him, such as the beefy editor who ushered him out of his office after a two-minute conversation, his hand on Spitzer's elbow, almost pushing him down a flight of stairs.[64]

To initiate the process, the surgeon general mailed all hospital administrators a letter informing them that no hospital could discriminate on the basis of race or deny staff privileges to qualified physicians who had been rejected by local medical societies because of race.[65] Satisfying these conditions placed hospital administrators on a collision course with physicians who viewed decisions about where to treat patients as their exclusive purview. As one SSA staffer fretted:

When, because of Medicare, pressures brought on hospitals' boards for them in turn, to bring pressure on physicians to send Negro patients to what have been predominantly "white hospitals" and white patients to what have been predominantly "Negro hospitals," this can be construed as an interference with the practice of medicine. And having persuaded physicians to use hospitals without regard to race, can we maintain that they should not respect the wishes of patients who prefer to share rooms with only persons of their own race? This would seem to be interference with the practice of medicine.[66]

According to Morton Lebow, public information officer for the OEHO, physicians from the Mobile Infirmary in Alabama continued referring black and white patients to separate hospitals. When that practice was challenged, an alarmed hospital administrator declared, "You don't mean to tell me that you expect us to tell our doctors where they can send their patients?"[67] Despite their misgivings about federal intervention in the practice of medicine, most doctors willingly complied because with Medicare they would be guaranteed payment for treating the elderly, a service they had often performed free.[68]

By May 30, 1966, the SSA had a list of all institutions that were in compliance with Title VI. The next step was to develop an "action list" of hospitals not yet cleared.[69] Ball declared, "I would like to keep the Public Health Service going during the next week in moving into every area where there is a significant problem and pressing quickly for solutions. Or, if we can no longer expect voluntary compliance, to immediately sue."[70] On July 1, 1966, Medicare was put into operation. Still fighting federal intervention, AMA president James Appel suggested that hospitals in communities that opposed integration be allowed to participate in Medicare by "switching the burden of bigotry to the patients. . . . A patient who refused to accept the hospital room offered could be placed in a segregated facility, but he would then lose his Medicare payment."[71] Appel's suggestion fell on deaf ears.

Most hospitals were eager to be approved so that they could begin receiving federal funds.[72] Although they "wanted no part of being watched over by the federal government," they "wanted in because of the financial rewards offered."[73] By July 21, 1966, only 320 hospitals were not certified for Medicare. Some southern hospitals avoided complying with Title VI by doing the "HEW shuffle" during on-site inspections, moving white and black patients into new beds in "integrated" rooms and wards for the study team's visit.[74] In Alabama a local man bragged to an investigator "that they had moved some comatose white patients into rooms with black patients" to fool the investigator.[75] Those who were best at revealing these practices were the local Public Health Service examiners. As the Public Health Service physician quoted earlier explained, "The most feared investigators were white southerners. They knew what they were looking for. We were dealing with deceit at all levels. They sniffed it out."[76]

Establishing compliance in these pockets of resistance was hindered by the difficulty of measuring of racial integration. What constituted an acceptable percentage of black or white patients? In Lynchburg, Virginia, hospital administrators were informed that 13 percent of the patients had to be black before the hospital could win approval. Hospital administrators complained that the quota was too large, given the low percentage of minorities in the service area.[77]

The most controversial issue was biracial room occupancy.[78] In Alabama, several hospitals refused to assign patients to rooms with people of a different race. In Mississippi, the only threats of violence were triggered by this issue.[79] The hospital administrator in Canton was visited by four local Klansmen, who threatened to bomb the hospital if patients were placed in integrated rooms. At another Mississippi hospital, FBI agents investigated allegations of civil rights violations. When the local Public Health Service manager entered the hospital in Meridian, Mississippi (a town where three civil rights workers were murdered), for a minor operation, he shared a room with the head of the local NAACP, a symbolic act that was widely criticized by the community. But after his release the hospital made other biracial room assignments.

The regional assistant commissioner of the SSA in Atlanta, James Murray, suggested ignoring room assignments initially and granting hospitals otherwise in compliance "provisional certification." Not only would this avoid dealing with the stickiest racial issue, it would ward off complaints that the government was interfering in physicians' medical decisions. This compromise was unacceptable to OEHO head Robert Nash, who insisted that "requiring hospitals to assign patients to rooms on a nondiscriminatory basis cannot in any way be considered interference with the practice of medicine."

Tearing down racial barriers did not necessarily lead to integration. Some black patients refused to go to white hospitals, fearing they would not receive proper care.[80] For example, in one Arkansas town, patients continued to go to racially separate hospitals even though both hospitals were officially desegregated. Local administrators begged Public Health Service officials, "Tell us what we are doing wrong and we will make it right. . . . Give us some guidelines . . . give us time . . . don't shut off our hospital beds."[81] This situation created a conundrum for SSA officials, for refusing approval of a hospital could mean denying care to

Medicare beneficiaries. In Mount Bayou, Mississippi, for example, the black hospital could not meet the quality standards for Medicare approval, while the white hospital was having Title VI difficulty.[82] As a result, Medicare beneficiaries had to travel long distances to hospitals in other counties. Further, many insurance companies had canceled hospital coverage for people 65 and older the day Medicare began operating. That meant that Social Security beneficiaries who lived in counties without an approved Medicare hospital would have no insurance coverage at all. This dilemma deprived "the most needy citizens of all—the lowest income, least educated, least resourceful . . . Negro and white alike—of the benefits the law was designed to provide."[83] It also created a public relations nightmare for the SSA. As one staff member explained:

> For a long time the people of this area have been fed a steady diet of anti-government propaganda heightened of course by their deep fears of the civil rights program, but until now they have not largely tended to associate social security . . . with all this. Now I believe there is a very strong feeling that social security has gone over to the enemy.[84]

Despite these problems, significant advances were made.[85] Many hospitals admitted their first black patients, made room assignments without regard to race, removed barriers in waiting rooms, operating rooms, and cafeterias, and offered staff privileges to black physicians for the first time.[86] By October, only 12 hospitals still were not certified.[87] A few holdouts avoided complying with Title VI but received reimbursement from Medicare by billing the government under an "emergency treatment" provision. This provision allowed Medicare patients to receive care from a noncomplying hospital in the event of a life-threatening situation. Instead of using the provision on an emergency basis, these hospitals used it routinely to furnish segregated care. After Mal Schechter, the Washington editor of the journal *Hospital Practice*, publicized the fact that 86 percent of the 21,000 emergency Medicare claims filed in 1967 came from the South (more than half from Alabama and Mississippi), this flexibility was eliminated. Within 18 months nearly every large southern hospital was receiving Medicare funds on a regular basis.[88]

Conclusion

For two-thirds of a century, southern politicians had resisted national health insurance for fear that federal financing of health care services would lead to federal monitoring of racial practices. Their agenda was compatible with the desires of physicians, who had their own reasons for opposing government intervention in the health care system. Medicare realized these fears by requiring hospitals to provide health care services without regard to race. As federal officials began certifying hospitals for Medicare eligibility on the basis of quality, they also forced the hospitals to prove that they were not discriminating. In investigating charges of discrimination, however, federal officials delved into every aspect of hospital operations, from patient room assignments to physician referral networks. Thus the dismantling of racial segregation also allowed federal officials to monitor internal hospital affairs, penetrating the barrier between providers and the federal government and undermining provider sovereignty in the pursuit of racial justice.

four

Don't Rock the Boat

Medicare had to be operating by July 1, 1966. Federal officials had less than a year to notify more than 19 million Social Security beneficiaries that they were eligible for benefits, inform hospitals and physicians of their new rights and responsibilities, and appoint "fiscal intermediaries" to handle claims and process payments. Most Americans knew that Congress had passed a new health insurance program for the elderly, but few understood what benefits Medicare would actually provide or who would be eligible to receive them.

The first task was to win over the AMA, whose cooperation would be crucial to Medicare's success. On July 3 President Lyndon Johnson agreed to meet with AMA officials who had come to complain about socialized medicine. A man of electrifying energy who could be both compassionate and cruel, Johnson was a consummate politician with an "uncanny instinct for the jugular of his adversaries."[1] As the doctors sat around the table, waiting politely for the president to speak, Johnson gave them the "treatment." He first told the assembled physicians, "Your country needs your help. Your President needs your help." Would they be willing to serve in Vietnam, treating wounded civilians? When the doctors immediately responded that they would, Johnson told an aide to get the press. In front of the assembled reporters, the president praised the doctors' willingness to help the Vietnamese. Then when reporters, primed by aides, asked the physicians if they would support Medicare, Johnson replied indignantly, "Of course, they'll support the law of the land." Turning to AMA president James Appel, he said, "You tell him." "Of course, we will," Appel meekly replied. A few weeks later the AMA publicly announced its intention to support Medicare.[2]

Although the battle appeared to have been won, in truth it had only begun. Appel was a moderate in AMA circles, and when Dr. Milford Rouse, former speaker of the House of Delegates, assumed office, he was less conciliatory. He made speeches attacking Medicare, refused to accept Medicare patients, and urged other doctors to do the same. On August 12, 1965, the Association of American Physicians and Surgeons published a *New York Times* op-ed piece telling physicians to boycott Medicare.[3] Some physicians defiantly flaunted their disdain for federal officials. Others complied, recognizing, as Ohio doctor Jack Schreiber did, that "Medicare's here to stay. We aren't bitter and we aren't soreheads. But we do plan to protect the doctor-patient relationship from outside interference."[4]

Notifying Beneficiaries

The task of notifying current Social Security beneficiaries as well as the thousands of people who were nearing 65 but not yet receiving benefits fell to SSA officials.[5] Their job was made infinitely more complex by the different requirements for Part A, the hospital benefit, and Part B, physicians' services. Everyone eligible for Social Security benefits would automatically receive Part A, but Part B was voluntary. People who didn't sign up for Part B coverage by March 31 would have to wait for the next enrollment period, which would not be for two years. Getting people signed up was a pressing priority, because most private insurance companies immediately dropped coverage of any services included in Medicare. Some canceled their coverage for people over 65 entirely.[6]

The SSA had had years to plan for Part A, but Part B was added at the last minute. To get people enrolled in Part B, the SSA embarked on a massive public information campaign. Press releases were sent to local newspapers and handed out to newspaper columnists. Posters were hung in Social Security offices, drugstores, and community centers telling people how to enroll. Messages were broadcast on popular radio shows, especially those that appealed to older audiences, such as *Bring Back the Bands* and the *Eddie Arnold Show*. Films were distributed to religious, fraternal, labor, and civil rights organizations.[7] Every Social Security beneficiary received at least three letters as reminders to sign up for Part B. The SSA also worked with the Office of Economic Opportunity, which ran Johnson's antipoverty programs, to do outreach in inner cities and among the homebound elderly. Special mailings were sent to nursing home administrators, urging them to tell their patients about Part B.[8] Most older people welcomed the new program, but some remained suspicious. John Sterusky became so annoyed after he received a sixth letter that he scrawled across it, "Rec'd 6 of these. Are you nuts? For the sixth time, NO."[9]

Despite this effort, thousands of people missed the deadline to enroll. Some discarded the notices, thinking they were junk mail. Others lost the letters or failed to enroll because they incorrectly presumed that their existing insurance policies would still cover physicians' services. Even with these slip-ups, in less than six months 88 percent of the people eligible for Part B had signed up.

Implementing Part A

In designing Medicare, federal officials had agreed that hospitals would be fully reimbursed for their costs, physicians would be paid their "usual and customary" fees, and private insurers would handle claims, inspect providers, and review billed costs.[10] SSA commissioner Robert Ball explained, "By and large, our posture at the beginning was one of paying full costs but not intervening very much in the way hospitals, or at least the better ones, conducted their business."[11] There would be no federal intervention in the sacred doctor-patient relationship. As Section 1801 of the Medicare legislation declared:

> Nothing in this title shall be construed to authorize any Federal officer or employee to exercise any supervision or control over the practice of medicine or the manner in which medical services are provided, or over the selection, tenure or compensation of any officer or employee of any institution, agency or person providing health services; or to exercise any supervision or control over the administration or operation of any such institution, agency or person.[12]

In keeping with this hands-off policy, groups of hospitals and nursing homes were allowed to choose their own "fiscal intermediaries" to administer Part A payments. The fiscal intermediaries were supposed to evaluate claims, determine whether charges were valid and consistent with prevailing rates, and make the payments from federal Medicare funds. To further appease the providers, any hospital that disagreed with the nomination of its group could pick a different intermediary. The SSA then had to negotiate contracts with the intermediaries to cover their administrative costs and work out the operating details.[13]

Medicare reinforced the cozy relationship between insurers and hospitals in several ways. Under the terms of the legislation creating Medicare, the SSA could contract with one national organization that would then subcontract with local organizations, an arrangement tailored for Blue Cross, whose various member plans were represented nationally by the Blue Cross Association (BCA). During the planning period, the BCA was paid a fee to participate in establishing Medicare regulations and contract provisions. When the BCA submitted a huge bill for start-up expenses, SSA officials complained, leading to a "tug-of-war."[14] But SSA officials grudgingly paid the bill. The AHA then nominated the BCA to administer Medicare and urged hospitals and nursing homes to nominate Blue Cross as their fiscal intermediaries.[15] As a result, 80 percent of the fiscal intermediaries chosen were Blue Cross organizations.[16]

During the numerous hearings held on Medicare, Congress had never debated the wisdom of allowing the private insurance industry to perform these critical administrative functions. The only time the issue was raised was on the Senate floor after the Medicare bill had passed both committees, when Senator Wayne Morse (D-Ore.) warned:

> These are non-governmental agencies whose basic commitment is not to the beneficiaries. . . . Blue Cross is essentially a creature and instrumentality of the hospitals. . . . while Blue Cross can legitimately serve as the agent of the hospitals in dealing with the government, it cannot possibly serve as the agent of the government.[17]

As soon as Medicare was enacted, the SSA began secret negotiations with the AHA and Blue Cross to determine the formula for reimbursing hospitals. The AHA "had a large voice" in these negotiations, worrying Senator Clinton Anderson that HEW was "going too far to win broad support."[18] SSA actuary Robert Myers, too, had doubts: "I had thought that Blue Cross, by being our fiscal intermediary, would be on our side in the necessary collective bargaining with the hospitals so as to see that we get an equitable and adequate rate structure. However, the approach . . . seems to be leaning in the other direction."[19] As negotiations proceeded, members of Congress complained that they could not get copies of minutes and reports. Finally, a set of general principles was released on May 2, 1966, just two months before Medicare would begin operating. The principles adopted specified that hospitals would be reimbursed retroactively for all "allowable" expenses plus a 2 percent bonus above their actual costs with no upper limit. Included as allowable costs were basic services, compensation for administrators and physicians who were hospital employees, hospital supplies, drugs prescribed in hospitals, depreciation on buildings and equipment that had been purchased with Hill-Burton funds, and loosely defined public relations costs including dues to professional organizations, professional conferences, lobbying, and even antiunion campaigns.[20] Alarmed, Senator Russell Long (D-La.), chairman of the Senate Finance Committee, expressed "grave concern" that program costs would far exceed original estimates.[21]

Medicare payments for nursing home care were implemented six months after the rest of the program began operating, on January 1, 1967. The legislation specified that Medicare would cover all charges for the first 20 days of skilled nursing care in an extended-care facility following a hospital stay, but only for the condition or illness that led to the hospitalization. For the next 80 days, Medicare would also pay for all but $5 a day. Over the objections of the SSA, the for-profit nursing home industry lobbied Congress and won support for an amendment allowing private nursing homes to be reimbursed for these allowable charges plus a 7.5 percent profit, which they argued was a "reasonable return on equity capital investment."[22] Then for-profit hospitals and nonprofit nursing homes began demanding the same return on their Medicare patients.[23] Unwilling to upset these providers, the SSA agreed. One of the few conditions imposed was that hospitals had to agree to accept the government payment and not charge patients an additional sum. One skeptical federal official noted, "We didn't want a hospital or physician to say, We'll take cost for all the aged that are poor but when we get a nice, juicy one, we'll charge our regular charges which are more."[24]

The sole cost containment provision in Medicare specified that participating hospitals had to appoint a utilization review board to ensure that hospital admissions were medically necessary, a provision that the AMA derided as "an example of governmental interference with the practice of medicine."[25] Since patients only entered hospitals on the recommendation of a physician, that involved monitoring physicians' traditional gatekeeping role. The SSA, reluctant to aggravate physicians, only rarely enforced utilization review standards.[26] Even so, physicians were furious that they could no longer admit patients simply by asking for a bed but now had to sign forms certifying that the admission was medically necessary. One doctor fumed, "The degree and the amount of federal control exerted on a local level through the power of the purse string is simply fantastic to behold."[27] Another doctor complained, "After a while, the federal government will be practicing medicine and doctors will just be the errand boys."[28] But the utilization review committees had no formal criteria for determining whether admissions were necessary and no power to deny payment. In most cases the review committees functioned ineffectively; in some cases they did not function at all.

Although the fiscal intermediaries were supposed to evaluate costs, most plans essentially abdicated this responsibility by subcontracting hospital audits to independent accounting firms such as Price, Waterhouse, which didn't challenge charges submitted for payment.[29] Blue Cross and other insurers simply became administrators, handling claims from patients but exerting no controls. In 1965 alone hospital daily charges jumped 16.5 percent, and between 1967 and 1973 Blue Cross administrative costs for Medicare Part A increased 201 percent.[30] Inflation in health care costs was also triggered by hospital supply companies that charged hospitals five times the regular price for such items as scissors, tape measures, and furniture. Investment analysts began telling clients that hospital supplies were a good investment because they were recession-proof.[31] Actuary Robert Myers decried this "intolerable and deliberate" draining of the Medicare trust fund, to no avail.[32]

Implementing Part B

Like Part A, Part B would also be administered by private insurance companies that would serve as "carriers" to handle claims and pay physicians' bills.[33] One hundred and thirty-six insurers submitted proposals.

Among them were nearly all the large commercial insurers. As a general rule, the SSA selected Blue Shield in areas where it was strong and commercial insurers where they had a large share of the market.[34] By July 1966 19 Blue Shield plans and 9 commercial companies had signed contracts to administer Part B. The commercials included the three powerhouses—Aetna Life, Mutual of Omaha, and Prudential.[35] In a few states, the state medical society was allowed to administer Part B. The Rhode Island Medical Society won the contract in its state, but the Mississippi Medical Society was rejected in favor of Travelers Life. Mississippi physicians, who were "disgruntled" by the decision, demonstrated their discontent "by not making much effort to cooperate or even communicate with [Travelers]."[36]

Part B payments were based on a fee-for-service formula that guaranteed physicians full payment for "prevailing" charges.[37] A charge was considered reasonable as long as it was consistent with the doctor's customary charge and not radically higher than the average charge for that service in the area. Each carrier was supposed to keep a file on each participating physician, showing what was charged for a particular service. Some carriers made a real attempt to monitor providers. For example, Travelers Life rejected a claim of $250 for removal of an eye and reduced the payment to $180 as consistent with prevailing charges in the area.[38] Other carriers were less responsible. More than two years after Medicare began operating, 14 carriers had yet to develop procedures for determining physicians' "customary" charges or whether charges billed to Medicare were "reasonable." By the time controls were put into effect, they were too late. As one Senate staffer complained, "They closed the barn door quite belatedly. Because of the length of the delay the carriers no longer have any way of telling what a physician's charges were before Medicare started."[39]

The fact that Medicare contained no controls on doctors' fees was speedily communicated to local medical societies, "not only to prepare doctors for July 1 but to help them adjust fees." As one aide cynically noted, the prospect of Medicare payments based on customary charges was "serving as an incentive to extremely sudden realization on the part of many physicians that their present fees [were] inadequate."[40] In the past, physicians had often charged what they thought a patient could pay. With Medicare they abandoned this practice and charged indigent patients the same as more affluent patients. Dr. Brendan Mylans defended this practice:

> I do not represent the ultra-conservative nit-wit branch of the American Medical Association. . . . However, in all fairness one must point out that . . . most physicians . . . even the most grasping, have treated some patients for nothing, or for a nominal sum. . . . However, now that the Government has assumed financial responsibility for the medical care of these patients, it is hardly fair to ask physicians to donate their services to the Government.

As one physician phrased it, "I am very glad to do charity work for my patients, but I certainly do not regard the Federal Government as an object of charity."[41] Some physicians made "gang" visits to nursing homes, seeing large numbers of patients without examining them individually, then charged Medicare for individual exams.[42] Unwilling to rock the boat because of "their preoccupation with having everything neatly in order by July 1," federal officials ignored these dubious practices.[43] Yet there were also legitimate reasons for costs to rise, as many older patients were now receiving medical care that they hadn't been able to afford previously.

Physicians also demanded the right to bill their patients directly and then let the patient be reimbursed by the insurance carrier. They preferred direct billing because there would be no government oversight and thus no limit on fees.[44] SSA officials objected that direct billing could create financial hardships for patients who might have to wait weeks or months to be reimbursed and advocated instead the "assignment" method of billing. Under the assignment method, patients would sign over their Medicare benefits to the physician, who would then be reimbursed by the government. The problem was that physicians who took assignment would not be allowed to charge more than what the insurance carrier deemed to be reasonable. Naturally, physicians objected to mandatory assignment on the grounds that it would lead to government regulation. One doctor mistakenly argued, "When the doctor sends a bill to the federal government [although the bill would actually go to the carrier], it will be scrutinized to see whether it's reasonable or not."[45] To avoid antagonizing doctors further, the SSA allowed direct billing, even though patients often had to pay the difference between what the physician charged and what the carrier allowed.

The entirely predictable result was that average fees for office visits immediately shot up. General practitioners' fees rose 25 percent, internists' 40 percent. Yet the fees of pediatricians, who treated children and thus had no Medicare patients, remained constant.[46] As one physician admitted:

> No health care program has ever strained the ethics of the medical profession as Medicare is doing. The temptation to chisel is enormous. . . . I'll admit that I try to take as much Medicare money from Uncle Sam as I possibly can. From what I've seen and heard, a lot of other doctors are doing the same. . . . Before Medicare I individualized the fee on every case. . . .Those days are gone forever. Now with Medicare patients, we doctors charge our "usual fee" for everything.[47]

With hospitals reimbursed for whatever they charged plus 2 percent, physicians paid their "customary" fees, suppliers totally unregulated, extended care facilities guaranteed 7.5 percent profits, a stepped-up demand for services, and insurance companies simply accommodating, there was neither the will nor the mechanism to contain costs.[48] Concerned that inflation was occurring even before Medicare took effect, in December 1965 Senator Anderson scheduled Finance Committee hearings to investigate the contractual arrangement between the government and the providers.[49] It was the first time Congress had ever conducted hearings on a program before it began. Testimony suggested that SSA officials were being overwhelmed by the provider groups as "Blue Cross, Blue Shield and other carriers . . . rushed to get state approval of increased rates before July 1."[50] When Senator Anderson proposed revising reimbursement formulas, he was barraged with complaints from hospitals and doctors. Four years later an investigation found that Medicare paid more than other Blue Shield contracts and that carrier performance was "erratic, inefficient, costly."[51]

Implementing Medicaid

Medicaid was not really a new program: it was basically an expansion of the Kerr-Mills program, which provided federal grants to the states to fund health care for the aged poor. Medicaid increased federal funds to the states but allowed states to decide how generous benefits would be or whether there would even be a state program. States that established Medicaid programs had to provide hospital care, physician services, and skilled nursing home services, but the amount of services required was not specified. State Medicaid plans had to include the *categorically needy*, which referred to recipients of old-age assistance (OAA), aid to the blind, and Aid to Families with Dependent Children (AFDC). States also could choose to include the *medically needy*, people whose income was too high to qualify for cash assistance but was insufficient to pay their medical expenses.[52] Most often, the medically needy were nursing home residents whose care costs exceeded their income.

Medicaid required the states to designate a single agency to administer the program. Many local Blue Cross plans, encouraged by Blue Cross of America, bid to implement Medicaid and won contracts in 23 states.[53] Other states administered the program themselves through state health departments.[54] Medicaid hospital payments were based on "reasonable costs" and thus completely open-ended. However, physicians were paid a set fee, as they had been in the state welfare medical programs before Kerr-Mills and in Kerr-Mills.[55] States that were already paying the health care expenses of the medically needy through Kerr-Mills could "buy in" to the Medicare program by paying the Part B premium and any coinsurance and deductibles. The buy-in allowed states to shift some of the health care costs of the elderly to the federal government. Since Medicare fees were unregulated, soon the "medical societies [were] plumping for States to buy in" because of the "inviting prospect of Part B fees."[56]

Sensing easy federal money, the states began pressuring HEW to implement Medicaid quickly. In the rush to begin operating Medicaid, some of the same administrative problems that plagued Medicare occurred, but with greater variation across states. Those that had smoothly operating Kerr-Mills programs, such as Pennsylvania and California, had plans ready before the federal guidelines were even written. The California program offered comprehensive benefits, including inpatient and outpatient care and a wide range of preventive and rehabilitative services. In other states the agencies responsible for administering Medicaid failed to determine "customary charges" for services, audit hospital books, or assist hospitals in setting up their utilization review programs. In states where Blue Cross administered Medicaid, auditors noted excessive and unaccountable payments for administrative costs.[57]

Within two years Medicaid was absorbing an increasing share of state revenues, crowding out spending for other social services. In New York, "medically needy" was defined so liberally that nearly half the state's residents could have qualified for benefits. In 1967 Congress sought to rein in costs by severely restricting the definition of "medically needy" to 133 1/3 percent of the AFDC eligibility level. States could continue to provide benefits to higher income individuals would receive no federal match. As a result, the potential number of Medicaid recipients dropped by 750,000 in 1968 and 900,000 in 1969 but also led to howls of protest from the states.[58] In 1971 new regulations allowed states to pay less than full "reasonable costs" for hospital care for the poor.[59] But when the New York legislature attempted to impose a ceiling on Medicaid expenditures, the hospitals sued and won a ruling that they had to be paid the full cost of services provided to Medicaid patients.[60]

Controlling Costs

By the end of the 1960s, the costs of the war in Vietnam and rising prices for energy and health care had created record budget deficits and inflation, ending two decades of economic growth and close to balanced budgets.[61] As the country's economic woes mounted, the health care system came under intense scrutiny for encouraging waste and inefficiency. No one could explain why there was a $49 a day difference in hospital charges between two hospitals in the same community serving similar patient populations, why patients in Philadelphia stayed in the hospital two days longer on average than patients in any other part of the country, or why there was no rational system of planning or coordination of resources with needs. In the Seattle area, for example, occupancy rates in some hospitals were below 50 percent, yet the city planned to build another 500 beds.[62]

When Richard Nixon became president in 1968, he proclaimed that the health care system faced a "massive crisis": "Unless action is taken . . . to meet that crisis within the next two or three years, we will have a breakdown in our medical care system."[63] The solution would not come from the commercial insurance companies, who never viewed their mission as cracking down on the providers but simply responded to cost increases by increasing coinsurance and deductibles, reducing the scope of benefits, or raising premiums.[64] Nor would a solution come from Blue Cross, whose primary mission seemed to be protecting the hospitals. When Pennsylvania's insurance commissioner held hearings to determine how hospital charges were calculated, Blue Cross officials refused to release their records: "We do not believe any responsible public purpose would be served by the indiscriminate release of the detailed information relating to salaries, other operating expenses and financial stability."[65]

Some concerted government response was required. The question was what form it would take. Although Nixon was a firm believer in the free market and ideologically opposed to wage or price controls, his economic advisors convinced him that inflationary pressures would continue to mount unless the government intervened in the wage- and price-setting process. Early in 1971 Nixon announced his New Economic Policy. It would involve a mandatory wage-price freeze for 90 days followed by a 2 to 3 percent yearly limit on average price increases and a 5.5 percent cap on wage hikes.[66] Medical care was singled out for special treatment, with physicians' fee increases capped at 2.5 percent annually and rises in hospital charges limited to 6 percent. Within a few months it appeared that the inflationary psychology had been broken. From August to November, the consumer price index rose by only 2.9 percent. But there were pressures to end the freeze from the start. Congress was bent on exempting some areas from control, and commercial insurers argued that the freeze on hospital charges and physicians' fees had halted new sales. More worrisome was that the administration might also freeze insurance premiums.[67] To allay these concerns, Nixon met personally with insurance company executives and promised not to include insurance rates in the price controls.[68]

The question was how to undo the controls without damaging the economy and creating another inflationary surge. In January 1973 the mandatory controls were replaced by voluntary guidelines. Immediately the stock market plunged and consumer prices soared. By April food prices were up 28 percent. Nixon restored the freeze in June for another 60 days, then began a process of dismantling all wage and price controls, industry by industry.[69] When the freeze was lifted for most goods and services, the controls remained on health care and three other key industries. Congress allowed these controls to expire in April, resulting immediately in another sharp increase in physician fees and hospital charges.

Some formal apparatus had to be established to monitor health care costs permanently. The utilization review boards had proved to be largely ineffectual. A second stab at monitoring costs was included in the 1972 amendments to the Social Security Act. The amendments mostly concerned the Social Security program, but they also made several important changes to Medicare. The most notable change was to extend Medicare to people who were eligible for disability insurance, a proposal that had been in the works since 1967 but had been vehemently opposed by the AMA, whose president, Carl Ackerman, argued that disabled persons who were financially needy could be covered under Medicaid.[70] Although the legislation passed both the House and Senate in 1970, it got hung up as part of broader negotiations over Medicare and was finally incorporated into the 1972 amendments. The amendments also allowed Medicare beneficiaries to choose coverage through a health maintenance organization. A little-noticed provision called for professional standards review organizations (PSROs) to be created to review hospital admissions and develop "standard practices."[71] Because the provision was attached to the amendments, it generated less controversy than it otherwise might have on its own.

The concept of PSROs had come out of a series of Senate Finance Committee hearings investigating the implementation of Medicare. During the hearings, it became evident that many of Medicare's problems stemmed from widespread abuses by providers and that Medicare's intermediaries and carriers had failed to prevent these practices.[72] One solution proposed was to create "program review teams" consisting of physicians, health care professionals, and consumers. The review teams would have authority to evaluate the care given to Medicare and Medicaid patients and deny payments for care deemed unnecessary. Upon learning of the proposal, the AMA countered that the monitoring should be done by state medical societies, a suggestion the Senate Finance Committee staff rejected as "totally self-serving." It would, in effect, turn "responsibility for review over to state medical societies with virtually no accountability."[73] Instead the Finance Committee proposed a stricter method of ensuring accountability through PSROs. The PSROs would be responsible for all medical care provided to Medicare patients to ensure that only medically necessary services were provided.[74] To guide the utilization review and identify inappropriate care, the PSROs would establish a set of professional standards or guidelines for medical care. Although the PSROs would include physicians, they would not be operated exclusively by state medical societies.

As the legislation moved through congressional committees, the AMA lobbied vigorously against it and succeeded in watering it down considerably. National norms and mandatory preadmission certification for elective surgery were eliminated, review of outpatient care was prohibited, a requirement was added that the majority of the committee members be physicians, and restrictions were placed on government control of the PSROs data. By 1974 more than 200 physician-staffed PSROs had been established. In most cases, responsibility for review was contracted to hospitals instead of an outside organization, further weakening their effectiveness.[75] Even though the PSROs had the authority to deny payments to physicians, they rarely applied sanctions because physicians generally were reluctant to challenge their colleagues.[76]

The following year, the medical component of the consumer price index rose 15 percent.[77] When HEW suggested more stringent regulations on PSROs in 1976, the Association of American Physicians and Surgeons sued the federal government, claiming the regulations were unconstitutional.[78] Persistent opposition from physicians caused the PSROs to flounder, and five years later no statistical profiles on length of stay for various diagnoses had been established and no sanctions against hospitals that deviated from national standards had been applied.[79]

In 1974 Congress also enacted a new health planning law, the National Health Planning and Resource Development Act. The legislation created a nationwide system of health systems agencies that would be run by consumer-dominated boards, not by physicians. Their task was to draw up three-year plans, review proposals for new projects, and ensure that new federal expenditures be demonstrably beneficial. The exclusion of physicians led AMA president Russell Roth to complain that physicians "had been relegated to a minor role."[80] His concerns were never realized, for although the health systems agencies were supposed to monitor the use of federal funds, they had no decision-making power and ultimately failed to exert any influence on cost increases.

Conclusion

Under Medicare the federal government poured virtually unlimited public resources into financing care for the aged and the poor, turning health care into a profitable enterprise for physicians, hospitals, and insurance companies. As what had been largely a charitable, ostensibly noncommercial enterprise became a growth industry, costs skyrocketed.

With the federal government unable to contain rising costs through price controls, PSROs, or health systems agencies, advocates of national health insurance now argued that the problem could be solved only by entirely revamping the health care system and placing responsibility in the hands of one purchaser, the federal government. However, the re-formers' task was infinitely more complex than it had been in the 1940s. The need to contain costs diminished the clarity of the message. What problems would national health insurance solve? It would surely need to rationalize the payment system as well as cover people under age 65 who had no health insurance. It would also need to confront an irratio-nal distribution of physicians across regions and between cities and rural areas. One hundred and thirty-four counties had no doctor. That meant that residents of towns such as Tilden, Illinois (population 1,000), had to go to neighboring towns to get medical care. When a little boy from Tilden was struck by a car while riding his bike, the town's mayor, Lawrence Campbell, personally rushed the child to the hospital, but all three doctors were out on call. The child died the following morning. Mr. Campbell later angrily declared, "I still feel that if that boy had immediate attention," his life might have been saved.[81] And any na-tional health insurance plan would have to revamp a hospital system that had grown haphazardly since World War II, with many hospitals operating like private corporations, pursuing gain and rewarding ex-pansion and utilization.[82] Could national health insurance accomplish all these tasks?

five

Cost Containment versus National Health Insurance

The year 1968 was a tumultuous one. In the first six months, protesters staged more than 200 demonstrations against the war in Vietnam. In April, riots erupted in 168 cities following the assassination of civil rights leader Martin Luther King Jr. In June presidential candidate Robert Kennedy was shot by an Arab nationalist angered over RFK's support for Israel. When Lyndon Johnson announced he would not run for reelection, the Democrats faced a bruising battle among three candidates—Georgia governor George Wallace, who played the race card to win the support of southern Democrats and blue collar workers, George McGovern, who sought to woo new constituencies of women and African Americans, and Hubert Humphrey, the consummate New Dealer. At the Democratic national convention in Chicago, 12,000 police and National Guardsmen waded into a crowd of protestors with rifles, bazookas, and flamethrowers. In the midst of chaos, the Democrats nominated Humphrey, who had to face not only his Republican challenger, former vice president Richard Nixon, but also Wallace, who had formed a third party. Wallace captured the Deep South, throwing the election to Nixon, who became president with only 43.4 percent of the vote.[1]

The chaos continued through Nixon's first year in office, with violent anti–Vietnam War protests culminating in May 1970, when National Guardsmen fired on student protestors at Kent State University, killing four and wounding nine. Outraged students on 250 campuses went on strike and then poured into Washington to lobby against the war. A group of construction workers, angry over the campus protests, struck back, attacking demonstrators in New York's financial district and storming City Hall.

With the country in turmoil, this would seem to be an inauspicious time to enact new social programs. Yet, contrary to popular perceptions, Nixon was not adverse to new social spending. During his first term in office, Congress had increased Social Security benefits significantly, added automatic cost-of-living increases, and extended Medicare to the disabled. President Nixon had also endorsed an ambitious welfare reform plan to replace Aid to Families with Dependent Children with a guaranteed annual income for the working and nonworking poor, a plan set up with incentives to encourage work among welfare recipients.[2] That plan was scrapped, but in 1972 old-age assistance was converted into a solely federal program called Supplemental Security Income (SSI), and SSI beneficiaries were granted automatic entitlement to Medicaid.[3]

In this climate, the liberal reformers who had supported Medicare felt cautiously optimistic that national health insurance would be next. Oscar Ewing declared, "Of course, it's inevitable; it's going to come because people need it."[4] Ig Falk remarked, "There is no turning back from the basic goals and policies incorporated in recently enacted public programs for health care; and . . . extension of those programs to more of the population is socially inevitable."[5] Even the director of the National Association of Blue Shield plans conceded, "The remarkable thing is the virtual absence at this point of publicly stated opposition in some form."[6]

Reviving National Health Insurance

The fight to resurrect national health insurance began in 1968 when Walter Reuther made a fiery speech before the American Public Health Association. Reuther charged that the existing health care system was disjointed, antiquated, and obsolete, a nonsystem of care.[7] The only way to remove economic barriers to care and contain health care costs was through national health insurance.[8] Confronting providers with a directness that Medicare reformers never would have dared to employ, Reuther envisioned a program that would strike at the heart of the fee-for-service payment system: "National health insurance must do more than simply pay doctor bills unilaterally determined by the medical profession or simply reimburse hospitals for costs unilaterally determined by them."[9]

Why did Reuther choose this moment to pursue national health insurance? After all, in the 1960s the trade unions had negotiated increasingly generous private health benefits and had won Medicare for retirees, which shored up collective bargaining. Why replace benefits that had been won through negotiations with a government program? One reason is that Reuther, unlike Meany, had never believed that collective bargaining alone could meet all workers' needs. Rather, he felt that many problems could be corrected only through political action. By the late 1960s collective bargaining had reached its limits, as the golden age of automobile manufacturing faded in the face of competition from foreign imports. Yet health care costs continued to rise, taking an increasingly large share of the total wage package negotiated in each new contract, a situation worsened by the expense of retirees' supplemental medigap benefits. Reuther had presumed that employers in the mass production industries would respond to the proliferation of negotiated benefits by turning to the government to assume some of the costs.[10] But he was wrong. Most large firms simply folded their pension and health insurance costs into their product prices and passed them on to consumers. In this context, it made sense for the unions to pursue a federal program.

Reuther also had personal reasons for leading a drive for national health insurance. Ever since the unification of the AFL and the CIO in 1955, Reuther had been at odds with George Meany over union goals and tactics. For example, Reuther believed that the labor movement had to focus on organizing the unorganized. He became a champion of Cesar Chavez, who was trying to bring the poorly paid migrant laborers into the United Farm Workers union. When Chavez organized a boycott of nonunion grapes, Meany made a donation but otherwise refused to endorse the boycott.[11] In the 1960 election Reuther organized a UAW campaign on John Kennedy's behalf, but Meany withheld his full support. Reuther was also more proactive than Meany on civil rights and more strongly against the Vietnam War. These political differences were exacerbated by different personal styles. Reuther led an almost ascetic life. He took few vacations, had little interest in food or drink, and believed that union leaders should share the lifestyle of the workers they represented. Meany drew a large salary, had gourmet tastes in wine and food, smoked expensive cigars, and played golf, a rich man's hobby. He held AFL-CIO annual meetings at a luxurious Miami beachfront hotel and spent his free time nightclubbing, lounging around the pool, and playing gin rummy. Reuther, outraged that labor meetings were held in Florida, refused to stay in the luxurious suite reserved for him and instead moved to a cheaper hotel. Meany's cronies liked to joke that Reuther was sleeping in a linen closet, squeezing his own orange juice.[12]

After a series of increasingly hostile disputes, in 1968 Reuther pulled the UAW out of the AFL-CIO. Although Reuther hoped to enlist other CIO unions in his crusade to revitalize the labor movement, he went alone. Weeks later he tried to create a new voice for organized labor by launching the Alliance for Labor Action. The only partner he could attract was the thuggish Teamsters union, which Reuther had previously tried to expel from the AFL-CIO for corruption and whose president, Jimmy Hoffa, was currently serving a prison sentence for jury tampering.[13]

Now Reuther needed to show what the UAW, marching alone, could achieve. He opened an office in Washington, D.C., and organized the Committee of 100 for National Health Insurance, a top-notch team of trade unionists, social activists, college professors, physicians, and liberal politicians, among them Representative Martha Griffiths (D-Mich.), whose district was the home of the UAW, and Senator Ted Kennedy (D-Mass.), the roguish youngest brother of the Kennedy clan.[14] Kennedy in particular, as a member of the Senate Labor and Public Welfare Committee and widely viewed as the heir apparent to the White House, seemed well positioned to lead the cause.[15] In Reuther's vision, the Committee for National Health Insurance, as it came to be called, would design a health insurance program that would salvage the best features of the current system but overcome the built-in waste and inefficiencies.

In 1969 committee members drafted their first model bill, an ambitious plan that would fold all public and private health plans into a single federal program, called Health Security. Wary of criticism that its plan might be labeled socialized medicine, the committee promised to reorganize the health care system "in an American way" without taking over hospitals or turning physicians into government employees.[16] Instead their plan would provide incentives for physicians to create prepaid group practices, and it would force doctors and hospitals to operate within a set national health budget. Despite the rhetoric to the contrary, the committee's proposal would usurp the market of the health insurance industry by converting private benefits into a public program.

When Kennedy assumed the chairmanship of the Senate Health Subcommittee in 1971, he introduced his Health Security bill. Basic changes were needed, Kennedy proclaimed, "if we are to escape the twin evils of a national health disaster or the total federalization of health care in the 1970s."[17] His grand plan went awry in July, however, when he ran his car off a bridge on Chappaquiddick Island, Massachusetts, while driving a young campaign worker home from a party. As Mary Jo Kopechne lay trapped in the sunken car, Kennedy left the scene, apparently to hide his involvement, leaving his passenger to drown. His power and prestige threatened, Kennedy suffered an instant "political decompression" in the Senate, losing on every key issue in the next ten months.[18]

Kennedy's fall from grace was brief. By spring, polls indicated he could be the Democratic front-runner for the presidency in 1972.[19] Using his subcommittee as a forum to promote national health insurance, Kennedy held splashy hearings in cities all over the country. Everywhere he went, the press slavishly followed. When the tour ended, his subcommittee issued a report entitled "The Health Care Crisis in America." Momentum seemed to be building for some action. That fall the National Governors' Conference endorsed a proposal for national health insurance.

The AMA remained a foe of any government program. Dr. Robert Heidt, president of the Cincinnati Academy of Medicine, wrote Nixon warning that most physicians had campaigned for his election but were discomforted "to hear of your possible plans for implementing national health insurance." He closed by declaring that he hoped the president's deliberations were guided by facts "rather than by self-aggrandizing bureaucrats."[20] But after its bitter defeat over Medicare, the AMA had discovered it was better to help craft a bill friendly to the profession than work against any reform.[21] Instead of launching an advertising campaign against Health Security, the AMA unveiled its own plan, Medicredit, that would enhance the private health insurance system.[22] Under Medicredit, low-income individuals would receive a voucher to purchase a basic health insurance package, middle-income people would get a tax credit for their insurance premiums, and the government would provide grants to the states to cover the very poor, much like Medicaid.[23] But none of the AMA's former allies offered support.

Hospital administrators had benefited from cooperating with the Social Security Administration in the period leading up to Medicare and appreciated the stable source of income Medicare provided. The American Hospital Association announced that it favored expanding Medicare into a national program. As AHA President George Graham explained, "I don't have a fear of government domination. We have to work with government."[24]

The insurance industry also opposed Medicredit, concerned that an infusion of federal funds into the insurance industry in the form of a subsidy would invite federal regulation.[25] Instead commercial insurers drew up their own bill, which ironically was similar to Eisenhower's plan for reinsurance, which they had rejected in the 1950s. Senate Finance Committee chairman Russell Long (D-La.) sponsored the catastrophic coverage bill, which would make each family responsible for covering its own medical expenses by purchasing a private insurance plan. Should these expenses reach catastrophic levels, then the government would pay the excess.[26]

President Nixon opposed any sort of compulsory federal health insurance program, but the deaths of his two brothers and the financial burden his family had to bear from his brother Harold's long illness had made a lasting impression. In 1947 he had surprised party conservatives by supporting a voluntary federal health insurance plan.[27] Now, not to be outdone by Kennedy, whom he regarded as a formidable political foe despite Kennedy's personal troubles, in February Nixon announced his own health program. As White House counsel John Erlichman noted in an internal memo: "I notice . . . that Teddy Kennedy has called for a national, compulsory health insurance program. As you know, this is a demagogic ploy since we can neither afford such a program nor would it be a good thing for the practice of medicine in this country."[28] Nixon's National Health Insurance Partnership Act took a regulatory approach that encouraged the private insurance market. It centered on an employer mandate where employers would either provide health insurance for their employees directly or pay taxes to insure them through a government program. Kennedy immediately fired off a response, labeling Nixon's plan "poorhouse medicine":

> President Nixon's National Health Insurance Partnership is . . . a
> partnership between the Administration and the private health

insurance industry. For the private insurance industry, the Administration plan offers a windfall of billions of dollars annually. The windfall is not entirely a surplus, since elements of the Administration's proposal appear to have originated with the insurance industry itself.[29]

The employer mandate won the endorsement of the Washington Business Group on Health, an organization whose primary mission was to bring together top-level executives to exchange ideas on cost-management techniques and help firms design benefits packages that could reduce health expenses. An organization with 200 member corporations, the Washington Business Group was headed by Willis Goldbeck. A man acknowledged by both admirers and critics to be ahead of business on most health issues, Goldbeck felt that if all employers were required by law to provide health benefits for their employees, it would help level the playing field between those employers who provided generous health benefits for employees and also subsidized their dependents and those who provided no insurance coverage. Another business group, the National Leadership Coalition for Health Care Reform, composed of executives from Chrysler, Bethlehem Steel, Lockheed, Safeway, Xerox, and Georgia Pacific, also endorsed a mandated benefits approach.[30]

Nixon's plan would also provide planning grants and loan guarantees for prepaid group practices called health maintenance organizations (HMOs).[31] The original HMO idea was proposed by David Ellwood, an "evangelical" Minneapolis physician who directed the American Rehabilitation Foundation.[32] Ellwood argued that the current health care cost crisis was caused by perverse incentives that encouraged costly treatment and penalized physicians who returned patients to health. He envisioned a system where primary care doctors would serve as gatekeepers who would evaluate patients before they saw specialists or received costly tests and high-technology care. Ellwood cleverly repackaged the prepaid health plans that had been in existence since the 1940s, called them HMOs, and sold them as a pro-market solution. HMOs would be nonprofit and would use any revenues saved to improve health care or increase the number of insured patients.[33]

At first glance, it is puzzling that a proposal to increase government intervention into the delivery of health care should come from Nixon, who had had the support of the AMA in the 1968 election and who had campaigned against federal intervention into the private sector. Yet Nixon's plan was a cool political calculation. National health insurance would clearly be an important issue in the upcoming elections, and White House aides needed an alternative to Kennedy's much grander proposal. Ellwood's plan did not require an immediate expenditure of large sums, and it involved the private sector. The White House approved the initiative, and in a special health message to Congress in February 1971, Nixon made HMOs the centerpiece of his health policy.[34]

By July, 22 different bills were on the table. At one end of the continuum was the AMA's Medicredit; at the other was Kennedy's plan to collapse all existing programs into a single government plan.[35] Yet despite all the activity in Congress, there was little public demand for national health insurance. Reformers' proposals couldn't compete for media attention with the war in Vietnam, which dominated the headlines every night, and there existed no grassroots force to carry the message to the public. Nelson Cruikshank had become president of the National Council of Senior Citizens, and the seniors who had supported Medicare were now primarily concerned with issues such as obtaining prescription drug benefits and monitoring legislation that might increase their health care costs.[36] As one Committee for National Health Insurance member conceded, there was no "massive public clamor to rearrange our present health care system."[37]

The trade union movement, in disarray since Reuther withdrew the UAW from the AFL-CIO, also failed to provide a firm base of support. On May 9, 1970, Reuther was killed when the twin-engine jet he was taking to inspect the UAW's new education center slammed into a tree and burst into flames.[38] The torch was passed to Leonard Woodcock, who vowed to continue the fight. Meany endorsed Health Security and devoted several radio addresses to the issue. In a 1969 speech, he blasted the medical profession:

> [T]here is something indecent about a small group of people making a lot of money out of the misery of other people. . . . This profiteering by the providers of medical care has had its worst effects in Medicare and Medicaid. . . . Some doctors and other health care practitioners have pounced on these programs as get-rich schemes for the medical profession. . . . And, instead of controls being placed

on fees and charges . . . the burden has fallen on the disadvantaged people the programs were supposed to help.[39]

But health care reform was a low priority for the AFL-CIO, which was absorbed in a battle with the Nixon administration over minority hiring in government-funded construction projects.[40] Health care reform could wait.

Reuther's Committee for National Health Insurance, hoping to stimulate public interest in the issues, outlined an ambitious public information campaign. They would prepare educational materials, hold a rally in Madison Square Garden, run newspaper ads across the country, and create a national speakers' bureau. They would also hire staff organizers to drum up political support and set up a "war room" where they would keep a district-by-district breakdown on the position of congressional candidates.[41] The public relations campaign never materialized, however, impeded by a lack of funds and foot soldiers. Instead the band of warriors toiled on, invisible, their hopes pinned on the fate of Ted Kennedy.

Although Congress took no action on any of the 1972 proposals for national health insurance, a battered, compromised experimental HMO pilot program was enacted the following year. The AMA did everything possible to block any HMO legislation. AMA lobbyists attempted to delay the Senate bill and defeat the House bill in committee.[42] Dr. Malcolm Todd, who was Nixon's personal physician when he was vice president, had ascended to the House of Delegates and was chairman of the Physicians' Committee to Reelect the President. Todd warned Nixon that "this HMO thing" kept coming up when physicians were approached to contribute to Nixon's campaign reelection fund.[43] However, HMOs had the support of corporate employers, who were disturbed by rising health care costs, and the measure was enacted over AMA opposition.

The Health Maintenance Organization and Resources Development Act of 1973 authorized $375 million in planning grants and loans to encourage the development of new HMOs. It also required companies that had 25 or more employees and that provided health insurance to offer an HMO option.[44] HMOs that received federal support would have to offer comprehensive benefits, charge their enrollees the same "community rate," and allow open enrollment at least once a year, regardless of an individual's health. These regulations made HMOs the most heavily regulated part of the health insurance system, placing them at a competitive disadvantage with other insurance plans and dampening their growth. A provision allowed Medicare beneficiaries to enroll in HMOs, but only two HMOs chose to participate.[45]

In the 1972 presidential race, Ted Kennedy, still uncertain of the effect of Chappaquiddick on his political future, announced he would not seek his party's nomination.[46] After Kennedy withdrew from the race, Wilbur Mills, the powerful chairman of the Ways and Means committee, began his own quixotic quest for the presidency, claiming in television interviews that he could defeat Nixon by sweeping the South and border states and winning the support of organized labor. Mills believed that segregation was a "dead issue" and was convinced that he could attract the African American vote. As he explained to a national audience, "I voted as I did over the years [against civil rights] because it was necessary to vote that way if I was to stay in Congress."[47]

During the 1972 election campaign, Kennedy and Mills announced that they would develop a joint national health insurance program in the spring.[48] When one of Nixon's informants leaked the news of the Kennedy and Mills plan, Nixon ordered HEW staff to meet with the Health Insurance Association of America and the AMA to devise an alternative proposal.[49] National health insurance might help the president: "Our media activities, once we find out what Mills is going to do, should start urging enactment of our health insurance proposal."[50] Nixon considered making his own major health policy statement in response but decided against it.[51] Instead he decided to emphasize the success of his wage and price controls in reducing inflation. His antiinflation measures had made "heartening progress in our fight against the increase in health care prices."[52] His staff agreed that this message was "fresher, more positive," giving the nation "one more reason why it would be wise to stay on our present course and not veer off in the directions offered by those who want a nationalized health program."[53] When Kennedy retorted that Nixon had done nothing for health care, Nixon reminded physicians that he had "introduced government action only when not to do so would result in no action at all." Further, he had "never involved the government in a manner that would seek to displace or in any way stunt the tremendous thrust and amazing ingenuity of America's traditionally private medical profession."[54]

Mills never won more than 5 percent of the vote in the primaries, and dropped out of the race after it was revealed that he had accepted $100,000 in illegal campaign contributions secretly funneled to him by Electronic Data Systems, a major processor of health insurance claims.[55] But Mills hinted that if a "draft Kennedy" movement materialized, he would be willing to run as vice president.[56] Although Kennedy and Mills got a plank included in the Democratic Party platform advocating compulsory national health care, the liberal George McGovern won a sufficient number of delegates during the primaries to capture the Democratic nomination.[57]

An astute observer of the national mood, Nixon recognized that the conservative Sunbelt was a growing force in American politics. During the campaign, he developed his "southern strategy," wooing former Wallace voters—white suburbanites, blue-collar workers, and ethnic middle-class Americans, especially those upset over school busing as a way to achieve racial balance. He appointed conservative justices to the Supreme Court, delayed school desegregation in Mississippi, and even courted the isolated Teamsters union by withdrawing his support for antistrike legislation that Republicans had been pushing.[58] One of Nixon's staunchest sources of support came from the AMA. Nixon's ally Malcolm Todd, now AMA president, advised him on how to mobilize physicians, who, he assured Nixon, were "not yet committed to socialized medicine for the U.S."[59] Nixon demolished McGovern in the election, winning 61 percent of the votes and carrying the entire (once solidly Democratic) Deep South as well as a majority of urban votes in traditional Democratic strongholds.

As Nixon embarked on his second term, an event that had occurred the previous June consumed his administration and eventually cost him the presidency. On June 17, 1972, police had arrested five men for breaking into the Watergate apartment complex in Washington, D.C. The men were in the process of attaching listening devices to telephones in offices of the Democratic National Committee. One of the men arrested was the security coordinator of the Committee to Re-elect the President. Another served on the staff of the White House Domestic Council. Although the burglary went almost unnoticed by the public, it generated furious activity at the White House, where incriminating documents were shredded and thousands of dollars paid in hush money.

When the burglars were tried in the spring of 1973, one of them, James McCord, implicated the administration. Further inquiry by the Senate indicated that there had been a cover-up at the highest level. One aide gave the shocking news that Nixon's conversations about the break-in had been tape-recorded. Hoping to quell growing public concern, Nixon appointed Harvard law professor Archibald Cox as special prosecutor. When Nixon ordered the Attorney General, Elliott Richardson, to deny Cox's request for the tapes, Richardson refused to carry out the order and resigned instead. Then the Solicitor General Robert Bork fired Cox. Outrage over what became known as the "Saturday Night Massacre" forced Nixon to appoint another special prosecutor, Leon Jaworski, who took him to court when he still refused to turn over the tapes.[60]

By the end of the year, Nixon's support on legislation in Congress had dropped to the lowest point of any president recorded. On 310 legislative votes taken that year, the White House won on only 51 percent.[61] Nixon might have weathered the scandal were it not for the seemingly endless war in Vietnam and the sorry state of the economy. Price increases ordered by the Organization of Petroleum Exporting Countries (OPEC) caused oil prices to rise 350 percent in 1973. Inflation shot up to a frightening 11 percent, causing a recession in the auto industry that then spread nationwide. As the Watergate scandal enveloped the administration, HEW secretary Caspar Weinberger was charged to draft a new health insurance bill to prove "that the government is not paralyzed."[62] Congress was likely to include health care on the agenda, Weinberger argued, and Nixon would be shut out if he did not have his own plan. At the end of 1973, Weinberger submitted a new proposal to the president, urging him to send it to Congress so that the administration could "regain the initiative in the health area."

Weinberger's plan had two parts. Both gave the insurance industry a central role. The first was the Comprehensive Health Insurance Plan, which involved an employer mandate and would be administered by private insurance companies. The second was the Assisted Health Insurance Plan, where states would contract with private insurance companies to cover low-income and high risk individuals.[63] Although administration officials worried about alienating their natural friends, "doctors, nurses, hospital administrators, insurance companies," they also did not want to appear to be "in their pocket."[64] One HEW staffer warned:

We should keep a low profile in dealing with the health special interest groups. . . . We don't want to publicly identify closely with organized medicine or the insurance industry. The key here is to work closely with these groups in developing an overall strategy for handling Congress.[65]

Nixon announced his national health insurance program in his 1974 State of the Union address. His nemesis, Ted Kennedy, labeled the plan a potential windfall for private insurance interests and announced he would oppose it.[66]

Behind the scenes, Committee for National Health Insurance members, undeterred by their failure to develop their public relations campaign, worked to formulate what they presumed would be Kennedy's new plan, one they understood had to be palatable to the private insurance industry. Conceding that it was politically impossible to exclude the insurers completely, they worried about how to control them so that they could not abuse the public interest. Ig Falk, who chaired the Technical Committee, suggested allowing private insurers to serve as fiscal intermediaries, as they did with Medicare.[67]

As the Committee for National Health Insurance toiled away in obscurity, Kennedy met secretly with Mills, and on April 2, 1974, with much fanfare, they announced their own plan, one that differed in some aspects from what committee members had in mind. Kennedy-Mills would replace the current system with a single national health insurance program that would provide a basic benefit package but otherwise preserve most aspects of the traditional health economy. It would include co-payments and deductibles, allow private insurers to serve as fiscal intermediaries, and leave room for lucrative supplementary benefits. Not unexpectedly, the AMA decried the "socialist" measure.[68] The National Federation of Independent Business called it "nothing more than a first step towards socialized medicine."[69] The AFL-CIO, furious at being excluded from the process, also denounced Kennedy-Mills as a sellout of fundamental principles. What was hardest to swallow was that Kennedy-Mills gave Blue Cross and commercial insurers a permanent role.[70] Even more odious was the sizable coinsurance and deductibles, which would place a heavy burden on low- and middle-income families.[71] The AFL-CIO told union members to press their elected representatives to delay voting on national health insurance until the following year, when they presumed a more liberal and veto-proof Congress would be in office, a reasonable hope given the toll Watergate was taking on the prospects of the Republican Party.

Nixon had his own problems with Watergate now escalating out of control.[72] In late April he finally released an edited version of the tapes, a move that satisfied neither the public nor the House Judiciary Committee. The House of Representatives began drafting articles of impeachment. By summer, new Watergate disclosures had become increasingly alarming. On July 24, the Supreme Court ordered Nixon to surrender the full tapes. Despite the uncertainty over the president's future, in August the House Ways and Means Committee met to mark up a compromise health bill, a plan Nixon seemed willing to consider to distract the public from the scandal. As White House staffer Frank Carlucci wrote to Nixon, "Last Thursday Secretary Weinberger described to you the general outlines of a proposed compromise health insurance bill offered by Chairman Mills. He understood that you wanted him to proceed to negotiate a bill within the compromise being offered."[73]

According to some observers, "The momentum for national health insurance in the Congress was greater than in virtually any other session . . . in American history."[74] The Nixon administration was eager to enact a popular program that could deflect attention from Watergate, and congressional support for health insurance was less partisan and ideological than it had been in the past. In May, an editorial in the *Washington Post* proclaimed, "The question is not *whether* the United States should have national health insurance, but *what kind* it should have."[75] Even insurance agents seemed resigned to the inevitable. In an address to members of the New Jersey and New York Insurance Associations, association president Charles Boteler told them, "We all know that national health insurance is inevitable."[76] These predictions turned out to be incorrect. On August 5 Nixon handed over the complete tapes, knowing they would damn him. Four days later he resigned.

Nixon's resignation left his successor, Vice President Gerald Ford, a nation whose faith in the presidency had been shaken and an economy headed toward recession. Still, in his first address to Congress, Ford singled out national health insurance as the major piece of domestic legislation Congress should pass that year. Senate Finance Committee chairman Long promised, "If the House sends us a bill, we will pass it."[77] Although Mills attempted to keep the ball rolling, Ways and Means became a target for lobbyists and contributions from special interests. When the committee met, AMA representatives attended the meeting and mustered 12 votes for an alternative plan similar to Medicredit with vouchers for the poor and tax credits for the middle class.[78] Labor leaders, who expected to unseat antireform Republicans in the 1974 elections, refused to support any compromise plan.[79] The insurance industry was opposed to several aspects of the measure. Further, few politicians were receiving mail on the issue from constituents, suggesting a distinct lack of public interest.[80] Unable to form a clear majority, Mills announced that the compromise measure would be tabled and that the committee would not resume consideration of national health insurance in the fall.[81]

If there were to be a future for national health insurance, it would no longer be negotiated by Mills. On October 7, the police stopped his Lincoln Continental, which was speeding with the lights off at 2 a.m. Mills staggered out, bleeding and drunk. Then his passenger, Annabel Battistella, a stripper who performed as Fannie Fox, jumped out of the car and leaped into the Tidal Basin. Mills won reelection to the House in November despite the scandal, but Democrats divested Ways and Means of its power to delegate committee assignments. Soon after Mills appeared drunk onstage at Fannie Fox's first appearance at a Boston strip club, he lost his chairmanship.[82]

During Ford's brief turn in office, the economy continued its tailspin with negative economic growth, inflation close to 12 percent and rising, and unemployment over 7 percent. The stalling economy forced Ford to retreat from his commitment to national health insurance.[83] By the end of the year, the campaign to whip inflation dominated. Following the collapse of national health insurance, Committee for National Health Insurance members regrouped to plan a strategy for the future. Gone were the grand ideas. Instead, conceding to political reality and abysmal economic forecasts, they agreed that a practical alternative would be a plan that would include all Americans but phase in benefits to various groups in a piecemeal fashion.[84] A phasing in of health insurance coverage might begin with mothers and children, then be extended to older workers and finally to the nonworking poor.[85]

In the 1976 election President Ford won the Republican Party nomination only after a bitter and divisive struggle with Ronald Reagan, the former actor turned politician and champion of the party's right wing.

Jimmy Carter, an obscure peanut farmer and one-term governor of Georgia, captured the Democratic Party nomination. The mild-mannered Carter beat Ford by a bare 2-million-vote margin. Now the economic problems that Ford had failed to address were in Carter's hands.

Shortly after he assumed office in 1977 Carter unveiled a timid anti-inflation program that relied almost exclusively on voluntary restraints by business and labor but included no mandatory controls or even any voluntary targets. Carter's modest goal was to reduce increases in the cost of living index by 2 percent. When these measures failed to have any effect, Carter waited until the end of 1978, then issued some toothless anti-inflation guidelines. The following month OPEC boosted oil prices by 14.5 percent. Gas prices soared, and by 1979 inflation hit 13 percent.[86]

Jimmy Carter Confronts the Hospital Industry

During the early months of his presidential campaign, Carter ignored health care. Later, as his candidacy appeared to be gaining ground, he met with labor leaders, whose support he would need to win the election.[87] The AFL-CIO, suspicious of Carter's credentials as a southern farmer and businessman, refused to support him, but he did win the endorsement of the UAW.[88] From the sidelines, Kennedy pushed the unions to get as much as they could from Carter, who reluctantly promised to pursue national health insurance.[89]

Shortly after Carter was sworn in as president, Kennedy began badgering him to fulfill his campaign commitment.[90] Carter promised Kennedy, "If you come up with a program, that's fine and you'll have my support if it preserves a role for the insurance companies."[91] Committee for National Health Insurance members, who would draft Kennedy's new measure, clearly understood the ground rules. The new technical director of the committee, Harvard professor Rashi Fein, acknowledged, "Private insurers had to have a role in it, and it was more than an intermediary or carrier."[92] Despite Carter's promise to Kennedy, inflation and energy costs remained the overriding issues on the national scene. Since 1966 the consumer price index had increased by 79.7 percent, hospital expenses 237 percent.[93] Before national health insurance could be considered, health care inflation had to be slowed.

The Carter administration's first attempt to rein in health care costs began in 1977 when Carter's HEW secretary, Joseph Califano, developed a seemingly simple plan for an across-the-board cap on hospital charges. One of those idealistic liberal reformers who had entered government service with the idea of making a revolution, Califano had served as Lyndon Johnson's chief advisor on domestic affairs during the 1960s. An intense and driven man who loved power and smoked four packs a day, Califano had been there to escort to class James Meredith, the first black student to be admitted into the University of Mississippi; he had worked with the Defense Department to dream up ways to bring down Fidel Castro. By comparison, hospital cost containment seemed a modest goal. The plan Califano devised would limit yearly rate increases to one and a half times any rise in the consumer price index, with a cap of 9 percent.[94] So that hospitals couldn't just shift costs from Medicare patients to privately insured patients to compensate, the cap would also apply to all private payers as well. As soon as the plan was announced, the hospital lobby began gearing up to thwart what one industry leader called its "most serious challenge."[95]

The AHA, which represented nonprofit community hospitals, formed its first political action committee and set aside a million-dollar advertising campaign fund. Then the for-profit hospitals swung into action. Investor-owned hospitals had expanded rapidly since Medicare had made hospitals such lucrative enterprises, and they were the biggest beneficiaries of inflation in the hospital sector. In just one year, from 1977 to 1978, the Hospital Corporation of America's profits rose 23.4 percent, the Medicore Company's 25.3 percent, and American Medical International's 52.3 percent. The Federation of American Hospitals, which represented for-profit hospitals, made hefty contributions to members of Congress who served on the committees that had jurisdiction over the measure, invited elected officials to speak before the group's convention, and featured interviews with favored politicians in its monthly magazine.[96]

The Federation of American Hospitals also formed a coalition with other hospital associations to devise an alternative to Califano's plan. Their Voluntary Cost Containment Program was directed by a national steering committee that, in turn, coordinated the activities of state-level committees. State committee members mailed over 23,000 letters to every hospital in the country warning that if they didn't get behind the

"Senate Emergency . . . Hospital Cost — Containment Bill"

The hospital industry opposed President Carter's efforts to enact hospital cost containment legislation. 1979, Jimmy Carter Presidential Library

voluntary effort, Carter would likely impose "inflexible and bureaucratic federal controls."[97] The Federation of American Hospitals also encouraged hospital administrators to tap the support they enjoyed in their communities. As Representative Willis Gradison (R-Oh.) noted, "Hospitals are where the babies are born and where lives are saved."[98] Hospitals were called on to enlist their network of trustees and state association executives to woo members of Congress who were wary of controls. The response of physicians and hospitals to the voluntary effort was "overwhelming."[99] According to one hospital administrator, "I filled out the forms. But we knew it was all bulls——t."[100]

Hospital cost containment received an equally hostile reception from the business community. All the key business groups—the National Association of Manufacturers, the Business Roundtable, the Chamber of Commerce, and the Washington Business Group on Health—opposed mandatory price controls.[101] The Washington Business Group on Health prepared a report that concluded that mandatory controls would interfere with voluntary efforts currently under way and would allow the federal government to undermine local hospital autonomy.[102] Although preliminary discussions with Blue Cross/Blue Shield officials had indicated "they were prepared to help out," that support never materialized.[103] Carter's only business support came from the Health Insurance Association of America, which agreed to a compromise plan: hospitals would be allowed to use voluntary measures to control costs, but a mandatory cap would be triggered if voluntary efforts failed to produce results.[104]

Califano's proposal never made it out of the Senate Finance Committee. Hospital opposition certainly was a factor, but equally damning was a lack of public concern. Although 65 percent of the public favored the proposed cap, cost containment was not a high priority for most people. Third-party payments from insurance companies to providers and low deductibles meant that most people did not feel the impact of higher health care costs with the same immediacy as they would an increase in the cost of groceries or gas. Secretary Califano did receive a few letters of complaint. One woman wrote protesting a $29,764 hospital bill for her sister's one-month stay; an uninsured Georgia woman described a $60,000 bill she had received for care of her premature infant.[105] But for the most part, no group that supported the president's bill lobbied legislators. Representative Bill Gradison noted, "I haven't received a single letter [on the subject]."[106]

Hospital cost containment also failed because there was dissension even among Carter's own team about whether a ceiling would achieve the desired result. Economists on the Council on Wage and Price Stability believed that a cap on hospital costs would not work, even if legislation could be enacted. One senior economist wrote, "The HEW proposed standards stand virtually no chance of being accepted either by physicians or by hospitals and will almost certainly be met with opposition."[107]

Although Carter seemed headed for defeat, he made hospital cost containment his number one inflation-fighting measure in his 1979 State of the Union address: "We must act now to protect all Americans from health care costs that are rising one million dollars per hour, 24 hours a day, doubling every five years. We must take control of the largest contributor to that inflation: skyrocketing hospital costs."[108] This time he made a concerted effort to enlist support from the hospital industry and business community. HEW officials held White House briefings for the major business organizations and a few sympathetic hospital organizations. One naively optimistic staffer was convinced that "business was more inclined to support hospital cost containment that year."[109] But even though business leaders were worried about health care costs, they were more concerned that hospital cost containment would lead to mandatory cost controls in other parts of the economy.[110] The administration also tried to win over the AFL-CIO, which had opposed the previous effort for fear that hospital cost containment might interfere with the newly won right to collective bargaining in the hospital industry.[111] To allay labor's concerns, Carter added a provision for a "wage pass-through" that would exclude wage increases of hospital employees from compliance measures, but union support remained lukewarm.[112] One staffer noted, "I get the feeling that even though some of these people said they would make calls, their heart is not really in the issue."[113] Finally, a compromise bill was hammered out in the Senate. The bill would allow the hospitals to pursue a voluntary strategy but would cap costs if they failed to reach their goals.[114]

The Senate victory caught industry lobbyists by surprise. One lobbyist who thought cost containment was dead had to scramble: "I was going to get a good night's sleep. I was going to get my clothes from the cleaners, but instead I'm up in the middle of the night to get a plane to Washington."[115] By noon the following day, hospital lobbyists were camped out in the capital, shuttling between offices. Carter's blitz of Congress, meetings with insurance industry executives and business leaders, and concessions to the trade unions proved to be no match for the hospital lobbyists.[116] The much weakened cost containment plan was defeated in the House by a resounding majority. Of the 234 House members who voted against it, 202 had received contributions from the AMA and the hospital organizations.[117] Bill Cable, who served as a congressional liaison under Carter, recalled: "Hospital cost containment was the toughest one I ever had to work on . . . we were so vehemently opposed and so successfully opposed by the hospital association and the hospital industry."[118] While the plan was under consideration, hospital charges rose just over 14 percent. After the industry killed the legislation, costs jumped 22 percent.[119]

Califano ran afoul of the hospital lobby again when he tried to solicit competitive bids for demonstration projects to find more efficient ways to operate Medicare. After bidders offered to process Medicare claims for half of what HEW was currently paying the preferred carriers, Blue Cross sued to stop HEW from awarding the bids. Blue Cross lost the suit but succeeded in blocking Califano's efforts to permit competitive bidding on a routine basis by working the crucial congressional committees. Then, when Califano attempted to force the Blue Shield plans that administered Medicare Part B to add board members who were not physicians, Blue Shield lobbied Congress and halted the order.[120]

"Staging In" Universal Coverage

While pursuing hospital cost containment, the Carter administration initially avoided any tie-in with national health insurance. Indeed, administration officials feared that opponents of national health insurance might view cost containment as a first step toward greater government interference.[121] When Ted Kennedy, brooding about Carter's inaction, spoke before the UAW convention in 1977, he told the cheering crowd that health reform "was in danger of becoming the missing promise" of the Carter administration and urged the president to get a proposal to Congress that year.[122] The next day Carter spoke to the same group, promising to have a bill ready before the end of 1978.[123] After consulting with his advisors, however, he decided against getting involved in too many issues at once. With school integration and welfare reform at the top of the political agenda, it would be at least a year before he could lay out principles for a national health insurance program.[124] When Califano finally began to craft core principles, the task proved to be a more daunting than anyone had expected. As Califano later admitted, "I did not anticipate how unprepared HEW was to develop a national health insurance proposal."[125]

Finally, more than a year later, Califano provided Carter with four options.[126] Carter discussed these options with Kennedy and labor leaders, who insisted that any plan include universal coverage, comprehensive benefits, and tough cost controls. Otherwise, the UAW would not back Carter in the 1980 election.[127] Carter countered with a more modest plan that would achieve universal coverage in stages. Phase 1 would cover all low-income children and provide "catastrophic" care for the aged for the expenses Medicare didn't cover. Other groups would be included later. Kennedy didn't object to phasing in as long as the decision to do so was made in advance. Otherwise, there would be a fight with Congress each time a new group was considered, a politically difficult maneuver. As Carter's advisor, Stuart Eisenstadt, recalled:

> I negotiated for days with Senator Edward Kennedy. . . . We agreed on virtually every program detail. . . . The unbridgeable difference was that President Carter and his economic advisors insisted that each subsequent phase after the first would be triggered only upon a presidential determination that inflation and fiscal conditions permitted it.[128]

Carter's decision was unacceptable to Kennedy, who scheduled a press conference to accuse Carter of a failure of leadership. With cameras rolling and supporters applauding, Kennedy announced that he would introduce his own proposal soon. Labor leaders condemned Carter's plan and vowed to assist Kennedy in enacting a real national health insurance bill.[129] Days later, five Democratic congressmen started a "Dump Carter—Draft Kennedy" movement, and a month later Kennedy announced that he would challenge Carter for the Democratic Party nomination. Kennedy lost early primaries in Iowa and New Hampshire but then won six primaries in the East and in California. Still, he lacked the delegates to beat Carter, and fellow Democrats worried that he was splitting the party and hurting Carter's reelection chances in 1980.

In May Kennedy staged another media event in the Senate Caucus Room, again crowded with supporters and television cameras. National health insurance, Kennedy announced, was "the last, best chance" to bring the health care system under control.[130] His Health Care for All Americans Act (written by the Committee for National Health Insurance) would guarantee universal coverage by requiring employers to pay health insurance premiums either into a quasi-public corporation, to a private insurance company, or to an HMO. The elderly and the disabled would continue to receive Medicare, and the federal government would assume responsibility for the poor.[131]

In response Carter announced his own national health plan, called HealthCare. The Carter proposal would require employers to offer private health insurance to full-time employees (and their dependents) for catastrophic health care expenses. It would also provide a subsidy for small businesses and expand Medicaid for low-income families. However, Carter's plan fell far short of meeting Kennedy and labor's criteria. It was premised on the passage of separate cost containment legislation, it did not guarantee universal coverage, and it preserved too large a role for private insurance companies.[132] Carter and Kennedy continued to negotiate behind the scenes and finally agreed on a compromise plan that would create two national consortia of insurance carriers, one consisting of Blue Cross and Blue Shield, the other of commercial insurers. These consortia would control costs through a national health budget, financed from premium payments, consumer payments, or government payments. As Ig Falk explained to Senator Kennedy, "skillful drafting" had resolved the problems and they now had a bill in sight "well worthy of your introduction."[133] The compromise plan would retain a viable role for the private sector but remain faithful to the essential principles of the Health Care for All Americans Act.[134]

As the economy continued its tailspin, Carter took drastic action to demonstrate that he was still in control. On July 17, 1979, he told members of his cabinet that their performance had been unsatisfactory. All offered to tender their resignations, and by the following week, he had accepted five. Among those fired was Califano, who Carter suspected favored Kennedy. Instead of demonstrating that he was in control, the firings suggested that Carter could not take criticism and was subject to emotional whims.[135]

National health insurance was now a dead issue. Even if it had an advocate within the administration, it could not compete for public attention with a crisis that began in November when Iranian militants overthrew the shah of Iran, stormed the United States Embassy in Tehran, and took 70 Americans hostage. Four days later, a blindfolded hostage was paraded on the embassy grounds near surging crowds chanting anti-American slogans. In retaliation, President Carter ordered a halt to oil imports from Iran and froze all Iranian assets in the United States. Gasoline prices again soared.[136] Carter's popularity temporarily surged as Americans rallied round the flag, then plummeted as the crisis dragged on with no solution in sight.

In the 1980 election, Ronald Reagan captured the Republican Party nomination by appealing to the old right of fiscal conservatives and the new right of social conservatives concerned with abortion, the Equal

Rights Amendment, and school prayer. In his campaign, Reagan promised to reverse the stresses of the Carter years. Carter had failed utterly to whip inflation. Unemployment, which had been low for most of his term, was on the rise. The hostage situation was unresolved.[137] If elected, Reagan would cut taxes, reduce unemployment, contain runaway social spending, strengthen free markets, and balance the budget. Two days before the election, the Iranian parliament voted to release the hostages if the United States accepted four conditions set down by their leader, Ayatollah Khomeini. Although Carter scurried to secure the hostages' release, no deal was struck.[138] Carter won only six states. Reagan's sweep was nationwide.[139] The hostages were finally released on January 20, the day Reagan was sworn in as president.

Discouraged Committee for National Health Insurance members conceded that national health insurance was dead. As Rashi Fein glumly concluded:

> Now that Ronald Reagan was President, there was absolutely no chance that he would buy into it. It did not behoove us to continue to support something [the compromise] which was not all that good, and whose great claim to fame was that it perhaps could be enacted. . . . If we stayed there, the next move would be further to the right, because this would now be the standard from which we would negotiate.[140]

Policy by Stealth: The Prospective Payment System

After his landslide victory President Reagan declared, "In this present crisis, government is not the solution to our problem, government is the problem."[141] His first year in office, he unveiled his own national recovery plan based on supply-side economic theory (or what critics called "voodoo economics"). The core idea of supply-siders was that tax cuts would generate economic growth.[142] Reagan kept his promise to reduce taxes, which instead of eliminating inflation tripled the national debt and ushered in a recession. He also kept his promise to reduce government spending. In his 1981 budget he eliminated the public service jobs program, cut 400,000 people from the food stamps program, reduced the federal subsidy for public housing residents, eliminated the minimum Social Security benefit, and ended benefits for older children of deceased workers.[143]

Medical costs, seemingly unresponsive to the forces that governed other parts of the economy, continued to outpace the consumer price index. President Reagan's first stab at health care costs was in keeping with his pledge to reduce government. His administration folded 22 separate health programs into four block grants for the states (maternal and child health, mental health, primary care, and preventive health).[144] Reagan also proposed capping the growth of the federal share of Medicaid funds at 5 percent, but Democrats felt that a 5 percent cap was too severe. In the end the administration retreated entirely from any Medicaid cuts.[145] From 1981 to 1982 the consumer price index increased by only 3 percent but hospital charges rose 20 percent and doctors' fees nearly 11 percent.[146] Still choosing not to confront the hospital lobby, the Reagan administration's only response was to increase the deductibles paid by Medicare beneficiaries.[147]

In 1982 Congress enacted the Tax Equity and Fiscal Responsibility Act (TEFRA), which contained several measures to control Medicare costs. Included were strict limits on Medicare reimbursement to hospitals and new incentives to encourage HMOs to enroll Medicare beneficiaries. The legislation also replaced the ineffectual PSROs with a second generation of peer review agencies, called peer review organizations. When the hospital industry and the AMA later convinced the Reagan administration that the peer review organizations should be dismantled in favor of a free market approach, the Washington Business Group on Health lobbied Congress and rescued them from the budget axe.[148] But the peer review organizations produced much the same results as the PSROs, rarely sanctioning physicians and generating no significant savings.[149] The sleeper in TEFRA was a requirement that HEW submit to Congress, within five months, a new prospective payment system for Medicare. This requirement was met by an indirect route via Social Security reform.

Since the late 1970s the Social Security trust fund had been teetering toward bankruptcy. In 1981 new projections indicated that there would be insufficient funds to pay benefits in just a few years.[150] To restore Social Security to solvency, President Reagan proposed an immediate cut of 31 percent in early retirement benefits (which would hit people ages 62 to 65) and a 10 percent cut in future benefits, even though polls showed that 65 percent of the public opposed further reductions in health and social welfare programs and even though more than 60 million people would be directly affected by the proposals.[151]

Reprisals from the public were swift and harsh. Hours after Reagan's proposals were announced, senior organizations began mobilizing. The National Council of Senior Citizens fired off 10,000 "seniorgrams" to activate its network of clubs. The AARP sent a legislative alert to 14,000 volunteer leaders, asking them to write their congressional representatives and to tell their friends and relatives to do the same. The Gray Panthers, a small intergenerational, antiestablishment organization, held candlelight vigils in the park across the street from the White House and staged rowdy public demonstrations around the country. Save Our Security, a coalition of 141 senior organizations, held a press conference to demonstrate seniors' opposition to the cuts.[152] Congressional offices were swamped with letters, cards, and phone calls.[153] Within days Reagan's public approval rating plummeted 16 points. Emboldened by the public outcry, Democrats who had acquiesced to Reagan's budget cuts railed against him, while Republicans, worried about the political costs of offending senior citizens, joined Democrats in attacking the proposals. That October, Congress restored the minimum Social Security benefit, promising never again to reduce benefits for current recipients, and Reagan abandoned all plans for benefit cuts in the near term.[154] Instead, he created the bipartisan National Commission on Social Security Reform to devise a politically feasible, long-range solution.

The National Commission on Social Security Reform began meeting in 1982. At each meeting senior citizens demonstrated in front of the hotel and lobbied individual commission members behind the scene. By November a crisis was declared when Social Security was forced to borrow from the Medicare and disability insurance trust funds to pay benefits on time. If some resolution was not reached, benefit checks would be delayed for the first time in history. Medicare had its own problems, however, with projections indicating that the Medicare trust fund would be depleted within five years.[155] The commission waited until after the 1982 congressional elections to hold its final meeting, but the meeting ended in a stalemate when members could not agree on a package of benefit cuts and tax increases.

Instead five commission members (among them Robert Ball and Alan Greenspan, who had served as President Ford's economic advisor) began meeting in secret with no records kept and no transcripts recorded. In January the five presented their recommendations to the full commission.[156] Their plan included delaying Social Security cost-of-living increases for six months, taxing benefits of upper-income Social Security beneficiaries, and raising the age of eligibility for full benefits from 65 to 67. The retirement age increase would be phased in incrementally, starting in 2000, 17 years in the future, so there would be no short-term political cost.[157] The Ways and Means Committee passed the bill by a large majority, and the final legislation was hammered out by a conference committee in March 1983.

The 1983 amendments to the Social Security Act also included a little-noticed provision that was slipped into the Ways and Means Committee bill at the last minute by members of the Health Subcommittee. With all the attention focused on the Social Security crisis, it elicited no debate and generated no controversy, even though it meant a radical restructuring of Medicare. As Paul Light noted, "It would have been a difficult fight on its own but had a free ride on the Social Security bill."[158]

The hospital cost control provision in the amendments would introduce a prospective payment system for Medicare. Instead of reimbursing hospitals after the fact, hospitals would receive a predetermined amount based on what treatment was provided. Prospective payment had been tested in a series of experiments in several states with large Medicaid populations.[159] The plan federal officials finally adopted for Medicare began as the New Jersey experiment. In New Jersey, as in many states, Blue Cross premiums were subject to the approval of the insurance commissioner. Every proposed premium rate increase met with public resistance and unfavorable publicity. Frustrated by having to pay rising hospital charges but forbidden from increasing premiums, Blue Cross turned against its former master, the hospital industry, and asked the state legislature to impose limits on hospital charges. The New Jersey Hospital Association vigorously lobbied against Blue Cross and instead promised to institute a "voluntary" review of hospital budgets. When the voluntary review had no effect on costs (because the reviewers were beholden to the Hospital Association), the legislature empowered the commissioners of health and insurance to actually set rates for Blue Cross patients. But hospitals circumvented the fixed rates by shifting costs to the commercial insurers, whose rates were not regulated. Within five years hospital charges paid by commercial insurers were 30 percent higher than Blue Cross charges. Commercial insurers were forced to raise their premiums and thus lose their competitive advantage over Blue Cross. As commercial insurers began to clamor for more regulation of hospital rates, the New Jersey Department of Health proposed an alternative—hospitals would be paid by the type of case treated, not by the number of patient days.[160] The plan antagonized both the hospitals and Blue Cross—the hospitals because they opposed any departure from cost-based reimbursement, Blue Cross because it gave commercial insurers an edge.

The 1983 amendments to the Social Security Act replaced the cost-plus hospital reimbursement system with this prospective payment system. The prospective payment system created fixed payment schedules for various diagnosis-related groups, called DRGs, regardless of the actual cost of treatment.[161] Hospitals could keep the difference from any cost savings but would not receive additional funds if their costs exceeded the limit. The American Hospital Association embraced prospective payment as a preferable alternative to the strict limits in TEFRA. According to an officer of the association, "Prospective payment was one of the things the hospitals went along with. . . . It was not a bad thing if the federal government did a good job of establishing the rates."[162] Although the prospective payment system only applied to Medicare, many states adopted it for their Medicaid populations as well. After 1983 the Washington Business Group on Health also helped some private companies adopt similar accounting procedures for their own health plans.[163]

The first year the prospective payment system was in operation, the average length of a hospital stay for Medicare beneficiaries declined by over 15 percent.[164] Within a few months, however, hospitals began reporting more high-cost cases, an example of what was called "DRG creep." As the hospital administrator quoted previously explained, "We were always one step ahead of the government."[165] Congress attempted to close the loopholes that allowed DRG creep, but hospitals objected, claiming that they were treating sicker patients, and the government backed down.[166] A few years later, in response to continued complaints from the AHA about the stringency of the DRG system, Congress boosted DRG rates.[167]

The prospective payment system not only changed the incentives in Medicare payments to hospitals but also rearranged the political coalitions within the health care system. Under the old cost-based reimbursement system, hospitals and physicians both benefited when more care was delivered. Now if the revenues expended in caring for patients exceeded the DRG limit, physicians were still the winners, but hospitals were the losers. Thus prospective payment placed hospitals at economic risk for the treatment decisions of physicians.[168] Prospective payment also indirectly put hospitals on a collision course with large, self-insured employers. The prospective payment system did not prohibit hospitals from shifting costs from Medicare patients to other payers, a decision that was bound to raise problems down the line. As hospitals compensated for limits on Medicare charges by increasing charges to younger patients, corporations wound up paying the bills. Once this practice became evident, the business community revolted. The National Association of Manufacturers began demanding that prospective payment regulations be tightened to prevent hospitals from "gaming the system." John Motley, lobbyist for the National Federation of Independent Business, argued, "Greater discipline on physicians is expected to have some spillover effect to the private sector."[169]

Although physicians' fees had increased at three times the rate of hospital payments during the 1980s, they aroused less concern because they represented a smaller portion of total costs. However, Dr. Arnold Redman, editor of the *New England Journal of Medicine*, warned physicians that the reprieve was temporary: "Doctors have to realize that they are the essence of the problem. Though they only get 20 percent of every dollar spent on medical care, they determine most of the other costs. And if they continue to dodge their responsibility, more government regulation is inevitable."[170] Sure enough, in 1984 Congress instituted a temporary freeze on Medicare payment increases to physicians. Then in 1985 Congress created a commission to develop a permanent fee schedule for physicians' services. Anticipating reform, the AMA decided that it would be better to be a part of the process than attempt to block any change. The AMA participated in the commission that drafted a plan and in 1989 agreed to replace fee-for-service payment with a predetermined fee schedule that would be phased in over a five-year period.

Under the new system, medical services were analyzed in terms of their complexity and time demands and then converted into fee schedules for office and hospital visits. Initially the fee schedules were set high, and physicians rallied against any proposed reductions. When the government proposed a 16 percent reduction in 1991, the AMA and other physicians' organizations created such a "firestorm of protest" that the regulation was revised.[171] Following complaints from physicians in 1998 that fees were too low, a more liberal fee schedule was adopted.[172] Even though the medical profession has had a continuing influence on the committees that set fees, both the prospective payment system and the new doctors' fee schedules were essentially "blunt instruments of prospective budgeting and price regulation" that shifted the balance of power from the providers toward the federal government.[173]

Conclusion

At the beginning of the 1970s, universal health insurance was at the forefront of national policy debates, but any chance it had was rapidly diminished by concerns about rising costs. For the next decade cost containment took center stage as the main issue on the health care agenda. As federal officials sought in vain to wrest control over charges and fees from providers, the medical lobby fought back, lobbying legislators and rallying local hospitals and community groups to fend off caps. The providers had important allies in their effort to defeat cost controls. They included business groups, who feared that controls in the health sector would lead to controls in other parts of the economy, and the trade unions, which had just won the right to bargain over wages for hospital employees and saw price controls as an antiunion measure.

A significant shift in power relations occurred with the introduction of the prospective payment system for Medicare, which restructured Medicare but did not tamper with wages or levy an overall cap on charges. But the gains of prospective payment were short-lived, as hospitals found ways to circumvent the controls and shift costs to other payers. When it became apparent that the federal government was incapable of restraining costs, corporate purchasers took matters in their own hands, rising in revolt against the hospitals and doctors.

six

The Revolt of the Corporate Purchaser

For nearly a century hospitals had viewed physicians as their main clients, and physicians accordingly made most of the decisions about what took place in hospitals. They admitted patients whenever they chose, kept them hospitalized for as long as they felt necessary, and ordered whatever tests they wanted. More was better. The longer patients stayed, the more tests were run, the more revenue hospitals took in. Stanford economist Alain Enthoven asserted, "Most physicians have no idea of the cost of the things they order—and no real reason to care."[1] Some people did care. Opal Burge of Hebron, Indiana, was shocked when she received a 208-page hospital bill with charges of over $250,000 for her husband's stay in an intensive care unit as he battled the emphysema that eventually took his life.[2] But most patients didn't object because they weren't paying the bill, at least not directly. Patients entered hospitals when they were sick and in pain, fearful of death, or elated over new life. Most were satisfied with the care they received, and if they thought about costs at all, they believed they were paying for receiving the best care in the world.

That arrangement lasted until the late 1970s. Then the actual customers, the employers who were paying the bills on behalf of their employees, began asking why patients faced long hospital stays for simple procedures, whether it was necessary to run so many expensive tests, and why a box of Kleenex cost 49 cents at Kmart but $19 on a patient's bedside table.[3] In the business world, the market ruled. When corporate executives made a business decision, whether about purchasing supplies or hiring personnel, they drove a hard bargain. Suppliers had to offer the lowest price to win a contract; prospective employees had to provide a resume listing their qualifications and prior experience. In making decisions about health care, however, these same businesses, now in the position of corporate purchasers of health care goods, were stymied. They had no way to determine whether physicians performing services were the best qualified or whether a charge for surgery, a birth, or emergency room care was reasonable. In fact, it was difficult to learn what the exact cost was. When employers sought answers to these questions, the insurers who were supposed to represent their interests refused to cooperate. In the 1980s, corporations decided it was time to use their purchasing power to challenge the providers' dominance over the health care system.

The Origins of the Corporate Revolt

By the early 1980s, the business community had become truly alarmed about the rising cost of health care. Between 1970 and 1982, while the gross domestic product grew by 208 percent, employer expenditures for health benefits grew by 700 percent.[4] Federal expenditures for Medicare slowed somewhat after the prospective payment system was introduced in 1983, but that had no effect on employers' expenditures. Indeed, the opposite was the case, as hospitals compensated for lost Medicare revenues by shifting costs onto private payers.[5] Every effort to cut Medicare payments translated into an increase in corporate costs.[6]

These trends affected small employers differently than large employers. Small firms had to purchase health insurance coverage for their employees in the small-group market. Some insurance carriers avoided this market entirely.[7] Those that did operate there used sophisticated forms of underwriting to skim off the more desirable employee groups and avoid paying for high-risk individuals. Insurers aggressively competed for groups of young and healthy employees, forcing many small firms, especially those with an older workforce, to cut back on coverage.

When the National Federation of Independent Business, the leading organization of small firms, surveyed its members in 1989, the most frequently voiced complaint was the rising cost of health benefits. Consider Ray Morgan, who owned a business in Algona, Iowa, with seven employees. Between 1988 and 1989, Morgan's premiums more than tripled, increasing from $837 to $2,685 a month, even though none of his employees had filed a major claim. Richard Ludwig, president of Lavelle Aircraft Company, a manufacturer with 150 employees, faced a similar dilemma. After premiums doubled between 1986 and 1989, he reluctantly cut benefits. Ludwig explained that, at $396,000 annually, "this is the single most expensive element of our business."[8] As health insurance became less affordable for small-business owners, they began curtailing benefits or dumping their employee health care coverage entirely.

State taxes on insurance premiums and state mandates requiring insurance companies to include certain services in all policies exacerbated the problem. By the mid-1980s there were more than 690 such mandates, ranging from wigs to mental health services to podiatry to acupuncture.[9] According to the National Federation of Independent Business, these mandates "seldom surfaced as a result of constituent demand" but rather were initiated by "well-organized special interest groups including the providers of services." With each new mandate, the number of providers performing the mandated services increased. For example, in Wisconsin after outpatient mental health services were included in state mandates, the number of mental health clinics grew from 40 to more than 900 in ten years. If state mandates were reduced, small firms could purchase a "catastrophic, bare bones policy."[10] Until that happened, the only option was to reduce benefits or drop coverage.

Blue Cross had once been a haven for small-business owners, but competition from commercial insurers had forced many Blue Cross plans to abandon community rating (where every subscriber paid the same rate) and adopt the underwriting practices used by commercial companies. One employer who had held a Blue Cross policy for more than a decade was notified that his group would now be "medically underwritten." Under the new contract terms, Blue Cross reserved the right to refuse coverage for any preexisting condition:

> Your group has been classified as medically underwritten for the contract period. . . . any participant from your group whose coverage becomes effective during the new contract period will be required to fill out and file a medical history questionnaire with us before qualifying for covered services . . . these subscribers may be permanently excluded from receiving . . . benefits for conditions which existed before they enrolled.[11]

In some states Blue Cross began selling stock and branching into the more lucrative life insurance business.[12] In recognition of the changed practices of the organization, in 1986 Congress removed Blue Cross' nonprofit tax exemption, ending its pretense of being a charitable community service organization.

Large firms had an alternative, thanks to the Employment Retirement Security Act of 1974 (ERISA). ERISA was the landmark legislation that created national standards for employee fringe benefit plans.[13] A provision added at the last minute exempted employer-provided fringe benefits from state laws governing these benefits, since fringe benefits were not technically "insurance." That gave firms with sufficient cash reserves or borrowing power an incentive to self-insure instead of purchasing coverage from an insurance company. Self-insured plans did not have to include any of the mandated benefits that ran up the costs of insurance in the small group market. Nor did they have to pay taxes on premiums. Self-insured firms also were exempt from state laws that regulated insurance companies and thus were free from liability in state court if their decisions regarding benefits harmed the people they insured.[14] What that meant was that patients could not sue if the company withheld payment for any health problem. When employees challenged these practices, the courts typically ruled in favor of the employer, as was the case of the Texas employee whose employer cut his health benefits from $1 million to $5,000 after he was diagnosed with AIDS.[15] In some instances, employers that self-insured were able to cut their overhead costs by 50 percent or better.[16]

In 1975, the year after ERISA was enacted, only 5 percent of employees were covered by self-insured plans, mainly those negotiated by labor unions; by 1985 that figure had climbed to 42 percent.[17] By the mid-1990s self-insurance covered nearly half of all workers and a much higher percentage of employees of large companies.[18] Employers, not insurance companies, had become the leading risk bearers.

Downsizing the Private Welfare State

Although being self-insured placed large firms in a more favorable position than small firms that had to purchase coverage from insurance companies, it did not immunize them from rising costs. So in the

1980s, as Marie Gottschalk noted, "business . . . set off on a long march to downsize the private welfare state."[19] Some employers dropped coverage altogether. In 1980 97 percent of medium and large employers offered health insurance benefits; by 1990 the figure was just 92 percent.[20] But dropping health insurance as a fringe benefit was not an option for most firms. In unionized industries, employers were locked into collective bargaining agreements with organized labor that prevented drastic cost-cutting measures. Nonunionized firms that stopped providing health benefits faced a tax penalty, poor employer-employee relations, and negative publicity. Most firms instead sought ways to reduce their costs.

One of the business leaders of the cost containment effort was Lee Iacocca, the brash and outspoken CEO of Chrysler. Iacocca, the son of Italian immigrants, had begun working for Ford after he completed his master's degree at Princeton University, working his way up to president in 1970. After the 1973 oil crisis, Ford experienced its first losing quarter since 1946 as the buying public turned to smaller, more fuel-efficient Japanese cars. Once the gas shortage eased, Americans resumed their love affair with large gas-guzzlers, and Ford was again operating in the black. But Iacocca had had a falling-out with Henry Ford when he insisted that the less profitable smaller vehicles had to be part of Ford's product line in the future. After being demoted twice, on July 14, 1978, he was summarily fired. His old friend Joe Califano called from his office in HEW to comfort him: "Lee, these things have a way of turning out okay. This just could be one the best things that ever happened to you."[21]

At first Iacocca didn't see it that way. But a few months after he left Ford, depressed and angered, he was approached by the Chrysler Corporation, which was in deep trouble as a result of decades of poor management. That year Chrysler posted losses of $160 million. Iacocca accepted the job of chairman and CEO and immediately began to survey management practices to determine how to turn the company around.[22] He didn't like what he saw. Chrysler was set up as a "cluster of little duchies" like Italy in the 1860s, each run by a prima donna.[23] Each of the 35 vice presidents had his own turf with no committee setup, no organizational chart, and no communication between departments. Iacocca fired 33 of the vice presidents, hired new accountants, and reorganized the way the company interacted with its dealerships. But before any of his innovations could take effect, the shah of Iran was deposed, the Americans were taken hostage, and the price of gas doubled—from 65 cents a gallon to over $1.30 a gallon—within a few weeks. People waited in long lines to fill their tanks. There were gas riots at some New York service stations. The market for station wagons, vans, and recreational vehicles dried up almost instantly.

Ideologically, Iacocca had always been "a free enterpriser, a believer in survival of the fittest."[24] With Chrysler close to bankruptcy, Iacocca reconsidered his lifelong opposition to government intervention in private business. He pleaded his case before Congress and won $1.5 billion in loan guarantees from President Carter. Sacrifices were in order. Iacocca first reduced his own salary of $360,000 to $1 a year, then cut other executives' pay by 10 percent. That made it easier to ask the rank-and-file workers to do their share. He put UAW president Doug Fraser on Chrysler's board of directors and wrested several concessions from the union. Autoworkers agreed to a $2-an-hour pay cut and promised not to strike when unprofitable plants were closed. Iacocca then turned to fringe benefits. Pensions took a huge share of the total wage package but were a non-negotiable item. Health care required close scrutiny. As Iacocca examined company records, he was amazed to discover that Blue Cross/Blue Shield was Chrysler's largest supplier, billing more than the company's suppliers of steel and rubber. Overall Chrysler paid about $600 million a year in health care costs, adding about $600 to the sticker price of each car.[25]

Iacocca determine he would find a way for Chrysler to exert its clout as a large purchaser of health services to weed out high-priced, inefficient providers. He first call was to his buddy Joe Califano, the man Carter had fired as HEW secretary. "Joe," Iacocca told him, "being fired by Jimmy Carter is the best thing that ever happened to you."[26] Iacocca invited Califano to his Waldorf Towers suite, and they talked for hours. Over dinner at Romeo Salta's on West 56th Street, Iacocca asked Califano for help. "You say you want to do something about health care costs. Why don't you chair the new health care committee of Chrysler's board of directors?"[27] Califano was hooked. Chrysler's was the first board of directors to appoint such a committee. If he couldn't get a handle on costs as HEW secretary, maybe he could do it through one of the largest corporations in the country.

To start the process, Califano asked Blue Cross/Blue Shield to provide detailed cost information, but Blue Cross stonewalled. When it became clear that Califano would persist, Blue Cross finally hired the Health Data Institute to audit Chrysler's health care expenditures. According to Califano, the audit revealed an "appalling degree of unnecessary care, inefficient practices and outright fraud." Some podiatrists were working on feet one toe at a visit and prolonging time off for employees on disability. Califano recalled the case of one employee certified as disabled because of foot surgery who was apprehended after a lengthy foot chase while attempting to steal parts from a Chrysler plant. Among the more egregious findings were that insurance payments to dermatologists were twice those to general practitioners and 25 percent higher than those to chest surgeons, that hospital stays for normal births were nearly double the national average, and that two-thirds of hospitalizations for "bed rest" for lower back pain were unnecessary.[28] Prescription drugs were also abused. One Chrysler employee received 51 prescriptions for 6,030 Valium pills over a 12-month period. Another got 136 prescriptions for 4,255 Percodan pills filled. As Iacocca complained, "As the system works now, the doctors and hospitals are killing us."[29]

Chrysler's first point of attack was services that could be easily monitored. Chrysler demanded that pharmacists substitute cheaper generic drugs for brand-name products, shifted business to laboratories that charged the lowest prices to run tests, and told physicians to drop their prices or lose Chrysler's business. Chrysler also won an agreement with the UAW for a hospital admission screening program and a "preferred provider" plan wherein workers would only see physicians on an approved list.[30] However, the UAW refused to accept co-payments and deductibles, which members would interpret as a reduction in benefits but which Iacocca saw as the heart of the problem: "The attitude [of workers] is always to let Uncle Lee pick up the tab. So what if you're charging me too much for the tests or the surgery—*I'm not paying for it.*"[31]

Other employers followed Chrysler's lead. In companies without unions, employees were forced to pay higher deductibles and co-payments and share the costs of premiums. Some employers resorted to "churning," switching policies just as the waiting period for employees with large medical expenses expired.[32] They also reduced benefits for expensive diseases such as cancer and AIDS or eliminated coverage for these conditions altogether. In 1980 72 percent of employers paid the total cost of their employees' health insurance; by 1990 just 51 percent did, and only 34 percent fully financed family coverage.[33] Cost sharing had a minimal impact on expenditures overall, however, because the majority of employees used few health care services. Those with serious health problems who used the most services were too concerned about their own health to be deterred from seeking care by high deductibles and co-payments.[34]

Employers also began to organize to use their purchasing power to negotiate better deals with providers. In Minneapolis a coalition of firms organized a purchasing cooperative in 1988 to bargain over prices. By 1992 the Buyers Health Care Cooperative had more than 400 employer members covering 380,000 employees. Co-op members conducted a computer analysis of hospital charges and then demanded that local hospitals implement clinical guidelines to reduce costs.[35] In California, the vice president of Plantronics took state data on hospital costs in his plant's hometown with him when he met with local hospital administrators, and he was able to negotiate a substantial discount. Hospitals were not always so cooperative, of course. In Lake County, Illinois, when a group of employers tried to negotiate directly with the local hospital, their actions triggered a reaction "something akin to the Mount Saint Helens' eruption."[36] However, several of the business leaders also served on the hospital board, and they forced the hospital to come to the bargaining table.

Employers also sought to mobilize politically to gain a more active voice in health policy decisions. In Massachusetts the CEO of Dennison organized 60 of the largest employers in the state and brokered changes in the state's rate-setting system that helped slow the rate of growth in hospital charges.[37] In Arizona a coalition of business leaders sponsored a series of ballot initiatives to curb hospital costs. But the hospitals attacked back, decrying "all out corporate warfare," and defeated the measures. The CEO of Meredith, one of the firms involved in the Arizona coalition, later ruefully recalled:

> Initially, we attempted to effect change through negotiation, discussion, debate, through participation of all of the interests with a vested stake in health care delivery. I know what the arguments are for a more conciliatory approach because I accepted them. . . . I am now convinced that we should have been more aggressive.[38]

The U.S. Chamber of Commerce, one of the oldest and largest business organizations in the country, had 2,700 state and local chapters, 65,000 member companies, and a staff of 1,400 in Washington, D.C., alone. With its large membership and vast networks, one might have expected it to be an effective voice for cost containment. The Chamber did influence some state policy decisions. For example, in California the Chamber joined forces with the Health Insurance Association of America to prevent the hospital lobby from watering down a new rate-setting system. More often, however, the Chamber was unable to reach consensus because of the clout of its provider members. When the Chamber formed a health policy committee, it was co-opted by the AHA, which then refused to allow consideration of any position contrary to the hospitals' interests. The Business Roundtable, an organization of the largest corporations in the country, experienced similar problems. When the Roundtable founded a Health Care Task Force in 1982, the drug manufacturer Eli Lilly seized control. Instead of focusing on cost containment, the task force dealt only with issues of interest to the pharmaceutical industry.

The Washington Business Group on Health was the one business group that was not beholden to providers. Its head, Willis Goldbeck, refused to allow any provider organizations into the inner circle, antagonizing the insurance companies, the AMA, and the AHA. Goldbeck had the behind-the-scenes support of the National Association of Manufacturers and other business groups that couldn't openly oppose their own provider members.[39] The Washington Business Group on Health had pushed for PSROs and for the prospective payment system for Medicare that changed how hospital charges were calculated.[40] Now Goldbeck turned to the issue of financial disclosure.

Eighteen states, at the urging of employers' associations, had enacted financial disclosure laws that required providers to release data on costs and physician practice patterns. These data helped businesses negotiate lower rates from providers. Despite the state laws, however, businesses found it difficult to get access to the data and even more difficult to interpret what they received. In 1984 Goldbeck helped Representative Ron Wyden (R-Ore.) write a bill that would give the Department of Health and Human Services the authority to make data on statewide health care charges easily accessible. Physicians and hospital groups lobbied against the Wyden measure, claiming that the data would be easy to misinterpret, but in 1985 Congress passed legislation that allowed employers to request information in state databases directly from the federal government. As states began collecting and reporting data on health care costs, the revelations fueled the fire. Analyses of expenditures showed huge regional variations in the number of tonsillectomies, coronary bypass surgeries, and hysterectomies performed for similar diagnoses, as well as significant discrepancies in prices charged by hospitals and physicians even in the same town.[41]

The Washington Business Group on Health also lobbied for a proposal to expand Medicare to pay for the "catastrophic" health care costs for Medicare beneficiaries, a plan that the business community endorsed because it would shift the burden of retiree health benefits from private companies to the government. In the previous decade, retiree health benefits had become a pressing concern for the large manufacturing companies.[42] The first retiree health benefits had been granted in 1953, when the Big Three auto manufacturers—General Motors, Ford, and Chrysler—agreed to provide retirees age 65 and older the same health benefits as active workers if they paid the full cost themselves. In 1961 the UAW won an agreement that the companies would pay the full cost of health benefits for workers and their dependents and half the cost for retirees. The same benefits were granted to early retirees, who were allowed to retire with reduced benefits at age 60 with 10 years of service and at age 55 with 30 years of service. With each new contract came more generous benefits, including fully paid retiree health benefits in 1964, prescription drugs for employees and their dependents in 1967 and for retirees in 1971, and eyeglass coverage for employees in 1976 and for retirees in 1979.[43] The United Steel Workers Association won a similar benefit package for its members.[44] Nonunionized firms followed suit, encouraged by provisions in the federal tax code that allowed firms to deduct retiree health benefits as a business expense. The enactment of Medicare shifted some of the costs of retiree benefits to the federal government, but firms were still responsible for costs for retirees under age 65 as well as the various co-payments and deductibles for retirees 65 and older that Medicare did not cover. In 1984 30 percent of Medicare beneficiaries received medigap coverage for these extra expenses from a past or current employer, with employers paying most of the cost.[45]

In 1967 the Supreme Court ruled that employers could use retiree health benefits to lure older workers into retirement without the risk of being sued for age discrimination. Following that decision, auto manufacturers responded to each slump in production by waiving the normal early retirement provisions. During the recessions in 1973–74 and 1981–82 "sweeteners" were added to the usual early retirement benefits to encourage older workers who would not otherwise be eligible to retire to do so.[46] By the 1980s what had been a relatively small business expense, retiree benefits, had grown into a huge liability, as the manufacturing workforce aged and the proportion of retirees relative to younger workers swelled.[47] In some industries there were more retirees than active workers. For example, when Iacocca took over Chrysler, there were three retirees for every two workers. Bethlehem Steel had 70,000 active workers and 54,000 retirees in 1980 but 37,000 active workers and 70,000 retirees five years later. This dilemma reached crisis proportions in 1986, when LTV filed for bankruptcy, terminating health insurance benefits for its 78,000 retirees.[48] The following year, troubled Kaiser Steel missed a $255,000 weekly premium payment. More than 4,300 retirees and 200 working employees over age 65 lost their health insurance.[49]

Congressional hearings were held, and *Fortune* magazine warned that retiree health benefits were "unfunded, out of control and growing more than twice as fast as inflation." If left unchecked, they could threaten not only profits but entire companies.[50] These events caused the Financial Accounting Standards Board, which regulates employee benefits, to take a hard look at retiree health plans. In 1987 the board issued a regulation that forced firms to include promised retiree health benefits on their balance sheets as a business expense, making these large and growing unfunded liabilities visible as part of the bottom line.[51] Not only had retiree health benefits become a huge business expense, they threatened to undermine investor confidence. As corporations sought a way to shed this responsibility, they seized upon a proposal to expand Medicare to cover many of these costs.

Shedding Retiree Health Benefits: The Medicare Catastrophic Coverage Act

The Medicare Catastrophic Coverage Act of 1988 is usually seen as a striking anomaly in Medicare history. It was enacted in the context of a rising budget deficit during the administration of Ronald Reagan, a conservative Republican who had campaigned on a promise to reduce government spending. Furthermore, it would increase Medicare expenditures and reverse the gains made by the prospective payment system. How, then, did catastrophic care ascend to the top of the domestic policy agenda and evade insurance industry opposition?

According to the accepted wisdom, the Catastrophic Coverage Act was the pet project of Otis Bowen, a warm and gregarious country doctor and former governor of Indiana.[52] Bowen had served on the 1981 Advisory Council on Social Security and had been offered a position as White House liaison to HEW but had declined because his wife, Beth, had terminal bone cancer. After Beth's death, Bowen married a widow who had been a lifelong friend he taught at the Indiana University School of Medicine. In 1985 Bowen was invited to become Secretary of Health, Education, and Welfare and was easily confirmed. Early in his tenure he began lobbying for President Reagan to include a catastrophic care initiative in his State of the Union address. Bowen had witnessed firsthand the distress of his elderly patients facing enormous health care bills after lengthy hospital stays. He also distrusted the insurance companies that sold medigap policies because of instances where they had refused to cover his patients' bills.

With midterm elections less than a year away, polls indicated that the president was particularly unpopular with the elderly. Catastrophic care legislation, Bowen argued, might soften his image.[53] Yet if Reagan wanted to cultivate elderly voters, catastrophic care seemed a curious choice of issues to pursue. By 1986 nearly 80 percent of people 65 and older already had supplemental medigap insurance that paid most of the costs Medicare did not cover.[54] Furthermore, under the prospective payment system the average hospital stay had dramatically declined, as hospitals released patients "quicker and sicker" to nursing homes or sent them home to recuperate. Only a small fraction of Medicare recipients (less than 1.5 percent) would ever stay in a hospital beyond the Medicare limit.[55] And Bowen's proposal excluded the most pressing concern of the elderly, which was long-term care. Instead of introducing catastrophic care legislation in his State of the Union address, which key administration officials opposed, Reagan ordered Bowen to head a study of the issue.

Bowen conducted his study with great fanfare, holding showy, well-publicized hearings all over the country. By October he had a proposal ready for the president to consider. It is not clear what the fate of Bowen's plan would have been had it not been for the Iran-contra crisis. The crisis began in the summer of 1986, when a group called Islamic Holy War seized three American hostages in Lebanon and demanded the release of 17 Kuwaiti prisoners who had been convicted of bombing American, French, and Kuwaiti installations. That October, halfway around the world in a seemingly unrelated incident, an American military cargo plane carrying a CIA operative was shot down over Nicaragua. Rumors spread that the Reagan administration had hatched a cockeyed plot to use funds from the illegal sale of arms to Iran to support the rebel Nicaraguan organization, called the contras. Four days before the congressional elections, the press reported that the administration had negotiated a secret arms deal with Iranian officials despite an official ban on providing arms to Iran. The deal was reportedly concocted by a small group within the National Security Council, led by Oliver North and personally approved by President Reagan.[56] The Iranians would receive 500 missiles in exchange for the release of one of the hostages. The funds from the sale would also be funneled to the Nicaraguan contras. Although President Reagan denied the plot, on November 3 one of the hostages, David Jacobsen, who directed the American University Hospital, was released.[57]

In the 1986 elections, the Democrats regained control of the Senate, an outcome that was particularly damaging to Reagan's image. Only 5 of 18 Republican senators the president had supported were elected. As the president's popularity plummeted, aides searched for an issue to deflect attention from Iran-contra and prove that the administration was not paralyzed. On November 19 Bowen introduced his proposal at a meeting of the White House Domestic Policy Council. Bowen's plan would expand Medicare coverage for acute hospital stays and cap an individual's out-of-pocket costs for physician services. As a sop to administration conservatives, it would also include federal tax credits to encourage the elderly to purchase private long-term care insurance.[58]

Bowen's report met with stunned silence. The chairman of Reagan's Council of Economic Advisors, Beryl Sprinkle, "a short, roly-poly man of single-minded conservative convictions," charged that the Bowen plan "would replace a competitive private market with a government monopoly."[59] Attorney General Edwin Meese complained that it would intrude into a market already served by private companies.[60] Medicare expansion on so grand a scale was a direct assault on the entire conservative agenda. Bowen countered that doing nothing would suggest that Reagan was insensitive to the elderly and the poor. Furthermore, he argued, the small amount of business the private insurance industry would lose would not destroy the market.

The next day Bowen announced his proposal at a news conference. Democrats in Congress applauded. Senator Ted Kennedy called Bowen "a great American" and told Republicans to "listen a little more" to Bowen and a "little less to the insurance industry."[61] If the president did not introduce Bowen's plan, he would do it himself. Four days later Bowen was summoned to the White House to meet with insurance executives. The executives expressed no opposition to Bowen's proposal for the simple reason that insurers had no desire to pay for lengthy hospital stays beyond the Medicare limit.(The medigap market was saturated and never had been that profitable to begin with. Expanding Medicare to cover catastrophic illness might also slow the trend toward self-insurance among large corporations. Although the Health Insurance Association of America favored an optional voucher program that would enable Medicare beneficiaries who had no medigap coverage to purchase private insurance, the executives made no attempt to defeat Bowen's plan.[62] According to a Health Insurance Association of America spokeswoman, "The companies can live with it. It's just that we feel the approach is misdirected."[63] Another industry representative noted, "We are not worried about losing the medigap market."[64] When one administration official asked, "How do you beat this proposal with private insurance?" the executives countered, "It's not a good business decision for us to get into that area."[65] There would still be numerous gaps in coverage, according to the vice president of Empire Blue Cross, including $2,000 a year for deductibles and co-payments. Nor would the Bowen plan cover Alzheimer's disease, which was "obviously a market for the private industry," noted Leonard Tondl of Mutual of Omaha, one of the insurers that had begun offering such coverage on an experimental basis. Conservative columnist Peter Ferrara acknowledged, "Insurance companies weren't interested in fighting. . . . Medigap just isn't that profitable."[66]

President Reagan was convinced by Bowen's arguments. He would support expanding Medicare on one condition—that it be financed entirely by the elderly. A bill was sent to Congress on February 24, 1987. What started as a relatively modest proposal expanded as it moved through the Democrat-controlled Congress. The final measure was much more generous than Bowen had originally proposed. It would cap the amount beneficiaries would have to pay for hospital and physician care at $2,146 per year and cover many other costs currently paid by individually purchased medigap policies or by employers, including prescription drugs, mammography screening, hospice care, and even caregiver support for the frail elderly.[67]

A decade earlier the hospital lobby had crushed Carter's proposal to cap the individual health care costs of all insured people, not just Medicare.[68] With the proposal narrowed to include just retirees, the hospital industry was less resistant. The AHA endorsed the measure as long as reimbursements to hospitals were not cut. The AMA supported it as long as fee-for-service was not challenged.[69] Blue Cross and Blue Shield supported it, as did the manufacturers of generic drugs. The Medicare Catastrophic Coverage Act's most enthusiastic boosters were the large manufacturers and the Washington Business Group on Health, which had been lobbying for relief from retiree health benefits.[70] The Catastrophic Coverage Act would solve part of the problem by shifting most of these costs to the federal government or to retirees themselves through higher taxes.

Bowen's original proposal was relatively modest and would be financed by a $59 annual charge, but cost estimates rose as new benefits were added. The one that aroused the most controversy was prescription drug coverage, which the AARP had relentlessly pursued. According to cynics, the AARP wanted drugs covered because it operated as a middleman for the nation's second largest mail order drug supply service, collecting a royalty on every prescription it filled. Adding drug coverage to Medicare would mean AARP would reap huge profits.[71] As one administration official complained, "They run the largest mail order drug operation in the business—they're going to make a fortune on it."[72] In reality AARP would lose business if seniors received prescription drugs for free.

The drug benefit aroused the fierce opposition of the Pharmaceutical Manufacturers Association (PMA). The PMA feared that if premiums failed to cover the program's costs, then the government would slap on price controls. To prevent an open-ended drug benefit from being included, the PMA organized a $3 million lobbying campaign. The PMA hired a public relations firm to phone the elderly and warn them that if the Medicare Catastrophic Coverage Act was enacted, they would be forced to pay higher taxes for benefits they already had.[73] The letter was signed by Dr. Francis Davis, president of Physicians for Quality Medical Care, a PMA front. In the letter Davis warned senior citizens that "if the House version passed instead of the Senate bill, senior citizens would be the losers," because only a few would benefit, "while higher premiums would be charged to all."[74] Seniors were urged to write their representatives supporting a watered-down Senate version that would phase in prescription drug coverage gradually and permit Medicare to stop paying for entire classes of drugs if costs rose too quickly.[75] Representative Pete Stark (D-Calif.) charged the PMA with being involved in "one of the sleaziest lobbying campaigns I've seen in some time." But the PMA had an ally in Bowen, who was dismayed that his bill had become a Christmas tree, with members of Congress vying to add new ornaments. Calling the drug benefit a "cruel hoax," Bowen argued that it would significantly raise the costs of the program. If the drug benefit was retained, he would recommend a presidential veto.

When it appeared that a prescription drug benefit would be included anyway, the PMA demanded a role in the negotiations. Representative Andrew Jacobs (D-Ind.), whose district was home to drug manufacturer Eli Lilly, offered an amendment to strike language encouraging the use of generic substitutes for brand-name drugs.[76] That amendment was rejected, but Jacobs won a victory. The final bill made no reference to cost controls. If prescription drug costs exceeded expectations, beneficiaries would pay higher premiums.

As word of the catastrophic coverage plan spread, most senior citizens' organizations initially supported it. The AARP actively lobbied for the proposal. When administration conservatives tried to convince the president to veto the measure, AARP helped persuade him to sign it.

Despite the positive response from many stakeholder groups usually opposed to government action, there were also early warnings that the proposal might receive a hostile reception. The Chamber of Commerce charged Bowen with "shoving Medicare further along a socialist path" and created a task force to develop a private sector approach.[77] The National Committee to Preserve Social Security and Medicare, an organization that was founded in 1982 to "save Social Security," also raised objections. This group had had a seedy reputation since an incident in 1983 when it had mailed a solicitation to thousands of older people promising that for a $10 contribution they would receive a printout of their Social Security earnings record, something the Social Security Administration provided for free. After its activities became the subject of congressional hearings in both chambers, it was named one of the nation's worst public interest groups by *Washington Monthly* magazine. During the 1986 elections, however, the National Committee had increased its staff from just a handful to more than 50, including 12 registered lobbyists, and persuaded 100,000 senior citizens to become active in local political campaigns.[78] In an effort to scuttle the bill, the group sent letters to more than 1.5 million people in September 1987, warning older people about the tax increase.[79]

As the Medicare legislation moved forward, the National Committee placed an ad in the *Washington Post* warning Congress: "Don't make a mistake that will harm and anger your senior constituents." After the measure passed the Senate in October 1987, the National Committee mailed a "legislative alert" to members of Congress asking them to vote against a conference bill. Most members of Congress discounted the National Committee, convinced that AARP spoke for the majority of senior citizens. Yet congressional staffers had begun sensing intense grassroots opposition. In a prescient statement, Peter Ferrera wrote, "AARP in any event will have its hands full next year as the elderly discover that what the organization has delivered for their dues is a major income tax increase exclusively on them, for benefits that are not the focus of their concern."[80] These warnings went unheeded.

On July 1, 1988, Congress passed the Medicare Catastrophic Coverage Act with huge bipartisan majorities in both House and Senate. President Reagan quickly signed the bill, and it was not until Congress adjourned that people began to understand its implications.[81] The Medicare Catastrophic Coverage Act would be a great benefit for the 20 percent of the elderly who had no medigap insurance and would guarantee that all Medicare beneficiaries had full prescription drug coverage.[82] But it would only modestly improve coverage for most older people, and it would significantly increase taxes for a large minority.[83] All Medicare beneficiaries would pay higher Part B premiums, and more affluent Medicare beneficiaries would pay an additional surcharge, up to $800 for a single person and $1,600 for a couple.[84] The clear winners were major corporations that were saddled with retiree health benefits. They would receive what the UAW called "a windfall reduction in liability," coupled with "a corresponding shift in cost through the increased Part B premium, to Medicare beneficiaries." The Employee Benefit Research Institute estimated that employers' liability for current retirees would drop by 30 percent.[85] Many retirees would now be paying a surtax and higher premiums to fund benefits their employers had formerly provided free. Employers did have to provide a rebate to retirees in the first year, a provision the AFL-CIO and UAW demanded, but only for that one year. After that, employers' expenses would be reduced with no rebate for retired employees.[86]

Retirees who had medigap benefits were furious.[87] Across the country, petition drives and other protests arose almost instantaneously, and their virulence surprised even congressional veterans. Senior citizens bombarded members of Congress with letters and phone calls denouncing the surtax and demanding long-term care benefits.[88] A 64-year-old former airline pilot organized the Seniors Coalition Against the Catastrophic Coverage Act from his retirement home in Las Vegas, claiming to have gathered 410,000 signatures on a repeal petition. Members of Congress were flooded with letters and phone calls. Senator Pete Wilson (R-Calif.) received 3,000 letters, 15,000 postcards, and an uncountable number of phone calls denouncing the surtax. Representative Claude Pepper received hundreds of surly letters from constituents such as Robert Landon, who wrote: "I did not complain when you decided to tax part of my Social Security but I strenuously object to your putting the bite on me again and having the gall to tell me that I can afford it."[89]

Senior citizens were stirred up by the National Committee to Preserve Social Security and Medicare, but other, more respectable seniors' groups whose members had retiree benefits also demanded repeal.[90] Federal employees were especially peeved at AARP. As Thomas Slater wrote, "As a federal retiree, I am furious that the American Association of Retired Persons (of which I am a member) would lobby for such an unfair law and angry that Congress passed it. . . . Repeal would make me happy."[91] Another retiree wrote:

Yes, my wife and I both pay the maximum surtax. But we already are paying $765.60 for Medicare and our gap insurance coverage costs $3,082 annually. Adding in the catastrophic surtax brings the cost for our health coverage to $5447.60 in 1989 and almost $6,000 two years hence.[92]

In an unpopular move AARP fired the head of California's Vote Project for supporting repeal legislation and tried to oust an AARP chapter president in Florida. More than 6,000 older people canceled their AARP membership.

Then the elderly took to the streets, an attention-getting move since people 65 and older are the least likely of all age groups to protest or take part in a demonstration.[93] In a scene replayed over and over on the nightly news, several dozen angry seniors accosted Representative Dan Rostenkowski (D-Ill.), chair of the House Ways and Means Committee, as he attempted to drive away from a meeting. Rostenkowski, a major supporter of the legislation, had maneuvered it through Congress, and now the elderly sought retribution. The demonstrators surrounded Rostenkowski's car, beating it with picket signs, pounding on the windows, and shouting "Coward!" "Recall!" and "Impeach!" A shaken Rostenkowski abandoned his car and fled the scene on foot.[94] As the protest mounted in intensity, members of Congress turned their wrath on the AARP. Representative Harris Fawell (R-Ill.) remarked, "They've clearly lost touch with their membership. Maybe they're too worried about selling prescription drugs to pay attention to costs and duplication of services."[95] On April 12 the Senate voted to hold hearings on the catastrophic law. The AARP refused to testify at the hearing, complaining that the witness lineup was stacked against the law.[96] As one senior citizen after another decried the legislation, a frustrated Senator Bob Packwood declared:

I will tell you who we have heard from. They all live in Sun City and they all have incomes of $30,000. I do not think it is unfair or unethical or immoral or wrong to ask those of us who are a little bit more privileged to give a little extra to take care of those who are a little less privileged.[97]

Senator Alan Simpson warned that members would regret a repeal vote: "We're not confused. We're terrorized. But when the older Americans . . .

find out we've been swung around by our tails by a small group of wealthy senior citizens, my guess is we'll see a firestorm."[98]

On October 4, 1989, in an unprecedented move, the House voted to repeal the program it had approved just 16 months earlier. Two days later the Senate voted to repeal the surtax, retaining only the long-term hospital benefit, which was subsequently eliminated, too.[99] Representative Henry Waxman (D-Calif.) said members voted to repeal the entire program because "the elderly were ungrateful. So let them stew in their own juices."[100] Representative Stark added, "The hell with it. . . . If seniors want long term care without helping to pay for it, they had better guess again."[101]

The repeal of the Medicare Catastrophic Coverage Act was a setback for the business community. In its wake, many firms began retreating from their commitment to their retirees. In April 1989 Pittston Coal declared it would no longer contribute to the miners' health and welfare funds. The United Mine Workers went on strike until Pittston finally agreed after a nine-month standoff to restore some of the benefits and replenish part of the miners' trust fund. Some firms, such as TRW, Pillsbury, and Quaker Oats, shifted more of the cost of retiree benefits onto current workers or retirees by increasing premiums, co-payments, and deductibles or by capping their own expenditures at a set amount.[102] By 1996 88 percent of employers required retirees over age 65 to pay some or all of the premiums that had formerly been provided for free.[103] Some firms established two-tier systems that provided full benefits for current workers and retirees but not for newly hired employees. Others pushed retirees into Medicare HMOs, a move that virtually eliminated their premium costs and transferred the risks of high costs onto Medicare.[104] The number of employers offering retiree benefits to early retirees, those age 55 to 64, dropped from 70 percent in the mid-1980s to 36 percent by 2000. There was an equally precipitous drop in retiree benefits for people 65 and older, with only 26 percent of Medicare-eligible retirees covered by an employer plan in 2000.[105] Thus, while some older people experienced short-term gains from the repeal of the Medicare Catastrophic Coverage Act, the long-term consequence was the loss of a fully financed prescription drug benefit and erosion of benefits for future retirees.

The decline of retiree health benefits represented a devastating loss for people such as 74-year-old Roman Makarewicz, who had worked for 42 years for the Pabst Brewing Company in Milwaukee. On August 6, 1996, with no warning, he and hundreds of other Pabst retirees received a letter announcing that the company was cutting its workforce by 200 and dropping retiree benefits as of September 1. Beer production had fallen by two-thirds in the past year, and Pabst could no longer afford to provide the coverage. Under Pabst's generous retiree health plan, Mr. Makarewicz had paid only $2 for each prescription. Now his prescription drug costs would soar. As he explained, "I've got high blood pressure. I've got to take a water pill. My medications alone are $114 a month. I've got arthritis in my knees. I can barely walk. Forty-two years you work in a place and then get stabbed in the back." His coworker, 70-year-old Gerald Holtslander, wearily agreed: "What are you going to do when they start changing the rules? A little guy can't do anything."[106]

In 2000 the Third Circuit Court of Appeals ruled that retirees who are eligible for Medicare could have a valid claim of age discrimination under the Age Discrimination in Employment Act if their employers provide them with coverage inferior to that offered to younger retirees, that is, those who are under 65 and thus not eligible for Medicare. In light of this decision more employers concluded that it was safer to eliminate retiree health benefits entirely than to risk being sued for age discrimination.[107]

During the 1980s employers had attempted to reduce their health care expenditures by shifting costs to employees, negotiating lower rates with providers, organizing to gain a voice in policy decisions, and supporting legislation that would transfer responsibility for retiree benefits to the federal government. When none of these tactics succeeded to any significant extent, in the late 1980s corporate purchasers turned with a vengeance to managed care.

The Ascendance of Managed Care

In the 1980s companies began experimenting with various piecemeal approaches to managing health care. Some companies, such as Pillsbury and Berol, began negotiating fees directly with physicians and hospitals before treatment or required employees to get approval for routine hospitalizations and obtain second opinions before undergoing certain operations.[108] Others, including Caterpillar, R. J. Reynolds, Chrysler, and aerospace giant Martin Marietta, began their own internal hospital utilization review programs or penalized employees who refused to switch to an HMO by imposing higher co-payments.[109] Berol built its own medical clinic with its own physicians, laboratory, and pharmacy.[110]

Corporate purchasers then turned to managed care in a more coordinated fashion. The shift began in earnest in 1987, when Edward Hennessy, the chairman of Allied Signal, frustrated by a 39 percent hike in health insurance costs in one year, declared, "Enough."[111] Hennessy asked an aide to show him the "most astronomical health care bills" of his employees, those $100,000 or higher. To his amazement, the aide wheeled in a cart with a three-foot-high stack of folders. That spring Hennessy invited a dozen of the nation's largest insurers to compete for a managed care contract. Cigna won the contract by promising to keep rate increases under 6 percent a year for the next three years.

Allied Signal rapidly became a model for the rest of corporate America.[112] Southwestern Bell adopted a managed care plan in 1987. Sears Roebuck switched to managed care in 1990. In 1989 the head of human resources at Wells Fargo organized a breakfast for dozens of area corporations to develop a managed care strategy. As a result of these efforts, the companies formed the Pacific Business Group on Health and began negotiating cheap managed care contracts.[113] The retreat from fee-for-service occurred rapidly. Between 1983 and 1994 the number of physicians employed in group practices, HMOs, and other organizational settings grew from 23 percent to 37 percent.

Managed care was not a single arrangement but rather involved a bewildering variety of forms. Some companies established HMOs with their own medical staff; others involved preferred provider organizations (PPOs) of independent physicians who contracted to provide services for a discounted rate in return for guaranteed patient volumes. Some self-insured firms created and ran their own managed care plans. Others hired specialized managed care firms to process employee claims. Regardless of the specifics, the central tenet of managed care was that doctors and hospitals should no longer be able to choose whatever treatment they preferred. Under managed care they were no longer solely in charge of medical decisions and no longer in control of the allocation of health care resources. Take Dr. Barry Levine, who taught at Harvard Medical School. One day he received a letter from Tufts Associated Health Plans, an HMO that covered some of Levine's patients. He was invited to what he thought would be a brainstorming session with HMO managers to solicit his advice. Instead Joe Gerstein, Tufts' medical director, informed him that he would have to discharge heart attack patients a half day earlier and use a shorter-acting anesthesia so his patients could go home sooner.[114]

The objective of managed care firms was to wrest control of services from physicians and hospitals and push providers to make "cost-efficient" choices.[115] Computer-generated data on patients' treatment and outcomes made it possible to identify subpar performance. Physicians were pressured to spend less time with each individual patient, to use fewer specialists, and to order fewer tests and procedures. When physicians challenged the decisions, statisticians pulled out their spreadsheets to demonstrate how the doctors' choice of treatment deviated from the norm. Some HMOs tethered physicians' incomes to patient treatment decisions. Physicians who kept costs under control were rewarded with incentive pay or bonuses as high as $150,000 a year, while those who failed to do so were threatened with "delisting." According to one national survey, over 70 percent of managed care plans used some type of physician profiling.[116] For the first time, the major health plans were not just clerks paying bills.

In the power grab by employers, physicians found their authority slipping away. When the House Subcommittee on Human Resources and Intergovernmental Relations held hearings on managed care in 1993, one physician after another decried the intrusion of managed care. Dr. Steven Kanig, a podiatrist from Albuquerque, complained:

> Managing care to ensure high quality and control cost is the avowed mission of these organizations [managed care firms]. Each is pursuing a strategy that is aimed at maximizing its competitive position. . . . Many physicians are concerned that the notion of quality has become just another marketing concept and has nothing to do with true quality of care. . . . It should not be assumed that primary gatekeepers automatically provide the most cost-effective care. And the expense of some of the health care parasite industries must be brought under control.[117]

His colleague Dr. Carol Merovka complimented HMOs for making it possible for more small businesses to afford to offer health benefits to their employees. And she appreciated the information HMOs provided that allowed physicians to practice more cost-effectively:

> I have never, as a training physician, had the opportunity to look at how much it cost to have a gallbladder ultrasound or a C.B.C. done, et cetera. . . . So by getting information from these HMOs, I have been able to now figure out when someone comes into my office how I can make tremendous cost savings that still allows me to provide quality care. And that information was not available to me until I participated as a physician in an HMO.[118]

Yet the information provided by her HMO included only a cost analysis; it had nothing to do with patient outcomes. Thus she declared in frustration:

> I need to get out from the burden of managed care. I find it to be very manipulative. I find it to be very obtrusive in the care that I would like to give to my patients. And I feel also that, for the most part, because it is so cost and HMO administrative driven, that the physicians have lost their voice in the process.[119]

Because HMO physicians are "very, very fragmented and disenchanted," not many of her colleagues "have the guts to stand up and say how intimidated they are, how unhappy they are."[120]

During the 1990s outraged physicians began fighting back against the speed-up of the production process, the loss of control over compensation, and the intrusion of nonmedical personnel into clinical decisions. They pursued their challenge to managed care through the courts, in the states, and in Congress, in many instances forming political alliances with consumers who were angered over the sometimes callous and clumsy treatment they received from managed care firms. Patients were forced to travel across town or further, far from family and friends, when they needed surgery. Sick children were given blood tests by cheaper but unfriendly technicians. Cancer patients had to fight to get costly treatments of unproven merit recommended by their doctors or even in some cases to obtain routine treatment.[121] One third-year medical student at the University of New Mexico described a notorious case in which his university's cancer center had to go to court to force an HMO to provide chemotherapy for a patient:

The unhappy ironic ending was that though the court ultimately ruled in the patient's favor, the litigation dragged so long that, by the time of the rule, the cancer had progressed beyond the point where the treatment could help. The patient died shortly after he won in court.[122]

In another case, Dr. Linda Peeno, who was a medical reviewer for Humana, testified that she had caused a death of a man when she denied a heart transplant:

> I was rewarded for this. It brought me an improved reputation in my job and contributed to my advancement afterward. The patient was a piece of computer paper. The "clinical goal" was to figure out a way to avoid payment. The diagnosis was to "DENY." Once I stamped "DENY" across his authorization form, his life's end was as certain as if I had pulled the plug on a ventilator. Not only did I demonstrate I could indeed do what was expected of me, I exemplified the "good" company doctor: I saved a half million dollars.[123]

By the mid-1990s polls showed that the insurance industry had become public enemy number one, even more despised than the tobacco industry.[124]

The AMA helped physicians in multispecialty groups acquire sufficient capital to organize their own HMOs and negotiate exclusive contracts with employers.[125] In 1996 podiatrists formed a union to bargain collectively with HMOs; other specialties considered the feasibility of starting their own unions. In the war with the HMOs, physicians won some battles but lost others. When a team of New Jersey anesthesiologists sued a hospital over the terms of a contract with an HMO, the hospital played hardball, hiring new anesthesiologists and taking patient assignments for these physicians out of the hands of the medical staff.[126] Some doctors, such as Daniel Fisher, packed up their equipment and quit practicing medicine. He explained his decision in a letter to his 2,651 patients:

> The system of HMOs, managed care, restricted hospitals and denial of needed medications has become so corrupt, so rotten, that I cannot stomach it any longer. The system is controlled by for-profit

HMOS with dividend hungry shareholders and high-salaried administrators. I was beginning to feel the pressure and change my
prescription habits from the best medicine I knew to the one that
would look best on my profile and hating myself for it.[127]

Physicians also lobbied state legislatures to regulate HMOs.[128] They
demanded that managed care companies publicly disclose the criteria
they used to determine whether to approve a given service and won
rulings requiring that nonmedical personnel could not deny services ordered by a physician.[129] At the urging of physicians' organizations, Rhode
Island and Virginia passed laws requiring that an independent reviewer
be available to assess HMO challenges to specialist referrals. New York
enacted a law requiring HMOs to reimburse patients for consultations
with physicians outside their HMO.[130] In response to pressure from physicians and consumers, three states passed laws restricting the ability of
HMOs to deny claims for emergency room use. In 1996 alone, 110 bills
were introduced in 36 states to extend hospital stays following a normal
birth.[131] Physicians also used their influence to get state insurance departments to issue regulations requiring HMOs to disclose financial incentives that encouraged physicians to withhold care.[132]

Following a series of takeovers and mergers in the early 1990s, managed care firms grew rapidly in size and market scope.[133] With their
billions in assets and influential lobbyists, these companies proved to
be formidable opponents. Recognizing their negative public image, they
used surrogates to fight their battles, mobilizing the Chamber of Commerce and the National Federation of Independent Business against
regulatory measures physicians proposed in the states.[134] As a result,
physicians' efforts to ban capitation payments (where they were paid a
flat amount for each patient) through either state or federal legislation
failed entirely.[135] When state and county medical societies pushed for
rules that would prohibit HMOs from excluding physicians from their
networks and force them to include "any willing provider," they were
blocked by a coalition of employers and HMOs in every one of 29 states
except Arkansas.[136]

Physicians also took their grievances to court in a series of class action suits.[137] They sued HMOs for antitrust relief, charging that insurance company mergers had consolidated power in the hands of a few
companies.[138] They brought suit against Cigna, one of the largest man-

aged care firms, on racketeering charges for underpaying patients' health claims, reaching a $50 million settlement in Illinois that was subsequently challenged in Florida.[139] Physicians won a major victory on June 20, 2002, when the Supreme Court upheld a lower-court decision giving patients the right to an independent review for denial of treatment.[140]

Physicians also pressed for "patients' rights" legislation that would allow patients who were denied care to sue their HMO.[141] When a patients' bill of rights was proposed in the Virginia General Assembly, the state's largest insurance company, Trigon Healthcare, a Blue Cross/Blue Shield giant, hired 33 lobbyists, including the governor's chief fundraiser, the wife of the executive director of the state Republican Party, a former state attorney general, and two Democratic Party campaign consultants. Lobbyists worked the General Assembly and held seminars around the state, targeting a provision that would allow patients to sue their health insurer for malpractice.[142] One legislator complained, "There was a great deal of lobbying, as much as I've seen in 35 years."[143] Although most of the bill remained intact, the key issue—the right to sue—was removed. The same organizations successfully employed similar tactics in Texas. Over the next few years, however, ten states gave injured patients the right to sue their HMO in state courts.[144]

The physicians took patients' rights to Congress, a tactic that antagonized self-insured firms, who opposed any feature that would weaken the ERISA preemption (which prevented self-insured firms from being sued in state courts). The Business Roundtable joined forces with the Chamber of Commerce, the National Association of Manufacturers, the Health Insurance Association of America, and Aetna to undermine public support for this provision.[145] The coalition paid for a $750,000 media blitz, widely airing ads that proclaimed that more federal regulation would increase premiums and cause more people to lose coverage.[146] Viewers first heard pitches from a worker, a small-business owner, and a mother and child and were then urged to call an 800 number to register their opposition. NAM also dispatched a memo to 200 lawmakers warning them against supporting the bill and threatening to stuff notes in workers' pay envelopes urging them to protest if it was enacted.[147] In 1999 the House of Representatives narrowly passed a patients' bill of rights, but the measure died in a conference committee.

The patients' bill of rights reappeared in 2001, when the Senate passed a new bill providing a host of protections for patients in self-insured health plans. The most significant provisions gave patients in these plans the right to sue when denial of treatment resulted in injury or death. AMA secretary-treasurer Donald Palmisano lauded the Senate bill as "a huge victory for patients" that "set a gold standard for protecting patients against managed care abuses."[148] While HMOs had stopped fighting other patient protections, they remained opposed to the issue of lawsuits. The bill appeared headed for passage in the House until President George W. Bush threatened to veto it after his advisors concluded that patients' rights were not a high public priority. Although 70 percent of the public said they favored a patients' bill of rights, patients' rights were ranked only seventh in importance, after education, energy exploration, and conservation.[149] It seemed unlikely that a presidential veto would trigger an explosive reaction. Instead, Bush negotiated behind the scenes for an amendment that would cap damages and move some kinds of lawsuits from state to federal courts. Democrats decried the amendment, claiming it "was slanted at every turn for the HMOs and against patients and doctors." The amended bill passed in the House on August 3, 2001, but died in a conference committee, exactly the outcome the HMOs wanted.[150]

In the wake of the failure of patients' rights, the courts began chipping away at the ERISA preemption of state regulations. In 2003 the U.S. Second Circuit Court of Appeals ruled in *Cicio v. Vytra Healthcare* that HMOs could be held liable if lack of patient care led to injury or death.[151] And although the patients' rights issue was dead in Congress, it was still alive in the states, with ten bills for patients' rights and managed care reform pending in 2003.

The costly wars between physicians and insurers resulted in a strategy shift on the part of HMOs and employers. The Coalition for Affordable Quality Health Care, an organization of HMOs, insurance companies, and trade associations, launched a $9 million campaign to improve the image of the managed care industry. Employers began offering their employees less restrictive managed care plans or giving them a choice of plans, and insurers began seeking less contentious relationships with providers.[152] Bending to the strength of the consumer movement, the American Association of Health Plans, the organization representing HMOs, also loosened restrictions on some of the more contentious issues, such as "drive-by" mastectomies and 24-hour hospital stays following a normal birth.[153]

Conclusion

From the New Deal to the 1970s, the chief obstacle to national health insurance was organized medicine. Then the excesses of the profession produced a counterreaction from the corporations that began to challenge the protected provider markets. Corporations tried a variety of tactics ranging from shifting costs to employees to negotiating with providers to organizing coalitions to influence policy debates. Ironically, the most effective challenge to the medical providers came from the private health insurance system, which physicians had helped to construct as an alternative to government intervention. It took the form of billion-dollar, for-profit managed care firms. Managed care helped to undermine physicians' claims of specialized knowledge by putting them at financial risk for their medical decisions and by placing decision-making power in the hands of nonphysicians.

The managed care wars changed the way most consumers received care. In the past health care had been rationed, but in implicit ways such as having lengthy waiting times to get appointments or being unable to see a specialist. Managed care engaged in explicit rationing by limiting patients' options, reducing their choice of health plans, or forcing them to see a physician who was a plan member. Even though most studies have found few differences in health outcomes between managed care and fee-for-service medicine, the visible constraints on choice created the perception that people were frequently denied access to lifesaving treatment or denied access to hospital care. Yet many people were willing to put up with constraints on choice in exchange for a promise of lower costs—a promise that hasn't materialized.[154]

The arousal of corporations and insurance companies also had consequences for national health insurance. It brought newly mobilized, powerful stakeholders into the political arena whenever health care reform was on the table. While corporations were primarily concerned with containing costs, insurers had a vested interest in preventing the federal government from creating competing products and in structuring any new programs in ways that would preserve the private market.

The true victims of the health care wars of the 1980s were neither physicians nor insurers. Rather, they were the millions of elderly people who did not try to overturn Rostenkowski's car, who did not write angry letters to their congressional representatives, and who did not testify before Congress against the Medicare Catastrophic Coverage Act. Not only did these people lose a benefit that would help defray the cost of the supplemental items that Medicare did not cover, such as prescription drugs (coverage for which employers were casting off with abandon), they also lost the sympathy of the key members of Congress whose support they would need if they hoped for any improvement in long-term care coverage. Since then, the long-term care market has moved in a direction that is similar to the pattern of health benefits for the younger population. That is, a small proportion of people purchase expensive policies on their own in the individual long-term care insurance market, a growing number are offered group long-term care benefits through an employer (but with the employer paying none of the costs), and the rest will do just what they have been doing—spending down their assets to qualify for Medicaid or hiring a smart lawyer to help them protect their estates.

seven

The Insurers Triumphant

The cost inflation of the 1980s proved to be damaging to the insurance industry in a number of ways. Not only did private insurance companies incur billions of dollars in underwriting losses, they also experienced an erosion of their economic base as the majority of large employers stopped using conventional insurance to cover their employees, moving to self-insurance instead.[1] Many insurance companies were forced out of the health care marketplace, leading to a rash of insurance company failures. In 1989 the House Committee on Oversight and Investigations concluded an inquiry into the causes of these failures. The inquiry uncovered "a remarkable record of greed and incompetence by the persons responsible for managing these companies." As evidence was presented, a sordid tale unfolded of "excessive underpricing, ridiculous management, self-dealing, non-existent records, and a general concern only for the welfare of the top corporate insiders." Worse, these activities were hidden "by contrived transactions, creative accounting and fraudulent reports to regulatory agencies."[2] The agencies that were supposed to monitor insurance company practices, the state insurance departments, were largely ineffectual, because in most states they lacked the personnel and authority to track and punish wayward insurers. In states where insurance commissioners were elected, their largest campaign contributions came from insurance companies. As one witness testified at another hearing, "In some cases the industry gets them elected."[3] Only one-third of insurance departments even had written rules regarding how to handle the 23,000 or so complaints that each department received on average each year, and half kept no records on the number of complaints about any specific insurance company.

Yet during the 1990s, the insurance industry emerged as the unchallenged master of the health care financing system, trumping physicians and hospitals and turning back challenges that might undermine their access to core markets. Industry leaders mobilized forces to fend off federal regulation, crush proposals for government-backed long-term care insurance and national health insurance, and spur the development of new private company products. At the century's end, the private insurance industry had vanquished any public sector alternative.

Long-Term Care for the Frail Elderly

In the mid-1980s the House Subcommittee on Health and Long Term Care held a series of hearings that highlighted the plight of the frail elderly. Once people became chronically ill with little hope of recovery, Medicare and most private insurance ended.[4] At that point the only option for most people was to deplete their life savings, then submit to what many considered humiliating scrutiny of their income and assets to determine their eligibility for Medicaid. Medicaid applicants faced a bewildering array of rules and regulations that varied from state to state. In some states Medicaid included the "medically needy," people who had minimal assets, low or moderate incomes (but were not desperately poor), and high medical expenses for nursing home care. Other states, those with no "medically needy" program, rejected applicants if their income was $1 over the Medicaid limit even when they owned nothing.[5] In such states anyone with Social Security benefits and a modest pension would likely be disqualified. For example, Ann Blake, a 55-year-old secretary, moved her incontinent 78-year-old mother from her home in Arkansas to a Florida nursing home, then applied for Medicaid, thinking the state would pay for her mother's care. Although Ann's mother owned no property and had a monthly income of just over $1,300, Florida's Medicaid income limit was $1,158 at that time. Her application was denied.[6] Ann was forced to take her mother out of the nursing home and set her up in a trailer in the backyard of her own modest home. Because most people had no idea what the Medicaid eligibility rules were in any particular state until they needed help, they often learned that they were ineligible when it was too late to make other arrangements.

Even people who were accepted for Medicaid often couldn't find a nursing home that would admit them when they needed care, because nursing home operators favored private-pay patients, who were charged higher rates. One study found that nearly 80 percent of nursing homes discriminated against Medicaid beneficiaries in their admission policies. Medicaid patients were often forced to wait two to three times as many days for admission as Medicare or private-pay patients.[7] As one Illinois nursing home administrator explained, "We refuse admission if someone is on Medicaid even if we have empty beds. It is a calculated risk. We would rather have the bed empty."[8] Nursing homes that accepted Medicaid patients usually provided poorer-quality care than those with higher proportions of private-pay patients.[9]

These problems were exacerbated by Medicare's prospective payment system, which reimbursed hospitals a flat amount depending on a patient's diagnosis, no matter how long the stay. Once the prospective payment system went into effect, hospitals transferred patients recovering from surgery or a heart attack to nursing homes as quickly as they could. Swamped with applications, nursing homes tightened their admission requirements.[10] The practice of releasing patients from hospitals quicker and sicker also placed pressure on the states, which through Medicaid paid for 41 percent of all nursing home care.[11] Rising Medicaid costs drained state coffers, consuming resources that might otherwise be used for education, infrastructure, and social services. In an effort to keep costs under control, some states resorted to freezing Medicaid reimbursement rates, a strategy that only worsened the dilemma for the frail elderly.[12] For example, Tennessee's preadmission screening program made it difficult even for very sick people to get nursing home care. One daughter was incredulous that her mother was deemed medically ineligible for nursing home care:

> She has been with me every day since she was sick. During the last two years, she has been in my house seven days a week, 24 hours a day. . . . She was in the emergency room, she had a leg ulcer and fell, which created another ulcer on her ankle. She has been treated for symptoms of congestive heart failure. She is a diabetic. She has had a few mini-strokes. . . . She is confused. She cannot cook for herself or get down into the bathtub. . . . But the

hospital said it did not see these things. It is hard to get them into a nursing home if they are not completely bedridden.[13]

In another case, a son who failed to find a nursing home placement for his mother explained his frustration with the system:

> My mother had a stroke and was getting where she could not take care of herself. She was paranoid. She could not cook meals very well or take care of her house. . . . If she did try to cook, she would burn things. She had bladder accidents . . . I went by every day after work to check on her. . . . Several times we had to redo paperwork.[14]

Despite his mother's precarious health, she was not considered sick enough to qualify for Medicaid.

As the long-term care system was squeezed to the limit, the elderly and their middle-aged children turned to the federal government to solve the problem. According to a poll conducted by the AARP in 1988, more than 75 percent of people age 45 and older supported a national long-term care program similar to Social Security. Governors, too, began to look to Washington for more help.

Long-term care was a market the private insurance industry had barely penetrated. Until the mid-1980s, the insurance industry had been uninterested in long-term care insurance, because expenses were too unpredictable and the elderly too poor to make the product viable. In 1985 fewer than three dozen companies offered any sort of long-term care coverage. The trend toward self-insurance among large firms had eroded the economic base of private insurance plans and left them with the less profitable business of claims processing and benefits management. To compensate for these losses, insurance companies began aggressively seeking new markets. As we saw in Chapter 6, one solution was to market managed care plans to employers.[15] Insurers also began exploring the untapped but potentially profitable long-term care market. In 1986 the Health Insurance Association of America created a Task Force on Long Term Care. The Task Force surveyed developments in the field and discovered that the generation of people who were approaching old age had higher median income, greater wealth, and "greater assets to protect and preserve" than any previous generation. Long-term care insurance presented a lucrative opportunity, because profits in the insurance industry are generated almost entirely from investment income. Policies that incur benefit expenses monthly, such as health insurance, are less profitable than policies whose payouts may be years in the future, such as life insurance.[16] The longer the duration of the policy, the higher the profits. People in their 50s and 60s who might not make claims for several decades and the upper-income "young" elderly who had assets to protect were the ideal "target market for a long term care insurance product."[17] By 1987 72 companies had leaped into the long-term care market.

At first the market was dominated by smaller, specialty companies that sold individual insurance policies. These individual policies were ripe for abuse. Most purchasers were frail elderly people in poor health, and the product was entirely unregulated. Previous investigations of sales practices in the medigap insurance market had found that agents frequently employed deception in explaining the limits and restrictions of their policies and often sold the elderly unnecessary policies for coverage they already had. For example, Mrs. Z. was sold similar medigap policies from three different agents. One 86-year-old Wisconsin woman bought 19 different policies from six agents representing nine companies.[18] Mrs. M's agent sold her a medigap policy, then changed companies four months later and sold her a new policy. Another agent sold the same client 11 different policies from three companies. As one former insurance agent testified, "The goal is to take advantage of what the older person doesn't know." The practice of paying high commissions the first year a policy was in effect encouraged "switching or twisting where agents get seniors to drop the insurance policy they sold them a short while ago to buy a new policy which is of no more value or less value. The agent is sitting pretty with another big, fat first-year sales commission of up to 60 percent of the premium paid by the victim."[19]

State insurance commissioners responded to complaints but only rarely initiated broader investigations of insurance companies. In most states there was no effort to determine whether fraudulent sales practices were isolated instances or systematic occurrences, and insurance companies were rarely fined or disciplined. To curb these abuses, in 1979 Congress enacted legislation that prohibited certain of the more unsavory marketing practices and allowed states to give a "seal of approval" to companies whose medigap policies met certain standards. The following year Congress established criminal penalties for agents who engaged in deceptive sales tactics and required insurers to provide minimum coverage and set minimum standards for loss ratios.[20] That meant that all medigap policies had to pay at least 60 cents on every premium dollar in benefits.[21] Yet a follow-up investigation in 1986 found that the elderly were no better off than they had been eight years before.[22] The regulatory measures had only been sporadically enforced, and little had been done to stop insurance scams. The majority of states allowed coverage gaps and loopholes to persist, and few states monitored how much of policyholders' premiums were actually paid out in benefits.

In 1991 Congress enacted stricter regulations for private medigap policies.[23] Insurance companies that offered supplemental medigap coverage law were prohibited from refusing any Medicare beneficiary who wished to purchase a policy, regardless of health.[24] The glitch was that older people had this protection only if a medigap policy was purchased within a six-month open enrollment period. When this six-month period ended, they could be denied coverage of a preexisting condition or be forced to pay higher rates.

The federal laws governing medigap policies, weak as they were, did not apply to long-term care insurance at all. As the insurance industry began expanding its offerings for long-term care, similar complaints surfaced. By 1989 20 states had begun investigations of sales practices for long-term care insurance in their legislative sessions.[25] In Congress the House Subcommittee on Health and Long Term Care conducted its own investigation and found numerous problems. Unscrupulous sales agents exaggerated what the policies covered and sold people duplicate policies. Insurance companies delayed paying benefits when people filed claims; some even disqualified policyholders entirely.[26] Most policies provided little protection against the cost of nursing home care, few were indexed to keep up with inflation, many excluded admissions for Alzheimer's disease (the main cause of nursing home admissions), and most allowed insurers to cancel coverage at any time. Some enterprising insurance companies created fictitious "groups" to sell insurance to the elderly. For example, in Massachusetts the insurance commissioner investigated a long-term care plan underwritten by the Pioneer Life Insurance Company through a group deceptively named the Association of Retired Americans.[27] As consumer advocate Bonnie Burns noted, "While there has been an explosion of companies willing to enter this market, there is no regulation to protect the consumer on whom this experiment is being conducted."[28]

Following the flurry of bad publicity, the larger insurance companies began entering the field, building upon their experience in marketing group health insurance to employers to craft better policies. Aetna offered a new plan for retired employees in Alaska that covered nursing home care and home care, the first policy sold through an employer group.[29] Prudential test-marketed a new product for AARP members.[30] As the idea of group long-term care insurance spread, other employers began offering long-term care policies to their employees. These policies were often negotiated by benefits managers who used the leverage afforded large groups to insist on automatic inflation adjusters, cheaper rates, a range of care options, and Alzheimer's coverage.

The insurance industry fiercely resisted any efforts by the federal government to regulate long-term care insurance, preferring to leave regulation to insurer-friendly state insurance departments.[31] In 1986 the National Association of Insurance Commissioners developed model legislation for long-term care policies in an effort to head off federal regulation. The Long Term Care Insurance Model Act and Regulation included inflation protection, a 30-day free-look period, and guarantees of refunds in case of a lapse or cancellation.[32] But only a few states adopted the model.[33]

With the industry seemingly incapable of policing itself and cash-strapped states unwilling to take on more of the long-term care burden, a federal program seemed to offer the most feasible solution. The plan came from Claude Pepper, who after his bitter 1950 defeat in the Senate race by George Smathers had returned to private law practice for a decade, then run for a seat in the House of Representatives when a new congressional district was carved out in Dade County following the 1960 census. As Pepper acquired seniority, he had moved up to become chairman of the powerful Rules Committee, which determined what bills would go to the floor for consideration by the entire House of Representatives. Age 87 himself, Pepper was the leading advocate of the elderly, whose major concern was long-term care. Representative Pepper's records were filled with letters such as the following from Robert Matteson:

When you're cornered, faced with odds so great you don't know how to surmount, the human nature in all of us tells us to seek help from persons who appear to be championing our needs and causes. I am 81, diabetic, faced with the possibility of a nursing home, with its grabbing everything I have left in this world, leaving me and my wife in poverty. This is the plight some witless jerk called our "Golden Years." There were occasions through the years when we paid our taxes more dutifully than willingly, but we paid them. So I'm saying to you, Mr. Pepper, please keep up your efforts to help us unfortunate people in the 80-year-class. Persuade the government, of which you are a part, to help us in extended catastrophic care.[34]

A desperate daughter wrote about her 84-year-old father, Valerio Dimaya, who had been hospitalized for several back fractures, then discharged to her care "with a catheter, a broken clavicle and without his dentures":

He can hardly eat a decent meal nor can he swallow well. Yet he was given huge pills for pain and for an antibiotic. The doctor says he doesn't know if it comes in liquid form. They just told me to find a home by looking in the phone book. No help was given. In the meantime, I'm paying for home care, caring for my three children as a single parent, teaching full time and attending school. Is there no real justice?[35]

Pepper had first introduced a bill to expand Medicare to cover home care services for disabled people of all ages on June 24, 1987. His ambitious proposal would have provided skilled nursing care, home health aides, rehabilitation therapy, and caregiver training.[36] Although the program would initially cover only care in the home, it would eventually be expanded "to cover nursing home care as well."[37] Careful to craft the bill so that physicians would not be threatened, Pepper won AMA support by allowing doctors to be the gatekeepers to the program. Anyone applying for benefits would first have to be certified by a physician as to need. Pepper's bill was killed in the House before it reached a floor vote, but Pepper, a shrewd political operator, threatened to bottle up the Medicare Catastrophic Coverage Act in his Rules Committee unless House Speaker Jim Wright promised to allow a floor vote on his home care bill. Wright also had to promise Pepper that he would appoint a commission to study long-term care and health insurance for the unemployed in the fall.[38]

On November 18, 1987, Pepper reintroduced his home care bill. For the insurance industry, Pepper's bill posed a direct threat to the developing long-term care market. Before the vote, the Health Insurance Association of America sent every member of Congress a letter declaring that "this bill is the wrong medicine for our country."[39] It represented "another example of an expensive government solution . . . that would lead to exploding public sector costs." It would create "an elaborate new layer of government regulation of the health care industry" and "preempt the nascent, but rapidly developing private insurance market."[40] The letter closed with a glowing endorsement of private long-term care insurance, which held "great promise in meeting the nursing home as well as home and community-based long term care needs of the chronically ill."[41]

The home care bill also aroused the opposition of business groups because it would be financed by removing the cap on the Medicare share of the payroll tax.[42] The Chamber of Commerce complained that the payroll tax increase would hurt small businesses and set a "dangerous precedent."[43] The National Federation of Independent Business warned that its members strongly opposed raising the payroll tax to finance long-term care and that it would consider the vote on Pepper's bill as "a Key Small Business Vote for the 100th Congress."[44] The National Association of Manufacturers recommended that Congress take measures instead to "encourage the insurance industry to continue to develop/market innovative insurance products for long term care."[45] The *Wall Street Journal* described the home care bill as "the welfare state on cocaine," supported by "the King Kong known as the senior citizen lobby that muscles in on an ever great share of the nation's wealth."[46]

President Reagan had supported the Medicare Catastrophic Coverage Act because the elderly would pay the costs themselves, but Pepper's bill would be funded by a payroll tax hike. Reagan promised to veto the bill should it reach his desk, declaring it would create "a group of underserved beneficiaries and underpaid providers" who "would constitute a potentially powerful lobby for the expansion of financing for benefits which . . . would add billions of dollars to the federal deficit."[47] In June 1988 99 Democrats joined with 144 Republicans to defeat the measure. Any member of Congress who voted in favor received a letter from the Health Insurance Association of America warning, "We want to take special notice of your vote last week on Rep. Pepper's home care bill."[48]

The defeat of the home care bill left the market open for the private insurance industry, but two problems stood in the way of success. The first was that in a number of states, many of the middle-class people who were the target market for long-term care insurance qualified for Medicaid payments for nursing home care. Many became eligible for Medicaid by "spending down" their assets after they entered a nursing home. For example, Margaret Stetler was in her early 80s and had diabetes and chronic heart failure. When she first entered a nursing home, she had over $40,000 in assets, which disqualified her for Medicaid. However, once she had spent down her assets, Medicaid picked up the cost of her care.[49] In other cases, middle-income elderly became eligible for Medicaid before they entered a nursing home by transferring their assets to their children. Although rules prohibited the transfer of assets three years prior to an application for Medicaid, asset transfers were allowed before then. Even within the three-year "look-back" period, there were loopholes that made it possible to shelter assets. An entire industry of Medicaid estate planners arose to help people find a way to qualify for Medicaid and preserve their estates for their children and grandchildren. In 1989 alone, membership in the National Academy of Elder Law Attorneys increased from 88 to 450.[50] Research found that somewhere between 33 and 40 percent of nursing home residents were eligible for Medicaid upon admission. Some had always been poor, but a significant number of this group had transferred assets to children three years prior to admission, often with the help of an elder-law attorney. In 1993 half of Medicaid applicants had transferred assets during the preceding 30 months. Of those who were ineligible for Medicaid when they first entered a nursing home, only one-third remained private payers. The other two-thirds spent down their savings to Medicaid levels within six months to a year. In 1990 the insurance industry began a campaign to tighten Medicaid eligibility rules to make it tougher for middle-class people to qualify for benefits.

The second reason the insurance industry had difficulty selling long-term care insurance was that the public had no confidence in the product. A Consumers Union study of 94 private long-term care insurance

In the 1990s rising health care costs moved national health insurance to the forefront of the political agenda. Library of Congress, Prints and Photographs Divisions, LC-USZ62-126890

policies found many were highly flawed, a situation made worse by "poorly trained and often unscrupulous agents" who misled consumers about the terms, benefits, and limitations of their coverage. So prevalent were these practices that there was a "need to reevaluate whether an agent-based distribution system [could] work for this product."[51] The House Select Committee on Aging similarly found numerous obstacles for people seeking to purchase coverage and substantial evidence of unscrupulous sales practices. One agent testified about the case of "Bob and Grace," who were frightened into purchasing a worthless policy:

> Bob and Grace didn't have much. They lived off a small pension and Social Security and had no significant savings. The agent pounded away at this poor elderly couples' fears. He told them a story of just having come from Miami where he had been with an elderly couple who didn't have insurance and were now actually living off cat food. Slapping his hand on the table, the agent said, "How would you like to spend the rest of your life eating Kal-Kan?" All the elderly gentleman remembered after that was writing out a check for $2,500.[52]

Another couple found the policy they had purchased to be worthless when they sought to collect the promised benefits:

> Mr. Fiery and I worked hard all our lives and were conservative with our spending. After about 5 years of faithfully paying premiums on the insurance, my husband took ill and had to be admitted to the hospital. After that the doctor said he needed care in a nursing home. While I was upset at the prospect of him not being at home, I was thankful that we had taken out the insurance policy to protect us financially for just this kind of thing. When I submitted the insurance forms for payment, the company said that John's care was not provided in a skilled nursing home as required by our policy. Well, the insurance agent didn't say one word about that when he sold us the insurance.[53]

One disgusted agent told of being approached by a company that specialized in long-term care policies:

> They offered me a guarantee of $50,000 minimum, a new 1987 car and gas to work for them. They told me [to say] that no matter

what people had in the way of insurance, it was trash and what I had was great. Their person told me, "Those old f——ts don't know any better anyway."[54]

When Congress attempted to set uniform federal standards to regulate long-term care insurance, the Health Insurance Association of America objected that federal regulation was unnecessary and that insurers needed protection in this new and risky market. Finally, in 1990 Congress established rules for the timely payments of claims, prohibited insurers from offering coverage that duplicated what Medicare already provided, and required insurance companies to adopt the National Association of Insurance Commissioners model policy.[55]

Although one might discount the home care bill as an overly ambitious publicity stunt that was doomed to fail, that interpretation ignores the fact that during this same period other countries succeeded in finding ways to help the frail elderly pay for long-term care. Germany, the Netherlands, and Australia all established arrangements for public long-term care insurance programs even as they were downsizing other entitlement programs.[56]

Reviving National Health Insurance

During the 1980s Congress had attempted to plug up some of the holes in the private health insurance system with the Consolidated Omnibus Reconciliation Act of 1985 (COBRA). COBRA required employers with 20 or more employees who provided group health insurance plans to offer temporary continuation of coverage for people who would otherwise lose it because of retirement, layoff, divorce, separation, or death. Through a tricky political maneuver the COBRA provision was embedded in the budget process, where secrecy prevailed and filibustering (a tactic used to kill controversial legislation) was prohibited, giving the business groups that opposed it no opportunity to mobilize.[57] But various restrictions coupled with high costs meant that only about 20 percent of people who were eligible for COBRA coverage actually took it.[58]

In the 1980s Congress had also enacted a series of measures that expanded Medicaid coverage for pregnant women and children and loosened the direct link between Medicaid and AFDC. States were allowed to base Medicaid eligibility on family income rather than welfare status and to include children in two-parent households.[59] In 1989 states were required to cover pregnant women and children under age 6 in families with incomes up to 133 percent of the federal poverty level. The following year states were required to cover children ages 6 to 18 in families with incomes up to the federal poverty level.[60] Some states took advantage of these new rules to subsidize coverage for entire families.[61] Oregon extended Medicaid eligibility to all state residents with income below the federal poverty level.[62] Tennessee's TennCare program made Medicaid available to families with income up to 400 percent of the federal poverty level.[63] As the eligibility criteria loosened, Medicaid coverage among children improved significantly.

Despite these efforts, by 1990 37 million Americans—mostly poor and low-income adults and children as well as some middle-income people—remained uninsured. More than twice as many had been uncovered for some period in the past two years.[64] Among the uninsured nearly 80 percent were fully employed, many in low-wage jobs with small firms or in occupations or industries that insurance companies deemed too risky.[65] About 1 million were classified as "medically uninsurable." These individuals could not obtain any health coverage because of poor health, a preexisting condition, or current employment in a hazardous occupation.[66] More than at any time in history, polls showed the public supported health care reform.[67]

Many key stakeholders also believed that some major change was necessary. They had the opportunity to air their views during hearings of the Pepper Commission.[68] Pepper Commission members were a who's who of health care policy, including Senator Ted Kennedy, Representative William Gradison, and Senator Jay Rockefeller, who succeeded Claude Pepper as chairman after Pepper's death in 1989. If commissioners could reach a consensus, much of the political work would have been done. After a rocky start with squabbles between those who wanted to emphasize long-term care and those who were most concerned with access to health care, commission members descended into partisan bickering. They finally split votes on a compromise plan called "pay or play" under which firms would have to either offer affordable insurance to their employees or pay into a federal fund for the uninsured.[69]

Although the Pepper Commission report ended up gathering dust on bookshelves, the testimony presented showed that while providers and business leaders favored some type of reform, there was no consensus among them about what the central problem was or what shape reform should take. The AMA conceded that action was needed to cover the uninsured but argued that it should be provided "to the greatest extent" through the private sector.[70] The AHA was most concerned about private insurers' increasingly rigid resistance to the cost-shifting tactics hospitals employed to compensate for cuts in public programs. To achieve universal coverage, which would make cost shifting unnecessary, the AHA advocated an employer mandate coupled with tax credits for small employers and an expanded Medicaid program for the poor.[71]

Large manufacturers also seemed to be leaning toward national health insurance. Chrysler's CEO, Lee Iacocca, had become less enamored of free markets and more willing to consider a government solution to help American manufacturers better compete in a global market.[72] Having to absorb health care in the sticker price of cars was taking its toll on the auto industry. As Iacocca explained:

> In the United States, employers pay most of the health-care bill. In other countries, that's mainly a governmental responsibility. I like our system better, but it does put a burden on the competitiveness of our products.[73]

John Butler, director of employee benefits at General Motors, expressed similar sentiments:

> At one time the unequivocal answer would be "no" to supporting national health insurance. Faced with a health care bill of $3 billion last year, GM is reconsidering its opposition. . . . In terms of our competition, I would say that is something we are looking at. I'm not saying we are endorsing it, just thinking about it.[74]

A survey of executives from Fortune 500 companies found that 80 percent believed that fundamental changes were needed in the health care system and that over 32 percent favored a public health insurance system.[75] Fifty-three percent of the executives also agreed that "the government should force all employers to pay for their workers' health care."[76] Many of these companies resented being charged indirectly for health care for the uninsured and for coverage of their employees' dependents when spouses worked for firms that did not provide coverage. In 1990 a number of large corporations including Bethlehem Steel, Chrysler, Lockheed, Westinghouse, and Xerox endorsed the idea of an employer mandate as a mechanism to control provider prices and fees.

Small firms mainly wanted the same tax and regulatory advantages as self-insured firms. Although they agreed that changes had to be made to control costs, they vehemently opposed an employer mandate or any measure that would raise taxes.[77] Their position was shared by the smaller commercial insurance companies that operated in the small-group and individual insurance market.[78] Like the small companies that they serviced, they wanted legislation that would level the playing field with self-insured firms regarding state mandates and taxes.[79]

The most important players in the game were the large managed care firms, which had grown rapidly in size and market scope following a series of takeovers and mergers.[80] By 1990 the eight largest insurance companies owned 45 percent of the 25 fastest-growing HMOs.[81] These multibillion-dollar firms did not initially stake out a public position on health care reform but just emphasized that they opposed government regulation of any sort.[82]

In 1991 national health insurance moved to the forefront of political debates when Senator John Heinz (D-Pa.) died in a plane crash and the governor of Pennsylvania appointed Harris Wofford, the 65-year-old former president of Bryn Mawr College, to replace him. Wofford was only supposed to serve until a special election could be held, but he decided to run for the regular Senate seat. The little-known Wofford was trailing far behind his opponent, Richard Thornburgh, the twice-elected, popular former governor and U.S. attorney general, until Wofford raised the topic of health insurance. It was a subject that he knew firsthand. His wife had a chronic medical condition, and each time he changed jobs they worried that she might be denied coverage. At one of his campaign stops, he declared, "The constitution says if you're charged with a crime, you have a right to a lawyer. Every American, if they're sick, should have the right to a doctor." The audience responded with thunderous applause and loud amens.[83] Wofford crushed Thornburgh in the election, and polls subsequently showed that voters identified health care as a key factor.[84]

Following the Wofford victory, dozens of bills were introduced in Congress, and business groups, insurance companies, and presidential hopefuls scrambled to develop their own plans. Senator Bob Kerrey (D-Neb.), the Vietnam war hero who had gained notoriety for his romance with movie star Debra Winger, advocated a program like Medicare for people of all ages. President George H. W. Bush, who until then had shown no interest in health care reform, called for greater regulation of the insurance industry, tax credits to help low-income families purchase insurance, and statewide purchasing pools for unhealthy people who were uninsurable in the private market. The candidate who came to own the issue, however, was Bill Clinton, the handsome, youthful, charismatic governor of Arkansas.

During the 1992 presidential campaign, Clinton promised to contain health care costs and guarantee universal coverage. Although he had endorsed the idea of "managed competition" where Americans would be "covered in big groups," he remained vague about what that would actually entail.[85] Clinton won the election, but with a scant 43 percent of the vote. Now he faced the challenge of meeting his campaign promise. On January 15, 1993, he made his first public announcement about health care reform, one that stunned the nation. He would create a task force to develop a plan and put his wife, Hillary Rodham Clinton, a smart, ambitious attorney, in charge. The announcement surprised White House staffers and heads of federal agencies. Many had been working on health care issues for decades. They understood the legislative process and expected to play a major part in health care reform. But their role would be peripheral. Day-to-day operations would be supervised by Ira Magaziner, an old friend who owned a consulting firm. A tall, unkempt man and a driven workaholic, Magaziner's main qualification for the job was a report on health care costs he had written for his home state of Rhode Island.

Some of Clinton's advisors urged him to get the task forces moving quickly to capitalize on the political momentum created by the election before opponents had time to organize. Others felt the budget deficit should take precedence. The deficit was the legacy of the Reagan administrations' economic policies. During the eight years Reagan was in office, the deficit nearly tripled, transforming the United States "from the world's number one creditor nation to the number one debtor." When George H. W. Bush succeeded Reagan in 1988, he went Reagan one better, racking up a deficit of $355 billion.[86] Clinton's economic advisors warned that health care reform would be expensive and should wait.[87] But Clinton had promised to have legislation within 100 days. Delay was out of the question. Magaziner immediately set to work. He created 8 cluster teams and 34 working groups, in all involving more than 630 health policy experts.[88] Some employees from the various federal agencies were included along with Democratic staffers, academics, and physicians. But the key stakeholder groups—insurance companies, business leaders, and provider organizations—though consulted, were not part of the task forces, leading many to feel resentful of the perceived "secrecy" surrounding the preparations. The first hitch came on February 24, 1993, when three groups from the health care industry sued the task force, claiming that Hillary Clinton was not a government employee and therefore could not chair or even attend closed task force meetings. As the First Lady recalled, "It was a deft political move, designed to disrupt our work . . . and foster an impression with the public and the news media that we were conducting secret meetings."[89] Eventually, the suit forced the release of 250 boxes of task force memos and reports, which proved to contain little of interest.

Despite Clinton's desire to get a quick start, the hundred days dragged on for seven months as other issues took precedence. The first delay came from a fight with the Republicans over the federal budget, followed by a protracted struggle with the trade unions over the North American Free Trade Agreement (NAFTA), which the unions viewed as an effort to shift production to low-wage countries with more lax environmental and labor standards. Before the election, Lane Kirkland, the aging president of the AFL-CIO, had told Clinton that the labor movement would be the "storm troopers" for national health insurance. Instead the AFL-CIO devoted its energies and resources to fighting NAFTA.[90]

Finally, on September 22 President Clinton made a prime-time address to the nation outlining his plan for health care reform. In his speech he decried spiraling health care costs, increasing red tape, and unaffordable prescription drugs and declared that Americans should never be at risk of losing their health insurance. Reforming the health care system was integral to improving the economy.[91] Then in a dramatic gesture, he held up a red, white, and blue "health security card" and promised to enact a program that would guarantee universal coverage and access to quality medical care. The details would follow in

October. Six days after the president's speech, the First Lady testified before five powerful congressional committees.[92] After her testimony, the White House planned a "rollout"—a series of speeches and events where the president would generate attention and support for his plan.[93] Instead on October 3, as the president was en route to California, his attention was diverted by an international emergency. American soldiers on a humanitarian mission in Somalia had been pinned down by factions led by Somali warlords after a botched raid on a warlord's headquarters. Two Black Hawk helicopters had been shot down. In the melee 18 Americans were killed and nearly 80 wounded. As the public watched a jeering mob drag the body of an American soldier through the streets, events planned to publicize health care reform were scrapped.[94] Not until October 27 were the Clintons able to relaunch the effort and regain momentum.

The question was how to proceed. One possibility was to hide health care reform in a budget bill, rather than going through normal political channels, where Senate Democrats would likely have difficulty mustering the 60 votes needed to stop a filibuster. This strategy had succeeded with COBRA, but Senator Robert Byrd (D-W.Va.), who chaired the Senate Appropriations Committee, balked, insisting there should be a public debate about so huge a measure.

Another option was to present Congress with general health care reform principles and work out the details later. But Rep. Dan Rostenkowski (D-Ill.), the "gruff and gritty old-school pol from Chicago" who chaired the Ways and Means Committee, insisted on a detailed bill spelling out every aspect of the plan.[95] Rostenkowski supported the concept of universal coverage but knew that higher taxes would be needed to finance it. The time it took to write the full bill gave numerous interest groups the opportunity to make demands in exchange for promises of support. By the time the final bill was released, it was 1,342 pages long, providing an easy target for Republican opponents to mock "big government."[96]

Health Security was the most ambitious policy proposal since the New Deal. It revolved around the concept of "managed competition." Managed competition was devised by concerned business leaders who began meeting in 1990 in Jackson Hole, Wyoming. Attending the meetings were several interested politicians: Dr. David Ellwood, the Minneapolis physician who had been involved in Nixon's HMO initiative;

Alain Enthoven, a Stanford economist; the president of the Blue Cross/ Blue Shield Association; and the executive vice president of Prudential, who represented the "gang of five," Aetna, Travelers, Cigna, MetLife, and Prudential—the large insurance companies that had moved aggressively into managed care. The Washington Business Group on Health was also brought on board. The Jackson Hole group, as it came to be called, hammered out a prototype for health care reform that was modeled around the existing relationship between corporate purchasers and managed care organizations and that favored the large insurers.[97] Under managed competition providers and insurers would be organized into networks that would integrate the financing and delivery of health care.[98] An independent agency would certify private insurance plans and set guidelines for a standard benefit package that all insurers would have to offer.

The Clintons' Health Security plan adopted many features advocated by the Jackson Hole group. It would establish a quasi-private system that relied on the market to drive down costs. The government would organize purchasing cooperatives called "health alliances" that would have the economic clout and expertise to bargain directly with health care providers. Firms with more than 5,000 employees could self-insure but would have to pay a new payroll tax to expand the public program for the uninsured if they chose this route.[99] But Health Security deviated from the recommendations of the Jackson Hole group in some respects. It would allow a national health board to establish regional and national spending limits, and it would give the board the authority to set limits on insurance premium hikes.

Health Security would solve a number of problems with the health care financing system. It would reform the small group and individual insurance market with its pervasive use of risk rating by prohibiting insurance companies from refusing coverage on the basis of age or health or terminating benefits for any reason.[100] It would end hospital cost-shifting because everyone would be covered. It would ease the burden of retiree health benefits by lowering the eligibility age for Medicare and capping the health care costs borne by any single firm. It would retain for the private insurance industry a market of supplemental products to cover health care expenses that were not included in the basic benefit package. And it would allow the large firms that had shifted into managed care to administer the purchasing cooperatives. But the controls on risk rating could cause smaller specialty insurance firms to lose 30 to 60 percent of their business, and health insurance agents would be put out of business entirely. Since no one would be denied coverage, insurance agents would no longer be selling individual coverage.[101]

The delays over the budget and NAFTA gave Clinton's opponents time to mobilize against him. The Health Insurance Association of America had begun to gear up even before Clinton took office. Eleven days after Clinton was sworn in, the association hired Bill Gradison (R-Oh.), the ranking Republican on the House Ways and Means Committee, as its president and chief lobbyist. A respected and knowledgeable Washington insider, Gradison resigned from Congress immediately to coordinate the opposition campaign, bringing with him the leading health policy counsel on Ways and Means, Charles Kahn, as executive vice president. According to Gradison:

> We had lots of time to get geared up. It gave us a lot more time to refine our message, raise our money, do internal staffing changes, and have training sessions with members of our association as to what they could do with their hometowns and their editorial boards.[102]

Gradison placed two public relations consultants on retainer, hired outside lobbyists, and initiated a $3 million advertising campaign. The first ads, which aired in spring 1993, only made vague statements about health care reform. Rather than denounce reform outright, these ads questioned government involvement in the health care system. The general message was "You will lose control" and, alternatively, that the private insurance industry could cover everyone.[103] In response, Hillary Clinton struck back, lashing out at the health insurance industry for "price gouging, cost shifting and unconscionable profiteering" and charging that insurance companies had brought the nation to the brink of bankruptcy."[104] After a hiatus during the summer, the Health Insurance Association of America unveiled a more aggressive round of attack ads in September. The ads featured a husband and wife, Harry and Louise, sitting at the kitchen table worrying about how the president's plan would affect their coverage. One ad said, "The government may force us to pick from a few health plans designed by government bureaucrats."[105] Another used language such as "mandatory," "billion dollar bureaucracy run by tens of thousands of new bureaucrats," and "government monopoly."[106] The Harry and Louise ads generated numerous media commentaries, counterresponses, spoofs, and cartoons. Although 52 percent of those who saw the ads felt they were completely untrue or more wrong than right, they helped frame Health Security in a way that shook public confidence.[107] As Ira Magaziner complained, "Every place I would go to a town hall meeting, a lot of people would have received letters or calls from these groups. They would ask questions like, why are you taking over the hospitals, which was not true. The same thing would happen on talk shows."[108]

The Health Insurance Association of America also organized the Coalition for Health Insurance Choices to enlist local business leaders in the struggle. The coalition printed a thick manual spelling out ways for insurers to get employees, vendors, and other sympathizers involved, and it set up a toll-free number to mobilize grassroots support, generating more than 135,000 calls. "SWAT teams" wrote letters, lobbied lawmakers, and held seminars to educate the public and local business leaders. The Lincoln National Life Insurance company of Fort Wayne, Indiana, had 150 such meetings.[109] CNA Financial, a Chicago-based insurer, sent brochures to its 70,000 agents and policyholders telling them to write to members of Congress, targeting 6 key senators and 11 representatives from five states.[110] Insurance agents proved to be highly effective allies, because they were located in every congressional district, tended to be active in their communities, and had extensive social networks. According to one of the targets, "I'm getting more lobbying from insurance agents . . . they really seem to be targeting the district."[111]

Aetna, MetLife, Cigna, Prudential, and Travelers had resigned from the Health Insurance Association of America in 1992 over its failure to support health care reform. These companies formed their own organization, the Alliance for Managed Competition.[112] Although Clinton's Health Security plan to create purchasing alliances revolved around the managed competition strategy that Alliance for Managed Competition members had helped design in Jackson Hole, they opposed certain features.[113] Notably, they feared that the alliances would not merely be purchasing cooperatives but would become regulatory bodies with much broader authority than the Jackson Hole group had originally envisioned. They also opposed the creation of a national health board that could have the authority to cap health spending on a nationwide basis.

Manufacturers with extensive retiree benefit commitments initially supported the Clinton plan because it would lower the age of eligibility for Medicare and cap any single firm's health care costs. One auto industry representative noted, "Absent some remedial measure such as that contained in the administration proposal, market forces will eventually force almost all employers to eliminate early retiree coverage."[114] Later, however, they reversed course and came out against the Health Security plan.[115] The shift in position was partly a response to the apparent success of managed care in containing costs. Employers' premiums had increased by 12 percent in 1990 and 8 percent in 1993; in 1994 they actually shrank by 1.1 percent.[116] Manufacturers also worried that the proposed alliances would be too comprehensive in scope, the basic benefit package too large, and the plan to limit lawsuits by employees too skimpy. Clinton also lost the pharmaceutical companies, who feared that the inclusion of prescription drugs would lead to the regulation of drug prices.

Small businesses opposed the employer mandate from the beginning, claiming it would impose an onerous tax burden. The National Federation of Independent Business joined the opposition campaign, dispatching a stream of faxes and action alerts from its Washington office to tens of thousands of small-business owners. Every week the federation polled its 600,000 members on their attitudes toward Health Security and sent their negative responses to members of Congress. The federation also conducted campaigns in states whose representatives served on key committees. For example, the federation targeted Montana Democrat Max Baucus, who sat on the Senate Finance Committee and whose initial public comments on Health Security had been favorable. After the federation staged public forums in Helena, Billings, and Missoula, Baucus wrote to small-business owners in Montana pledging to vote against any bill that could hurt them.[117] The federation also worked the media, using the powerful radio talk shows to generate opposition. When Hillary Clinton pulled into Portland, Oregon, in the Health Security Express, a bus caravan inspired by the freedom riders of the 1960s, a vocal group of protestors surrounded the bus. As she tried to speak, she was drowned out by booing and heckling. Even though she wore a bulletproof vest, she felt for the first time that her life was in danger:

The call to arms [of the radio talk show hosts] attracted hundreds of hard-core right wingers: militia supporters, tax protesters, clinic blockaders. . . . After the speech ended and we were driving away from the stage, hundred of protesters swarmed the limousine. What I could see from the car was a crowd of men who seemed to be in their twenties and thirties. I'll never forget the look in their eyes and their twisted mouths as they screamed at me while the agents pushed them away.[118]

By mid-fall 1993 Clinton had lost the support of all the major business groups, not only the National Federation of Independent Business, but also the Chamber of Commerce, the Business Roundtable, and the National Association of Manufacturers.

Whereas in the 1940s the AMA had been the most vocal political opponent of the Truman plan, in the 1990s physicians were nearly invisible in public debates over Health Security. One reason was that the AMA was no longer the sole voice of the medical profession. Rather, the profession had splintered into hundreds of special-purpose medical associations.[119] Another was that the AMA had become more diverse, with women and minorities making up a larger percentage of the membership. These changes not only made consensus more difficult to achieve but also meant that the threat of being ostracized for publicly disagreeing was less severe.

Initially, the AMA endorsed the concept of universal coverage as long as it didn't mean stringent cost controls or regulations that would give managed care an advantage. Some doctors' organizations, such as the American Academy of Family Physicians and the American Academy of Pediatrics, gave the Clinton plan full support. Others, such as the American College of Physicians, opposed some features but supported the employer mandate, while the American College of Surgeons supported a single-payer system like Medicare, arguing that it would preserve patient choice and physician autonomy.[120] These disagreements made it impossible for physicians to convey a clear message about where the medical profession stood on health care reform. Tellingly, the various accounts of Clinton's failed effort scarcely mention the AMA or physicians.[121]

Republicans, who had initially cooperated with the Clinton administration, adopted a new hard-line stance in the fall. In October the Republican National Committee released its own television ads, calling Health Security a "costly, bureaucratic nightmare" and flooding the airwaves in every city Hillary Clinton visited. In December, William Kristol, a Republican strategist, wrote Republican congressional leaders urging them to kill health care reform. Kristol argued that the Clinton plan was "a serious political threat to the Republican party." Its demise would be "a monumental setback for the President."[122]

The campaign against health care reform was virtually indistinguishable from presidential campaigns in the scale of field organizing, sophistication, and public relations tactics.[123] Various industry groups hired nearly 100 law and public relations firms to lobby. Among the key lobbyists were some household names, including former senator Paul Tsongas (D-Mass.), former congressmen Tom Downey (D-N.Y.), and Vin Weber (R-Minn.). When Senator Christopher Dodd (D-Conn.), who sat on the Labor and Human Resources Committee, was up for reelection in 1992, he received $375,000 from the political action committees of Aetna, Cigna, MetLife, Prudential, and Travelers, as well as $24,000 in contributions from individual insurance officers. In return, Dodd publicly lambasted a Democratic National Committee television spot that accused the insurance industry of obstructing health care reform.[124] The Alliance for Managed Competition bankrolled reelection campaigns for three Connecticut incumbents, Senator Joseph Lieberman and Representatives Barbara Kennelly and Nancy Johnson. Lieberman, who favored a more conservative, less regulatory approach, collected more than $265,000 from health insurance interests during the first quarter of 1994. Kennelly, who served on Ways and Means, received $101,400 from health and insurance industry PACs. To ensure that Kennelly got the message, Aetna employees were told to contact her and "voice your opposition to . . . price controls."[125] In March 1994, alliance executives met with Representative Jim Cooper (D-Tenn.), who was running for the Senate. In the first quarter of 1994, Cooper raised nearly $2.4 million, with a substantial portion coming from the health care sector.[126] In return Cooper sponsored the alliance's preferred plan, which relied mainly on the private market and the tax code to drive down costs. Overall, the Center for Public Integrity estimated that 650 organizations spent at least $100 million to defeat the Clinton plan. Its supporters raised only $15 million.[127] Hillary Clinton bitterly recalled,

"Even a popular President armed with a bully pulpit could not match the hundreds of millions of dollars spent to distort an issue through negative and misleading advertisements and other means."[128]

Polls conducted shortly after Clinton's first announcement showed that 67 percent of the public approved of Health Security. By February 1994, public approval had dwindled to 44 percent.[129] That summer the Senate Finance Committee voted for a compromise plan, but it was never brought to the floor. As the First Lady wrote, "Health care faded with barely a whimper."[130] In the 1994 elections the Republican Party ran on a Contract with America platform against the welfare state and big government, and the debacle over the Health Security plan was widely credited with giving the Republican Party control of the House of Representatives for the first time in 40 years.[131]

The Aftermath

After the demise of Health Security, health policy making moved toward shoring up the private health insurance system by tightening regulations to make private insurance more secure and by expanding coverage for certain groups, namely, children and the elderly. The policy change that received the most publicity was the Personal Responsibility and Work Opportunity Act of 1996, better known as the welfare reform bill. During his presidential campaign, Bill Clinton had pledged to reform the welfare system. With Health Security in tatters, he needed to show he could fulfill at least one of his promises. The Personal Responsibility and Work Opportunity Act replaced AFDC, the New Deal cash assistance for poor mothers and their children, with Temporary Assistance to Needy Families (TANF). TANF had stiffer work requirements, a two-year time limit, and a cap on benefit amounts regardless of family size; combined, these features made it tougher to qualify for cash benefits.[132] The intent of welfare reform was to discourage long-term welfare stayers and encourage work, not to reduce health benefits for poor families. To prevent mothers who lost cash benefits from also losing their health coverage, TANF was purposely decoupled from Medicaid. States were given greater flexibility to expand Medicaid eligibility beyond the traditional welfare limits. Under the new rules, mothers who left TANF could continue receiving Medicaid for up to 12 months. Then at the end of a year they could be reevaluated to see if they might qualify under some other criteria.[133] Among women who left welfare for work, one-third continued on Medicaid, one-third obtained private health coverage, and one-third became uninsured.[134] In some instances, they lost coverage when they left TANF and failed to provide the information needed to redetermine their eligibility for Medicaid. In other cases, they incorrectly believed that they no longer qualified for Medicaid because they were ineligible for TANF.[135] Sometimes they were just rejected outright.

In 1997 a new child benefit, the State Children's Health Insurance Program (SCHIP), was enacted. SCHIP increased funds to the states to insure low-income children. Under SCHIP states could cover children from families with incomes up to 200 percent of the poverty level, either by expanding Medicaid or by creating a separate program.[136] Since SCHIP was enacted, children's uninsurance rates have decreased sharply. From 2001 to 2003, the percentage of low-income children enrolled in either SCHIP or Medicaid rose from 38 percent to 49 percent.[137] SCHIP rules were later amended to allow uninsured parents to be covered along with their children. While several states extended coverage to low-income parents, federal law prohibits Medicaid from covering people who are not parents. Childless adults are excluded entirely.

Despite these gains, many eligible children remain uninsured.[138] Rates of uninsurance are especially high among Hispanic children, with more than 25 percent lacking coverage.[139] One problem in insuring low-income children is how to inform parents who have never been TANF recipients that their children are eligible for benefits. Another problem is that children may inadvertently lose coverage when a parent leaves TANF or when they "age out" of Medicaid and should be transferred to SCHIP but are not.[140] A third problem is that SCHIP does not offer stable coverage. More children were covered after new regulations were adopted in 2002 that required every state to provide Medicaid coverage to all children under age 19 whose family income fell below the federal poverty level.[141] However, the recession of 2001–2 caused state coffers to dwindle. In response, many states tightened Medicaid and SCHIP eligibility criteria and limited new enrollments.[142] By 2003 three states had halted SCHIP enrollments entirely, resulting in long waiting lists for hundreds of children.[143]

A less publicized health policy event was the Health Insurance Portability and Accountability Act of 1996. The brainchild of Senators Ted Kennedy and Nancy Kassebaum (R-Kan.), the Health Insurance Portability and Accountability Act was intended to make the private insurance market more secure and narrow the conditions under which companies could refuse coverage. In the original version, insurance companies would have to guarantee that people could renew their coverage, new employees would be automatically accepted into currently covered groups, experience rating would be prohibited, and it would be more difficult for insurers to exclude an applicant based on a preexisting condition.[144] It was this feature that aroused the most opposition from insurers. The Health Insurance Association of America strenuously objected that allowing people who lost group coverage for any reason to purchase an individual policy from the same company would trigger a "meltdown of the individual insurance market."[145] Individual enrollment lacked the risk-spreading advantage of large group plans and attracted subscribers in poorer health.[146]

What finally passed was a watered-down bill that eliminated some of the more egregious practices of the small group market. HIPAA did give employees who lost group coverage and exhausted their COBRA eligibility the right to convert these policies to individual coverage. HIPAA also prohibited insurers from charging different premiums for individuals within groups and required insurers that operated in the small group market to guarantee renewal to any group.[147] Upon signing the bill, President Clinton proclaimed that it "seals the cracks that swallow as many as 25 million Americans who can't get insurance or who fear they'll lose it."[148] But HIPAA did not say that these policies had to be offered at an affordable price and contained loopholes that allowed insurers to avoid covering people who might run up expensive health care bills. After HIPAA some insurers threatened to cut commissions of agents who sold policies to undesirable individuals or conveniently "lost" the paperwork for qualified applicants. Some insurers have offered the required coverage, but at prohibitive costs.

HIPAA did not dramatically change the nature of the small group market or guarantee that people would not be rejected for coverage because of health. That left people such as Jody and Matt Miller confronting nearly the same obstacles they faced before HIPAA was enacted. The Millers, a couple in their early 40s, had COBRA coverage for

18 months from a group plan that Matt had held at Occidental College while he was writing a book. Although they could have remained with the group plan, the cost was $1,300 a month. Because Jody was thinking of starting her own business and Matt was a self-employed writer, their insurance agent advised them to purchase individual policies now while they were still young and healthy. It would be much harder to obtain such coverage when they were older. The Millers applied to Blue Cross but to their shock and dismay were both rejected. The reason? Jody had once been treated for minor neck spasms and used a nasal spray for sinus problems when she traveled. Matt had had a speck in his field of vision several years earlier. These minor health problems made them high risks according to the calculation of insurance company underwriters.[149]

The other significant change to result from HIPAA has been in private long-term care insurance. Long-term care insurance had grown sluggishly until the mid-1990s, because most people avoided thinking about the prospect of entering a nursing home until a health crisis forced them to do so. By then they were ineligible for coverage or so old that the cost was prohibitive: a 75-year-old who purchased a standard policy in 1995 would pay $8,146 yearly compared to $2,560 for a 65-year-old.[150] The Republican's Contract with America had included a provision that would make premium expenses for long-term care insurance tax deductible.[151] Using tax incentives to encourage the purchase of private insurance would not only stimulate the market but also signal to consumers that the government considered long-term care insurance a worthwhile product.[152] This provision was included in HIPAA. HIPAA allowed people who itemize deductions on their income taxes to deduct a portion of long-term care insurance premiums. It also made employer contributions toward the cost of group long-term care insurance a tax-deductible business expense. After HIPAA long-term care insurance sales increased an average of 21 percent a year, with the biggest increase occurring in group insurance plans offered by employers.[153] Between 1999 and 2001 alone, the number of employers offering long-term care insurance to their employees increased by 46.8 percent.[154] As insurance companies expanded benefits to include coverage for home care, Alzheimer's disease, and residence in assisted-living facilities, long-term care insurance also became an increasingly important part of retirement planning.

Recent experiences suggest that even with expanded regulation, consumers face uncertainty with this product. Some companies, eager to get a foothold in the new market, offered unrealistically low rates and then had to stop writing policies as expenses exceeded premium revenues. For example, Conseco, after increasing its market share through acquisitions and product launches, decided to discontinue new sales following a class action suit by 700,000 clients alleging they had been misled about the likelihood of premium increases. Although marketing materials had promised that premiums would remain stable, rates increased between 10 and 40 percent a year, sometimes several years in a row. One company representative explained, "It's not like life insurance where there's thousands of years' worth of mortality research. With long term care, the nature of the coverage has changed faster than the actuaries can calculate it."[155] To deter insurance companies from offering unrealistically low rates, insurance commissioners in several states began requiring insurers to disclose the company's history of rate increases to prospective clients.

The expansion of private long-term care insurance is a positive development for more affluent middle-income people, those who make enough money to itemize their tax deductions. Purchasing a long-term care policy not only gives them a tax advantage but also provides alternatives to a nursing home when care is needed. Having a home care option has become especially important since the Balanced Budget Act of 1997. The Balanced Budget Act cut Medicare payments for home care visits and tightened up eligibility criteria, making it more difficult for Medicare beneficiaries to qualify for benefits.[156] Presuming that the companies that sell long-term care insurance stay in business and presuming that these policies pay what they promise, which for middle-aged people may involve a 20- or 30-year wait, they will add an element of protection and predictability for this particular segment of the older population. That these promises will be kept is a better bet for people who purchase their policies through an employer group, where they have the protection of experienced benefit analysts, than for individual policy holders.

The Balanced Budget Act of 1997 also created Medicare+Choice, which allowed risk-based HMOs and PPOs to participate in Medicare. Some policy makers viewed Medicare+Choice as a vehicle to provide richer benefits to Medicare beneficiaries compared to what was available in the traditional fee-for-service program, especially prescription drug coverage; others felt Medicare+Choice would reduce costs by generating competition among various plans or even set the stage for the full privatization of Medicare.[157] By 2001 just 16 percent of people 65 and older had chosen the HMO option, while hundreds of plans, affecting more than 2 million people, withdrew from the program due to low reimbursement rates.[158]

The most recent health policy event was enactment of the Medicare Modernization Act of 2003, which provides Medicare beneficiaries with a prescription drug benefit. Hailed as the biggest overhaul of Medicare since its inception, the new program picks up 75 percent of a beneficiary's drug costs up to $2,250 a year.[159] Then in a confusing twist, coverage stops until a beneficiary has spent another $3,600, creating a "doughnut hole."[160] After that Medicare pays 95 percent of any additional drug costs.

The legislation also offers HMOs new incentives to participate in the Medicare program in the wake of the failed Medicare+Choice program. Medicare Advantage gives HMOs payment rates that are 25 percent higher than those paid in the traditional fee-for-service program. Also included are tax incentives to encourage higher-income elderly to purchase private health insurance policies as a substitute for Medicare and $70 billion in subsidies to employers so they won't drop prescription drugs from their retiree health plans (although many analysts doubt that the incentives are sufficient to have that effect). The final caveat is that the federal government is prohibited from negotiating drug prices, the same hands-off concession that was granted to providers in exchange for their cooperation in Medicare. Who concocted this scheme?

The no-price-negotiation feature came from the Pharmaceutical Research and Manufacturers of America (PhRMA), with its 620 lobbyists. In the first six months of 2003, the PhRMA pumped $8 million into a lobbying campaign against price controls. As PhRMA spokesman Jeff Trewhitt said, "We are lobbying anyone who will listen at the 11th hour, and the message is very clear."[161] The "doughnut hole" was a concession to the American Association of Health Plans, which represents managed care firms. In the past, the elderly who chose Medicare HMOs over the traditional Medicare program were motivated mainly by a desire to have their prescription drugs covered. If Medicare assumed all drug costs, then HMOs would be a less attractive alternative. The result was a benefit that paid some of the costs for low spenders, covered most of the costs for people with catastrophic drug expenditures, and preserved the free market for the middle class.[162]

Conclusion

The 1990s is mostly remembered for the failure of Clinton's Health Security plan. The Clinton plan generated hundreds of books and articles seeking to explain the outcome. Some pundits blamed proximal events: the plan's complexity had fueled opponents' claims that it was a misconceived big government effort; the Clinton administration had been unable to nurture durable political alliances as reformers had in 1965; organized labor failed to mobilize a broad spectrum of support. Others blamed more enduring features of American politics—the institutional structure of the state, antistatist values, or racist sentiments.[163]

The focus on this single policy case has obscured the effect of the less dramatic but equally consequential health policy measures that were enacted. On one hand, public policy moved to shore up the private insurance market through increased regulation of insurers and through tax incentives for the purchase of private long-term care insurance. On the other hand, barriers to coverage for low-income families and children were lowered through a loosening of the eligibility criteria in Medicaid and enactment of a new benefit, SCHIP, for children. Yet variations in eligibility criteria across states, an inherent feature of Medicaid, and low cutoff levels in many states meant that most low-income adults and all childless, poor adults were still uninsured.

| Why the United States Has
No National Health Insurance
and What Can Be Done About It

Across the entire span of the twentieth century, all attempts to enact a health care reform plan that would guarantee universal coverage have been defeated. The AALL compulsory state health insurance plan in the 1910s, Roosevelt's proposal for national health insurance in the New Deal, Truman's plan in the post–World War II era, Nixon's National Health Insurance Partnership and Kennedy's Health Care for All Americans Act in the 1970s, and Clinton's Health Security plan in the 1990s met the same ignominious fate. These events had significant consequences for the financing of health care, for the ironic outcome in each instance was federal action that entrenched a private alternative to a public program. In the Progressive Era the failed AALL bill stimulated the first commercial insurance plans. In the 1940s Truman's loss occurred alongside court decisions that encouraged the spread of private group insurance. Nixon's National Health Insurance Partnership Act of 1972 led instead to federal support for private HMOs. The defeat of Claude Pepper's home care bill in the 1980s spurred the development of private long-term care products. The failure of President Clinton's Health Security plan in the 1990s led to regulatory measures that shored up the private health insurance system and stimulated the purchase of long-term care products. Even the enactment of Medicare in 1965 preserved a profitable market segment for private insurers in the form of supplemental medigap policies while removing a needy constituency, the aged, from debates over coverage for people of working age.

(The health care financing system that emerged over the past 100 years is a patchwork of public and private programs that provides some people with secure coverage but leaves others with sporadic periods of being uninsured and 45 million with no health insurance at all.) The recent decline in the number of employers who offer health insurance to their employees—from 67 percent to 63 percent in just the two-year period from 2001 to 2003—has shaken confidence in the future viability of employment-based benefits.[1] The drop in retiree benefits has been even more precipitous, as I noted in Chapter 6, from 70 percent in 1985 to 36 percent by 2000.[2] My task has been to explain how this unwieldy and inefficient financing system came to be and consider what lessons history provides about how to reverse the tide.

Theories of the Welfare State Revisited

Antistatist Values

Some health policy experts hold that antistatist values have been the principal barrier to major health care reform. Does the evidence support this assertion? Antistatist themes have fueled every proposal for government-financed health care services. In the 1910s the socialist threat hovered over the AALL campaign for compulsory health insurance. In the 1940s the AMA decried Truman's national health insurance plan as an un-American plot that would destroy the doctor-patient relationship, create a large health bureaucracy, and pave the way for a communist takeover. Then in the 1990s the haunting specter of big government reappeared to undermine support for President Clinton's Health Security proposal. But if antistatist values were a potent causal force, then why did the public fail to respond in the 1960s when the AMA promoted the same tired themes against Medicare?

One reason is that Medicare appeared on the national agenda in a supportive political climate.[3] The civil rights movement had legitimated federal intervention for the pursuit of racial justice, the communist threat was no longer a domestic issue but had shifted to a distant war in Vietnam, and President Johnson had declared a war against poverty. In the 1960s government was perceived to be a force that could serve the greater public good. A second reason is that there was an organized counterforce, the National Council of Senior Citizens, to challenge AMA claims and demonstrate that the aged were a worthy and deserving constituency.

The evidence suggests that antistatism does provide enduring symbols that are available in political debates over the welfare state.[4]

Antistatist themes help to dramatize the issues(limit the potential range of options)considered legitimate choices, and justify inaction.[5] But alternative values of community and social responsibility can also be invoked to support government intervention. What has mattered more than the rhetoric is the constellation of interest groups vying for power and the organizational strength of the contending groups—the AMA versus the AFL-CIO in the 1950s and again in the 1960s, the Health Insurance Association of America and the National Federation of Independent Business versus senior citizens' organizations in the 1980s, and the Health Insurance Association of America and the National Federation of Independent Business allied against a loosely knit and largely ineffectual coalition of social reformers in the 1990s.

Weak Labor

Other health policy experts attribute the failure of health care reform to a weak labor movement. There is some truth to this assertion. For the first half of the twentieth century, the AFL, the largest trade union, rejected outright the idea that workers should form a separate labor party, a strategic choice that weakened labor's ability to pursue national welfare benefits. Not only did it mean that did the trade unions had no direct way to influence policy decisions, it also meant that they were often divided over labor's proper sphere of influence. On one side of these disputes were leaders such as Samuel Gompers and George Meany, who preferred to pursue the class struggle by negotiating better wages and working conditions in collective bargaining agreements. On the other side were leaders such as Walter Reuther, who believed that the unions could work with government to create a European-style corporate state. These internal divisions over strategy and tactics made it impossible for workers to speak with one voice.

Yet there is also evidence that counters the "weak labor" thesis. Once the AFL and the CIO united into a single union in 1955, they mobilized first for disability insurance and then for Medicare. These programs were important to the labor movement because they shifted the cost of insuring disabled workers and retirees to the public purse and thus allowed unions to pursue wage increases and other benefits for working members in their negotiated contracts. The success of disability insurance and Medicare demonstrates that organized labor does not have to form a separate political party to advance social welfare programs.

This brief historical moment of labor unity and strength was over by the late 1960s, when the trade unions once again split into warring factions, with the UAW going it alone after Reuther withdrew that union from the AFL-CIO. Once the AFL-CIO opposed Senator Kennedy's compromise plan for a basic benefit package that, in retrospect, would have been a wise course to pursue, the unions never again exerted their weight on behalf of universal coverage. When President Clinton proposed his Health Security plan, promised trade union support failed to materialize because of what the unions saw as his unfriendly trade policies, leaving no organized force to counter the opposition.

Racial Politics

A third explanation for why the United States has no national health insurance emphasizes the racial politics of the South. From the New Deal until the 1960s, southern politicians did conspire with conservative Republicans to block national health insurance but, interestingly, not disability insurance. What made disability insurance acceptable to them was a compromise hammered out by Nelson Cruikshank and his colleagues that the program would be run by state health departments, not federal officials. The grip of the South on national social welfare legislation weakened considerably in the 1960s and was broken in the Democratic sweep of the 1964 election. The enactment of Medicare, in turn, gave federal officials the leverage to force southern health care facilities to integrate.

While overt racial barriers such as separate white and colored entrances, wards, waiting rooms and cafeterias were removed in the wake of Medicare, racial dynamics have not disappeared entirely from policymaking processes. As job-based benefits have become a surrogate for national policy, racial inequality in access to benefits has become a secondary effect of employment.[6] Racial politics has also been transmitted through coded messages implying that minorities are undeserving beneficiaries of social programs. Such messages permeated the welfare reform debate of 1996, in which welfare recipients were implicitly portrayed as black, promiscuous, and lazy, even though the majority of AFDC recipients were white. They also provided a subtle subtext in debates over Clinton's Health Security plan.[7]

State Structures and Policy Legacies

A fourth explanation for why the United States has no national health insurance emphasizes the effect of American political institutions and the legacies of past policy decisions.[8] Over the course of the twentieth century, a constellation of interest groups did emerge around the health care financing system, jockeying for position every time health care reform was under consideration—trade unions, small businesses, large manufacturers, senior citizens, welfare recipients, and the privately insured middle class. Thus one might argue that trade unions' weak support for national health insurance in the 1940s was driven by the legacy of wartime and postwar policies that encouraged collective bargaining for fringe benefits. One might also argue that Medicare created a senior citizens' movement that was subsequently primed to oppose any benefit cuts or tax increases, or that the financing mechanism in Medicare gave the hospital industry a vested interest in opposing subsequent efforts to impose price controls. Such an argument cannot explain why the unions pursued disability insurance and Medicare, why the most pressing concern of the elderly—long-term care—was never addressed in the political process, or how a prospective payment system for Medicare was able to transcend hospital industry opposition. By attempting to account for nearly everything, theorists who focus on policy legacies can neither predict the direction of policy decisions (i.e., positive or negative) nor explain how the preferences and expectations of various groups get translated into actual political decisions.

Stakeholder Mobilization

The evidence presented in the preceding chapters shows only one historical constant across every case, namely, that each attempt to guarantee universal coverage has been resisted by powerful special interests who have used every weapon on hand to keep the financing of health services a private endeavor. For the first half of the twentieth century, the antireform coalition was led by physicians, who feared that government financing of medical services would lead to government control of medical practice. Physicians appeared to have the deciding voice in health policy debates because their political goals were compatible with those of key allies. These allies included hospital administrators, who had created Blue Cross in the 1930s as a way to finance hospital care and dampen demand for a government solution; large manufacturers, who viewed fringe benefits as a way to fend off trade unionism; and insurers, who viewed compulsory health insurance as unwelcome competition. Even the trade unions, suspicious of state power, championed the medical societies when compulsory state health insurance was on the agenda in the Progressive Era.

The support of these groups alone might not have given organized medicine veto power over national health insurance. Physicians also needed the backing of key elected officials, those who controlled key congressional committees and who were willing to convert their preferences into negative votes. For three decades, physicians worked to secure the victory of friends such as Senator Robert Taft and to vanquish enemies such as Senator Claude Pepper. In the 1950 election, the AMA's rhetorical pyrotechnics had real political consequences, helping to restructure the balance of power in Congress and reshape the political landscape in a more conservative direction.

Not only did these early victories convince public officials that physicians were an omnipotent political force, they also lulled physicians into a false sense of security. It took more than a decade to disabuse both groups of these beliefs. The first indicator that the AMA could win only when it had these powerful coalition partners occurred in the 1950s when the AFL-CIO wooed southern Democrats and co-opted the insurance industry in the fight for disability insurance. Then, in the 1960s, labor leaders joined with senior citizens to vanquish the AMA, their victory secured by the defection of hospital administrators and insurance companies. The contest over Medicare helped the Democrats sweep the House and Senate in the 1964 election and gave northern Democrats a majority without the South for the first time since the New Deal, shattering organized medicine's power base.

The Medicare triumph made reformers more optimistic about the prospects for national health insurance. With the AMA licking its wounds and trying to restore its tarnished image, and with millions of working-age adults and children without coverage, it appeared that the 1970s would be a propitious time to act. But as the AMA moved off center stage, the insurance industry moved to the forefront of health policy debates. From the 1970s to the 1990s, the Health Insurance Association of America lobbied against national health insurance and long-term care insurance for the frail elderly, mobilizing small-business groups such as the National Federation of Independent Businesses and insurance agent associations to their cause. The only significant legislation enacted during this period, the Medicare Catastrophic Coverage Act of 1988, had the blessing of the insurance industry. The changing composition of the antireform coalition, dominated first by physicians and then by insurers, has obscured the persistence of stakeholder mobilization as the primary impediment to national health insurance.

Prospects for Reform

What is the likelihood of achieving universal coverage in the future? Some people argue that the prospects are nil, because universal coverage is inherently incompatible with employment-based health insurance. But Germany organizes and finances health benefits through the labor market yet covers everyone.[9] Past experience suggests that any plan for the federal government to become the single payer of health care services would be certain to elicit the opposition of those who benefit from existing arrangements but that the government's role can be expanded to cover the inevitable gaps that occur when coverage is purchased from an industry that, by its nature, is designed to exclude people with the highest health risks.[10]

The public is not averse to taking action. According to one recent poll conducted by America's Health Insurance Plans, the national trade association for health insurers, 59 percent of respondents agreed that the government could do a better job than the private sector in ensuring that more Americans have access to quality care.[11] Other surveys show that people would be willing to spend more tax dollars to improve health care coverage.[12] The question is what course to pursue.

There is no magic bullet. That much is apparent. Rather, the first step should be to continue the process of Medicaid expansion that began in the 1980s. Medicaid has developed in a piecemeal fashion over more than half a century. It originated with state payments to vendors (doctors and hospitals) for health care for the poor, which were converted into the Kerr-Mills program in 1960. When Medicaid was enacted in 1965, eligibility was tied to receipt of welfare benefits and thus to the rules governing welfare eligibility, as had been the case with Kerr-Mills, but the states retained considerable discretion over benefits and eligibility criteria. Federal guidelines specify that states must cover certain mandatory groups. These include pregnant women and children under age six from families with incomes below 133 percent of the poverty level, older children in families with incomes up to the poverty level, most elderly and disabled recipients of SSI (the federal welfare benefit for the very poor), and parents whose income falls below state welfare eligibility levels. States may also choose to cover people in each of these categories at higher income levels.[13] The result is 50 state programs, all with their own rules, enrollment procedures, and income guidelines.

Due to its historic ties to welfare, Medicaid still bases eligibility on family status. According to federal law, childless couples and single adults are not eligible for Medicaid unless the state has obtained a waiver from the Department of Health and Human Services. As a result, only parents are eligible for Medicaid in 42 states.[14]

Medicaid income cutoff levels also vary according to family status. In most states children are eligible for Medicaid or SCHIP if family income is below 200 percent of the federal poverty level. For parents, however, the income cutoff is 70 percent of the poverty level ($10,835 for a family of three in 2004). The result is that in many low-income families, the children are insured but not their parents, or younger children are insured but not their older brothers and sisters. That's the case with Sara and Oscar's family. Sara used to work cleaning houses, but when her third child was born, she calculated that a babysitter, bus fare, and lunch would eat up all her wages. Now she's a stay-at-home mom. Her husband, Oscar, is a driver for a courier service, but lately competition from other companies has cut into his hours and wages. Sara, her third child (who is now 2), and her fourth child (a 1-month-old infant) are covered by Medicaid, but Oscar and the couple's two older children, ages 11 and 14, are uninsured.[15]

Achieving a uniform level of coverage across the states requires changes in federal law to reduce variation across income classes and family types. The first step is to require all states to base Medicaid eligibility on income, not family status.[16] Such a change would extend coverage to the two-thirds of the uninsured population who are poor or near poor and whose income just exceeds current state eligibility levels. For example, Medicaid could be expanded to include parents and childless adults with incomes up to 200 percent of the poverty level ($38,800 for a family of four in 2003).[17] Only 32 percent of this group were insured in 2003.[18]

Medicaid modernization is the direction policy has been headed in the past two decades anyway. The chief obstacle to further expansion is cost. With state budgets periodically in crisis and shortfalls in 2004 totaling nearly $70 billion, governors are unlikely to welcome additional federal mandates unless they are accompanied by fiscal relief.[19] That relief might take the form of an exchange where the federal government would pick up all the costs of covering children if the states would expand coverage of low-income adults, or it could involve a change in the way the federal match is calculated.

Medicaid expansion would improve coverage among some of the uninsured but would do nothing for low-income families above the cutoff point, who live paycheck to paycheck. Patty, a mother of two who cuts pork in a meat processing plant, rotates her bills from month to month:

> What we do is call this one and say "I'm going to be late" and pay that one. Then we'll skip this one, two or three times and pay that one, and then I'll call you back and make arrangements with this one, and we do it like that every month.[20]

In families such as Patty's, where housing, food, child care, and transportation expenses consume the entire household income, health insurance is an unaffordable luxury. Nor would Medicaid expansion help middle-income people who have been labeled uninsurable by medical underwriters. Coverage for these individuals and families could be increased through federal vouchers, with the amount of the voucher determined by household income. The vouchers could be used to buy into the Federal Employees Health Benefits Program, which currently is open only to federal employees and their families and which offers subscribers a choice of 350 health plans. If uninsured people were allowed to buy into the federal employee program, they would have the risk-spreading advantages that people who work for large firms now enjoy. To prevent the inclusion of high-risk people from raising premiums for all federal employees (and thus arousing the antagonism of federal employees' unions), a separate risk pool could be created, with insurers bidding for the right to provide coverage to this group.

Allowing people to buy into the federal program would be a boon to early retirees—people in their 50s and early 60s—whose coverage has declined from 66 percent (among large employers) in 1988 to only 38 percent by 2003. Older adults are far more likely than younger people to report being in fair or poor health and to have a chronic illness such as heart disease, arthritis, or diabetes. Without the risk-spreading advantages of an employer plan, early retirees are forced into the individual insurance market, where they have a hard time purchasing coverage at any price because of aggressive screening by insurers.[21] Many are people like Bill, a former Kodak executive, who along with hundreds of other Kodak employees was downsized out of his job after 32 years with the company. It felt to Bill "like a mass burial. You expected to reach a top job level, say, from 50 to 62, where you'd make a significant contribution to the company. Instead the best thing they think we can contribute at 50 is to get out."[22] Like many older workers who were forced into early retirement, Bill had a generous pension package. But fewer and fewer of these packages include health insurance. In 2004 Sears Roebuck announced that it would no longer provide retiree health benefits for new hires or for current employees under age 40. Aetna cut its subsidy for retiree health benefits for all future retirees. Lucent made deep cuts in retiree health benefits and significantly raised retiree contributions.[23] Opening the federal plan to these people would help stem the erosion of retiree health benefits.

Permitting people to buy into the federal health plan has the added value of being able to reduce racial disparities in coverage, which are largely a by-product of employment patterns. The effectiveness of the federal health program in achieving this goal has already been proven. In 2002–3 nearly 60 percent of Hispanic nonelderly adults were uninsured for some time, compared to 43 percent of African Americans and 23 percent of whites.[24] Both African Americans and Hispanics are less likely than whites to be employed in the kind of companies that offer health benefits, but African Americans have a significant advantage over Hispanics because they are more likely to work for a state or the federal government.[25]

Another idea that merits consideration is to establish a stop-loss plan, also called a premium rebate pool. This idea, which was endorsed by presidential candidate John Kerry in the 2004 election, is actually a revival of the reinsurance concept that originated during the Eisenhower administration in the 1950s and was proposed by Senator Russell Long in the 1970s, with the backing of the insurance industry. Under Senator Kerry's proposal, the federal government would reimburse eligible health plans (including self-insured plans) for some percentage of their "catastrophic" cases—say, 75 percent of any costs that exceed $50,000.[26] A stop-loss program is already operating, in effect, with the Federal Emergency Management Agency (FEMA), which provides financial help to businesses and individuals that face catastrophic losses that their insurance policies do not cover.[27] Reinsurance is also working well in the Netherlands, where it covers the cost of catastrophic care and long-term care for the frail elderly and disabled. By eliminating the highest-cost cases, reinsurance there makes it possible for all other health insurance policies to cover basic health costs at predictable levels.[28]

The bulk of the problem today involves employees in small firms, a situation that has been gradually worsening. In 2004 nearly all large firms with 200 or more employees offered health coverage, but only 52 percent of the smallest companies (three to nine workers) did so.[29] If a federal stop-loss benefit was adopted in the United States, small employers would be able to offer the "bare bones" policy that many have advocated, and insurers could design basic plans, knowing that any excessively high expenses would be repaid through the premium rebate pool. Since most health care costs are incurred by a few individuals, insurers currently have pronounced incentives to use aggressive underwriting tactics to identify high-risk people. If the variation in costs across individuals could be significantly reduced through reinsurance, then insurers could offer reasonably priced coverage that would lower health care premiums for everyone. To be effective, certain conditions would have to be imposed. For example, employers that participate in the program would have to cover all workers in the firm and adopt various cost containment strategies such as disease management programs.[30] A side benefit would be to reduce the incentives employers have to discriminate against older workers and people with disabilities in their hiring decisions. To reduce start-up costs, stop-loss insurance could be phased in gradually, applying first only to small businesses that purchase health insurance in the small-group market (or would like to if costs could be kept under control). Later phases could include catastrophic long-term care costs for the elderly and then self-insured firms.

A less desirable option is to provide tax credits against the purchase of a private health insurance plan. Past experiments with tax credits have found them to be ineffective in extending coverage to the groups that need it most. In 1990 Congress gave tax incentives to low-income families to purchase coverage for their children. Children's health coverage failed to increase, because the tax credit was small, covering less than a quarter of average premiums. Many people were not even aware that their children were eligible, and there were widespread abuses by unscrupulous insurers. Three years later, Congress repealed the legislation.[31] Current tax credit proposals are equally meager. For example, in 2004 President George W. Bush proposed a tax credit of $1,000 per adult and $500 per child, with a $3,000 maximum, against the cost of health premiums. However, the average cost of a family policy in 2003 was $9,068. Further, tax credits would do little to help the 61 percent of people with incomes below the poverty level ($18,660 a year for a family of four) who were uninsured in 2003.[32] Nor would they help people with incomes up to 250 percent of the poverty level, who pay no income taxes anyway. The likely effect of a tax credit would be to reduce costs for already insured families but do nothing to extend coverage to the uninsured.

Every one of the options suggested above has been under consideration for more than half a century. The challenge is not in identifying feasible choices but in mustering the political will. What will it take to summon the political will to make significant progress toward universal coverage? We can look to the past to envision what might be possible in the future. At first glance, it might appear that opponents of health care reform were so often victorious because they had superior resources.[33] Yet closer scrutiny suggests that their success depended even more on their organizational strength. The AMA, the Health Insurance Association of America, the Federation of American Hospitals, the Chamber of Commerce, and the National Federation of Independent Business had in common a national leadership, state level organizations, and a local network—whether it consisted of physicians, hospital staff, small-business owners, or insurance agents—capable of marshaling a grassroots effort. In the notable instances when ordinary citizens defeated elite stakeholders, their success was predicated on their organizational capacity. Civil rights activists, trade unions, and senior citizens succeeded because they coordinated their efforts through organizations that mirrored the federated structure of American government.[34]

These events indicate that the best strategy for groups involved in health care reform is to forge a three-tiered coalition. At the top there must be a national leadership responsible for mapping out a grand plan to disseminate ideas, recruit members nationwide, and cultivate political insiders (influential congressional committee chairs and civil servants) who can introduce bills and devise ways to attach health care initiatives to less visible budget measures.[35] These activities could be coordinated by Washington insiders, those think tanks and policy institutes that have policy expertise but no grassroots force. At the middle level, the coalition must involve intermediate institutions such as state labor federations or senior citizens' clubs, whose leaders can coordinate activities, tap into indigenous social networks, and disseminate the organizations' models and ideas.[36] Recruitment could focus on organizations that represent employers and trade unions frustrated by rising health care costs (up 14 percent in 2004 alone), older people who fear losing their health coverage along with their jobs, as well as low-income uninsured people, especially those who live in districts of key members of Congress. Finally, the coalition needs local chapters that can funnel money to higher levels and mobilize grassroots activists to engage in social action to influence state and local politics. Such a structure ties leaders to one another, links local groups to larger issues, and affords opportunities for political leverage at the local, state, and national levels.

The challenge facing reformers in the current political climate is how to craft a message that can unify the various needy population groups that might form such a coalition. Current institutional arrangements have splintered the public into constituencies whose concerns vary according to the source and amount of their existing coverage. Privately insured families seek more secure benefits, the elderly want support for long-term care, and the uninsured want affordable coverage. Despite these differences, what unites these seemingly disparate groups is the shared risk of being uninsured that touches every family and every individual across the life course. That is the message that people understand. The public is willing. The time to act is now.

Notes

Introduction

1. Jamie Court and Francis Smith, *Making a Killing: HMOs and the Threat to Your Health* (Monroe, Me.: Common Courage Press, 1999), p. 1.
2. Personal interview, author's files.
3. Timothy Stoltzfus Jost, *Disentitlement? The Threats Facing Our Public Health Care Programs and a Rights-Based Response* (New York: Oxford University Press, 2003), p. 24.
4. Anna Dixon and Elias Mossialos, *Health Care Systems in Eight Countries: Trends and Challenges* (London: European Observatory on Health Care Systems, 2002), pp. 48, 65; Jon Ivar Elstad, *Recent Developments in the Norwegian Health Care System: Pointing in What Direction?* (Oslo: Norsk Institute for Forskning om Oppvekst, 1997).
5. Antonia Maioni, *Parting at the Crossroads: The Emergence of Health Insurance in the United States and Canada* (Princeton, N.J.: Princeton University Press, 1998).
6. Justin Keen, Donald Light, and Nicholas May, *Public-Private Relations in Health Care* (London: King's Fund Publishing, 2001), p. 33; Mary Ruggie, *Realignments in the Welfare State: Health Policy in the United States, Britain, and Canada* (New York: Columbia University Press, 1996), p. 193.
7. Dixon and Mossialos, *Health Care Systems in Eight Countries*, p. 18.
8. Donald Light, "The Practice and Ethics of Risk-Related Health Insurance," *Journal of the American Medical Association* 267, 18 (1992): 2503–4; see also Thomas Bodenheimer, "Should We Abolish the Private Health Insurance Industry?" *International Journal of Health Services* 20, 2 (1990): 213.
9. U.S. Census Bureau, *Health Insurance Coverage: 2003* (Washington, D.C.: Census Bureau, 2004).
10. Kathleen Stoll and Kim Jones, "One in Three: Non-Elderly Americans Without Health Insurance 2002–2003," Families USA Foundation, Washington, D.C., 2004, p. 3.
11. Ibid., p. 5.
12. John Broder, "Problem of Lost Health Benefits Is Reaching the Middle Class," *New York Times*, November 25, 2002, p. 1A.
13. "Second Class Medicine," *Consumer Reports*, September 2000, p. 50.
14. Mark Steinberg and Mark Merlis, "Working Without a Net: The Health Care Safety Net Still Leaves Millions of Low-Income Workers Uninsured," Families USA Foundation, Washington, D.C., 2004, p. 3.

15. "Second Class Medicine," p. 46.

16. Diane Rowland, "Health Care and the Uninsured," testimony before the House of Representatives, Ways and Means Committee, Washington, D.C., March 9, 2004; H. E. Freeman, L. H. Aiken, R. J. Blendon, and C. R. Corey, "Uninsured Working-Age Adults: Characteristics and Consequences," *Health Services Research* 24 (1990): 812–23; A. C. Monheit, M. M. Hagan, M. L. Berk, and P. J. Farley, "The Employed Uninsured and the Role of Public Policy," *Inquiry* 22 (1986): 348–64; Linda Bilheimer and David Colby, "Expanding Coverage: Reflections on Recent Efforts," *Health Affairs,* January/February 2001, p. 83; John Holahan and Niall Brennan, "Who Are the Adult Uninsured?" National Survey of America's Families, series B, no. B-14, Urban Institute, Washington, D.C., March 2000, p. 4; L. A. Faulkner and H. H. Schauffler, "The Effect of Health Insurance Coverage on the Appropriate Use of Recommended Clinical Preventive Services," *American Journal of Preventive Medicine* 13, 6 (1997): 453–58.

17. Peter Szilagyi, Jack Zwanger, Lance Rodewald, Jane Holl, Dana Mukamel, Sarah Trafton, Laura Shone, Andrew Dick, Lynne Jarrell and Ricard Raubertas, "Evaluation of a State Health Insurance Program for Low-Income Children," *Pediatrics* 105, 2 (2000): 363.

18. Institute of Medicine, *Insuring America's Health: Principles and Recommendations* (Washington, D.C.: Institute of Medicine, 2004), pp. 6–8.

19. "Cover the Uninsured Week, May 10–16, Kicks Off in Detroit," press release, PR Newswire, www.prnewswire.com, May 10, 2004.

20. Institute of Medicine, *Insuring America's Health,* pp. 6–8.

21. Hillary Rodham Clinton, *Living History* (New York: Simon and Schuster, 2003), p. 145.

22. Gerard F. Anderson, Uwe E. Reinhardt, Peter S. Hussey, and Varduhi Petrosyan, "It's the Prices, Stupid: Why the United States Is So Different from Other Countries," *Health Affairs* 22, 3 (2003): 89–105.

23. David Rothman, "A Century of Failure: Health Care Reform in America," *Journal of Health Policy Politics, Policy and Law* 18, 2 (1993): 273.

24. For a similar argument, see Colin Gordon, *Dead on Arrival: The Politics of Health Care in the Twentieth Century* (Princeton, N.J.: Princeton University Press, 2003).

25. Paul Starr, *The Social Transformation of American Medicine* (New York: Basic Books, 1982), p. 5.

26. Ibid., pp. 14–15.

27. Ibid., p. 168.

28. Beatrix Hoffman, *The Wages of Sickness: The Politics of Health Insurance in Progressive America* (Chapel Hill: University of North Carolina Press, 2001), p. 69.

29. Quoted in ibid., p. 81.

30. Edwin E. Witte, *The Development of the Social Security Act* (Madison: University of Wisconsin Press, 1962), pp. 174–81; Gordon, *Dead on Arrival,* pp. 16–18.

31. Gordon, *Dead on Arrival,* p. 15.

32. Statement on Truman Health Plan, *Journal of the American Medical Association* 146, 1 (1949): 114.

33. Starr, *The Social Transformation of American Medicine,* p. 231.

34. Hoffman, *The Wages of Sickness,* p. 69.

35. Florence Calvert Thorne, *Samuel Gompers, American Statesman* (New York: Philosophical Library, 1957), p. 63; Hoffman, *The Wages of Sickness*, pp. 115, 136.

36. Chamber of Commerce, *You and Socialized Medicine* (pamphlet), p. 3, Taft Papers, Library of Congress, Box 640, Legislative Files, File: Health Legislation, 1945.

37. Amie Forand Oral History, Columbia University Oral History Collection, p. 43.

38. Lawrence R. Jacobs, *The Health of Nations: Public Opinion and the Making of American and British Health Policy* (Ithaca, N.Y.: Cornell University Press, 1993), p. 52.

39. Edward Chase, "The Doctors' Bonanza," April 15, 1967, Anderson Papers, Library of Congress, Box 731, File: Finance Committee, Medicare.

40. Abraham Ribicoff, *The American Medical Machine* (New York: Saturday Review Press, 1972), p. 73.

41. Donald Light, "The Restructuring of the American Health Care System," in *Health Politics and Policy*, edited by Theodor J. Litman and Leonard S. Robins (Albany, N.Y.: Delmar, 1997), p. 51; Clark C. Havighurst, "Health Care as a (Big) Business: The Antitrust Response," *Journal of Health Politics, Policy and Law* 26, 5 (2001): 938–55; Donald Light, "Countervailing Powers: A Framework for Professions in Transition," in *Health Professions and the State in Europe*, edited by Terry Johnson, Gerry Larkin, and Mike Saks (London: Routledge, 1995), pp. 24–41.

42. Joseph Califano Jr., *America's Health Care Revolution: Who Lives? Who Dies? Who Pays?* (New York: Random House, 1986), p. 10.

43. Betty Leyerle, *Moving and Shaking American Medicine: The Structure of a Socioeconomic Transformation* (Westport, Conn.: Greenwood Press, 1984), p. 76.

44. Arnold Birenbaum, *Managed Care: Made in America* (Westport, Conn.: Praeger, 1997), p. 41.

45. Robert Schwartz, "How Law and Regulation Shape Managed Care," in *Managed Care: Financial, Legal, and Ethical Issues*, edited by David Bennahum (Cleveland: Pilgrim Press, 1999), p. 25; Birenbaum, *Managed Care*, p. 31.

46. "Clinton Health Plan Spells Change for Insurers," *Bestwire*, A. M. Best Co., September 20, 1993; "Lobbyism Axed Health Care Reform," *Houston Chronicle*, September 23, 1994, p. A18.

47. Seymour Martin Lipset, *American Exceptionalism: A Double-Edged Sword* (New York: W. W. Norton, 1996), p. 22; Seymour Martin Lipset and Gary Marks, *It Didn't Happen Here: Why Socialism Failed in America* (New York: W. W. Norton, 1999).

48. Lawrence R. Jacobs, "Health Reform Impasse: The Politics of American Ambivalence Toward Government," *Journal of Health Politics, Policy and Law* 18, 3 (1993): 630; Theodore Marmor, *The Politics of Medicare*, 2nd ed. (New York: Aldine de Gruyter, 2000), p. 101.

49. Roy Lubove, *The Struggle for Social Security, 1900–1935* (Pittsburgh: University of Pittsburgh Press, 1986), p. 2.

50. Jacobs, "Health Reform Impasse," p. 630.

51. Theda Skocpol, *Boomerang: Health Care Reform and the Turn Against Government in U.S. Politics* (New York: W. W. Norton, 1996), pp. 163–64, 171.

52. Theda Skocpol, *Protecting Soldiers and Mothers: The Political Origins of Social Policy in the United States* (Cambridge, Mass.: Harvard University Press, 1992), p. 16.

53. Vincente Navarro, "Why Some Countries Have National Health Insurance, Others Have National Health Services, and the U.S. Has Neither," *Social Science and Medicine* 28, 9 (1989): 887.

54. Skocpol, *Protecting Soldiers and Mothers*, p. 74; Lubove, *The Struggle for Social Security*, 41.

55. Nelson Lichtenstein, "Labor in the Truman Era: Origins of the Private Welfare State," in *The Truman Presidency*, edited by Michael J. Lacey (New York: Cambridge University Press, 1989), p. 131; Marie Gottschalk, *The Shadow Welfare State: Labor, Business, and the Politics of Health Care in the United States* (Ithaca, N.Y.: Cornell University Press, 2000), p. 167.

56. Jill Quadagno, *The Transformation of Old Age Security: Class and Politics in the American Welfare State* (Chicago: University of Chicago Press, 1988), p. 78.

57. Robert C. Lieberman, *Shifting the Color Line: Race and the American Welfare State* (Cambridge, Mass.: Harvard University Press, 1998).

58. Lee J. Alston and Joseph P. Ferrie, *Southern Paternalism and the American Welfare State: Economics, Politics, and Institutions in the South, 1865–1965* (New York: Cambridge University Press, 1999); Lieberman, *Shifting the Color Line*.

59. Kenneth Finegold and Theda Skocpol, *State and Party in America's New Deal* (Madison: University of Wisconsin Press, 1995); Edwin Amenta, *Bold Relief: Institutional Politics and the Origins of Modern American Social Policy* (Princeton, N.J.: Princeton University Press, 1998).

60. Jacob Hacker, "The Historical Logic of National Health Insurance: Structure and Sequence in the Development of British, Canadian and U.S. Medical Policy," *Studies in American Political Development* 12 (1998): 57–130; Lipset, *American Exceptionalism*, p. 6; Lipset and Marks, *It Didn't Happen Here*, p. 13; Louis Hartz, *The Liberal Tradition in America* (New York: Harcourt Brace, 1955), p. 147.

61. Hacker, "The Historical Logic of National Health Insurance," p. 59.

62. Maioni, *Parting at the Crossroads*, p. 23.

63. Daniel Beland and Jacob S. Hacker, "Ideas, Private Institutions, and American Welfare State 'Exceptionalism': The Case of Health and Old-Age Insurance, 1915–1965," *International Journal of Social Welfare* 13 (2004): 45.

64. Paul Pierson, "Increasing Returns: Path Dependence and the Study of Politics," *American Political Science Review* 94, 2 (2000): 252.

65. Jacob S. Hacker, *The Divided Welfare State: The Battle over Public and Private Social Benefits in the United States* (New York: Cambridge University Press, 2002), p. 26.

Chapter One

1. Ronald Radosh, *Debs* (Englewood Cliff, NJ: Prentice-Hall, 1971), p. 57, 59.

2. Ibid., 4; Robert Zieger, *John L. Lewis, Labor Leader* (Boston: Twayne, 1988), p. 16.

3. H. Wayne Morgan, *Eugene V. Debs, Socialist for President* (Syracuse, N.Y.: Syracuse University Press, 1962), p. 166.

4. John C. Farrell, *Beloved Lady: A History of Jane Addams' Ideas on Reform and Peace* (Baltimore, Md.: John Hopkins University Press, 1967), p. 126; Theda

Skocpol, *Protecting Soldiers and Mothers: The Political Origins of Social Policy in the United States* (Cambridge, Mass.: Harvard University Press, 1992), p. 265.

5. Beatrix Hoffman, *The Wages of Sickness: The Politics of Health Insurance in Progressive America* (Chapel Hill: University of North Carolina Press, 2001), p. 26.
6. Farrell, *Beloved Lady*, p. 59.
7. Florence Calvert Thorne, *Samuel Gompers, American Statesman* (New York: Philosophical Library, 1957), p. 12.
8. Hoffman, *The Wages of Sickness*, p. 69.
9. Colin Gordon, *Dead on Arrival: The Politics of Health Care in the Twentieth Century* (Princeton, N.J.: Princeton University Press, 2003), p. 213.
10. Paul Starr, *The Social Transformation of American Medicine* (New York: Basic Books, 1982), p. 253.
11. Hoffman, *The Wages of Sickness*, p. 37.
12. Quoted in ibid., p. 86.
13. Ibid., p. 105.
14. Quoted in ibid., p. 106.
15. Ibid., p. 2.
16. Ibid., pp. 115, 136.
17. Ibid., p. 113.
18. Isidore Falk Oral History, Columbia University Oral History Collection, p. 47.
19. Nelson Cruikshank Oral History, Columbia University Oral History Collection, p. 9; Gordon, *Dead on Arrival*, p. 15.
20. Falk Oral History, p. 55.
21. Albert Woodward, "The U.S. Health Insurance Industry: An Alternative View," *International Journal of Health Services* 8, 3 (1978): 493.
22. Donald Light, "The Restructuring of the American Health Care System," in *Health Politics and Policy*, edited by Theodor J. Litman and Leonard S. Robins (Albany, N.Y.: Delmar, 1997), p. 49.
23. Quoted in Michael B. Katz, *The Price of Citizenship: Redefining America's Welfare State* (New York: Henry Holt, 2001), p. 3. See Wilbur Cohen Oral History, Columbia University Oral History Collection, p. 55.
24. Quoted in Mark Peterson, "From Trust to Political Power: Interest Groups, Public Choice and Health Care," *Journal of Health Politics, Policy and Law* 26, 5 (2001): 1148; Starr, *Social Transformation of American Medicine*, p. 253.
25. Cited in Theodore Marmor, *The Politics of Medicare*, 2nd ed. (New York: Aldine de Gruyter, 2000), p. 6.
26. Oscar Ewing Oral History, August 26, 1966, Columbia University Oral History Collection, p. 7.
27. Alanson Willcox Oral History, Columbia University Oral History Collection, p. 5.
28. Cohen Oral History, p. 55.
29. Jill Quadagno, *The Transformation of Old Age Security: Class and Politics in the American Welfare State* (Chicago: University of Chicago Press, 1988), p. 42; Michael B. Katz, *The Price of Citizenship: Redefining America's Welfare State* (New York: Metropolitan Books, 2001), p. 10.
30. Woodward, "The U.S. Health Insurance Industry: An Alternative View," p. 494.

31. Sylvia A. Law, *Blue Cross: What Went Wrong* (New Haven, Conn.: Yale University Press, 1976), pp. 8–9.
32. Ibid., p. 10.
33. Ibid., pp. 8–9.
34. U.S. Congress, House Committee on Expenditures in Executive Departments, Investigation of the Participation of Federal Officials in the Formation and Operation of Health Workshops, Hearings Before the Subcommittee on Publicity and Propaganda, 80th Congress, 1st Session, May 28–June 18, 1947, p. 40.
35. Walter Reuther, "The Health Care Crisis: Where Do We Go from Here?" *American Journal of Public Health* 59, 1 (1969): 17.
36. Falk Oral History, p. 59.
37. Quoted in Gordon, *Dead on Arrival*, p. 216.
38. Rashi Fein, *Medical Care, Medical Costs: The Search for a Health Insurance Policy* (Cambridge, Mass.: Harvard University Press, 1986), p. 27.
39. Claude Denison Pepper with Hays Gorey, *Pepper: Eyewitness to a Century* (San Diego: Harcourt Brace Jovanovich, 1987), pp. xiii, 45.
40. Claude Pepper Oral History, Columbia University Oral History Collection, p. 17.
41. Ibid., p. 17.
42. Channing Frothingham, "Rx for National Health," *Social Progress*, November/December 1948, Pepper Library, Florida State University, Tallahassee, Series S201, Box 93, File 1.
43. Quoted in Starr, *Social Transformation of American Medicine*, p. 279.
44. Quoted in Bernard Asbell, *When F.D.R. Died* (London: Jonathan Cape, 1961), p. 164.
45. Sean J. Savage, *Truman and the Democratic Party* (Lexington: University Press of Kentucky, 1997), p. 8.
46. Ibid., p. 8.
47. Harry S. Truman, *Memoirs of Harry S. Truman*, vol. 2: *Years of Trial and Hope* (Garden City, N.Y.: Doubleday, 1956), p. 19.
48. Nelson Cruikshank Oral History, Columbia University Oral History Collection, p. 6.
49. Monty Poen, *Harry S. Truman Versus the Medical Lobby: The Genesis of Medicare* (Columbia: University of Missouri Press, 1979), pp. 60–61.
50. Arthur Herman, *Joseph McCarthy: Reexamining the Life and Legacy of America's Most Hated Senator* (New York: Free Press, 2000), p. 39; John E. Haynes, *Red Scare or Red Menace? American Communism and Anticommunism in the Cold War Era* (Chicago: Ivan Dee, 1996); Harvey Klehr, John E. Haynes, and Fridrikh I. Firsov, *The Secret World of American Communism* (New Haven, Conn.: Yale University Press, 1995).
51. Holly J. McCammon, Karen E. Campbell, Ellen M. Granberg, and Christine Mowery, "How Movements Win: Gendered Opportunity Structures and U.S. Women's Suffrage Movements, 1866 to 1919," *American Sociological Review* 66 (2001): 68.
52. Richard Gid Powers, *Not Without Honor: The History of American Anticommunism* (New Haven, Conn.: Yale University Press, 1998), p. 84.
53. Ibid., p. 86.
54. Haynes, *Red Scare or Red Menace*, p. 66.
55. Ibid., p. 68.

56. Iwan Morgan, *Nixon* (London: Oxford University Press, 2002), pp. 45–46.
57. *Message from the President of the United States, National Health and Disability Insurance Program, 80th Congress, 1st Session* (Washington, D.C.: U.S. Government Printing Office, 1947), p. 3.
58. Harry S. Truman to Watson B. Miller, March 19, 1946, Federal Security Administration, Administrator's Records, Harry S. Truman Presidential Library, Independence, Missouri, RG 235, Box 31, File 031.2.
59. Ewing Oral History, p. 35.
60. Frothingham, "Rx for National Health."
61. Oscar R. Ewing, *The Nation's Health: A Report to the President*, September 1948, Pepper Library, Series 201, File 92, Folder 10.
62. Louis L. Knowles and Kenneth Prewitt, eds., *Institutional Racism in America* (Englewood Cliffs, N.J.: Prentice-Hall, 1969); M. Meltsner, "Equality and Health," *Pennsylvania Law Review* 115, 1 (1966): 22–38.
63. Truman, *Memoirs*, p. 19.
64. Savage, *Truman and the Democratic Party*, p. 155.
65. "The Voluntary Way Is the American Way," 1949, Taft Papers, Box 643, Legislative Files 1924–53, File: Health—National Program for Medical Care (S. 1679–S. 1581).
66. Address of Representative Forest Harness Before the Conference of Executive Secretaries of the Indiana State Medical Association, February 15, 1948, National Archives, Washington, D.C., RG 233, Records of the U.S. House of Representatives, 80th Congress, Committee on Expenditures in Executive Departments, Box 462, File: Federal Security Agency: Correspondence, Hearings, Reports.
67. Lawrence Jacobs, *The Health of Nations* (Ithaca, N.Y.: Cornell University Press, 1993).
68. Harness Address, note 50.
69. Investigation of the Participation of Federal Officials in the Formation and Operation of Health Workshops, p. 10.
70. Forest A. Harness, "Our Most Dangerous Lobby," *Reader's Digest*, December 1947, RG 233, Records of the U.S. House of Representatives, National Archives, Washington, D.C., 80th Congress, Committee on Expenditures in Executive Departments, Box 447, File: AAA in Nebraska.
71. Notes on Conference—Miss Huffman and NM—8/4/47, National Archives, Washington, D.C., RG 233, Records of the U.S. House of Representatives, 80th Congress, Committee on Expenditures in Executive Departments, Box 462, File: Federal Security Agency: Correspondence, Hearings, Reports.
72. Executive Session—Confidential, RG 233, Records of the U.S. House of Representatives, 80th Congress, Committee on Expenditures in Executive Departments, Box 462, File: Federal Security Agency: Correspondence, Hearings, Reports.
73. Falk Oral History, p. 268.
74. Poen, *Harry S. Truman Versus the Medical Lobby.*
75. Testimony of Senator Robert A. Taft, National Health Program of 1949, May 24, 1949, U.S. Senate, Subcommittee on Health of the Committee on Labor and Public Welfare, Washington, D.C., p. 637.
76. Address of Robert Taft to Wayne County Medical Society, October 7, 1946, Taft Papers, Box 643, Legislative Files, 1924–53, File: Health—National Program for Medical Care (S. 1679–S. 1581).

77. Philip A. Klinkner and Rogers M. Smith, *The Unsteady March: The Rise and Decline of Racial Equality in America* (Chicago: University of Chicago Press, 1999), p. 222.
78. Nelson Cruikshank Oral History, p. 28.
79. "The President's Message and the Compulsory Health Insurance Bill," *Journal of the American Medical Association,* May 7, 1949, 111.
80. Robert C. Lieberman, *Shifting the Color Line: Race and the American Welfare State* (Cambridge, Mass.: Harvard University Press, 1998), p. 34; Jill Quadagno, *The Color of Welfare: How Racism Undermined the War on Poverty* (New York: Oxford University Press, 1994), p. 21.
81. Summary of the Voluntary Health Insurance Bill, Pepper Library, Series S201, Box 93, File 1.
82. Comparison of the Three Major Health Bills Before the 81st Congress, Pepper Library, Series S201, Box 93, File 1.
83. Daniel Mitchell, "Earl Warren's Lost Cause: How the United State Might Have Had Canadian-Style Health Insurance," *WorkingUSA,* summer 2002, pp. 19–20.
84. R. L. Sensenich, President's Address, Minutes of the Annual Session of the House of Delegates, American Medical Association, Atlantic City, June 6–10, 1949, reprinted in *Journal of the American Medical Association,* June 18, 1949, p. 613.
85. Address of Clem Whitaker, Minutes of the Annual Session of the House of Delegates, American Medical Association, Atlantic City, June 6–10, 1949, reprinted in *Journal of the American Medical Association,* June 18, 1949, p. 696.
86. Ibid.
87. John Flynn, *The Road Ahead: America's Creeping Revolution* (New York: Devin-Adair, 1949).
88. "Statement on Truman Health Plan," *Journal of the American Medical Association* 146, 1 (1949): 114.
89. Chamber of Commerce, *You and Socialized Medicine* (pamphlet), p. 3, Taft Papers, Box 640, Legislative Files, File: Health Legislation, 1945.
90. Marjorie Shearon, "Freedom of Choice Under the Wagner-Murray-Dingell Bill S. 1050," November 18, 1945, p. 7, Taft Papers, Box 640, File: Health Legislation.
91. "Socialized Medicine: A Medical OPA," p. 2, 1949, Taft Papers, Box 643, File: Health—National Program for Medical Care (S. 1679–S. 1581).
92. Caldwell Esselstyn Oral History, Columbia University Oral History Collection, p. 7.
93. Clem Whitaker and Leone Baxter, "A Simplified Blueprint of the Campaign Against Compulsory Health Insurance," 1949, National Education Campaign, American Medical Association, pp. 3–4, Taft Papers, Box 643, Legislative Files, File: National Program for Medical Care (S. 1679–S. 1581).
94. Ibid., pp. 4–12.
95. Letter from Marjorie Shearon to Senator Taft, January 9, 1945, Taft Papers, Box 643, File: Health: Social Security Legislation 1945–46.
96. "The Voluntary Way Is the American Way," Taft Papers, Box 643, File: Health—National Program for Medical Care (S. 1679–S. 1581), 1949.
97. Whitaker and Baxter, "A Simplified Blueprint," p. 2.
98. "Proposal for Action to Be Taken by Federal and State Governments and by Private Groups to Develop a National Health Program," February 6, 1946, Taft Papers, Box 643, File: Health—Social Security Legislation 1945–46.

99. Edward O'Connor, Statement Before the Senate Subcommittee on the Committee on Labor and Public Welfare, June 29, 1949, Pepper Library, Series S202E, Box 4, File 1.

100. Proposal for National Health Insurance in S. 1679, Statement of Ray D. Murphy, Vice President and Actuary of the Equitable Life Assurance Society to the United States before the Senate Committee on Labor and Public Welfare, June 1949, pp. 8–9, Pepper Library, Series S202E, Box 4, File 1.

101. Chamber of Commerce, *You and Socialized Medicine.*

102. "Socialized Medicine: A Medical OPA," p. 3.

103. Chamber of Commerce, *You and Socialized Medicine.*

104. Ibid.

105. Ewing Oral History, p. 41.

106. Michael Davis Oral History, Columbia University Oral History Collection, p. 49.

107. Ewing Oral History, p. 65.

108. Gallup Polls, *Public Opinion, 1935–71* (Bloomington, Ind.: Phi Delta Kappa, 1973), 2:801.

109. Letter from President Harry Truman to Ben Turoff, April 12, 1949, Truman Library, Correspondence Files, Textual Records, Series A.

110. Elmer Henderson, "A Fancy Package of Untruths," *Journal of the American Medical Association*, November 11, 1950, p. 11.

111. "11,000 Papers Get AMA Memo on Ad Payoff," *In Fact*, September 25, 1950, p. 2.

112. Bernard DeVoto, "Letter for a Family Doctor," *Harper's*, January 1951, p. 59, Pepper Library, Series S201, Box 92, Folder 10.

113. Esselstyn Oral History, p. 16.

114. Dr. Bernard Meyer, Physician's Forum, Testimony on Senate Bills 1456, 1581, and 1679, June, 22, 1949, Pepper Library, Series S202E, Box 4, Folder 1.

115. R. M. Cunningham Jr., "Can Political Means Gain Professional Ends?" *Modern Hospital* 77, 6 (1951): 51, Pepper Library, Series S201, Box 93, Folder 1.

116. "AMA Health Stand Scored by Ewing," 1949, Taft Papers, Box 643, File: Health—National Program for Medical Care (S. 1679–S. 1581).

117. Ewing Oral History, p. 57; Memo from Marjorie Shearon to Senator Robert Taft, January 17, 1946, Taft Papers, Box 643, File: Health—Social Security Legislation 1945–46.

118. Quotes from Address of Guy George Gabrielson, March 29, 1950, Pepper Library, Series S431C, Box 19, Folder 5.

119. Taft Papers, Box 643; Haynes, *Red Scare or Red Menace?*

120. Klehr, Haynes, and Firsov, *The Secret World of American Communism*, p. 49; Powers, *Not Without Honor*, p. 242.

121. Cunningham, "Can Political Means Gain Professional Ends?" pp. 53–54.

122. Ibid.

123. Stanley Kelley, *Professional Public Relations and Political Power* (Baltimore: Johns Hopkins University Press, 1956), chap. 3.

124. Letter from Louis Orr, M.D., to Dr. Arthur Schwartz, April 10, 1950, Pepper Library, Series S201, Box 93, File 1.

125. Cruikshank Oral History, p. 265.

126. Pepper Oral History, p. 52.

127. Ibid., p. 28.

128. Ibid., p. 52.

129. Pepper, *Pepper: Eyewitness to a Century*, pp. 193, 202.

130. Falk Oral History, p. 228.
131. The Medical Lobby's 1952 Platform, Bulletin 7, November, 1951, Committee for the Nation's Health, Pepper Library, Series S201, Box 93, Folder 1.
132. Sheri David, "Eisenhower and the American Medical Association: A Coalition Against the Elderly," in *Dwight D. Eisenhower: Soldier, President, Statesman*, edited by Joann Krieg (Westport, Conn.: Greenwood Press, 1987), p. 59.
133. Truman, *Memoirs*, p. 24.
134. Roswell Perkins Oral History, Columbia University Oral History Collection, p. 7.
135. Alan Pond Oral History, Columbia University Oral History Collection, pp. 11, 123.
136. Jacob S. Hacker, "Boundary Wars: The Political Struggle over Public and Private Social Benefits in the United States," doctoral dissertation, Yale University, 2000, p. 310.
137. Perkins Oral History, p. 36.
138. Ibid., p. 84.
139. Pond Oral History, p. 64.
140. Hacker, "Boundary Wars," p. 238; Pond Oral History, p. 3.
141. Perkins Oral History, pp. 36–37.
142. Pond Oral History, p. 9; Perkins Oral History, pp. 37, 42, 79.
143. Perkins Oral History, p. 43.
144. Ibid., pp. 44, 66.
145. Ibid., p. 58.
146. Ibid., p. 59.
147. Stephen Ambrose, *Eisenhower, the President* (New York: Simon and Schuster, 1984), p. 199.

Chapter Two

1. Melvyn Dubofsky and Warren Van Tine, *John L. Lewis: A Biography* (New York: Quadrangle/New York Times Book Company, 1977), p. 426.
2. Saul Alinsky, *John L. Lewis* (New York: G. P. Putnam's Sons, 1949), p. 344.
3. Ibid.
4. Robert Zieger, *John L. Lewis, Labor Leader* (Boston: Twayne, 1988), p. 153.
5. Alinsky, *John L. Lewis*, p. 329.
6. Ibid., p. 344.
7. Marie Gottschalk, *The Shadow Welfare State: Labor, Business, and the Politics of Health Care in the United States* (Ithaca, N.Y.: Cornell University Press, 2000), p. 46; Jennifer Klein, "The Business of Health Security: Employee Health Benefits, Commercial Insurers, and the Reconstruction of Welfare Capitalism, 1945–1960," *International Labor and Working Class History* 58 (2000): 198.
8. Health Insurance Plans in the United States, Report of the Committee on Labor and Public Welfare, U.S. Senate, Report No. 359, Part 1, 82nd Congress, 1st Session, May 28, 1951, p. 2.
9. Beth Stevens, "Blurring the Boundaries: How the Federal Government Has Influenced Welfare Benefits in the Private Sector," in *The Politics of Social Policy in the United States*, edited by Margaret Weir, Ann Shola Orloff, and Theda Skocpol (Princeton, N.J.: Princeton University Press, 1988), p. 125.

10. Archie Robinson, *George Meany and His Times: A Biography* (New York: Simon and Schuster, 1981), p. 18.
11. Jennifer Klein, *For All These Rights: Business, Labor and the Shaping of America's Public-Private Welfare State* (Princeton, N.J.: Princeton University Press, 2003), p. 177.
12. Ibid., p. 178.
13. Klein, "The Business of Health Security," p. 295; Louis Reed, "Private Health Insurance: Coverage and Financial Experience," *Social Security Bulletin* 30 (1967): 3–22; Stevens, "Blurring the Boundaries," pp. 133–34.
14. Stevens, "Blurring the Boundaries," p. 133.
15. Klein, "The Business of Health Security," 295.
16. Elizabeth Fones-Wolf, *Selling Free Enterprise: The Business Assault on Labor and Liberalism, 1945–60* (Urbana: University of Illinois Press, 1994).
17. Klein, "The Business of Health Security," p. 299.
18. Nelson Lichtenstein, "Labor in the Truman Era: Origins of the Private Welfare State," in *The Truman Presidency*, edited by Michael J. Lacey (New York: Cambridge University Press, 1989), p. 129.
19. Nelson Cruikshank Oral History, Columbia University Oral History Collection, p. 50.
20. U.S. Congress, House Committee on Expenditures in Executive Departments, Investigation of the Participation of Federal Officials in the Formation and Operation of Health Workshops, Hearings before the Subcommittee on Publicity and Propaganda, 80th Congress, 1st Session, May 28–June 18, 1947, p. 40.
21. Alan Derrickson, "Health Security for All?" *Journal of American History* 80 (1994): p. 1358; Lichtenstein, "Labor in the Truman Era," p. 139.
22. Gottschalk, *The Shadow Welfare State*, p. 52; Nelson Lichtenstein, "From Corporatism to Collective Bargaining: Organized Labor and the Eclipse of Social Democracy in the Postwar Era," in *The Rise and Fall of the New Deal Order, 1930–1980*, edited by Steve Fraser and Gary Gerstle (Princeton, N.J.: Princeton University Press, 1989), pp. 122–52.
23. Judith Stepan-Norris and Maurice Zeitlin, "Union Democracy, Radical Leadership, and the Hegemony of Capital," *American Sociological Review* 60 (1995): 829–50; Judith Stepan-Norris and Maurice Zeitlin, *Left Out: Reds and America's Industrial Unions* (Cambridge: Cambridge University Press, 2002).
24. Stevens, "Blurring the Boundaries," p. 141.
25. Michael Brown, "Bargaining for Social Rights: Unions and the Reemergence of Welfare Capitalism," *Political Science Quarterly* 112, 4 (1997–98): 653.
26. Stevens, "Blurring the Boundaries," p. 141.
27. Alan Derickson, "Health Security For All?" *Journal of American History* 80 (1994): 1351.
28. Cruikshank Oral History, p. 9.
29. Colin Gordon, "Why No National Health Insurance in the U.S.: The Limits of Social Provision in War and Peace, 1941–1948," *Journal of Policy History* 9, 3 (1997): 277–310.
30. Quoted in Lichtenstein, "Labor in the Truman Era," p. 138.
31. Frank Cormier and William J. Eaton, *Reuther* (Englewood Cliffs, N.J.: Prentice-Hall, 1970), p. 321.
32. Edward D. Berkowitz, *Mr. Social Security: The Life of Wilbur Cohen* (Lawrence: University Press of Kansas, 1995), p. 55.

33. Kathryn Ellickson Oral History, Columbia University Oral History Collection, p. 72.
34. Cruikshank Oral History, p. 56.
35. Arthur Hess Oral History, Columbia University Oral History Collection, p. 88; M. G. Gluck and Virginia Reno, eds., *Reflections on Implementing Medicare: Implementation Aspects of National Health Care Reform* (Washington, D.C.: National Academy of Social Insurance, 2001), p. 20.
36. Hess Oral History, p. 36.
37. Ibid., p. 39.
38. Isidore S. Falk Oral History, Columbia University Oral History Collection, p. 193.
39. Ibid., p. 88; Gluck and Reno, *Reflections on Implementing Medicare*, p. 20.
40. E. H. O'Connor, "The Doctors' Case Against Compulsory Disability Insurance," Conference of Medical Service, Chicago, February 11, 1951, pp. 1–2, 8, Pepper Library, S201, Box 93, File 1.
41. Cruikshank Oral History, p. 44.
42. Edward Berkowitz, "Disability Insurance and the Limits of American History," *Public Historian* 8, 2 (1986): 65–82.
43. Cruikshank Oral History, p. 56.
44. Oscar Ewing Oral History, Columbia University Oral History Collection, p. 77.
45. Sylvia A. Law, *Blue Cross: What Went Wrong* (New Haven, Conn.: Yale University Press, 1976), p. 12.
46. Ewing Oral History, p. 77.
47. Elizabeth Wickenden Oral History, Columbia University Oral History Collection, p. 162. The Social Security Board was now called the Social Security Administration.
48. Joseph Stetler Oral History, Columbia University Oral History Collection, p. 17.
49. Leonard Woodcock Oral History, Columbia University Oral History Collection, p. 2.
50. Ibid., p. 3.
51. Gottschalk, *The Shadow Welfare State*, p. 58.
52. Cruikshank Oral History, p. 75.
53. Ellickson Oral History, p. 277.
54. Ibid., p. 124.
55. Ibid., p. 122.
56. Ibid., p. 128.
57. Amendments to Title II of the Social Security Act; Ellickson Oral History.
58. Ellickson Oral History, p. 45.
59. Nelson H. Cruikshank, *The Cruikshank Chronicles: Anecdotes, Stories, and Memoirs of a New Deal Liberal*, edited by Alice Hoffman and Howard Hoffman (Hamden, Conn.: Archon Books, 1989), p. 157.
60. Amie Forand Oral History, Columbia University Oral History Collection, p. 20.
61. Lisbeth Bamberger Schorr and Leonard Lesser Oral History, Columbia University Oral History Collection, p. 70.
62. *Congressional Quarterly Almanac, 1960* (Washington, D.C.: Government Printing Office, 1960), p. 154.
63. Schorr and Lesser Oral History, p. 18.
64. Ibid., pp. 66, 3.

65. Gallup *Poll Reports, 1935–68* (Princeton, New Jersey: American Institute of Public Opinion, 1969), p. 337.
66. Ivan Nestingen Oral History, Columbia University Oral History Collection, pp. 69–70.
67. Cruikshank, *The Cruikshank Chronicles*, p. 155.
68. Stetler Oral History, p. 27, 30.
69. Perkins Oral History, p. 81.
70. Walter McNerney Oral History, Columbia University Oral History Collection, p. 15.
71. David Sheri, "Eisenhower and the American Medical Association: A Coalition Against the Elderly," in *Dwight D. Eisenhower: Soldier, President, Statesman,* edited by Joanne P. Krieg (Westport, Conn.: Greenwood Press, 1987), p. 61.
72. Dora L. Costa, *The Evolution of Retirement: An American Economic History, 1880–1990* (Chicago: University of Chicago Press, 1998).
73. Robert Myers Oral History, Columbia University Oral History Collection, pp. 36, 40.
74. Stetler Oral History, p. 43.
75. The AMA accused the AFL-CIO of fighting Kerr-Mills in the states, an accusation union leaders did not entirely deny. According to Ellickson, the AFL-CIO did not fight it but did compile material to show that it was inadequate. They provided cost estimates and when the insurance companies attacked their estimates, they tried "to find out how the insurance industry had developed their cost estimates" (Ellickson Oral History, p. 62).
76. Letter from Clinton P. Anderson to Mrs. Leslie Hines, November 23, 1964, Anderson Papers, Library of Congress, Box 680, File: Finance, Social Security, Medical Care for the Aged.
77. *Medical Assistance for the Aged, the Kerr-Mills Program 1960–1963, Report by the Subcommittee on Health of the Elderly to the Special Committee on Aging, U.S. Senate* (Washington, D.C.: Government Printing Office, October 1963), p. 6.
78. Ibid., p. 4.
79. Ibid., p. 4.
80. Cohen Oral History, p. 27.
81. Ellickson Oral History, p. 61.
82. *Blue Cross and Private Health Insurance Coverage of Older Americans, A Report by the Subcommittee on Health of the Elderly, Senate Special Committee on Aging, July 1964* (Washington, D.C.: Government Printing Office, 1964), p. 22.
83. Ibid., p. 42.
84. *Blue Cross and Private Health Insurance Coverage,* p. 33.
85. Ellickson Oral History, p. 246.
86. Cruikshank Oral History, p. 320.
87. Letter from Martha Botts to Clinton Anderson, September 26, 1964, Anderson Papers, Box 681, File: Finance, Social Security, Medicare—Con.
88. Letter from Ned Flightner to Clinton Anderson, September 17, 1964, Anderson Papers, Box 681, File: Finance, Social Security, Medicare—Con. See also letter from L. W. Dempsey, who complained, "This is the very best and first Socialistic peace of legislation ever considered by an elected congress under a Republic. These men who are interested in this for political gain in office had shed there [sic] oath of office. To protect that Republic. And our United States Constitution. From socialism."

89. Letter from Mrs. J. L. Flinchum to Clinton Anderson, November 13, 1964, Anderson Papers, Box 681, File: Finance, Social Security, Medicare—Con.
90. Letter from Clinton Anderson to Mrs. Andrew F. Bott, October 21, 1964, Anderson Papers, Box 681, File: Finance, Social Security, Medicare—Con.
91. Esselstyn Oral History, p. 4–5.
92. Ibid., p. 6.
93. Schorr and Lesser Oral History, p. 103.
94. Esselstyn Oral History, p. 25.
95. Ibid., p. 39.
96. Schorr and Lesser Oral History, p. 103.
97. Peter Corning, *The Evolution of Medicare: From Idea to Law*, Social Security Administration, Office of Research and Statistics, Research Report 29 (Washington, D.C.: U.S. Department of Health, Education and Welfare, 1969), p. 91.
98. Esselstyn Oral History, p. 35.
99. Cruikshank Oral History, p. 321.
100. Gerald Markowitz and David Rosner, "Seeing Common Ground: A History of Labor and Blue Cross," *Journal of Health Politics, Policy and Law* 16, 4 (1991): 700.
101. Wickenden Oral History, p. 134.
102. Blue Carstenson Oral History, Columbia University Oral History collection, pp. 213, 212.
103. Ibid., pp. 76–79.
104. Letter from F. L. Chatham to Clinton P. Anderson, December 15, 1964, Anderson Papers, Box 680, File: Finance, Social Security, Medical Care for the Aged.
105. Stetler Oral History, p. 52.
106. Carstenson Oral History, p. 97.
107. Ibid., p. 204.
108. Ibid., pp. 163–66.
109. Statement by AFL-CIO Executive Council on Hospital Insurance for the Aged, February 23, 1965, RG 233, Records of the House of Representatives, 89th Congress, Committee on Ways and Means, Legislative Files, Box 22, File: HR 6675—8 of 94.
110. Corning, *The Evolution of Medicare*, p. 93.
111. Carstenson Oral History, p. 47.
112. Cohen Oral History, p. 27.
113. Irving Bernstein, *Guns or Butter: The Presidency of Lyndon Johnson* (New York: Oxford University Press, 1996).
114. Theodore Marmor, *The Politics of Medicare*, 2nd edition (New York: Aldine de Gruyter, 2000), p. 38.
115. Richard Harris, *A Sacred Trust* (New York: New American Library, 1966), p. 39.
116. Carstenson Oral History, p. 185.
117. Forand Oral History, p. 43.
118. Wickenden Oral History, p. 169.
119. "Washington News," *Journal of the American Medical Association* 186, 9 (1963): 16–17.
120. "Washington News," *Journal of the American Medical Association* 187, 3 (1964): 17.
121. Stetler Oral History, p. 49.

122. Carstenson Oral History, p. 14.
123. Ewing Oral History, p. 66.
124. Ellickson Oral History, p. 71.
125. Robert Dallek, *Flawed Giant: Lyndon Johnson and His Times, 1961–1973* (New York: Oxford University Press, 1998), p. 49.
126. Joseph Califano Jr., *The Triumph and Tragedy of Lyndon Johnson* (New York: Simon and Schuster, 1991), p. 9.
127. "Washington News," *Journal of the American Medical Association* 187, 7 (1964): 17.
128. *Blue Cross and Private Health Insurance Coverage,* note 50, p. 29.
129. Ibid., pp. 10–11.
130. Irwin Unger, *The Best of Intentions: The Triumphs and Failures of the Great Society Under Kennedy, Johnson, and Nixon* (New York: Doubleday, 1996).
131. Carstenson Oral History, p. 52.
132. Ibid., p. 55.
133. Cruikshank Oral History, p. 79.
134. Wickenden Oral History, p. 148.
135. Julian Zelizer, *Taxing America: Wilbur Mills, Congress, and the State, 1974–1975* (Cambridge: Cambridge University Press, 1998).
136. Carstenson Oral History, p. 57.
137. Robert Myers with Richard Vernaci, *Within the System: My Half Century in Social Security* (Winsted, Conn.: ACTEX, 1992), p. 161.
138. Berkowitz, "Disability Insurance," p. 192.
139. Alanson Willcox Oral History, Columbia University Oral History Collection, p. 43.
140. Ibid., p. 67.
141. Cohen Oral History, p. 32.
142. McNerney Oral History, p. 24.
143. Law, *Blue Cross.*
144. Wickenden Oral History, p. 52.
145. "After Medicare, What?" editorial comment, *National Underwriter*, January 9, 1961, p. 22.
146. Corning, *The Evolution of Medicare*, p. 102.
147. Eldercare Act of 1965, AFL-CIO Department of Social Security, March 1, 1965, RG 233, Records of the House of Representatives, 89th Congress, Committee on Ways and Means, Legislative Files, Box 21, File: HR 6675—3 of 94.
148. "Eldercare Branded Empty Propaganda," *AFL-CIO News*, February 20, 1965, RG 233, Records of the House of Representatives, 89th Congress, Committee on Ways and Means, Legislative Files, Box 21, File: HR 6675–3 of 94.
149. Wickenden Oral History, p. 169.
150. Letter from Leo H. Irwin, Chief Counsel, U.S. House of Representatives, to John Slack, June 18, 1965, RG 233, Records of the House of Representatives, 89th Congress, Committee on Ways and Means, Legislative Files, Box 21, File: HR 6675–4 of 94.
151. Bernstein, *Guns or Butter*, p. 171.
152. Quoted in Berkowitz, "Disability Insurance," p. 196.
153. Gluck and Reno, *Reflections on Implementing Medicare*, p. 2.
154. Lawrence R. Jacobs, *The Health of Nations: Public Opinion and the Making of American and British Health Policy* (Ithaca, N.Y.: Cornell University Press, 1993).

155. Schorr and Lesser Oral History, p. 26.
156. McNerney Oral History, p. 34.
157. Schorr and Lesser Oral History, p. 30.
158. Ibid., p. 74.
159. Ellickson Oral History, p. 64.
160. Schorr and Lesser Oral History, p. 75.
161. Ibid., p. 27.
162. Bernstein, *Guns or Butter*, p. 176.
163. Letter from Irwin to Slack, June 18, 1965.
164. Cruikshank Oral History, pp. 371–72.
165. Cruikshank, *The Cruikshank Chronicles*, p. 170.
166. Stetler Oral History, p. 8.
167. Cohen Oral History, p. 27.
168. Stetler Oral History, p. 14.

Chapter Three

1. Hugh Davis Graham, *The Civil Rights Era: Origins and Development of National Policy* (New York: Oxford University Press, 1990), pp. 3–5.
2. Quoted in Howard Schuman, Charlotte Steeh, Lawrence Bobo, and Maria Krysan, *Racial Attitudes in America* (Cambridge, Mass.: Harvard University Press, 1997), p. 10.
3. David R. James, "The Transformation of the Southern Racial State: Class and Race Determinants of Local-State Structures," *American Sociological Review* 53 (1988): 193.
4. Memo from Alanson Willcox to the Secretary, March 4, 1964, National Archives, College Park, Maryland, MRG 235, Box 7: Hospital Construction, File: Segregation and Discrimination.
5. Isidore Falk Oral History, Columbia University Oral History Collection, p. 279.
6. Ibid., p. 279.
7. Rufus Miles Jr., *The Department of Health, Education and Welfare* (New York: Praeger, 1974), p. 112.
8. Karen Kruse Thomas, "The Blueprint of Segregation: The Influence of Southern State Health Policy on the Federal Hill-Burton Hospital Construction Program, 1939–54," paper presented to the Southern Historical Association, Baltimore, November 9, 2002, p. 10.
9. Memo from Harrison to Siegel, January 18, 1954, note 45, National Archives, College Park, Maryland, RG 235, Box 7, File: Segregation and Discrimination.
10. Letter from Dr. Hubert Eaton to Dr. Boisfeuillet Jones, October 13, 1962; letter from Boisfeuillet Jones, Special Assistant to the Secretary, to Dr. Hubert Eaton, November 13, 1962, National Archives, College Park, Maryland, RG 235, Box 7, File: Segregation and Discrimination.
11. Thomas, "The Blueprint of Segregation," p. 2; Memo from Alanson Willcox to the Secretary, March 4, 1964, National Archives, College Park, Maryland, RG 235, Box 7, File: Segregation and Discrimination.
12. Malvin Schechter, "Segregated Blood: A Backlash Backfires," *Hospital Practice*, July 1969, p. 21.

13. David Barton Smith, "Addressing Racial Inequities In Health Care: Civil Rights Monitoring and Report Cards," *Journal of Health Politics, Policy and Law* 23, 1 (1998): 75-105.
14. Thomas, "The Blueprint of Segregation," p. 9.
15. Ibid., p. 17.
16. Quoted in Schuman, Steeh, Bobo, and Krysan, *Racial Attitudes in America*, p. 20.
17. Memo from Darrell Lane to Parke Banta, June 10, 1954; memo: Hospital Survey and Construction—Nondiscrimination Requirements Under Present Statute, January 31, 1956, National Archives, College Park, Maryland, RG 235, Box 7, File: Segregation and Discrimination.
18. Memo from Edward Rourke, October 11, 1961, National Archives, College Park, Maryland, RG 235, Box 7, File: Segregation and Discrimination.
19. Hospital Construction Program—Nondiscrimination—Constitutional Question, November 16, 1956, National Archives, College Park, Maryland, RG 235, Box 7, File: Segregation and Discrimination.
20. Memo from Gladys Harrison to Parke Banta, January 31, 1956, National Archives, College Park, Maryland, RG 235, Box 7, File: Segregation and Discrimination.
21. Memo from Alanson Willcox to Jack Haldeman, February 12, 1963, National Archives, College Park, Maryland, RG 235, Box 7, File: Segregation and Discrimination.
22. Karen Kruse Thomas, "The Wound of My People: Segregation and the Modernization of Health Care in North Carolina, 1935–1975," doctoral dissertation, University of North Carolina, 1999, p. 10.
23. Augustus K. Jones Jr., *Law, Bureaucracy, and Politics: The Implementation of Title VI of the Civil Rights Act of 1964* (Washington, D.C.: University Press of America, 1982).
24. Aldon D. Morris, *The Origins of the Civil Rights Movement: The Implementation of Title VI of the Civil Rights Act of 1964* (New York: Free Press, 1986).
25. Correspondence Between Catherine Patterson, Burke Marshall, and Alanson Willcox, October 4, October 23, October 25, 1963, National Archives, College Park, Maryland, RG 235, Box 1, File: Alabama.
26. Letter from Horace Reed to T. Fletcher Little, May 2, 1962, National Archives, College Park, Maryland, RG 235, HEW, Box 7, Hospital construction, File: Segregation and Discrimination.
27. David Barton Smith, *Health Care Divided: Race and Healing a Nation* (Ann Arbor: University of Michigan Press, 1999), pp. 75–76.
28. Letter from Reginald Hawkins to Alanson Willcox, July 27, 1963, National Archives, College Park, Maryland, RG 235, Box 7, File: Segregation and Discrimination.
29. Schuman, Steeh, Bobo, and Krysan, *Racial Attitudes in America*, pp. 25–26.
30. Smith, "Addressing Racial Inequities in Health Care," p. 81.
31. Memo from Office of General Counsel to Carl Harper, Regional Attorney, December 31, 1959, National Archives, College Park, Maryland, RG 235, Box 7, File: Segregation and Discrimination.
32. Memo from Carl Harper to Edward Rourke, Assistant General Counsel, Office of General Counsel, May 4, 1962, National Archives, College Park, Maryland, RG 235, Box 7, File: Segregation and Discrimination.

33. Letter from James S. Carr, Deputy Regional Attorney to Edward Burke, Assistant General Counsel to HEW, October 16, 1962, National Archives, College Park, Maryland, RG 235, Box 7, File: Segregation and Discrimination.
34. "Negroes' Suit Demands Full Grady Hospital Integration," *Atlanta Constitution*, September 25, 1962, p. 1, National Archives, College Park, Maryland, RG 235, Box 7, File: Segregation and Discrimination.
35. Letter from James S. Carr, Deputy Regional Attorney to Edward Burke, Assistant General Counsel to HEW, October 16, 1962, National Archives, College Park, Maryland, RG 235, Box 7, File: Segregation and Discrimination.
36. Memo from General Counsel to Marion E. Gardner, *Wood v. Hogan*, Lynchburg General Hospital, June 25, 1962, National Archives, College Park, Maryland, RG 235, Box 7, File: Segregation and Discrimination.
37. Letter from Virgil A. Wood to Robert F. Kennedy, June 8, 1962, National Archives, College Park, Maryland, RG 235, Box 7, File: Segregation and Discrimination.
38. Adam Clayton Powell, "Hospital Integration and Job Opportunity: Equality Goals for 1963," *Journal of the National Medical Association,* July 1963, pp. 338–41.
39. Memo from Edward Rourke to Luther Terry, April 6, 1964, National Archives, College Park, Maryland, RG 235, Box 7, File: Segregation and Discrimination.
40. Kenneth Wing, "Title VI and Health Facilities: Forms Without Substance," *Hastings Law Journal* 30 (1978): 138.
41. Letter from Alanson Willcox to Reginald Hawkins, August 20, 1964, National Archives, College Park, Maryland, RG 235, Box 7, File: Segregation and Discrimination.
42. Memo from Alanson Willcox to Wilbur Cohen, August 14, 1963, National Archives, College Park, Maryland, RG 235, Box 7, File: Segregation and Discrimination.
43. Conduct Required Under State Statutes Which Is Inconsistent with the Nondiscrimination Assurances in the Hill-Burton, Mental Retardation Facilities and Community Mental Health Centers Construction Programs, June 26, 1964, National Archives, College Park, Maryland, RG 235, Box 7, File: Segregation and Discrimination.
44. Memo from Gladys Harrison to Parke Banta, January 31, 1956, Appendix I, State Statutes, National Archives, College Park, Maryland, RG 235, Box 7, File: Segregation and Discrimination.
45. Conduct Required Under State Statutes Which Is Inconsistent with the Nondiscrimination Assurances in the Hill-Burton, Mental Retardation Facilities and Community Mental Health Centers Construction Programs, June 26, 1964, National Archives, College Park, Maryland, RG 235, Box 7, File: Segregation and Discrimination.
46. Letter from Senator Harrison Williams to Jack Haldeman, February 4, 1963, National Archives, College Park, Maryland, RG 235, Box 7, File: Segregation and Discrimination.
47. Memo from Lisle Carter to Alanson Wilcox, June 18, 1962, National Archives, College Park, Maryland, RG 235, Box 7, File: Segregation and Discrimination.

48. Memo from James Quigley to Alanson Wilcox, July 10, 1963, National Archives, College Park, Maryland, RG 235, Box 7, File: Segregation and Discrimination.

49. *Congressional Record*, April 3, 1957, pp. 4480–82.

50. Smith, "The Racial Integration of Health Facilities," p. 858.

51. Title VI of the Civil Rights Act, December 14, 1965, National Archives, College Park, Maryland, RG 47, Box 300. File: PA 16 Title VI Compliance.

52. Jeremy Rabkin, "Office for Civil Rights," in *The Politics of Regulation*, edited by James Q. Wilson (New York: Basic Books, 1980), p. 310.

53. Jones, *Law, Bureaucracy, and Politics*, p. 122.

54. Memo from Robert Nash to James Murray, Medicare and Civil Rights, March 19, 1966, National Archives, College Park, Maryland, RG 47, Box 300, File: PA 16 Title VI Compliance.

55. Miles, *The Department of Health, Education, and Welfare*, p. 64.

56. M. G. Gluck and Virginia Reno, eds., *Reflections on Implementing Medicare: Implementation Aspects of National Health Care Reform* (Washington, D.C.: National Academy of Social Insurance, 2001), p. 7.

57. Title VI of Civil Rights Act of 1965, National Archives, College Park, Maryland, RG 47, Box 300, File: PA 16, Title VI Compliance, p. 1.

58. Robert C. Lieberman, *Shifting the Color Line: Race and the American Welfare State* (Cambridge, Mass.: Harvard University Press, 1998), p. 71.

59. Commissioner's Bulletin, National Archives, College Park, Maryland, RG 47, Box 300, File: PA 16, Title VI Compliance.

60. Telephone interview with Dr. Richard Smith, career service officer in the Public Health Service and Special Projects officer, February 17, 1999.

61. Letter from Robert Ball to the Secretary, Nov. 1, 1965, National Archives, College Park, Maryland, RG 47, Box 330, File: PA Title VI Compliance.

62. Memo from Robert Ball to the Under Secretary, October 13, 1965, National Archives, College Park, Maryland, RG 47, Box 300, File: PA 16, Title VI Compliance.

63. Memo from Robert Ball to the Secretary, March 14, 1966, National Archives, College Park, Maryland, RG 47, Box 300, File: PA 16, Title VI Compliance.

64. Telephone interview with Carlton Spitzer, April 11, 2003; Carlton E. Spitzer, "A Crusader for Civil Rights and Racial Equality," Special to the *Star-Democrat*. Spitzer Files, manuscript sent to author.

65. Hospital Application for Participation; Guidelines for Compliance with Title VI, National Archives, College Park, Maryland, RG 47, Box 300, File: PA 16, Title VI Compliance.

66. Letter from James Murray to Robert Ball, February 15, 1966, National Archives, College Park, Maryland, RG 47, Box 300, File PA 16, Title VI Compliance.

67. Memoirs of Morton Lebow, Public Information Office, Office of Equal Health Opportunity, prepared for the author, p. 2.

68. Letter from Roy Swift to Robert Ball, undated, National Archives, College Park, Maryland, RG 47, Box 298, File: PA Title VI Compliance.

69. Memo from Louis Zawatzky to Jack Futterman, January 18, 1966, National Archives, College Park, Maryland, RG 47, Box 300, File: PA 16, Title VI Compliance.

70. Note from Robert Ball to Irv Wolkstein, July 2, 1966, National Archives, College Park, Maryland, RG 47, Box 300, File: PA 16, Title VI Compliance.

71. "AMA Head Urges Doctors Not to Thwart Medicare Program That Starts Friday," *Wall Street Journal*, June 27, 1966, Anderson Papers, Library of Congress, Box 702, File: Finance Committee, Medicare—General.
72. Edward Berkowitz, *Mr. Social Security: The Life of Wilbur J. Cohen* (Lawrence: University Press of Kansas, 1995).
73. Lebow Memoirs, p. 1; memo from Roy Swift, Corrected Number of Southern Counties with No Medicare Hospitals, July 25, 1966, National Archives, College Park, Maryland, RG 47, Box 298, File: PA 16 Hospital Compliance Report; Title VI Compliance Problems, RG 47, Box 298, File: PA 16 Hospital Compliance Report.
74. Robert Nash, "Compliance of Hospitals and Health Agencies with Title VI of the Civil Rights Act," *American Journal of Public Health* 58 (1968): 246–51.
75. Lebow Memoirs.
76. Telephone interview with Dr. Richard Smith, career service officer in the Public Health Service and Special Projects officer, February 17, 1999.
77. Memo from Roy Swift to Robert Ball, May 27, 1966, Observations on Title VI Compliance Efforts, National Archives, College Park, Maryland, RG 47, Box 298, File: PA 16 Hospital Compliance Report.
78. Letter from Robert Nash to James Murray, March 10, 1966, National Archives, College Park, Maryland, RG 47, Box 300, File: Title VI Compliance.
79. Memo from James Murray to Robert Ball, Medicare and civil rights, February 15, 1966, National Archives, College Park, Maryland, RG 47, Box 300, File: PA 16, Title VI Compliance.
80. Telephone interview with Dr. Richard Smith, career service officer in the Public Health Service and Special Projects officer, February 17, 1999.
81. "Federal Compliance Complaint Is Puzzle for Officials of Two Hospitals in Lincoln," *Elk Valley Times*, June 29, 1966, National Archives, College Park, Maryland, RG 47, Box 298, File: PA 16 Hospital Compliance Report.
82. Taborian Hospital, National Archives, College Park, Maryland, RG 47, Box 298, File: PA 16 Hospital Compliance Report.
83. Report of Title VI Issues, Natchez, Mississippi, July 15, 1966, National Archives, College Park, Maryland, RG 47, Box 298, File: PA Title VI Compliance.
84. Letter from Roy Swift to Robert Ball, undated, National Archives, College Park, Maryland, RG 47, Box 298, File: PA Title VI Compliance.
85. Berkowitz, *Mr. Social Security*.
86. Malvin Schechter, "Medicare and Desegregation," *Hospital Practice*, January 1967, p. 14.
87. Determination of Inability to Secure Compliance by Voluntary Means, December 30, 1966, National Archives, College Park, Maryland, RG 47, Box 298, File: PA 16 Hospital Compliance Report.
88. Malvin Schechter, "Emergency Medicare and Desegregation: A Special Report," *Hospital Practice*, July 1968, pp. 14–15; Malvin Schechter, "Emergency Medicare and Desegregation: Subterfuge Ends," *Hospital Practice*, January 1970, p. 17; memo from Peter Libassi to Robert Ball, July 25, 1966, National Archives, College Park, Maryland, RG 47, Box 298, File: PA 16 Hospital Compliance Report; Interview with Robert Ball, October 24, 1997.

Chapter Four

1. Joseph A. Califano Jr., *The Triumph and Tragedy of Lyndon Johnson: The White House Years* (New York: Simon and Schuster, 1991), pp. 9–10.

2. Robert Dallek, *Flawed Giant: Lyndon Johnson and His Times, 1961–1973* (New York: Oxford University Press, 1998), p. 210.
3. Marilyn Moon, *Medicare Now and in the Future* (Washington, D.C.: Urban Institute Press, 1993), p. 30.
4. Claude Pepper Oral History, Columbia University Oral History Collection, p. 45.
5. M. G. Gluck and Virginia Reno, eds., *Reflections on Implementing Medicare: Implementation Aspects of National Health Care Reform* (Washington, D.C.: National Academy of Social Insurance, 2001), pp. 35–37.
6. Telephone conversation between Art Fogleson and Martin Cohen of HIP, New York. August 9, 1966, National Archives, College Park, Maryland, RG 47, Office of the Commissioner, Box 298, File: PA 16, Enrollment April through December 1966.
7. Memo from Roy Swift to Bob Ball, September 12, 1966, National Archives, College Park, Maryland, RG 47, Office of the Commissioner, Box 298, File: PA 16, Enrollment April through December 1966.
8. Edward Berkowitz, "Disability Insurance and the Limits of American History," *Public Historian* 8, 2 (1986): 210.
9. Beneficiary Notice to John Sterusky, National Archives, College Park, Maryland, RG 47, Office of the Commissioner, Box 298, File: PA 16 Enrollment April through December 1966.
10. Robert Stevens and Rosemary Stevens, *Welfare Medicine in America* (New York: Free Press, 1974), p. 50; Letter from Leo H. Irwin, Chief Counsel, U.S. House of Representatives, to John Slack, June 18, 1965, National Archives, Washington, D.C., RG 233, Records of the House of Representatives, 89th Congress, Committee on Ways and Means, Legislative Files, Box 21, File: HR 6675–4 of 94; Lawrence R. Jacobs, *The Health of Nations: Public Opinion and the Making of American and British Health Policy* (Ithaca, N.Y.: Cornell University Press, 1993).
11. Quoted in Berkowitz, "Disability Insurance," 203.
12. Quoted in Jonathan Oberlander, *The Political Life of Medicare* (Chicago: University of Chicago Press, 2003), p. 109.
13. Letter from Robert Ball to Bowman Doss, President, Nationwide Mutual Insurance Company, February 11, 1966, National Archives, College Park, Maryland, RG 47, Office of the Commissioner, Box 298, File: PA 16 Contracts. Agreements for Carrying Out Title XVII of the Social Security Act, 1966; Robert Ball, Report to Social Security Administration Staff on the Implementation of the Social Security Amendments of 1965, November 15, 1965, in Gluck and Reno, *Reflections on Implementing Medicare*, p. 39.
14. Memo from Jay Constantine to Senator Anderson, April 14, 1966, Anderson Papers, Library of Congress, Box 702, File: Finance Committee, Medicare—General.
15. Memo from Arthur Hess to Robert Ball, May 18, 1966, National Archives, College Park, Maryland, RG 47, Office of the Commissioner, Box 298, File: PA 16 Contracts, Agreements for Carrying Out Title XVII of the Social Security Act, 1966. Although most of the planning involved the SSA and the BCA, some commercial insurers also participated.
16. Letter from Robert Ball to Bowman Doss, President, Nationwide Mutual Insurance Company, February 11, 1966, National Archives, College Park, Maryland, RG 47, Office of the Commissioner, Box 298, File: PA 16 Contracts, Agreements for Carrying Out Title XVII of the Social Security Act, 1966.

17. *Congressional Record*, July 8, 1965, pp. 159, 70–71.
18. Memo to Senator Anderson, February 9, 1966, Anderson Papers, Box 702, File: Finance Committee, Medicare—Correspondence.
19. Memo from Robert Myers to Robert Ball, February 10, 1966, Anderson Papers, Box 702, File: Finance Committee, Medicare—General.
20. Sylvia A. Law, *Blue Cross: What Went Wrong?* (New Haven, Conn.: Yale University Press, 1976), pp. 72–73. One scandal came to light in 1971 when memos were published from Blue Cross officials describing a task force aimed at persuading key members of Congress that BCA should have a prominent role in any national health insurance program that might be enacted. Medicare tax dollars were being used to fund a campaign against proposals by some members of Congress.
21. Law, *Blue Cross: What Went Wrong*, pp. 63–64.
22. "Nursing Home Costs Will Soar Highly," undated newspaper clipping, Anderson Papers, Box 732, File: Finance Committee, Medicare—Correspondence.
23. "Hospitals to Demand Profit-Return Parity," *Washington Post*, August 30, 1966, Anderson Papers, Box 701, File: Finance Committee, Medicare—Title 19.
24. Alanson Willcox Oral History, Columbia University Oral History Collection, p. 96.
25. Elizabeth Wickenden Oral History, Columbia University Oral History Collection, p. 144.
26. Joseph Califano Jr., *America's Health Care Revolution: Who Lives? Who Dies? Who Pays?* (New York: Random House, 1986), pp. 98–100.
27. Letter from C. J. Jannings to Clinton Anderson, September 29, 1964, Anderson Papers, Box 681, File: Social Security, Medicare—Con.
28. "Physicians Rebel Against Medicare Forms in Ohio; Revolt Soon May Hit Other States," *Wall Street Journal*, undated, Anderson Papers, Box 702, File: Finance Committee, Medicare—General.
29. Law, *Blue Cross: What Went Wrong*, p. 91.
30. Thomas Bodenheimer, "Should We Abolish the Private Health Insurance Industry?" *International Journal of Health Services* 20, 2 (1990): 211.
31. Law, *Blue Cross: What Went Wrong*, p. 89.
32. Memo from Jay Constantine to Senator Anderson, March 2, 1966, Anderson Papers, Box 702, File: Finance Committee, Medicare—General.
33. Paul Starr, *The Social Transformation of American Medicine* (New York: Basic Books, 1982), p. 375.
34. Berkowitz, "Disability Insurance," p. 216.
35. Memo to Wilbur Cohen and Robert Ball, status of definitive contracts, June 28, 1966, National Archives, College Park, Maryland, RG 47, Box 298, File: PA 16 Contracts, Agreements for Carrying Out Title XVII of the Social Security Act, 1966.
36. Visit to headquarters of Mississippi State Medical Society, National Archives, College Park, Maryland, RG 47, Office of the Commissioner, Box 298, File: Contracts, Agreements for Carrying Out Title XVII of the Social Security Act, 1966.
37. Oberlander, *The Political Life of Medicare*, p. 110.
38. Visit to Headquarters of Traveler's Life Insurance Company's Medicare Center, National Archives, College Park, Maryland, RG 47, Office of the

Commissioner, Box 298, File: Contracts, Agreements for Carrying Out Title XVII of the Social Security Act, 1966.

39. Re: Part B of Medicare, Memo from Jay Constantine to Senator Anderson, October 4, 1968, Anderson Papers, Box 732, File: Finance Committee, Medicare—Correspondence.

40. Re: Part B of Medicare, Memo from Jay Constantine to Senator Anderson, October 4, 1968, Anderson Papers, Box 732, File: Finance Committee, Medicare—Correspondence.

41. Letter from Brendan Mylans to Senator Anderson, January 5, 1968. Anderson Papers, Box 732, File: Finance Committee, Medicare—Correspondence.

42. Edward Berkowitz, *Robert Ball and the Politics of Social Security* (Madison: University of Wisconsin Press, 2004), p. 225.

43. Memo from Howard to Senator Anderson, February 9, 1966, Anderson Papers, Box 702, File: Finance Committee, Medicare—Correspondence.

44. "AMA Urges Doctors to Choose Alternative of Billing Patients Directly for Medicare," *Wall Street Journal*, June 30, 1966, Anderson Papers, Box 702, File: Finance Committee, Medicare—Correspondence.

45. "Payments Plague Medicare," newspaper clipping, Anderson Papers, Box 732, File: Finance Committee, Medicare—Correspondence.

46. Edward Chase, "The Doctors' Bonanza," April 15, 1967, Anderson Papers, Box 731, File: Finance Committee, Medicare.

47. William A. Nolen, M.D., "Are Doctors Profiteering on Medicare?" *Medical Economics*, 1967, p. 98, Anderson Papers, Box 702, File: Finance Committee, Medicare—General.

48. Starr, *The Social Transformation of American Medicine*, p. 381.

49. Letter from Clinton P. Anderson to Russell Long, December 6, 1965, Anderson Papers, Box 702, File: Finance Committee, Medicare—Correspondence.

50. Memo from Jay Constantine to Senator Anderson, January 29, 1966, Anderson Papers, Box 702, File: Finance Committee, Medicare—Correspondence.

51. Quoted in Berkowitz, "Disability Insurance," p. 226.

52. Stevens and Stevens, *Welfare Medicine in America*, p. 66.

53. Law, *Blue Cross: What Went Wrong*, p. 46.

54. Memo from George Rawson to Arthur Hess, April 11, 1966, National Archives, College Park, Maryland, RG 47, Office of the Commissioner, Box 298, File: PA 16 Enrollment April through December, 1966. Once again the South was the laggard. The only southern state participating in Medicaid was Arkansas.

55. Starr, *The Social Transformation of American Medicine*, p. 372.

56. Memo from George Rawson to Arthur Hess, April 11, 1966, National Archives, College Park, Maryland, RG 47, Box 298, File: PA 16 Enrollment April through December, 1966.

57. Law, *Blue Cross: What Went Wrong*, p. 48.

58. Colleen Grogan and Eric Patashnik, "Between Welfare Medicine and Mainstream Entitlement: Medicaid at the Political Crossroads," *Journal of Health Politics, Policy and Law* 28, 5 (2003): 841.

59. Ibid., p. 242.

60. Law, *Blue Cross: What Went Wrong*, p. 102.

61. Julian E. Zelizer, *Taxing America: Wilbur Mills, Congress, and the State, 1945–1975* (Cambridge: Cambridge University Press, 1998), p. 262.
62. Reported in Abraham Ribicoff, *The American Medical Machine* (New York: Saturday Review Press, 1972), p. 93.
63. Quoted in Democratic Advisory Council of Elected Officials, Domestic Affairs Task Force Summary, Health Security, p. 9, files of Rashi Fein, Department of Social Medicine, Harvard Medical School, Cambridge, Massachusetts.
64. "Hospital Costs to Climb Again This Year Blue Cross President Tells House Panel," *Wall Street Journal*, March 6, 1967, p. 1.
65. Ribicoff, *The American Medical Machine*, p. 98.
66. Rowen, *Self-Inflicted Wounds*, pp. 72–73.
67. Memo from George Crawford to Peter Flanigan, September 23, 1971, Nixon Presidential Materials, National Archives, College Park, Maryland, Subject File IS, Box 2, File 6/1/72–8/9/74.
68. Memo from George Crawford to Peggy Harlow, October 7, 1971, Nixon Presidential Materials, Subject File IS, Box 2, File 6/1/72–8/9/74.
69. Rowen, *Self-Inflicted Wounds*, pp. 81–83.
70. "Hospital Costs to Climb Again This Year," p. 1.
71. Law, *What Went Wrong?* p. 130.
72. Oberlander, *The Politics of Medicare*, p. 116.
73. Oberlander, *The Politics of Medicare*, p. 117.
74. Julian Zelizer, *Taxing America: Wilbur D. Mills, Congress and the State, 1945–1075* (Cambridge, England: Cambridge University Press, 1998), p. 342.
75. Oberlander, *The Politics of Medicare*, pp. 118–19.
76. Kant Patel and Mark Rushefsky, *Health Care Politics and Policy in America* (Armonk, N.Y.: M. E. Sharpe, 1999), p. 400; Starr, *The Social Transformation of American Medicine*, p. 400.
77. Issue Report No. 1, The Health Crisis, July 18, 1974, Democratic Study Group, U.S. House of Representatives, files of Rashi Fein, Department of Social Medicine, Harvard Medical School, Boston.
78. Starr, *The Social Transformation of American Medicine*, p. 407.
79. Carolyn Tuohy, *Accidental Logics: The Dynamics of Change in the Health Care Arena in the United States, Britain, and Canada* (New York: Oxford University Press, 1999), p. 131; Law, *Blue Cross: What Went Wrong*, p. 122.
80. Russell B. Roth, M.D., "A Bankrupt Law," *American Medical News*, November 22, 1976, p. 10; Hacker, *The Divided Welfare State*, p. 253.
81. Ribicoff, *The American Medical Machine*, p. 14.
82. Democratic Advisory Council of Elected Officials, Domestic Affairs Task Force Summary, Health Security, p. 7, files of Rashi Fein, Department of Social Medicine, Harvard Medical School, Boston.

Chapter Five

1. Stephen E. Ambrose, *Nixon: The Triumph of a Politician, 1962–1972* (New York: Simon and Schuster, 1989), p. 220.
2. Jill Quadagno, *The Color of Welfare: How Racism Undermined the War on Poverty* (New York: Oxford University Press, 1994), Chapter 6.
3. Disabled SSI recipients who return to work but continue to be medically disabled may remain eligible for Medicaid. States have three options as

to how to treat SSI recipients in regard to Medicaid eligibility. They may cover all SSI recipients under Medicaid, they may provide Medicaid to SSI recipients only if the recipient completes a separate application with the state agency that administers Medicaid. or they may impose more rigid eligibility criteria for Medicaid than for SSI. Thus access to health insurance for the disabled partly depends on residence.

4. Oscar Ewing Oral History, Columbia University Oral History Collection, p. 59.
5. Isidore S. Falk, "Beyond Medicare," *American Journal of Public Health* 59, 3 (1969): 619.
6. A Grid to Evaluate the Mounting Debate About National Health Insurance, p. 5, files of Rashi Fein, Department of Social Medicine, Harvard Medical School, Boston.
7. Walter P. Reuther, "The Health Care Crisis: Where Do We Go From Here?" *American Journal of Public Health* 59, 1 (1969): 14.
8. National Health Insurance, interview with Walter P. Reuther, Chairman, Committee of One-Hundred for National Health Insurance, pp. 7–8, files of Rashi Fein.
9. Statement by AFL-CIO Executive Council on National Health Insurance, February 17, 1970, p. 1, files of Rashi Fein.
10. Nelson Lichtenstein, *The Most Dangerous Man in Detroit: Walter Reuther and the State of American Labor* (New York: Basic Books, 1995), p. 297.
11. John Barnard, *Walter Reuther and the Rise of the Auto Workers* (Boston: Little, Brown, 1983), p. 182.
12. Ibid., pp. 78–79.
13. Lichtenstein, *The Most Dangerous Man in Detroit*, pp. 430–33; Frank Cormier and William Eaton, *Reuther* (Englewood Cliffs, N.J.: Prentice-Hall, 1970), p. 419.
14. Theo Lippman Jr., *Senator Ted Kennedy* (New York: W. W. Norton, 1976), p. 236.
15. National Health Insurance, interview with Walter P. Reuther, Chairman, Committee of One-Hundred for National Health Insurance, p. 4, files of Rashi Fein.
16. Memo from Carry to Rashi Fein, July 6, 1970, files of Rashi Fein.
17. "Health Security for America," *Congressional Record*, Proceedings and Debates of the 92nd Congress, First Session, p. 1.
18. William H. Honan, *Ted Kennedy: Profile of the Survivor* (New York: Quadrangle Books, 1972), p. 105.
19. Anthony Summers, *The Arrogance of Power: The Secret World of Richard Nixon* (New York: Viking, 2000), p. 379.
20. Letter from Dr. Robert Heidt to President Nixon, July 13, 1970. White House Central Files, Subject Files, (HE) Health, Box 4, File: (GEN) HE 7/1/70–12/31/70, National Archives, Nixon Presidential Materials Staff, College Park, Maryland.
21. Richard Lyons, "Nixon National Health Insurance Program," *New York Times*, January 9, 1974, p. 1.
22. Quadagno, *The Color of Welfare*.
23. Design and Cost Estimates of a Tax Credit System to Finance Medical Care, May 16, 1969, American Medical Association, Washington, D.C., p. 4, files of Rashi Fein, Department of Social Medicine, Harvard Medical School, Boston.

24. A Grid to Evaluate the Mounting Debate, p. 2.
25. Income Tax Credits to Assist in the Purchase of Voluntary Health Insurance, File: Tax Credit for Health Insurance (Nixon Task Force), files of Rashi Fein.
26. A Grid to Evaluate the Mounting Debate, p. 4.
27. Iwan W. Morgan, *Nixon* (London: Arnold, 2002), p. 71.
28. Cited in Norbert Israel Goldfield, *National Health Reform American Style: Lessons from the Past: A Twentieth Century Journey* (Tampa, Fla.: American College of Physician Executives, 2000), p. 109.
29. Statement of Senator Edward M. Kennedy on the President's Health Message, February 18, 1971, files of Rashi Fein.
30. Paul Starr, "Transformation in Defeat: The Changing Objectives of National Health Insurance, 1915–1980," *American Journal of Public Health* 72, 19 (1982): 85.
31. "Health Maintenance Organizations Promoted by Nixon," *New York Times*, October 10, 1972, p. 1A; Paul Starr, *The Social Transformation of American Medicine* (New York: Basic Books, 1982), p. 396.
32. Quoted in Lawrence D. Brown, *Politics and Health Care Organization: HMOs as Federal Policy* (Washington, D.C.: Brookings Institution, 1983), p. 206.
33. David Bennahum, "The Crisis Called Managed Care," in *Managed Care: Financial, Legal, and Ethical Issues*, edited by David Bennahum (Cleveland: Pilgrim Press, 1999), p. 3; Jake Spidle, "The Historical Roots of Managed Care," in *Managed Care: Financial, Legal, and Ethical Issues*, edited by David Bennahum (Cleveland: Pilgrim Press, 1999), p. 16.
34. Brown, *Politics and Health Care Organization*, p. 219. Lippman, *Senator Ted Kennedy*, p. 233.
35. National Health Insurance, American Hospital Association, files of Rashi Fein.
36. "National Council of Senior Citizens Says False Claims Being Made," *New York Times*, November 7, 1972, p. 21.
37. Don Wenger, chairman of the board, Ironside Corporation, "J'Accuse: Health Field Fiscal Foolishness," January 5, 1972, HE, Box 2, File: EX HE 1/1/72–1/31/72, Nixon Presidential Materials, National Archives, College Park, Maryland.
38. Lichtenstein, *The Most Dangerous Man in Detroit*, p. 437.
39. Archie Robinson, *George Meany and His Times: A Biography* (New York: Simon and Schuster, 1981), p. 283.
40. Letter from David S. Turner to Members of the U.S. Congress, October 5, 1970, Pepper Library, Florida State University, Tallahassee, Series 3098, Box 52, File 1; AFL-CIO Executive Council Statement, February 17, 1970, p. 1 (note 22); Katherine Ellickson Oral History, Columbia University Oral History Collection, p. 135; Goldfield, *National Health Reform American Style*, p. 114.
41. Minutes of Meeting of Technical Committee of Committee for National Health Insurance, August 31, 1972, files of Rashi Fein.
42. Minutes of Meeting of Technical Committee of Committee for National Health Insurance, August 31, 1972, files of Rashi Fein.
43. Brown, *Politics and Health Care Organization*, p. 257.
44. Kennedy HMO Proposal, HE, Box 2, File: EX HE 3/1/72–3/31/72, Nixon Presidential Materials.

45. Memo from Minority Staff of the Subcommittee on Health and Long-Term Care, Hearing on Medicare HMOs, April 24, 1985, Pepper Library, Series S302A, Box 25, File 1; Lawrence David Weiss, *Private Medicine and Public Health: Profit, Politics, and Prejudice in the American Health Care Enterprise* (Boulder, Colo.: Westview Press, 1997), p. 90.
46. Summers, *The Arrogance of Power*, p. 380.
47. Julian Zelizer, *Taxing America: Wilbur D. Mills, Congress and the State, 1945–1975* (Cambridge: Cambridge University Press, 1998), p. 331.
48. Lippman, *Senator Ted Kennedy*, p. 238.
49. Memo from Ken Cole to Dick Nathan, July 29, 1971, IS, Box 2, File 6/1/72–8/9/74, Nixon Presidential Materials.
50. News Media, HE, Box 2, File 5/1/72, Nixon Presidential Materials.
51. Memo from Ray Waldman, September 7, 1972, Re: Human Resources Committee of the National Governors' Conference, HE, Box 2, File 5/1/72, Nixon Presidential Materials; see also memo from Jim Cavanaugh to Ken Cole, September 22, 1972.
52. Memo from David Parker to H. R. Haldeman, October 10, 1972, HE, Box 2, File 5/1/72, Nixon Presidential Materials.
53. Memo from Dave Gergen to Tod Hullin, Proposed President's Statement, October 29, 1972, HE, Box 2, File 5/1/72, Nixon Presidential Materials.
54. President Nixon's Rx: Health Care: With Government Help—But Without Government Takeover, Staff Member and Office Files, Patrick J. Buchanan, Box 11, File: Health Care, Nixon Presidential Materials.
55. Zelizer, *Taxing America*, p. 319.
56. Ambrose, *Nixon*, p. 554.
57. Joint Statement of Representative Wilbur D. Mills and Senator Edward M. Kennedy Before the Democratic Platform Committee, June 17, 1972, HE, Box 2, File 5/1/72, Nixon Presidential Materials; Barnard, *Walter Reuther and the Rise of the Auto Workers*, pp. 41–43.
58. Ambrose, *Nixon*, p. 584.
59. Schedule proposal, Greeting: Dr. Malcolm Todd, August 6, 1973, HE, Box 2, File 8/1/73, Nixon Presidential Materials.
60. Summers, *The Arrogance of Power*, p. 459.
61. Richard Madden, "93rd Congress' 2nd Session Set for Jan. 21," *New York Times*, January 21, 1974, p. 16.
62. Quoted in Flint Wainess, "The Ways and Means of National Health Care, 1974 and Beyond," *Journal of Health Politics, Policy and Law* 24, 2 (1999): 313.
63. Memo for the President from Caspar Weinberger, November 2, 1973, White House Central Files, Subject Files, HE (Health) Box 2, File: EX HE 8/1/73, Nixon Presidential Materials.
64. Quoted in Wainess, "The Ways and Means of National Health Care," p. 315.
65. Game Plan on the Health Issue, HE, Box 3, File 1/1/73–5/31/74, Nixon Presidential Materials.
66. Harold M. Schnaeck Jr., "Pres. Nixon Sends to Congress His National Health Insurance Proposal," *New York Times*, February 7, 1974, p. 34.
67. Isadore S. Falk, A Modification of the Health Security Program (S. 3; H.R. 22) to Provide for Functional Participation by the Insurance Industry, July 13, 1972, files of Rashi Fein.

68. David Dranove, *The Economic Evolution of American Health Care: From Marcus Welby to Managed Care* (Princeton, N.J.: Princeton University Press, 2000), p. 30.

69. Quoted in Cathie Jo Martin, "Together Again: Business, Government and the Quest for Cost Control," *Journal of Health Politics, Policy and Law* 18, 2 (1993): 369.

70. Author's interview with Rashi Fein, Boston, March 7, 2001.

71. "Kennedy's Collapse: Health Professionals for Political Action," *Notes on Health Politics* 2, 7 (1974), files of Rashi Fein.

72. John Herbers, "Weinberger Says Democrats Failed to Move on Health Insurance Issue," *New York Times*, February 27, 1974, p. 1.

73. Memo from Frank Carlucci to the President, received August 29, 1974, IS, Box 2, File 6/1/72–8/9/74, Nixon Presidential Materials.

74. Wainess, "The Ways and Means of National Health Care," p. 307.

75. "The Health Insurance Debate," *Washington Post*, May 26, 1974, p. C6.

76. Remarks by Charles M. Boteler Jr., President of the National Association of Mutual Insurance Agents, IS, Box 2, File 6/1/72–8/9/74, Nixon Presidential Materials.

77. "Chances of NHI Passage Rise as Ford Takes Over," *American Medical News*, August 19, 1974, p. 1, Pepper Library, S303A, Box 1, File 15.

78. Wainess, "The Ways and Means of National Health Care," p. 326.

79. Howard Wolinsky and Tom Brune, *The Serpent on the Staff: The Unhealthy Politics of the American Medical Association* (New York: Putnam, 1994), p. 31.

80. "Rep. Mills' NHI Plan Is Shelved," *American Medical News*, August 26, 1974, p. 1, Pepper Library, S303A, Box 1, File 15.

81. A Digest of Congressional Activities Relating to the Topic of National Health Insurance, Pepper Library, Series 301, Box 286, File 8.

82. Zelizer, *Taxing America*, pp. 351–52.

83. Rashi Fein, *Medical Care, Medical Costs: The Search for a Health Insurance Policy.* (Cambridge, Mass.: Harvard University Press, 1986), p. 150.

84. Memo from Max W. Fine to Leonard Woodcock, August 28, 1974, Subject: An Alternative Bill, files of Rashi Fein.

85. Memo from Dick Shoemaker to Bert Seidman, November 21, 1974, Subject: Hip Pocket NHI Program, files of Rashi Fein.

86. Hobart Rowen, *Self-Inflicted Wounds: From LBJ's Guns and Butter to Reagan's Voodoo Economics* (New York: Times Books, 1994), pp. 169, 196.

87. Burton Hersh, *The Shadow President: Ted Kennedy in Opposition* (South Royalton, Vt.: Steerforth Press, 1997), p. 25.

88. Taylor Dark, "Organized Labor and the Carter Administration: The Origins of Conflict," in *The Presidency and Domestic Policies of Jimmy Carter*, edited by Herbert Rosenbaum and Alexej Ugrinsky (Westport, Conn.: Greenwood Press, 1994), p. 766.

89. Joseph Califano Jr., *Governing America: An Insider's Report from the White House and Cabinet* (New York: Simon and Schuster, 1981), p. 89; Gary M. Fink, "Fragile Alliance: Jimmy Carter and the American Labor Movement," in *The Presidency and Domestic Policies of Jimmy Carter*, edited by Herbert Rosenbaum and Alexej Ugrinsky (Westport, Conn.: Greenwood Press, 1994), p. 794.

90. Califano, *Governing America*, p. 89.

91. Author's interview with Rashi Fein, Boston, March 7, 2001.

92. Ibid.
93. Hospital Cost Containment Nearing a Vote, Background Report by Office of Medical Liaison, White House Press Office, October 29, 1979, p. 3, Carter Library, Atlanta, Records of Chief of Staff Landon Butler, Box 101, File: Hospital Cost Containment, 1/24/79–10/29/79.
94. Califano, *America's Health Care Revolution*, p. 10; Michael G. Krukones, "Campaigner and President: Jimmy Carter's Campaign Promises and Presidential Performance," in *The Presidency and Domestic Policies of Jimmy Carter*, edited by Herbert Rosenbaum and Alexej Ugrinsky (Westport, Conn.: Greenwood Press, 1994), p. 133.
95. John Inglehart, "The Hospital Lobby Is Suffering from Self-Inflicted Wounds," *National Journal*, October 1, 1977, p. 1526, Carter Library, Records of Chief of Staff Landon Butler, Box 101, File: Hospital Cost Containment, 1/24/79–10/29/79.
96. Ibid., p. 1528.
97. "The Voluntary Effort," American Hospital Association, American Medical Association, Federation of American Hospitals, January 30, 1978, Carter Library, Staff Offices, Peter Bourne, Special Assistant to the President, Box 33, File: Hospital Cost Containment 10/1/77–2/2/78.
98. Inglehart, "The Hospital Lobby," p. 1526.
99. Letter from John Alexander McMahon, James Sammons, and Michael Bromberg, American Hospital Association, to the President, February 2, 1978, Carter Library, Staff Offices, Peter Bourne, Special Assistant to the President, Box 33, File: Hospital Cost Containment 10/1/77–2/2/78.
100. Author's interview with anonymous hospital administrator, May 2, 2003.
101. Inglehart, "The Hospital Lobby," p. 1527.
102. Letter from Stuart Eisenstadt to Walter Wristo, Citibank, May 22, 1979, Carter Library, Office of the Deputy of the Chief of Staff, Stephen Selig's Subject File, 1979–1981, Box 175, File: Hospital Cost Containment, 3/21/79–9/28/79.
103. Note to Stuart Eisenstadt, Ann Wexler, and Landon Butler from Dick Warden, September 11, 1978, Carter Library, Records of Chief of Staff Landon Butler, Box 100, File: Hospital Cost Containment, 9/12/78–10/15/78.
104. Memo from Landon Butler to Steve Selig, September 21, 1978, Carter Library, Records of Chief of Staff Landon Butler, Box 100, File: Hospital Cost Containment, 9/12/78–10/15/78.
105. Excessive Hospital Bills: Letters from the Public, Carter Library, White House Press Office, White House Office Subject File, Box 61, File: Hospital Cost Containment 7/78.
106. "A GOP View on Hospital Costs," *National Journal*, October 1, 1977, p. 1528, Carter Library, Records of Chief of Staff Landon Butler, Box 101, File: Hospital Cost Containment, 1/24/79–10/29/79.
107. Memo from Zachary Dyckman to Alfred Karn, Special Assistant to the President on Inflation, Carter Library, Domestic Policy Staff Files, Subject File, 1976–1981, Box 216, File: Hospital Cost Containment.
108. State of the Union Address, 1979, Carter Library. See also Hospital Cost Containment Nearing a Vote, Background Report by Office of Medical Liaison, White House Press Office, October 29, 1979, p. 3, Carter Library, Records of Chief of Staff Landon Butler, Box 101, File: Hospital Cost Containment, 1/24/79–10/29/79.

109. Hospital Cost Containment/Business Strategy, Memo from Richard Reiman to Richard Moe, February 9, 1979, Carter Library, Office of the Deputy of the Chief of Staff, Stephen Selig's Subject File, 1979–1981, Box 175, File: Hospital Cost Containment, 5/12/78–2/13–79.

110. Outreach Strategy—Hospital Cost Containment, Memo from Anne Wexler to Dick Moe, February 2, 1979, Carter Library, Records of Chief of Staff Landon Butler, Box 101, File: Hospital Cost Containment, 1/24/79–10/29/79.

111. Author's telephone interview with anonymous American Hospital Association officer, September 3, 2003.

112. Background Report, AFL-CIO Executive Council on Hospital Cost Containment, Bal Harbour, Florida, February, 1979, Carter Library, Records of Chief of Staff Landon Butler, Box 101, File: Hospital Cost Containment, 2/24/79–6/15/79.

113. Update—Hospital Cost Containment, Memo from Steve Selig to Anne Wexler, March 28, 1979, Carter Library, Office of the Deputy of the Chief of Staff, Stephen Selig's Subject File, 1979–1981, Box 175, File: Hospital Cost Containment, 3/21/79–9/28/79.

114. "Administration Launches Last-Ditch Fight to Get Hospital Cost Control," *Congressional Quarterly*, September 16, 1978, p. 2480.

115. "Hospital Cost Control Legislation Dies," *Congressional Quarterly*, October 21, 1978, p. 3074.

116. President's Daily Diary, February 13, April 11, April 24, May 7, 1979; May 23, 1979, Carter Library.

117. Califano, *Governing America*, p. 147.

118. Exit interview with Bill Cable, congressional liaison during the Carter administration, February 21, 1981, Carter Library.

119. Califano, *America's Health Care Revolution*, p. 147.

120. Ibid., pp. 127–28.

121. Health Cost Containment Task Force—Proposed Strategy, Memo from Richard Moe from Hamilton Jordan, Frank Moore, March 1, 1979, Carter Library, Office of the Chief of Staff, Subject File, 1977–1980, Box 46, File: Health/Hospital Costs.

122. Califano, *Governing America*, p. 98.

123. Hersh, *The Shadow President*, p. 25.

124. Califano, *Governing America*, pp. 98–99.

125. Ibid., pp. 92–93.

126. Fink, "Fragile Alliance," p. 795.

127. National Health Insurance, Memo from Landon Butler to Hamilton Jordan, September 6, 1979, Carter Library, Office of the Chief of Staff, Subject File, 1977–1980, Box 46, File: Health/Hospital Costs.

128. Stuart Eisenstadt, "President Carter, the Democratic Party, and the Making of Domestic Policy," in *The Presidency and Domestic Policies of Jimmy Carter*, edited by Herbert Rosenbaum and Alexej Ugrinsky (Westport, Conn.: Greenwood Press, 1994), p. 13.

129. Fink, "Fragile Alliance," p. 796.

130. Statement of Senator Edward Kennedy on Introduction of a New National Health Insurance Outline, October 2, 1978, files of Rashi Fein.

131. Health Care for All Americans Act of 1979; see also Press Release, Committee for National Health Insurance, August 18, 1980, files of Rashi Fein; see also Memo from Douglas Fraser to Members of the Committee for

National Health Insurance Committee of One Hundred, October 4, 1979, files of Rashi Fein.

132. Executive Committee Meeting, Committee for National Health Insurance, March 20, 1978, files of Rashi Fein, folder: Committee for National Health Insurance, Kennedy-Carter Discussions; see also Public Papers of the Presidents of the United States, Jimmy Carter, Book 1—January 1 to June 22, 1979 (Washington, D.C.: Government Printing Office, 1980), pp. 1029–30.

133. Letter from I. S. Falk to Senator Edward Kennedy, August 9, 1979, files of Rashi Fein.

134. Confidential memo, April 4, 1978, Proposed basic principles for a White House National Health Insurance proposal, files of Rashi Fein, Department of Social Medicine, Harvard Medical School, Boston, folder: Committee for National Health Insurance, Kennedy-Carter Discussions.

135. Betty Glad, *Jimmy Carter, in Search of the Great White House* (New York: W. W. Norton, 1980), pp. 447–48.

136. "Iran Outlines Demands for Hostages Release," *Washington Post*, November 14, 1979, p. A1.

137. E. J. Dionne, Jr., *Why Americans Hate Politics* (New York: Simon and Schuster, 1991), p. 132.

138. "Significant Dates in the Hostage Crisis," *New York Times*, January 21, 1981, p. A7.

139. "Reagan Takes Oath as 40th President," *New York Times*, January 20, 1980, p. A1.

140. Author's interview with Rashi Fein, Boston, March 7, 2001.

141. "Reagan Takes Oath as 40th President."

142. Rowen, *Self-Inflicted Wounds*, p. 208.

143. Jill Quadagno, "Generational Equity and the Politics of the Welfare State," *Politics and Society* 17 (1989): 356.

144. Gordon, *Dead on Arrival*, p. 38.

145. Helen Slessarev, "Racial Tensions and Institutional Support: Social Programs During a Period of Retrenchment," in *The Politics of Social Policy in the United States*, edited by Margaret Weir, Ann Shola Orloff, and Theda Skocpol (Princeton, N.J.: Princeton University Press, 1988), p. 360.

146. Califano, *America's Health Care Revolution*, p. 148.

147. Charlene Harrington, "Social Security and Medicare: Policy Shifts in the 1980s," in *Fiscal Austerity and Aging: Shifting Government Responsibility for the Elderly*, edited by Carroll Estes, Robert Newcomer, and Associates (Beverly Hills, Calif.: Sage, 1983), pp. 92–93.

148. Linda Demkovich, "On Health Issues, This Business Group Is a Leader, But Is Anyone Following?" *National Journal*, June 18, 1983, pp. 1278–80.

149. Jonathan Oberlander, *The Political Life of Medicare* (Chicago: University of Chicago Press, 2003), p. 119.

150. In 1977 Congress raised payroll taxes, the second increase in six years, and enacted modest, less visible cuts by changing the formula for calculating benefits. Edward Berkowitz, *America's Welfare State: From Roosevelt to Reagan* (Baltimore, Johns Hopkins University Press, 1991), p. 72.

151. Paul Charles Light, *Artful Work: The Politics of Social Security Reform* (New York: Random House, 1985), p. 122.

152. Lawrence Alfred Powell, Kenneth J. Branco, and John B. Williamson, *The Senior Rights Movement: Framing the Policy Debate in America* (New York: Twayne, 1996), p. 160.

153. Minutes of the Board of Directors, Committee for National Health Insurance, June 21, 1982, files of Rashi Fein.
154. Light, *Artful Work*, p. 124.
155. Carolyn Rinkus Thompson, "The Political Evolution of the Medicare Catastrophic Health Care Act of 1988," doctoral dissertation, Johns Hopkins University, 1990, pp. 66–67.
156. Light, *Artful Work*, pp. 180–83.
157. Paul Pierson, *Dismantling the Welfare State: Reagan, Thatcher, and the Politics of Retrenchment* (Cambridge: Cambridge University Press, 1994), p. 67; Light, *Artful Work*, p. 119.
158. Light, *Artful Work*, p. 189.
159. Dranove, *The Economic Evolution of American Health Care*, p. 50.
160. James Morone and Andrew Dunham, "Slouching Towards National Health Insurance: The Unanticipated Politics of DRGs," *Bulletin of the New York Academy of Medicine* 62, 6 (1986): 264; Donald Light, "The Restructuring of the American Health Care System," in *Health Politics and Policy*, edited by Theodor J. Litman and Leonard S. Robins (Albany, N.Y.: Delmar, 1997), p. 55.
161. The hospital cost containment program, which had begun as an experiment in New Jersey, was now applied to the entire Medicare program; see Chapter 4.
162. Author's telephone interview with anonymous American Hospital Association officer, September 3, 2003.
163. Betty Leyerle, *Moving and Shaking American Medicine: The Structure of a Socioeconomic Transformation* (Westport, Conn.: Greenwood Press, 1984), p. 38; Linda Bergthold, *Purchasing Power in Health: Business, the State, and Health Care Politics* (New Brunswick, N.J.: Rutgers University Press, 1990), pp. 42–44.
164. Jeff Goldsmith, "Death of a Paradigm: The Challenge of Competition," *Health Affairs* 3, 3 (1984): 7.
165. Author's interview with anonymous hospital administrator, May 2, 2003.
166. Califano, *America's Health Care Revolution*, p. 119.
167. Ibid., p. 120.
168. Goldsmith, "Death of a Paradigm," p. 8.
169. Testimony of John Motley III, Director of Federal Governmental Relations, National Federation of Independent Business before the U.S. Bipartisan Commission on Comprehensive Health Care (Pepper Commission), October 24, 1989, p. 177, Pepper Library, Series 302, Box 63, File 8.
170. "Holding Down Medicare Costs," *Chicago Tribune*, January 21, 1985, Section 1, p. 10.
171. Miriam Laugesen and Thomas Rice, "Is the Doctor In? The Evolving Role of Organized Medicine in Health Policy," *Journal of Health Policy, Politics and Law* 28, 2–3 (2003): 306.
172. Kant Patel and Mark Rushefsky, *Health Care Politics and Policy in America* (Armonk, N.Y.: M. E. Sharpe, 1999), pp. 115–16.
173. Oberlander, *The Political Life of Medicare*, p. 124.

Chapter Six

1. Alain C. Enthoven, *Health Plan: The Only Practical Solution to the Soaring Cost of Medical Care* (Reading, Mass.: Addison-Wesley, 1980), p. xvii.

2. Joseph Califano Jr., *America's Health Care Revolution: Who Lives? Who Dies? Who Pays?* (New York: Random House, 1986), p. 5.

3. Linda Bergthold, *Purchasing Power in Health: Business, the State, and Health Care Politics* (New Brunswick, N.J.: Rutgers University Press, 1990), p. 4; Betty Leyerle, *Moving and Shaking American Medicine: The Structure of a Socioeconomic Transformation* (Westport, Conn.: Greenwood Press, 1984), p. 31.

4. Bergthold, *Purchasing Power in Health*, p. 2; Jill Quadagno, David MacPherson, and Jennifer Reid Keene, "The Effect of a Job Loss on the Employment Experience, Health Insurance, and Retirement Benefits of Workers in the Banking Industry," in *Ensuring Health and Income Security for an Aging Workforce*, edited by Peter P. Budetti, Richard V. Burkhauser, Janice Gregory, and Allan Hunt (Ann Arbor, Mich.: W. E. Upjohn Institute for Employment Research, 2001), p. 219.

5. Jonathan Oberlander, *The Political Life of Medicare* (Chicago: University of Chicago Press, 2003), p. 55.

6. Carolyn Tuohy, *Accidental Logics: The Dynamics of Change in the Health Care Arena in the United States, Britain, and Canada* (New York: Oxford University Press, 1999), p. 130.

7. Testimony of the Blue Cross and Blue Shield Association on Health Coverage for the Uninsured before the before the U.S. Bipartisan Commission on Comprehensive Health Care (Pepper Commission), p. 3, October 24, 1989, Pepper Library, Florida State University, Tallahassee, Series 302, Box 63, File 8.

8. Letter from Richard Ludwig to Senator John Heinz, October 11, 1989, Pepper Library, Series 302, Box 63, File 8.

9. Jacob S. Hacker, *Blurring the Boundaries: The Battle over Public and Private Social Benefits in the United States* (Cambridge: Cambridge University Press, 2002), p. 256.

10. Testimony of John Motley, Director of Federal Governmental Relations, National Federation of Independent Business, before the Pepper Commission, pp. 3–6, October 24, 1989, Pepper Library, Series 302, Box 63, File 8.

11. Letter from Muriel Mathis, Account Executive, Blue Cross and Blue Shield, September 20, 1989, Pepper Library, Series 302, Box 63, File 8.

12. Thomas Bodenheimer, "Should We Abolish the Private Health Insurance Industry?" *International Journal of Health Services* 20, 2 (1990): 206.

13. Karen Titlow and Ezekiel Emanuel, "Employer Decisions and the Seeds of Backlash," *Health Affairs* 24, 5 (1999): 943.

14. Daniel Fox and Daniel Schaffer, "Health Policy and ERISA: Interest Groups and Semipreemption," *Journal of Health Politics, Policy and Law* 14, 2 (1989): 245, 252; Arnold Birenbaum, *Managed Care: Made in America* (Westport, Conn.: Praeger, 1997), p. 39; Timothy Stoltzfus Jost, *Disentitlement: The Threats Facing Our Public Health-Care Programs and a Rights-Based Response* (New York: Oxford University Press, 2003), p. 185. Corporations also often purchased reinsurance against large, unpredictable claims that they might not be able to pay through their reserve funds.

15. Leyerle, *The Private Regulation of American Health Care*, p. 28. The shift toward self-insurance was not only a response to the failure of many insurers to develop and use effective cost containment data, but also was motivated by a desire to provide equal coverage of employees in different states and avoid state premium taxes.

16. Jeff Goldsmith, "Death of a Paradigm: The Challenge of Competition," *Health Affairs* 3, 3 (1984): 9.
17. Birenbaum, *Managed Care: Made in America*, p. 39; Bodenheimer, "Should We Abolish the Private Health Insurance Industry," p. 205.
18. Birenbaum, *Managed Care: Made in America*, p. 39.
19. Marie Gottschalk, *The Shadow Welfare State: Labor, Business, and the Politics of Health Care in the United States* (Ithaca, N.Y.: Cornell University Press, 2000), p. 121.
20. Robert Blendon, Jennifer Edwards, and Ulrike Szalay, "Managed Care: Key to Health Insurance Reform?" *Health Affairs*, winter 1991.
21. Califano, *America's Health Care Revolution*, p. 11.
22. Lee Iacocca with William Novak, *Iacocca: An Autobiography* (New York: Bantam Books, 1984), pp. 92, 114, 126, 144.
23. Ibid., p. 152.
24. Ibid., p. 192.
25. Ibid., p. 306.
26. Califano, *America's Health Care Revolution*, p. 11.
27. Gottschalk, *The Shadow Welfare State*, p. 100.
28. Califano, *America's Health Care Revolution*, p. 23.
29. Iacocca, *Iacocca*, p. 308.
30. Califano, *America's Health Care Revolution*, p. 29; Melissa Hardy, Lawrence Hazelrigg, and Jill Quadagno, *Ending a Career in the Auto Industry: 30 and Out* (New York: Plenum Press, 1996), p. 87.
31. Iacocca, *Iacocca*, p. 307.
32. Donald Light, "The Practice and Ethics of Risk-Related Health Insurance," *Journal of the American Medical Association* 267, 18 (1992): 2505.
33. Blendon, Edwards, and Szalay, "Managed Care: Key to Health Insurance Reform?"
34. Betty Leyerle, *The Private Regulation of American Health Care* (Armonk, N.Y.: M.E. Sharpe, 1994), pp. 109–10; Titlow and Emanuel, "Employer Decisions and the Seeds of Backlash," p. 943.
35. Leyerle, *The Private Regulation of American Health Care*, pp. 105–6; Tuohy, *Accidental Logics*, p. 137.
36. Quoted in Bergthold, *Purchasing Power in Health*, p. 55.
37. Susan Goldberger, "The Politics of Universal Access: The Massachusetts Health Security Act of 1988," *Journal of Health Politics, Policy and Law* 15, 4 (1990): 857; Bergthold, *Purchasing Power in Health*, pp. 5, 107; Richard Kronick, "The Slippery Slope of Health Care Finance: Business Interests and Hospital Reimbursement in Massachusetts," *Journal of Health Politics, Policy and Law* 15, 4 (1990): 888.
38. Quoted in Bergthold, *Purchasing Power in Health*, p. 54.
39. Testimony of Bruce Miller, Vice President, Motorola, Inc. on behalf of the National Association of Manufacturers before the U.S. Bipartisan Commission on Comprehensive Health Care (Pepper Commission), October 24, 1989, p. 173, Pepper Library; Linda Demkovich, "On Health Issues, This Business Group Is a Leader, But Is Anyone Following?" *National Journal*, June 18, 1983, p. 1278–80.
40. Bergthold, *Purchasing Power in Health*, p. 43.
41. Lawrence D. Brown, "Dogmatic Slumbers: American Business and Health Policy," *Journal of Health Politics, Policy and Law* 18, 2 (1993): 349.

42. Jennifer Klein, *For All These Rights: Business, Labor, and the Shaping of America's Public-Private Welfare State* (Princeton, N.J.: Princeton University Press, 2003), p. 255.

43. Califano, *America's Health Care Revolution*, pp. 13–15.

44. Gottschalk, *The Shadow Welfare State*, p. 110.

45. Oberlander, *The Political Life of Medicare*, p. 49.

46. Robert Clark, Linda Shumaker Ghent, and Alvin Headen, "Retiree Health Insurance and Pension Coverage: Variations and Firm Characteristics," *Journal of Gerontology* 49, 2 (1994): S53; Hardy, Quadagno, and Hazelrigg, *Ending a Career in the Auto Industry*, p. 44.

47. Jill Quadagno and Melissa Hardy, "Private Pensions, State Regulation and Income Security for Older Workers: The U.S. Auto Industry," in *The Privatization of Social Policy? Occupational Welfare and the Welfare State in America, Scandinavia, and Japan*, edited by Michael Shalev (London: Macmillan, 1996), p. 141.

48. Gottschalk, *The Shadow Welfare State*, p. 127.

49. John Neilsen, "Sick Retirees Could Kill Your Company," *Fortune*, March 2, 1987, p. 98.

50. Quoted in Carolyn Rinkus Thompson, "The Political Evolution of the Medicare Catastrophic Health Care Act of 1988," doctoral dissertation, Johns Hopkins University, 1990, p. 131.

51. Neilsen, "Sick Retirees Could Kill Your Company," pp. 98–99.

52. Oberlander, *The Political Life of Medicare*, pp. 53–54; Thompson, "The Political Evolution of the Medicare Catastrophic Health Care Act," p. 132.

53. Richard Himelfarb, *Catastrophic Politics: The Rise and Fall of the Medicare Catastrophic Coverage Act of 1988* (University Park: Pennsylvania State University Press, 1995), p. 19; Paul Charles Light, *Artful Work: The Politics of Social Security Reform* (New York: Random House, 1985), p. 122.

54. Himelfarb, *Catastrophic Politics*, pp. 12–14.

55. Martha Holstein and Meredith Minkler, "The Short Life and Painful Death of the Medicare Catastrophic Coverage Act," *International Journal of Health Services* 21 (1991): 1016; Fernando M. Torres-Gil, "The Politics of Catastrophic and Long-Term Care Coverage," *Journal of Aging and Social Policy* 1 (1989): 65; Steven Rathgeb Smith, "The Role of Institutions and Ideas in Health Care Policy," *Journal of Health Politics, Policy and Law* 20, 2 (1995): 386.

56. "Reagan Tries to Silence Reports of Iran Arms Deal," *Los Angeles Times*, November 6, 1986, Part 1, p. 1.

57. "U.S. Looks for Sign in Captors' Move," *New York Times*, November 4, 1986, p. A11.

58. Quoted in Thompson, *The Political Evolution of the Medicare Catastrophic Health Care Act*, p. 76.

59. Hobart Rowen, *Self-Inflicted Wounds: From LBJ's Guns and Butter to Reagan's Voodoo Economics* (New York: Random House, 1994), p. 211; Robert Pear, "Lawmakers Assail Reagan over Plan for Major Illness," *New York Times*, January 29, 1987, p. A2.

60. Quoted in Himelfarb, *Catastrophic Politics*, p. 22; Julie Rovner, "Reagan Sides with Bowen on Medicare Plan," *Congressional Quarterly*, February 14, 1987, p. 297.

61. Robert Englund, "The Catastrophic Health Care Blunder," *American Spectator*, November 1988, p. 28.

62. Himelfarb, *Catastrophic Politics*, p. 19.
63. Steven Prokesch, "Medicare Expansion Under Fire," *New York Times*, February 12, 1987, p. 1A.
64. Quoted in Debra Street, "Maintaining the Status Quo: The Impact of the Old-Age Interest Groups on the Medicare Catastrophic Coverage Act of 1988," *Social Problems* 40 (1993): 437.
65. Englund, "Catastrophic Blunder," p. 28.
66. Cited in Thompson, "Political Evolution of the Medicare Catastrophic Health Care Act," p. 199.
67. Street, "Maintaining the Status Quo," 435.
68. "The Hospital Lobby Is Suffering from Self-Inflicted Wounds," *National Journal*, October 1, 1977, p. 1526. See also Hospital Costs Containment, Background Report by Office of Media Liaison, The White House Press Office, March 5, 1979, Carter Library, Atlanta, Records of Chief of Staff Butler, Box 101, File: Hospital Cost Containment, 2/24/79–10/29/79.
69. Street, "Maintaining the Status Quo," p. 436.
70. Statement of William S. Hoffman, Director, Social Security Department, UAW, on the subject of Medicare Catastrophic Health Insurance before the Subcommittee on Health, Committee on Ways and Means, U.S. House of Representatives, Washington, D.C., March 10, 1987, Pepper Library, Series 309A, Box 155A, File 1.
71. Himelfarb, *Catastrophic Politics*, pp. 38–39.
72. Englund, "Catastrophic Blunder," p. 30.
73. Julie Rovner, "Catastrophic Costs Conferees Irked by Lobbying Assaults," *Congressional Quarterly*, March 26, 1988, pp. 777–78.
74. Ibid.
75. Spencer Rich, "Drug Makers Fight New Outpatient Benefit," *Washington Post*, September 14, 1987, p. A4.
76. Julie Rovner, "House OKs Medicare Expansion," *Congressional Quarterly*, July 25, 1987, p. 1639.
77. Cited in Thompson, *Political Evolution of the Medicare Catastrophic Health Care Act*, p. 172.
78. Michelle Murphy, "Elderly Lobby Continues to Thrive," *Congressional Quarterly*, March 26, 1988, pp. 778–79.
79. Quoted in Himelfarb, *Catastrophic Politics*, p. 52.
80. Peter J. Ferrera, "The Hidden Costs of Health Coverage for the Elderly," *Wall Street Journal*, April 26, 1988, Pepper Library, Series 302A, File 42, Box 7.
81. Mike Causey, "Spreading the Burden," *Washington Post*, January 5, 1989.
82. Marilyn Moon, *Medicare Now and in the Future*, 2nd ed. (Washington, D.C.: Urban Institute, 1993), p. 108.
83. Englund, "The Catastrophic Health Care Blunder," p. 26; Oberlander, *The Political Life of Medicare*, p. 68
84. Himelfarb, *Catastrophic Politics*, pp. 12–14; Henry J. Pratt, *Gray Agendas: Interest Groups and Public Pensions in Canada, Britain, and the United States* (Ann Arbor: University of Michigan Press, 1993), p. 194; E. M. Abramson, "Planning Ahead for the New Medicare Catastrophic Coverage Act," *Washington Post*, November 7, 1988; "Tax-Snatchers," *Washington Post*, May 2, 1988, Pepper Library, Series 302A, File 42, Box 7.
85. Statement of William S. Hoffman, Director, Social Security Department, UAW, on the subject of Medicare Catastrophic Health Insurance before

the Subcommittee on Health, Committee on Ways and Means, U.S. House of Representatives, Washington, D.C., March 10, 1987, Pepper Library, Series 309A, Box 155A, File 1.

86. Ibid.
87. *Statement of Alan Reuther, Associate General Counsel, UAW, Before the Senate Finance Committee Hearings on Medicare Catastrophic Coverage, July 11, 1989, First Session* (Washington, D.C.: Government Printing Office, 1989), p. 39.
88. Letter from Robert L. Landon to Claude Pepper, October 10, 1988, Pepper Library, Series 309A, Box 155A, File 1; Street, "Maintaining the Status Quo," p. 437; Mike Causey, "A System Gone Haywire," *Washington Post*, January 23, 1989; letter to the editor from Lloyd Unsell, *Washington Post*, October 31, 1989, p. A22; Susan A. MacManus with Patricia A. Turner, *Young v. Old: Generational Combat in the 21st Century* (Boulder, Colo.: Westview Press, 1996), p. 176.
89. Letter from Robert L. Landon to Claude Pepper, October10, 1988, Pepper Library, Series 309A, Box 155A, File 1.
90. Street, "Maintaining the Status Quo," p. 437.
91. Mike Causey, "A System Gone Haywire," *Washington Post*, January 23, 1989.
92. Letter to the editor from Lloyd Unsell.
93. MacManus and Turner, *Young v. Old*, p. 176.
94. Himelfarb, *Catastrophic Politics*, p. 74.
95. Quoted in Pratt, *Gray Agendas*, p. 195.
96. Julie Rovner, "Surtax Reduction a Possibility But Critics Demand Repeal," *Congressional Quarterly*, April 22, 1988, p. 902.
97. Julie Rovner, "Catastrophic Coverage Law Narrowly Survives Test," *Congressional Quarterly*, June 10, 1989, p. 1402.
98. Julie Rovner, "Both Chambers in Retreat," *Congressional Quarterly*, October 7, 1989, p. 2635.
99. Stephen Crystal, "Health Economic, Old-Age Policies and the Catastrophic Medicare Debate," *Journal of Gerontological Social Work* 15 (1990): 21–31; Christine Day, "Older American Attitudes Toward the Medicare Catastrophic Coverage Act of 1988," *Journal of Politics* 55 (1993): 167–77.
100. Julie Rovner, "The Catastrophic Costs Law: A Massive Miscalculation," *Congressional Quarterly*, October 4, 1989, p. 2715.
101. Julie Rovner, "Catastrophic Insurance Law: Costs vs. Benefits," *Congressional Quarterly*, December 3, 1988, p. 3452.
102. Gottschalk, *The Shadow Welfare State*, p. 128; *Retiree Health Benefits: Employer-Sponsored Benefits May Be Vulnerable to Further Erosion*, Report to the Chairman, Committee on Health, Education, Labor and Pensions, U.S. Senate (Washington, D.C.: General Accounting Office, 2001), p. 2.
103. *Retiree Health Trends and Implications of Possible Medicare Reforms* (Washington, D.C.: Kaiser Family Foundation, 2001), p. 1; *Retiree Health Benefits*, p. 10.
104. James Causey, "Pabst to Cut Retiree Benefits," *Milwaukee Journal Sentinel*, August 6, 1996, p. 1.
105. *Retiree Health Benefits*, p. 6; Titlow and Emanuel, "Employer Decisions and the Seeds of Backlash," p. 942
106. Causey, "Pabst to Cut Retiree Benefits," p. 1.
107. *Retiree Health Benefits: Employer-Sponsored Benefits May Be Vulnerable to Further Erosion*, pp. 16–17.

108. George Anders, *Health Against Wealth: HMOs and the Breakdown of Medical Trust* (Boston: Houghton Mifflin, 1996), p. 24.
109. Califano, *America's Health Care Revolution*, pp. 33–34.
110. Leyerle, *The Private Regulation of American Health Care*, p. 21.
111. Anders, *Health Against Wealth*, p. 16.
112. Ibid., p. 30.
113. Ibid., p. 32.
114. Ibid., p. 36.
115. Leyerle, *The Private Regulation of American Health Care*, p. 6.
116. Tuohy, *Accidental Logics*, p. 147; Bodenheimer, "Should We Abolish the Private Health Insurance Industry," p. 208.
117. Statement of Steven P. Kang, M.D., President-Elect, Greater Albuquerque Medical Association, at the Hearings of the Human Resources and Intergovernmental Relations Subcommittee of the Committee on Government Operations, U.S. House of Representatives, 103rd Congress, 1st Session, September 26, 1993, pp. 16–17.
118. Statement of Carol Merovka, M.D., Past President, Greater Albuquerque Medical Association, at the Hearings of the Human Resources and Intergovernmental Relations Subcommittee of the Committee on Government Operations, U.S. House of Representatives, 103rd Congress, 1st Session, September 26, 1993, pp. 28–29.
119. Ibid., p. 30.
120. Ibid., p. 29.
121. Peter Jacobson, "Who Killed Managed Care? A Policy Whodunit," *Saint Louis University Law Journal* 47 (2003): 365–96.
122. Testimony by Cornelia Lange at the Hearings of the Human Resources and Intergovernmental Relations Subcommittee of the Committee on Government Operations, U.S. House of Representatives, 103rd Congress, 1st Session, October 5, 1993, pp. 52–53.
123. Jamie Court and Francis Smith, *Making a Killing: HMOs and the Threat to Your Health* (New York: Common Courage Press, 1999), p. 6.
124. "Prez Rips Health Biz Insurers," *Daily News* (New York), July 8, 1998, p. 26.
125. Birenbaum, *Managed Care*, p. 128.
126. Ibid., p. 135.
127. Court and Smith, *Making a Killing*, p. 8.
128. Anders, *Health Against Wealth*, p. 210; see Chapter 7.
129. Birenbaum, *Managed Care*, p. 121; Clark C. Havighurst, "How the Health Care Revolution Fell Short," *Law and Contemporary Problems* 65, 4 (2002): 61–62.
130. Birenbaum, *Managed Care*, pp. 137, 139.
131. Ibid., p. 139.
132. Gillian Fairfield, David Hunter, David Mechanic, and Flemming Rosleff, "Managed Care: Implications of Managed Care for Health Systems, Clinicians and Patients," *British Medical Journal* 314 (June 1997): 1895.
133. Jerry Geisel, "HMOs See Glory Days Under Clinton," *Business Insurance*, December 18, 1992, p. 6.
134. Anders, *Health Against Wealth*, p. 19.
135. Schwartz, "How Law and Regulation Shape Managed Care," p. 31.
136. Anders, *Health Against Wealth*, p. 216; Birenbaum, *Managed Care*, p. 140.

137. Quoted in Leyerle, *The Private Regulation of American Health Care*, p. 115; Clark C. Havighurst, "Consumers Versus Managed Care: The New Class Actions," *Health Affairs*, 20, 4 (2001): 12.

138. Miriam Laugesen and Thomas Rice, "Is the Doctor In? The Evolving Role of Organized Medicine in Health Policy," *Journal of Health Politics, Policy and Law* 28, 2–3 (2003): 291.

139. Catherine Wilson, "Mediation to Continue in Cigna's Racketeering Suit," *Miami Herald*, April 29, 2003, p. 8B.

140. "Court, 5–4, Upholds Authority of States to Protect Patients," *New York Times*, June 20, 2002, p. 1A.

141. Tom Daschle and Edward Kennedy, "For Patients, a Better Bill of Rights," *Washington Post*, July 13, 1999, p. A19.

142. Donald Baker, "Insurance Proposals Bring Out Lobbyists," *Washington Post*, February 21, 1999, p. C1.

143. Ibid.

144. Fred Barnes, "Patients' Bill of Goods," *Weekly Standard*, August 6, 2001, p. 11.

145. Dan Morgan, "Health Care Lobby Targets GOP Senators on Air," *Washington Post*, July 5, 1999, p. A3.

146. Bennett Roth, "Congress Will Contend Again over Health Issues," *Houston Chronicle*, December 13, 1997, p. A1.

147. Amy Goldstein, "House Approves GOP's Health Insurance Tax Breaks," *Washington Post*, October 7, 1999, p. A12.

148. "AMA Calls on Congress to Vote on Patients' Rights Before August Recess," PR Newswire, www.prnewswire.com, July 19, 2001.

149. Barnes, "Patients' Bill of Goods," p. 11.

150. Robert Pear, "Measure Defining Patients' Rights Passes in House," *New York Times*, August 3, 2001, p. A1; "House Approves Patients' Bill of Rights," United Press International, August 2, 2001.

151. Melanie Eversley, "Georgia Congressman Revives Patients' Rights Bill," *Atlanta Journal and Constitution*, March 9, 2003, p. A1.

152. Robert Hurley, Joy Grossman, Timothy Lake, and Lawrence Casalino, "A Longitudinal Perspective on Health Plan-Provider Risk Contracting," *Health Affairs* 21 (2002): 144–53; Debra Draper, Robert Hurley, Cara Lesser, and Bradley Strunk, "The Changing Face of Managed Care," *Health Affairs* 21, 1 (2003): 14; Suzanne Felt-Lisk and Glen Mays, "From the Field: Back to the Drawing Board: New Directions in Health Plan Care Management Strategies," *Health Affairs* 21, 5 (2003): 216.

153. Birenbaum, *Managed Care*, p. 144.

154. David Mechanic, "The Rise and Fall of Managed Care," *Journal of Health and Social Behavior* 45 (Extra Issue) (2004): 76–86.

Chapter Seven

1. Jeff Goldsmith, "Death of a Paradigm: The Challenge of Competition," *Health Affairs* 3, 3 (1984): 10.

2. U.S. House of Representatives, Committee on Energy and Commerce, Subcommittee on Oversight and Investigations, Hearings on Insurance Company Failures, 101st Congress, 1st Session, August 3, 1989, p. 587.

3. Nursing Home Insurance: Exploiting Fear for Profit? Joint Hearing before the Subcommittee on Health and Long-Term Care and the Subcommittee

on Housing and Consumer Interests, Select Committee on Aging, U.S. House of Representatives, 100th Congress, 1st Session, August 6, 1987, p. 42.

4. Claude Pepper, "Long-Term Care Insurance: The First Step Toward Comprehensive Health Insurance," *Journal of Aging and Social Policy* 1 (1989): 10–11.

5. Jill Quadagno, Madonna Harrington Meyer, and Blake Turner, "Falling Through the Medicaid Gap: The Hidden Long Term Care Dilemma," *Gerontologist* 31 (1991): 521–26.

6. Madonna Harrington Meyer, "Universalism vs. Targeting as the Basis of Social Distribution: Gender, Race and Long Term Care in the U.S.," doctoral dissertation, Florida State University, Tallahassee, 1991, p. 105.

7. Madonna Harrington Meyer and Michelle Kesterke Storbakken, "Shifting the Burden Back to Families?" in *Care Work: Gender, Labor and the Welfare State*, edited by Madonna Harrington Meyer (New York: Routledge, 2000), p. 219.

8. Ibid., p. 221.

9. Joseph Angelelli, Vincent Mor, Orna Intrator, Zhanlian Feng, and Jacqueline Zinn, "Oversight of Nursing Homes: Pruning the Tree or Just Spotting Bad Apples?" *Gerontologist* 43 (2003): 74.

10. Martha Holstein and Meredith Minkler, "The Short Life and Painful Death of the Medicare Catastrophic Coverage Act," *International Journal of Health Services* 21 (1991): 1016; Fernando M. Torres-Gil, "The Politics of Catastrophic and Long-Term Care Coverage," *Journal of Aging and Social Policy* 1 (1989): 68; Steven Rathgeb Smith, "The Role of Institutions and Ideas in Health Care Policy," *Journal of Health Politics, Policy and Law* 20, 2 (1995): 386.

11. Charlene Harrington, "Social Security and Medicare: Policy Shifts in the 1980s," in *Fiscal Austerity and Aging: Shifting Government Responsibility for the Elderly*, edited by Carroll L. Estes, Robert Newcomer, et al. (Beverly Hills, Calif.: Sage, 1983), p. 93; Torres-Gil, "The Politics of Catastrophic and Long-Term Care Coverage," p. 74.

12. Harrington, Meyer, and Storbakken, "Shifting the Burden Back to Families?" p. 219.

13. Ibid., p. 225.

14. Ibid., p. 224.

15. Jeff Goldsmith, "Death of a Paradigm: The Challenge of Competition," *Health Affairs* 3, 3 (1984): 9–10; Thomas Bodenheimer, "Should We Abolish the Private Health Insurance Industry?" *International Journal of Health Services* 20, 2 (1990): 205.

16. Jon Gabel and Alan Monheit, "Will Competition Plans Change Insurer-Provider Relationships?" *Milbank Memorial Fund Quarterly* 61 (1983): 610–40.

17. Laurence F. Lane, "The Potential of Private Long Term Care Insurance," p. 17, Pepper Library, Florida State University, Tallahassee, Series 302A, File 60, Box 5.

18. *Abuses in the Sale of Health Insurance to the Elderly in Supplementation of Medicare*, House of Representatives, Select Committee on Aging (Washington, D.C.: U.S. Government Printing Office, 1977), pp. 102–3.

19. Nursing Home Insurance: Exploiting Fear for Profit, p. 38.

20. Richard Himelfarb, *Catastrophic Politics: The Rise and Fall of the Medicare Catastrophic Coverage Act of 1988* (University Park: Pennsylvania State University Press, 1995), p. 13.

21. Bodenheimer, "Should We Abolish the Private Health Insurance Industry," p. 214.
22. Private Long-Term Care Insurance: Unfit for Sale? Report by the Chairman of the Subcommittee on Health and Long-Term Care of the Select Committee on Aging, U.S. House of Representatives, 101st Congress, 1st Session, May 1989, p. 1.
23. Donald Light, "The Practice and Ethics of Risk-Related Health Insurance," *Journal of the American Medical Association* 267, 18 (1992): 2506.
24. *Retiree Health Benefits: Employer-Sponsored Benefits May Be Vulnerable to Further Erosion*, Report to the Chairman, Committee on Health, Education, Labor and Pensions, U.S. Senate (Washington, D.C.: General Accounting Office, 2001), p. 24.
25. Lane, "The Potential of Private Long Term Care Insurance," pp. 18–19.
26. Nancy Benac, "Lies, Abuses Cited in Long-Term Health Policy Sales," Associated Press, n.d., Pepper Library, Series 302A, File 42, Box 7.
27. Letter from Roger Singer, Commissioner of Insurance, Commonwealth of Massachusetts, to Claude Pepper, August 4, 1987, Pepper Library, Series S302A, Box 60, File 1.
28. Statement of Bonnie Burns, Medicare Specialist and Consumer Advocate, Before the Subcommittee on Health and Long-Term Care, House of Representatives, August 6, 1987, Pepper Library, Series 507A, Box 100, File 3.
29. "Insurance for Elderly Increasing," *Washington Post*, March 18, 1987, Pepper Library, Series S302A, Box 60, File 5.
30. "Catastrophic Health Insurance: Filling the Long-Term Care Gap," Statement of the American Association of Retired Persons Before the House Select Committee on Aging, Subcommittee on Health and Long Term Care, July 2, 1987.
31. Private Long-Term Care Insurance: Unfit for Sale, pp. 2–4.
32. Robert Pear, "Wide Abuse Cited in Nursing Home Insurance," *New York Times*, June 26, 1991, p. A1.
33. "Long Term Care Insurance," Statement of Michael Zimmerman, Human Resource Division of GAO, Before the Subcommittee on Health and Long-Term Care, House of Representatives, August 6, 1987, Pepper Library, Series S307A, Box 100, File 3.
34. Letter from Robert T. Matteson to Hon. Claude Pepper, May 25, 1988. Pepper Library, Series S302A, Box 60, File 1.
35. Letter from Janet Dimaya Ramos to Senate Commission on Aging, September 28, 1985. Pepper Library, Series S302A, Box 27, File 7.
36. The bill would also establish a home care quality assurance program that would create peer review organizations. The PROs would be responsible for monitoring the quality of home care services, conduct unannounced inspections of home care agencies, and impose penalties on noncomplying organizations.
37. Letter from Claude Pepper and Edward Roybal to House of Representatives, May 31, 1988, Pepper Library, Series 302A, File 42, Box 3.
38. "Catastrophic Health Insurance: The Long-Term Care Gap," statement of Claude Pepper, chairman of the Subcommittee on Health and Long-Term Care of the House Committee on Aging, July 2, 1987, Pepper Library, Series 307A, Box 100, File 1.
39. Health Insurance Association of America Comments on H.R. 3436, April 26, 1988, p. 1, Pepper Library, Series 302A, File 42, Box 7.

40. Ibid., pp. 2–4.
41. Ibid., p. 17.
42. Letter to Claude Pepper from Coordinating Committee for Long Term Care, April 22, 1988, Pepper Library, Series 302A, File 42, Box 7.
43. Letter from Albert Bourland, vice president for Congressional relations, Chamber of Commerce, May 23, 1988, Pepper Library, Series 302A, File 42, Box 7.
44. Letter from John Motley, director, Federal Government Relations, National Federation of Independent Business, June 2, 1988, Pepper Library, Series 302A, File 42, Box 7.
45. Letter from Jerry Jasinowski, executive vice president, National Association of Manufacturers, May 17, 1988, Pepper Library, Series 302A, File 42, Box 7.
46. "Elderly Lobby Peppers the House on Health Bill," *Wall Street Journal*, May 6, 1988, Pepper Library, Series 302A, File 42, Box 7.
47. Letter from Otis R. Bowen, Secretary of Health and Human Services, June 8, 1988, Pepper Library, Series 302A, File 42, Box 7.
48. Letter from Linda Kenckes, vice president, federal affairs, Health Insurance Association of America, Pepper Library, Series 302A, File 42, Box 7; "Long-Term Care Bill Derailed—For Now," *Congressional Quarterly*, June 11, 1988, p. 1604.
49. "Faces of Medicaid," Kaiser Commission on Medicaid and the Uninsured, Kaiser Family Foundation, Washington, D.C., April 2004, p. 7.
50. Colleen Grogan and Eric Patashnik, "Universalism Within Targeting: Nursing Home Care, the Middle Class, and the Politics of the Medicaid Program," *Social Service Review* 77, 1 (2003): 61.
51. Testimony of Gail Shearer, Consumers Union, before the Subcommittee on Health and Environment, Energy and Commerce Committee and the Subcommittee on Health and Long-Term Care, Select Committee on Aging, U.S. House of Representatives, Hearings on Abuses in the Sale of Long Term Care Insurance to the Elderly, n.d., Pepper Library, Series 302A, Box 28, File 7.
52. Private Long Term Care Insurance: Unfit for Sale, p. 2.
53. Ibid., p. 3.
54. Testimony of John Gilmore before the Subcommittee on Health and Long Term Care, Select Committee on Aging, U.S. House of Representatives, 101st Congress, 1st Session, May 1989, mimeograph, Pepper Library, Series 309A, Box 100, File 3.
55. Justin Keen, Donald Light, and Nicholas May, *Public-Private Relations in Health Care* (London: King's Fund Publishing, 2001), p. 120.
56. Hans Riedel, "Private Compulsory Long Term Care Insurance in Germany," *Geneva Papers on Risk and Insurance* 28, 2 (2003): 275–93.
57. Linda Bergthold, *Purchasing Power in Health: Business, the State, and Health Care Politics* (New Brunswick, N.J.: Rutgers University Press, 1990), p. 41; Mark A. Peterson, "Clinton's Plan Goes to Congress—Now What," *Journal of Health Politics, Policy and Law* 14, 2 (1994): 265.
58. Karen Pollitz, "Extending Health Insurance Coverage for Older Workers and Early Retirees," in *Ensuring Health and Income Security for an Aging Workforce*, edited by Peter B. Budetti, Richard V. Burkhauser, Janice M. Gregory, and H. Allan Hunt (Kalamazoo, Mich.: Upjohn Institute for Employment Research, 2001), p. 239.

59. Cindy Mann, Diane Rowland, and Rachel Garfield, "Historical Overview of Children's Health Care Coverage," *The Future of Children* 13, 1 (2003): 35.
60. Ibid., p. 36.
61. Linda Bilheimer and David Colby, "Expanding Coverage: Reflections on Recent Efforts," *Health Affairs,* January/February 2001, p. 84.
62. Marsha Gold, Jessica Mittler, Anna Aizer, Barbara Lyons, and Cathy Schoen, "Health Insurance Expansion Through States in a Pluralistic System," *Journal of Health Politics, Policy and Law* 26, 3 (2001): 593.
63. Leighton Ku and Bowen Garrett, "How Welfare Reform and Economic Factors Affected Medicaid Participation: 1984–1996," Discussion Paper, Urban Institute, Washington, D.C., 2000, p. 11.
64. H. E. Freeman, L. H. Aiken, R. J. Blendon, and C. R Corey, "Uninsured Working-Age Adults: Characteristics and Consequences," *Health Services Research* 24 (1990): 812–23.
65. Keen, Light, and May, *Public-Private Relations in Health Care*, pp. 115–16; Light, "The Practice and Ethics of Risk-Related Health Insurance," pp. 2503–4.
66. Statement of the American Medical Association Before the Bipartisan Commission on Comprehensive Health Care, Re: Providing Adequate Health Insurance Coverage to the Uninsured and Underinsured, October 24, 1989, p. 73, Pepper Library, Series 302, Box 63, File 8; Light, "The Practice and Ethics of Risk-Related Health Insurance," p. 2507; see also Bodenheimer, "Should We Abolish the Private Health Insurance Industry?" p. 213.
67. Mark Schlesinger, "Reprivatizing the Public Household? Medical Care in the Context of American Public Values," *Journal of Health Politics, Policy and Law* 29, 4–5 (2004): 969–2004.
68. "Catastrophic Health Insurance: The Long-Term Care Gap," Statement of Claude Pepper, Chairman of the Subcommittee on Health and Long-Term Care, of the House Committee on Aging, July 2, 1987, Pepper Library, Series 307A, Box 100, File 1.
69. Pepper Commission, Health Legislation and Regulation, F&G, vol. 16, no. 9, March 7, 1990, Pepper Library, Series 302A, Box 63, File 1.
70. Statement of the American Medical Association Before the Bipartisan Commission on Comprehensive Health Care, p. 73.
71. Statement of Paul Rettig Before the Bipartisan Commission on Comprehensive Health Care, October 24, 1989, Pepper Library, Series 302, Box 63, File 8.
72. Marie Gottschalk, *The Shadow Welfare State: Labor, Business and the Politics of Health Care in the United States* (Ithaca, N.Y.: ILR Press, 2000), p. 106.
73. Lee Iacocca with Sonny Kleinfield, *Talking Straight* (New York: Bantam Books, 1988), p. 260.
74. "GM Weighs National Health Care," *Detroit News*, March 16, 1988, pp. 1–2C.
75. Cited in Cathie Jo Martin, "Together Again: Business, Government and the Quest for Cost Control," *Journal of Health Politics, Policy and Law* 18, 2 (1993): 369.
76. Peter Swenson and Scott Greer, "Foul Weather Friends: Big Business and Health Care Reform in the 1990s in Historical Perspective," *Journal of Health Politics, Policy and Law* 27, 4 (2002): 605.

77. Statement of John Motley III, National Federation of Independent Business, Before the Bipartisan Commission on Comprehensive Health Care, October 24, 1989, Pepper Library, Series 302, Box 63, File 8.

78. Testimony of Charles Kahn, Executive Vice President of the Health Insurance Association of America, Before the House Subcommittee on Health and the Environment, Hearings on H.R. 1200, American Health Security Act of 1993, U.S. House of Representatives, Washington, D.C., February 1, 1994.

79. Testimony of Carl Schramm, President of the Health Insurance Association of America, before the Bipartisan Commission on Comprehensive Health Care, October 24, 1989, pp. 3–11, Pepper Library, Series 302, Box 63, File 8.

80. Jerry Geisel, "HMOs See Glory Days Under Clinton," *Business Insurance*, December 18, 1992, p. 6.

81. Alain Enthoven, *Health Plan: The Only Practical Solution to the Soaring Cost of Medical Care* (Reading, Mass.: Addison-Wesley, 1980); "Clinton Plan Rewards Big Insurers," letter to the editor, *New York Times*, November, 7, 1993.

82. Statement by Samuel Havens, Group Health Association of America, before the Bipartisan Commission on Comprehensive Health Care, October 24, 1989, Pepper Library, Series 302, Box 63, File 8.

83. Haynes Johnson and David Broder, *The System: American Politics at the Breaking Point* (Boston: Little, Brown, 1997), p. 60.

84. Jacob S. Hacker, *The Road to Nowhere: The Genesis of President Clinton's Plan for Health Security* (Princeton, N.J.: Princeton University Press, 1997), pp. 27–28.

85. Cited in ibid., p. 105.

86. Rowen, *Self-Inflicted Wounds*, p. 214.

87. Bob Woodward, *The Agenda: Inside the Clinton White House* (New York: Simon and Schuster, 1994), p. 164.

88. Johnson and Broder, *The System*, p. 96.

89. Hillary Rodham Clinton, *Living History* (New York: Simon and Schuster, 2003), p. 154.

90. Theda Skocpol, *Boomerang: Health Care Reform and the Turn Against Government in U.S. Politics* (New York: W. W. Norton, 1996), p. 78.

91. Clinton, *Living History*, pp. 115–16.

92. Woodward, *The Agenda*, p. 169.

93. Clinton, *Living History*, p. 190.

94. Johnson and Broder, *The System*, p. 188.

95. Clinton, *Living History*, p. 189.

96. Ibid., p. 193.

97. Hacker, *The Road to Nowhere*, p. 53.

98. Ibid., p. 56; Carolyn Tuohy, *Accidental Logics: The Dynamics of Change in the Health Care Arena in the United States, Britain and Canada* (New York: Oxford University Press, 1999), p. 75.

99. Jim Duffett, "Private Health Insurers Cost Too Much," *Chicago Sun-Times*, December 18, 1993, p. 16.

100. Darrell M. West, Diane Heith, and Chris Goodwin, "Harry and Louise Go to Washington: Political Advertising and Health Care Reform," *Journal of Health Politics, Policy and Law* 21, 1 (1996): 41.

101. "Insurance File: Diagnosis for a Reformed Health System," *Lloyd's List International*, November 2, 1993, p. 4.
102. Darrell M. West and Burdette Loomis, *The Sound of Money: How Political Interests Get What They Want* (New York: W. W. Norton, 1999), p. 79.
103. Raymond Goldsteen, Karen Goldsteen, James Swan, and Wendy Clemena, "Harry and Louise and Health Care Reform: Romancing Public Opinion," *Journal of Health Politics, Policy and Law* 26, 4 (2001): 1329; Johnson and Broder, *The System*, pp. 90–92.
104. Skocpol, *Boomerang*.
105. Dana Priest, "First Lady Lambasts Health Insurers," *Washington Post*, November 2, 1993, p. A1.
106. Goldsteen, Goldsteen, Swan, and Clemena, "Harry and Louise and Health Care Reform," p. 1332.
107. West and Loomis, *The Sound of Money*, p. 100.
108. West, Heith, and Goodwin, "Harry and Louise Go to Washington," p. 61.
109. Center for Public Integrity, "Well-Heeled: Inside Lobbying for Health Care Reform: Part II," *International Journal of Health Services* 25 (1995): 613.
110. Christopher Connell, "Health Insurers Mount Attack on Clinton Plan," Associated Press, October 18, 1993.
111. Center for Public Integrity, "Well-Heeled," p. 609.
112. Martin, "Together Again," 383.
113. Tuohy, *Accidental Logics*, p. 81.
114. Gottschalk, *The Shadow Welfare State*, p. 130.
115. Johnson and Broder, *The System*, p. 317.
116. Swenson and Greer, "Foul Weather Friends," p. 610.
117. Johnson and Broder, *The System*, p. 221.
118. Clinton, *Living History*, p. 246.
119. Miriam Laugesen and Thomas Rice, "Is the Doctor In? The Evolving Role of Organized Medicine in Health Policy," *Journal of Health Politics, Policy and Law* 28, 2–3 (2003): 296.
120. Tuohy, *Accidental Logics*, pp. 153–54.
121. Johnson and Broder, *The System*; Skocpol, *Boomerang*; Hacker, *The Road to Nowhere*, p. 28.
122. Quoted in Clinton, *Living History*, p. 230.
123. Johnson and Broder, *The System*, p. 195.
124. Center for Public Integrity, "Well-Heeled," p. 607.
125. Ibid., p. 608.
126. Gottschalk, *The Shadow Welfare State*, p. 153; Center for Public Integrity, "Well-Heeled," pp. 594–95.
127. Clinton, *Living History*, p. 233.
128. Ibid., p. 230.
129. West and Loomis, *The Sound of Money*, p. 93.
130. Clinton, *Living History*, p. 247.
131. Skocpol, *Boomerang*, p. 171.
132. TANF did allow states some flexibility in instituting these new regulations. John Holahan and Niall Brennan, "Who Are the Adult Uninsured?" National Survey of America's Families, Series B, No. B-14, Urban Institute, Washington, D.C., March 2000, p. 2.
133. Ku and Garrett, "How Welfare Reform and Economic Factors Affected Medicaid Participation," p. 12; Leighton Ku and Brian Bruen, "The Continuing

Decline in Medicaid Coverage," Assessing the New Federalism, Series A, No. A-37, Urban Institute, Washington, D.C., 1999, p. 3.

134. Bowen Garrett and John Holahan, "Welfare Leavers, Medicaid Coverage and Private Health Insurance," National Survey of America's Families, Series B, No. B-13, Urban Institute, Washington, D.C., 2000, p. 1.

135. Marilyn Ellwood and Carol Irvin, "Welfare Leavers and Medicaid Dynamics: Five States in 1995," Mathematica Policy Research, Cambridge, Mass., April 14, 2000, p. 2; Garrett and Holahan, "Welfare Leavers," p. 1.

136. Ku and Bruen, "The Continuing Decline in Medicaid Coverage, " p. 2; Ruth Almedia and Genevieve Kenney, "Gaps in Insurance Coverage for Children: A Pre-CHIP Baseline," Assessing the New Federalism, Series B, No. B-19, Urban Institute, Washington, D.C., 2000, p. 2. After 2002 states were required to provide Medicaid coverage to all children under age 19 whose family income fell below the federal poverty level. See Mann, Rowland, and Garfield, "Historical Overview of Children's Health Care Coverage," p. 36; Gabrielle Lessard and Leighton Ku, "Gaps in Coverage for Children in Immigrant Families," *The Future of Children* 13, 1 (2003): 101.

137. B. C. Strunk and J. D. Reschovsky, "Trends in U.S. Health Insurance Coverage, 2001–2003: Results from the Community Tracking Survey," Robert Wood Johnson Foundation Tracking Report No. 9, August 2004.

138. P. J. Cunningham, "SCHIP Making Progress: Increased Take-Up Contributes to Coverage Gains," *Health Affairs* 22, 4 (2003): 163–72; Holahan and Brennan, "Who Are the Adult Uninsured?" p. 1.

139. Gulnur Scott and Hanyu Ni, "Access to Health Care Among Hispanic/ Latino Children: United States, 1998–2001," *Advance Data from Vital and Health Statistics* 344 (2004): 3.

140. Mann, Rowland, and Garfield, "Historical Overview of Children's Health Care Coverage," p. 36.

141. Ibid., p. 36; Lessard and Ku, "Gaps in Coverage for Children in Immigrant Families," p. 101.

142. Gold, Mittler, Aizer, Lyons, and Schoen, "Health Insurance Expansion Through States in a Pluralistic System," pp. 598, 600.

143. Mann, Rowland, and Garfield, "Historical Overview of Children's Health Care Coverage," p. 42.

144. Testimony of Charles Kahn, Executive Vice President of the Health Insurance Association of America, Before the House Subcommittee on Commerce, Consumer Protection and Competitiveness, U.S. House of Representatives, November 16, 1993.

145. Robert Pear, "Insurers Fighting a Bipartisan Bill for Health Care," *New York Times*, February 2, 1996, p. A1.

146. David G. Smith, *Entitlement Politics: Medicare and Medicaid, 1995–2001* (New York: Aldine de Gruyter, 2002), p. 159.

147. Katherine Swartz and Betsey Stevenson, "Health Insurance Coverage of People in the Ten Years Before Medicare Eligibility," in *Ensuring Health and Income Security for an Aging Workforce*, edited by Peter B. Budetti, Richard V. Burkhauser, Janice M. Gregory, and H. Allan Hunt (Kalamazoo, Mich.: Upjohn Institute for Employment Research, 2001), pp. 13–40; Timothy Stoltzfus Jost, *Disentitlement? The Threats Facing Our Public Health-Care Programs and a Rights-Based Response* (New York: Oxford University Press, 2003), pp. 188–89.

148. "Pulling Back on Health Care," editorial, *Washington Post*, April 13, 1998, p. A22.
149. Jody Miller and Matt Miller, "Singled Out," *New York Times Magazine*, April 18, 2004, p. 48, 50.
150. Jennifer Mellor, "Filling in the Gaps in Long Term Care Insurance," in *Care Work: Gender, Labor and the Welfare State*, edited by Madonna Harrington Meyer (New York: Routledge, 2000), p. 205.
151. Ibid., p. 208.
152. Joshua Weiner, "Financing Reform for Long Term Care: Strategies for Public and Private Long Term Care Insurance," in *From Nursing Homes to Home Care*, edited by Marie Cowart and Jill Quadagno (New York: Haworth Press, 1996), p. 116.
153. Testimony by Bertram Scott, Executive Vice President, TIAA-CREF, before the Senate Special Committee on Aging Hearing on Offering Retirement Security to the Federal Family: A New Long Term Care Initiative, April 10, 2002.
154. Sally Roberts, "More Employers Offering Long Term Care Programs," *Business Insurance*, September 29, 2003, p. T4.
155. "For More Insurers, It's LTC Ya Later," Crain Communications, *Investment News*, September 1, 2003, p. 1.
156. William D. Spector, Joel W. Cohen, and Irena Pesis-Katz, "Home Care Before and After the Balanced Budget Act of 1997," *Gerontologist* 44, 1 (2004): 40.
157. Gail Wilensky, "The Balanced Budget Act of 1997: A Current Look at its Impact on Patients and Providers," Statement before the Subcommittee on Health and Environment, Committee on Commerce, U.S. House of Representatives, Washington, D.C., July 19, 2000, p. 2.
158. "The Future of Retiree Health Benefits: Challenges and Options," Testimony of Patricia Neuman, Henry J. Kaiser Foundation, Before the Subcommittee on Employer-Employee Relations, U.S. House of Representatives, November 1, 2001, p. 4; Marsha Gold and Timothy Lake, *Medicare+Choice in California: Lessons and Insights*, Henry J. Kaiser Family Foundation, Washington, D.C., September 2002, p. 1.
159. Jacob Hacker and Theodore Marmor, "Medicare Reform: Fact, Fiction and Foolishness," *Public Policy and Aging Report* 13, 4 (2004): 1.
160. Jonathan Oberlander, "The Politics of Medicare Reform," *Washington and Lee Law Review* 60, 4 (2003): 1135.
161. Quoted in William Weissert, "Medicare Rx: Just a Few of the Reasons Why It Was So Difficult to Pass," *Public Policy and Aging Report* 13, 4 (2004): 3–4.
162. I owe this insight to William Weissert.
163. Skocpol, *Boomerang*, pp. 163–64, 71; Gottschalk, *The Shadow Welfare State*, pp. 157–58; Marie Gottschalk, "It's the Health-Care Costs, Stupid: Ideas, Institutions and the Politics of Organized Labor and Health Policy in the United States," *Studies in American Political Development* 14, 2 (2000): 234; Lawrence R. Jacobs and Robert Shapiro, "Don't Blame the Public for Failed Health Care Reform," *Journal of Health Politics, Policy and Law* 20, 2 (1995): 413; James Morone, "Nativism, Hollow Corporations and Managed Competition: Why the Clinton Health Care Reform Failed," *Journal of Health Politics, Policy and Law* 20, 2 (1995): 392–93; Sven Steinmo and Jon Watts,

"It's the Institutions, Stupid! Why Comprehensive National Health Insurance Always Fails in America," *Journal of Health Politics, Policy and Law*
20, 2 (1995): 330; Vincente Navarro, "Why Congress Did Not Enact Health
Care Reform," *Journal of Health Politics, Policy and Law* 20, 2 (1995): 458.

Chapter Eight

1. Strunk and Reschovsky, "Trends in U.S. Health Insurance Coverage," p.
   1. This figure actually overstates the amount of employment-based coverage, because it includes Medicare beneficiaries who have supplemental medigap benefits from a former employer, employees who purchase a
   group health insurance package through an employer but pay all of the
   costs themselves, and government employees whose insurance is paid
   with tax dollars. Once these groups are excluded from estimates, only 43
   percent of the population is insured through a private employer. See
   Olveen Carrasquillo, David Himmelstein, Steffie Woolhandler, and David
   Bor, "A Reappraisal of Private Employers' Role in Providing Health Insurance," *New England Journal of Medicine* 340, 2 (1999): 111.
2. *Retiree Health Benefits: Employer-Sponsored Benefits May Be Vulnerable to
   Further Erosion*, Report to the Chairman, Committee on Health, Education, Labor and Pensions, U.S. Senate (Washington, D.C.: General Accounting Office, 2001), p. 6.
3. Holly J. McCammon, Karen E. Campbell, Ellen M. Granberg, and Christine Mowery, "How Movements Win: Gendered Opportunity Structures
   and U.S. Women's Suffrage Movements, 1866 to 1919," *American Sociological Review* 66 (2001): 51.
4. Margaret R. Somers, "What's Political or Cultural About Political Culture and the Public Sphere? Toward an Historical Sociology of Concept
   Formation," *Sociological Theory* 13, 2 (1995): 123.
5. Murray Edelman, *Constructing the Political Spectacle* (Chicago: University
   of Chicago Press, 1995); Anne E. Kane, "Theorizing Meaning Construction in Social Movements: Symbolic Structures and Interpretation During the Irish Land War, 1879–1882," *Sociological Theory* 15, 3 (1997): 249–76;
   Deborah Stone, *Policy Paradox: The Art of Political Decision Making* (New
   York: W. W. Norton, 1997), p. 11; Nicholas Pedriana and Robin Stryker,
   "Political Culture Wars 1960s Style: Equal Employment Opportunity—
   Affirmative Action Law and the Philadelphia Plan," *American Journal of
   Sociology* 103 (1997): 634–91.
6. Jan E. Mutchler and Jeffrey A. Burr, "Racial Differences in Health and
   Health Care Service Utilization in Later Life: The Effect of Socioeconomic
   Status," *Journal of Health and Social Behavior* 32, 4 (1991): 351.
7. Gwendolyn Mink, *Welfare's End* (Ithaca, NY: Cornell University Press,
   1998), p. 23; James Morone, "Nativism, Hollow Corporations, and Managed Competition: Why the Clinton Health Care Reform Failed," *Journal
   of Health Politics, Policy and Law* 20, 2 (1995): 393.
8. Paul Pierson, "Increasing Returns: Path Dependence and the Study of
   Politics," *American Political Science Review* 94, 2 (2000): 252.
9. Volker Amelung, Sherry Glied, and Angelina Topan, "Health Care and
   the Labor Market: Learning from the German Experience," *Journal of Health
   Politics, Policy and Law*, 28, 4 (2003): 693–94.

10. Justin Keen, Donald Light, and Nicholas May, *Public-Private Relations in Health Care* (London: King's Fund Publishing, 2001), pp. 116–17.
11. "Findings from 17 State Survey," America's Health Insurance Plans, April 12, 2004.
12. Timothy Stoltzfus Jost, *Disentitlement? The Threats Facing Our Public Health Care Programs and a Rights-Based Response* (New York: Oxford University Press, 2003), p. 272.
13. "Bush Administration Medicaid/SCHIP Proposal," May, 2003, Kaiser Commission on Medicaid and the Uninsured, Henry J. Kaiser Family Foundation, Washington, D.C., 2003, p. 4
14. Kathleen Stoll and Kim Jones, "One in Three: Non-Elderly Americans Without Health Insurance 2002–2003," Families USA Foundation, Washington, D.C., 2004, p. 10.
15. "Challenges and Tradeoffs in Low-Income Family Budgets: Implications for Health Coverage," Kaiser Commission on Medicaid and the Uninsured, Henry J. Kaiser Family Foundation, Washington, D.C., 2004, p. 3.
16. Judith Feder, Larry Levitt, Ellen O'Brien, and Diane Rowland, "Covering the Low-Income Uninsured: The Case for Expanding Public Programs," *Health Affairs* 20, 1 (2001): 28.
17. Kenneth E. Thorpe, "Federal Costs and Savings Associated with Senator Kerry's Health Care Plan," Rollins School of Public Health, Emory University, Atlanta, Georgia, August 2, 2004.
18. "Job Loss, Rising Premiums Take Toll on Employer Health Coverage in 2003," Robert Wood Johnson Foundation news release, August 20, 2004.
19. "Bush Administration Medicaid/SCHIP Proposal," p. 2.
20. "Challenges and Tradeoffs in Low-Income Family Budgets," p. 4.
21. "The State of Retiree Health Benefits: Historical Trends and Future Uncertainties," Testimony of Patricia Neuman to the Special Committee on Aging, U.S. Senate, Washington, D.C., May 17, 2004, p. 2.
22. Quoted in Gail Sheehy, *New Passages: Mapping Your Life Across Time* (New York: Random House), p. 261.
23. "The State of Retiree Health Benefits," p. 1.
24. Stoll and Jones, "One in Three," p. 6.
25. Carrasquillo, Himmelstein, Woolhandler, and Bor, "A Reappraisal of Private Employers' Role," p. 112.
26. Kenneth E. Thorpe, "The Impact of Sen. John Kerry's Health Care Proposal on Health Care Costs," Rollins School of Public Health, Emory University, Atlanta, Georgia, June 2004, p. 1.
27. Ibid., p. 3.
28. Keen, Light, and May, *Public-Private Relations in Health Care*, p. 132.
29. "Employer Health Benefits: 2004 Summary of Findings," Kaiser Commission on Medicaid and the Uninsured, Kaiser Family Foundation, Washington, D.C., 2004, p. 1.
30. Thorpe, "The Impact of Sen. John Kerry's Health Care Proposal on Health Care Costs," p. 3.
31. Linda Bilheimer and David Colby, "Expanding Coverage: Reflections on Recent Efforts," *Health Affairs,* January/February 2001, p. 86.
32. John Holahan and Niall Brennan, "Who Are the Adult Uninsured?" National Survey of America's Families, series B, no. B-14, Urban Institute, Washington, D.C., March 2000, p. 2.

33. Colin Gordon, *Dead on Arrival: The Politics of Health Care in Twentieth-Century America* (Princeton, N.J.: Princeton University Press, 2003), p. 11.
34. Doug McAdam and Yang Su, "The War at Home: Antiwar Protests and Congressional Voting, 1965–1973," *American Sociological Review* 67, 5 (2002): 696–721.
35. Constance Nathanson, "The Skeptic's Guide to a Movement for Universal Health Insurance," *Journal of Health Politics, Policy and Law* 28, 2–3 (2003): 443–72; Paul Pierson, *Dismantling the Welfare State: Reagan, Thatcher and the Politics of Retrenchment* (Cambridge: Cambridge University Press, 1994), p. 22.
36. Theda Skocpol, Marshall Ganz, and Ziad Munson, "A Nation of Organizers: The Institutional Origins of Civic Volunteerism in the United States," *American Political Science Review* 94, 3 (2000): 528.

Index

J. I. PACKER

EVANGELISM

& THE

SOVEREIGNTY

OF GOD

InterVarsity Press
Downers Grove, Illinois

InterVarsity Press
P.O. Box 1400, Downers Grove, IL 60515-1426
World Wide Web: www.ivpress.com
E-mail: mail@ivpress.com

InterVarsity Press® is the book-publishing division of InterVarsity Christian Fellowship/USA®, a student movement active on campus at hundreds of universities, colleges and schools of nursing in the United States of America, and a member movement of the International Fellowship of Evangelical Students. For information about local and regional activities, write Public Relations Dept., InterVarsity Christian Fellowship/USA, 6400 Schroeder Rd., P.O. Box 7895, Madison, WI 53707-7895.

Cover photograph: R. Harris / Photo Researchers, Inc.

ISBN 0-8308-1339-X

Printed in the United States of America ∞

Library of Congress Catalog Card Number: 67-28875

27	26	25	24	23	22	21	20	19	18	17	16	15	14	13	12
17	16	15	14	13	12	11	10	09	08	07	06	05	04	03	02

CONTENTS

FOREWORD

THE nucleus of the following discourse was an
address given at the Pre-Mission Conference
of the London Inter-Faculty Christian Union
on October 24th, 1959. It has been expanded in the
hope of giving it a wider usefulness. Its origin, and
the practical nature of its subject-matter, accounts
for its homiletical style.

Lest its purpose be misconceived, may I say at the
outset what it is not.

It is not a blueprint for evangelistic action today,
though it sets out relevant principles for determining any evangelistic strategy.

It is not a contribution to the current controversy
about modern evangelistic methods, though it lays
down relevant principles for settling that controversy.

It is not a critique of the evangelistic principles of
any particular person or persons, though it provides
relevant principles for evaluating all evangelistic
activities.

What is it, then? It is a piece of biblical and
theological reasoning, designed to clarify the relationship between three realities: God's sovereignty,
man's responsibility, and the Christian's evangelistic
duty. The last of these is its proper subject; divine
sovereignty and human responsibility are discussed

7

only so far as they bear on evangelism. The aim of the discourse is to dispel the suspicion (current, it seems, in some quarters) that faith in the absolute sovereignty of God hinders a full recognition and acceptance of evangelistic responsibility, and to show that, on the contrary, only this faith can give Christians the strength that they need to fulfil their evangelistic task.

It must not be thought that on all the points with which I deal I am trying to lay down some sort of 'I.V.F. orthodoxy'. The limits of 'I.V.F. orthodoxy' are set out in the Fellowship's doctrinal basis. Beyond those limits, members of the Fellowship are free, in John Wesley's phrase, to 'think and let think', and no opinion on any subject can be regarded as the only one permissible. On the subject now to be dealt with, it may well be that some members of the Fellowship will think differently from the present writer. Equally, however, an author has a right to his own opinion, and he cannot be expected to conceal his views when he believes them to be biblical, relevant, and (in the strict sense) edifying.

J. I. PACKER

INTRODUCTION

ALWAYS and everywhere the servants of Christ are under orders to evangelize, and I hope that what I shall say now will act as an incentive to this task. I hope, too, that it will serve a further purpose. There is in Christian circles at the present time much heart-searching and dispute about ways and means of evangelism. I want to speak about the spiritual factors involved in evangelizing, and I hope that what I say may help towards resolving some of the current disagreements and debates.

Evangelism is my proper subject, and I am to speak of it in relation to the sovereignty of God. That means that I shall not be speaking of the sovereignty of God further than is necessary for right thinking about evangelism. Divine sovereignty is a vast subject: it embraces everything that comes into the biblical picture of God as Lord and King in His world, the One who 'worketh all things after the counsel of his own will' (Eph. i.11), directing every process and ordering every event for the fulfilling of His own eternal plan. To deal with such a subject in full, one would have to take soundings in the depths, not merely of providence, but also of predestination and the last things, and that is more than we can or need do here. The only aspect of divine

sovereignty that will concern us in these pages is
God's sovereignty in grace : His almighty action in
bringing helpless sinners home through Christ to
Himself.

In examining the relationship between God's
sovereignty and the Christian's task of evangelism,
I have a specific aim in view. There is abroad today
a widespread suspicion that a robust faith in the
absolute sovereignty of God is bound to undermine
any adequate sense of human responsibility. Such a
faith is thought to be dangerous to spiritual health,
because it breeds a habit of complacent inertia. In
particular, it is thought to paralyse evangelism by
robbing one both of the motive to evangelize and of
the message to evangelize with. The supposition
seems to be that you cannot evangelize effectively
unless you are prepared to pretend while you are
doing it that the doctrine of divine sovereignty is not
true. I shall try to make it evident that this is nonsense. I shall try to show further that, so far from
inhibiting evangelism, faith in the sovereignty of
God's government and grace is the only thing that
can sustain it, for it is the only thing that can give
us the resilience that we need if we are to evangelize
boldly and persistently, and not be daunted by
temporary setbacks. So far from being weakened
by this faith, therefore, evangelism will inevitably
be weak and lack staying power without it. This, I
hope, will become clear as we proceed.

CHAPTER I

DIVINE SOVEREIGNTY

I DO not intend to spend any time at all proving
to you the general truth that *God is sovereign in
His world*. There is no need; for I know that, if
you are a Christian, you believe this already. How
do I know that? Because I know that, if you are a
Christian, you pray; and the recognition of God's
sovereignty is the basis of your prayers. In prayer,
you ask for things and give thanks for things. Why?
Because you recognize that God is the author and
source of all the good that you have had already,
and all the good that you hope for in the future.
This is the fundamental philosophy of Christian
prayer. The prayer of a Christian is not an attempt
to force God's hand, but a humble acknowledgment
of helplessness and dependence. When we are on
our knees, we know that it is not we who control the
world; it is not in our power, therefore, to supply
our needs by our own independent efforts; every
good thing that we desire for ourselves and for others
must be sought from God, and will come, if it comes
at all, as a gift from His hands. If this is true even
of our daily bread (and the Lord's Prayer teaches
us that it is), much more is it true of spiritual benefits. This is all luminously clear to us when we are
actually praying, whatever we may be betrayed into
saying in argument afterwards. In effect, therefore,

what we do every time we pray is to confess our own impotence and God's sovereignty. The very fact that a Christian prays is thus proof positive that he believes in the Lordship of his God.

Nor, again, am I going to spend time proving to you the particular truth that *God is sovereign in salvation.* For that, too, you believe already. Two facts show this. In the first place, you give God thanks for your conversion. Now why do you do that? Because you know in your heart that God was entirely responsible for it. You did not save yourself; He saved you. Your thanksgiving is itself an acknowledgment that your conversion was not your own work, but His work. You do not put it down to chance or accident that you came under Christian influence when you did. You do not put it down to chance or accident that you attended a Christian church, that you heard the Christian gospel, that you had Christian friends and, perhaps, a Christian home, that the Bible fell into your hands, that you saw your need of Christ and came to trust Him as your Saviour. You do not attribute your repenting and believing to your own wisdom, or prudence, or sound judgment, or good sense. Perhaps, in the days when you were seeking Christ, you laboured and strove hard, read and pondered much, but all that outlay of effort did not make your conversion your own work. Your act of faith when you closed with Christ was yours in the sense that it was you who performed it; but that does not mean that you saved yourself. In fact, it never occurs to you to suppose that you saved yourself.

As you look back, you take to yourself the blame for your past blindness and indifference and obstinacy and evasiveness in face of the gospel message; but you do not pat yourself on the back for having been at length mastered by the insistent Christ. You would never dream of dividing the credit for your salvation between God and yourself. You have never for one moment supposed that the decisive contribution to your salvation was yours and not God's. You have never told God that, while you are grateful for the means and opportunities of grace that He gave you, you realize that you have to thank, not Him, but yourself for the fact that you responded to His call. Your heart revolts at the very thought of talking to God in such terms. In fact, you thank Him no less sincerely for the gift of faith and repentance than for the gift of a Christ to trust and turn to. This is the way in which, since you became a Christian, your heart has always led you. You give God all the glory for all that your salvation involved, and you know that it would be blasphemy if you refused to thank Him for bringing you to faith. Thus, in the way that you think of your conversion and give thanks for your conversion, you acknowledge the sovereignty of divine grace. And every other Christian in the world does the same.

It is instructive in this connection to ponder Charles Simeon's account of his conversation with John Wesley on Dec. 20th, 1784 (the date is given in Wesley's *Journal*): ' "Sir, I understand that you are called an Arminian; and I have been sometimes called a Calvinist; and therefore I suppose we are to draw daggers. But before I consent to begin the combat, with your permission I will ask you a few questions. ... Pray, Sir, do you feel yourself a depraved creature, so depraved that you would never have thought of turning to God, if God had not first put it into your heart?" "Yes," says the veteran, "I do indeed." "And do you utterly despair of recommending yourself to God by anything you can do; and look for salvation solely through the blood and righteousness of Christ?" "Yes, solely through Christ." "But, Sir, supposing you were at first saved by Christ, are you not somehow or other to save yourself afterwards by your own works?" "No, I must be saved by Christ from first to last." "Allowing, then, that you were first turned by the grace of God, are you not in some way or other to keep yourself by your own power?" "No." "What, then, are you to be upheld every hour and every moment by God, as much as an infant in its mother's arms?" "Yes, altogether." "And is all your hope in the grace and mercy of God to preserve you unto His heavenly kingdom?" "Yes, I have no hope but in Him." "Then, Sir, with your leave I will put up my dagger again; for this is all my Calvinism; this is my election, my justification by faith, my final perseverance : it is in substance all that I hold, and as I hold it; and therefore, if you please, instead of searching out terms and phrases to be a ground of contention between us, we will cordially unite in those things wherein we agree." [1]

There is a second way in which you acknowledge

[1] *Horae Homileticae*, Preface: I. xvii f.

that God is sovereign in salvation. You pray for the conversion of others. In what terms, now, do you intercede for them? Do you limit yourself to asking that God will bring them to a point where they can save themselves, independently of Him? I do not think you do. I think that what you do is to pray in categorical terms that God will, quite simply and decisively, save them: that He will open the eyes of their understanding, soften their hard hearts, renew their natures, and move their wills to receive the Saviour. You ask God to work in them everything necessary for their salvation. You would not dream of making it a point in your prayer that you are not asking God actually to bring them to faith, because you recognize that that is something He cannot do. Nothing of the sort! When you pray for unconverted people, you do so on the assumption that it is in God's power to bring them to faith. You entreat Him to do that very thing, and your confidence in asking rests upon the certainty that He is able to do what you ask. And so indeed He is: this conviction, which animates your intercessions, is God's own truth, written on your heart by the Holy Spirit. In prayer, then (and the Christian is at his sanest and wisest when he prays), you *know* that it is God who saves men; you *know* that what makes men turn to God is God's own gracious work of drawing them to Himself; and the content of your prayers is determined by this knowledge. Thus, by your practice of intercession, no less than by giving thanks for your conversion, you acknowledge and confess the sov-

ereignty of God's grace. And so do all Christian
people everywhere.

There is a long-standing controversy in the Church
as to whether God is really Lord in relation to human
conduct and saving faith or not. What has been said
shows us how we should regard this controversy.
The situation is not what it seems to be. For it is
not true that some Christians believe in divine sovereignty while others hold an opposite view. What
is true is that all Christians believe in divine sovereignty, but some are not aware that they do, and
mistakenly imagine and insist that they reject it.
What causes this odd state of affairs? The root
cause is the same as in most cases of error in the
Church—the intruding of rationalistic speculations,
the passion for systematic consistency, a reluctance
to recognize the existence of mystery and to let God
be wiser than men, and a consequent subjecting of
Scripture to the supposed demands of human logic.
People see that the Bible teaches man's responsibility
for his actions; they do not see (man, indeed, cannot
see) how this is consistent with the sovereign Lordship of God over those actions. They are not content
to let the two truths live side by side, as they do in
the Scriptures, but jump to the conclusion that, in
order to uphold the biblical truth of human responsibility, they are bound to reject the equally biblical
and equally true doctrine of divine sovereignty,
and to explain away the great number of texts that
teach it. The desire to over-simplify the Bible by cutting out the mysteries is natural to our perverse
minds, and it is not surprising that even good men

should fall victim to it. Hence this persistent and troublesome dispute. The irony of the situation, however, is that when we ask how the two sides pray, it becomes apparent that those who profess to deny God's sovereignty really believe in it just as strongly as those who affirm it.

How, then, do you pray? Do you ask God for your daily bread? Do you thank God for your conversion? Do you pray for the conversion of others? If the answer is 'no', I can only say that I do not think you are yet born again. But if the answer is 'yes'—well, that proves that, whatever side you may have taken in debates on this question in the past, in your heart you believe in the sovereignty of God no less firmly than anyone else. On our feet we may have arguments about it, but on our knees we are all agreed. And it is this common agreement, of which our prayers give proof, that I take as our starting-point now.

CHAPTER II

DIVINE SOVEREIGNTY AND HUMAN RESPONSIBILITY

OUR aim in the present study is to think out the nature of the Christian's evangelistic task in the light of this agreed presupposition that God is sovereign in salvation. Now, we need to recognize right at the outset that this is no easy assignment. All theological topics contain pitfalls for the unwary, for God's truth is never quite what man would have expected; and our present subject is more treacherous than most. This is because in thinking it through we have to deal with an *antinomy* in the biblical revelation, and in such circumstances our finite, fallen minds are more than ordinarily apt to go astray.

What is an antinomy? *The Shorter Oxford Dictionary* defines it as 'a contradiction between conclusions which seem equally logical, reasonable or necessary'. For our purposes, however, this definition is not quite accurate; the opening words should read 'an *appearance* of contradiction'. For the whole point of an antinomy—in theology, at any rate—is that it is not a real contradiction, though it looks like one. It is an *apparent* incompatibility between two apparent truths. An antinomy exists when a pair of principles stand side by side, seemingly irreconcilable, yet both undeniable. There are cogent reasons for believing each of them; each rests on clear and solid evidence; but it is a mystery to you how they can be squared with each other. You see that each must be true on its own, but you do not see how they can both be true together. Let me give an example. Modern physics faces an antinomy, in this sense, in its study of light. There is cogent evidence to show that light consists of waves, and equally cogent evidence to show that it consists of particles. It is not apparent how light can be both waves and particles, but the evidence is there, and so neither view can be ruled out in favour of the other. Neither, however, can be reduced to the other or explained in terms of the other; the two seemingly incompatible positions must be held together, and both must be treated as true. Such a necessity scandalizes our tidy minds, no doubt, but there is no help for it if we are to be loyal to the facts.

It appears, therefore, that an antinomy is not the same thing as a paradox. A paradox is a figure of speech, a play on words. It is a form of statement that seems to unite two opposite ideas, or to deny something by the very terms in which it is asserted. Many truths about the Christian life can be expressed as paradoxes. A Prayer Book collect, for instance, declares that God's 'service is perfect freedom' : man goes free through becoming a slave. Paul states various paradoxes of his own Christian experience : 'sorrowful, yet always rejoicing . . . having nothing, and yet possessing all things'; 'when I am weak, then am I strong' (2 Cor. vi.10, xii.10). The point of a paradox, however, is that what creates the appearance of contradiction is not the facts, but the words. The contradiction is verbal, but not real, and a little thought shows how it can be eliminated and the same idea expressed in non-paradoxical form. In other words a paradox is always *dispensable*. Look at the examples quoted. The Prayer Book might have said that those who serve God are free from sin's dominion. In 2 Cor. vi.10 Paul might have said that sorrow at circumstances, and joy in God, are constantly combined in his experience, and that, though he owns no property and has no bank balance, there is a sense in which everything belongs to him, because he is Christ's, and Christ is Lord of all. Again, in 2 Cor. xii.10, he might have said that the Lord strengthens him most when he is most conscious of his natural infirmity. Such non-paradoxical forms of speech are clumsy and dull beside the paradoxes which they would replace, but they express precisely the same meaning. For a paradox is merely a matter of how you use words; the employment of paradox is an arresting trick of speech, but it does not imply even an appearance of contradiction in the facts that you are describing.

Also it should be noted that a paradox is always *comprehensible*. A speaker or writer casts his ideas into paradoxes in order to make them memorable and provoke thought about them. But the person at the receiving end must be able, on reflection, to see how to unravel the paradox, otherwise it will seem to him to be really self-contradictory, and therefore really meaningless. An incomprehensible paradox could not be distinguished from a mere contradiction in terms. Sheer paradox would thus have to be written off as sheer nonsense.

By contrast, however, an antinomy is neither dispensable nor comprehensible. It is not a figure of speech, but an observed relation between two statements of fact. It is not deliberately manufactured; it is forced upon us by the facts themselves. It is unavoidable, and it is insoluble. We do not invent it, and we cannot explain it. Nor is there any way to get rid of it, save by falsifying the very facts that led us to it.

What should one do, then, with an antinomy? Accept it for what it is, and learn to live with it. Refuse to regard the apparent inconsistency as real; put down the semblance of contradiction to the deficiency of your own understanding; think of the two principles as, not rival alternatives, but, in some way that at present you do not grasp, complementary to each other. Be careful, therefore, not to set them at loggerheads, nor to make deductions from either that would cut across the other (such deductions would, for that very reason, be certainly unsound). Use each within the limits of its own sphere of reference (*i.e.*, the area delimited by the evidence from which the principle has been drawn). Note what connections exist between the two truths and their two frames of reference, and teach yourself to think of reality in a way that provides for their peaceful coexistence, remembering that reality itself has proved actually to contain them both. This is how antinomies must be handled, whether in nature or in Scripture. This, as I understand it, is how

modern physics deals with the problem of light, and
this is how Christians have to deal with the antinomies of biblical teaching.

The particular antinomy which concerns us here
is the apparent opposition between divine sovereignty and human responsibility, or (putting it
more biblically) between what God does as King and
what He does as Judge. Scripture teaches that, as
King, He orders and controls all things, human
actions among them, in accordance with His own
eternal purpose.[1] Scripture also teaches that, as
Judge, He holds every man responsible for the
choices he makes and the courses of action he pur-
sues.[2] Thus, hearers of the gospel are responsible for
their reaction; if they reject the good news, they are
guilty of unbelief. 'He that believeth not is condemned already, because he hath not believed . . .'[3]
Again, Paul, entrusted with the gospel, is responsible
for preaching it; if he neglects his commission, he is
penalized for unfaithfulness. 'Necessity is laid upon
me; yea, woe is unto me, if I preach not the gospel!'[4]
God's sovereignty and man's responsibility are
taught us side by side in the same Bible; sometimes,
indeed, in the same text.[5] Both are thus guaranteed
to us by the same divine authority; both, therefore,

---

[1] See Gn. xlv.8, l.20; Pr. xvi.9, xxi.1; Mt. x.29; Acts iv.27f;
Rom. ix.20 f.; Eph. i.11, etc.

[2] See Mt. xxv; Rom. ii.1–16; Rev. xx.11–13, etc.

[3] Jn. iii.18; cf. Mt. xi.20–24; Acts xiii.38–41; 2 Thes. i.7–10,
etc.   [4] 1 Cor. ix.16; cf. Ezk. iii.17 ff., xxxiii.7 ff.

[5] E.g., Lk. xxii.22 : 'the Son of man goeth (to his death), *as
it was determined;* but *woe unto that man by whom he is
betrayed!' Cf.* Acts ii.23.

are true. It follows that they must be held together, and not played off against each other. Man is a responsible moral agent, though he is *also* divinely controlled; man is divinely controlled, though he is *also* a responsible moral agent. God's sovereignty is a reality, and man's responsibility is a reality too. This is the revealed antinomy in terms of which we have to do our thinking about evangelism.

To our finite minds, of course, the thing is inexplicable. It sounds like a contradiction, and our first reaction is to complain that it is absurd. Paul notices this complaint in Romans ix. 'Thou wilt say then unto me, Why does he (God) yet find fault? For who hath resisted his will?' (Rom. ix.19). If, as our Lord, God orders all our actions, how can it be reasonable or right for Him to act also as our Judge, and condemn our shortcomings? Observe how Paul replies. He does not attempt to demonstrate the propriety of God's action; instead, he rebukes the spirit of the question. 'Nay but, O man, who art thou that repliest against God?' What the objector has to learn is that he, a creature and a sinner, has no right whatsoever to find fault with the revealed ways of God. Creatures are not entitled to register complaints about their Creator. As Paul goes on to say, God's sovereignty is wholly just, for His right to dispose of His creatures is absolute.[6] Earlier in the Epistle, he had shown that God's judgment of sinners is also wholly just, since our sins richly deserve His sentence.[7] Our part, he would tell us, is to acknowledge these facts, and to adore God's

[6] Rom. ix.20 f.   [7] Rom. i.18 ff., 32, ii.1–16.

righteousness, both as King and as Judge; not to speculate as to how His just sovereignty can be consistent with His just judgment, and certainly not to call the justice of either in question because we find the problem of their relationship too hard for us! Our speculations are not the measure of our God. The Creator has told us that He is both a sovereign Lord and a righteous Judge, and that should be enough for us. Why do we hesitate to take His word for it? Can we not trust what He says?

We ought not in any case to be surprised when we find mysteries of this sort in God's Word. For the Creator is incomprehensible to His creatures. A God whom we could understand exhaustively, and whose revelation of Himself confronted us with no mysteries whatsoever, would be a God in man's image, and therefore an imaginary God, not the God of the Bible at all. For what the God of the Bible says is this: 'My thoughts are not your thoughts, neither are your ways my ways... as the heavens are higher than the earth, so are my ways higher than your ways, and my thoughts than your thoughts' (Is. lv. 8 f.). The antinomy which we face now is only one of a number that the Bible contains. We may be sure that they all find their reconciliation in the mind and counsel of God, and we may hope that in heaven we shall understand them ourselves. But meanwhile, our wisdom is to maintain with equal emphasis both the apparently conflicting truths in each case, to hold them together in the relation in which the Bible itself sets them, and to recognize that here is a mystery which we cannot expect to solve in this world.

This is easily said, but the thing is not easily done. For our minds dislike antinomies. We like to tie up everything into neat intellectual parcels, with all appearance of mystery dispelled and no loose ends hanging out. Hence we are tempted to get rid of antinomies from our minds by illegitimate means : to suppress, or jettison, one truth in the supposed interests of the other, and for the sake of a tidier theology. So it is in the present case. The temptation is to undercut and maim the one truth by the way in which we stress the other : to assert man's responsibility in a way that excludes God from being sovereign, or to affirm God's sovereignty in a way that destroys the responsibility of man. Both mistakes need to be guarded against. It is worth reflecting, therefore, on the way in which these temptations arise in connection specifically with evangelism.

There is, first, the temptation to *an exclusive concern with human responsibility*. As we have seen, human responsibility is a fact, and a very solemn fact. Man's responsibility to his Maker is, indeed, the fundamental fact of his life, and it can never be taken too seriously. God made us responsible moral agents, and He will not treat us as anything less. His Word addresses each of us individually, and each of us is responsible for the way in which he responds—for his attention or inattention, his belief or unbelief, his obedience or disobedience. We cannot evade responsibility for our reaction to God's revelation. We live under His law. We must answer to Him for our lives.

Man without Christ is a guilty sinner, answerable

to God for breaking His law. That is why he needs
the gospel. When he hears the gospel, he is responsible for the decision that he makes about it. It sets
before him a choice between life and death, the most
momentous choice that any man can ever face.
When we present the gospel to an unconverted man,
it is very likely that, without fully realizing what he is
doing, he will try to blind himself to the gravity of
this issue, and thereby to justify himself in shrugging
the whole thing off. Then we have to use every legitimate means in our power to bring home to him the
seriousness of the choice that confronts him, and to
urge him not to let himself treat so solemn a matter
in an irresponsible way. When we preach the promises and invitations of the gospel, and offer Christ to
sinful men and women, it is part of our task to
emphasize and re-emphasize that they are responsible to God for the way in which they react to the
good news of His grace. No preacher can ever make
this point too strongly.

Similarly, we ourselves have a responsibility for
making the gospel known. Christ's command to His
disciples, 'Go ye . . . and make disciples . . .' (Mt.
xxviii.19, RSV), was spoken to them in their representative capacity; this is Christ's command, not merely
to the apostles, but to the whole Church. Evangelism
is the inalienable responsibility of every Christian
community, and every Christian man. We are all
under orders to devote ourselves to spreading the
good news, and to use all our ingenuity and enterprise to bring it to the notice of the whole world. The
Christian, therefore, must constantly be searching his

conscience, asking himself if he is doing all that he might be doing in this field. For this also is a responsibility that cannot be shrugged off.

It is necessary, therefore, to take the thought of human responsibility, as it affects both the preacher and the hearer of the gospel, very seriously indeed. But we must not let it drive the thought of divine sovereignty out of our minds. While we must always remember that it is our responsibility to proclaim salvation, we must never forget that it is God who saves. It is God who brings men and women under the sound of the gospel, and it is God who brings them to faith in Christ. Our evangelistic work is the instrument that He uses for this purpose, but the power that saves is not in the instrument: it is in the hand of the One who uses the instrument. We must not at any stage forget that. For if we forget that it is God's prerogative to give results when the gospel is preached, we shall start to think that it is our responsibility to secure them. And if we forget that only God can give faith, we shall start to think that the making of converts depends, in the last analysis, not on God, but on us, and that the decisive factor is the way in which we evangelize. And this line of thought, consistently followed through, will lead us far astray.

Let us work this out. If we regarded it as our job, not simply to present Christ, but actually to produce converts—to evangelize, not only faithfully, but also successfully—our approach to evangelism would become pragmatic and calculating. We should conclude that our basic equipment, both for personal dealing and for public preaching, must be twofold. We must have, not merely a clear grasp of the meaning and application of the gospel, but also an irresistible technique for inducing a response. We should, therefore, make it our business to try and develop such a technique. And we should evaluate all evangelism, our own and other people's, by the criterion, not only of the message preached, but also of visible results. If our own efforts were not bearing fruit, we should conclude that our technique still needed improving. If they were bearing fruit, we should conclude that this justified the technique we had been using. We should regard evangelism as an activity involving a battle of wills between ourselves and those to whom we go, a battle in which victory depends on our firing off a heavy enough barrage of calculated effects. Thus our philosophy of evangelism would become terrifyingly similar to the philosophy of brainwashing. And we would no longer be able to argue, when such a similarity is asserted to be a fact, that this is not a proper conception of evangelism.[8] For it *would be* a proper conception of evangelism, if the production of converts was really our responsibility.

This shows us the danger of forgetting the practical implications of God's sovereignty. It is right to recognize our responsibility to engage in aggressive evangelism. It is right to desire the conversion of unbelievers. It is right to want one's presentation of

---

[8] As D. M. Lloyd-Jones argues, in *Conversions: Psychological and Spiritual* (I.V.F., 1959), against the thesis of Dr William Sargant.

the gospel to be as clear and forcible as possible. If
we preferred that converts should be few and far
between, and did not care whether our proclaiming
of Christ went home or not, there would be something wrong with us. But it is not right when we take
it on us to do more than God has given us to do. It
is not right when we regard ourselves as responsible
for securing converts, and look to our own enterprise
and techniques to accomplish what only God can
accomplish. To do that is to intrude ourselves into
the office of the Holy Ghost, and to exalt ourselves
as the agents of the new birth. And the point that we
must see is this: *only by letting our knowledge of
God's sovereignty control the way in which we plan,
and pray, and work in His service, can we avoid becoming guilty of this fault.* For where we are not
consciously relying on God, there we shall inevitably
be found relying on ourselves. And the spirit of self-
reliance is a blight on evangelism. Such, however, is
the inevitable consequence of forgetting God's
sovereignty in the conversion of souls.

But there is an opposite temptation that threatens
us also: namely, the temptation to *an exclusive concern with divine sovereignty.*

There are some Christians whose minds are constantly taken up with thoughts of the sovereignty of
God. This truth means a great deal to them. It has
come to them quite suddenly, perhaps, and with the
force of a tremendous revelation. They would say
that it has caused a real Copernican revolution in
their outlook; it has given a new centre to their entire personal universe. Previously, as they now see,

man had been central in their universe, and God had
been on the circumference. They had thought of
Him as a Spectator of events in His world, rather
than as their Author. They had assumed that the
controlling factor in every situation was man's
handling of it rather than God's plan for it, and they
had looked upon the happiness of human beings as
the most interesting and important thing in creation,
for God no less than for themselves. But now they
see that this man-centred outlook was sinful and
unbiblical; they see that, from one standpoint, the
whole purpose of the Bible is to overthrow it, and
that books like Deuteronomy and Isaiah and John's
Gospel and Romans smash it to smithereens in
almost every chapter; and they realize that henceforth God must be central in their thoughts and
concerns, just as He is central in reality in His own
world. Now they feel the force of the famous first
answer in the Westminster *Shorter Catechism*:
'Man's chief end is to glorify God, and (by so
doing, and in so doing,) to enjoy him for ever.'
Now they see that the way to find the happiness
that God promises is not to seek it as an end in
itself, but to forget oneself in the daily preoccupation of seeking God's glory and doing His will
and proving His power through the ups and downs
and stresses and strains of everyday life. They see
that it is the glory and praise of God that must
absorb them henceforth, for time and for eternity.
They see that the whole purpose of their existence is
that with heart and life they should worship and
exalt God. In every situation, therefore, their one

question is: what will make most for God's glory? what should I do in order that in these circumstances God may be magnified?

And they see, as they ask this question, that, though God uses men as means for achieving His purposes, in the last analysis nothing depends on man; everything depends, rather, on the God who raises men up to do His will. They see, too, that God is handling every situation before His servants come on the scene, and that He continues to handle it and work out His will in it through each thing that they do—through their mistakes and failures, no less than through their personal successes. They see, therefore, that they need never fear for the ark of God, as Uzzah feared for it, for God will maintain His own cause. They see that they need never make Uzzah's mistake, of taking too much on them, and doing God's work in a forbidden way for fear that otherwise it would not get done at all.[9] They see that, since God is always in control, they need never fear that they will expose Him to loss and damage if they limit themselves to serving Him in the way that He has appointed. They see that any other supposition would in effect be a denial of His wisdom, or His sovereignty, or both. They see, also, that the Christian must never for one moment imagine himself to be indispensable to God, or allow himself to behave as if he were. The God who sent him, and is pleased to work with him, can do without him. He must be ready to spend and be spent in the tasks that God sets him; but he must never suppose that

9 2 Sa. vi.6 f. Uzzah transgressed the prohibition of Nu. iv.15.

the loss to the Church would be irreparable if God should lay him aside and use someone else. He must not at any point say to himself, 'God's cause would collapse without me and the work I am doing'—for there is never any reason to think this is so. It is never true that God would be at a loss without you and me. Those who have begun to understand the sovereignty of God see all this, and so they seek to efface themselves in all their work for God. They thus bear a practical witness to their belief that God is great, and reigns, by trying to make themselves small, and to act in a way which is itself an acknowledgment that the fruitfulness of their Christian service depends wholly on God, and not upon themselves. And up to this point they are right.

They are, however, beset by exactly the opposite temptation to that discussed above. In their zeal to glorify God by acknowledging His sovereignty in grace, and by refusing to imagine that their own services are indispensable to Him, they are tempted to lose sight of the Church's responsibility to evangelize. Their temptation is to reason thus: 'Agreed, the world is ungodly; but, surely, the less we do about it, the more God will be glorified when at length He breaks in to restore the situation. The most important thing for us to do is to take care that we leave the initiative in His hands.' They are tempted, therefore, to suspect all enterprise in evangelism, whether organized or on the personal level, as if there were something essentially and inescapably man-exalting about it. They are haunted by the fear of running ahead of God, and feel that there is nothing more urgent than to guard against the possibility of doing this.

Perhaps the classic instance of this way of thinking was provided two centuries ago by the chairman of the ministers' fraternal at which William Carey mooted the founding of a missionary society. 'Sit down, young man,' said the old warrior; 'when God is pleased to convert the heathen, He will do it without your aid, or mine!' The idea of taking the initiative in going out to find men of all nations for Christ struck him as improper and, indeed, presumptuous.

Now, think twice before you condemn that old man. He was not entirely without understanding. He had at least grasped that it is God who saves, and that He saves according to His own purpose, and does not take orders from man in the matter. He had grasped too that we must never suppose that without our help God would be helpless. He had, in other words, learned to take the sovereignty of God perfectly seriously. His mistake was that he was not taking the Church's evangelistic responsibility with equal seriousness. He was forgetting that God's way of saving men is to send out His servants to tell them the gospel, and that the Church has been charged to go into all the world for that very purpose.

But this is something that we must not forget. Christ's command means that we all should be devoting all our resources of ingenuity and enterprise to the task of making the gospel known in every possible way to every possible person. Unconcern and inaction with regard to evangelism are always, therefore, inexcusable. And the doctrine of divine sovereignty would be grossly misapplied if we should invoke it in such a way as to lessen the urgency, and immediacy, and priority, and binding constraint, of the evangelistic imperative. No revealed truth may be invoked to extenuate sin. God did not teach us the reality of His rule in order to give us an excuse for neglecting His orders.

In our Lord's parable of the talents,[1] the 'good and faithful' servants were those who furthered their master's interests by making the most enterprising lawful use that they could of what was entrusted to them. The servant who buried his talent, and did nothing with it beyond keeping it intact, no doubt imagined that he was being extremely good and faithful, but his master judged him to be 'wicked', 'slothful', and 'unprofitable'. For what Christ has given us to use must be put to use; it is not enough simply to hide it away. We may apply this to our stewardship of the gospel. The truth about salvation has been made known to us, not for us simply to preserve (though we must certainly do that), but also, and primarily, for us to spread. The light is not meant to be hidden under the bushel. It is meant to shine; and it is our business to see that it shines. 'Ye are the light of the world . . .' says our Lord.[2] He who does not devote himself to evangelism in every way that he can is not, therefore, playing the part of a good and faithful servant of Jesus Christ.

Here, then, are two opposite pitfalls: a Scylla and Charybdis of error. Each is the result of partial

[1] Mt. xxv.14–30.   [2] Mt. v.14–16.

vision, which means partial blindness; each reveals
a failure to face squarely the biblical antinomy of
the responsibility of man and the sovereignty of God.
Both unite to warn us not to pit these truths against
each other, nor to allow either to obscure or over-
shadow the other in our minds. Both unite to warn
us also against reacting from one extreme of error
into the other. If we did that, our last state might
well be worse than the first. What are we to do,
then? To direct our course along the narrow channel
that leads between Scylla and Charybdis; in other
words, to avoid both extremes. How? By making it
our business to believe both these doctrines with all
our might, and to keep both constantly before us for
the guidance and government of our lives.

We shall proceed now according to this maxim.
In what follows, we shall try to take both doctrines
perfectly seriously, as the Bible does, and to view
them in their positive biblical relationship. We shall
not oppose them to each other, for the Bible does
not oppose them to each other. Nor shall we qualify,
or modify, or water down, either of them in terms
of the other, for this is not what the Bible does
either. What the Bible does is to assert both truths
side by side in the strongest and most unambiguous
terms as two ultimate facts; this, therefore, is the
position that we must take in our own thinking.
C. H. Spurgeon was once asked if he could reconcile
these two truths to each other. 'I wouldn't try,' he
replied; 'I never reconcile friends.' Friends?—yes,
friends. This is the point that we have to grasp. In
the Bible, divine sovereignty and human responsi-

bility are not enemies. They are not uneasy neighbours; they are not in an endless state of cold war
with each other. They are *friends*, and they work
together. I hope that what I am to say now about
evangelism will help to make this clear.

CHAPTER III

EVANGELISM

W E shall now try to answer from Scripture the following four questions concerning the Christian's evangelistic responsibility. What is evangelism? What is the evangelistic message? What is the motive for evangelizing? By what means and methods should evangelism be practised?

I. WHAT IS EVANGELISM?

It might be expected that evangelical Christians would not need to spend time discussing this question. In view of the emphasis that Evangelicals always, and rightly, lay on the primacy of evangelism, it would be natural to assume that we were all perfectly unanimous as to what evangelism is. Yet in fact much of the confusion in present-day debates about evangelism arises from lack of agreement at this point. The root of the confusion can be stated in a sentence. It is our widespread and persistent habit of defining evangelism in terms, not of a message delivered, but of an effect produced in our hearers.

For illustration of this, look at the famous definition of evangelism which the Archbishops' Committee gave in its report on the evangelistic work of the Church in 1918. 'To *evangelise*', declared the Committee, 'is *so to present Christ Jesus in the power*

*of the Holy Spirit, that men shall come to put their
trust in God through Him, to accept Him as their
Saviour, and serve Him as their King in the fellowship of His Church.'*

Now this is in many ways an excellent definition.
It states admirably the aim and purpose of the evangelistic enterprise, and rules out many inadequate
and misleading ideas. To start with, it makes the
point that evangelizing means *declaring a specific
message.* According to this definition, it is not evangelism merely to teach general truths about God's
existence, or the moral law; evangelism means *to
present Christ Jesus,* the divine Son who became
man at a particular point in world-history in order
to save a ruined race. Nor, according to this definition, is it evangelism merely to present the teaching
and example of the historical Jesus, or even the truth
about His saving work; evangelism means *to present
Christ Jesus* Himself, the living Saviour and the
reigning Lord. Nor, again, is it evangelism, according to this definition, merely to set forth the living
Jesus as Helper and Friend, without reference to
His saving work on the cross; evangelism means *to
present* Jesus as *Christ,* God's anointed Servant, fulfilling the tasks of His appointed office as Priest and
King. 'The man Christ Jesus' is to be presented as
the 'one mediator between God and men',[1] who
'suffered for sins ... that he might bring us to God',[2]
the One *through whom,* and through whom alone,
men may *come to put their trust in God,* according
to His own claim : 'I am the way, the truth, and the

[1] 1 Tim. ii.5.   [2] 1 Pet. iii.18.

life : no man cometh unto the Father, but by me."[3]
He is to be proclaimed as the *Saviour*, the One who
'came into the world to save sinners'[4] and 'redeemed
us from the curse of the law, being made a curse for
us'[5]—'Jesus, which delivereth us from the wrath to
come.'[6] And He is to be set forth as *King*: 'for to
this end Christ died, and lived again, that he might
be Lord of both the dead and the living'.[7] There is
no evangelism where this specific message is not
declared.

Again, the definition makes the point that evangelizing means declaring this specific message *with
a specific application*. It is not evangelism, according
to this definition, to present Christ Jesus as a subject
for detached critical and comparative study. Evangelism, according to this definition, means presenting Christ Jesus and His work in relation to the needs
of fallen men and women, who are without God as
a Father and under the wrath of God as a Judge.
Evangelism means presenting Christ Jesus to them
as their only hope, in this world or the next. Evangelism means exhorting sinners to *accept* Christ
Jesus *as their Saviour*, recognizing that in the most
final and far-reaching sense they are lost without
Him. Nor is this all. Evangelism also means summoning men to receive Christ Jesus as all that He is
—Lord, as well as Saviour—and therefore to *serve
Him as their King in the fellowship of His Church*,
the company of those who worship Him, witness
to Him, and work for Him here on earth. In other

---

[3] Jn. xiv.6. [4] 1 Tim. i.15. [5] Gal. iii.13.
[6] 1 Thes. i.10, RV. [7] Rom. xiv.9, RV.

words, evangelism is the issuing of a call to turn, as
well as to trust; it is the delivering, not merely of a
divine invitation to receive a Saviour, but of a divine
command to repent of sin. And there is no evangelism where this specific application is not made.

The definition under review establishes these vital
points well. But on one fundamental matter it goes
astray. It puts a consecutive clause where a final
clause should be. Had it begun : 'to evangelise is
to present Christ Jesus to sinful men *in order that*,
through the power of the Holy Spirit, they *may*
come . . .', there would be no fault to find with it.
But it does not say this. What it does say is quite
different. 'To evangelise is *so* to present Christ Jesus
in the power of the Holy Spirit, *that* men *shall*
come . . .' This is to define evangelism in terms of an
effect achieved in the lives of others; which amounts
to saying that the essence of evangelizing is producing converts.

But this cannot be right, as we pointed out at an
earlier stage. Evangelism is man's work, but the
giving of faith is God's. It is true, indeed, that every
evangelist's aim is to convert, and that our definition
perfectly expresses the ideal which he longs to see
fulfilled in his own ministry; but the question
whether or not one is evangelizing cannot be settled
simply by asking whether one has had conversions.
There have been missionaries to Moslems who
laboured for a lifetime and saw no converts; must
we conclude from this that they were not evangelizing? There have been un-evangelical preachers
through whose words (not always understood in the

sense intended) individuals have been soundly converted; must we conclude from this that these preachers were evangelizing after all? The answer, surely, is no in both cases. The results of preaching depend, not on the wishes and intentions of men, but on the will of God Almighty. This consideration does not mean that we should be indifferent as to whether we see fruit from our witness to Christ or not; if fruit is not appearing, we should seek God's face about it to find out why. But this consideration does mean that we ought not to define evangelism in terms of achieved results.

How, then, should evangelism be defined? The New Testament answer is very simple. According to the New Testament, evangelism is just preaching the gospel, the evangel. It is a work of communication in which Christians make themselves mouthpieces for God's message of mercy to sinners. Anyone who faithfully delivers that message, under whatever circumstances, in a large meeting, in a small meeting, from a pulpit, or in a private conversation, is evangelizing. Since the divine message finds its climax in a plea from the Creator to a rebel world to turn and put faith in Christ, the delivering of it involves the summoning of one's hearers to conversion. If you are not, in this sense, seeking to bring about conversions, you are not evangelizing; this we have seen already. But the way to tell whether in fact you are evangelizing is not to ask whether conversions are known to have resulted from your witness. It is to ask whether you are faithfully making known the gospel message.

E.S.G.—2*

For a complete picture of what the New Testament means by evangelism, we need not look further than the apostle Paul's account of the nature of his own evangelistic ministry. There are three points to note about it.

1. *Paul evangelized as the commissioned representative of the Lord Jesus Christ.* Evangelism was a task that had been specifically entrusted to him. 'Christ sent me . . . to preach the gospel.'[8] Now, see how he regarded himself in virtue of this commission. In the first place, he saw himself as Christ's *steward*. 'Let a man so account of us (myself, and my fellow-preacher Apollos),' he wrote to the Corinthians, 'as of ministers of Christ, and (in that capacity) stewards of the mysteries of God.'[9] 'A dispensation of the gospel (*i.e.*, a commission to dispense it : "a stewardship", RV) is committed unto me.'[1] Paul saw himself as a bondslave raised to a position of high trust, as the steward of a household in New Testament times always was; he had been 'approved of God to be intrusted with the gospel',[2] and the responsibility now rested on him to be faithful to his trust, as a steward must be,[3] guarding the precious truth that had been committed to him (as he later charges Timothy to do[4]), and distributing and dispensing it according to his Master's instructions. The fact that he had been entrusted with this stewardship meant, as he told the Corinthians, that 'necessity is laid upon me; yea, woe is unto me, if I preach not the

---

[8] 1 Cor. i.17.   [9] 1 Cor. iv.1, RV.   [1] 1 Cor. ix.17.
[2] 1 Thes. ii.4, RV; *cf.* 1 Tim. i.11 f.; Tit. i.3.
[3] *Cf.* 1 Cor. iv.2.   [4] 1 Tim. vi.20; 2 Tim. i.13 f.

gospel!'[5] The figure of stewardship thus highlights Paul's *responsibility* to evangelize.

Again, Paul saw himself as Christ's *herald*. When he describes himself as 'appointed a preacher' of the gospel,[6] the noun he uses is *kēryx*, which means a herald, a person who makes public announcements on another's behalf. When he declares, 'we preach Christ crucified',[7] the verb he uses is *kēryssō*, which denotes the herald's appointed activity of blazoning abroad what he has been told to make known. When Paul speaks of 'my *preaching*', and 'our *preaching*', and lays it down that, after the world's wisdom had rendered the world ignorant of God, 'it pleased God by the foolishness of *preaching* to save them that believe',[8] the noun he uses is *kērygma*, meaning, not the activity of announcing, but the thing announced, the proclamation itself, the message declared. Paul, in his own estimation, was not a philosopher, not a moralist, not one of the world's wise men, but simply Christ's herald. His royal Master had given him a message to proclaim; his whole business, therefore, was to deliver that message with exact and studious faithfulness, adding nothing, altering nothing, and omitting nothing. And he was to deliver it, not as another of man's bright ideas, needing to be beautified with the cosmetics and high heels of fashionable learning in order to make people look at it, but as a word from God, spoken in Christ's name, carrying Christ's authority, and to be authenticated in the

[5] 1 Cor. ix.16; *cf.* Acts xx.20, 26 f.; 2 Cor. v.10 f.; Ezk. iii.16 ff., xxxiii.7 ff. [6] 2 Tim. i.11; 1 Tim. ii.7, RV mg. [7] 1 Cor. i.23. [8] 1 Cor. ii.4, xv.14, i.21.

hearers by the convincing power of Christ's Spirit.
'When I came to you,' Paul reminds the Corinthians,
'I ... came ... declaring unto you the testimony of
God.' I came, Paul is saying, not to give you my own
ideas about anything, but simply to deliver God's
message. Therefore, 'I determined not to know any
thing among you, save Jesus Christ, and him crucified'—for it was just this that God sent me to tell
you about. 'And my speech and my preaching
(*kērygma*) was not with enticing words of man's
wisdom, but in demonstration of the Spirit and of
power; that your faith should not stand in the wisdom of men, but in the power of God.'[9] The figure
of the herald thus highlights the *authenticity* of
Paul's gospel.

Thirdly, Paul considered himself Christ's *ambassador*. What is an ambassador? He is the authorized
representative of a sovereign. He speaks, not in his
own name, but on behalf of the ruler whose deputy
he is, and his whole duty and responsibility is to
interpret that ruler's mind faithfully to those to
whom he is sent. Paul used this figure twice, both
times in connection with his evangelistic work. Pray
for me, he wrote from prison, 'that I may open my
mouth boldly, to make known the mystery of the
gospel, for which I am an *ambassador* in bonds: that
therein I may speak boldly, as I ought to speak.'
God, he wrote again, has 'committed unto us the
word of reconciliation. We are *ambassadors* therefore on behalf of Christ, as though God were intreat-

* 1 Cor. ii.1-5. The argument is not affected if for 'testimony' we read 'mystery' in verse 1, as RV does.

ing by us : we beseech you on behalf of Christ, be ye reconciled to God.'[1] Paul called himself an ambassador because he knew that, when he proclaimed the gospel facts and promises, and urged sinners to receive the reconciliation effected at Calvary, it was Christ's message to the world that he was declaring. The figure of ambassadorship thus highlights the *authority* that Paul had, as representing his Lord.

In his evangelism, then, Paul consciously acted as the slave and steward, the mouthpiece and herald, the spokesman and ambassador, of the Lord Jesus Christ. Hence, on the one hand, his sustained boldness and unshakable sense of authority in face of ridicule and indifference; hence, on the other hand, his intransigent refusal to modify his message in order to suit circumstances. These two things, of course, were connected, for Paul could regard himself as speaking with Christ's authority only as long as he remained faithful to the terms of his commission and said neither less nor more than he had been given to say.[2] But while he preached the gospel that Christ had entrusted to him, he spoke as Christ's commissioned representative, and could therefore speak authoritatively, and claim a right to be heard.

But the commission to publish the gospel and make disciples was never confined to the apostles. Nor is it now confined to the Church's ministers. It is a commission that rests upon the whole Church collectively, and therefore upon each Christian individually. All God's people are sent to do as the

[1] Eph. vi.19 f.; 2 Cor. v.19 f., RV.   [2] *Cf.* Gal. i.8 ff.

Philippians did, and 'shine as lights in the world;
holding forth the word of life'.[3] Every Christian,
therefore, has a God-given obligation to make
known the gospel of Christ. And every Christian
who declares the gospel message to any fellow-man
does so as Christ's ambassador and representative,
according to the terms of his God-given commission.
Such is the authority, and such the responsibility,
of the Church and of the Christian in evangelism.

2. The second point in Paul's understanding of
his own evangelistic ministry follows on from the
first. *His primary task in evangelism was to teach
the truth about the Lord Jesus Christ.*

As Christ's ambassador, Paul's first job was to
'get acrosss' the message that his Sovereign had
charged him to deliver. Christ sent me, he declared,
—to do what?—'to preach the gospel'.[4] The Greek
word here is *euangelizomai*, meaning publish the
euangelion, literally the 'good news'. For that is what
Paul's gospel was. Good news, Paul proclaimed, has
come into the world—good news from God. It is
unlike anything that the world, Jewish or Gentile,
had guessed or expected, but it is something that the
whole world needs. This good news, the 'word of
God' in the usual New Testament sense of that
phrase,[5] 'the truth' as Paul often calls it,[6], is a full
and final disclosure of what the Creator has done,
and will do, to save sinners. It is a complete unfold-

---

[3] Phil. ii.15 f.   [4] 1 Cor. i.17.
[5] *Cf.* Acts iv.31, viii.14, xi.1, xiii.46; 2 Cor. ii.17; Col. i.25;
1 Thes. ii.13; 2 Tim. ii.9.
[6] *Cf.* 2 Cor. iv.2; Gal. ii.5, 14; 2 Thes. ii.10 ff.; 2 Tim. ii.18,
25, iii.8.

ing of the spiritual facts of life in God's apostate
world.

What was this good news that Paul preached?
It was the news about Jesus of Nazareth. It was the
news of the incarnation, the atonement, and the
kingdom—the cradle, the cross, and the crown—of
the Son of God. It was the news of how God 'glorified his servant Jesus'[7] by making Him Christ, the
world's long-awaited 'Prince and . . . Saviour'.[8] It
was the news of how God made His Son Man; and
how, as Man, God made Him Priest, and Prophet,
and King; and how, as Priest, God also made Him
a sacrifice for sins; and how, as Prophet, God also
made Him a Lawgiver to His people; and how, as
King, God has also made Him Judge of all the
world, and given Him prerogatives which in the
Old Testament are exclusively Jehovah's own—
namely, to reign till every knee bows before Him,
and to save all who call on His name. In short, the
good news was just this : that God has executed His
eternal intention of glorifying His Son by exalting
Him as a great Saviour for great sinners.

Such was the gospel which Paul was sent to
preach. It was a message of some complexity, needing to be learned before it could be lived by, and
understood before it could be applied. It needed,
therefore, to be *taught*. Hence Paul, as a preacher
of it, had to become a teacher. He saw this as part
of his calling; he speaks of 'the gospel : whereunto
I am appointed a preacher . . . *and a teacher*'.[9]

<hr>

[7] Acts iii.13, RV.   [8] Acts v.31.   [9] 2 Tim. i.10 f.

And he tells us that teaching was basic to his evangelistic practice; he speaks of 'Christ . . . whom we preach . . . *teaching every man* in all wisdom'.[1] In both texts the reference to teaching is explanatory of the reference to preaching. In other words: it is by teaching that the gospel preacher fulfils his ministry. To *teach* the gospel is his first responsibility: to reduce it to its simplest essentials, to analyse it point by point, to fix its meaning by positive and negative definition, to show how each part of the message links up with the rest—and to go on explaining it till he is quite sure that his listeners have grasped it. And therefore when Paul preached the gospel, formally or informally, in the synagogue or in the streets, to Jews or to Gentiles, to a crowd or to one man, what he did was to *teach* —engaging attention, capturing interest, setting out the facts, explaining their significance, solving difficulties, answering objections, and showing how the message bears on life. Luke's regular way of describing Paul's evangelistic ministry is to say that he *disputed*,[2] or *reasoned* (*dialegomai:* RSV renders 'argued'),[3] or *taught*,[4] or *persuaded* (*i.e.,* sought to carry his hearers' judgments).[5] And Paul himself refers to his ministry among the Gentiles as primarily a task of instruction: 'unto me . . . was this grace given, to preach unto the Gentiles the unsearchable riches of Christ; and *to make all men see* what is the

---

[1] Col. i.28.   [2] Acts ix.29.
[3] Acts xvii.2, 17, RV, xviii.4, xix.8 f., RV, xxiv.25.
[4] Acts xviii.11, xxviii.31.
[5] Acts xviii.4, xix.8, 26, xxviii.23; *cf.* xxvi.28.

dispensation of the mystery . . .'[6] Clearly, in Paul's view, his first and fundamental job as a preacher of the gospel was to communicate knowledge—to get gospel truth fixed in men's minds. To him, teaching the truth was the basic evangelistic activity; to him, therefore, the only right method of evangelism was the teaching method.

3. *Paul's ultimate aim in evangelism was to convert his hearers to faith in Christ.*

The word 'convert' is a translation of the Greek *epistrephō*, which means—and is sometimes translated—'turn'. We think of conversion as a work of God, and so from one standpoint it is; but it is striking to observe that in the three New Testament passages where *epistrephō* is used transitively, of 'converting' someone to God, the subject of the verb is not God, as we might have expected, but a preacher. The angel said of John the Baptist: 'Many of the children of Israel shall he *turn* to the Lord their God.' [7] James says: 'Brethren, if any of you do err from the truth, and one *convert* him; let him know, that he which *converteth* the sinner . . . shall save a soul from death . . .'[8] And Paul himself tells Agrippa how Christ had said to him: 'I send thee (to the Gentiles) to open their eyes, and to *turn* them from darkness to light, and from the power of Satan unto God', and how he had obeyed the heavenly vision by proclaiming to both Jews and Gentiles 'that they should repent and *turn* to God'.[9] These passages represent the converting of others as the

[6] Eph. iii.8, RV. [7] Lk. i.16. [8] Jas. v.19 f.
[9] Acts xxvi. 17 ff.

work of God's people, a task which they are to perform by summoning men to turn to God in repentance and faith.

When the Scriptures speak in this way of converting, and of saving, too, as a task for God's people to
perform, they are not, of course, calling in question
the truth that, properly speaking, it is God who
converts and saves. What they are saying is simply
that the conversion and salvation of others should
be the Christian's objective. The preacher should
work to convert his congregation; the wife should
work to save her unbelieving husband.[1] Christians
are sent to convert, and they should not allow themselves, as Christ's representatives in the world, to
aim at anything less. Evangelizing, therefore, is not
simply a matter of teaching, and instructing, and
imparting information to the mind. There is more
to it than that. Evangelizing includes the endeavour
to elicit a response to the truth taught. It is communication with a view to conversion. It is a matter,
not merely of informing, but also of inviting. It is
an attempt to *gain,* or *win,* or *catch,* our fellow-men
for Christ.[2] Our Lord depicts it as fishermen's work.[3]

Paul, again, is our model here. Paul, as we saw,
knew himself to be sent by Christ, not only to open
men's minds by teaching them the gospel (though
that must come first), but also to turn them to God
by exhorting, and applying the truth to their lives.
Accordingly, his avowed aim was not just to spread
information, but to save sinners : 'that I may by all

[1] 1 Cor. vii.16.   [2] See 1 Cor. ix.19 ff.; 1 Pet. iii.1; Lk. v.10.
                       [3] Mt. iv.19; *cf.* xiii.47.

means save some'.[4] Thus, there was in his evangelistic preaching both instruction—'God was in Christ
reconciling the world unto himself'—and entreaty
—'we beseech you on behalf of Christ, be ye reconciled to God'.[5] His responsibility extended, not only
towards the gospel which he was charged to preach
and preserve, but also towards the needy people to
whom he was sent to impart it, and who were perishing without it.[6] As an apostle of Christ, he was more
than a teacher of truth; he was a shepherd of souls,
sent into the world, not to lecture sinners, but to love
them. For he was an apostle second, and a Christian
first; and, as a Christian, he was a man called to love
his neighbour. This meant simply that in every
situation, and by every means in his power, it was
his business to seek other people's good. From this
standpoint, the significance of his apostolic commission to evangelize and found churches was simply
that this was the particular way in which Christ was
calling him to fulfil the law of love to his neighbour.
He might not, therefore, preach the gospel in a
harsh, callous way, putting it before his neighbour
with a contemptuous air of 'there you are—take it
or leave it', and excusing himself for his unconcern
about people on the grounds of his faithfulness to
the truth. Such conduct would be a failure of love
on his part. His business was to present truth in a
spirit of love, as an expression and implementation
of his desire to save his hearers. The attitude which
informed all Paul's evangelism was this: 'I seek not

[4] 1 Cor. ix.22, RV; cf. Rom. xi.14.   [5] 2 Cor. v.19 f., RV.
[6] Cf. Rom. i.13 ff.

yours, but you . . . and I will very gladly spend and be spent for you.'[7]

And all our own evangelism must be done in the same spirit. As love to our neighbour suggests and demands that we evangelize, so the command to evangelize is a specific application of the command to love others for Christ's sake, and must be fulfilled as such.

Love made Paul warm-hearted and affectionate in his evangelism. 'We were gentle among you,' he reminded the Thessalonians; 'being affectionately desirous of you, we were willing to have imparted unto you, not the gospel of God only, but also our own souls, because ye were dear unto us.'[8] Love also made Paul considerate and adaptable in his evangelism; though he peremptorily refused to change his message to please men,[9] he would go to any lengths in his presentation of it to avoid giving offence, and putting needless difficulties in the way of men's accepting and responding to it. 'Though I was free from all men,' he wrote to the Corinthians, 'I brought myself under bondage to all, that I might gain the more. And to the Jews I became as a Jew, that I might gain Jews; to them that are under the law, as under the law . . . that I might gain them that are under the law; to them that are without law, as without law . . . that I might gain them that are without law. To the weak I became weak, that I might gain the weak; I am become all things to all men, that I may by all means save

[7] 2 Cor. xii.14 f.　　　　[8] 1 Thes. ii.7 f.
[9] *Cf.* Gal. i.10; 2 Cor. ii.17; 1 Thes. ii.4.

some.'[1] Paul sought to save men; and because he sought to save them, he was not content merely to throw truth at them; but he went out of his way to get alongside them, and to start thinking with them from where they were, and to speak to them in terms that they could understand, and above all to avoid everything that would prejudice them against the gospel, and so put stumbling-blocks in their path. In his zeal to maintain truth he never lost sight of the needs and claims of people. His aim and object in all his handling of the gospel, even in the heat of the polemics which contrary views evoked, was never less than to win souls, by converting those whom he saw as his neighbours to faith in the Lord Jesus Christ.

Such was evangelism according to Paul: going out in love, as Christ's agent in the world, to teach sinners the truth of the gospel with a view to converting and saving them. If, therefore, we are engaging in this activity, in this spirit, and with this aim, we are evangelizing, irrespective of the particular means by which we are doing it.

We saw earlier how wrong our thinking would go if we defined evangelism too broadly, and fell into assuming that the production of converts was our personal responsibility. We would now point out that there is an opposite mistake which we must also avoid: the mistake, that is, of defining evangelism too narrowly. One way of making this mistake

[1] 1 Cor. ix.19 ff., RV; cf. x.33.

would be to define evangelism institutionally, in terms of holding some particular type of evangelistic meeting—a meeting, let us say, run on informal lines, at which testimonies are given, choruses are sung, and an appeal is made at the close for some outward sign of having received Christ, such as raising the hand, or standing, or walking to the front. Should we equate the Church's evangelistic responsibility with the holding of such meetings, or the Christian's evangelistic responsibility with bringing unconverted people to such meetings, we should be grievously astray, as the following considerations will show.

1. In the first place, there are many ways of bringing the gospel before the unconverted in order to win them, besides getting them to meetings of this type. There is, to start with, the way of personal evangelism, by which Andrew won Peter, and Philip won Nathanael, and Paul won Onesimus.[2] There is the home meeting, and the group Bible study. Also, and most important, there are the regular services Sunday by Sunday in local churches. Insofar as the preaching at our Sunday services is scriptural, those services will of necessity be evangelistic. It is a mistake to suppose that evangelistic sermons are a special brand of sermons, having their own peculiar style and conventions; evangelistic sermons are just scriptural sermons, the sort of sermons that a man cannot help preaching if he is preaching the Bible biblically. Proper sermons seek to expound and apply what is in the Bible. But what is in the Bible

[2] Jn. i.40 ff., 43 ff.; Phm.10

is just the whole counsel of God for man's salvation; all Scripture bears witness, in one way or another, to Christ, and all biblical themes relate to Him. All proper sermons, therefore, will of necessity declare Christ in some fashion, and so be more or less directly evangelistic. Some sermons, of course, will aim more narrowly and exclusively at converting sinners than do others. But you cannot present the Lord Jesus Christ as the Bible presents Him, as God's answer to every problem in the sinner's relationship with Himself, and not be in effect evangelistic all the time. The Lord Jesus Christ, said Robert Bolton, is 'offered most freely, and without exception of any person, every Sabbath, every Sermon, either in plaine, and direct terms, or implyedly, at the least.'[3] So it is, inevitably, wherever the Bible is preached biblically. And there is something terribly wrong in any church, or any man's ministry, to which Bolton's generalization does not apply. If in our churches 'evangelistic' meetings, and 'evangelistic' sermons, are thought of as special occasions, different from the ordinary run of things, it is a damning indictment of our normal Sunday services. So that if we should imagine that the essential work of evangelism lies in holding meetings of the special type described out of church hours, so to speak, that would simply prove that we had failed to understand what our regular Sunday services are for.

2. Secondly, imagine a local church, or fellowship of Christians, who are giving themselves whole-

[3] *Instructions for a Right Comforting Afflicted Consciences,* 3rd. ed. (1640), p. 185.

heartedly to evangelism by the means mentioned above—personal work, home meetings, and gospel preaching at their ordinary services—but have never had occasion to hold, or to join in, evangelistic meetings of the special sort that we are considering. If we equated the Christian duty of evangelism with running and supporting such meetings, we should have to conclude that this church or fellowship, because it eschewed them, was not evangelizing at all. But that would be like arguing that you cannot really be an Englishman unless you live at Frinton-on-Sea. And it would surely be a little odd to condemn people for not evangelizing just because they do not join in meetings of a type of which there is no trace in the New Testament. Was no evangelizing done, then, in New Testament times?

3. In the third place, it needs to be said that a meeting, or service, is not necessarily evangelistic just because it includes testimonies, and choruses, and an appeal, any more than a man is necessarily English because he wears striped trousers and a bowler hat. The way to find out whether a particular service was evangelistic is to ask, not whether an appeal for decision was made, but what truth was taught at it. If it transpired that insufficient of the gospel was preached to make the appeal for response intelligible to the congregation, the right of the meeting to be called evangelistic would be very doubtful.

We say these things, not to grind a polemical axe, but simply in the interests of clear thinking. It is no part of our purpose to belittle evangelistic meetings and campaigns as such. We are not suggesting that there is no place at all for special evangelistic meetings; that, in face of the rampant paganism of the modern world, would be excessively foolish. The only point we are making here is that there is a place for other forms of evangelistic action too; indeed, under certain circumstances, a prior place. Because God has used meetings, and series of meetings, of this type in the past, there is a certain surface plausibility about the idea that they constitute the normal and natural, and necessary, and indeed only, pattern of evangelism for the present and the future. But this does not follow. There can be evangelism without these meetings. They are in no way essential to the practice of evangelism. Wherever, and by whatever means, the gospel is communicated with a view to conversion, there you have evangelism. Evangelism is to be defined, not institutionally, in terms of the kind of meeting held, but theologically, in terms of what is taught, and for what purpose.

What principles should guide us in assessing the value of different methods of evangelism, and how much the Christian duty to evangelize really involves for us, we shall discuss at a later stage.

II. WHAT IS THE EVANGELISTIC MESSAGE?

We shall have to deal with this fairly summarily. In a word, the evangelistic message is the gospel of Christ, and Him crucified; the message of man's sin and God's grace, of human guilt and divine forgiveness, of new birth and new life through the gift of the Holy Spirit. It is a message made up of four essential ingredients.

1. The gospel is a message about *God*. It tells us who He is, what His character is, what His standards are, and what He requires of us, His creatures. It tells us that we owe our very existence to Him, that for good or ill we are always in His hands and under His eye, and that He made us to worship and serve Him, to show forth His praise and to live for His glory. These truths are the foundation of theistic religion, and until they are grasped the rest of the gospel message will seem neither cogent nor relevant. It is here, with the assertion of man's complete and constant dependence on his Creator, that the Christian story starts.

We can learn again from Paul at this point. When preaching to Jews, as at Pisidian Antioch,[4] he did not need to mention the fact that men were God's creatures; he could take this knowledge for granted, for his hearers had the Old Testament faith behind them. He could begin at once to declare Christ to them, as the fulfilment of Old Testament hopes. But when preaching to Gentiles, who knew nothing of the Old Testament, Paul had to go further back, and start from the beginning. And the beginning from which Paul started in such cases was the doctrine of God's Creatorship, and man's creaturehood. So, when the Athenians asked him to explain what his talk of Jesus and the resurrection was all about, he spoke to them first of God the Creator, and what He made man for. 'God . . . made the world . . . he giveth to all life, and breath, and all things; and hath made . . . all nations . . . that they should seek

[4] Acts xiii.16 ff.

the Lord.'[5] This was not, as some have supposed, a piece of philosophical apologetic of a kind that Paul afterwards renounced, but the first and basic lesson in theistic faith. The gospel starts by teaching us that we, as creatures, are absolutely dependent on God, and that He, as Creator, has an absolute claim on us. Only when we have learned this can we see what sin is, and only when we see what sin is can we understand the good news of salvation from sin. We must know what it means to call God Creator before we can grasp what it means to speak of Him as Redeemer. Nothing can be achieved by talking about sin and salvation where this preliminary lesson has not in some measure been learned.

2. The gospel is a message about *sin*. It tells us how we have fallen short of God's standard; how we have become guilty, filthy, and helpless in sin, and now stand under the wrath of God. It tells us that the reason why we sin continually is that we are sinners by nature, and that nothing we do, or try to do, for ourselves can put us right, or bring us back into God's favour. It shows us ourselves as God sees us, and teaches us to think of ourselves as God thinks of us. Thus it leads us to self-despair. And this also is a necessary step. Not till we have learned our need to get right with God, and our inability to do so by any effort of our own, can we come to know the Christ who saves from sin.

There is a pitfall here. Everybody's life includes things which cause dissatisfaction and shame. Everyone has a bad conscience about some things in his

[5] Acts xvii.24 ff. See also Acts xiv.15 ff.

past, matters in which he has fallen short of the standard which he set for himself, or which was expected of him by others. The danger is that in our evangelism we should content ourselves with evoking thoughts of these things and making people feel uncomfortable about them, and then depicting Christ as the One who saves us from these elements of ourselves, without even raising the question of our relationship with God. But this is just the question that has to be raised when we speak about sin. For the very idea of sin in the Bible is of an offence against God, which disrupts a man's relationship with God. Unless we see our shortcomings in the light of the law and holiness of God, we do not see them *as sin* at all. For sin is not a social concept; it is a theological concept. Though sin is committed by man, and many sins are against society, sin cannot be defined in terms of either man or society. We never know what sin really is till we have learned to think of it in terms of God, and to measure it, not by human standards, but by the yardstick of His total demand on our lives.

What we have to grasp, then, is that the bad conscience of the natural man is not at all the same thing as conviction of sin. It does not, therefore, follow that a man is convicted of sin when he is distressed about his weaknesses and the wrong things he has done. It is not conviction of sin just to feel miserable about yourself and your failures and your inadequacy to meet life's demands. Nor would it be saving faith if a man in that condition called on the Lord Jesus Christ just to soothe him, and cheer him up, and make him feel confident again. Nor should we be preaching the gospel (though we might imagine we were) if all that we did was to present Christ in terms of a man's felt wants. ('Are you happy? Are you satisfied? Do you want peace of mind? Do you feel that you have failed? Are you fed up with yourself? Do you want a friend? Then come to Christ; He will meet your every need ...'— as if the Lord Jesus Christ were to be thought of as a fairy godmother, or a super-psychiatrist.) No; we have to go deeper than this. To preach sin means, not to make capital out of people's felt frailties (the brainwasher's trick), but to measure their lives by the holy law of God. To be convicted of sin means, not just to feel that one is an all-round flop, but to realize that one has offended God, and flouted His authority, and defied Him, and gone against Him, and put oneself in the wrong with Him. To preach Christ means to set Him forth as the One who through His cross sets men right with God again. To put faith in Christ means relying on Him, and Him alone, to restore us to God's fellowship and favour.

It is indeed true that the real Christ, the Christ of the Bible, who offers Himself to us as a Saviour from sin and an Advocate with God, does in fact give peace, and joy, and moral strength, and the privilege of His own friendship, to those who trust Him. But the Christ who is depicted and desired merely to make the lot of life's casualties easier by supplying them with aids and comforts is not the real Christ, but a misrepresented and misconceived

Christ—in effect, an imaginary Christ. And if we taught people to look to an imaginary Christ, we should have no grounds for expecting that they would find a real salvation. We must be on our guard, therefore, against equating a natural bad conscience and sense of wretchedness with spiritual conviction of sin, and so omitting in our evangelism to impress upon sinners the basic truth about their condition—namely, that their sin has alienated them from God, and exposed them to His condemnation, and hostility, and wrath, so that their first need is for a restored relationship with Him.

It may be asked: what are the signs of true conviction of sin, as distinct from the mere smart of a natural bad conscience, or the mere disgust at life which any disillusioned person may feel?

The signs seem to be three in number.

(i) Conviction of sin is essentially an awareness of *a wrong relationship with God* : not just with one's neighbour, or one's own conscience and ideals for oneself, but with one's Maker, the God in whose hand one's breath is and on whom one depends for existence every moment. To define conviction of sin as a sense of need, without qualification, would not be enough; it is not any sense of need, but a sense of a particular need—a need, namely, for restoration of fellowship with God. It is the realization that, as one stands at present, one is in a relationship with God that spells only rejection, and retribution, and wrath, and pain, for the present and the future; and a realization that this is an intolerable relationship to remain in, and

therefore a desire that, at whatever cost and on whatever terms, it might be changed. Conviction of sin
may centre upon the sense of one's guilt before God,
or one's uncleanness in His sight, or one's rebellion
against Him, or one's alienation and estrangement
from Him; but always it is a sense of the need to get
right, not simply with oneself or other people, but
with God.

(*ii*) Conviction of sin always includes conviction
of *sins* : a sense of guilt for particular wrongs done
in the sight of God, from which one needs to turn,
and be rid of them, if one is ever to be right with
God. Thus, Isaiah was convicted specifically of sins
of speech,[6] and Zacchaeus of sins of extortion.[7]

(*iii*) Conviction of sin always includes conviction
of *sinfulness* : a sense of one's complete corruption
and perversity in God's sight, and one's consequent
need of what Ezekiel called a 'new heart',[8] and our
Lord a new birth,[9] *i.e.* a moral re-creation. Thus, the
author of Psalm li—traditionally identified with
David, convicted of his sin with Bathsheba—confesses, not only particular transgressions (verses 1–4),
but also the depravity of his nature (verses 5–6), and
seeks cleansing from the guilt and defilement of both
(verses 7–10). Indeed, perhaps the shortest way to
tell whether a person is convicted of sin or not is to
take him through Psalm li, and see whether his heart
is in fact speaking anything like the language of the
psalmist.

3. The gospel is a message about *Christ*—Christ
the Son of God incarnate; Christ the Lamb of God,

[6] Is. vi.5.   [7] Lk. xix.8.   [8] Ezk. xxxvi.26.   [9] Jn. iii.3 ff.

dying for sin; Christ the risen Lord; Christ the perfect Saviour.

Two points need to be made about the declaring of this part of the message.

(i) *We must not present the Person of Christ apart from His saving work.*

It is sometimes said that it is the presentation of Christ's Person, rather than of doctrines about Him, that draws sinners to His feet. It is true that it is the living Christ who saves, and that a theory of the atonement, however orthodox, is no substitute. When this remark is made, however, what is usually being suggested is that doctrinal instruction is dispensable in evangelistic preaching, and that all the evangelist need do is paint a vivid word-picture of the Man of Galilee who went about doing good, and then assure his hearers that this Jesus is still alive to help them in their troubles. But such a message could hardly be called the gospel. It would, in reality, be a mere conundrum, serving only to mystify. Who was this Jesus? we should ask; and what is His position now? Such preaching would raise these questions while concealing the answers. And thus it would completely baffle the thoughtful listener.

For the truth is that you cannot make sense of the historic figure of Jesus till you know about the *incarnation*—that this Jesus was in fact God the Son, made man to save sinners according to His Father's eternal purpose. Nor can you make sense of His life till you know about the *atonement*—that He lived

as man so that He might die as man for men, and
that His passion, His judicial murder, was really His
saving action of bearing away the world's sins. Nor
can you tell on what terms to approach Him now
till you know about the *resurrection, ascension,* and
heavenly session—that Jesus has been raised, and
enthroned, and made King, and lives to save to the
uttermost all who acknowledge His Lordship. These
doctrines, to mention no others, are essential to the
gospel. Without them, there is no gospel, only a
puzzle story about a man named Jesus. To oppose
the teaching of doctrines about Christ to the presenting of His Person is, therefore, to put asunder
two things which God has joined. It is really very
perverse indeed; for the whole purpose of teaching
these doctrines in evangelism is to throw light on the
Person of the Lord Jesus Christ, and to make clear
to our hearers just who it is that we want them to
meet. When, in ordinary social life, we want people
to know who it is that we are introducing them to,
we tell them something about him, and what he has
done; and so it is here. The apostles themselves
preached these doctrines in order to preach Christ,
as the New Testament shows. In fact, without these
doctrines you would have no gospel to preach at all.

(*ii*) But there is a second and complementary
point. *We must not present the saving work of Christ
apart from His Person.*

Evangelistic preachers and personal workers have
sometimes been known to make this mistake. In
their concern to focus attention on the atoning death

of Christ, as the sole sufficient ground on which sinners may be accepted with God, they have expounded the summons to saving faith in these terms: 'Believe that Christ died for your sins.' The effect of this exposition is to represent the saving work of Christ in the past, dissociated from His Person in the present, as the whole object of our trust. But it is not biblical thus to isolate the work from the Worker. Nowhere in the New Testament is the call to believe expressed in such terms. What the New Testament calls for is faith in (*en*) or into (*eis*) or upon (*epi*) Christ Himself—the placing of our trust in the living Saviour, who died for sins. The object of saving faith is thus not, strictly speaking, the atonement, but the Lord Jesus Christ, who made atonement. We must not in presenting the gospel isolate the cross and its benefits from the Christ whose cross it was. For the persons to whom the benefits of Christ's death belong are just those who trust His Person, and believe, not upon His saving death simply, but upon *Him*, the living Saviour. 'Believe on *the Lord Jesus Christ*, and thou shalt be saved,'[1] said Paul. 'Come unto *me* . . . and *I* will give you rest,'[2] said our Lord.

This being so, one thing becomes clear straight away : namely, that the question about the extent of the atonement, which is being much agitated in some quarters, has no bearing on the content of the evangelistic message at this particular point. I do not propose to discuss this question now; I have done

[1] Acts xvi.31.   [2] Mt. xi.28.

that elsewhere.[3] I am not at present asking you whether you think it is true to say that Christ died in order to save every single human being, past, present, and future, or not. Nor am I at present inviting you to make up your mind on this question, if you have not done so already. All I want to say here is that even if you think the above assertion is true, your presentation of Christ in evangelism ought not to differ from that of the man who thinks it false.

What I mean is this. It is obvious that if a preacher thought that the statement, 'Christ died for every one of you', made to any congregation, would be unverifiable, and probably not true, he would take care not to make it in his gospel preaching. You do not find such statements in the sermons of, for instance, George Whitefield or Charles Spurgeon. But now, my point is that, even if a man thinks that this statement would be true if he made it, it is not a thing that he ever needs to say, or ever has reason to say, when preaching the gospel. For preaching the

[3] In my introduction to the 1959 reprint of *The Death of Death in the Death of Christ*, by John Owen. Owen's book is a classical discussion of the complex of questions which the controversy about 'limited atonement' involves. The central issue does not concern the value of the atonement, considered in itself, nor the availability of Christ to those who would trust Him as their Saviour. All agree that no limit can be set to the intrinsic worth of Christ's death, and that Christ never casts out those who come to Him. The cleavage is over the question, whether the intention of the Father and the Son in the great transaction of Calvary was to save any more than actually are saved. There is no room here to open up this elaborate question; and in any case, nothing in the text depends one way or the other on the answer that one gives to it.

gospel, as we have just seen, means inviting sinners
to come to Jesus Christ, the living Saviour, who, by
virtue of His atoning death, is able to forgive and
save all those who put their trust in Him. What has
to be said about the cross when preaching the gospel
is simply that Christ's death is the ground on which
Christ's forgiveness is given. And this is all that has
to be said. The question of the designed extent of
the atonement does not come into the story at all.

The fact is that the New Testament never calls
on any man to repent on the ground that Christ died
specifically and particularly for him. The basis on
which the New Testament invites sinners to put
faith in Christ is simply that they need Him, and
that He offers Himself to them, and that those who
receive Him are promised all the benefits that His
death secured for His people. What is universal and
all-inclusive in the New Testament is the invitation
to faith, and the promise of salvation to all who
believe.[4]

Our task in evangelism is to reproduce as faithfully as possible the New Testament emphasis. To go
beyond the New Testament, or to distort its view-
point or shift its stress, is always wrong. And therefore—if we may at this point speak in the words of
James Denney—'we do not think of separating
(Christ's) work from Him who achieved it. The New
Testament knows only of a living Christ, and all

---

[4] See Mt. xi.28 ff., xxii.9; Lk. ii.10 f., xii.8; Jn. i.12, iii.14
ff., vi.40, 54, vii.37, xi.26, xii.46; Acts ii.21, x.43, xiii.39; Rom.
i.16, iii.22, ix.33, x.4 ff.; Gal. iii.22; Tit. ii.11; Rev. xxii.17;
cf. Is. lv.1.

apostolic preaching of the gospel holds up the living Christ to men. But the living Christ is Christ who died, and He is never preached apart from His death, and from its reconciling power. It is *the living Christ, with the virtue of His reconciling death in Him*, who is the burden of the apostolic message ... The task of the evangelist is to preach *Christ ... in His character as the Crucified*.'[5] The gospel is not, 'believe that Christ died for everybody's sins, and therefore for yours,' any more than it is, 'believe that Christ died only for certain people's sins, and so perhaps not for yours.' The gospel is, 'believe on the Lord Jesus Christ, who died for sins, and now offers you Himself as your Saviour.' This is the message which we are to take to the world. We have no business to ask them to put faith in any view of the extent of the atonement; our job is to point them to the living Christ, and summon them to trust in Him.

It was because they had both grasped this that John Wesley and George Whitefield could regard each other as brothers in evangelism, though they differed on the extent of the atonement. For their views on this subject did not enter into their gospel preaching. Both were content to preach the gospel just as it stands in Scripture: that is, to proclaim 'the living Christ, with the virtue of His reconciling death in Him', to offer Him to sinners, and to invite the lost to come to Him and so find life.

4. This brings us to the final ingredient in the

'*The Christian Doctrine of Reconciliation*, p. 287; my italics.

gospel message. The gospel is a summons to *faith and repentance*.

All who hear the gospel are summoned by God to repent and believe. 'God . . . commandeth all men every where to *repent*,' Paul told the Athenians.[6] When asked by His hearers what they should do in order to 'work the works of God', our Lord replied: 'This is the work of God, that ye *believe* on him whom he hath sent.'[7] And in 1 John iii.23 we read: 'This is his *commandment*, That we should believe on the name of his Son Jesus Christ . . .' Repentance and faith are rendered matters of duty by God's direct command, and hence impenitence and unbelief are singled out in the New Testament as most grievous sins.[8] With these universal commands, as we indicated above, go universal promises of salvation to all who obey them. 'Through his name *whosoever believeth* in him shall receive remission of sins.'[9] '*Whosoever will*, let him take the water of life freely.'[1] 'God so loved the world, that he gave his only begotten Son, that *whosoever believeth* in him should not perish, but have everlasting life.'[2] These words are promises to which God will stand as long as time shall last.

It needs to be said that faith is not a mere optimistic feeling, any more than repentance is a mere regretful or remorseful feeling. Faith and repentance are both acts, and acts of the whole man. Faith is more than just credence; faith is essentially the

---

[6] Acts xvii.30.   [7] Jn. vi.29.
[8] *Cf.* Lk. xiii.3, 5; 2 Thes. ii.11 f.   [9] Acts x.43.
[1] Rev. xxii.17.   [2] Jn. iii.16.

casting and resting of oneself and one's confidence on the promises of mercy which Christ has given to sinners, and on the Christ who gave those promises. Equally, repentance is more than just sorrow for the past; repentance is a change of mind and heart, a new life of denying self and serving the Saviour as king in self's place. Mere credence without trusting, and mere remorse without turning, do not save. 'The devils also believe, and tremble.'[3] 'The sorrow of the world worketh death.'[4]

Two further points need to be made also.

(i) The demand is for *faith as well as repentance*. It is not enough to resolve to turn from sin, and give up evil habits, and try to put Christ's teaching into practice by being religious and doing all possible good to others. Aspiration, and resolution, and morality, and religiosity, are no substitutes for faith. Martin Luther and John Wesley had all these long before they had faith. If there is to be faith, however, there must be a foundation of knowledge: a man must know of Christ, and of His cross, and of His promises, before saving faith becomes a possibility for him. In our presentation of the gospel, therefore, we need to stress these things, in order to lead sinners to abandon all confidence in themselves and to trust wholly in Christ and the power of His redeeming blood to give them acceptance with God. For nothing less than this is faith.

(ii) The demand is for *repentance as well as faith*. It is not enough to believe that only through Christ and His death are sinners justified and accepted, and

[3] Jas. ii.19.   [4] 2 Cor. vii.10

that one's own record is sufficient to bring down God's condemning sentence twenty times over, and that, apart from Christ, one has no hope. Knowledge of the gospel, and orthodox belief of it, is no substitute for repentance. If there is to be repentance, however, there must, again, be a foundation of knowledge. A man must know that, in the words of the first of Luther's Ninety-five Theses, 'when our Lord and Master, Jesus Christ, said "Repent", He called for the entire life of believers to be one of repentance,' and he must also know what repentance involves. More than once, Christ deliberately called attention to the radical break with the past that repentance involves. 'If any man will come after me, let him *deny himself*, and take up his cross daily, and follow me ... whosoever will *lose his life for my sake*, the same (but only he) shall save it.'[5] 'If any man come to me, and *hate not* his father, and mother, and wife, and children, and brethren, and sisters, yea, and his own life also (*i.e.*, put them all decisively second in his esteem), *he cannot be my disciple* ... whosoever he be of you that forsaketh not all that he hath, *he cannot be my disciple*.'[6] The repentance that Christ requires of His people consists in a settled refusal to set any limit to the claims which He may make on their lives. Our Lord knew —who better?—how costly His followers would find it to maintain this refusal, and let Him have His way with them all the time, and therefore He wished them to face out and think through the implications of discipleship before committing themselves. He

[5] Lk. ix.23 f.   [6] Lk. xiv.26, 33.

did not desire to make disciples under false pretences. He had no interest in gathering vast crowds of professed adherents who would melt away as soon as they found out what following Him actually demanded of them. In our own presentation of Christ's gospel, therefore, we need to lay a similar stress on the cost of following Christ, and make sinners face it soberly before we urge them to respond to the message of free forgiveness. In common honesty, we must not conceal the fact that free forgiveness in one sense will cost everything; or else our evangelizing becomes a sort of confidence trick. And where there is no clear knowledge, and hence no realistic recognition of the real claims that Christ makes, there can be no repentance, and therefore no salvation.

Such is the evangelistic message that we are sent to make known.

III. WHAT IS THE MOTIVE FOR EVANGELIZING?

There are, in fact, two motives that should spur us constantly to evangelize. The first is love to God and concern for His glory; the second is love to man and concern for his welfare.

1. The *first* motive is primary and fundamental. The chief end of man is to glorify God. The biblical rule of life is: 'do all to the glory of God.'[7] Men glorify God by obeying His word and fulfilling His revealed will. Similarly, the first and great commandment is: 'Thou shalt love the Lord thy God.'[8] We show love to the Father and the Son, who have so richly loved us, by keeping Their commandments.

[7] 1 Cor. x.31. [8] Mt. xxii.37 f.

'He that hath my commandments, and keepeth them, he it is that loveth me,' said our Lord.[9] 'This is the love of God,' wrote John, 'that we keep his commandments.'[1] Now, evangelism is one of the activities that the Father and the Son have commanded. 'This gospel of the kingdom,' Christ tells us, 'shall' (according to Mark, 'must') 'be preached in all the world for a witness.'[2] And before His ascension Christ charged His disciples in the following categorical terms: 'Go ye . . . and make disciples of all the nations.' To this command He added at once a comprehensive promise: 'and lo, I am with you alway, even unto the end of the world.'[3] The comprehensiveness of this promise shows us how wide is the application of the command to which it is appended. The phrase 'even unto the end of the world' makes it clear that the 'you' to whom the promise was given was not solely and exclusively the eleven disciples; this promise extends to the whole Christian Church throughout history, the entire community of which the eleven were, so to speak, founder members. It is, therefore, a promise for us no less than for them, and a promise of great comfort too. But if the promise extends to us, then the commission with which it is linked must extend to us also. The promise was given to encourage the eleven, lest they be overwhelmed at the size and difficulty of the task of world evangelism that Christ was laying upon them. If it is our privilege to appropriate the promise, then it is also our responsibility to accept the

<hr>

[9] Jn. xiv.21.   [1] 1 Jn. v.3.
[2] Mt. xxiv.14; Mk. xiii.10.   [3] Mt. xxviii.19 f., RV.

commission. The task laid upon the eleven is the Church's constant task. And if it is the Church's task in general, then it is your task and my task in particular. If, therefore, we love God and are concerned to glorify Him, we must obey His command to evangelize.

There is a further strand to this thought. We glorify God by evangelizing, not only because evangelizing is an act of obedience, but also because in evangelism we tell the world what great things God has done for the salvation of sinners. God is glorified when His mighty works of grace are made known. The psalmist exhorts us to 'shew forth his salvation from day to day. Declare his glory among the heathen, his wonders among all people.'[4] For a Christian to talk to the unconverted about the Lord Jesus Christ and His saving power is in itself honouring and glorifying to God.

2. The *second* motive that should prompt us to assiduous evangelism is love to our neighbour, and the desire to see our fellow-men saved. The wish to win the lost for Christ should be, and indeed is, the natural, spontaneous outflow of love in the heart of everyone who has been born again. Our Lord confirms the Old Testament demand that we should love our neighbour as ourselves.[5] 'As we have therefore opportunity,' writes Paul, 'let us do good unto all men.'[6] What greater need has any man than the need to know Christ? What greater good can we do to any man than to set before him the knowledge of Christ? Insofar as we really love our neighbour as

'Ps. xcvi.2 f.　　⁵Mk. xii.31; Lk. x.27 f.　　⁶Gal. vi.10.

ourselves, we shall of necessity want him to enjoy the salvation which is so precious to us. This, indeed, should not be a thing that we need to think about, let alone argue about. The impulse to evangelize should spring up spontaneously in us as we see our neighbour's need of Christ.

Who is my neighbour? When the lawyer, confronted with the demand of love for one's neighbour, asked our Lord this question, Christ replied by telling the story of the Good Samaritan.[7] What that story teaches is simply this: that any fellow human being whom you meet who is in need is your neighbour; God has put him there so that you may help him; and your business is to show yourself neighbour to him by doing all that you can to meet his need, whatever it may be. 'Go, and do thou likewise,' said our Lord to the lawyer. He says the same to us. And the principle applies to all forms of need, spiritual no less than material. So that when we find ourselves in contact with men and women who are without Christ, and so face spiritual death, we are to look on them as our neighbours in this sense, and ask ourselves what we can do to make Christ known to them.

May I stress again: if we ourselves have known anything of the love of Christ for us, and if our hearts have felt any measure of gratitude for the grace that has saved us from death and hell, then this attitude of compassion and care for our spiritually needy fellow-men ought to come naturally and spontaneously to us. It was in connection with

[7] Lk. x.29 ff.

aggressive evangelism that Paul declared that 'the love of Christ constraineth us'.[8] It is a tragic and ugly thing when Christians lack desire, and are actually reluctant, to share the precious knowledge that they have with others whose need of it is just as great as their own. It was natural for Andrew, when he found the Messiah, to go off and tell his brother Simon, and for Philip to hurry to break the good news to his friend Nathanael.[9] They did not need to be told to do this; they did it naturally and spontaneously, just as one would naturally and spontaneously share with one's family and friends any other piece of news that vitally affected them. There is something very wrong with us if we do not ourselves find it natural to act in this way : let us be quite clear about that. It is a great privilege to evangelize; it is a wonderful thing to be able to tell others of the love of Christ, knowing that there is nothing that they need more urgently to know, and no knowledge in the world that can do them so much good. We should not, therefore, be reluctant and backward to evangelize on the personal and individual level. We should be glad and happy to do it. We should not look for excuses for wriggling out of our obligation when occasion offers to talk to others about the Lord Jesus Christ. If we find ourselves shrinking from this responsibility, and trying to evade it, we need to face ourselves with the fact that in this we are yielding to sin and Satan. If (as is usual) it is the fear of being thought odd and ridiculous, or of losing popularity in certain circles, that holds us back, we need to ask

[8] 2 Cor. v.14.   [9] Jn. i.40 ff.

ourselves in the presence of God : Ought these things to stop us loving our neighbour? If it is a false shame, which is not shame at all, but pride in disguise, that keeps our tongue from Christian witness when we are with other people, we need to press upon our conscience this question : Which matters more—our reputation, or their salvation? We cannot be complacent about this gangrene of conceit and cowardice when we weigh up our lives in the presence of God. What we need to do is to ask for grace to be truly ashamed of ourselves, and to pray that we may so overflow in love to God that we shall overflow in love to our fellow-men, and so find it an easy and natural and joyful thing to share with them the good news of Christ.

By now, I hope, it is becoming clear to us how we should regard our evangelistic responsibility. Evangelism is not the only task that our Lord has given us, nor is it a task that we are all called to discharge in the same way. We are not all called to be preachers; we are not all given equal opportunities or comparable abilities for personal dealing with men and women who need Christ. But we all have some evangelistic responsibility which we cannot shirk without failing in love both to our God and to our neighbour. To start with, we all can and should be praying for the salvation of unconverted people, particularly in our family, and among our friends and everyday associates. And then we must learn to see what possibilities of evangelism our everyday situation holds, and to be enterprising in our use of them. It is the nature of love to be enterprising. If you love someone, you are constantly trying to think out what is the best you can do for him, and how best you can please him, and it is your pleasure to give him pleasure by the things you devise for him. If, then, we love God—Father, Son, and Spirit—for all that They have done for us, we shall muster all our initiative and enterprise to make the most that we can of every situation for Their glory—and one chief way of doing this is to seek out ways and means of spreading the gospel, and obeying the divine command to make disciples everywhere. Similarly, if we love our neighbour, we shall muster all our initiative and enterprise to find ways and means of doing him good. And one chief way of doing him good is to share with him our knowledge of Christ. Thus, if we love God and our neighbour, we shall evangelize, and we shall be enterprising in our evangelism. We shall not ask with reluctance how much we have to do in this realm, as if evangelizing were a distasteful and burdensome task. We shall not enquire anxiously after the minimum outlay of effort in evangelism that will satisfy God. But we shall ask eagerly, and pray earnestly to be shown, just how much it is in our power to do to spread the knowledge of Christ among men; and once we see what the possibilities are, we shall give ourselves wholeheartedly to the task.

One further point must be added, however, lest what we have said be misapplied. It must never be forgotten that the enterprise required of us in evangelism is the enterprise of love: an enterprise that springs from a genuine interest in those whom we seek to win, and a genuine care for their well-being, and expresses itself in a genuine respect for them and a genuine friendliness towards them. One sometimes meets a scalp-hunting zeal in evangelism, both in the pulpit and on the personal level, which is both discreditable and alarming. It is discreditable, because it reflects, not love and care, nor the desire to be of help, but arrogance, and conceit, and pleasure in having power over the lives of others. It is alarming, because it finds expression in a ferocious psychological pommelling of the poor victim which may do great damage to sensitive and impressionable souls. But if love prompts and rules our evangelistic work, we shall approach other people in a different spirit. If we truly care for them, and if our heart truly loves and fears God, then we shall seek to present Christ to them in a way that is both honouring to Him and respectful to them. We shall not try to violate their personalities, or exploit their weaknesses, or ride roughshod over their feelings. What we shall be trying to do, rather, is to show them the reality of our friendship and concern by sharing with them our most valuable possession. And this spirit of friendship and concern will shine through all that we say to them, whether in the pulpit or in private, however drastic and shattering the truths that we tell them may be.

There is a famous old book on personal evangelism by C. G. Trumbull, entitled *Taking Men Alive*. In the third chapter of that book, the author tells us of the rule that his father, H. C. Trumbull, made for himself in this matter. It was as follows:

'Whenever I am justified in choosing my subject of conversation with another, the theme of themes (Christ) shall have prominence between us, so that I may learn of his need, and, if possible, meet it.' The key words here are: *'whenever I am justified in choosing my subject of conversation with another'.* They remind us, first, that personal evangelism, like all our dealings with our fellow-men, should be courteous. And they remind us, second, that personal evangelism needs normally to be founded on friendship. You are not usually justified in choosing the subject of conversation with another till you have already begun to give yourself to him in friendship and established a relationship with him in which he feels that you respect him, and are interested in him, and are treating him as a human being, and not just as some kind of 'case'. With some people, you may establish such a relationship in five minutes, whereas with others it may take months. But the principle remains the same. The right to talk intimately to another person about the Lord Jesus Christ has to be earned, and you earn it by convincing him that you are his friend, and really care about him. And therefore the indiscriminate buttonholing, the intrusive barging in to the privacy of other people's souls, the thick-skinned insistence on expounding the things of God to reluctant strangers who are longing to get away—these modes of behaviour, in which strong and loquacious personalities have sometimes indulged in the name of personal evangelism, should be written off as a travesty of personal evangelism. *Impersonal* evangelism would be a better name for them! In fact, rudeness of this sort dishonours God; moreover, it creates resentment, and prejudices people against the Christ whose professed followers act so objectionably. The truth is that real personal evangelism is very costly, just because it demands of us a really personal relationship with the other man. We have to give ourselves in honest friendship to people, if ever our relationship with them is to reach the point at which we are justified in choosing to talk to them about Christ, and can speak to them about their own spiritual needs without being either discourteous or offensive. If you wish to do personal evangelism, then—and I hope you do; you ought to —pray for the gift of friendship. A genuine friendliness is in any case a prime mark of the man who is learning to love his neighbour as himself.

IV. BY WHAT MEANS AND METHODS SHOULD EVANGELISM BE PRACTISED?

There is today a controversy in some evangelical circles about evangelistic methods. Some are criticizing, and others are defending, the type of evangelistic meeting that has been a standard feature of English and American evangelical life for almost a century. Meetings of this type are well known, for they are very characteristic. They are deliberately made brisk and bright, in the hope that people who have little interest in the Christian message, and who may never have been inside a Christian church, may nevertheless find them an attraction. Everything is accordingly planned to create an atmosphere of warmth, good humour and happiness. The meeting normally includes a good deal of music—choir items, solo items, choruses, and rousing hymns, heartily sung. Heavy emphasis is laid on the realities of Christian experience, both by the choice of hymns and by the use of testimonies. The meeting leads up to an appeal for decision, followed by an after-meeting or a time of personal counselling for the further instruction of those who have made, or wish to make, a decision in response to the appeal.

The main criticisms that are made of such meetings—whether they are wholly justified we would not venture to say—are as follows. Their breezy slickness (it is said) makes for irreverence. The attempt to give them 'entertainment value' tends to lessen the sense of God's majesty, to banish the spirit of worship, and to cheapen men's thoughts of their Creator; moreover, it is the worst possible preparation of the potential converts for the regular Sunday services in the churches which they will in due course join. The seemingly inevitable glamourizing of Christian experience in the testimonies is pastorally irresponsible, and gives a falsely romanticized impression of what being a Christian is like. This, together with the tendency to indulge in long-drawn-out wheedling for decisions and the deliberate use of luscious music to stir sentiment, tends to produce 'conversions' which are simply psychological and emotional upheavals, and not the fruit of spiritual conviction and renewal at all. The occasional character of the meetings makes it inevitable that appeals for decision will often be made on the basis of inadequate instruction as to what the decision involves and will cost, and such appeals are no better than a confidence trick. The desire to justify the meetings by reaping a crop of converts may prompt the preacher and the counsellors to try and force people through the motions of decision prematurely, before they have grasped what it is really all about, and converts produced in this way tend to prove at best stunted and at worst spurious and, in the event, gospel-hardened. The way ahead in evangelism, it is said, is to break completely with this pattern of evangelistic action, and to develop a new pattern (or, rather, restore the old one which existed before this type of meeting became standard), in which the evangelizing unit is the local church rather than a group or cross-section of churches, and the evangelistic meeting finds its place among the local church's services—a pattern, indeed, in which the local church's services function continually as its evangelistic meetings.

The usual reply is that, while the things stigmatized are certainly real abuses, evangelistic meetings of the standard pattern can be, and frequently are, run in a way that avoids them. Such meetings, it is said, have proved their usefulness in the past; experience shows that God uses them still; and there seems to be no sufficient reason for abandoning them. It is argued that, while so many churches in each major denomination are failing in their evangelistic responsibility, these meetings may well be the only opportunity for presenting the gospel to vast multitudes of our fellow-men and women. The way ahead, therefore, it is maintained, is not to abolish them, but to reform them where abuses exist.

The debate continues. No doubt it will remain with us for some time to come. What I want to do here is not to go into this controversy, but to go behind it. I want to isolate the key principle that should guide us in our assessment both of these and any other methods of evangelism that may be practised or proposed.

What is this key principle? The following line of thought will make it clear.

Evangelism, as we have seen, is an act of communication with a view to conversion. In the last analysis, therefore, there is only one *means* of evangelism : namely, the gospel of Christ, explained and applied. Faith and repentance, the two complementary elements of which conversion consists, occur as a response to the gospel. 'Belief cometh of hearing,' Paul tells us, 'and hearing by the word of Christ'[1]—or, as *The New English Bible* expands the verse, 'faith is awakened by the message, and the message that awakens it comes through the word of Christ'.

Again, in the last analysis, there is only one *agent* of evangelism : namely, the Lord Jesus Christ. It is Christ Himself who through His Holy Spirit enables His servants to explain the gospel truly and apply it powerfully and effectively; just as it is Christ Himself who through His Holy Spirit opens men's minds[2] and hearts[3] to receive the gospel, and so

[1] Rom. x.17, RV.   [2] Lk. xxiv.45.   [3] Acts xvi.14.

draws them savingly to Himself.[4] Paul speaks of
his achievements as an evangelist as 'those (things)
which *Christ wrought through me*, for the obedience
of the Gentiles, by word and deed . . . *in the power
of the Holy Ghost*'.[5] Since Augustine the point has
often been made that Christ is the true minister of
the gospel sacraments, and the human celebrant acts
merely as His hand. We need to remember the
equally basic truth that Christ is the true minister of
the gospel word, and the human preacher or witness
acts merely as His mouth.

So, in the last analysis, there is only one *method*
of evangelism: namely, the faithful explanation
and application of the gospel message. From which it
follows—and this is the key principle which we are
seeking—that the test for any proposed strategy, or
technique, or style, of evangelistic action must be
this: will it in fact serve the word? Is it calculated
to be a means of explaining the gospel truly and
fully and applying it deeply and exactly? To the
extent to which it is so calculated, it is lawful and
right; to the extent to which it tends to overlay and
obscure the realities of the message, and to blunt the
edge of their application, it is ungodly and wrong.

Let us work this out. It means that we need to
bring under review all our evangelistic plans and
practices—our missions, rallies, and campaigns; our
sermons, talks, and testimonies; our big meetings,
our little meetings, and our presentation of the
gospel in personal dealing; the tracts that we give,
the books that we lend, the letters that we write—

[4] Jn. xii.32.   [5] Rom. xv.18 f., RV.

and to ask about each of them questions such as the
following:

Is this way of presenting Christ calculated to impress on people that the gospel is *a word from God*?
Is it calculated to divert their attention from man
and all things merely human to God and His truth?
Or is its tendency rather to distract attention from
the Author and authority of the message to the
person and performance of the messenger? Does it
make the gospel sound like a human idea, a
preacher's plaything, or like a divine revelation, before which the human messenger himself stands in
awe? Does this way of presenting Christ savour of
human cleverness and showmanship? Does it tend
thereby to exalt man? Or does it embody rather the
straightforward, unaffected simplicity of the messenger whose sole concern is to deliver his message,
and who has no wish to call attention to himself, and
who desires so far as he can to blot himself out and
hide, as it were, behind his message, fearing nothing
so much as that men should admire and applaud
him when they ought to be bowing down and hum-
bling themselves before the mighty Lord whom he
represents?

Again: is this way of presenting Christ calculated
to promote, or impede, the work of the word in
men's *minds*? Is it going to clarify the meaning of
the message, or to leave it enigmatic and obscure,
locked up in pious jargon and oracular formulae?
Is it going to make people think, and think hard,
and think hard about God, and about themselves in
relation to God? Or will it tend to stifle thought by

playing exclusively on the emotions? Is it calculated to stir the mind, or put it to sleep? Is this way
of presenting Christ an attempt to move men by the
force of feeling, or of truth? Not, of course, that
there is anything wrong with emotion; it is strange
for a person to be converted without emotion; what
is wrong is the sort of appeal to emotion, and playing
on emotion, which harrows people's feelings as a
substitute for instructing their minds.

Again : we have to ask, is this way of presenting
Christ calculated to convey to people the *doctrine* of
the gospel, and not just part of it, but the whole of it
—the truth about our Creator and His claims, and
about ourselves as guilty, lost, and helpless sinners,
needing to be born again, and about the Son of God
who became man, and died for sins, and lives to
forgive sinners and bring them to God? Or is it likely
to be deficient here, and deal in half-truths, and
leave people with an incomplete understanding of
these things, and hurry them on to the demand for
faith and repentance without having made it clear
just what they need to repent of, or what they ought
to believe?

Again : we have to ask, is this way of presenting
Christ calculated to convey to people the *application*
of the gospel, and not just part of it, but the whole
of it—the summons to see and know oneself as God
sees and knows one, that is, as a sinful creature, and
to face the breadth and depth of the need into which
a wrong relationship with God has brought one, and
to face too the cost and consequences of turning to
receive Christ as Saviour and Lord? Or is it likely to

be deficient here, and to gloss over some of this, and to give an inadequate, distorted impression of what the gospel requires? Will it, for instance, leave people unaware that they have any immediate obligation to respond to Christ at all? Or will it leave them supposing that all they have to do is to trust Christ as a sin-bearer, not realizing that they must also deny themselves and enthrone Him as their Lord (the error which we might call only-believism)? Or will it leave them imagining that the whole of what they have to do is to consecrate themselves to Christ as their Master, not realizing that they must also receive Him as their Saviour (the error which we might call good-resolutionism)? We need to remember here that spiritually it is even more dangerous for a man whose conscience is roused to make a misconceived response to the gospel, and take up with a defective religious practice, than for him to make no response at all. If you turn a publican into a Pharisee, you make his condition worse, not better.

Again: we have to ask, is this way of presenting Christ calculated to convey gospel truth in a manner that is appropriately *serious?* Is it calculated to make people feel that they are indeed facing a matter of life and death? Is it calculated to make them see and feel the greatness of God, and the greatness of their sin and need, and the greatness of the grace of Christ? Is it calculated to make them aware of the awful majesty and holiness of God? Will it help them to realize that it is a fearful thing to fall into His hands? Or is this way of presenting Christ so light and casual and cosy and jolly as to make it hard for the hearers to feel that the gospel is a matter of any consequence, save as a pick-me-up for life's misfits? It is a gross insult to God, and a real disservice to men, to cheapen and trivialize the gospel by one's presentation of it. Not that we should put on an affected solemnity when speaking of spiritual things; there is nothing more essentially frivolous than a mock seriousness, and nothing more likely to make hypocrites out of our hearers. What is needed is this : that we, who would speak for Christ, should pray constantly that God will put and keep in our hearts a sense of His greatness and glory, and of the joy of fellowship with Him, and of the dreadfulness of spending time and eternity without Him; and then that God will enable us to speak honestly, straightforwardly, and just as we feel about these matters. Then we shall be really natural in presenting the gospel—and really serious too.

It is by asking questions of this sort that we must test and, where necessary, reform our evangelistic methods. The principle is that the best method of evangelism is the one which serves the gospel most completely. It is the one which bears the clearest witness to the divine origin of the message, and the life-and-death character of the issues which it raises. It is the one which makes possible the most full and thorough explanation of the good news of Christ and His cross, and the most exacting and searching application of it. It is the one which most effectively engages the minds of those to whom witness is borne, and makes them most vividly aware that the gospel is God's word, addressed personally to them in their own situation. What that best method is in each case, you and I have to find out for ourselves. It is in the light of this principle that all debates about evangelistic methods must be decided. For the present, we leave the matter there.

CHAPTER IV

DIVINE SOVEREIGNTY AND EVANGELISM

W̲E start this final section by summing up what we have learned so far about evangelism.

Evangelism, we have learned, is a task appointed to all God's people everywhere. It is the task of communicating a message from the Creator to rebel mankind. The message begins with information and ends with an invitation. The information concerns God's work of making His Son a perfect Saviour for sinners. The invitation is God's summons to mankind generally to come to the Saviour and find life. God commands all men everywhere to repent, and promises forgiveness and restoration to all who do. The Christian is sent into the world as God's herald and Christ's ambassador, to broadcast this message as widely as he can. This is both his duty (because God commands it, and love to our neighbour requires it) and his privilege (because it is a great thing to speak for God, and to take our neighbour the remedy—the only remedy—that can save him from the terrors of spiritual death). Our job, then, is to go to our fellow-men and tell them the gospel of Christ, and try by every means to make it clear to them; to remove as best we can any difficulties that they may find in it, to impress them with its seriousness, and to urge them to respond to it. This is our abiding responsibility; it is a basic part of our Christian calling.

But now we come to the question that has loomed over us from the outset. How is all this affected by our belief in the sovereignty of God?

We saw earlier that divine sovereignty is one of a pair of truths which form an antinomy in biblical thinking. The God of the Bible is both Lord and Lawgiver in His world; He is both man's King and man's Judge. Consequently, if we would be biblical in our outlook, we have to make room in our minds for the thoughts of divine sovereignty and of human responsibility to stand side by side. Man is indubitably responsible to God, for God is the Lawgiver who fixes his duty, and the Judge who takes account of him as to whether or not he has done it. And God is indubitably sovereign over man, for He controls and orders all human deeds, as He controls and orders all else in His universe. Man's responsibility for his actions, and God's sovereignty in relation to those same actions, are thus, as we saw, equally real and ultimate facts.

The apostle Paul forces this antinomy upon our notice by speaking of God's will (*thelēma*) in connection with both these seemingly incompatible relations of the Creator to His human creatures, and that within the limits of a single short Epistle. In the fifth and sixth chapters of Ephesians, he desires that his readers may be found 'understanding what the *will* of the Lord is' (v. 17) and 'doing the *will* of God from the heart' (vi.6). This is the will of God as Lawgiver, the will of God that man is to know and obey. In the same sense, Paul writes to the Thessalonians: 'This is the *will* of God, even your sanctification, that ye should abstain from fornication.'[1] In the first chapter of Ephesians, however, Paul speaks of God's having chosen him and his fellow-Christians in Christ before the world began 'according to the good pleasure of his *will*' (verse 5); he calls God's intention to sum up all things in Christ at the end of the world 'the mystery of his *will*' (verse 9); and he speaks of God Himself as 'him who worketh all things after the counsel of his own *will*' (verse 11). Here God's 'will' is clearly His eternal purpose for the disposal of His creatures, His will as the world's sovereign Lord. This is the will that God actually fulfils in and through everything that actually happens—even man's transgressions of His law.[2] Older theology distinguished the two as God's will of *precept* and His will of *purpose*, the former being His published declaration of what man ought to do, the latter His (largely secret) decision as to what He Himself will do. The distinction is between God's *law* and His *plan*. The former tells man what he should be; the latter settles what he will be. Both aspects of the will of God are facts, though how they are related in the mind of God is inscrutable to us. This is one of the reasons why we speak of God as incomprehensible.

Now, our question is: Supposing that all things do in fact happen under the direct dominion of God,

---

[1] 1 Thes. iv.3; *cf.* Mt. vii.21,xii.50;Jn.vii.17; 1 Jn. ii.17, etc.
[2] See, *e.g.*, Gn. xlv.5 ff., l.20. God's *thelema* is spoken of in this sense in Rom. i.10, xv.32; Rev. iv.11, etc.

and that God has already fixed the future by His decree, and resolved whom He will save, and whom not—how does this bear on our duty to evangelize?

This is a question that troubles many evangelical Christians today. There are some who have come to believe in the sovereignty of God in the unqualified and uncompromising way in which (as we judge) the Bible presents it. These are now wondering whether there is not some way in which they could and should witness to this faith by modifying the evangelistic practice which they have inherited from a generation with different convictions. These methods, they say, were devised by people who did not believe what we believe about God's absolute sovereignty in salvation; is that not of itself reason enough for refusing to use them? Others, who do not construe the doctrine of divine sovereignty in quite this way, nor take it quite so seriously, fear that this new concern to believe it thoroughly will mean the death of evangelism; for they think it is bound to undercut all sense of urgency in evangelistic action. Satan, of course, will do anything to hold up evangelism and divide Christians; so he tempts the first group to become inhibited and cynical about all current evangelistic endeavours, and the second group to lose its head and become panicky and alarmist, and both to grow self-righteous and bitter and conceited as they criticize each other. Both groups, it seems, have urgent need to watch against the wiles of the devil.

The question, then, is pressing. It was the Bible itself that raised it, by teaching the antinomy of God's

dual relation to man; and we look now to the Bible to
answer it.

The biblical answer may be stated in two proposi-
tions, one negative and one positive.

1. *The sovereignty of God in grace does not affect
anything that we have said about the nature and
duty of evangelism.*

The principle that operates here is that the rule of
our duty and the measure of our responsibility is
God's revealed will of precept, and not His hidden
will of event. We are to order our lives by the light
of His law, not by our guesses about His plan. Moses
laid down this principle when he had finished teaching Israel the law, the threats, and the promises of
the Lord. 'The secret things belong unto the Lord
our God: but those things which are revealed belong unto us . . . that we may do all the words of this
law.'[3] The things that God is pleased to keep to
Himself (the number and identity of the elect, for
instance, and when and how He purposes to convert
whom) have no bearing on any man's duty. They
are not relevant in any way for the interpreting of
any part of God's law. Now, the command to evangelize is a part of God's law. It belongs to God's
revealed will for His people. It could not, then, in
principle be affected in the slightest degree by anything that we might believe about God's sovereignty
in election and calling. We may well believe that (in
the words of Article XVII of the Church of England) God 'hath constantly (*i.e.*, firmly, decisively)

* Dt. xxix.29.

decreed by his counsel secret to us, to deliver from curse and damnation those whom he hath chosen in Christ out of mankind, and to bring them by Christ to everlasting salvation, as vessels made to honour'. But this does not help us to determine the nature of the evangelistic task, nor does it affect our duty to evangelize universally and indiscriminately. The doctrine of God's sovereignty in grace has no bearing on these things.

Therefore we may say :

(*i*) The belief that God is sovereign in grace does not affect the *necessity* of evangelism. Whatever we may believe about election, the fact remains that evangelism is necessary, because no man can be saved without the gospel. 'There is no difference between the Jew and the Greek,' proclaims Paul; 'for the same Lord over all is rich unto all that call upon him. For whosoever shall call upon the name of the Lord (Jesus Christ) shall be saved.' Yes; but nobody will be saved who does not call upon the name of the Lord, and certain things must happen before any man can do this. So Paul continues : 'How then shall they call on him in whom they have not *believed*? and how shall they believe in him of whom they have not *heard*? and how shall they hear without a *preacher*?'[1] They must be told of Christ before they can trust Him, and they must trust Him before they can be saved by Him. Salvation depends on faith, and faith on knowing the gospel. God's way of saving sinners is to bring them to faith through bringing them into contact with the gospel. In God's

[1] Rom. x.12 ff.

E.S.G.—4

ordering of things, therefore, evangelism is a necessity if anyone is to be saved at all.

We must realize, therefore, that when God sends
us to evangelize, He sends us to act as vital links in
the chain of His purpose for the salvation of His
elect. The fact that He has such a purpose, and that
it is (so we believe) a sovereign purpose that cannot
be thwarted, does not imply that, after all, our
evangelizing is not needed for its fulfilment. In our
Lord's parable, the way in which the wedding was
furnished with guests was through the action of the
king's servants, who went out as they were bidden
into the highways and invited in all whom they
found there. Hearing the invitation, the passers-by
came.[5] It is in the same way, and through similar
action by the servants of God, that the elect come
into the salvation that the Redeemer has won for
them.

(*ii*) The belief that God is sovereign in grace does
not affect the *urgency* of evangelism. Whatever we
may believe about election, the fact remains that
men without Christ are lost, and going to hell
(pardon the use of this tarnished phrase : I use it
because I mean it). 'Except ye repent,' said our Lord
to the crowd, 'ye shall *all* . . . *perish*.'[6] And we who
are Christ's are sent to tell them of the One—the
only One—who can save them from perishing. Is
not their need urgent? If it is, does that not make
evangelism a matter of urgency for us? If you knew
that a man was asleep in a blazing building, you
wou'd think it a matter of urgency to try and get to

[5] Mt. xxii.1 ff.   [6] Lk. xiii.3, 5.

him, and wake him up, and bring him out. The world is full of people who are unaware that they stand under the wrath of God : is it not similarly a matter of urgency that we should go to them, and try to arouse them, and show them the way of escape?

We should not be held back by the thought that if they are not elect, they will not believe us, and our efforts to convert them will fail. That is true; but it is none of our business, and should make no difference to our action. In the first place, it is always wrong to abstain from doing good for fear that it might not be appreciated. In the second place, the non-elect in this world are faceless men as far as we are concerned. We know that they exist, but we do not and cannot know who they are, and it is as futile as it is impious for us to try and guess. The identity of the reprobate is one of God's 'secret things' into which His people may not pry. In the third place, our calling as Christians is not to love God's elect, and them only, but to love our neighbour, irrespective of whether he is elect or not. Now, the nature of love is to do good and to relieve need. If, then, our neighbour is unconverted, we are to show love to him as best we can by seeking to share with him the good news without which he must needs perish. So we find Paul warning and teaching 'every man' :' not merely because he was an apostle, but because every man was his neighbour. And the measure of the urgency of our evangelistic task is the greatness

' Col. i.28.

of our neighbour's need and the immediacy of his danger.

(*iii*) The belief that God is sovereign in grace does not affect the *genuineness* of the gospel invitations, or the *truth* of the gospel promises. Whatever we may believe about election, and, for that matter, about the extent of the atonement, the fact remains that God in the gospel really does offer Christ and promise justification and life to 'whosoever will'. '*Whosoever* shall call upon the name of the Lord shall be saved.'[8] As God commands all men everywhere to repent, so God invites all men everywhere to come to Christ and find mercy. The invitation is for sinners only, but for sinners universally; it is not for sinners of a certain type only, reformed sinners, or sinners whose hearts have been prepared by a fixed minimum of sorrow for sin; but for sinners as such, just as they are. As the hymn puts it:

> 'Let not conscience make you linger,
>   Nor of fitness fondly dream;
> All the fitness He requireth
>   Is to feel your need of Him.'[9]

The fact that the gospel invitation is free and unlimited—'*sinners* Jesus will *receive*'—'come *and welcome* to Jesus Christ'[1]—is the glory of the gospel as a revelation of divine grace.

There is a great moment in the Holy Communion service of the Church of England when the minister

[8] Rom. x.13.
[9] From Joseph Hart's *Come, ye sinners* (*Christian Praise*, 196). The whole hymn is a magnificent statement of the gospel invitation.   [1] Title of a book by John Bunyan.

utters the 'comfortable words'. First the congregation confesses its sins to God in language of extreme strength ('our manifold sins and wickedness . . . provoking most justly thy wrath . . . the burden of them is intolerable. Have mercy upon us, have mercy upon us . . .'). Then the minister turns to face the people and proclaims to them the promises of God.

'Hear what comfortable words our Saviour Christ saith unto *all* that truly turn to him.

'Come unto me *all* that travail and are heavy laden, and I will refresh you.

'So God loved the world, that he gave his only-begotten Son, to the end that *all* that believe in him should not perish, but have everlasting life.

'Hear also what Saint Paul saith.

'This is a true saying, and worthy of *all* men to be received, that Christ Jesus came into the world to save sinners.

'Hear also what Saint John saith.

'If *any man* sin, we have an Advocate with the Father, Jesus Christ the righteous; and he is the propitiation for our sins.'[2]

Why are these words 'comfortable'? Because they are God's words, and they are all true. They are the essential gospel. They are the promises and assurances which Christians who approach the Lord's Table should come trusting. They are the word which the sacrament confirms. Note them carefully. Note first their *substance*. The object of faith which they present is not mere orthodoxy, not mere truth about Christ's atoning death. It is not less than that,

[2] Mt. xi.28; Jn. iii.16; 1 Tim. i.15; 1 Jn. ii.1; italics mine.

but it is more than that. It is the living Christ Himself, the perfect Saviour of sinners, who carries in
Himself all the virtue of His finished work on the
cross. 'Come *unto me . . . He* is the propitiation for
our sins.' These promises direct our trust, not to the
crucifixion as such, but to Christ crucified; not to
His work in the abstract, but to Him who wrought it.
And note second the *universality* of these promises.
They offer Christ to *all* who need him, *all* 'that truly
turn to him', *any man* who has sinned. None are shut
out from mercy save those who shut themselves out
through impenitence and unbelief.

Some fear that a doctrine of eternal election and
reprobation involves the possibility that Christ will
not receive some of those who desire to receive Him,
because they are not elect. The 'comfortable words'
of the gospel promises, however, absolutely exclude
this possibility. As our Lord elsewhere affirmed, in
emphatic and categorical terms: 'Him that cometh
to me I will *in no wise* cast out.'[3]

It is true that God has from all eternity chosen
whom He will save. It is true that Christ came
specifically to save those whom the Father had given
Him. But it is also true that Christ offers Himself
freely to all men as their Saviour, and guarantees to
bring to glory everyone who trusts in Him as such.
See how He Himself deliberately juxtaposes these
two thoughts in the following passage:

'I came down from heaven, not to do mine own
will, but the will of him that sent me. And this is the
Father's will which hath sent me, that of *all which*

[3] Jn. vi.37.

he hath given me I should lose nothing, but should raise it up again at the last day. And this is the will of him that sent me, that *every one which seeth the Son, and believeth on him,* may have everlasting life: and I will raise him up at the last day.'[4] 'All which he hath given me'—here is Christ's saving mission defined in terms of the whole company of the elect, whom He came specifically to save. 'Every one which seeth the Son, and believeth on him'— here is Christ's saving mission defined in terms of the whole company of lost mankind, to whom He offers Himself without distinction, and whom He will certainly save, if they believe. The two truths stand side by side in these verses, and that is where they belong. They go together. They walk hand in hand. Neither throws doubt on the truth of the other. Neither should fill our minds to the exclusion of the other. Christ means what He says, no less when He undertakes to save all who will trust Him than when He undertakes to save all whom the Father has given Him.

Thus John Owen, the Puritan, who wrote in defence of both unconditional election and limited atonement, is able—is, indeed, constrained—to address the unconverted as follows:

'Consider the infinite condescension and love of Christ, in his invitations and calls of you to come unto him for life, deliverance, mercy, grace, peace and eternal salvation. . . . In the declaration and preaching of them, Jesus Christ yet stands before

[4] Jn. vi. 38 ff.

sinners, calling, inviting, encouraging them to come
unto him.

'This is somewhat of the word which he now
speaks unto you: Why will ye die? why will ye
perish? why will ye not have compassion on your
own souls? Can your hearts endure, or can your
hands be strong, in the day of wrath that is
approaching? . . . Look unto me, and be saved;
come unto me, and I will ease you of all sins, sor-
rows, fears, burdens, and give rest to your souls.
Come, I entreat you; lay aside all procrastinations,
all delays; put me off no more; eternity lies at the
door . . . do not so hate me as that you will rather
perish than accept of deliverance by me.

'These and the like things doth the Lord Christ
continually declare, proclaim, plead and urge upon
the souls of sinners . . . He doth it in the preaching
of the word, as if he were present with you, stood
amongst you, and spake personally to every one of
you . . . He hath appointed the ministers of the
gospel to appear before you, and to deal with you
in his stead, avowing as his own the invitations which
are given you in his name, 2 Cor. v.19, 20.'[5]

So indeed it is. The invitations of Christ are words
of God. They are true. They are meant. They are
genuine invitations. They are to be pressed upon the
unconverted as such. Nothing that we may believe
about God's sovereignty in grace makes any difference to this.

(iv) The belief that God is sovereign in grace does

[5] From *The Glory of Christ* (*Works*, ed. W. Goold, 1850,
I.422).

not affect the *responsibility of the sinner* for his reaction to the gospel. Whatever we may believe about election, the fact remains that a man who rejects Christ thereby becomes the cause of his own condemnation. Unbelief in the Bible is a guilty thing, and unbelievers cannot excuse themselves on the grounds that they were not elect. The unbeliever was really offered life in the gospel, and could have had it if he would; he, and no-one but he, is responsible for the fact that he rejected it, and must now endure the consequences of rejecting it. 'Everywhere in Scripture,' writes Bishop J. C. Ryle, 'it is a leading principle that man can lose his own soul, that if he is lost at last it will be his own fault, and his blood will be on his own head. The same inspired Bible which reveals this doctrine of election is the Bible which contains the words, "Why will ye die, O house of Israel?"—"Ye will not come unto me, that ye might have life."—"This is the condemnation, that light is come into the world, and men loved darkness rather than light, because their deeds were evil." (Ezk. xviii.31; Jn. v.40, iii.19.) The Bible never says that sinners miss heaven because they are not elect, but because they "neglect the great salvation", and because they will not repent and believe. The last judgment will abundantly prove that it is not the want of God's election, so much as laziness, the love of sin, unbelief, and unwillingness to come to Christ, which ruins the souls that are lost.'[6] God gives men what they choose, not the opposite of what they choose. Those who choose death, therefore, have

[6] *Old Paths,* p. 468.

E.S G.—4*

only themselves to thank that God does not give them life. The doctrine of divine sovereignty does not affect the situation in any way.

So much for the first and negative proposition. The second is positive.

2. *The sovereignty of God in grace gives us our only hope of success in evangelism.* Some fear that belief in the sovereign grace of God leads to the conclusion that evangelism is pointless, since God will save His elect anyway, whether they hear the gospel or not. This, as we have seen, is a false conclusion based on a false assumption. But now we must go further, and point out that the truth is just the opposite. So far from making evangelism pointless, the sovereignty of God in grace is the one thing that prevents evangelism from being pointless. For it creates the possibility—indeed, the certainty—that evangelism will be fruitful. Apart from it, there is not even a possibility of evangelism being fruitful. Were it not for the sovereign grace of God, evangelism would be the most futile and useless enterprise that the world has ever seen, and there would be no more complete waste of time under the sun than to preach the Christian gospel.

Why is this? Because of the spiritual inability of man in sin. Let Paul, the greatest of all evangelists, explain this to us.

Fallen man, says Paul, has a blinded mind, and so is unable to grasp spiritual truth. 'The natural (unspiritual, unregenerate) man receiveth not the things of the Spirit of God : for they are foolishness unto him : neither can he know them, because they

are spiritually discerned."⁷ Again, he has a perverse
and ungodly nature. 'The carnal mind (the mind of
the unregenerate man) is enmity against God; for
it is not subject to the law of God, neither indeed can
be.' The consequence? 'So then they that are in the
flesh cannot please God.'⁸ In both these passages
Paul makes two distinct statements about fallen man
in relation to God's truth, and the progression of
thought is parallel in both cases. First Paul asserts
unregenerate man's failure, as a matter of fact. He
'receiveth not the things of the Spirit of God'; he 'is
not subject to the law of God'. But then Paul goes
on to interpret his first statement by a second, to the
effect that this failure is a necessity of nature, something certain and inevitable and universal and un-
alterable, just because it is not in man to do otherwise than fail in this way. 'Neither *can* he know
them.' 'Neither indeed *can* be.' Man in Adam has
not got it in him to apprehend spiritual realities, or
to obey God's law from his heart. Enmity against
God, leading to defection from God, is the law of
his nature. It is, so to speak, instinctive to him to
suppress and evade and deny God's truth, and to
shrug off God's authority and to flout God's law
—yes, and when he hears the gospel to disbelieve
and disobey that too. This is the sort of person that
he is. He is, says Paul, '*dead* in trespasses and sins'⁹
—wholly incapacitated for any positive reaction to
God's Word, deaf to God's speech, blind to God's
revelation, impervious to God's inducements. If you
talk to a corpse, there is no response; the man is

⁷ 1 Cor. ii.14.   ⁸ Rom. viii.7 f.   ⁹ Eph. ii. 1.

dead. When God's Word is spoken to sinners, there is equally no response; they are 'dead in trespasses and sins'.

Nor is this all. Paul also tells us that Satan (whose power and ill will he never underestimates) is constantly active to keep sinners in their natural state. Satan 'now worketh in the children of disobedience'[1] to ensure that they do not obey God's law. And 'the god of this world hath blinded the minds of them which believe not, lest the light of the glorious gospel of Christ . . . should shine unto them.'[2] So that there are two obstacles in the way of successful evangelism : the first, man's natural and irresistible impulse to oppose God, and the second, Satan's assiduity in shepherding man in the ways of unbelief and disobedience.

What does this mean for evangelism? It means, quite simply, that evangelism, described as we have described it, cannot possibly succeed. However clear and cogent we may be in presenting the gospel, we have no hope of convincing or converting anyone. Can you or I by our earnest talking break the power of Satan over a man's life? No. Can you or I give life to the spiritually dead? No. Can we hope to convince sinners of the truth of the gospel by patient explanation? No. Can we hope to move men to obey the gospel by any words of entreaty that we may utter? No. Our approach to evangelism is not realistic till we have faced this shattering fact, and let it make its proper impact on us. When a schoolmaster is trying to teach children arithmetic, or

[1] Eph. ii.2.   [2] 2 Cor. iv.4.

grammar, and finds them slow to learn, he assures himself that the penny must drop sooner or later, and so encourages himself to keep on trying. We can most of us muster great reserves of patience if we think that there is some prospect of ultimate success in what we are attempting. But in the case of evangelism there is no such prospect. Regarded as a human enterprise, evangelism is a hopeless task. It cannot in principle produce the desired effect. We can preach, and preach clearly and fluently and attractively; we can talk to individuals in the most pointed and challenging way; we can organize special services, and distribute tracts, and put up posters, and flood the country with publicity—and there is not the slightest prospect that all this outlay of effort will bring a single soul home to God. Unless there is some other factor in the situation, over and above our own endeavours, all evangelistic action is foredoomed to failure. This is the fact, the brute, rock-bottom fact, that we have to face.

Here, I suspect, we find the canker that is really weakening evangelism in evangelical circles today. Everyone seems to agree that our evangelism is not in a healthy state, but there is no agreement as to the nature of the malady, or what should be done to cure it. Some, as we have indicated, appear to think that the basic trouble is the current revival in many places of faith in the sovereignty of divine grace—a faith which finds expression in a fresh emphasis on the doctrines of unconditional election and effectual calling. Their remedy, it seems, would be to try and refute, or suppress, these doctrines, and to discourage people from taking them seriously. Since, however, so many of the greatest evangelists and missionaries of past days have held precisely these doctrines, it is, to say the least, not obvious that the diagnosis is right, or the suggested remedy appropriate. Moreover, it seems clear that evangelism was languishing between the two world wars, long before this fresh emphasis began to be made. Others, as we have also hinted, appear to locate the trouble in the kind of evangelistic meetings that are commonly held, and to think that if we cut out the jollity and made them more sombre, and abolished appeals and counselling rooms and after-meetings, our evangelism would automatically be reinvigorated. But this also is not obvious. I suspect that the root of the trouble with our evangelism today lies deeper than either of these diagnoses goes. I suspect that what is really responsible for this sense of evangelistic malaise is a widespread neurosis of disillusionment, an unacknowledged failure of nerve, springing from a long-standing failure to reckon with the fact that evangelism, regarded as a human enterprise, must be expected to fail. Let me explain.

For about a century now, it has been characteristic of evangelical Christians (rightly or wrongly— we need not discuss that here) to think of evangelism as a specialized activity, best done in short sharp bursts ('missions' or 'campaigns'), and needing for its successful practice a distinctive technique, both for preaching and for individual dealing. At an early stage in this period, Evangelicals fell into the way of assuming that evangelism was sure to succeed if it was regularly prayed for and correctly run (*i.e.*, if the distinctive technique was used). This was because in those early days, under men like Moody, Torrey, Haslam and Hay Aitken, evangelistic campaigns usually were successful—not because they were always well planned and run (by twentieth-century standards, they often were not), but because God was working in Britain in those days in a way in which He is evidently not working now. Even then, however, it was noticeable that the second mission in any place would rarely be as productive as the first, or the third as the second. But during the past fifty years, as our country has drifted further and further from its Christian moorings, the law of diminishing returns has set in much more drastically. Evangelistic campaigns have become less and less fruitful. And this fact has unnerved us.

Why has it unnerved us? Because we were not prepared for it. We had come to take it for granted that good organization and efficient technique, backed by a routine of prayers, was itself sufficient to guarantee results. We felt that there was an almost magical potency in the special meeting, the special choir and soloist, and the special preacher. We felt convinced that the thing that would always bring life into a dead church, or a dead town, was.an intensive evangelistic mission. With the top of our minds, many of us still think that, or profess to think it. We tell each other that it is so, and make our plans on this basis. But with the bottom of our minds, in our heart of hearts, we have grown discouraged, and disillusioned, and apprehensive. Once we thought that well-planned evangelism was sure to succeed, but now we find ourselves afraid each time that it is going to fail, as it has failed so often before. Yet we are afraid to admit our fears to ourselves, for we do not know what to make of a situation in which our planned evangelism fails. So we repress our fears, and our disillusionment becomes a paralysing neurosis, and our evangelistic practice becomes a jaded and half-hearted routine. Basically, the trouble is our unconfessed doubts as to the worthwhileness of what we are doing.

Why have we these doubts? Because we have been disillusioned. How have we been disillusioned? By the repeated failure of the evangelistic techniques in which we once reposed such confidence. What is the cure of our disillusionment? First, we must admit that we were silly ever to think that any evangelistic technique, however skilful, could of itself guarantee conversions; second, we must recognize that, because man's heart is impervious to the word of God, it is no cause for surprise if at any time our evangelism fails to result in conversions; third, we must remember that the terms of our calling are that we should be faithful, not that we should be successful; fourth, we must learn to rest all our hopes of fruit in evangelism upon the omnipotent grace of God.

For God does what man cannot do. God works by His Spirit through His Word in the hearts of sinful men to bring them to repentance and faith. Faith is a gift of God. 'Unto you *it is given* in the behalf of Christ . . . to believe on him,' writes Paul to the

Philippians.[3] 'By grace are ye saved through faith,' he tells the Ephesians, 'and that not of yourselves; it is *the gift of God*.'[4] So, too, repentance is the gift of God. 'Him (Christ) did God exalt,' Peter told the Sanhedrin, '. . . to be a Prince and a Saviour, for to *give* repentance to Israel, and remission of sins.'[5] When the Jerusalem church heard how Peter had been sent to evangelize Cornelius, and how Cornelius had come to faith, they said : 'Then hath God also to the Gentiles *granted* repentance unto life.'[6] You and I cannot make sinners repent and believe in Christ by our words alone; but God works faith and repentance in men's hearts by His Holy Spirit.

Paul terms this God's work of 'calling'. The old theologians named it 'effectual calling', to distinguish it from the ineffective summons that is given when the gospel is preached to a man in whose heart God is not at work. It is the operation whereby God causes sinners to understand and respond to the gospel invitation. It is a work of creative power : by it, God gives men new hearts, freeing them from slavery to sin, abolishing their inability to know and do God's truth, and leading them actually to turn to God and trust Christ as their Saviour. By it, also, God breaks Satan's hold upon them, delivering them from the domain of darkness and transferring them into 'the kingdom of his dear Son'.[7] It is thus a calling that creates the response which it seeks, and

[3] Phil. i.29.
[4] Eph. ii.8. Whether the gift of God in this text is the act of believing, or the fact of being-saved-through-believing (commentators divide), does not affect our point.
[5] Acts v.31, RV.   [6] Acts xi.18.   [7] Col i.13.

confers the blessing to which it invites. It is often
termed the work of 'prevenient grace', because it
precedes any motion Godward in the heart of sinful
man. It has been described (perhaps misleadingly)
as a work of 'irresistible grace', simply because it
effectively dethrones the disposition to resist grace.
The Westminster Confession analyses it as an activity of God in and upon fallen men, 'enlightening
their minds spiritually and savingly to understand
the things of God; taking away their heart of stone,
and giving unto them an heart of flesh; renewing
their wills, and by his almighty power determining
them to that which is good; and effectually drawing
them to Jesus Christ; yet so as they come most freely,
being made willing by his grace.'[8]

Christ Himself taught the universal *necessity* of
this calling by the Word and the Spirit. '*No man* can
come to me, except the Father which hath sent me
draw him.'[9] He also taught the universal *efficacy* of
it. '*Every man* ... that hath heard, and hath learned
of the Father, cometh unto me.'[1] And with this He
taught the universal *certainty* of it for all whom
God has chosen. '*All* that the Father giveth me shall
come to me :'[2] they shall hear of Me, and they shall
be moved to trust Me. This is the Father's purpose,
and the Son's promise.

Paul speaks of this 'effectual calling' as the out-
working of God's purpose of election. To the
Romans, he says : 'Whom (God) did foreknow, he

---

[8] Westminster Confession, X.i; *cf.* 2 Cor. iv.6; 1 Cor. ii.10
ff.; Ezk. xxxvi.26 f.; Jn. vi.44 f.; Phil. ii.13.
    [9] Jn. vi.44.   [1] Verse 45.   [2] Verse 37.

also did predestinate to be conformed to the image of his Son ... moreover whom he did predestinate, them he also *called* : and whom he *called*, them he also justified : and whom he justified, them he also glorified.'³ To the Thessalonians he writes : 'God hath from the beginning chosen you to salvation through sanctification of the Spirit and belief of the truth : whereunto he *called* you by our gospel, to the obtaining of the glory of our Lord Jesus Christ.'⁴ The author of the call, the apostle tells us, is God; the mode of calling is by the gospel; and the issue of the call is a title to glory.

But if this is so, then we see at once why it was that Paul, who faced so realistically the fact of fallen man's slavery to sin and Satan, was able to avoid the disillusionment and discouragement that we feel today as it dawns upon us more and more clearly that, humanly speaking, evangelism is a hopeless task. The reason was that Paul kept his eyes firmly fixed on the sovereignty of God in grace. He knew that God had long before declared that 'my word ... that goeth forth out of my mouth ... shall not return unto me void, but it shall accomplish that which I please, and it shall prosper in the thing whereto I sent it.'⁵ He knew that this was no less true of the gospel than of any other divine utterance. He knew, therefore, that his own preaching of the gospel would not in the long run prove fruitless. God would see to that. He knew that wherever the word of the gospel went, God would raise the dead. He knew that the word would prove a savour of life to

³ Rom. viii.29 f.   ⁴ 2 Thes. ii.13 f.   ⁵ Is. lv.11.

some of those who heard it. This knowledge made
him confident, tireless, and expectant in his evangelism. And if there were on occasion hard spells,
with much opposition and little visible fruit, he did
not panic or lose heart. For he knew that if Christ
had opened the door for him to make known the
gospel in a place, that meant that it was Christ's
purpose to draw sinners to Himself in that place.
The word would not return void. His business,
therefore, was to be patient and faithful in spreading the good news till the time of harvest should
come.

There was a time at Corinth when things were
hard; there had been some converts, certainly, but
opposition was mounting and even Paul, the daunt-
less, was wondering whether it was worth persevering there. 'Then,' we are told, 'spake the Lord
(Jesus) to Paul in the night by a vision, Be not
afraid, but speak, and hold not thy peace : for I am
with thee, and no man shall set on thee to hurt thee :
for I have much people in this city.'[6] As if to say :
go on preaching and teaching, Paul, and let nothing
stop you; there are many here whom I mean to
bring to Myself through your testimony to My
gospel. 'This confirms S. Luke's emphasis upon the
prevenient choice of God,' comments Rackham.[7]
And Luke's emphasis reflects Paul's conviction,
based upon Christ's own assurance to him. Thus the
sovereignty of God in grace gave Paul hope of success as he preached to deaf ears, and held up Christ

[6] Acts xviii.9 f.
[7] *The Acts of the Apostles,* p. 327; *cf.* Acts xiii.48.

before blind eyes, and sought to move stony hearts. His confidence was that where Christ sends the gospel there Christ has His people—fast bound at present in the chains of sin, but due for release at the appointed moment through a mighty renewing of their hearts as the light of the gospel shines into their darkness, and the Saviour draws them to Himself.

In a great hymn which he wrote shortly after his conversion (possibly the day after), Charles Wesley spoke of what had happened like this:

> 'Long my imprisoned spirit lay
>   Fast bound in sin and nature's night;
> Thine eye diffused a quickening ray,—
>   I woke, the dungeon flamed with light;
> My chains fell off, my heart was free,
> I rose, went forth, and followed thee.'[8]

That is not only a vivid statement of experience; it is also a piece of excellent theology. This is precisely what happens to unconverted men and women wherever the gospel is preached. Paul knew that; hence his confidence and expectancy when evangelizing.

Paul's confidence should be our confidence too. We may not trust in our methods of personal dealing or running evangelistic services, however excellent we may think them. There is no magic in methods, not even in theologically impeccable methods. When we evangelize, our trust must be in God who raises the dead. He is the almighty Lord who turns men's hearts, and He will give conversions

[8] From *And can it be* (*Christian Praise*, 235).

in His own time. Meanwhile, our part is to be faithful in making the gospel known, sure that such labour will never be in vain. This is how the truth of the sovereignty of God's grace bears upon evangelism.

What effects should this confidence and certainty have upon our attitude when evangelizing? Three at least.

(i) It should make us *bold*. It should keep us from being daunted when we find, as we often do, that people's first reaction to the gospel is to shrug it off in apathy or even contempt. Such a reaction should not surprise us; it is only to be expected from the bondslaves of sin and Satan. Nor should it discourage us; for no heart is too hard for the grace of God. Paul was a bitter opponent of the gospel, but Christ laid His hand on Paul, and Paul was broken down and born again. You yourself, since you became a Christian, have been learning constantly how corrupt and deceitful and perverse your own heart is; before you became a Christian, your heart was worse; yet Christ has saved you, and that should be enough to convince you that He can save anyone. So persevere in presenting Christ to unconverted people as you find opportunity. You are not on a fool's errand. You are not wasting either your time or theirs. You have no reason to be ashamed of your message, or half-hearted and apologetic in delivering it. You have every reason to be bold, and free, and natural, and hopeful of success. For God can give His truth an effectiveness that you and I cannot give it. God can make His truth triumphant to the conversion of the most seemingly hardened unbeliever. You and I will never write off anyone as hopeless and beyond the reach of God if we believe in the sovereignty of His grace.

(ii) This confidence should make us *patient*. It should keep us from being daunted when we find that our evangelistic endeavours meet with no immediate response. God saves in His own time, and we ought not to suppose that He is in such a hurry as we are. We need to remember that we are all children of our age, and the spirit of our age is a spirit of tearing hurry. And it is a pragmatic spirit; it is a spirit that demands quick results. The modern ideal is to achieve more and more by doing less and less. This is the age of the labour-saving device, the efficiency chart, and automation. The attitude which all this breeds is one of impatience towards everything that takes time and demands sustained effort. Ours tends to be a slapdash age; we resent spending time doing things thoroughly. This spirit tends to infect our evangelism (not to speak of other departments of our Christianity), and with disastrous results. We are tempted to be in a great hurry with those whom we would win to Christ, and then, when we see no immediate response in them, to become impatient and downcast, and then to lose interest in them, and feel that it is useless to spend more time on them; and so we abandon our efforts forthwith, and let them drop out of our ken. But this is utterly wrong. It is a failure both of love for man and of faith in God.

The truth is that the work of evangelizing demands

more patience and sheer 'stickability', more reserves
of persevering love and care, than most of us
twentieth-century Christians have at command. It
is a work in which quick results are not promised;
it is a work, therefore, in which the non-appearance
of quick results is no sign of failure; but it is a work
in which we cannot hope for success unless we are
prepared to persevere with people. The idea that a
single evangelistic sermon, or a single serious conversation, ought to suffice for the conversion of anyone who is ever going to be converted is really silly.
If you see someone whom you meet come to faith
through a single such sermon or talk, you will normally find that his heart was already well prepared by
a good deal of Christian teaching and exercise of
spirit prior to your meeting with him. The law that
operates in such cases is 'one soweth, and another
reapeth'.[9] If, on the other hand, you meet a person
who is not thus prepared, a person who as yet has
no conviction of the truth of the gospel and perhaps
no idea, or even a false idea, of what the gospel
actually is, it is worse than useless to try and stam-
pede him into a snap 'decision'. You may be able to
bully him into a psychological crisis of some sort,
but that will not be saving faith, and will do him no
good. What you have to do is to take time with
him, to make friends with him, to get alongside
him, to find out where he is in terms of spiritual
understanding, and to start dealing with him at
that point. You have to explain the gospel to him,
and be sure that he understands it and is con-

[9] Jn. iv.37.

vinced of its truth, before you start pressing him to an active response. You have to be ready to help him, if need be, through a spell of seeking to repent and believe before he knows within himself that he has received Christ, and Christ has received him. At each stage you have to be willing to go along with him at God's speed, which may seem to you a strangely slow speed. But that is God's business, not yours. Your business is simply to keep pace with what God is doing in his life. Your willingness to be patient with him in this way is the proof of your love to him no less than of your faith in God. If you are not willing thus to be patient, you need not expect that God will favour you by enabling you to win souls.

Whence comes the patience that is so indispensable for evangelistic work? From dwelling on the fact that God is sovereign in grace and that His word does not return to Him void; that it is He who gives us such opportunities as we find for sharing our knowledge of Christ with others, and that He is able in His own good time to enlighten them and bring them to faith. God often exercises our patience in this, as in other matters. As He kept Abraham waiting twenty-five years for the birth of his son, so He often keeps Christians waiting for things that they long to see, such as the conversion of their friends. We need patience, then, if we are to do our part in helping others towards faith. And the way for us to develop that patience is to learn to live in terms of our knowledge of the free and gracious sovereignty of God.

(iii) Finally, this confidence should make us *prayerful*.

Prayer, as we said at the beginning, is a confessing of impotence and need, an acknowledging of helplessness and dependence, and an invoking of the mighty power of God to do for us what we cannot do for ourselves. In evangelism, as we saw, we are impotent; we depend wholly upon God to make our witness effective; only because He is able to give men new hearts can we hope that through our preaching of the gospel sinners will be born again. These facts ought to drive us to prayer. It is God's intention that they should drive us to prayer. God means us, in this as in other things, to recognize and confess our impotence, and to tell Him that we rely on Him alone, and to plead with Him to glorify His name. It is His way regularly to withhold His blessings until His people start to pray. 'Ye have not, because ye ask not.'[1] 'Ask, and it shall be given you; seek, and ye shall find; knock, and it shall be opened unto you : for every one that asketh receiveth; and he that seeketh findeth; and to him that knocketh it shall be opened.'[2] But if you and I are too proud or lazy to ask, we need not expect to receive. This is the universal rule, in evangelism as elsewhere. God will make us pray before He blesses our labours in order that we may constantly learn afresh that we depend on God for everything. And then, when God permits us to see conversions, we shall not be tempted to ascribe them to our own gifts, or skill, or wisdom,

[1] Jas. iv.2.   [2] Mt. vii.7 f.

or persuasiveness, but to His work alone, and so we shall know whom we ought to thank for them.

The knowledge, then, that God is sovereign in grace, and that we are impotent to win souls, should make us pray, and keep us praying. What should be the burden of our prayers? We should pray for those whom we seek to win, that the Holy Spirit will open their hearts; and we should pray for ourselves in our own witness, and for all who preach the gospel, that the power and authority of the Holy Spirit may rest upon them. 'Pray for us,' writes Paul to the Thessalonians, 'that the word of the Lord may run and be glorified.'[3] Paul was a great evangelist who had seen much fruit, but Paul knew that every particle of it had come from God, and that unless God continued to work both in him and in those to whom he preached he would never convert another soul. So he pleads for prayer, that his evangelism might still prove fruitful. Pray, he pleads, that the word of the gospel may be glorified through my preaching of it, and through its effect in human lives. Pray that it may be used constantly to the conversion of sinners. This, to Paul, is an urgent request, just because Paul sees so clearly that his preaching can save nobody unless God in sovereign mercy is pleased to bless it and use it to this end. Paul, you see, does not hold that, because God is sovereign in saving sinners, therefore prayer is needless, any more than he holds that, because God is sovereign in saving sinners, evangelistic preaching is needless. Rather, he holds that, just because the sal-

[3] 2 Thes. iii.1, RV.

vation of sinners depends wholly upon God, prayer
for the fruitfulness of evangelistic preaching is all
the more necessary. And those today who, with
Paul, believe most strongly that it is the sovereign
agency of God, and that alone, that leads sinners to
Christ, should bear witness to their faith by showing
themselves most constant and faithful and earnest
and persistent in prayer that God's blessing may rest
on the preaching of His word, and that under it
sinners may be born again. This is the final bearing
of belief in the sovereignty of God's grace upon
evangelism.

We said earlier in this chapter that this doctrine
does not in any way reduce or narrow the terms of
our evangelistic commission. Now we see that, so far
from contracting them, it actually expands them.
For it faces us with the fact that there are two sides
to the evangelistic commission. It is a commission,
not only to preach, but also to pray; not only to talk
to men about God, but also to talk to God about
men. Preaching and prayer must go together; our
evangelism will not be according to knowledge, nor
will it be blessed, unless they do. We are to preach,
because without knowledge of the gospel no man
can be saved. We are to pray, because only the
sovereign Holy Spirit in us and in men's hearts can
make our preaching effective to men's salvation, and
God will not send His Spirit where there is no
prayer. Evangelicals are at present busy reforming
their methods of evangelistic preaching, and that is
good. But it will not lead to evangelistic fruitfulness

unless God also reforms our praying, and pours out on us a new spirit of supplication for evangelistic work. The way ahead for us in evangelism is that we should be taught afresh to testify to our Lord and to His gospel, in public and in private, in preaching and in personal dealing, with boldness, patience, power, authority, and love; and that with this we should also be taught afresh to pray for God's blessing on our witness with humility and importunity. It is as simple—and as difficult—as that. When all has been said that has to be said about the reformation of evangelistic methods, it still remains that there is no way ahead but this, and if we do not find this way, we shall not advance.

Thus the wheel of our argument comes full circle. We began by appealing to our practice of prayer as proof of our faith in divine sovereignty. We end by applying our faith in divine sovereignty as a motive to the practice of prayer.

What, then, are we to say about the suggestion that a hearty faith in the absolute sovereignty of God is inimical to evangelism? We are bound to say that anyone who makes this suggestion thereby shows that he has simply failed to understand what the doctrine of divine sovereignty means. Not only does it undergird evangelism, and uphold the evangelist, by creating a hope of success that could not otherwise be entertained; it also teaches us to bind together preaching and prayer; and as it makes us bold and confident before men, so it makes us humble and importunate before God. Is not this as it should be? We would not wish to say that man cannot evangelize at all without coming to terms with this doctrine; but we venture to think that, other things being equal, he will be able to evangelize better for believing it.

We're Going to Need More Wine

P9-DBX-731

"I love this woman and her book."

"I have gotten the pleasure to know Gabrielle over the years and besides the fact that
she loves to drink, I've always taken comfort in how much we have in common.
The predilection to go from talking about the latest humiliating sexual position to a debate on
politics or racism, that's exactly what this book felt like to me, an honest conversation with
Gabrielle about her life. I appreciate her integrity, love her humor and openness about her life.
I also love the fact that she's older than me. . . . Go, girl."

"A hilarious and moving memoir from a natural storyteller.
Gabrielle Union explores love, family, trauma, and racial identity in a book that somehow
manages to be both heartbreakingly honest and laugh-out-loud funny."

"*We're Going to Need More Wine* is a collection of funny and emotional essays. . . .
Union gets real about everything."

"[Union] delivers more than just laughs in this moving essay collection."

"[A] thought-provoking, funny, tell-it-like-it-is essay collection."

"[Gabrielle Union has] written a book of essays as raw and honest as anyone has ever
produced. . . . As witty, warm, and assured on the page as she is in person, this book lives somewhere
between Nora Ephron and Eve Babitz, with a touch of Audre Lorde's radical awareness."

"With honesty and humor, Union bares her soul and shares her levels of insecurity, the difficulties
of being a black woman in Hollywood, and the way fame has changed her life. She embraces many
multilayered issues in these intimate essays, giving readers glimpses of insight into her soul."

"Union invites readers into her world with honesty, grit, and grace. A much-needed addition to
the endless catalog of celebrity memoirs."

WE'RE GOING TO
NEED MORE WINE

WE'RE GOING TO NEED MORE

wine

STORIES THAT ARE FUNNY, COMPLICATED, AND TRUE

GABRIELLE UNION

DEY ST.

An Imprint of WILLIAM MORROW

HarperCollins books may be purchased for educational, business,
or sales promotional use. For information, please email the Special
Markets Department at SPsales@harpercollins.com.

A hardcover edition of this book was published in 2017 by Dey
Street Books, an imprint of William Morrow.

FIRST DEY STREET BOOKS PAPERBACK EDITION PUBLISHED 2019.

Designed by Renata De Oliveira

Library of Congress Cataloging-in-Publication Data has been
applied for.

ISBN 978-0-06-269399-0

19 20 21 22 23   LSC   10 9 8 7 6 5

I dedicate this book to those who have been humiliated and wanted to hide away forever. To those who have been broken and superglue wasn't enough to help. To those who have felt frozen in fear and shame. To those who have kept smiling as their throats were closing up. To those who thought they had all the answers but realized they were sorely ignorant. I see you. I gotchu. And to my parents, who I never understood until I became an adult who followed her heart . . . I'm sorry and I love you. I get it now.

contents

INTRODUCTION

This kind of feels like a first date.

I have that same feeling you get five minutes before you meet the other person, when you're giddy about where things might go. But also wary, because you've been on enough bad dates to know exactly how this can go awry. They order the salmon and pronounce the *l* and you're like, How the hell has my life come to this?

No pressure, but I have thought of you the whole time I've been writing this book. I have never shared these stories outside of a close circle of people, the friends you can tell all your secrets to because you know all of theirs. So I want this to be like one of those nights out with someone you can be real with. We're sitting across from each other over drinks, and we're in the middle of this ridiculous, hyperventilating laugh/cry because even I can't believe I did some of these things, foolishness that made perfect sense at the time but sounds ludicrous now. "Oh no, it gets worse," I say, taking a sip as everyone in the restaurant looks over at us losing it. These are the stories that require reinforcements. If I'm going to really get into them, we need to flag the waiter and tell him not to be a stranger and to keep pouring, because we're gonna need more wine tonight.

Thinking of you this past year, I jotted down notes, sent texts to myself, and went back to look at some of the books that meant something to me and left me better for reading them. One of the things I marked to share was a line from James Baldwin.

"The very time I thought I was lost, My dungeon shook and my chains fell off."

Baldwin was quoting a spiritual about the strength that comes from survival. I have felt lost plenty, stuck in the dungeons I was thrown into, and some I even locked myself into. I felt the chains of growing up trying to be someone I wasn't, and then living in Hollywood, a town that rewards pretending. The dungeon represents so many parts of my life and all of our lives. I don't think I'm special, or that my pain makes me unique. I've had a couple of moments—okay, months, maybe years—where the idea of disappearing and never being seen again seemed like an appealing option. I've been lucky that someone was always there to give me hope, whether it was a member of my support group at UCLA's Rape Crisis Center or my dog Bubba crawling under my bed to find me hiding from life after public humiliation. They rescued me from my dungeons, and later I had to do the work to shake off the shackles that I had put on myself. I hemmed myself in with shame, and also with the fear of not being chosen by men. I remember the moment I realized I was free, looking in a mirror and saying, "I choose my motherfucking self."

We'll get to that. Right now, I should just tell you at the outset that I have trust issues. I have to wonder if I will pay a consequence for telling my truth. We're entering a full-on relationship where I have all this hope that my words are going to be interpreted the way I intend. I don't want you to have to guess about my intentions. I want to make you laugh/cry as we tackle some big stuff. And if you don't agree with me, I want you to be able to say, "At least that bitch is honest." Oh, yeah, you should know that I cuss. You never knew that, did you? Having a publicist has served me well. Let's press on, nothing to see here.

It was terrifying putting myself back into some of the scenes you'll find here. But it was also the essential work of finding my authentic self. As I retraced the steps and missteps of my life, I began to stop avoiding memories that triggered emotional flashbacks, and I chose to embrace them as revelations. Each revealed a bread crumb that I had dropped along the way, leading me further on my path to understanding who I truly am.

Reading all these stories together, I wondered if I was really brave enough to share all of this. Then I remembered another quote I wrote down. This one comes from Carrie Fisher.

"Stay afraid, but do it anyway."

So cheers. Here's to us being afraid and doing it anyway.

one

LADIES AND GENTLEMEN, MISS PLEASANTON

It is a peculiar sensation, this double-consciousness, this sense of always looking at one's self through the eyes of others, of measuring one's soul by the tape of a world that looks on in amused contempt and pity. One ever feels his two-ness—an American, a Negro; two souls, two thoughts, two unreconciled strivings; two warring ideals in one dark body, whose dogged strength alone keeps it from being torn asunder.

—W. E. B. Du Bois, *The Souls of Black Folk*

When I was in the second grade, my parents moved us from Omaha, Nebraska, to Pleasanton, California. My parents had spent a year living in San Francisco just after they got married, and my arts-loving mother had lived for the city's culture and open spirit. So when my father announced he was getting transferred to go back to the Bay Area, she rejoiced. My mother pushed for Oakland, where we would be around other black families and still close to all that San Francisco had to offer. But my father, obsessed with keeping up with the Joneses, had bigger plans. He had a white work friend who had moved to Pleasanton, a half-hour drive and a world away from Oakland. "If it's good enough for Dave," he said, "it's good enough for us."

In Omaha, we were part of the largest African American extended family in Nebraska. In Pleasanton, we would be the chocolate chip in the cookie. My mother didn't want that for her daughters—me, my older sister, Kelly, and my younger sister, Tracy. Well, she lost that battle. Everything she feared came to pass.

The residents of Pleasanton divided themselves into housing developments. And where you lived said everything about who you were. We bought a house in Val Vista, which was working middle class with upper-middle-class goals. Val Vista was considered just below Valley Trails in the Pleasanton development caste system. But neither of those neighborhoods was nearly as good as the Meadows, across town, where they had green belts that connected all the cul-de-sacs and the streets. When you told someone where you lived, it was shorthand for the truth of your family's economic situation: good, average, or untouchable.

Since birth my family has called me Nickie, from my middle name, Monique. It took a little less than a year in Pleasanton for someone to call me nigger. It was during third-grade recess at Fairlands Elementary, and it came from Lucas. He was one of the Latino kids bused in from Commodorsky, the low-income housing development. He rode with Carmen, Lori, and Gabriel, or, as everyone called them, the Commodorsky kids. One day, Lucas decided my name made for great racist alliteration.

"Nickie's a nigger!" he said, pointing at me with a huge

smile of revelation, like he'd found me in a game of hide and seek. For one day to my face, and who knows how many days behind my back, "Nigger Nickie" caught on like wildfire. The kids chanted it, trying on the word as a threat ("Nigger!") and a question ("Nigger?"), and then as singsong: "Nig-ger Nic-kie. Nig-ger Nic-kie."

I couldn't afford to stand out like that ever again. So I became obsessed with observing the Commodorsky kids, clocking all the shit they did that everyone—meaning the white ones—made fun of. I wanted to be the exact opposite. And I was clocking the white kids, too, of course. I looked at them and thought, That's where I'm going to. And when I saw the Commodorsky kids, all I could think was, That's where I'm running from.

With every single move I made and every word I spoke, I stayed hyperalert to what I called the Black Pitfalls. What were the things that would make me appear blacker? I only ate chicken with a knife and fork, and never in front of white people. Certainly not KFC. And no fruit on a rind. You were not gonna see a toothy-grin-and-watermelon scene from me.

I had been warned, of course. My parents gave me the pep talk when I started school, the same speech all black parents give their kids: You're gonna have to be bigger, badder, better, just to be considered equal. You're gonna have to do twice as much work and you're not going to get any credit for your accomplishments or for overcoming adversity. Most black people grow accustomed to the fact that we have to excel just to be seen as existing, and this is a lesson passed down from generation to generation. You can either be Super Negro or the forgotten Negro.

It's actually very accurate advice. But the problem with putting it on a kid is that if you're not as good as—or eight times as good as—you feel like you are less than. Not just in academics or in sports: every kid cares about something and wants to receive love and praise for that particular quality or ability. You are always chasing, always worrying about being exposed as the dumb black kid. The foolish nigger. On one hand, it puts your shoulder to the wheel, so you're always pushing, working, striving. But one misstep and it's over. An A minus can feel like Hiroshima. It's catastrophic because you feel exposed. It's still an A, but what it feels like is "Dumb nigger." "You're a joke." "Of course you missed it, *nigger*." I had that fear as a kid, with every worksheet. Do you remember the timed tests with multiplication? I became psychotic about those. I would see "4 x 16 = _____" and hear my father's voice: "Bigger, badder, better." By the way, it's taking everything I have not to tell you I know the answer is 64. Which leads me to 64 being a perfect square, which leads me down the rabbit hole of listing other perfect squares . . . and who cares?

I did. This insane need to stay beyond reproach by being perfect also applied to getting a bathroom pass. Other kids would ask the teacher for one and she would say, "You've got five minutes," tapping her watch. She never gave me a time because I was the fastest piss in the West. I always timed myself—literally counting each second—because I wanted to come back with so much time left on the five-minute mental clock that she didn't even need to give me a deadline.

The following year, Tarsha Liburd showed up on the bus from Commodorsky. Her family had moved there from Oakland. She was black—described by everyone as "*so* black"—and she had these corduroys she wore all the time. Tarsha had a big, grownup ass as a third grader, and the top of her butt would always be bursting out of those cords.

I didn't tell my mother there was another black girl at school, but she heard about it. "You better be nice to her," she said, "because they're all going to be mean to her."

Because Tarsha had become a walking, lumbering punch line of people pointing at her crack, I convinced myself that if I just ignored her, I would be doing right by her. I wouldn't join in on making fun of her—she was simply invisible to me.

At lunchtime, the girls at my table called a meeting. One girl looked right at me. "Are you going to be friends with Tarsha Liburd?"

Tarsha was sitting close by, so I quietly said, "No." But I made a face showing that the very idea was preposterous. Why would I have anything to do with that girl?

Another girl stared at me and said, loud enough for Tarsha to hear: "If you don't like Tarsha Liburd, raise your hand." And everyone put up two hands and looked at me.

I heard my mother's voice and felt Tarsha's eyes on me. I raised my hand just to my shoulder, a half-hearted vote against her.

"Well, I don't know her," I said. I waved my hand side to side by my shoulder, hoping it would be read as "waffling" to Tarsha and "above it all" to the table.

A day went by. I was in my Gifted and Talented education program, doing calligraphy, thank you very much, when a voice came over the intercom.

"Please send Nickie to the principal's office."

I naturally thought I was getting an *award*. My smug self just paused, elegantly finished my line of calligraphy, and packed my books. I waltzed to the principal's office, practicing a look of "who, me?" gratitude.

Principal McKinley, a burly Irish man with kind eyes, peered at me, taking my measure. "Nickie, did you raise your hand when asked if you don't like Tarsha Liburd?"

"No," I said. "I did this." I showed my discreet half wave. "Because, I, I, um . . ." I started to cry. Bawl. In my head, I was already four steps ahead, my mom disappointed in me for being mean to the other black girl.

Principal McKinley told me he was putting my name in the Blue Book. Which was, to my third-grade understanding, an unholy text containing the names of bad children. Teachers said it could follow you and you might not get into the college of your choice. The principal then told me that if I behaved for the rest of the year, he would have my name erased from it. But I didn't believe him. Even years later, when I was applying to colleges, there was a small part of me that wondered, Is my name still in the Blue Book?

I was the only person to get in trouble for this conversation, and it had to have come from Tarsha. I wasn't mad at her. I was very aware that I had done the wrong thing, but I also knew why I'd done it. It was survival of the fittest—*Lord of the Flies* in suburbia—and I had to eat.

Tarsha remained invisible to me through elementary school. At the time I told myself she was invisible because she just didn't have much of a personality. I know now that I was only justifying my refusal to connect with her. I was afraid to take the risk of being black by standing next to her.

FROM SECOND GRADE TO SIXTH GRADE, JODY MANNING AND I WERE NECK and neck when it came to grade point average. Her family lived in the Meadows—one of the richest neighborhoods in Pleasanton—and they just had nice stuff. Their house, in my mind, felt like a museum. It felt rich. When I was little, one of my barometers for wealth was if the family had Welch's grape juice. I noticed that all the rich kids drank it after school. The Mannings definitely had Welch's. The Unions had grape drink.

After school and at recess, we started playing *Days of Our Lives*. Everyone chose a character and we just invented scenarios. Jody Manning was Marlena, Scott Jenkins was Roman Brady, and my friend Katie was Hope. I'd like to tell you that this is where I discovered a love of acting. No. Maybe because I always had to be Abe the policeman. He was the only black guy on *Days*. Black Lexie didn't come on for a couple more years. So I was Abe the policeman.

As if it weren't enough that she got to play Marlena, Jody and her sister also always had coordinating, full Esprit outfits. And it wasn't from the Esprit outlets where you got like the sweatshirt and paired it with Garanimals trash. They were just perfect, those Mannings, and Jody set a high bar for competition in class. I remember we once did a presentation together in the sixth grade. The job was to come up with an ad campaign for a product, and we were assigned Bumble Bee tuna. I was the talent, thank you. Our catchphrase was just saying "Bumble Bee tuna" emphatically. Everyone was saying it at recess, so we got an A plus.

In case you are not already reaching for the Nerd Alert button, around this time, I started reading three newspapers a day. And that became an obsession, like times tables and square roots. I would figure out exactly down to the minute how long I could be in the shower, how long it would take me to get ready, and still have time to read the newspapers. The first two, the *Tri-Valley Herald* and the *Valley Times,* were exactly how they sound. Here's an actual headline in the *Valley Times,* which I cut out and laminated for my civics class: MEXICANS ROB THE MALL. Meanwhile, the "Mexicans" were from, like, the next town over, and they probably knocked over a Sunglass Hut.

So those papers didn't take me that long. But then I would read the *Oakland Tribune,* which was much more involved. On the rare occasion that I didn't finish, I would take whatever was left and I would go through it in my first-period class, usually an English class. If I didn't, I just couldn't focus. I honestly don't know what came first—a love of reading the newspapers, or wanting to be Super Negro, the magical special black person who has all the knowledge and is never caught out there looking ignorant. "She is so knowledgeable" is what I lived for. "That black girl is really something."

My other job was to be popular, which I approached with the same strategy as my studies. Meaning it was everything.

Sleepovers were the thing among the girls, and you had to be there or else you would be "discussed." I had all the sleepover worries preteens have about pranks and fears that I would smell by morning. But my hair was also a problem. I didn't want to go through the normal ritual that I did at home, wrapping my hair with a scarf, because it would draw attention to my blackness and therefore my difference. When in Rome, do as the white girls do. So I would put my hair in a ponytail or a bun and try to keep as still as possible all night—as we call it, "sleeping pretty." But eventually slumber takes over and you become a human being. By the time I woke up in the morning, my hair would be unruly.

"Oh my God, you look like Buckwheat!" someone invariably said, pointing to the mass of hair on my head. Eddie Murphy's *SNL* version of Buckwheat was still fresh and popular, all hair and teeth and "Ohtay!"

"Do Buckwheat!"

And I would do it. I would go into the "Buckwheat Got Shot" routine, with my hands in the air like Eddie's. Every time I said, "Ohtay," the girls would die.

Now that I was willingly their clown, the directives began.

"Act like you put your finger in a socket."

"Pretend you're a Kewpie doll."

I pulled my hair up to make it stand on end. Making them laugh gave me the illusion of agency and control. Minstrelsy makes the audience comfortable. Now that I am on the other side of it, and proud of my blackness, they wouldn't know what to do with me. People don't know what to do with you if you are not trying to assimilate.

Nevertheless, I did manage to create real, lasting friendships with other girls during this period. And we liked to have fun. We had our first kegger in seventh grade, right before school let out for summer. We were farting around in a park and we saw these older kids hide their pony keg in the bushes. We waited for them to leave, snuck over, got their pony keg, and rolled it right on over to my friend Missy Baldwin's house. None of us knew how to open it, so we hammered a screwdriver into the side until we made a hole and were able to drain the beer into a bucket.

And then we had all this beer! So we called people—meaning boys—and they biked over to Missy's house. There was just this trove of Huffys and BMXs dropped in her front yard as kids raced to the back practically shouting, *"Beer!"* The house got trashed and kids put her lawn furniture into her pool. This wasn't even at night and it was in a planned community. But her parents were hippies and were like, "Missy. Man, that's not cool."

That wouldn't have worked with my parents, but they had

no idea where I was anyway. They put in long days at their tele-communications jobs—my dad in San Jose, my mom in Oak-land, both a one-hour commute away. My older sister, Kelly, who acted as if she had birthed herself, was given a very long leash, but she had a lot of responsibility, too. If anything happened, my sister had to take care of it. If I had a dentist appointment, she would have to take time off from school activities to play chauf-feur. Class projects, homework—she was my Google before there was Google. In high school, she loved sports but didn't have my natural athleticism. She quickly recognized the gifts she had and segued into being a team manager and coaching youth basketball. Everything she wore was from Lerner, and she became a manager there at sixteen. There she was in her blazers with the huge shoul-der pads. I idolized her, but also took her guidance and intelli-gence for granted.

She and Tracy, my little sister, had the caregiver-child rela-tionship because of the eleven years between them. I was in the middle, completely under my family's radar. So I created a family of my friends. They were everything to me, and as a result, I was hardly ever home.

I only drank with friends, enjoying the game of getting the alcohol as much as drinking it. We'd steal from our parents or con older relatives into buying it for us. We used to play a drink-ing game called vegetable. Each person would choose a vegeta-ble and try to say it without showing our teeth, and then we'd give someone another vegetable to say. You'd always pick some-thing tough, like "rhubarb" or "asparagus" or "russet potatoes." If you showed your teeth—by laughing, for instance—you had to pound a Keystone Light or whatever contraband we'd gotten our hands on that evening. And it doesn't take a lot to laugh when you're drunk on cheap beer and high, which, oftentimes, we were.

But there were little matters of etiquette in these situations that reminded me of my place. When you shared a can of beer, the directive was always "Don't nigger-lip it." It meant don't get your mouth all over it.

Another common term was "nigger-rig." To nigger-rig something was to MacGyver it or fix it in a half-ass way—to wit, opening a pony keg with a screwdriver. Sometimes people would catch themselves saying "nigger" in front of me.

"Oh there's niggers and there's, you know, cool black people," they'd say to excuse it. "You're not like them."

In my English class in ninth grade, we read *The Adventures of Huckleberry Finn* aloud. The teacher made us take alternating paragraphs in order of where we sat in class. We were seated alphabetically by name, so as a "U" I was in the back of the class. Twain uses the word "nigger" exactly 219 times in the book. I would count the paragraphs to read ahead and see if there were any "niggers" in what I had to say. Each time a kid said "nigger," the whole class turned their heads to watch my response. Some turned to look at me just before they read it aloud, wincing in an apology that only made me more aware of the blackness I was trying so hard to escape. Others turned to smile as they said it, aiming "nigger" right at me.

But most times it felt like kids at my school simply forgot I was black. Perversely, I was relieved when they did. I had so completely stopped being black to these people that they could speak to me as a fellow white person.

"Nigger" wasn't the only slur slung around at the few people of color who dotted the overwhelmingly white student population.

But being so focused on my own situation, I wasn't always proficient in racist slang. Sure, I could decipher jokes about the Latino kids and the couple of Asian girls, but it took me a long time to realize people weren't calling our classmate Mehal a "kite." In Pleasanton you were either Catholic or Mormon, and Mehal was proudly Jewish. She invited us all to her bat mitzvah. Nobody went. Our belief system was "Jews killed Jesus, Jews are bad." Mehal flew the flag, and so she was out, but when we found out Eric Wadamaker was Jewish, it was like he'd had a mask ripped off at the end of *Scooby-Doo.*

"You know Waddy's a Jew?"

"Whaaaat? But he's so cool."

The pressure to assimilate infused every choice we made, no matter our race. Kids who didn't use the slurs certainly didn't speak up against classmates or parents using them. They adopted the language or they kept silent. Because to point out inequality in the town would mean Pleasanton was not perfect. And Pleasanton had to be perfect.

WHEN I WAS THIRTEEN, MY PARENTS BEGAN SENDING ME BACK TO OMAHA alone to spend summers with my mother's mother. It was at my request; my older sister was going off to college and I was looking for more freedom. As soon as the plane landed, I heard a sound like the sprinklers of California when they started up, that sharp *zzt-zzt,* but at a constant hum. It was the sound of insects. Cicadas provided the backdrop to my Omaha summers.

My grandmother brought my cousin Kenyatta to the airport to meet me that first year. A year younger than me, she was effortlessly cool. My grandmother raised Kenyatta while her mother, Aunt Carla, was in and out of jail. Grandma also raised Kenyatta's little brother. Aunt Carla was never out for more than a year and a half. She was awesome, don't get me wrong; she just had a problem with drugs. Kenyatta was very thin, like me, with really big eyes and chocolate-brown skin. Her lips literally looked like four bubbles, briefly joining on the edge of bursting. "Those lips," boys always said in admiration, making kissing faces at her.

Kenyatta gave me access to the cool black kids in the neighborhood. She had all these tough friends, some of whom had already been to juvie. They were all pretty and all having sex.

She had told her friends her cousin from California was coming, so a bunch of them waited outside Grandma's house to meet me. To them California was three things: beaches, celebrities, and gangs. They came ready to talk to me about what I had seen of the Crips and the Bloods.

"Hi there," I said, getting out of the car.

Their faces sank. It was over.

"Oh, Jesus," her friend Essence said. "Your cousin is white, Kenyatta."

"You're an Oreo," said this boy Sean.

It wasn't a surprise, but it wasn't something to get upset about. I had hoped to get off the plane and slip into a new life. Be a Janet Jackson doing Charlene on *Diff'rent Strokes,* or, my greatest wish, Lisa Bonet on *The Cosby Show.* The cool black girl that Pleasanton could never appreciate. But I was still just me. Luckily, I was under Kenyatta's protection. They could tease me, but only so much.

"Did you bring the tapes?" she asked.

"Yeah," I said, opening my carry-on to pull out two cassettes. She had asked me to tape California radio stations so her crew could press play and be transported to the beaches with the celebrities and the gangbangers.

We all went upstairs and crowded into her room, which would now also become my room. My grandmother had crammed two twin beds in there, so we all sat down. Kenyatta couldn't get that tape in her boom box fast enough.

Everyone leaned in as she pressed play. Crowded House's "Don't Dream It's Over" filled the room.

"What the fuck is this?" asked Sean.

"It's the radio back home," I said. "This is what they play in California."

"Do they play L.A. Dream Team?" asked Kenyatta. "World Class Wreckin' Cru?"

I pretended to know who they were, then remembered the radio station's tag line. "Um," I said. "They play the hits."

I'd taped 120 minutes of the Top 40 of Pleasanton. At first they gave it a chance. Heart. Whitesnake. They gave up at Tiffany.

Kenyatta put in a New Edition tape, and my heart leapt. I was obsessed with them, the few black boys who showed up on MTV. We girls bonded right there, talking about Bobby Brown leaving the group and Johnny Gill coming in. And which one of us Ralph Tresvant would pick out of a crowd.

I could hold my own talking about New Edition, but I felt real green on being black. And *everyone* was black in my grandmother's North Omaha neighborhood. Beyond New Edition, I wasn't up on *anything* when it came to being black. My grandma lived on the edge of what was considered "a bad area," and it was its own world, without white people. The way people talked about white folks when there were no white folks around was dramatically different—just as white folks spoke differently about black people when they thought black people weren't around, except in Pleasanton, where they forgot I was black because I blended in so well. I began studying my cousin Kenyatta and her friends to relearn blackness. Otherwise, I would be dismissed as "corny," which was the death kiss in Omaha. To be corny there was the equivalent of being labeled a "nerd" in Pleasanton—you could not come back from it. No boy would even consider coming near you. Being off-limits and forever friend-zoned was a given as the black girl in Pleasanton. But in Omaha, I had a shot at getting boys to like me the way I liked them. I couldn't blow it.

I earned respect pretty quickly, and I'm sure a lot of that had to do with being Kenyatta's cousin. Mostly I did it by keeping a poker face and not saying anything, no matter how surprised or confused I was by something people did or said. Nobody tried to mess with me.

I liked North Omaha from the jump—the dampness in the air, and how the sun never really shone. Somehow, though, the few white folks we saw on trips to the mall were all kind of tanned in this ruddy color that white people turn when they're overheated. Everyone just lived out on their blocks, hanging back, chilling, talking shit, flirting. Every so often, the sky would suddenly turn black and everyone would start running because there was a tornado coming. As soon as it blew by, everyone came back outside to the streets.

It was Midwest summer, when there's nothing to do. We were kids with no jobs, so every morning the conversation went like this: "Where are we gonna go today?" "What boy's house can we walk to?" "Whose parents aren't home?" "Who has a car?" Just finding somebody with a car was incredibly rare. In Pleasanton, everybody had a car. But in Omaha, people got around through what they called "jitneys": elderly people that you knew your whole life would say, "Hey, call me if you need me to get to the store. Just give me three dollars."

Teenagers even drank differently in North Omaha. It wasn't the binge drinking of mixed drinks in plastic cups, like in Pleasanton. If you were kicking back on the stoop you had a forty or a wine cooler. The penny candy store was right next to the liquor store, so when we hung out in front of the candy store, folks might have thought we were there to get candy, but we were really waiting on a mark. When you found one, you would shoulder-tap the guy. "Heeeey, can you get me a forty of Mickey's big mouth?" (Mickey's "big mouth" is a malt liquor also known as a "grenade," for the shape of the bottle it comes in.) It was never tough.

It was a very exciting time in my life, and there was a bit of danger that felt glamorous. The summer I was thirteen, crack started to show up in North Omaha. My aunt Carla also got out of jail. I saw her as effortlessly cool and admired her gift for always having guys around. She was staying with a boyfriend, even though she always had a home at my grandmother's if she needed it. The guys who she introduced me to were always really nice, and only later would you find out that so-and-so was involved in one of the largest drug busts in the history of the Midwest. Aunt Carla came over to Grandma's soon after she was sprung and saw a letter from my parents. They were sending me eighty dollars' cash a week that summer to give to my grandmother. Selfish me kept that cash, of course.

"Let me hold that eighty dollars," Aunt Carla said, "and on Friday, I'll give you three hundred dollars and we'll go to Red Lobster."

"Sure," I said, handing her the money. It was Monday, and I

knew I'd have another eighty dollars the next week, so it wasn't a big deal.

Wednesday my aunt came over again. "Give me your sizes," she said. "I wanna get you some back-to-school clothes."

"I want Guess jeans," I said, and then reeled off my sizes along with a list of additional asks.

Lo and behold, Friday came and Aunt Carla showed up in a limo, carrying shopping bags full of clothes for Kenyatta and me.

"Now let's go to Red Lobster," she said, handing me my three hundred dollars.

It was my first time in a limo. Kenyatta and I opened the windows and waved to everyone we passed on the ride to dinner. At the restaurant, we feasted—ordering the lobster and shrimp combo and eating every Cheddar Bay biscuit in sight. When we emerged rubbing our stomachs, the limo was gone.

"I only had it for the way over," Aunt Carla said, slotting a coin in the nearby pay phone as she took a drag on a cigarette. Her friend eventually showed up in a Buick, and as we started the drive home, she said, "I need to stop at Kmart. Stay in the car," she told us.

She went inside to write a few bad checks while we waited.

"You girls doing good?" said the driver.

We both nodded.

He proceeded to pull out a crack pipe and smoke up. The windows were closed, so we couldn't help but be hotboxed. We didn't feel any secondhand effects, but I would always immediately recognize that smell as an adult, traveling the country and going to clubs.

We were familiar with crack already, because our friends were dealers. We'd seen plenty of crack pipes and even watched people weigh it for parceling. North Omaha was rapidly changing, and every summer, the changes escalated. The L.A.-based dealers had begun to spread out across the country to get a piece of the local drug trade everywhere. Gang members came to North Omaha, selling a lifestyle as if they were setting up franchises. But it was all so bizarre to watch. North Omaha is made up of a bunch of families that have been there for generations. You walk down the street and somebody can identify what family you belong to by your facial features. All of a sudden here come these powerful gangs, splitting up families as kids randomly chose different gang sets.

A lot of my cousins and neighborhood kids that I'd grown up with during my summer visits, boys and girls, began to claim allegiance to L.A. gangs that they didn't know anything about. It started as a saccharine, almost Disney-like version of gang life. When I returned at fourteen, every young person was touched by some sort of criminal enterprise, with varying degrees of success. Some kids got one rock of cocaine and announced, "I'm a drug dealer." Then there were kids who as teenagers were doing, in terms of drug dealing, very well for themselves. They had their own apartments and flaunted their wealth.

At the end of the day, I didn't look at crack so negatively, because I saw our little friends making money off it. Drug dealing felt like any other job to me. I only knew young dealers and the random ones that my aunt knew. I didn't see the underbelly. The violence, the desperation, the addiction. All I knew was, I gave my aunt eighty dollars and she gave me three hundred dollars back. That was integrity. I later found out Aunt Carla asked her friend who was a booster—a shoplifter by profession, thank you—to get those school clothes for me at the mall. I didn't think less of her or those clothes. I thought Aunt Carla was smart. And

I went to Red Lobster in a limo. If someone smoked crack on the way home, that was a small price to pay for the adventure. A footnote, really. What remains is that she kept her word. In retrospect, I guess it's naïve to think this would all end well, but I saw honor among thieves.

In the midst of this, I was still Nickie, trying to get boys to like me, specifically Kevin Marshall. The summer I was fourteen, Kenyatta and I invited two boys over to my grandmother's with the promise of alcohol. Andy Easterbrook and beautiful Kevin. I was truly, madly, deeply, over the moon in love with Kevin. He was caramel colored, with green eyes, and a great athlete. He wasn't supposed to like a chocolate girl like me. And he liked me.

First order of business: coming through on that promised alcohol. Kenyatta and I decided to steal my aunt Joanne's wine coolers. This was the biggest mistake of the summer! God, if there was anybody who counted their wine coolers it was Aunt Joanne. But when you're a kid and you see two four-packs and there are boys to impress, you take one or two and say, "There's still some left." Boy, did we pay for that.

Next, we had to sneak Andy and Kevin into the house without Grandma knowing. Now, Grandma was always in her rocking chair, and she had to get out of it in order to see the door. So we knew that we would have a fighting chance to sneak the boys up the stairs while Grandma was working up enough momentum to propel her ass out of the chair. Even better, we knew she couldn't go upstairs because of her knees.

But as the wine cooler situation makes clear, Kenyatta and I were dumb as fuck. We ran in, pushing the boys in front of us and yelling, "Hi, Grandma! Bye, Grandma!" as we raced up the stairs. My grandma was slow and her knees were shit, but she wasn't deaf. She kept yelling, "Who all is in here?" because you can surely tell the difference between two sets of feet and four heading up the stairs. Especially boys racing to get alcohol.

So, Grandma simply refused to go to sleep. She got up from her chair and she sat in the couch next to the front door. She knew whoever we'd snuck in eventually had to come down because there was no bathroom upstairs. Somebody's gotta pee. Someone's gotta leave. And she was gonna be there to see it.

Of course, she also knew we were smoking weed up there. We were making this big attempt to hide it, blowing the smoke through the window screens. But you couldn't open the screens, and the mesh was so small that the smoke just stayed in the room. So our play to hide our business didn't work at all.

Between the wine coolers and the Mickey's big mouth they gallantly brought, the boys had to pee soon enough. They filled the empty bottles, but then had to go again. So then they had the bright idea to pour the bottled pee out through the screen. All that weed smoke not making it through the tiny mesh should have shown us that this was not a good idea. Between kid logic and the weed, it made perfect sense at the time. The piss just pooled in the gutter of the window. Hot urine in the windowsill—ah, the romance and brilliance of the teenage years.

When Grandma finally relented and went to bed in what felt like nine hours, the boys left.

"I know you had boys up there," she said to us the next morning. "I know you were smoking that weed."

"No we didn't," I said.

Aunt Joanne kept saying, "And I know you took my wine coolers!"

"No, we didn't," I said.

"Did Grandma take them?" offered Kenyatta.

"You know," I said, "other people come over here."

It's one of my greatest shames that some of my last memories of my grandmother when she was cognizant were just bald-faced lies. In a short while, she would have dementia and not know who I was. But I have to tell you, I would have done anything for Kevin Marshall. My parents let me go back to Omaha that Christmas, and the only reason I went was to have a chance to see Kevin Marshall and get a real kiss.

And I got it. Kevin Marshall tongue-kissed me on the corner of Forty-ninth and Fort, right by the bus stop.

I'm pretty, I thought. Kevin Marshall, this light-skinned boy with green eyes who is not supposed to find me attractive, found me pretty enough to kiss. On the level playing field of Omaha, a guy like Kevin was a huge get, having his pick of the pecking order of skin color that is in place in black and brown communities across the world. And he had picked a chocolate girl like me.

Then I thought, Maybe black boys like me.

THE NEXT SUMMER, WHEN I WAS FIFTEEN, I EASED BACK INTO MY BLACK-ness even more quickly. But North Omaha had changed more, too. It was no longer the Disney version of gang culture, it was real. The buzz in the air now seemed more scary than exhilarating. Boys would pick Kenyatta and me up to go for a ride, and we'd end up going over the bridge to Council Bluffs because they needed to pick up some money or deliver a package. It continually felt like the beginning of a bad movie. These were not bad people. These were regular kids who got swept up in the frenzy of having to be in a gang and do gang shit to impress each other. Drive-by shootings started happening, and kids began to get killed. Something very bad was coming.

My cousin was dating this guy named Ryan. He and his friend Lucky were always around. Lucky always had cornrows that never appeared freshly braided. They drove vintage El Caminos, restored status symbols they called "Old Schools." You saw these cars, lovingly and expensively restored by masters, and knew these guys had money. One night Ryan did a drive-by, shooting someone in the neck and paralyzing him. We saw a police sketch on the news and my grandma said, "Doesn't that look like your friend Ryan?"

"Nope," said Kenyatta.

"No way," I said, thinking, Yep, that's Ryan.

He came to the door later that night, after Grandma went to sleep. Kenyatta let him in quickly, and we sat on the steps leading upstairs. Ryan had the gun, and he placed it on the ground by his feet. We all stared at it.

"Can I hold it?" Kenyatta asked.

He picked it up by the handle and she held it, aiming away from us. She looked at it with a mixture of admiration and fear. This gun had been fired and it had paralyzed someone. The whole town was looking for Ryan, and here he was.

"Can I?" I asked.

Kenyatta handed it to me, and I held it like you would a caterpillar, with my fingers splayed out not to touch anything. It was so heavy. I thought, That's why he accidentally shot that kid. It's probably just too big a gun for him to aim.

"Can I stay here?" asked Ryan.

It hadn't occurred to me he would ask that, but it obviously had to Kenyatta, who nodded quickly. "We'll put you in the basement," she said. "Grandma won't know." And we did. For three weeks, we brought him food. Peanut butter sandwiches we made covertly, leftovers from dinner. Beer when we had it. We kept him company, talking about what was going on in the neighborhood. I watched some detective show where they accused this woman of "harboring a fugitive." I felt like I had a secret. I was protecting a good guy who made a mistake.

Police knew it was Ryan who had done the shooting, and it became clear to him that this hideout plan wouldn't last. He turned himself in. He went to prison. Lucky was killed the following summer, leading everyone to think they were the first one to say, "Guess he wasn't so lucky." Another friend got shot and had to wear a colostomy bag for the rest of his life. Kevin joined a gang, then his best friend Dennis died. A girl I knew stabbed a jitney driver rather than pay him five dollars. He lived. He'd known her since she was a baby and was able to tell police exactly where she lived, who her grandfather was, hell, who her great-grandmother was. Another boy that I thought was so cute shot up a Bronco Burgers. The mom of one of our friends decided she had to get her son out of Omaha. She sent him to Denver, and he got mixed up with gangs there. He got killed, too.

None of these people changed. The environment around them did. They were all good people who made choices that ended up having insane consequences. But their hearts never changed. They were playing roles assigned to them, the same way I did in Pleasanton.

WHEN I WOULD GO BACK TO PLEASANTON AT THE END OF THOSE Nebraska summers, I didn't share any of those stories. The kids I went to school with didn't deserve to hear them. They were mine, and I knew I could never convince my friends of the innate goodness of Kenyatta, Kevin, and Lucky, anyway. Of Ryan, even. So I would simply become the invisible black girl again. I checked my language, the cadence of my walk, and the confidence of just being in my skin. The older I got, the more resentful I became of these reentry periods. People in California noticed my attitude was different. I was quicker to anger at slights. I wouldn't play Buckwheat.

I especially struggled back home after the summer of hiding Ryan. I don't know if my older sister, Kelly, noticed, or if I just got lucky, but she took me under her wing. By then she was in college, starting out at USC before transferring to San Jose State. Immediately at USC, she found a very cool group of black friends. I was so jealous. When she got away from the house, she stopped having to be my mother-sister. She was just Kelly, and our relationship changed for the better.

When I was fifteen, she took me to a black frat party at San Jose State. It was like she gave me the keys to this kingdom of cool black people who valued education and fun. They were just worldly, and cool and dope and sexy. In the way that Omaha gave me an outlet for my Pleasanton frustration, my sister's world of college became a new outlet. I looked around at these students and saw black excellence. I met an Alpha Phi Alpha brother named Darryl, who talked to me for a long time that night. He even gave me his number. I gave him a fake number in return because I had lied about my age and this was a *man*. But I held onto that piece of paper for years.

That night made me see the either/or schism I was trapped in. Between Pleasanton and Omaha, I was caught in a dual consciousness: who I had to be when I was around my own people, and who I had to be in high school. Now, it's easy to see how caught I was in that back-and-forth mental chess match of trying to be okay in both worlds. "Two warring ideals in one dark body," as Du Bois wrote; the dark body of a young girl. Each was me, but the constant code-switching—changing my language, demeanor, and identity expression to fit in—left me exhausted.

"You were fly, dope, and amazing from birth," I would tell that girl now. "From the second you took your first breath, you were worthwhile and valid. And I'm sorry you had to wait so long to learn that for yourself."

two

SEX MISEDUCATION

In the fifth grade, the girls were all ushered into the school multi-purpose room, where it was explained to us that WE COULD GET PREGNANT AT ANY MOMENT. Well, at least our period would strike any minute, which meant we could hypothetically conceive a child.

The problem is, Miss Brackett forgot to include the part about *how* we would get pregnant. She just left it at "it could just *happen*." No one was brave enough to ask questions. And if you don't know *how* you get pregnant, just that it MIGHT HAPPEN AT ANY MOMENT, it's a little scary. I would lie awake at night in my room, clutching my bed-in-a-bag twin sheets to my chin and wondering what could happen to impregnate me. If you were raised Catholic like I was, you already know from Sunday school that nothing really has to happen. You could go to sleep and wake up carrying Baby Jesus. I've seen countless paintings of the Annunciation, where Mary "accepts" the news that she is pregnant. But my favorite is Dante Gabriel Rossetti's at the Tate Britain in

London. Mary is in bed, giving the angel Gabriel a bleary-eyed look of "Are you fucking kidding me right now?"

That's how we felt. Are you kidding me with this "at any moment you could become a mom!" stuff? We lived in a primarily Catholic and Mormon town, so our moms definitely weren't chatting among themselves about periods. When any of my friends' moms talked to them, it was to simply hand them some pads. I certainly wasn't going to talk to my older sister about it, and because I could barely decode Tampax commercials, I looked for information in books. Naturally, my friends and I turned to *Are You There God? It's Me, Margaret,* Judy Blume's classic 1970 menstruation how-to, disguised as a preadolescent narrative. Among us ten- and eleven-year-olds, the book became required reading, and we ferreted out dog-eared copies from the local library, big sisters, and a few progressive mothers. Some girls, like me, just skipped to the blood pages. They'd hand me a copy and I'd fan through the pages to the good parts. Then I'd pass the wisdom on to the next girl. "Here," I'd say, pointing. "Then here."

We needed answers because it was all so scary—the idea of bleeding randomly and accepting it as natural seemed completely unnatural. After all, when you skinned your knee, you ran for a Band-Aid. "Where's the Bactine? I have to cover this!" But when it came to our periods, we were supposed to be celebratory? Like our moms would suddenly initiate us into their blood cult? This was a horror movie set in the leafy surroundings of Pleasanton Middle School.

It came for Melody first. In fifth grade, during homeroom. She bled right through her pants. She looked down in shock, the blood slowly blossoming in the crotch and back of her pants, and

Lucas, the boy who'd called me a nigger in the second grade, saw it first and reliably pounced.

"Melody is having her period!" he yelled out, disgusted and delighted. "Let's jump her!" He and a few of his lackeys hooted with laughter, while the rest of us looked on in horror and panic. Now an initiate into the blood cult of adult women, Melody, of course, COULD GET PREGNANT AT ANY MOMENT. (Where was the teacher? Don't ask. Faculty lounge? Smoke break?) After a few excruciating moments, Melody unfroze and ran screaming. No one followed her.

That included me. I felt ashamed. I was her friend, but for much of the school year, it was like being friends with a leper. Nobody else got her period for the longest time, but soon enough all the girls in fifth grade became familiar with Melody's month-to-month schedule, and when she was absent, we spoke gravely of her condition, dramatically shushing each other when a boy came within hearing range.

By seventh grade, Melody was no longer alone in her period drama, as all of us were getting picked off like flies. One of our friends would stay home from school or race to the nurse's office, and then we would know: "It came for her." No one I knew was excited about it. You looked forward to it the way you looked forward to food poisoning.

I knew that at any moment, it would be my turn to stand up and everyone would point in my direction. I remember we all wore dark colors in case it happened. I began carrying my jean jacket with me at all times, ready for the big moment. I pinned concert buttons all over it of the Top 40 stuff I loved—Stray Cats, Def Leppard, New Edition, Billy Joel—and tied it around my waist to conceal the inevitable evidence when the time came. We asked each other so many questions, because unless we'd been struck, none of us had answers. "Like, what happens? You put this pad on, and then what? You're just bleeding and sitting in it?"

I finally became a woman in a bathroom stall at Macy's, halfway through seventh grade. I was at Stoneridge Mall with a few friends. I felt a little dampness down below, started silently panicking and screaming, then whispered to my friends, "Oh my God, I think it's happening!" We speed-walked to the restroom, and my friend Becky, always prepared, handed me a pad. I went into the stall a girl and came out an adult.

When I got home, I tried to pretend as if nothing had happened. I balled up my bloody underwear and jeans and stuffed them deep in the closet of the bathroom I shared with my older sister, Kelly. I felt cramped and sore, but I just didn't want to have the mortifying "talk" with anyone. I don't know why I didn't throw the clothes away. I guess it felt wasteful? Kid logic is just dumb. Weeks later, my mom found them while cleaning the house.

"I found your . . ." She paused. "Soiled underwear." Ugh, to this day, the word "soiled" still makes me cringe. She handed me some pads—offering no instructions, no sitting on the couch and patting the cushion next to her—and that was that.

But I kept worrying about my next period, and I was terrified of being humiliated at school. Every month was a guessing game. "When will it happen? Will everyone find out? Will guys try to jump me and make me pregnant?" At first, I didn't know how to use the pads, and for a full year I continually had accidents because my pads were riding high. Not only did I not know how pads worked, I didn't understand how my vagina worked, either. And that's because, dear reader, I thought my clitoris was my vagina.

I started masturbating early, at age five or six. So I knew where the fun was. I knew where my clitoris was. My vagina? Not so much. I'd lived my life thinking, Of course sex is painful, because it's where you pee from! And of course childbirth is painful, because you pee out a baby! Even though I'd seen a number of anatomy diagrams, I knew where I masturbated, so I assumed that was my vagina.

I only discovered my vagina in the eighth grade, after a year of accidents. My girlfriend Danielle—Big D—and I were swimming at a local sports complex called AVAC, short for Amador Valley Athletic Club, and of course I got my period. In the water, I noticed a wispy trail of blood. It was coming from me. It was especially mortifying because AVAC was as fancy as a country club, with the best of everything. I frantically climbed out of the pool with Big D following, and locked myself in a bathroom. She talked to me through the door.

"Nick, it's okay," Big D said, concern in her voice but cool as ever. She had a bookie dad and was never prudish like most of the other girls I knew then.

"I have to go home!" I said, frantically.

"Oh, just put in a tampon," said Big D.

"I'm not a whore!" I shrieked. We just assumed tampons made you break your hymen, so if you used them instead of pads, you were no longer a virgin. And at that stage, if you weren't a virgin in Pleasanton, you were considered a whore.

"What?" said Big D. The record scratched.

"I've never used one," I whispered.

"Open the door," she said, and I did, but just a crack. She passed me a plastic-wrapped cylinder, and I took it from her, grateful.

"Now lay on the floor," I heard her voice say, coaching me through it. "Put your knees up, and just slowly put it in."

I did as commanded, laying out my plush AVAC towel and trying to put the tampon in what I thought was my vagina. "It's too big," I said.

"What?"

"It's too big."

"Let me in."

I unlocked the door. She came in, like the straight man in a screwball comedy.

"Where are you trying to put it?" she asked.

I was trying to put a tampon in my urethra.

"Um, that's not your vagina," Big D explained, slowly.

I let that sit for a beat.

"What?" I said, as casually as I possibly could.

Now I see *That's Not Your Vagina* being a great title for this little one-act play, but then I didn't see the humor.

So there we were, on the floor of a bathroom at AVAC, and Big D just slid that tampon right on up so fast I didn't think quickly enough to be freaked out. And I was all, "Where are you going?" as if she was doing a Jacques Cousteau deep dive. And she's going down. And I was like, "There's something more down there? What an amazing discovery!" Finding my vagina was a moment of "Interesting. Did. Not. Know. That." Big D was exactly the friend I needed to get me through the moment as quickly as possible. We never once spoke of it again until we were adults, not out of shame, but from a sense of "What happens in an AVAC bathroom stays in an AVAC bathroom." Only recently, when I brought it up to her, did it seem even remotely nuts.

But how was I supposed to know where my vagina was? From a young age, most girls are not given the most basic information about their bodies. And we grow into smart women who often don't go to doctors on a regular basis because we are too busy putting others in our lives first, and don't share personal medical information with each other, either. People talk about our bodies solely as reproductive systems, and we remain just as clueless as The Virgin Mary's learning she was but a vessel for something greater.

THANK GOD FOR JUDY BLUME, BECAUSE AT LEAST SHE ARMED ME WITH THE basic facts of menstruation. Nowadays, girls can Wikipedia everything—or more likely, study porn clips online.

But back then, all we had was Judy Blume. She also gifted us with *Forever*. We all knew and loved *Forever,* because it had the Sex Scene. And outside of porn (which was damn hard to procure in those pre-Internet days), *Forever* was the only depiction of sex we had ever seen. High school senior Katherine meets fellow student Michael, who nicknames his penis "Ralph" and teaches her how to rub one out, before they go "all the way" in his sister's bedroom.

We were smart enough to know that *Forever*—not the cheesy VHS porn tapes that my trusty friend Becky had discovered in her parents' room—taught us the more accurate portrait of how sex would unfold in our own lives. (Thank you, Judy!) *Forever* gave us the truth. It was about wanting to have sex, preparing to have sex, having sex, and what happens afterward. Judy Blume was our tutor.

During our freshman year, my friend Julie had sex at a house party with a boy she liked. They had planned to do it, but both were too fearful to go buy condoms. He told her he had a plan, so just before the big deed, he pulled out a plastic baggie. You read that right. A Ziploc.

A month or so later, a bunch of us were hanging out on one of the school lawns. None of us wanted to just go home and be bored, so we decided to be bored together. We were talking about how we couldn't wait for summer when Julie started crying. She leaned forward into the circle.

"I think I'm pregnant," she whispered.

We sort of fell into her, muffling her cries. I asked her twice if she was sure. It was such a stupid question, but I didn't want what she was saying to be true. My friend Barbara instead snapped into action. She was always very advanced and finger-snapping efficient with her asymmetrical bob and mod clothes.

"Okay, how much money do you have?" she said.

Julie shrugged.

"Okay," she said, looking at us all. "How much money do *we* have?"

Barbara said we needed about $350. That's what she decided was the going rate for an abortion.

Over the next couple of days, like some very special *Magic School Bus* episode, we all, a bunch of fourteen- and fifteen-year-olds, went to our parents to make a bunch of fake requests for money to buy new uniforms or to go on nonexistent field trips. In a couple of days, we got $350. The next hurdle was scheduling the abortion within the confines of the school day. To accomplish this, the lot of us cut class to go to the Planned Parenthood in Pleasanton. There was a lone protester outside. She wasn't crazy, as far as protesters go, but it was strangely terrifying. She had a sign and was just there, staring at a bunch of teenagers who didn't want anyone to see us.

Imagine five terrified fourteen- and fifteen-year-old girls sitting in a waiting room, hugging our backpacks. There was a basket of condoms on a little side table by the door. As we waited for Julie, I was eyeing those condoms. And sitting in a Planned Parenthood waiting for my friend's abortion to be over, I was still afraid of what the people working there would think if they saw me taking a condom.

Julie came out and we all hugged her. She didn't cry, she just wanted to get on with her life. She led the way out the door, walking fast and with her eyes focused forward. I trailed behind, and in one fell swoop I dumped the entire basket of condoms into my bag.

No one called shotgun. We let Julie sit in the passenger seat. As soon as the car doors closed, I opened my bag to show everyone the condoms.

"Everyone take some," I ordered.

They wouldn't. Everyone was afraid of getting caught by their parents with condoms.

"Fine," I said. "I'll hold them. But come to me, okay?"

That's how it went. I became the condom dispensary, bringing them to school and to parties whenever I got the heads-up. Adults weren't looking out for us. They assumed that we knew we could get pregnant and wouldn't risk it by actually having sex. But even when you know better, it doesn't mean you're going to do better. That's a lie parents tell themselves so they don't have to admit their kids have sex. And they do. They will either live with fear and baggies and abortions, or live with knowledge and condoms.

My dad found my stash, of course, and flipped out.

"They're for my friends," I screamed. That didn't help. I used the "What were you doing snooping in my room?" tactic, which actually worked for once. I think he was terrified.

These days, kids are mostly just honest with adults, which is just weird. I recently met a young woman in a teen empowerment seminar. "I told him I wanted to suck his dick so I sucked his dick," she said. "It's no big deal."

Um, yeah . . . No?

Now, when I try to talk to our boys or I talk to young girls, here's what I say:

"Are you ready to own your sexuality in a way that you can experience pleasure as well as give it? And be truly grown-up about it?"

But what kids are doing now, the way they process it and act on it, is so different. They would probably read *Forever* and it would be so pedestrian to them. "What kind of baby-book bullshit is this?"

But I see their "raw honesty" and I raise them.

"If you're such good friends that you gave him a blow job," I asked that one girl, "did he eat your pussy?"

"No," she said, looking at her friends.

"Well, make sure he does that next time."

"Okay."

"And then have him eat your ass," I said, "and see where that goes."

"Whoa."

"It's called reciprocation. Otherwise, it's a very unequal friendship. And I wouldn't want that kind of friendship. If you're gonna do it, then shit, really do it."

I WANT PEOPLE TO MAKE INFORMED, JOYFUL CHOICES ABOUT SEX. BE-
cause I love sex. In the heyday of my twenties and thirties, I loved
the variety. Now that I am married, I am in a monogamous relationship. But I used to think monogamy was for suckers who
didn't have options. "Some choose monogamy," I would say, "but
most people have it foisted upon them."

I just didn't see the point back then. I did, however, see the
point in *publicly* declaring oneself to be in a monogamous relationship. It was never lost on me that society thinks a woman
should be allotted one dick to use and she should be happy with
it for the rest of her life. But I always saw sex as something to be
enjoyed. Repeatedly. With as many different partners as possible.

In interviews I am often asked what sage advice I have to offer
young women. I admit the advice I give in *Redbook* is different
than what I tell people over drinks. There is a gorgeous, perfect,
talented young actress who I talked to at a party a few weeks ago.

"Look, you can't take your pussy with you," I said. "Use it.
Enjoy it. Fuck, fuck, fuck, until you run out of dicks. Travel to
other countries and have sex. Explore the full range of everything,
and feel zero shame. Don't let society's narrow scope about what
they think you should do with your vagina determine what you
do with your vagina."

As I talked, the look on her face was the slow-clap moment
in movies. There was the beginning of the realization that I was
really saying this, then the rapturous joy of a huge smile as she
knew I meant every word. Enough with teaching people to pretend that sex is only for procreation and only in the missionary
position and only upon taking the marital oath. If you're having
consensual sex with another adult, enjoy it.

So repeat after me: I resolve to embrace my sexuality and my freedom to do with my body parts as I see fit. And I will learn about my body so I can take care of it and get the pleasure I deserve. I will share that information with anyone and everyone, and not police the usage of any vagina but my own. So help me Judy Blume.

three

BLACK GIRL BLUES

Here is a secret to talking to teenagers: they open up best when you're not sitting across the table staring at them. For the past year I have mentored a class of teens around age fourteen. I find they share the most about what's going on in their lives when we're taking a walk. Recently, I took them out on a particularly gorgeous, sunny day. As this one boy Marcus got a bit ahead of me, he did this stop-and-start fast walk, like some sort of relay race. He would stop in the shade of a tree, then sprint through the direct sunlight to stand at the next tree.

"What are you doing?" I finally asked.

"I don't want to get any blacker," said Marcus.

"You're literally running from your blackness, Marcus," I said. "You know? It's a bit much. I'm not going to win any mentoring awards if you keep this up."

I checked in on him at lunch—the other secret to getting teenagers to talk is food. He explained that the relay race was all about girls. The girls he considered the hottest in school only liked the guys who look like Nordic princes. And that's not him.

"You're perfect," I said. "Look at my husband. He is *not* light skinned, and he has not exactly lacked for female attention. So many girls are gonna love you exactly the way you are. I'm not light."

"You get lighter sometimes," said Marcus. "I've noticed."

I scoffed. "If you want to stay inside on a soundstage with no windows for months on end," I said, "you too can look jaundiced. It's because I work inside."

"Yeah, well. It's possible then. So I'm just gonna stay out of the sun."

This kid I'm supposed to be mentoring had been sold the same ideal I had when I was young. I too went through periods where I stayed in the shade. I was obsessed with putting on sunblock, and in late summer I would insist on showing people my tan lines. "Look, this is my original color," I would say, proffering my shoulder to a white girl. "Look how light I am." I was really saying, "I have a chance to get back to that shade, so please excuse my current darkness."

I learned to apologize for my very skin at an early age. You know how you tell little girls, even at their most awkward stages, "You're so pretty" or "You're a princess"? My family played none of those games. The collective consensus was, "Oof, this one."

I was so thin that I looked like a black daddy longlegs spider with buckteeth. This is not overly earnest, false-humility celebrity speak, I swear. In case I didn't know that, the world presented a relentless barrage of images and comments making it clear to me and all my peers that most of us would never get within spitting distance of classic beauty. But I thought that at least my parents should think I was cute. When they would gather my sisters and me for a family photo, they would check each face for perfection. There was always a pause when they got to me. "Ah, Nickie, what a personality you have. You are *funny*."

In my family, light skin was the standard of beauty. This was true both in my dad's family, who were all dark-skinned, and my mom's family, who were very light. My mom was the most beautiful woman in the world to me—and I looked nothing like her.

With my dad, I simply wasn't his version of pretty. His ideal is very specific: short, light skin, long hair. I checked none of the above. Of my sisters, I looked the most like my father, and I think he wanted no part of that. As for my mother, only now do I understand that she made a decision to never praise my looks because she grew up being told her looks would be enough. They weren't. Young Theresa Glass was encouraged to build a foundation on the flower of her beauty and simply trust that it would remain in bloom long enough to win the security of a good man. Her thoughts on the books she read voraciously would only spoil the moment. "Shh," they said. "Just be pretty. When you get a man, talk all you want."

So my mom was the nineteen-year-old virgin who married the first guy who said he loved her. And by the time she had me, she'd realized that marriage was *not* the end-all. He didn't want to hear her thoughts, either. Looks had gotten her no-fucking-where.

I couldn't lighten my skin to be considered beautiful like her, but I thought that if I fixed my hair, I had more of a fighting chance at being told I was pretty. At age eight, I begged my Afro-loving mother to let me start straightening my hair with relaxer, which some called *crainy crack*. Twice a month on Saturdays, she begrudgingly took my sisters and me on the hour-long drive from Pleasanton to my cousin's salon in Stockton for the "taming" of my hair.

My mother had rocked an Angela Davis Afro in the seventies and did not approve of these trips to the salon. Yet she repeatedly caved to our demands that we straighten our hair, a political act of surrender on her part, or simply maternal fatigue. Either way, my desire to be seen and validated by my white peers when it came to my hair had the power to override her beliefs as a mother.

I cut out pictures from magazines to show my cousin what I wanted. If I was the Before, the straight-haired, light-skinned women in these pictures could be my happily ever After. One day when I was twelve, I brought a picture of Troy Beyer, the biracial actress who played Diahann Carroll's daughter on *Dynasty*. She was basically Halle Berry before there was Halle. I didn't even know that she was biracial, and I didn't know what work went into making her gorgeous straight hair fall so effortlessly around her light-skinned face. I just wanted to be that kind of black girl.

"This is what I want," I said.

My cousin looked confused, but shrugged and went to work. The deal with relaxer was that it was usually left on for about fifteen minutes to straighten hair. It's a harsh chemical, and the way I understood it was that no matter how much it itched or burned, the more I could stand it, the better. If fifteen minutes means it's working, then thirty minutes means I'm closer to glory. At thirty-five minutes I might turn white!

But the other thing with relaxers is that the hairdresser has to rely on you telling them when the chemicals start to burn. So if you're saying, "I'm good, I'm fine," they're all, "Shit, leave it on, then."

The burn is incredible, let me tell you. You start to squirm around in your seat. You're chair dancing—because your head feels like it's on fire. Eventually, you have to give in because you can't take it anymore. Not this time. In my world, if there were degrees of "good blackness," the best black girl was light skinned with straight hair and light eyes. I don't have light eyes and I don't have light skin, but at least I could get in the game if my hair was straight. No pain, no gain.

This day I was going to break my record. I would withstand any temporary pain to finally be pretty.

"You good?" my cousin said about fifteen minutes in.

I nodded. I wasn't. It didn't matter.

A few more minutes went by. I could feel the chemicals searing my scalp. I closed my eyes and gritted my teeth. I told myself this pain was only temporary. When people at school saw me, I would be so grateful and proud of my strength. Every single minute counted.

"You good?" she said again.

I nodded. Finally, I began to bawl, then weep, then scream. My cousin raced me to the bowl to rinse me out.

"Dammit, why didn't you tell me?" I ended up with lesions on my scalp where the relaxer gave me chemical burns. I was willing to disfigure myself in order to be deemed "presentable" and "pretty." To be truly seen. At twelve, I had not been once called pretty. Not by friends, not by my family, and certainly not by boys. My friends all had people checking them out and had their isn't-that-cute elementary school boyfriends. I was completely and utterly alone and invisible.

What was it like for my mother to sit there for hours upon hours, watching these black girls she wanted to raise to be proud black women become seduced by assimilation? And then to see her child screaming and squirming with open sores on her scalp because she wanted her hair to be as soft and silky as possible. My hair turned out like that of any other black girl with a tight curl pattern who'd gotten their hair relaxed and styled: medium length, slightly bumped under, except with lesions that would later scab.

Even after I was burned, with each trip to my cousin's salon, I carried with me the hope that this would be the week I was going to look like the pictures. That misguided goal remained unattainable, of course, but I could always tell the difference in the way people treated me when I came fresh from getting my hair done professionally.

"Oh my God, your hair looks so straight."

"Your hair looks so nice that way!"

Translation: You look prettier the closer you get to white. Keep trying.

If I didn't have my hair done professionally for school picture day, I didn't want to give out the prints when they arrived. There are years where my school photo is simply missing from the albums because they were given to me to take home. If I didn't look within a mile of what I thought of as "okay," I just didn't give the photos to my mother. I was not going to give her the opportunity to hand that eight-by-ten glossy to my grandmother so she could frame it next to photos of my cousins who had lighter skin and straight hair.

I would tear the photos into pieces, scattering images of myself in different garbage cans to eliminate even the chance of piecing my ugliness together. "No," I said to myself, "you're not gonna document this fuckery."

BECAUSE I'VE DONE SO MANY BLACK FILM PRODUCTIONS, HAIR HAS NOT always been the focal point of my performance. But on white productions, it is like another actor on set with me. A problem actor. First of all, they never want to hire anyone black in hair and makeup on a white film. Hair and makeup people hire their friends, and they naturally want to believe their friend who says they can do *anything*. "Oh yeah, I can do black hair," they say. Then you show up, and you see immediately that they don't have any of the proper tools, the proper products, and you look crazy. If you ever see a black person on-screen looking nuts? I guarantee they didn't have a black person in hair and makeup.

I figured this out right away on one of my very first modeling jobs, when I was about twenty-two. It was for a big teen magazine, and they said, "Come with your hair clean."

I actually washed my hair. Now, if you ask any black performer who has been around in Hollywood for more than a minute, "Come in clean" means you come in with your hair already *done*. That way, they can't screw you up. You come in pressed, blown out, or flat-ironed. Otherwise, you're just asking for trouble.

I didn't know that. My dumb novice ass showed up for my first big modeling shoot fresh from the shower. This white woman was literally trying to round brush my hair and then use just a curling iron to get the edges straight.

"You don't look like how you looked in your modeling photos," the hairdresser said. She hair-sprayed my hair and then put heat on it. My eyes got wide. She was going to break my hair right off of my head. I said nothing and did anything but look in the mirror. I didn't have enough confidence to say, "You don't know what you're doing. Step away from my hair."

She did her damage, then leaned back to take in her efforts.

"You look beautiful!" In fact, I looked nuts. Then I had to do the shoot, and proceeded to be documented for life looking like a crazy person. It was the bad school photos all over again—but I couldn't tear up all those magazines.

When I started acting, my hairstyle determined how people saw and cast me. I played a teenager for a hundred years, so I kept a flip. That flip said "All-American Nice Girl from the Right Side of the Tracks." As I was booking more jobs and meeting more and more hair and makeup people who didn't know what they were doing, I made a choice to grow out my relaxer. Now, the trope in African American hair-story narratives is that this is when I became "woke." It's not. I grew out my relaxer because my hair was so badly damaged, it was split to the scalp. If you're on a production that does not believe in diversity in the hair and makeup trailer, it's a lot easier to let them style a weave than let them touch your real hair. I was also then getting a lot of attention from the type of black men that every black woman is supposed to covet, and a good number of those particular men had been conditioned to love long hair. These two things went hand in hand—I was being chosen and validated.

I stopped using my own hair probably after *7th Heaven,* in the nineties. I have always had very good weaves, so when I cut my weave for *Daddy's Little Girls* and *Breakin' All the Rules,* people thought I was just "crazy experimental with my hair." No, I am just crazy experimental with hair that I can purchase. After a certain point, when my natural hair was long and healthy, I just put it up in a bun. I didn't politicize my choice. It was another option, that's it.

Then, because of work, wigs became so much easier to use and offered me more flexibility. My hair is braided down underneath, and every night I pop the wig off. Sometimes I leave the set rocking my own braids like Cleo from *Set It Off*. I still wash my hair and rebraid it. Then I can pop that wig back on and go to work. The less time I have to be in hair and makeup, the better.

Still, I struggle with the questions: Does this wig mean I'm not comfortable in my blackness? If I wear my hair natural, do I somehow become more enlightened? It is interesting to see the qualities ascribed to women who wear their hair in braids or in natural hairstyles, even among black people. We have so internalized the self-hatred and the demands of assimilation that we ourselves don't know how to feel about what naturally grows out of our head.

Being in an all-black production is no guarantee that your hair won't be a source of drama. Recently, I was in one and there was pushback about getting a natural no-heat hairstyle. I thought it would be an interesting option for my character.

"Well, we want her to be like, really pretty . . ."

"Honey, my face is where the action is," I said. "Natural hair *is* pretty, but my face is the moneymaker."

When I did *Top Five* with Chris Rock, the character needed to have her hair blond. I knew that if there were paparazzi photos from the set posted online, it would start an avalanche of "Gabrielle Wants to Be White" blog posts. So I got in front of it and posted a selfie on Instagram captioned, "New day, new job . . . new do." I thought the message was clear: This is for a role. Don't come at me with your @'s. I pressed Share and that was that.

Well, that didn't work. "Why did you do this?" was written over and over again. I felt judged. A person I never met wrote, "What happened to my baby?" I felt completely outside myself in a way that was not comfortable at all. There is an idea that if you choose to have blond hair as a black woman, you are morally deficient. I didn't just have to read it on social media, I could *feel* it in interactions I had away from the set.

It would be naïve of me to say that hair is just an accessory. I recognize that black hair has been politicized, and not by us. We have since reclaimed that politicization. We have ascribed certain characteristics to people who rock a natural look versus weaves and wigs. If you choose to have natural hair, or even to promote the *idea* of natural hair, you are somehow a better black person than someone with a weave or someone who straightens their hair. You have transcended pettiness and escaped the bonds of self-esteem issues. But I have traveled around the world and I know this to be true: there are assholes who wear natural hair, and assholes who wear weaves. Your hair is not going to determine or even influence what kind of person you are.

GROWING UP, I WAS ALSO OBSESSED WITH MY NOSE—AND NOSE JOBS. I still kind of am. I first became aware of rhinoplasty when people started making fun of Michael Jackson getting his first big one. I was on the playground and a kid asked, "How does Michael Jackson pick his nose?"

He didn't wait for me to answer. "From a catalog!" he yelled.

I paused. "Wait, that's a thing? I don't have to live with this nose if I don't want it?" It wasn't just Michael. Growing up, it felt like every black star, people who you thought were beyond perfect the way they were, changed their nose. The successful people, who used to have noses like you, suddenly didn't. It only made me more self-conscious. I would stare into the mirror, thinking about how as soon as these people got the chance to fix their mess of a nose, they did.

Like them, I wanted a finer, more European nose. I used to call my nose the Berenstain Bear nose, because I thought it looked exactly like the noses on that family of cartoon bears. As a kid I tried the old clothespin trick. I would walk around my house with my nose pinched in a clothespin, hoping it would miraculously reshape my nose. I had a method, attaching it just so and mouth-breathing while I did my homework. It didn't work.

There was a whole period of time in high school where I would do this weird thing with my face to create the illusion that my nose was thinner. I'd curl my upper lip under itself and do a creepy smile to pull down my nasal folds. I thought I was a nasal illusionist, but I ended up looking like Jim Carrey's Fire Marshall Bill on *In Living Color*.

The reality is that growing up in Pleasanton and coming up in Hollywood, nobody ever said one word about my nose. I imagined people talking about my nose, but it was really just noise that originated in my own mind. People have since accused me of having a nose job, however, which made me even more convinced that people thought that I had a nose I should want to fix.

So here is the truth: I have never had a nose job. I am, in fact, the Fugitive of nose jobs. Like Dr. Richard Kimble, blamed for killing his wife, I too stand accused of a crime I didn't commit. It's a constant on social media. Catch me in the right light, or after a contouring makeup session some might deem aggressive, and the comments section lights up. "Nose job." "Fillers." "She fucked up her face." The next day I'll post another shot with my nose fully present and accounted for and people will literally say, "She let the fillers wear off." It takes everything I have not to write these people and say, "Do you have any idea how fillers work?"

Okay, I will admit I have researched. I have even fantasized about putting myself in the able hands of Dr. Raj Kanodia, Beverly Hills sculptor to the stars. A white friend went to Dr. Raj, and afterward I took her chin in my hand, literally holding her face to the light like it was a beautiful work of art. We actresses talk and share secrets, so I know people who feel they owe their careers to his work. But that won't be me. I can't even get the slightest tweak, because I will be slammed. I am stuck getting all the flack for a nose job without any of the benefits.

Maybe one day, when I'm a real grown-up, I will wear my hair natural and I won't contour my nose. Hell, I'll just be me. And hopefully people will accept me the way I am.

THE BALLAD OF NICKIE AND LITTLE SCREW

Here I am, three decades later, and it is as if I am seeing him for the first time. He just suddenly appeared, striding across the massive fields at Sports Park. It was the summer before ninth grade, and those of us who played sports year-round hung out at the park constantly.

He wore a yellow polo shirt that matched a stripe in the plaid of his Bermuda shorts. And of course he had his baseball hat on, with sandy blond-brown hair sticking out from underneath. Now, that wouldn't be a color anyone would want. You would sit in the salon chair, take in its dullness, and say, "Get rid of this." His teeth weren't at all straight, with gaps dotting his crooked smile. Everyone else in Pleasanton got braces in elementary school—I was considered late to the game in fifth grade—so his gappy grin made him special. He walked bow-legged, a Marky Mark swagger to every watched step.

Lucy laid claim to him first. She was "the Mexican" in our group of friends. As he walked, she told us everything she knew about Billy Morrison. Everyone called him Little Screw because his older brother's nickname was Screw. Screw looked like someone had put a palm on his face and turned it counterclockwise, ever so slightly. The rumor was he'd gotten hold of a bad batch of drugs when he was a kid, and as a teenager his face just grew that way, but that was probably just a stupid rumor. Screw and Little Screw's parents had a tire store franchise and had just moved from Fremont. They were flush enough to move into the Meadows development, but saying "Fremont" in Pleasanton was an insult, so they had baggage. You heard the imaginary organ play a sudden "dunh dunnnnh" behind that phrase. There were a lot of Mexicans in Fremont, people said, and maybe even Filipinos. And poor white people. Little Screw had gone to a private Christian school before his family moved up and moved out. And over and over this is what I heard about him:

"You know . . . he had a black girlfriend . . ."

It was always whispered with an air of "*this* is how wild this guy is." I had stopped being black to these folks years ago, so it was said sotto voce for the shock of it, certainly not for my benefit. But it meant I had a chance with Billy. Little Screw might be able to like me.

As brown people, Lucy and I had heretofore been ineligible for the dating dramas of middle school. We were always "the friend." The town was made up of Mormons and Catholics, and to this day remains deeply conservative. Lucy, at least briefly, had luck with Jeremy Morley of the Mormon Morleys, which seemed like this unbelievable coup. But mostly we were always "the friend." At the school dances, I would always have to ask somebody to dance, blurting out "JUSTASFRIENDS" before they thought I had some twisted idea. And certainly no one ever asked me. When we danced as a group and a slow dance came on, the unlucky one would end up with me. During Poison's "Every Rose Has Its Thorn" or whatever slow dance, I'd look wistfully over the guy's shoulder, suspecting he was looking at everyone else and rolling his eyes. Dancing with me was an act of charity, a Make-A-Wish mercy dance.

I didn't have a model for what I was feeling until I saw the black eunuchs from Mel Brooks's *History of the World, Part 1*. In the movie there is an extended boner joke with Gregory Hines hiding among the sexless, castrated guards allowed to be in the maidens' chambers. He fails the eunuch test while the real ones pass with flaccid colors. In my heart, I was Gregory Hines with a hard-on, but to everyone else I was the eunuch. You can be the trusted confidante or witty sidekick, there and in the mix. But remember, you don't appeal to *anybody*. Not to the whites, but also not to the very few people of color, either. The two African American boys in my grade wanted nothing to do with me. And the other two black girls steered clear of me and each other, to avoid amplifying our blackness. Because anyone brown would say, "Well, if I hang with you, then we'll become superbrown." So I was a eunuch. A social eunuch.

For all of freshman year, Billy was an electric current moving through my group of friends. We would trade Billy sightings. Someone would say they spotted him at lunch or in the hall. "What did he have on?" we would ask in response. "Was he wearing his hat?" He wasn't in any AP or honors classes, so

I would only see him at sporting events. He played baseball—
because of course he didn't play soccer like every other Ken doll
in Pleasanton—so we made sure to go to every game. When he
played basketball, we admired the muscles of his arms and his tic
of pulling his shirt away from his chest after he scored. He never
looked around, never held up his arms in victory if he sank a basket. He just continued on as if he'd wandered into a pickup game
that he might leave at any time.

When I would run into Billy, it was usually at the Sports Park
between games. I would have my bag of softball equipment and
he would be lugging his baseball equipment.

"Did you win?" he'd ask.

"Yeah," I'd say. "You?"

"Yeah."

"Cool," I'd say.

"Yeah, cool."

Walking away, I would feel high just from that brief encounter.

Billy hung out with all the athletes, but he was close friends
with Mike, whose dad was the basketball coach. Mike's whole family was made up of great athletes—the sports dynasty of Pleasanton.
To run afoul of any of them was social death. Billy's friendship with
Mike ended abruptly one night at basketball practice, when Billy
got into it with Mike's dad and told him, "Suck my balls."

And that was that.

But Billy seemed exempt from the social hierarchy. The incident just added to the legend of Little Screw. Billy was two years
older than us and already driving. His car was the only freshman's
car in the parking lot. He had a GMC truck. It was black with
gold trim, with BILLY emblazoned on the back in tan paint. I
wanted it to read BILLY AND NICKIE so badly. He was such a badass

in that ride. His parents were always away, either taking an RV trip or busy with their store in Fremont, so he and his brother had more freedom than most kids. They threw huge parties, and my friends and I always went. Our parents all worked long hours, so they never really had a line on where we were or what we were doing. I routinely used the "I'm staying at so-and-so's house" line when I was really out partying. There was only one parent who cared where we really were: Alisa's mom, Trudy. You never name-dropped Alisa in any of these schemes because Trudy would go looking for her and ruin everything.

It was Lucy who lost her virginity to Billy first. I was so jealous, but I masked it. "Tell me everything," I said, as if I was happy for her. I wanted to be the one so much that I didn't even hear her describing what had gone down. I was too busy thinking, He had a black girlfriend, Lucy is Mexican . . . I have a shot. The door is clearly open.

Little Screw and Lucy didn't go out or even have sex again. He just moved on to Alice, another Mexican girl. Billy claimed her. He called Alice "my girlfriend." I had to figure out what secret pull she had. She lived near me in Val Vista, considered next-to-last in the Pleasanton development caste system. Alice was on the traveling soccer team, and she was big on wearing her warm-up pants to school, along with slides or Birkenstocks with socks. She always had a scrunchie to match her socks, usually neon pink. She would wear part of her hair up, the rest falling in curls.

A rumor went around that she was a freak in bed. "You know, she rides guys," someone told me, "and then leans back and plays with their balls." If you've never had sex, that sounds like some acrobatic Cirque du Soleil–level shit.

Everyone was having sex by this point except me. Freshman

year ended and I went to Omaha, where I at least had a chance with boys. The real test that summer was when I went to a co-ed basketball camp. The black guys there had a thing for me, though I was too focused on basketball to do anything. "You're like a white girl without the hassle," one guy told me. He meant it as a compliment, and on some level, I probably took it as one. Nonetheless, they saw me. I was a viable option.

Being the eunuch in Pleasanton, I was still in the middle of the long, long process of being Friend to Billy. I wish I could say it was strategic. The rare times he would go to some kid's bonfire, I would slide on over to him as casually as I could. Southern rock was massive then, so there was always a lot of Lynyrd Skynyrd and Allman Brothers to be heard. At every party, Steve Miller's "The Joker" was played at least twice. You'd find young Nickie, standing next to a fire, talking to a white boy in a Skynyrd T-shirt emblazoned with the Confederate flag. These young bucks, scions of upper-middle-class families, wishing they were back in Dixie. Away, away. And then there was Billy, looking as out of place as me. He was more into driving around playing Sir Mix-a-Lot. I'd hang on to every word he said. He would complain about Alice, and I would chime in, coaching from the sidelines as only a friend could do.

"Just tell her how you feel," I'd say, thinking, Just tell *me* how you feel.

They broke up, and my determination to be noticed by Billy only grew. At one of the parties at his house around November of sophomore year, Billy gave me a sign. He looked at me in such a way that I just knew.

"We should hang," he said.

I felt *invincible*.

HERE'S HOW IT WENT: ON SATURDAY, NOVEMBER 12, 1988, BILLY AND I made a plan for him to pick me up at my house after I went to a Warriors game to celebrate my little sister's birthday. I still remember the score: the Warriors beat the Portland Trail Blazers, 107–100. I borrowed my friend Danielle's light blue denim skirt, and as my parents slept upstairs and I waited for Billy to pull up in his GMC, I checked myself in the mirror roughly fifty-six times. When he finally showed, I walked out the front door and left it unlocked.

We drove to his house and he led me straight to his parents' bedroom. Remember how it felt as a kid when you went into your friends' parents' bedrooms? They just felt grand. Holy shit, I remember thinking, I'm so not supposed to be in here. We're in here and we're going to fuck.

I lay down and the panic set in. He'd already had sex with Alice, the ball-fondling sex acrobat, so in my mind I saw Alice smirking at me, always so sure of herself in those fucking soccer warm-ups, that neon scrunchie barely able to hold the glory of her hair.

In comparison, I was *so* black, I was *so* not cool, and I was *so* inexperienced.

Billy started to kiss me. My mind was racing. What if my vagina looked like a fucking dragon? I had another friend who was really into trimming and shaving her pubic hair. This same girl would even sometimes shave her vagina using a mirror. She would then brag-slash-explain to all of us using very adult words: "Well, if you don't know yourself . . ."

And I don't know myself! At all! And now Billy's going to see me and even I don't know what he's going to see. Then it occurs to me: Oh my God, he is going to have sex with black pussy.

I knew, even though I was so inexperienced, that in inter-racial porn there is a lot of "Give me that black pussy" talk. And I had always thought it sounded so dirty. Now I realize that in fact *I* have black pussy. Did he have sex with that black girlfriend back in Fremont? I hadn't thought about my vagina in relation to other vaginas he'd seen. And I hadn't done anything to mine in preparation. So now, I thought, he is going to see this black *Teen Wolf* pussy. It's going to look different, smell different, be differ-ent. He is going to be repulsed. And if this doesn't go well it will be because he is rejecting my black pussy.

We got under the covers and I pulled up my skirt to fumble out of my underwear, doing as inelegant a job as possible. We left our shirts on.

"I'm a virgin," I said.

He smiled. I later found out that this was his thing. He was the Deflowerer. It's not why he had sex with me, but he was known for being a lot of people's first time.

He didn't even look at my vagina. He started to put his dick in and then he looked at me, trying to gauge: "Am I killing you?" I was silent. It was uncomfortable, but it wasn't, like, crazy painful.

And then it was. I start making this bug-eyed look that I knew could not be sexy. I flashed through every book I'd ever read that included a sex scene and landed upon the words, "Look him in the eye." So I tried that. Weird. It's too much to maintain eye contact with a guy when you're sixteen years old and mortified.

He was very gentle and so determined, like he was solving a math problem. But he still hadn't laid eyes on my vagina. I was still wearing Danielle's skirt and I started to panic, because I real-ized that when I gave it back to her it was going to smell like sex.

She would know. Because at first you don't want anyone to know, but then you want the whole fucking world to know.

I waited for all the things I had read about to happen, while trying to mask the pain, horror, and humiliation.

It started to not hurt anymore. Maybe even feel good. And then, with a strange sound, it was over. Where was the magic? Where was the cuddling? The fireworks and the I-love-yous? *Something. Anything?*

He got up to flush the condom, and I saw his bare butt for the first time, watching that bow-legged walk across the room. He was a dude strutting around in a white Hanes tee and tube socks. I let out a contented sigh. He was just so sure of himself that it was infectious. I had just lost my virginity.

When he came back to the bed, we locked eyes, and all my newfound self-assuredness disappeared. I felt ridiculous. I felt exposed. He hadn't seen my black pussy, but did it feel different to him? Did he like it? Did he hate it? Is that why he came so fast?

He leaned on my side of the mattress.

"We're gonna have to wash these sheets."

"Huh?"

"You bled all over the sheets."

There was no sweetness. It was simply a statement of fact, like a detective at a crime scene. I got up, and I saw what he saw. It *was* a crime scene, there on those light gray sheets. The books never described it that way. The books never said there would be this much blood.

Inside, I wanted to die. In fact, I decided I *was* dying. A little of humiliation, and a little physically. I crossed some weird boundary, turned around, and found that the door had vanished behind me. I was stuck in a weird space of middle earth.

I had unleashed my black pussy on the world, and look what happened. Here's this perfect man, and I've ruined the sheets of his parents' bed. I wanted to crawl into a ball and call my best girlfriend and write it in my diary—all at once. And now I had to wait for a whole laundry cycle?

Yes, I did. We sat there in his living room, barely talking. And as we waited for the dryer to ding, I felt myself slip-sliding right back into the friend zone. I was already mourning all the flirtation, the touching, the little signals of interest.

He drove me across town, back to my house. When we finally pulled up, he jerked his head toward the car door like I didn't understand how it worked. I sat. I waited.

"Y'all right?" he said.

The car was still running.

"Yeah, yeah."

He nodded. I wanted him to kiss me the way Molly Ringwald got kissed. In my head I was screaming, "I want you to be Jake Ryan! Kiss me like that!"

He didn't.

I let myself out of the car and closed the door softly.

As I walked to my house, I pretended not to watch him drive away.

BILLY GOT BACK WITH ALICE SHORTLY AFTER WE HAD SEX.

When Billy showed interest in me, I felt myself vibrating with sexual energy. I wasn't Gregory Hines in the eunuchs' chamber anymore. What's more, people could see it. Everyone around me knew that I was a viable option. My confidence swelled—and promptly deflated when he moved on to someone else. For a few weeks, I remembered looking around, scanning the halls and classrooms for signs of other interested suitors. "Anybody else? Anybody? No?"

No. I was back to eunuch status. But now I'd had a taste. I knew what was on the other side.

I wanted a do-over. Later that school year, I got it. It was in February. Billy and I had sex on the ground outside an industrial park. I drank a Mickey's big mouth. This time, I thought, it was for real.

That one didn't do the trick either. We did have a pseudo-romance of sorts and hooked up many more times. Throughout my teens, I never dated a guy without cheating at least once with Billy. Even now, I google him. I'll be with someone from Pleasanton and he'll come up in conversation. The other person might say, "I wonder what he's . . ." and immediately it's "Hold, please," as I start typing. Or if I'm with a mutual friend from home and they have a laptop open, I direct them: "Go to his Facebook." I don't want to actually connect. I just want to be a voyeur. I want to see how his kids turned out. I want to see if they're ballsy like him.

But it doesn't matter. As many times as we hooked up, there would never be BILLY AND NICKIE painted on the back of that GMC. I was never his Chosen One.

five

OPEN HOUSE

When I was little, my mom would take me with her to open houses. We'd drive out to Oakland and San Francisco—cities she loved far more than our town of Pleasanton—and we'd wander from house to house. These were homes that we no way in hell could afford, but we toured them just to see how other people lived. People who were not us.

I was eight when we toured a huge San Francisco Victorian, all light wood and curving staircases with a bay window that actually looked out on the bay. I ran to the window to take in all the blue of the water.

"Your world is only as small as you make it, Nickie," she said.

That was the same year she took me to see Nikki Giovanni recite poetry at the Oakland Children's Museum. We sat high up in coliseum seating, listening as Nikki talked about dragonflies and strawberry patches. My mother kept nudging me into listening. "Isn't this wonderful?" she asked again and again.

Mom was always taking my sisters and me to events like this.

She loved the ballet and would take us to see *The Nutcracker* at Christmas. She would buy tickets for the Alvin Ailey dance company whenever they were in the Bay Area. On every one of these excursions, she would inevitably start talking to a stranger. My sisters and I called them Random Acts of Conversation, rolling our eyes. "Where are you from?" she would ask the rando she had found, whose existence we would then be dragged into acknowledging. "Oh, wow," she would say.

Mom was so bored and lonely in the small world of Pleasanton. When my parents moved there, my father simply stopped including her when he went out. And Cully Union, an extremely social person who could also talk to anybody—except his wife Theresa—went out a lot.

My parents both had telecommunications jobs, he at AT&T and she at Pacific Bell. Back in Nebraska, they also worked a night shift cleaning a day-care center so I could receive free care when I was little. My father was obsessed with upward mobility and after he got his BA degree from the University of Nebraska at Omaha, he later got an advanced degree going to night school. My mother was pursuing her master's at Holy Name, a Catholic college in Oakland. My dad thought that her studies would help her move up the ranks at Pacific Bell. But learning for my mother was about her love of literature. Her time at Holy Name was meaningful for her. To this day, she talks about two classmates, a Chinese American and Mexican American who took her out to try Thai food for the first time. When my father realized her higher education was in the humanities and would not result in more money for the household, he stopped funding it. He hadn't cared to know what she was studying, because Dad is always oblivious to things he isn't interested in. She never completed her master's.

Meanwhile, he was funding his second life. Around my junior year of high school, I discovered a green ATM card in a drawer. I brought it to my older sister, Kelly.

"There's a lot of money in that one," she said.

It was the card Dad used to finance his life with another woman. Kelly was aware of the reality long before I was. She had gotten a sales job with AT&T, working out of the Oakland office while my dad was in San Jose. Kelly's job took her up and down the bay, and whenever she was close to San Jose my dad would say, "Let's link up and have lunch."

But it came with the caveat, "Just let me know before you come to the office."

One day she surprised him. Dad was in a meeting in the conference room, and someone gave Kelly a folder to leave on his desk. He had a glass desktop, under which he kept several family photos. Where there was usually one photo of my mom and dad, this time there were instead several photos of my dad with another woman.

"She looked so much like Mom," Kelly told me. "But she's not Mom."

Kelly said that once she discovered the reason for the green ATM card, she would ask Dad to lend it to her—basically daring him to say no. After a while, I told him he also needed to give me the card.

"Take out twenty dollars," he'd say, expressionless.

I'd take out two hundred.

Then Kelly found the secret photo album. She always did know where to snoop, although my father didn't put much effort into hiding it. It was right under the bed, almost in plain sight. The other woman had put together an old-school family photo album of all their trips together, thick and loaded with time-stamped pictures in plastic sheaths. My sister and I examined the dates, realizing he had been lying to us for years about his whereabouts.

Kelly pointed at a photo of my father with this woman who was not our mother in front of a waterfall, wearing leis.

"February 14," I said.

"That was the conference . . ." Kelly said.

"In Parsippany!" we said together.

"You were in Kona, asshole," I said, turning to the next page.

Kelly had been right. My mother and this other woman were the *same* woman: short, light-skinned, with freckles. They each had short blond hair.

He had a type.

I started calling the green ATM cash "Hawaii money." My dad never acknowledged in any way that Kelly and I knew about the other woman or what this card was for. Life simply continued, with him feeling he still retained his full authority over us. During my senior year, my soccer team was in a tournament against our archrival Fremont. Dad loved those soccer games, sitting in the all-white audience with a megaphone, watching his daughter outrun everyone. That day, I shanked a penalty kick in Sudden Death. Game over. I looked to my dad. He put the megaphone down and wrapped his hands around his neck. His eyes bugged out and closed, his tongue lolled.

Then he stopped, looked me right in the eye and mouthed the word "Choke."

The parents to the left and right of him saw the act and laughed. He laughed with them, his chosen people.

"Fuck you!" I yelled, stomping off the field. Up until that

point, I had never sworn at my dad in my entire life. Only once did I allow myself to look back at him: his bemused expression showed the slightest bit of pride. Like, "Look at you, kiddo."

FOR THE LAST FIVE YEARS OF THEIR MARRIAGE, MY PARENTS DID NOT speak to each other. Not to say "Excuse me" in the kitchen during the morning rush, or even a reflexive "Bless you" after a sneeze. This was during my senior year of high school and into my college years. My mother slept on the couch in the living room, like a boarder. My sisters and I all led separate lives.

One morning, it looked like my mother caught a glimmer of hope. She discovered two tickets Dad had bought for the ballet. It was the kind of thing my father would never want to do, much less with his wife.

So Mom took off early from work that day, had her hair done, and bought a new outfit. It goes to show how much my mother worked, because I remember distinctly how bizarre it was to see her at home while the sun was out, in the middle of the week.

Dad came home shortly after her. She sat on the couch, pretending to read a magazine and waiting patiently as he moved about the house. She didn't let on that she knew about his ballet surprise, even though she was completely done up. I can imagine her, in her mind, practicing her surprised face.

He strode over to the side table, where the tickets were. He bent over, picked them up, and strutted out the door. My mother's face took on a faraway look. She pretended none of this humiliation had happened.

The next morning, I didn't ask him where he'd been. Inside, I felt humiliated on my mother's behalf, but on the outside, I showed the passive politeness of a fellow boarder in this house.

I CALLED RECENTLY AND I ASKED HER ABOUT THOSE TICKETS.

"You know, what I want you to know more than anything," she said, "is that everything you remember is what you remember."

After a long pause, she sighed. "The tickets," she said. "I just thought . . . perhaps."

The word hung in the miles between us. I myself say "maybe" when I don't want something to happen. I reserve "perhaps" for when I get asked about things I hope for.

"Those weren't the first tickets to something that I would have liked to go to, nor the last," she said. "I was ready, in case he, on this day, thought to take me. But I was also prepared for him not to take me."

"When did you know he was cheating?"

"I didn't," she said.

"Mom," I said.

"We never had the conversation once in our entire marriage," she said. "I wasn't looking for it. I loved my *house*. I loved the swimming pool. I loved my life with you girls. I loved having money in the bank. I loved having the creature comforts that we worked so hard for. My feeling about him was 'I'm happy, and as long as you don't disrupt that, I don't care what you do.'"

Everything you remember is what you remember.

My mother told me that on Sunday nights Dad was always out late. So she began to go out herself, something I don't remember at all. I only recall Mom waiting at home for Dad. She would leave after Tracy and I were in bed. I was probably sneaking out the same nights.

"There were a lot of live jazz places that your dad didn't go to," she said. "One of my good friends from work, her husband was in a band, and I would meet up with her."

Her girlfriends considered her bait to draw men in. "A blond black woman, I don't care if you're rail thin or four hundred pounds, you're gonna get a lot of attention," my mother told me. "And I always got a lot of attention." She never acted on it, she said, but relished the idea that she was pulling them in for the team.

"Most of the time I wouldn't run into any of your dad's friends," she said. "And most of the time it wouldn't get back to him. But sometimes it did, and that was okay, too."

He knew more than she realized. Our longtime neighbors who lived across the street, a Filipino family, socialized with Dad and the other woman. Turns out the wife was always spying on my mom. "I saw Theresa leave last night," she would narc to my dad. "Where did she go?" My dad was always Mr. Neighborly, acting like the mayor of our street, and my mom was more interested in reading a book inside than chatting in the driveway. Other couples also became complicit as they began to double-date with my father and my mother's stand-in. I guess she just seemed like a better fit for their friend Cully. They wanted Mom out.

I watched Dad try to make the ride bumpier for Mom. I could tell he hoped he could buck her off, but she was not going.

"He always was a great provider," she told me. "He made sure we had a really nice home and that my children were well taken care of."

It was, she said, a lesson from an epic fight she had had with her own mother. As a teenager, Mom worked in a hospital as a cleaner. My grandmother happened to be there one day and Mom complained about how much she hated the job.

"Shut up," my grandmother told her. "Shut your mouth and get your check. When you find a different job, then you leave. But otherwise, keep your head down, shut your mouth, and get that check."

Mom paused. "We had a good life."

THE NIGHT MY DAD FINALLY GOT HIS WISH, HE WAS HOME FROM WORK before Mom. I was visiting from UCLA. Tracy was at the house and Dad said something cruel to us girls, who knows what, and we both started crying. He left and my mother came home to the chaos of daughters in tears. Tracy screamed that Dad was mean. Mom calmed us down and eventually, we went to bed.

My mother stood alone in the kitchen. My father had left her a note saying that he wouldn't be home until late. He had spelled her name wrong: "Teresa." They'd been married nearly thirty years.

He didn't know that my mother had called the bank that day. She'd tried to pay their property taxes and the check bounced. Their bank account was overdrawn. She remembered the night before, when my father announced that he wasn't paying for braces for my little sister. "She doesn't really need them," he'd said.

He had just been on another business trip.

Something in my mother finally broke.

She turned the note over and took a pen.

"I am leaving you," she wrote.

She went to her brother's house. My uncle was living in Fremont with a roommate, and then my mom became his roommate. Tracy stayed with my dad and finished high school, but there was a point when she was living with my mom in Fremont and going to high school in Pleasanton.

My mom insists she only found out about the affair when she met someone who knew Dad from AT&T.

"You have a beautiful home," she said.

"You've been to my house?"

"Yes," she said. "Cully was the chair of the tennis tournament last year." The lady described the house, and also the other woman. She had been standing next to Dad, acting as if our house was her house.

I wasn't ever formally introduced to the other woman. She just appeared, now with a name. Toni.

My parents divorced my senior year of college. The divorce was final in early June. He married the other woman on June 9. I graduated from UCLA on June 16. Dad skipped my college graduation, because Toni insisted on an immediate Hawaii honeymoon. I don't blame her. My graduation was going to be a family moment shortly after the family had been dismantled.

But of course I had to go to Dad's wedding. By then, they had moved to Phoenix, Arizona. It was never clear when they bought their new house. But it didn't matter. They had, and this wedding was on. My dad had invited his mother—whom we all called Mama Helen—to fly in from Omaha, but he had neglected to tell her the reason why. He couldn't tell her he was getting remarried, because, well, he hadn't told Mama Helen he'd gotten divorced.

It was Mama Helen's first flight, and she brought hard-boiled eggs and chicken packed in little baggies. She smelled up the plane, and since she was hard of hearing, she also spent the whole flight yelling.

Phoenix in June was *hell* degrees. When we arrived at Dad and Toni's house, we came upon a crew of aunts and girl cousins making homemade wedding souvenirs. Before she had time to figure out what was going on, someone rushed over and took Mama Helen out dress shopping "for an occasion."

My sisters and I joined our aunts at the table. Half of them had only just found out about the wedding themselves. Somebody looked up from the tchotchkes we were making and asked, "Did anybody tell Mama Helen?"

My father was called in.

"Did you tell Mama Helen you're getting married?" an aunt asked.

"I'm gonna tell her," he said.

"Does she know you're divorced?" said someone else.

"I'm gonna tell her. I'm gonna tell her."

The place went up in guffaws. "Oh, shit!" said a cousin, as the rest did impressions of my dad's frightened face.

When he finally got the nerve to tell his mother, shortly before the ceremony, Mama Helen's solidarity with my mom was like Sister Souljah. It was fascinating because, mind you, this woman was never a fan of my mother's. She called her "piss-colored" for the bulk of the marriage. But this whole deal didn't sit right with her. Not at all.

She decided to speak her mind at the church. My soon-to-be stepmother had a family member who was the pastor. He went on and on about this blessed union. That's when Mama Helen piped up from the front pew in her deaf-lady voice.

"She's a whore," she said to no one in particular, meaning the entire church. "Home-wrecker."

NOW, OUR BOYS CALL TONI NANA, AND SHE IS A LOVELY GRANDMOTHER. She and my dad still take their trips to Hawaii. People move on.

After the divorce, Mom left Pleasanton to move back to

Omaha. She was ready to start over. Instead of an easy retirement, she chose to help a relative who had a problem with drugs. This relative repeatedly got pregnant, and one by one, these babies came to live with my mother shortly after their births. This retirement-age woman adopted these children, now aged nine, eight, and six. Two beautiful girls and the youngest, a boy. My mother refused to let them be separated from each other.

She busts her ass to keep up with these kids. She has discovered emojis, this seventy-year-old woman, and she'll send me a wineglass with an exclamation point. She is also queen of the wink-and-tongue-out face.

I see you, Mom. I see what you are doing for these kids, and how you keep them together. I give you respect, because nobody is going to give you praise for doing what black women have done forever, raising kids who are not their own.

Nowadays, I catch myself starting conversations the way she used to. I think back to when we Union girls confronted her about this need to connect with strangers. It was just that she is a decent human being with a genuine curiosity about other human beings. She already knew what made my father tick, and the people of Pleasanton for that matter. They held no surprise.

"There are so many more people than you realize," she told us girls, "people who look up to the same sun and the moon and the stars. It's your birthright to explore this world."

It's only as small as you make it.

six

WHO HATES YOU MOST?

The cast of *Being Mary Jane* was holed up in a conference room while the crew investigated a gas leak on our Atlanta soundstage. Eventually we each reached the end of memes and Snapchat filters on our phones, so to kill time we started trading stories.

"Okay, who in your life has hated you the most?" someone asked.

People talked about a costar they'd gotten fired, an ex they brazenly cheated on. Amateur hour. Basic stuff. I knew I had the winner: a girl from high school named Queeshaun.

Queeshaun was best friends with Angela Washington, who was dating Jason Kidd when I met him. This was my junior year of high school, while I was technically dating Tyrone Reed, a stoner rebel from a nearby town. Tyrone had gotten his arm broken by the police, so obviously his cast had FUCK THE POLICE written on it in huge block letters. He would lean the cast out of his convertible VW bug when he drove around town. So rebellious.

Jason Kidd was the best high school player in the country, six foot four as a junior, and already famous among sports fans and college recruiters alike. His high school, St. Joseph's, could seat eight hundred in their gym. With Jason on the team, they were forced to move their games to a venue that seated five thousand, and people still got turned away.

I was in a Saturday afternoon girls' basketball tournament, and I stayed to watch the guys play. I was performing a bit, throwing out tips to the players, even Jason. It worked. Jason sat at the end of the bench, a towel around his neck. He knew everyone in that place was watching him, but he suddenly lifted his eyes to look right at me. It wasn't eye sex, just "I see you."

At half time, I went to the bathroom and there was Angela. I knew her from playing ball, because she was a star player for Livermore High. Our teams often competed against each other. Standing at the sinks, we talked about the game.

"That Jason is amazing," I said.

"Yeah," she said, "he is."

She walked out and went right over to Jason and I realized, Oh, she is totally his girlfriend. There went that idea.

At the end of the game, she left with Jason's parents, and he went over to the team bus. He lingered behind so I could catch up, and when I did, he asked for my number. We then proceeded to talk all hours for the rest of the weekend, and made a pact that on Monday I would break up with Tyrone and he would break up with Angela. We did so, with a generous round of "It's not you, it's me" for everyone.

I got right into being Jason's girlfriend and I wanted *everyone* to know it. I would go to my beloved Kim's Nails in Oakland, getting the letters of his name spelled out with a heart on my nails. J-A-S-O-N-K-I-D-D-♥. Don't judge me. I felt like a boss bitch.

The Friday before Christmas break, my school had a pep rally during lunchtime. My girlfriend Paige was a cheerleader, so I was right there, sitting with friends on a lunch table right at the front watching them perform. Fantasy Direct, a group of high-school-age DJs, was running the music. They were black and Latino, and from neighboring towns. But one, Hector, lived across the street from me.

Suddenly, this big black girl walked in with a determined stomp in her step. She had dookie braids, a pink ribbon woven into each one. She immediately stuck out to me, of course, because you know there were no other black girls around. Way across the room, I saw her go up to Hector, who then pointed in my direction. I looked behind me, thinking, Who could she possibly be looking for?

Then she started stalking through the crowd, about four or five people deep, around my lunch table. As she got closer, she lunged through a wall of people to get to me. But I still didn't understand that I was the target.

This girl is just really angry, I thought. Somebody is going to get their ass kicked. Meanwhile, the white people were practically clearing a path for her, just assuming that the black girl was there for the other black girl.

"I'm gonna whoop yo' ass, bitch!" she yelled at the top of her lungs, pointing right at me. "I'm gonna whoop yo' ass!"

I swear, I looked around like, "This couldn't possibly be about me." Eventually, the school security dragged her off school grounds by the shoulders. "I'm gonna get you, Nickie Union!" she yelled as they pulled her out the door. "I'm gonna come back after school and kick your ass!"

I was shaking as if I'd had a near-death experience. I had no idea who in the world this bitch was, and now all these white girls were staring at me.

"Oh my God," went the chorus. "Oh my God, are you okay? That was, like, so terrifying."

So I marched over to Hector and asked him why he sent her over to me.

"Oh, Queeshaun?" he said. "You don't know her?" He acted with total innocence. "She asked where you were. We thought you invited her."

"Hector, you know who comes to my house," I said. "And not a one looks like this bitch. Thanks a lot."

I immediately went to a pay phone and called my big sister Kelly. "COME GET ME NOW," I demanded, and I sat in the parking lot for the half hour it took for her to drive from San Jose State, where she was going to school. When I saw her, I stood up, waving like some castaway flagging down a helicopter.

"Where the hell is she?" she said, flying out of the car and darting her eyes around sniper style.

"She left," I said. "But she'll be back."

"We're gonna wait for her."

"Uh, no!" I started screaming. "Take me home!" I was not giving this girl a chance to come back and kill me.

"Nickie, you have to face her," she said. "Otherwise you're a coward."

"You stay, then," I said, getting into the car and locking the door. I waved. "Tell me how it goes!"

When my mom got home I kept talking about how I was

traumatized by "the day's events." I practically needed a fainting couch after what I had been through. But my teen/girlfriend priorities kicked in, and I asked my mom to take me to the mall because I still needed to get a Christmas gift for Jason.

We went to a Structure and I picked out the brighter of two Cosby-esque sweaters. I was smug as hell, having turned the day around. As we were getting ready to leave, I half-heartedly hummed along to the mall Muzak's "Jingle Bells." My mom and I went down the main escalator and I decided that crazy Queeshaun chick had the whole Christmas break to figure out she had me mixed up with another girl.

Midway down, my self-satisfied haze cracked. I saw my nightmare come to life in the form of Queeshaun standing at the bottom of the escalator, talking to, of all people, my freshly minted exboyfriend Tyrone, with his FUCK THE POLICE cast. They both looked up, and I immediately began trying to run up the down escalator.

"Nickie," my mom yelled, grabbing me by the back of my coat to stop me.

"Mom, that's her," I yelled. "That's her."

She turned and stared at Queeshaun, who couldn't believe her luck.

"I can't believe," Mom said, "you are scared of a girl wearing a bullet bra."

I had no idea what Queeshaun's bra had to do with me, since I was going to die at the bottom of that escalator. "I'm gonna whip yo' fuckin' ass for Angela," Queeshaun yelled, as we slowly moved toward her. "I don't care if your mama's here. I'mma whip yo' mama's ass, too."

As we reached bottom, Tyrone tried to drag Queeshaun away with his one good arm. I took the opportunity to run past them, but my mom stayed behind and got right in Queeshaun's face. Once Queeshaun said "I'll fight your mama," my mother—who is absolutely not this person—started nodding like Clair Huxtable about to school Theo, right there in front of Mrs. Field's Cookies. Mom wasn't about to fight this girl, though Queeshaun certainly would have come to blows with my mother. As Tyrone held Queeshaun back, my mother stood as tall and straight as can be. She was trying to show me the importance of standing your ground. Meanwhile, I was halfway down to McDonald's, yelling back, "Just come on!"

Finally, Mom relented and followed me. The whole car ride home I was shaking, but my mom had no sympathy whatsoever.

"That girl," she said. "She's got that fool bullet bra on. I can't believe you would be afraid of a girl like that."

"Mom. She came up to my school to kill me and she just tried again. Of course I'm scared."

"You should never be afraid of anyone. Certainly not the likes of her."

By the time we got home from the mall, Queeshaun had left a string of messages on our answering machine. This was one of those old-school answering machines, and my dad walked in to hear Queeshaun's threats.

"We'll just call her parents," he said. He then made a big deal of looking her family up in the phone book and calling her mother.

Satan's mom was not impressed.

"What are you gonna do? They're kids," she said. "Let our daughters handle it."

He hung up and right away, Queeshaun started burning up our phone. Cully Union told her to stop, and when she wouldn't, we just let her run out the answering machine tape. "Your monkey-ass dad is a snitch, bitch," she said. "I'm gonna kick his ass, too."

Dad being Dad, he decided to bring the whole answering machine to the police station. He played the tape for the all-white Pleasanton PD, and at first they were concerned. Then, as Queeshaun's insults and craziness took on the feel of a stereotypical crazy black woman comedy sketch, they couldn't stifle their laughter.

"Yo' monkey-ass daddy is a motherfucking punk nigger snitch" put them over the edge.

"Wait," a blond cop finally said, trying not to smile. "You don't even know her?"

"No," I said. "I swear."

"Why would she do this?"

"Apparently I hurt her feelings, because I started dating her best friend's boyfriend. Excuse me, ex-boyfriend."

That did it. The whole station erupted into guffaws.

"Look," said the blond guy. "This is not enough for us to go on. If she physically touches you, call us."

If she physically touched me, I knew I'd be dead. I took a break from imagining my funeral, lavish with tears, and called Jason to ask him about Queeshaun. He told me Queeshaun was rich and had a huge house. That came as a shock. It made no sense that someone rich would have dookie braids and want to kill me. One or the other I guess I could have comprehended, but both were overkill. The irony is that my initial assessment of her was exactly that of my white peers: If she has dookie braids, she must be poor. If she is a big black girl, she must be angry. Although in this case, this bitch really did want to kill me.

Jason thought it was funny that she was acting so crazy. "She's harmless," he said.

"Say that at my funeral," I told him. "This bitch is nuts."

Jason and I were still dating right into league basketball season. My team was set to play Angela's twice, and of course the first game was on her home turf of Livermore High. Angela stared at me on the court, and Queeshaun looked like she could barely contain herself in the stands, where she was sitting not so far from my "monkey-ass dad." I had begged Jason to come, but he couldn't because he also had a game. My sister was supposed to get off early from her job at the Limited so she could be there to protect me, but no such luck. My whole team was terrified, because everyone and her white mother had heard about Queeshaun.

I was a mess the whole game, unable to function as my hands shook in the layup line. Then I airballed so bad that my coach benched me. We lost, of course, and my teammates and I lingered inside as our coach went to bring the bus. Queeshaun paced back and forth, whispering to Angela. We knew that as soon as we left the gym, Queeshaun would follow us out and go in for the kill.

The stalling tactic was becoming embarrassing when suddenly the gym doors burst open. In walked my sister Kelly, in full Foxy-Brown-bent-on-vengeance mode. My hero, she had sped over straight from work, still in her black Limited blazer with the huge shoulder pads. I'd always loved my brilliant, take-charge sister, but never more than in that moment.

"Queeshaun?" she yelled. "You here?"

"Yep," Queeshaun said, stepping right up to Kelly.

"You so much as touch my sister, I will kill you."

And that did it. Queeshaun lunged forward. A couple of girls pulled her back. My sister was ride or die. She came over to me and threw her arm around my shoulder. "If you touch my sister," she said to all of Livermore, "I will kick every single one of your asses."

"That's right," I said, suddenly bold with my bodyguard beside me. "What she said."

She took me home. In the car, I did impressions of her Action Jackson performance. "I will spit on your grave, Queeshaun!"

The next time I played against Angela was completely a different story. Jason was there. Even better, Queeshaun wasn't. That let me talk trash straight to Angela, who was having her worst game of the season just as I had my best. I was so pleased with myself.

Jason and I were not at our best point, however. Instead of getting his full name across my nails, I was getting a subtle J and K painted. It was the nineties version of "It's complicated."

That spring I was at Kim's Nails with friends one afternoon, and just as the nail tech started in on the K, in walked Queeshaun. Did this bitch have a homing device on my freaking car? Her eyes snapped open from the surprise of seeing me, then narrowed with fury as she saw the J-K.

"Hold still," said the tech, as my hand started to shake.

"I told you the next time I saw you I was going to kick yo' ass, bitch!" My K not even finished, my friends threw down money and hustled me out the back door. It felt like I'd been in a stickup.

That seemed like the end. Cut to: the last day of junior year, and four of us were celebrating by sitting in Paige's car and oh-so-glamorously drinking Purple Passion in the parking lot of a strip mall. Lucy was in the front with Paige and I sat in the backseat with another friend, Sook, our doors open as we listened to the radio.

The song of the summer, Mariah's "Vision of Love," came on, and Paige turned it up *loud*, probably to drown us all out as we sang along. Just as I was pretending to hit that Mariah note, this meaty hand reached in and grabbed me by the arm, trying to drag me out of the car.

It was goddamned Queeshaun.

"I'm gonna kick your ass, bitch!" she screamed.

"What the fuck is wrong with you?" I yelled, as Sook held tight to my legs.

Paige pressed the gas, driving off with half of my body out the door. She did circles in the parking lot, swerving to try to shake Queeshaun as Mariah continued to belt. Sook managed to pull me in bit by bit, just like in the movies. It was kill or be killed. I tried to slam the car door on Queeshaun as Paige hit the gas to get the hell out of that parking lot.

Queeshaun started to run, that's how desperate she was to kick my ass! Finally, she tripped, let go, and hit the pavement. Hard.

"OH MY GOD," we said in one collective teen scream. Paige stopped the car.

"Is she dead?" I said.

Queeshaun instantly leapt up, and we all screamed. Again. First she moved toward us, then doubled back to get in her car. The bitch was *giving chase*. What was this zombie bitch?

We stopped at a light and she caught up to us, bumper to bumper. Paige pressed the gas, running the red to get away. Queeshaun stayed right on us. We went into the Meadows development, hoping to lose her in the cul-de-sacs. Paige even killed her lights and gunned it, relying on her knowledge of the twists and turns of suburban subdivisions. We finally shook her, and we saw a house party. We decided it was safer to hide out there.

We didn't mention Queeshaun to a single soul. On the one hand, we did kind of almost kill her and wanted deniability. On the other, she was like Beetlejuice—just saying her name could summon her.

When we left the party an hour later, there she was, sitting in her car, waiting for us. She'd spotted Paige's car. Of course she had. Now I had to choose between the social suicide of running back into the house and having Queeshaun follow me to beat me up in a Meadows party, or take my chances with the girls. It was that same fear of being associated with someone who looked like Queeshaun. I somehow got a pass, but I couldn't bring an agitated scary black girl to a party, because then I would be the scary black girl, too. Also, fighting was just unheard of in polite upper-middle-class suburban planned communities. It was more about emotional warfare.

"Get to the car," I whispered to Paige.

I stood by the door to the house party as the girls ran to the car.

"Come on, bitch," I said.

Queeshaun got out of her car and slammed the door. For a second, we stood frozen facing each other. Just as she started her charge onto the lawn, I cut left, fast, racing to Paige's car like I was doing the one-hundred-meter for the gold. By the time Queeshaun realized she'd been tricked and ran to get back in her car, we were tearing down the road.

We drove around Pleasanton all night. Each of us refused to go to our houses, afraid that Queeshaun would be lying in wait. Paige eventually parked at Foothill High, and we watched the sun begin to rise to Roxette's "It Must Have Been Love."

"Man," Sook said, as if she had been thinking one single thought through the whole song. "That Queeshaun really hates you."

Paige reenacted Queeshaun's rise up from the ground. "That is some Freddy Krueger–level crazy," she said to a mad chorus of laughter.

A few years later I met Freddy Washington, who is Angela's little brother, at UCLA. I asked Freddy if Angela still blamed me for Jason Kidd breaking up with her.

"No," he said. "Angela doesn't care."

"Oh, good," I said, relieved.

"But Queeshaun?" Freddy added with a sinister chuckle. "That crazy bitch still talks about you."

I flashed to her in a room with photos of me all over a wall. "Soon, Nickie Union," she said. "Soon."

MY *BEING MARY JANE* CASTMATES AGREED I WON THE CONTEST.

"Whatever happened to that girl?" my costar Lisa Vidal asked.

"No idea." Everyone grabbed his or her phone again, in a race to find Queeshaun. A particularly savvy Facebooker found a woman by her name. He held up his screen.

There she was. My high school nightmare, still looking like she would kick my ass in a second. She was presenting an office look, and I imagined all the coworkers she terrorized. From my reaction, everyone could tell it was her.

Lisa grabbed the phone to get a better look and screamed. "She's living in Atlanta!"

"Oh my God, she followed me here," I said, only half kidding.

The door to the conference room swung open and every single one of us seasoned professionals *jumped.* We all expected to see Queeshaun standing there, yelling her trusty catchphrase: "I told you the next time I see you I'mma kick yo' ass!"

"We're all clear, guys," said the production assistant, eyeing us with suspicion.

We were safe. For now.

seven

CODE 261

I worked there with all my friends that summer after freshman year of college. It was an easy job. You didn't have to help *anyone*, that's the beauty of Payless shoe stores. The customers help themselves and you just have to ring them up. So you can kind of fuck around all day and get paid.

It was near the end of July, the time of the big Garth Brooks concert. Everyone had tickets and they needed someone to cover. It was assumed that I didn't like Garth. Black girls don't want to see country music. But I would have loved to see Garth. *No Fences* was one of my favorite albums, and I knew every single word to "Friends in Low Places." But of course, Nickie can work that night. The black girl and the Goth girl—they'll cover.

I was nineteen.

Someone was hitting Payless stores that summer, but we didn't know a thing. He was a former employee, black. The management and police had positively identified him because he robbed the same store where he used to work. They had a description, even his driver's license information. Then he hit a second store. Mind you, Payless would send you a storewide alert to change the price of a shoe or tell you how to display new sandals. They had the ability to warn us about this guy, tell us to be on the lookout for this former employee. They had pictures and a driver's license. And since our store was in a predominantly white community, if a black guy walked in, we would pick up on him right away. And yet, we weren't told a thing. Not a peep about the robberies.

Our store had even been hit before, but by someone else. Goth Girl had been there then, but no one got hurt. Every other Payless store that had ever been robbed now had security measures, like cameras and panic buttons. Not ours. And we were right by the freeway, such an easy mark.

So a black man walks into a Payless just before closing . . .

When he first walked in, I was in the back of the store straightening up a display of fake Timberlands in the men's department. When it was two to the store, one person worked the register, one worked the floor. He came up behind me and asked me about the boots. I don't remember what he asked, because I took one look at him and I immediately wanted to run. I didn't. I ignored my instincts. Part of that was the racial component of where I lived. I was very aware of how my coworkers and the people in the community viewed black people. So my instincts said, "Run. Run. This is a bad situation." But my racial solidarity and my "good home training" as a "polite" woman said, "Stay put. Don't feed a stereotype. Don't be rude."

He went back to the front and I started vacuuming. This was at eight forty-five. We weren't supposed to vacuum until the store actually closed at nine, but this was a trick staffers did to tell customers that it was closing time, get the fuck out.

The vacuum was so loud, and I heard Goth Girl scream to me to come to the register. Something in her voice told me to run. Again, I didn't. I overruled my instincts and walked to the front, where he was holding a gun on her. He motioned to me with the gun to get behind the register. As Goth Girl gave him the money, he was incredulous that there was only a couple of hundred. As a former employee, he knew there should be more.

"I already did the drop," she said, referring to walking the pouch of money to the nearby bank. It was another way we cut closing corners to clock out early. She sounded more annoyed than frightened. She had been there during the previous robbery and wasn't hurt. And being an entitled young person, she had the luxury of being angry.

"Go in the back," he said when he had emptied the cash into his bag.

Goth was in front of me, and the gun was in my back as he marched us to the storeroom. The gun was in *my* back, and she was still cursing him out, kicking boxes all the way in.

"This is such bullshit," she said as he closed the storeroom door behind us. "I can't believe this is happening."

"Take off your clothes."

Goth was still pissed. "I'm not taking my clothes off."

Mind you, I was naked in a second. It never even occurred to me to say no.

We'll be naked and dead when they find us, I thought.

And then he told us to both get in the bathroom.

Okay, I thought, maybe he'll just put us in the bathroom. Maybe he's doing this to buy time so he can leave.

So we crammed into the tiny little bathroom. And then, seconds later, he ordered me out.

He threw me to the ground and was suddenly on me, spreading my legs as he kept the gun on my head.

As he raped me, I began to hover over myself. I could see the whole room. I looked at that poor crying girl as she was being raped and thought, Things like this happen to bad people. Things like this don't happen to people like me. My psyche, my body, my soul, simply could not take it. Though people say things like "I saw my whole life flash before my eyes," I can tell you that this didn't happen to me. I didn't see my life. I was just very much present at the scene, watching this man rape me with a gun to my head.

He turned me over to go for it doggy style. He put the gun down, placing it right next to me. I wasn't looking at him, obviously, but staring at his gun.

"Can you hand me the gun?"

He said it just like that, as he ripped into me. He said it so very casually. "Can you hand me the gun?" It wasn't even "Gimme the gun." It wasn't forceful or gruff. It was like he was asking for the salt.

"Can you hand me the gun?"

And in that moment, when he asked me to give him the gun, the me that was hovering above and the me getting raped became *one*. I was back in my body, and I grabbed that motherfucking gun.

I moved forward, turned, and landed on my back. And I shot at him.

I can go right back to that moment now. The sound of the gunshot reverberating in my ears, every muscle in my hurting body tensed, the smell of gunpowder filling the air.

And the realization that I missed. And that I was probably going to die very soon.

He jumped on me, trying to yank the gun out of my fist. He bashed my face as he turned the gun toward me with his other hand.

My finger was wedged between the trigger and the base of the gun. It felt like he was going to rip my finger off, but I wouldn't let go. I flashed on scenes from movies, so I kept trying to pull the trigger seven times. I just thought that if I clicked it seven times, I would save myself. I was trying to turn the gun away from my face *and* holding on to it *and* trying to pull the trigger all at the same time.

I kept screaming for Goth to come out and help me. She didn't come out.

Finally, he ripped the gun out of my hand. He pointed the barrel at my head as he stood over me.

"Now I'm gonna have to kill you, bitch."

I looked down, begging, my face a mess of blood and tears. I clutched a gold-plated chain necklace my boyfriend Alex had given me.

"You can have this," I sputtered. "Take it. It's worth more than the money you got. Take it."

He had already taken everything else from me. This necklace was all I had to offer for my life.

He didn't take the necklace. I didn't dare look at him. And as quickly as it all happened, he was calm. And again, he said, very casually.

"How do I get out of here?"

I pointed to the back exit, whimpering, snorting tears and the thick blood back into my nose.

He went out and I was left alone. I never saw him again.

I called for Goth. I didn't ask why she hadn't come out. I knew why. In those moments, you do what you need to do to stay alive, I guess. Self-preservation is a motherfucker.

I DON'T REMEMBER WHICH ONE OF US CALLED 911, BUT THE POLICE GOT there fast. I am grateful I was raped in an affluent neighborhood with an underworked police department. And an underutilized rape crisis center. And overly trained doctors and nurses and medical personnel. The fact that one can be grateful for such things is goddamn ridiculous.

Two cops arrived initially, and then there were more. Many more. If they had been writing a manual for police officers and medical personnel on how to handle a rape case with care and compassion, I would have been the perfect test case on procedure. They were wonderful. And I know this now because I have spent time lobbying Congress and state legislatures about the treatment of rape victims. I've seen the worst-case scenarios, and they are devastating. Now, I can appreciate the care with which I was handled. Now, I know it rarely happens that way. And it *really* rarely happens that way for black women. I am grateful I had the experience I did, wrapped up in the worst experience of my life. Now.

Then, I was hysterical. I'm not a hysterical person. I'm not even a weepy person. And I was hysterical. I looked up, and suddenly my dad and my older sister, Kelly, were just there at the store. Later, I would find out they were running errands and saw the police cars lined up outside the Payless where I worked. But in that moment, it just seemed surreal to suddenly have them there.

"Calm down," my dad kept saying, over and over again, as he touched my shoulder. I couldn't speak to tell him what happened and I couldn't imagine telling him anyway.

The cops were radioing dispatch and other officers using police codes, a jumble of numbers wrapping around my head. None of them meant anything.

But Kelly was majoring in criminal justice. And I saw her face when she recognized the police code for rape: 261.

She whispered in Dad's ear. And the way he looked at me after, oh my God, is still a nightmare. I sued Payless for negligence, but I wanted to sue them for my dad looking at me like that. I HATED THAT. To this day, I HATE IT.

The look was: Damaged. Victim. Guilt. Fear. Like, I was my dad's prize. He didn't acknowledge it in words, but I was his favorite because I was the most like him. As far as he was concerned, I followed the rules. I was the kid you bragged about. I got great grades. Was the perfect athlete. Blah blah blah. And in that moment I was *damaged*. It was as if someone had broken his favorite toy.

I was taken to the hospital. After having my dad see me in that moment, my boyfriend Alex came to the hospital. And he too was destroyed. We'd been together about a year. His family was Greek and Mexican, and they were completely opposed to us being together. They called him a nigger lover.

"But you're an interracial couple!" he would answer.

"Why do you have to go to the extreme?" was the response.

Yet in the moment of Alex finding out I'd been raped and his parents having to deal with their child being crushed, they finally realized that our thing was real. I was, to put it mildly, very resentful that it took my being raped for them to not have a problem with interracial dating. But anyway.

My mom arrived, quiet and scared. I flashed to the advice my mom had given my older sister and me for how to handle anyone who wanted to mug us or worse.

"You know what you do, right?"

We would say in unison with matching eye rolls: "What do we do, Mom?"

"You say 'Shit, shit bastard!' That's what you do."

Shit, shit bastard. She thought a woman spewing out a string of nonsense swears would shock an assailant into confused submission. To this day my sisters and I will just text those words to each other, or leave "Shit, shit bastard" on each other's voice mails.

She didn't know what to say to me. I'm sure she was shocked because it happened to the one daughter she didn't think she had to worry about. I had always been the strongest one, taking care of myself. They had never seen me show fear. You move your kids to this all-white community and force them to go to these all-white schools. You think you've priced yourself out of this shit. You've done all these things and then this happens.

A FEW DAYS LATER, THE GUY STRUCK AGAIN IN A NEIGHBORING CITY. YOU could see him on the security camera at Payless this time. He walked in, saw the camera, and walked right back out. But then I guess he was just amped up to keep this crime spree going and he walked into a Clothestime store. I knew the girl there. He'd become more brazen, bolder, and he hurt her even more than he hurt me. By then the manhunt was reaching fever pitch. Within the week, he turned himself in. Because they knew who he was, the cops had started watching his mother's house, and she got him to surrender.

My dad was the one who went to every arraignment. Every single court hearing. I remember Dad saying, "I want him to see me." He is one of those parents who can rule with a look. Discipline with a glare. And he really thought that the same glare that got us to stop jumping on the bed, or to eat our vegetables, was going to work on someone who'd raped women. But he was there. Glaring.

"*Now* I feel bad," my rapist would say. "Not when I was smashing her crying face or leaving her in a heap. Nope. But her father's glare. That did it. That's what made me see the evil I had done." Dad took it personally, so this wasn't about justice for me. It was a personal affront to him. It happened to me, but it was an affront to him.

To this day, my dad has the article from the newspaper about my rape in his wallet. Twenty-four years. He has never explained to me why he carries it around, but I know it's a reminder that someone dared to fuck with him. "How dare you even think you could do this to *me*?"

Because of that article, everybody knew. They didn't print my name, but there were very few black people my age in Pleasanton. And just in case, for the people who didn't know, Lisa Goodwin went to a party and to get sympathy for herself, told *my* story but made it about how it affected *her*.

I had to testify in front of a grand jury, but I didn't have to see him. The most traumatizing part was going into the courthouse and seeing other criminals. I could see them coming off the transport van in shackles. Coming face-to-face with criminals, being in the courthouse with rapists and murderers and child molesters, was, for somebody in the throes of post-traumatic stress, all too much. I got into the elevator and in two seconds, I literally sprinted back out. Wrong combination of people. I heard my mom apologize because I guess she probably thought it looked rude.

He took a plea deal of thirty-three years. So we never had to go to a *trial*. I hope he's still in jail. I haven't looked to see if he's out. I do know he is aware of who I've become. My father said they mentioned it in one of the parole proceedings. My dad goes to those, too.

I have seen enough episodes of *Oz* that I really believe in prison justice. I believe there are certain things that prisoners do very well. And their handling of rapists is one of them. So . . . I feel pretty solid about that. Whatever he's endured brings me joy. I hope it happens every day of his life. A few times a day. I'm perfectly okay with that.

People always ask, "Do you wish you'd had better aim?" I mean, obviously you pull the trigger of a gun to stop, maim, or kill. That was my goal in that split second. But I don't think I'm a killer. I don't think I could live with killing anyone, even in self-defense. I think I would be even more tortured by that.

The other question I get asked is "What were you wearing?" I got raped at work and people still want to know what role I played in what happened to me.

I HAD ALREADY TRANSFERRED FROM THE UNIVERSITY OF NEBRASKA AND was supposed to start UCLA in August. But I couldn't do the grand jury and be in Los Angeles, so I deferred and did a semester of my sophomore year at a junior college in Fremont. During that time, I opted to sue Payless for not providing a safe environment.

Timing became the most important thing in my life. I timed everything I did to try to reduce the space for something else to happen to me. If I could limit the time I was in, say, a restaurant, then that would narrow the likelihood of me being murdered if the restaurant was held up in a hostage situation. That's how my brain began to function.

There were times when I was studying in the library, and I lost track of time and let it get dark out. Then I had to get from the library to my car. I'd run to my car, jump in, slam the door, and slump into the seat in a heap of tears. I'd shake, my arm numb as if I were having a heart attack—and I had to sit and wait. My car at the time was a stick shift and I couldn't stop my foot from shaking to put my car in gear, so I had to just sit. But sitting meant a carjacking was possible.

I moved from the fear of one random act of violence to another, because I'd seen the devil up close. Once you've been the victim of a violent crime and you have seen evil in action, you know the devil lives and breathes in people all day, every day.

The first therapist I saw was a bust. I saw him about two weeks after I was raped. He very quickly diagnosed me with post-traumatic stress disorder and insisted on trying to hypnotize me. A person who has just been raped isn't into that mind control shit, I assure you. He tried several times, and I would scrunch my face, pretending, but in my mind I'd be organizing my closet. I was also struck that he thought I was so Humpty Dumpty broken that he couldn't even talk to my conscious self. It's like he was looking past me to say, "Let me talk to your manager. I need to see someone who's really in charge here."

One of the first weeks of classes at UCLA, I saw an ad in the *Daily Bruin* for mental health services.

I visited the clinic and realized that the UCLA Rape Crisis Center was a part of mental health services. And through the Rape Crisis Center, there was group therapy. And you could meet other rape survivors. And so I got rid of Mr. Hypnotism and started seeing a therapist through UCLA.

In group, I was the only stranger rape. The rest of the students had been raped by acquaintances or family members. Some studies have estimated that 90 percent of rapes perpetrated against college-age women are acquaintance rapes. You want to know something weird? I felt grateful that my rapist was a stranger. It felt like a luxury not knowing the person. Because there was no gray area. There was no question of "Who are they going to believe, him or me?"

I was also the only one in the group who'd gone through the criminal justice system. Some of these women still had classes with these guys. One woman, I think she was an engineering student, was raped by her lab partner. But she had to go right back. I don't remember if she was the one who ended up dropping out. I know she wanted to, because the engineering department was so small and she felt trapped.

Group therapy was the only place I could feel "not crazy." I was around other young people with the same stresses I have, the same fears and triggers. You know that feeling you get when somebody first rubs your feet? It's like a jolt through your whole body, then an instant exhale.

Each time we met, I exhaled. Because when you've been raped, you really feel like you're on an island. Rape is the most underreported crime there is. And it's shrouded in secrecy and shame. You think no one will be able to relate to you because of what you've been through. Then to be in this room, where *everyone* could relate, changed everything. *Wow, that girl is getting straight As. That girl got a great internship. This girl is engaged.* It gave me the calm I so desperately needed. I saw the possibility of hope.

My therapist was lovely. "Let's talk," she said to me the first time we met. "Just talk." Unlike my previous therapist, she didn't treat me as someone irrevocably broken. She gave me glue, some Band-Aids, and Bactine, and said, "You've got this."

At UCLA, my life was like that cartoon where someone is walking along and magically a new plank is placed before them with each new step. It felt like there was nothing beneath me, but then each visit, each story, each memory was like another plank. I had no idea where those planks were taking me, but I was hoping that healing was on the other side. Being able to function was on the other side. Not having to literally run in panic all the time was on the other side.

And then, before I got to the other side, I went and got famous.

THERE'S A VISE AROUND MY CHEST AND MY ARMS ARE NUMB. IF I HAD TO swim for my life, I would die right now. It's like a slow-moving heart attack. Those dreams where something is happening but you can't move—that's my life.

And this is twenty-four years later.

I am in the car outside Target. I am talking myself into going in. I have a list clutched in my hand, because it's a sort of security blanket of order. I have to be as efficient as possible, get in and get out. And it's also something to stare at if I am being stared at. In my head I rehearse the walk to the door, and I gauge how well I did choosing one of the times that the store is less crowded. I won't feel safe, not even when I am back in my car. I will feel only safe when I am home. When every door is locked and checked.

After I was raped, in 1992, I didn't leave my house for a whole year unless I had to go to court or to therapy. I simply did not leave. That spiraled into me not going anywhere that I could be robbed. Anyplace where there was money exchanged, I simply avoided. The other day I was telling my husband that I couldn't remember the last time that I actually went into a bank. The idea of being in there while it was robbed—that shallow-breathing-inducing fear of "I could be robbed right now"—is too much for me. Anytime I go to a restaurant with someone, I joke, "Sorry, the Malcolm X in me can't sit with my back to the door." But I can't. I cannot enjoy a meal if my back is to the door.

Twenty-four years.

That feeling of surveillance, of being hunted, never goes away. Fear influences everything I do. I saw the devil up close, remember. And I see now how naïve I was. Of course I can never truly have peace again. That idea is fiction. You can figure out how to move through the world, but the idea of peace? In your soul? It doesn't exist.

I often get asked if my fears have decreased as I move further from the rape. No. It's more about me moving from becoming a rape victim to a rape survivor. I am selective about who I allow into my life. I can spot people who make me feel anxious or fearful, and they are not welcome.

But with the accessibility of our culture, I can't keep boundaries. It could be the guy who grabs me, yelling, "YOU KNOW YOU WANT TO GET THIS PICTURE!" People will grab me as I'm walking through a crowd. They may turn it into a joke, but they are also not taking no for an answer. No one understands how much female celebrities are physically touched and grabbed and shoved and fondled. We all talk about it. I can't tell you how many times people—men and women—feel your body. "Oh, you're just a little bitty thing," I hear, with someone squeezing my thigh. Men take pictures and get you under the armpit so they can feel the side of your boob. But we're supposed to just take it.

I was talking to someone about this recently. "You have a lot of rape energy around you," he said. "Something happening to you that you had no power to stop. And it keeps happening."

The first time I said no, my ex-husband Chris and I were on a casino floor in Vegas. We were having a huge argument and I was crying. I stared down at the incredibly tacky carpet of giant red and green flowers surrounded by gilded latticework. I followed the loop of the lace over and over with my eyes, hoping to disappear into the rug. But I felt something. Even before I heard the yell, I sensed I was in someone's sights.

"Bring it on!"

It was a cheerleading squad first marching, then running toward me. They were in full regalia, head to toe, clearly in town for a cheerleading competition.

"It's already been brought!" they yelled.

I was still sobbing as they surrounded us. "I am so sorry," I said, practically heaving. "It's not a good time, girls."

They looked so disappointed, curling their lips to smile at me, willing my ugly cry away.

When they finally walked away, I felt a wave of panic that I'd let these people down. I wanted to call them back. "I can do this!" I wanted to yell. "I can be what you need!" I still think about that moment.

I can remember each time I said no, because I have panic attacks about backlash. When my husband Dwyane and I are together, we've got double the attention. Don't get me wrong—I'm incredibly grateful to represent something so very positive to a group of people, but the flipside is that each interaction is anxiety producing for me and an opportunity for me to disappoint yet again. I have such a fear of not fulfilling the ever-changing wants and needs and expectations of strangers that I become terrified of what should be basic encounters. Going into a bar with friends, I'm like a rabbit that has wandered into a yard where a pack of wild dogs lives. One minute, I'm just hanging, chilling with all the other rabbits. Then something picks up my scent, and I've gotta flee.

When we're out with the boys we raise, Zaire, Dahveon, and Zion, we try to say, "Hey, guys, it's family time." Not so long ago, we were all at brunch in Miami and an entire family came over. Mind you, we were in the middle of a family discussion, and also just really enjoying being together. It was one of the very few times I was not completely on edge out in public, looking around, checking for the emergency exits.

Zaire, who was twelve at the time, took the lead and jokingly said, "Not a good time."

The mom looked at me. "Is this what you're allowing?"

"We're just trying to enjoy breakfast," I said in my sweetest actress voice.

She grabbed my arm. Like you would grab a kid who is about to fall in the pool. She used full force. She wanted my attention.

"That's a shame," she hissed.

This woman snatched me, right in front of my family. I try to teach the kids about boundaries and sticking up for yourself and not letting people show you disrespect, and then I am grabbed in front of them.

"*What* is a shame?" I asked. There was no answer.

It happened so fast. It was so shocking.

D intervened. *"Not now,"* he told the woman.

It is twenty-four years later. My instinct in so many situations when I feel threatened is to *run*. As fast as I can. But just as that night at Payless, my good home training keeps me frozen in fear.

And then, sometimes, we humans perceive each other.

I will be in the ladies' room, washing my hands next to another woman. She will take a few glances, which I notice, and as I'm readying myself to walk out the door, she'll say, "Me, too."

She doesn't have to tell me what she means. I nod. I have been doing rape advocacy and sharing my own story since the beginning of my career. We don't hug. We don't cry. She nods back at me. Just two women in a moment of mutual respect, acknowledging the truth and consequences of our experience. Feeling, in that moment, less alone on our respective islands.

eight

BLACK WOMAN BLUES

"You know, you are really pretty for a dark-skinned girl."

The woman placed her hand on mine as she said this. We had just met. This black lady had stopped me at the airport to say she enjoyed *Being Mary Jane*. She delivered her remark about beauty with a tone of assurance, yet surprise.

For years, whenever I heard this I would tighten my lips into an impassive smirk, tilt my head as if I didn't really understand what the person was saying, and move the conversation elsewhere. Or simply end it. I know, it sounds like I was just called pretty. I get that it can be confusing. The phrase is used in the black community as if a unicorn had just been spotted prancing across 125th Street. Through God all things are possible, and it's even possible that He sometimes makes dark-skinned women who aren't ugly. Somehow, some way, I escaped the curse of my melanin and Afrocentric features to become a credit to my skin tone. "We found one!"

An ex-friend I came up with in Hollywood used to say, "I just think it's great that you are so dark and still able to book jobs." She was the slightest shade lighter than me. I let it go until I simply let her go, but recently, I've grown tired of ignoring these remarks and what they mean about all darker-skinned women. Issues of colorism run so deep in the African American community, but more and more I see it spring up on social media as #teamlightskin versus #teamdarkskin. It's an age-old us-against-us oversimplification that boils down to the belief that the lighter your skin tone, the more valuable and worthy you are. The standard of beauty and intelligence that has historically been praised by the oppressor has been adopted by the oppressed.

This value system has become ingrained in us. As a teen, I became obsessed with the attention of boys, and equally fixated, if not more so, on the light-skinned girls who, I felt, would walk into a room and immediately snatch that attention away. I disliked them on sight.

My mother is light skinned, and she grew up having girls say to her face: "You think you're so much better than me." Mom and her sisters saw their light skin as a burden. They were called piss colored and listened to chants of "light, bright, and damn near white." My mother told me that she married a darker-skinned black man because she didn't want her kids to have "light-skin problems." I can imagine my grandmother's face when Mom brought home Cully Union.

My mother felt the burden, but I witnessed the privilege. Inheriting my father's skin, but growing up in proximity to my mother's lightness and to the lightness of my cousins, I saw how people across the whole color spectrum responded differently to them than they did to me. In my view, there was simply no comparison in our plights. It was impossible not to grow to resent that.

We darker girls should not be pitted against our lighter-skinned sisters, but our pain at being passed over also shouldn't be dismissed by people saying, "Love the skin you're in." You can love what you see in the mirror, but you can't self-esteem your way out of the way the world treats you. Not when we are made to feel so unloved and exiled to the other end of the beauty spectrum.

I e-mailed a young friend of mine telling her that I wanted to write about colorism. She replied immediately. "Sometimes it makes me feel crazy," she told me, "because when I bring up the issue it's met with confusion or disbelief." This gorgeous young woman blessed with darker skin had tried to self-esteem herself into fulfillment for years, but her experience with colorism left her feeling hopelessly alone. My friend had no problem getting a date, but finding amazing black men who truly love darker-skinned women proved to be a challenge. "The truth is, there are just certain men that are not and will never check for you," she says. "At least not seriously."

Perhaps more isolating, whenever she has raised the issue of colorism with friends or men, she is told that she is creating and encouraging division within the community. "People tell me I'm just imagining these feelings," she said; they think she's exaggerating the effects of colorism she experiences professionally and socially.

She's not. She is not imagining this shit, and she is not alone. For decades, sociologists like Margaret Hunter have collected real empirical evidence that we are color struck. Darker-skinned people face a subset of racial inequalities related to discipline at school, employment, and access to more affluent neighborhoods. In one study, Hunter found that a lighter-skinned woman earned, on average, twenty-six hundred dollars more a year than her darker sister. In her 2002 study of the color stratification of women, Hunter also presented real statistical evidence showing that light-skinned African American women had "a clear advantage in the marriage market and were more likely to marry high-status men than were darker-skinned women."

I have my own case study. My first husband was dark skinned, and I was the darkest-skinned woman he ever dated. Once he got a little success in football, he told me, "I wanted the best." What he considered the best, a sign that he had "made it," was dating light-skinned girls. It showed he had the ability to break through class and color barriers. He chose to marry me because I was famous and had money. For him, that trumped color.

"The number-one draft pick or the up-and-coming action hero will never choose me, because I'm dark skinned," my friend said. On the other hand, she has sometimes felt fetishized by men who briefly date her solely for the visual. "After Lupita got big, I noticed it was trendy to like me," she said. "On that note, white men *love* me. It's almost like a validation for them. 'Look at this black woman on my arm, natural hair, black skin, natural ass . . . See, I'm down!'

"It's hard to gauge who really likes me," she continued, "and who just wants to use me as an accessory. I've been told repeatedly that I'm not worthy, so when someone says that I *am,* it feels like a setup."

When black men are just honest with me, they admit that their vision of success most often does not include *expanding* on their blackness. "It's lightening up my gene pool," one guy boldly told me. "If I have a baby with you, we're gonna have a black-ass baby." When Serena Williams, whose fiancé is white, announced her pregnancy, a light-skinned black guy with twenty-one thousand followers announced on Twitter: "Can't blame her for needing a lil' milk in her coffee to offset those strong genes for generations to come."

That's some shit, and it hurts. We talked about the disconnect between the adoration so many black men shower on their mothers and grandmothers and their refusal to spend the rest of their lives with a woman who resembles their hue. "Why isn't the same type of woman good enough or even worth considering?" she asked me. "And do they even know they're doing this?"

There is another question I have to ask. Aren't these men also acutely aware of what it is to move through this world in the body of a dark brown boy? These men grow up seeing how people with lighter skin are respected and treated differently. Dark skin is weaponized and continually used against us day to day. What if it's not simply preference or acquiring a status symbol, but a learned tactic of survival?

I say this as someone who was certainly guilty of being color struck when I began dating. In my junior year of high school, I knew I was cute because I began pulling people that dark-skinned black girls were not supposed to pull. That was the barometer of my beauty: who and what I was winning in spite of my blackness. These boys were all top athletes, and I saw the admiration my dad had for me as I was dating them. My dad would go to their games and invite neighbors over to meet them. The more he bragged, the more validated I was that I was doing something right. "If I don't pull somebody that other people want and that crowds actually *cheer for . . ."* The stakes got higher and higher.

Eventually I didn't necessarily need to be the girlfriend. I just needed these guys to choose me in the moment, over someone else. That line of thinking can get you very sexually active very quickly. And it just kind of got away from me. You find yourself, a couple of Keystone Lights in, kissing some random guy in the bathroom of a house party. Some guy you don't know at all, who maybe isn't even your type, but just looked your way . . . and you needed that validation fix.

For the longest time, I wouldn't date anyone darker than me. It was so ingrained in me that I didn't see it as an active choice that I was friend-zoning anyone with more melanin than me. In my early twenties, someone finally did an intervention. I was having lunch with my older sister and one of her guy friends, Eric, at a soul food spot, of all places. I was wearing a T-shirt emblazoned with ERASE RACISM. I was making some point about power structures in relationships, feeling woke as fuck.

"Well, let's talk about how you're color struck," said Eric.

"Excuse me?" I said.

"I've known you since you were, what, twelve, thirteen?" he said. "The guys you've said you had crushes on and the guys that you dated, none of them are darker than you. A lot of them are a *lot* lighter than you. Have you thought about why that is?"

"Look," I said, "I actually don't think about that stuff. Love sees no color."

"Bullshit," he said. "To say 'love sees no color' is dumb as fuck. If that beautiful love of yours were kidnapped, you wouldn't go to the police and say, 'Help, a lovely soul was snatched off the street . . .'"

"No," I said, making a face in the hope that we'd just drop it.

"You'd give a thorough-ass description," he said. "Height, weight, scars, and you'd start with skin color and tone. You actually do see each other, quite clearly, and that's amazing."

I pretended to be really intent on my mac and cheese.

"Love sees everything," Eric said. "You're making a choice. And when you make that choice of putting yourself in a position to fall in love with a very specific person who looks nothing like yourself, that does actually say something about your choices."

So I got real. Right there, in my now ridiculous Erase Racism shirt, I opened up about my choices. I talked about feeling passed over for white and lighter-skinned girls and the rush I felt every time I got someone they were supposed to get. As I spoke, I realized it had so little to do with the actual guy. It wasn't my preference for light-skinned guys. It was all about their preference for me.

People underestimate the power of conversation. That lunch intervention gave me permission to like other people. If I could truly love my own skin, then I was not going to see darker skin as a threat to my worthiness and my value. Then it was come one, come all.

Shortly after, I met my cousin's former football teammate Marlin, whose nickname was literally Darkman. Marlin was midnight black, with a perfect smile and a gorgeous body. I met him at this massive sports bar called San Jose Live, and he had such enthusiasm about the music playing that with every new song he was like, "That's my jam!" He was a hard dancer, meaning that you'd feel like a rag doll keeping up, but he was sweet. We ended up dating for two years, until I met my first husband and broke up with him. My first husband was chocolate brown, beefy, and covered in tattoos. He didn't look like anyone I had dated, either.

When I got divorced and I went flying through my bucket list of dicks, they came in all shapes and sizes. This new approach was liberating. I felt open like a twenty-four-hour Walmart on freaking Black Friday.

Once I dated black men, I felt like I could breathe. Exhale and inhale deeply, without the anxiety of being examined by others to ensure that I was the "right kind of black" to even qualify to date interracially. When I dated nonblack men, there was always the *Get Out* fear of meeting their parents. My college boyfriend's parents were nice to my face but called him a nigger lover and accused him of screwing up his life dating a black girl. Now I no longer had to endure the constant evaluations of my character, looks, and accomplishments from his friends and from strangers witnessing a white man being publicly affectionate with me. It drove me crazy to watch them look at us, puzzling out the equation of why I would be worthy of his touch. I could breathe.

I think that might be the biggest reason so many people root for me and Dwyane. He chose an undeniably black woman. When you have struggled with low self-esteem, to have anyone root for you feels good. To have women rooting for you who have been in your shoes and felt the pain you felt, feels likes a thousand little angel wings beating around you.

OF COURSE COLORISM ISN'T JUST CONFINED TO BEING AFRICAN AMERIcan. Or even American. In 2011, I went to Vietnam to film the *Half the Sky* documentary with Nicholas Kristof, a Pulitzer Prize–winning columnist for the *New York Times*. We were there to delve into issues around education and young women, but when we landed, I immediately saw all these surgical masks. I wondered what I was walking into. Was there some kind of viral outbreak? If so, I was going to need one of those masks. It was also oppressively hot, yet people wore long-sleeved shirts with every inch of skin covered by fabric.

Oh, I thought, it might just be the usual, run-of-the-mill epidemic of colorism. I started asking questions, because I think it's important to have that conversation and examine our value systems. I noticed I wasn't getting a straight answer through the translator. People acted like they had no idea what I was talking about. When I finally met a blunt local teenager who could speak English, I jumped on the chance to ask about all the covering up.

"Oh," she said immediately, "nobody wants to get darker."

It was that simple. I could tell it immediately dawned on her that she'd just told a black person that nobody wants to get dark. So she switched to "they."

"They want their color to be just like him," she continued, pointing to a crew member traveling with me. "White."

"So what happens if you happen to get dark?" I asked.

"Like the people who work in the fields?" she asked. "They think it's ugly."

It smacked me right between the eyes. "They think it's ugly," I repeated, letting the phrase hang in the air.

"Yeah, but if it's vacation dark, it's more like a sign of wealth," she said. "If you're just *dark* dark, it's a sign that you're poor and you work in the sun doing manual labor. And no one wants to be associated with that."

I have now had these conversations with girls all over the world, from Asia to South America, Europe to Africa. When I am traveling, I see billboards on the streets with smiling light-skinned models promising the glory of brightening and lightening therapies. Take Fair & Lovely, an extremely profitable Unilever lightening cream that the company boasts has been transforming lives for the better since 1975. Sold in forty countries, this melanin suppressor is the best-selling "fairness cream" in the world. Seriously, Unilever says that *one in ten* women in the world use it. In India, the ads have changed with time from the original focus on getting a man—"if you want to be fair and noticed"—to becoming lighter in order to get a *job*. One career girl ends the commercial looking at her new face in the mirror. "Where have *you* been hiding?" she asks herself.

We're right here and we're hiding in plain sight.

"FOR A BLACK GIRL YOU SURE ARE PRETTY!"

This is the white cousin of "pretty for a dark-skinned girl." To fully understand colorism, we have to acknowledge the root. Just as dark-skinned girls are often only deemed deserving of praise *despite* their skin tone, black women as a whole are often considered beautiful despite their blackness.

I have heard this often, coming from left field at work or meeting someone new. One time that sticks out was when I heard it in the parking lot of my twentieth high school reunion in Pleasanton a few years back. The guy was drunk and so was I, since I'd grabbed vodka as soon as I walked in to dull the effects of standing out so much. I wasn't sure if it was my fame or my blackness that made everyone say, "Oh, there she is." I had forgotten that long before I was ever on-screen, I already was famous in Pleasanton. I was the black one.

We were in the parking lot, figuring out where to go for the second hang. It was not lost on me that I was with the same crew that went to all the bonfires. The guy said it out of nowhere as if he perceived me for the first time and had to qualify his regard with a caveat.

"Why do you say, 'for a black girl'?"

"I don't know," he said. He told himself, and me, that he just didn't know black girls, so he was color-blind. The same way I had done when I was actually color struck. It was good to go back to Pleasanton and see that I wasn't imagining what I felt as a kid. Once you're an adult, you can read the room in the context of the larger world. For some of these people, and definitely this guy, I was still the only black friend they had. That twenty years during which they could have found at least one replacement for me? Yeah, they never got to it. I looked around at the people gathered, standing around just like we did at the bonfires. How many black people had these people ever had in their homes? Did they work with any at all?

That's the thing, though. Having more black people around increases opportunities to learn and evolve, but that alone doesn't undo racist systems or thought processes. That is the real work we all have to do. I always want there to be a point to what I am saying, and I don't want to bring up the issue of colorism just to bring it up, or simply teach white readers about strife within the black community. At the very least, I of course want my friend to know she is not alone in her feelings about colorism. But I want to expect more than that. For years, we have advised women of color—light and dark—that the first step to healing is to acknowledge that colorism exists. Well, if we have hashtags about which teams people are on, black children staying out of the sun to avoid getting darker, and research studies that show the darker your skin, the greater your economic disadvantage, then we know colorism is a fact. We're ready for the next step, and we can't shrink from it just because it's hard and uncomfortable.

So let's aim higher than merely talking about it. Let's also expand that conversation beyond the black women who experience the damaging effects of colorism and stop telling them, "Love the skin you're in."

This cannot be a group hug of women validating women. Men must mentor girls as they grow into women, guiding them to find their own validation so they don't seek it elsewhere in negative ways. Tell your daughter or niece she is great and valued not in spite of who she is, but because she is exactly who she is. Because dark skin and Afrocentric features are not curses. We are beautiful. We are amazing and accomplished and smart.

Okay, smart is never a given with anyone, but we *are* here. And we don't need black ladies in airports and white guys in parking lots grading us on a curve, thank you very much.

nine

MISTLETOE GIRL #2 TELLS ALL

Ask any actor, and they will tell you the teacher who had the biggest influence on them as they crafted their technique. You'll hear names like Stanislavsky, Strasberg, Adler, Hagen, and, of course, my own teachers, Screech and Mr. Belding.

I made my screen debut with two lines as Mistletoe Girl #2 on *Saved by the Bell: The New Class.* And, yes, I was in awe of Dustin Diamond, aka Screech, and Dennis Haskins, aka Mr. Belding. All the other kids on set were as green as I was, but these two were veterans as the only holdovers from the original show. In this room, they were stars.

The show taped in front of a live studio audience, but during rehearsals the studio was empty. So any scene I wasn't in, which was the majority of them, I would go take a seat in the audience instead of going to my dressing room. I didn't just watch Dustin Diamond and Dennis Haskins act; I studied how they interacted with the director and how they treated the rest of the cast and the crew. Dustin had been doing comedy for years, so he had this slapstick ability that he would reserve and then tweak for scenes. I didn't realize that was a skill set you had to actually work at. Also, he was older than the teenagers on the show, and I knew I was going to be older than the people I was working with as long as I kept getting cast as a high schooler. Do you keep your distance as the adult? How much do you joke around? I literally just didn't know anything. And Dennis was all about dirty humor as soon as work was done, so I definitely learned that you could choose who you wanted to be on set.

I actually played two different black girls on the show, coming back later as Jennifer, a girl obsessed with collecting coins. She also inexplicably dressed like a 1950s housewife heading to a garden party, but then she went to the Sadie Hawkins dance in a hot red dress. I guess her closet had some serious range. I fortunately started my career off doing a lot of multicamera half-hour shows where I had the ability to sit in the audience and watch people work. One of my favorites to study was Sherman Hemsley on *Goode Behavior*, a house-arrest comedy. Yeah, a house-arrest sitcom. I tested to be a series regular as Sherman's granddaughter, but I didn't get the part. However, the producers brought me back to play her best friend. The whole time I was on set I was thinking, That's George Jefferson! I sat in the audience, listening to the notes he was given and watching how he tweaked his performance to suit them. It was a master class in comedic timing. Now, it wasn't my cup of tea, but he made it sound like it was. He had just the right rhythm to wait for the laugh and then zero in for the punch line.

My go-to acting technique was to smile a lot. The guy who

played Juan Epstein on *Welcome Back, Kotter,* Robert Hegyes, was one of the assistant directors. He saw me watching every scene and took a seat next to me out in the audience.

"I have two pieces of advice for you," he said.

I nodded and braced for the inevitable: "One, you're creepy. Two, stop staring at the talent."

"I can tell you're basically waiting for your line," he said. "It's 'Blah blah blah, now me.'"

He was right. Whenever I did a scene, I smiled a lot at the other actor to show I was listening, and almost nodded when it was about to be my turn, as if to say, "That's my cue."

"Always remember to listen to what the other actors are saying, and react. Just listen and react."

"Got it," I said. "Listen and react." I really did get it. One thing about me, I don't mind notes if they are helpful.

"The other thing to remember is this: you are always going to be able to find people who don't want to watch you fail."

He saw a young person who he knew was learning and took time to pull me aside and help me. Throughout my career, all kinds of people have been generous enough to help me and challenge me so they can see me be the best version of me. Hollywood is indeed dog-eat-dog, but there are groups of great people who are just nice. I held on to that, because this business also has a lot of rejection. When I first started auditioning for television shows, the main game was at Warner Bros., where everyone would hang out to audition for a shot on one of the million teen shows on the WB. I spent a lot of time doing guest spots on these series, playing high schoolers. In those rooms, there would be hundreds of other actors like me, dressed young even though we were all in our early to mid-twenties, but also honest-to-gosh kids. You could tell who they were because their mothers and fathers were grilling them on the material so hard that eventually the kid would have a crying meltdown. Mind you, this would be for a two-line gig on *Nick Freno: Licensed Teacher*.

As I got older and I spent more and more time on these sets, I realized these parents had given up everything else in their lives. So those two lines could decide whether or not they get to stay one more month at the Oakwood Apartments in Burbank, or had enough money to eat. A guy I met in those rooms, a successful actor now, told me what it was really like.

"Do you know me and my mom and my sisters were living out of my car during pilot season?" he asked me once. "We would get to the studio early and wash up in the bathroom there."

His mom had a trick when things got really bad. They would show up for the audition early and say that a younger sister had an accident. "Is there a trailer where we could wash her pants out?" she'd ask. Then they would go in the trailer and wash the family's clothes with hand soap.

"That's kind of ingenious," I said.

"It shows how badly they wanted it."

I was lucky in that I just wanted it for me. I became eligible to join the Screen Actors Guild (SAG) with an AT&T commercial directed by Forest Whitaker. I thought the ad was going to make me an ongoing AT&T spokesperson and thus rich, but the company scrapped it. But it was a union job, and if you are not union, that first job you book makes you union eligible. You cannot take a second union job without paying your dues. I was counting on paying my SAG dues with an ongoing gig on *Moesha*. I was supposed to play a head cheerleader, a nemesis to Brandy's Moesha. But they decided to not make the role recurring, and that was it. A job that was supposed to be a few episodes became just one: "Nah, we're good." I took that as being fired. How else was I supposed to take it? That always stayed with me. There's always someone bigger, badder, better. Don't save your best for when you think the material calls for it. Always bring your full potential to every take, and be on top of your job, or they will replace you.

PROBABLY 50 PERCENT OF THE FAN MAIL I'VE RECEIVED IN MY ENTIRE CAreer is because of one episode of *Star Trek: Deep Space Nine*. I played N'Garen in the "Sons and Daughters" episode, and Trekkies tell me that it was a pivotal one because it reintroduced Worf's son. My character had an interest in astrophysics, and as a rookie weapons officer for the Klingon Defense Force I took out a Jem'Hadar cruiser. Hadar's gonna hate.

The pivotal thing for me was that it was a job. I was twenty-four and I didn't want to play high schoolers forever. A Klingon, I thought, showed range.

We filmed at Stage 18 of Paramount's back lot, which was made to look like the IKS *Rotarran* hanging out on the Cardassian border. I see you, Trekkies. I'm not even going to make a Kardashian joke.

It took an obscene amount of time to turn me into a Klingon, and I would sit there for hours in the makeup chair, depleted of small talk because it took so long that there was simply nothing left to discuss. The hair and makeup room was huge, housing Ferengi ears and ridged Bajoran noses. My wig was standard Klingon, but fuller and somewhat braided, and for makeup I had just a hint of rose red on the lips. The look said warrior, but approachable. The irony of the situation was that the role was kind of high school: I was one of five new recruits, and Worf's son totally got bullied in the cafeteria. I was the mean girl of the squad.

The direction I kept getting was "Klingons don't smile." All day long I would get caught on camera with a grin. "Gabrielle, Klingons don't smile."

At lunchtime, I would stay in my makeup and a bunch of us Klingon recruits would go to Lucy's El Adobe Café on Melrose, across from Paramount Studios. The first time we went in, I expected *some* reaction.

"You must get a lot of Klingons, huh?" I asked.

"All kinds of people," said the waitress.

I ordered the ground beef tacos. As we Klingon day players sat there looking at the wall of autographed celebrity photos, I ate as much of the salsa as I could. To this day, I love their salsa.

On the last day, after working nineteen hours and escorting a convoy of Klingon cargo vessels to Donatu V, I was beat. They said I had to wait until the makeup department was ready so I could take my Klingon face off. I had an hour and a half to kill before they'd get to me. So I went back to Lucy's and sat alone in a booth with a book. Ricardo Montalbàn smiled down at me from an autographed picture. He was Khan on the original series and in *Star Trek II: The Wrath of Khan,* so it seemed like a sign. When the waiter came over, I ordered a margarita.

"Can I see some ID?"

He held my California license up to my Klingon face and squinted. "I don't know," he said. "You look different."

"It's me," I said.

"I know," he said. "I'm just kidding."

"Sorry," I said. "Klingons don't smile."

PRETTY SOON AFTER MY *DEEP SPACE NINE* GIG, I LANDED MY FIRST FILM: *10 Things I Hate About You.* Like a bunch of Klingon recruits, we all bonded that first night at the hotel in Tacoma, Washington. There wasn't a mean girl or boy among us, and we made a pact that this was going to be the best summer ever. There was Julia Stiles, wise beyond her New York years, and Joseph Gordon-Levitt, who was recognized everywhere he went as a star of NBC's *Third Rock from the Sun.* He and David Krumholtz—whom we affectionately called Krummy—bonded deep over their intellectual love of hip-hop. Larisa Oleynik was another child star, with her own show on Nickelodeon, and Andrew Keegan was the cast heart-throb. Susan May Pratt was a Michigan girl, and we clicked over our shared love of the Midwest and having a really, really good time. We were both the oldest. Playing a high schooler in your twenties isn't exactly mutton dressed as lamb, but it still makes you feel like people's big sister.

It was my first movie, this modern high school take on *Taming of the Shrew,* but we were all fish out of water. There was a "no favored nation" clause in all our contracts, which meant every cast member was treated equally. We all got the same type of hotel room, same rental car, and same type of trailer. That first week we had the run of Tacoma. It's a really beautiful port city, so we would go waterskiing and take camping trips. I made it my mission to make everyone laugh through a trip to Mount St. Helens. We were tight.

The new guy, someone named Heath Ledger from Australia, was set to show up a week into shooting. We were so afraid he was going to be a drag. Would he fit in? Would he be a jerk? Would he light up?

The first night after he arrived, he met us in the bar at the top of the hotel. Only Susan and I were over twenty-one, so the cast sent us up as ambassadors to check him out.

We found him, all of nineteen years old, drinking a scotch on the rocks and holding hands with his girlfriend, who appeared to be at least thirty-seven. He was stunning, with long dark hair falling in curls. Then he opened his mouth and he was James Bond.

"Hello, ladies," he said. He had this twinkle.

Susan and I looked at each other. Oh, this was going to work out just fine.

He talked about Shakespeare and art, all in an impossibly nondickhead way. He was two years out of Perth, which he described as "a wonderful place to grow up in as a kid, and a wonderful place to leave as a teenager." He was wise and sexy beyond his years.

We went downstairs to report our findings.

"What's he like?" everyone asked.

"He's a man," I said to the crew. "You're gonna love him."

And we did. Heath didn't have to try to ingratiate himself into our circle, which by then had turned our hotel into a sort of college dorm of smoking weed and big discussions about life. We were all within two floors of each other, and we would always end up in each other's rooms at the end of shooting, hanging out and listening to music. Heath would play the didgeridoo, a long cylindrical wind instrument he carried everywhere in a leather case. The sound is somewhere between a foghorn and an extended belch, but his passion for it was infectious. When hotel guests complained about the noise and the smell of weed, we acted very offended.

We also had a routine of eating together every night, and we'd often drive our little rental cars over to this joint that was like the local version of a Dave & Buster's for burgers and video games. The whole experience felt like the best summer camp.

When the cast moved up to Seattle, Julia's mom and Larisa's mom didn't want to stay, so they signed them over to me as the adult in charge. Bad move. (Sorry, moms!)

"First order of business," I told the girls, "is getting you fake IDs." Welcome to the Gabrielle Union Finishing School for Young Ladies.

We all went out as a pack in Seattle. Heath, ever the gentleman, held every door and our hands as we navigated the stairs of U-Dub college bars in our high heels. For me, it was fun to experience all of these adventures through their underage eyes. The rush of fake IDs! Beer! Throwing up! To add to the joy, there were lots of budding little romances among the cast, which were harmless and without drama.

When we wrapped, we knew for sure we would all see each other again, just like summer camp reunions. But that never happened. We were never all in the same place again. We all went right into new films except baby Larissa, who went straight off to college. I would see Julia on a plane, maybe Krummy. Andrew was such a club guy that I'd run into him here and there.

I don't want to overstate my own bond with Heath, because every single one of us shared it. Whenever I ran into him in L.A. after *10 Things*, it was like we had just wrapped yesterday. We would both reel off names of people from the movie that we had seen and share updates on their lives. There was never the weird Hollywood distance that creeps in. You usually get so close on a set and then it's out of sight, out of mind. You forget you were family for a while. Not this cast. Heath and I would hug and say, "Take care." His loss was a death in the family that all of us felt equally.

I'D PRETTY MUCH CORNERED THE MARKET ON OUTSPOKEN-BLACK-HIGH-schooler roles when I was invited to do a table read for a project called *Cheer Fever*. Honestly, the only reason I took the table read was that I had really wanted to get a role in *Sugar and Spice*, a bank-robbing-cheerleader film. I didn't get a spot in that one because, guess what, they didn't want to go black on any of the characters. And it bombed. It bombed so bad that I love telling people I didn't get the job, because it's like saying the Craigslist Killer never got back to you.

I was intrigued by the concept of *Cheer Fever*, which would of course become *Bring It On*, because it highlighted the rampant appropriation of black culture. Here, the idea was that a white high school squad, the San Diego Toros, get ahead by stealing cheer routines from a black team, the East Compton Clovers.

But when I got the script for the table read, my character, Isis, was a combination of Foxy Brown and eight other blaxploitation characters squeezed into a skintight cheerleader uniform. There were all these made-up slang words. Now, I am not the most Ebonically gifted person, but I recognize a made-up word when I see it.

The initial script had one word in particular, or, I should say, a collection of letters, that I just tripped over as I was reading it in my living room. I couldn't figure out what it said, so I showed it to my husband at the time. Chris peered at it like a word problem and then recoiled.

"Oh, God," he said.

"What?" I said. "What does it say?"

"I think they transcribed a *Martin* episode."

Martin Lawrence used to have these comic exclamations of disbelief as a realization dawned on him. It's an improv riff that he mastered, but they had tried to spell it out. The full line was

"Ossaywhattawhattawhat? Me-ow. *Me* gonna ow *you*. My nails are long, sharp, and ready to slash."

Clearly they were going for an Oscar. I love campy humor as much as the next person, but I didn't want to be picketed by the NAACP. The original script had Isis and Kirsten Dunst's character, Torrance, ending up cheering together at UC Berkeley. If you know what it takes to get into the UC system, you know Isis is not an ignorant fool. She's a leader, she's a great student, she's taking AP classes, and she's got high SAT scores. I wanted Isis to be presented as a tough leader who was not going to let these girls steal from her without some cheer justice for the act of cultural appropriation.

The director, Peyton Reed, was on board, and every morning we would meet in my trailer to rewrite dialogue to make it more believable. I could not, however, make my cheerleading skills seem at all believable. The actresses on the white squad, the Toros, had started filming earlier and had about three weeks of cheerleading camp to boot. Our squad, the Clovers, had nine days to learn the same number of routines. The Clovers consisted of three members of the girl group Blaque, several college cheerleaders, and me. Of course the pros and the girls from Blaque got it quickly, but me? I am not by any stretch a dancer, or someone who picks up eight counts quickly. So pretty much every day I would come into cheerleading camp smelling of Icy Hot, like somebody's old uncle.

Hi-Hat was our choreographer, and the poor thing knew I was hopeless. She just looked at me like, "Well, just do your best." I know she was thinking, This bitch is never gonna get it.

So they did a lot of close-ups of me during the routines. Wide shots were out because I don't match anybody.

One day I finally broke Hi-Hat. She threw up her hands.

"Do what you're gonna do," she said. "Just commit to it so it will look good."

Kirsten had a house with her mom out in La Jolla during that shoot, but the rest of the cast was staying in a San Diego hotel, going to all the bars and clubs around town. Everyone was horny, and there were a lot of marriages that didn't make it to the end of production. Normally I would be right in there for the fun, but I kind of felt like the cruise director. I was older and knew the area. There were a lot of people who weren't quite twenty-one yet and I couldn't get a million fake IDs. So the only place I could take them was Tijuana.

"How do you know TJ so well?" one cheerleader asked me, five tequilas in.

"I was on travel soccer in high school," I said. It's true. My soccer team was made up of the biggest female hellions in California. One time we walked across the border the night of an away game. We returned with one tattoo and six marines.

Kirsten was still in high school, and compared to me then she was *so* young. She was super nice and we would go out of our way to include her whenever we could. Her mom hosted barbecues, and we would all go because we wanted Kirsten to feel like part of the gang. You went, you ate, and you turned to the person next to you. "What bar are we going to?"

The movie came out and surprised everyone. We made ninety million dollars, and it's become a cult classic. Soccer dads will come up to me and start doing the cheers, the "Brrr, It's Cold in Here" routine, then ask me if they're doing it right. I have to answer, "Dude, I have no idea. Sorry."

I worked hard to make Isis a real character. It is interesting to me that when people reenact my scenes, they turn me back into that "Me-ow" caricature the director and I consciously took steps to avoid. They snap their fingers and say, "It's already been broughten."

That line is actually from a later spoof of teen movies, but perception is reality. Isis was an educated leader who refused to have her cheers stolen, but these people genuinely believe she was the villain.

A bunch of us did a cast reunion and photo shoot for a magazine a couple of years back. Kirsten was there and I mentioned how people say the "It's already been broughten" line at me even though it wasn't in the scene she and I played.

"It wasn't?" she said, laughing. "I thought it was."

Perception is reality.

SOMETIMES IT'S THE DIRECTOR'S PERCEPTION OF YOU THAT CAN RUIN A project. I get asked about *Friends* a lot because people know there were only two black people on the show who didn't play something like a waiter or Chandler's coworker. That leaves Aisha Tyler and me. For some reason, people get our plotlines confused. Aisha played the woman pursued by Joey and Ross. I played the woman pursued by Joey and Ross. Okay, I get it now.

When I was on, it was their seventh season, when *Friends* started to have more stunt guest stars. Susan Sarandon, Kristin Davis, Winona Ryder, Gary Oldman, and me.

I heard I got the gig on a Tuesday, the morning after my CBS hospital drama *City of Angels* was canceled. The best part of that show, by the way, was working with Blair Underwood—the sixth grader in me was dying. The worst part was having to yell "Pump in epinephrine!" and screwing it up each time. (*You* try it.) I had heard CBS gave great Christmas gifts, so my goal was to try to hang on until Christmas. We didn't make it.

When I drove onto the Warner Bros. lot I was not scheming to become best friends with the Friends. I was so okay with that. By then I had done 1,001 guest roles and I understood how these shows worked. If you're a regular, especially megastars grinding through your seventh season, you have so much on your plate that going out of your way to befriend your guest star is the last thing on the priority list.

But they were all really nice and totally professional. I thought, Okay, this could be cool. They had it down to a science and needed only three or four days to bang out an episode. My first scene was on the street outside Central Perk, with me unloading the back of a car, announcing that I am moving into the neighborhood. (Briefly, apparently.) The director was a regular, he did a lot of episodes. He went over the scene with David Schwimmer, Matt Perry, and the extras. Then he turned to me, and his tone completely changed.

"Do you know what a mark is?" he said in a singsong voice. "You stay on that so the camera can see you."

It was like he was talking to a toddler. He assumed on sight that I didn't know a single thing.

"Don't worry," I said. "I know."

Of course I knew what a mark was. Did he talk to other guest stars like this? The same thing happened in my next scene, this one with Matt LeBlanc.

"Okaaaay," the director continued in the singsong voice he reserved for me. He mimed how I should hold a lamp. "You could do thiiiiiis," he said. "Or thiiiiiiis."

His tone was so condescending, as if I had just wandered in off the street or won a contest for a *Friends* walk-on. It's funny, because I was standing there with Matt LeBlanc. I had four films under my belt that had either opened at number one at the box office or at number two behind blockbusters like the freaking *Matrix*. Matt, meanwhile, had made a movie with a monkey. Yet the director was talking to me, his guest star, as if I hadn't accomplished a single thing.

It's telling, I think, that my scenes were not in the usual *Friends* settings. First, I was outside Central Perk, a street set that fans know to be pretty rarely used on the show. Then Joey and Ross went inside Central Perk to discuss me, and then I showed up again with both of them at an obviously fake bar. My black face didn't darken the door of their favorite café, and certainly not the Friends' apartments. In their ninth year, Aisha Tyler had the weight of integrating the *Friends* set and storyline like some sort of Ruby Bridges of Must-See TV. They let her character, Charlie Wheeler, stay for nine episodes. In 2003, *Entertainment Weekly* suggested it was odd that the two black girls were given the exact same storyline. "The déjà vu wouldn't be that notable except that *Friends'* depiction of New York City is notoriously lily-white." Executive producer David Crane took umbrage. "The other story line [with Union] was quick and funny, where the two guys didn't realize they were dating the same girl," he told the magazine. "Charlie Wheeler [Tyler] is a brilliant paleontologist who should be dating someone like Ross, but hooks up with Joey first." Got it.

By 2016, the whitewashing of the Friends' world was so apparent in reruns and streaming that series cocreator Marta Kauffman had to acknowledge the situation to the *Washington Post*. "That is a criticism we have heard quite a bit," Kauffman said. "When we cast the show, we didn't say to ourselves, 'This is going to be an all-white cast.'"

But it was. I didn't call the director on the way he treated me, which I regret. I thought, *No wonder you don't have black talent on this show.* He assumed I didn't know anything and he felt comfortable dismissing me with condescending directives. It's actually not enough to just point out that there were so few black actors on the show. We need to look at why, *and* why it was assumed that I knew nothing. Bias, whether implicit or explicit, hits every industry. To be a black person is to understand what it is to be automatically infantilized and have it be assumed that you don't have the talent or the skill set required to do your job. It's the reason Dr. Tamika Cross, a chief resident and OB/GYN, was stopped from helping a man who fell unconscious on her flight. When they asked if there was a doctor who could help, Tamika went into action. And was denied.

"Oh, no, sweetie," Dr. Cross recalled the flight attendant saying. "Put your hand down, we are looking for actual physicians or nurses or some kind of medical personnel; we don't have time to talk to you."

To compare myself to a doctor is a leap, I know, but it's just how people talk to us. So no, I couldn't possibly know where my mark was.

My short time on the *Friends* set was a lesson, though. I had grown as an actress, raised my salary quote, and proved I could open films. But it wasn't enough. I thought about that speech Dad gave me before I started elementary school: "You're gonna have to be bigger, badder, better, just to be considered equal. You're gonna have to do twice as much work and you're not going to get any credit."

It was still true, even in the land of make-believe.

ten

CRASH-AND-BURN MARRIAGE

Have you ever had a dream where you're in a car and you're heading right for a wall? You're trying to hit the brakes, but you just speed closer and closer to your doom? Well, you are cordially invited to my first wedding.

May 5, 2001, was a hot day, even for New Orleans. My bridesmaids were all hungover, their faces puffy and shiny from frozen daiquiris and hurricanes, a peril of having your wedding during Jazz Fest. Just before the ceremony, they were rock-paper-scissoring to see who got to go down the aisle with the Heisman winners. The loser had to walk with the groom's friend who was just sprung from jail. He'd made bail in a murder case and was still wearing prison braids, as fuzzy as his alibi.

Their game of rock-paper-scissors was a convenient distraction from what I was pretty sure could be a heart attack. But once they all walked, it was just me, myself, and my anxiety, standing at the beginning of an aisle that now seemed a country mile long. At the end was Chris, someone I had no business marrying.

I took a step, and my shaking started with the first chords of "Endless Love." I was on the edge of sobs, but not the usual wedding tears of a bride overcome by emotion. Everyone could tell, especially my father. He looped his arm through mine to escort me, which is to say drag me, down the aisle.

"Stop it," he hissed in my ear. "Stop this right now. You're back at Foothill High School. You're the point guard; you're leading your team. Stop this foolishness."

I nodded, trying to turn my ugly-cry into a game face. Two guests I didn't recognize jumped in front of the videographer to take photos. They paused a beat, each lowering their disposable cameras and smiling as if giving direction. Like maybe I'd get the idea and be happy. Chris and I hadn't thought to write the number of guests allowed on the response card, so our wedding planner had simply seated, say, fifteen people on a card that went to one cousin. "The girl from *Bring It On* is marrying that football player, so invite the whole block," I imagine them saying. "Well, yeah, he got cut from the Jacksonville Jaguars, but he's hoping to be a Raider."

As Dad held me up down the aisle, I saw that the pastor that Chris's mother had insisted we use was not there. My family is Catholic, but Chris wouldn't commit to doing the Pre-Cana classes you have to take in order to get married by a priest. His mother's suddenly precious pastor had skipped the rehearsal. I thought if he was a no-show, that would be my out. Then I saw him, blending in and chatting with the groomsmen. Mingling at my wedding ceremony.

I had asked one of my closest guy friends, Dulé Hill, to do

a reading. He was playing Charlie on *The West Wing* at the time, and I had been his girlfriend on the show. Dulé thought this marriage was a terrible mistake, so as he read from Corinthians, he kept sighing dramatically, pausing to look at me like, "Are you getting this?"

"Love is patient," he said, "*love* is kind."

After an eye roll, he continued, ticking off all the boxes on what was wrong with my relationship.

"It does not envy, it does not boast, it is not proud. It does not dishonor others."

Long pause. Tick. Tick. Tick.

I heard a plane in the distance.

"It is not self-seeking, it is not easily angered, it keeps no record of wrongs."

If Chris and I had kept no record of wrongs, we would have had nothing to talk about. His endless cheating had given me permission to cheat, too. I was just less sloppy about it, so he wasn't aware. While he dealt in volume, I dealt in quality. A note for the novice cheater: never, ever cheat with someone who has less to lose than you. You want someone who will be more inclined to keep his or her mouth shut.

"Who gives this woman to be married to this man?" the pastor asked, his voice thick with Louisiana country. Chris suddenly turned his back on me. I remember it in slow motion, him stepping down from the altar and moving toward his groomsmen.

I was being left at the altar, I thought. This was really happening. I had missed my chance to run, and now *he* was Julia freaking Roberts, the Runaway Groom riding off on a horse. He knows, I thought. He knows I cheated on him and he won't marry trash.

Chris leaned in with his groomsmen, taking a huddle. They stamped their feet in unison, all turning back to me with a football chant of "We do!"

It was a joke. Chris had planned this. He wasn't leaving me. He didn't know I was trash. I was saved from shame and washed with relief. I could endure a toxic marriage, but the humiliation of being left, of being publicly rejected—that would have been too much.

The pastor began the vows. "Do you, Gabriel, take Christopher to be your lawfully wedded husband?"

Wait, I thought. "Gabriel"? This guy just mispronounced my name at my own wedding? But I was raised to never correct people. Certainly not a pastor. All I needed to do was say my name the right way when I repeated the vows. But because I was a good Catholic girl, I said it wrong.

"I, Gabriel, take . . ."

A groan went up from the bridesmaids. I glanced back at their disbelieving faces, then over at Dulé, ready with the faintest shake of his head. I smiled at Chris, which is something I always do to another actor when I am nervous in a scene and just want to get through it. I had a hard time looking at him, so my eyes settled on his forehead.

The pastor pronounced us man and wife, and our exit song down the aisle was Natalie Cole's "This Will Be." It's a cockeyed ode to bliss that now seems a little too on the nose irony-wise. Our videographer walked backward in front of us, capturing the exact moment one of our groomsmen, a huge guy named Zeus, clapped us on the back.

"Y'alls is married now," he said, riffing on a *Color Purple* line with a voice full of forced wonder and excitement.

On the video, which I have watched only once, you see my face fall. It was the beginning of the end.

SO WHAT GOT ME THERE? WELL, MY ROOMMATE IN 1999 HAD A THING FOR linebackers in the AFC Central Division. Her taste was very specific, and I can't fault her for it because they were actually all great guys. One in particular hosted a three-day party in Jacksonville, Florida, every April. My roommate and I went one year with some friends, and on the first night there was a bowling party. I immediately clocked this guy in the next lane, definitely not my type. He was a running back, short and built, and a Jacksonville Jaguars teammate had given him the nickname "Little Thicky." That was an accurate description. He had on these baggy jeans, and he'd cut off the hems to shorten them. Later, when I was shopping for him, I learned that 38-28 is in fact a mean size to find.

"What are you, Huck Finn?" I asked, looking down at his frayed cuffs.

"My name's Chris."

"Where's Jim? He out watching the raft?"

He gave it right back, trash-talking my game. He was legit funny, a country boy from Kenner, Louisiana, where they take turtles out of the swamp to cook them. He liked drinking dark liquor and playing cards, and he reminded me of the kind of men who married into my family. The contrast was that he also had tattoos all over his arms, two earrings, and an easy cartoon cat smile. When we were all leaving, he got on a Ducati, and that sealed it. As a child of *Grease 2*, I was always on the lookout for a Cool Rider.

I found myself thinking about him, and the next night he showed up at the house where most of us were staying. One of my girlfriends was like, "He's *downstairs*!" He had come back, so that meant he was interested, too. It's funny, in retrospect, how excited I was.

We spent the rest of the party weekend joined at the hip, hanging out and trading potshots. A big part of our courtship was ragging on each other. Sure, later we would use it as a weapon, having learned what to say to wound and what would be the kill shot. But in the beginning, it was good fun. It felt like a mutual chase.

We would visit each other in Jacksonville and L.A. for weekends. My career was starting to rise, so the arrangement was good. I could focus on work and auditions while he did his training. We had dreams. "After football, I'm one class away from my kinesiology degree from Michigan," he told me. "I want to go into sports medicine."

In July, after three months of dating, Chris bought an engagement ring, but he held on to it until my birthday, at the end of October. I flew to Jacksonville to celebrate. I spent the whole day at the spa, and when I got back to his house, there was a rose petal path from the front door to the bedroom. At the end was Chris, down on one knee. He had a bucket of KFC on the floor, and he was eating KFC potato wedges with one hand while holding a ring in the other. When I tell this story to new girlfriends, they always ask, tentatively, if there was some sentimental thing about KFC. No, I have to tell them; in the first of a list of many ignored red flags, I guess he was eating and I had surprised him.

The ring felt big and special, and so many of my friends were already married. I'd won something under the wire, I thought. I was the girl who called everyone to share my news, but I remember feeling more and more apprehensive with each call. I'm the opposite of impetuous. I am a "measure sixteen times, then cut once" person. And then torture myself in the middle of the night about how I kind of did a half-assed job on that sixteenth measurement. So I got defensive when the general response was "Are you sure?" and "As long as you're happy . . ." People thought it was a terrible idea, given that I'd only known him a few months and had only seen him on random weekends. People on the other side of marriage know what happens when you've never spent any real time together. I had no idea what that reality actually looked like, but I told myself I was just efficient.

The next day I had to fly up to Wilmington to audition for *Dawson's Creek*. It was a quick trip, there and back in one day. Back in Jacksonville, I let myself into Chris's place while he was still at practice and got on his computer to check my e-mail.

Kids, this was medieval times, when olde-timey laptops used to have messages pop up on the screen like they were breaking in with a special report. And there it was:

"Yo, you still got that girl coming in next weekend? Nigga, she's Greek. Nigga, she's Greek."

This was from his best friend. Now, I am not Greek. Nor do I know why his friend was so insistent about this woman's Greek identity. All I knew was that I was going to be back in L.A. the weekend of Greekfest. And this was literally not even twenty-four hours after he had proposed to me.

I packed my bag and kept my ring on just so he could see me take it off when I threw it at him. When he walked in the door, I nailed it, throwing the diamond right at him. Chris entered the scene in full apology mode, as his boy had tipped him off. I guess my reply—something like "Yes, what was her name again?"—gave away that the person typing wasn't Chris. He bent to pick up the ring and was crawling on the ground, begging.

"You *just* proposed," I yelled.

"I didn't know if you were going to say yes," he said.

"So you lined up a backup?" I yelled. "Who do you think you're kidding?"

But for someone with an intense fear of public humiliation, who, just hours ago, felt lucky to have been chosen, I had no choice but to stay. I didn't have it in me to call all those people twenty-four hours later to say, "You were right." Because then everyone would know just how naïve and foolish I really was.

The judgment, I imagined, would be on a grand scale. My publicist had also announced our engagement to the press, and I felt like there was no turning back. People had taken time to ask my publicist for details on how we met and I had already crafted a quote about our happiness. "Yeah, about what I said," I dreaded saying. "Uh, please respect our privacy during this difficult time?" Now I know the headline would have been "Eighth Lead of *She's All That* Calls Off Engagement," but in my mind, the story was far bigger.

I stalled, putting off sending out the Save the Dates and stretching the engagement from 1999 all the way to 2001. When the Jaguars cut him in 2000, my girlfriends told me that I should, too. But I couldn't kick him while he was down. I also believed he had a real skill set that would be attractive to another team. The Raiders were interested, and by the time we finally got married, he was doing off-season training with them. He was technically on the team and got a small stipend for working out, but he didn't have a contract. We married in May, and at the end of August he got cut from the Raiders and never played football again. And for the rest of our marriage, never had another check. From a job. Ever again.

What about that kinesiology degree he was so close to getting? Funny, I asked the same question.

"Yeah, about that," he said. "I'm actually a year and a half away. And if you're an ex-athlete on scholarship and don't tell the university that you want to come back in a certain amount of time, they don't budget for you. I'd be paying for it. Since I don't live in Michigan, I'd be paying out-of-state tuition."

So the Bank of Gabrielle Union was officially open. And doing a brisk business.

I TRIED. NOT MUCH, MIND YOU. BUT I DID TRY. WE WERE LIVING IN A cookie-cutter split-level town house in the Tarzana neighborhood of L.A., and he decided he needed office space for a company that (as far as I could tell) existed mainly in his mind. He'd convinced a few people to hire him as a marketing-type consulting person of some sort and he was adamant he needed a plush office to be taken seriously. So I got him one by the Fox lot in Century City. He needed to have that office feng-shuied, by the way. Never been to Asia, but he needed it to be feng-shuied to be on trend. I thought, If this is what will make you happy and productive, you do you. Neither happened.

I started handing him ways to make me happy, gradually making them simpler and simpler. "What was the name of that soul food place we saw on Sepulveda?" I'd ask. "Maybe we should go there some night."

He upped his game, however, as a prolific cheater. I was resigned to it, more annoyed by his moping around than his cheating. I'd hear the garage door and tense up, not sure what mood he'd be in. I distinctly remember yelling, "I don't care who sucks your dick, just come home and be nice to me."

Yet I would suddenly decide to get randomly, epically jeal-ous. I was doing laundry one day and going through his pockets. Since it wasn't his money he was running around with, he could always be counted upon to put cash or credit cards through the wash. Sitting cross-legged on our bedroom floor, I found a piece of paper reading ANGELINA, 818-whatever-whatever.

The ragey-rage set in. I knew he was fucking other people, but finding that number set me off. I decided to stash the number on top of the armoire in our bedroom, where it sat, waiting for the perfect moment for me to go ballistic when he accused me of something. Exhibit A: You're a dick. Prosecution rests. Case closed.

It took a couple of weeks, but sure enough, he handed me just the right opportunity to go for it. I pulled down the number.

"Is this the bitch?" I screamed, sounding like Rowdy Roddy Piper from the WWF. "Angelina? Is this the bitch you're fucking?"

He laughed. Right in my face. I became unhinged, fueled by embarrassment and anger.

"You think you're gonna call this bitch?" I screamed. "YOU THINK YOU'RE GONNA CALL THIS BITCH?"

Reader, I put the paper in my mouth. I chomped and chewed until I could swallow.

"You're not calling this bitch," I said, coughing a little.

Chris paused. "Angelina is the name of the soul food restau-rant you asked me to find."

I blinked. "Well," I said.

"How does that taste?"

Another time we went nine days straight without speaking. Ghosts in a split-level house, finding reasons not to be in the same room. In the midst of this, I had a red-carpet premiere that involved some sort of love theme, so I needed a date. Reporters had been picking up a "trouble in paradise" vibe with us, and I thought I had to keep up appearances.

Hours before the event, he was downstairs watching TV and I was upstairs thinking, How do I even get him to talk to me? And I hatched a plan I am not proud of. "I bet if I was injured he would have to talk to me."

I went to the middle landing and then down a couple steps. By that time, I had done a couple of action movies, so I knew how to fake a fall without being injured. I tucked and rolled, slamming the wall where I knew he was sitting on the other side.

"Baby!" he said, running to me.

"Don't you baby me," I said, screaming and pretending to fight back tears. I pulled out the performance of my life. "You don't even want to talk to me and now I've got to go to this premiere all alone and I'm *injured*."

He went to the premiere. We smiled for the cameras. We played our roles.

My drama moves weren't always successes. Like the night I ran away from home. Yes, my adult home. You know the moment in the movies where the girl runs off and the guy runs after her? Well, I tried my hand at that. Midfight, I literally ran out of my own house in shorts and a T-shirt. No wallet, no phone. I just started running, assuming Chris was going to run after me. But I forgot that I was in decent shape, so I just kept going.

I ended up on the backside of a park, one where he played basketball. He'll come find me here, I thought. I propped myself against a tree and waited. Just so we could have this scene of "Thank you for finding me . . ."

He never came. Instead, I fell asleep, sitting against a tree.

I woke up to the tingling feeling of a trail of ants climbing up my arm.

Hello, rock bottom, I thought.

It was after 4 A.M. and the sun was just starting to creep up. I had run so far from home that now I had to walk back. Step after step of utter Charlie Brown defeat. I held on to the glimmer of hope that Chris would be waiting at the door, frantic. I planned out my apology to the police, who I was certain would be swarming my house after Chris's call about a missing person. "I just needed some air."

When I got home Chris was fast asleep up in our room, snoring to the heavens. He could not be bothered.

You are right to wonder if we sought professional help. There were indeed forays into couples therapy. The first one, we had the luxury of choice. We were on the *Titanic,* asking to see the bar menu. We decided we wanted a black woman, and a Christian woman at that. We thought she would shame us into being together. Fifteen minutes into our first session, before we even got to any of the tough stuff, she stopped us.

"This isn't gonna work," she said. "You guys don't belong together."

We'd been dumped.

"How dare she?" I scoffed before we even got in the car.

"Who does she think she is?" snapped Chris.

Oh, we were going to show that woman. Things got better for a bit, in that every once in a while we would have a great night where we laughed. Maybe this is enough, I thought.

Our friends didn't think so. One sent us to another therapist named Sally, whom our friend credited with saving her marriage. Like the good Christian sister therapist before her, Sally also marveled how we ever got past the dating stage, but she was committed.

We lied to Sally constantly. Chris and I were both terrified of being judged. When one of us would go out on a limb and share some uncomfortable truth, the other person would act blindsided. My eyes would widen like I couldn't begin to comprehend where any of this was coming from. I wanted Sally to like me, so I couldn't tell her the truth. I wanted to win.

Sally called me on my competitiveness pretty early in our sessions. "You think in terms of winning and losing," she said. "But if you're winning, who's losing?"

"Him!"

"That's your husband," she said slowly, like this might be news to me. "You're not supposed to want him to lose."

"Wow," I said. "You don't know me, huh?"

Chris decided to stop coming to the appointments. I kept right on like the good student I was, needing that A.

"Now that we're here alone, you need an exit strategy," she said, leaning in. "Why don't you give yourself six months to mentally, physically, financially, prepare to leave."

Sally was talking truth now. I kept going alone, and I started to get a plan together. There was an actual date in my calendar, and the date came and went. I knew the milk was not just spilled all over the floor, it had been left out to curdle. And I was spooning it up, saying, "I can still eat cereal with this."

THEN CAMERON CAMERA ENTERED MY LIFE. THAT'S NOT HER REAL NAME— her working name was even dopier—and I resent protecting the identity of a woman who tried to extort me after sleeping with my husband, but I am not sure of the etiquette.

Chris and I went to a summer potluck with a bunch of couples. There was this woman there, serving up Sexy Librarian and being very flirty with all the husbands. At one point, a bunch of guys were missing, and I found her showing them all her Web site, Cameron Camera, where people paid to watch her in various stages of undress. Great potluck, everyone! Gentlemen, hide your hard-ons!

A lot of people wanted to go out after the potluck night, including Chris, but I had a girlfriend drive me home. He ended up hooking up with Cameron Camera in our SUV. And of course she left an earring, probably one she got ten-for-a-dollar at a pharmacy for just such occasions. That gave her the excuse to call him at his office—the one I got feng-shuied—which gave him the excuse to have sex with her again. "Since you came all the way out to Century City, the least I can do is fuck you."

Cameron Camera laid low for quite some time, surfacing when she heard I had the *Honeymooners* movie coming out. She contacted a bunch of tabloids and entertainment news shows, saying she was ready to sell proof that Gabrielle Union's husband was cheating.

A friend at one of the shows gave my team a heads-up. Before telling me about the woman, they hired Marty Singer, legal guard dog and bad cop to the stars. I was downstairs in my dining room when my cell phone rang. At the other end were my agent, my manager, my publicist, and special guest star Marty.

"Listen," my manager said, "this is a really hard conversation to have . . ."

Oh God, I thought, they're dropping me.

"I'll just say it," he said. "Someone is shopping around a story that Chris is cheating on you. She has photos."

"Oh," I said quietly, then louder. "Oh." And I laughed. I howled.

"Gabrielle . . ." said my publicist.

"Which woman?" I asked. Chris was upstairs, and I spoke to the ceiling. "Trust me, this isn't a problem."

"Her name is Cameron," said my publicist.

"Oh, Cameron Camera with the nudie site," I said, blurting it out like a charades answer to show how cool I was with this. "She's not even cute. I'm so sorry she bothered you. Please don't worry."

"It might not be so easy," my agent said. "You have a movie coming out. We need to know what the pictures are so we can warn the studio."

"Like if it's kissing, whatever," said my manager. "If it's her hand up his ass . . ."

"Got it," I said. "Hand up the ass is a problem."

"So we need to see what she has," said Marty. "Set up a sting and put a price on those photos. In the meantime, talk to Chris and see what she has on him."

Like he was waiting for his cue, Chris came down the stairs. The same ones I'd "fallen down" a few months before.

"You didn't notice the flashbulbs?" I asked.

"What?"

"When she was taking pictures of you guys fucking, you didn't notice the flash going off?"

"What?" Maybe he was in straight denial or, like me, was trying to figure out which woman it could have been.

"Cameron Camera, remember her?" I said, casually, like I was jogging his memory. "You fucked her last summer? Well, she waited for just the right moment. Now she's gone to all these people saying she has proof that you cheated. Anything you want to say?"

Just like how we began, when he got caught with the Greek, he went right into groveling.

"Get out!" I screamed. "I'm about to have to pay a bitch for fucking my husband. *And* I have to pay Marty Singer to help me pay her! Your dick keeps costing me money!"

He was panicked, but not about losing a wife. If I left, the cash flow would go with me, and with it the illusion of his success.

I became fixated on the word "sting," which they set up that week for 7 A.M. in a coffee shop. All the intrigue made the situation sound at least slightly more exciting than just asking, pretty please, to see exactly what position the woman was in with my husband. I kept my phone in my hand all morning, but Cameron Camera never showed. Either she didn't really have proof and didn't think we'd ask to see it in exchange for the money, or she just wanted to feel relevant.

My marriage was obviously over, but I was still desperately afraid of people labeling me a failure, so I didn't want to jump right into the divorce, either. Carrie Fisher had a line I love about why she and Paul Simon ended their marriage: "Things were getting worse faster than we could lower our standards." I realized that I needed to really take stock of the situation between Chris and me, and make a decision based not in anger but in what I really wanted and how I really felt.

So one night, I was sitting up in our bed when he came in the room.

"Let's talk," I said.

"Yeah," he said.

"Listen," I said, "if we're gonna have this conversation, let's be brutally honest."

"Okay," he said, sitting down next to me. "The truth."

We went through it, question by question, bringing up even the most obscure things from years prior. "When you said you got into a fight at Mel's Diner in Hollywood," I asked, "was that true?"

"No," he said. "I was with somebody."

"You went through the motions of tearing your shirt?"

"Yeah."

"I knew it," I said, laughing. "The way it was torn, I knew it."

He brought up an actor I had done a film with.

"Did you sleep with him?" he asked.

"No," I said.

"Were you in love with him?"

"Yes," I said. "Yes, I was. But you would have been in love with him, too."

There was something about the permission to be honest that allowed us to reestablish the friendship we had in the beginning. That night we decided to split up, and yet in the months after, we became sort of best friends again. We hung out more in those months than when we were married. Before, we had been that downer couple that ruined the party when we showed up. It was that uncomfortable to be in our presence. But as separated people, our friends were like, "Hey, we can hang!"

When we announced the separation, my team gave a statement to the AP at 9 A.M. West Coast time. By 9:15, my publicist and manager started what they called "The Divorce List." Reps for athletes and celebrities were calling to see if they could set up a date. Some were reaching out directly.

My manager called to tell me I was popular.

"Who?" I said, pretending to be disgusted but feeling flattered. "Who wouldn't give me a *day?*"

He reeled off the first two, naming an aging sportscaster and then maybe a fading music producer who held on to his Jheri curl two decades too long.

"Okay," I said. "I'm good. Please stop."

The honeymoon period of my divorce from Chris was short-lived, and I did the laundry list of dumb things you do when you want your ex to like you. I invested in a company he started with one of my friends. I paid rent for six months on a new home for him and cosigned for a Porsche. Then he abandoned the Porsche at the Burbank airport and I inherited a bunch of bills and parking tickets. The business failed, so there went that money, too. And like my money, I have never seen him again.

Chris moved to Atlanta, where I shoot *Being Mary Jane*. I reached out to him once and said, "Let's get together." I meant it, but he owes me so much money, I'm afraid he thought it was a trap. He never showed.

He needn't worry. My sting days are behind me.

eleven

PRESCRIPTION FOR A BREAKUP

Are you experiencing heartbreak accompanied by nutty behavior?

Symptoms include, but are not limited to, obsessively clocking your ex's social media and light stalking of the new girl's Instagram. You may also be having moderate to severe instances of driving past their house and hiding in their bushes. You have been given a diagnosis of generally crazy, unproductive behavior.

I am here to help. What I can prescribe is not medication, but an easy-to-follow syllabus and wine list. This is a list of pro tips best used NOW.

PRO TIP: WATCH *SPLENDOR IN THE GRASS*

Shot in luscious Technicolor, *Splendor in the Grass* is Warren Beatty's first film and one of Natalie Wood's best. She plays Deanie, a pre-Depression Kansas girl who understandably falls in lust and love with Warren's Bud. He loves her, too, but has sex with been-there-done-that Juanita instead. Deanie wants to have sex with Bud so badly that repressing the desire drives her insane. Everyone who I make watch this film remembers this one doozy Deanie tosses out during her mad scene in the bathtub: "Did he spoil me? No. No, Mom! I'm not spoiled! I'm not spoiled, Mom! I'm just as fresh and I'm virginal like the day I was born, Mom!"

My mom loved Natalie Wood, so I grew up watching this film and her others, like *West Side Story* and *Rebel Without a Cause*. Junior year of high school, I needed *Splendor in the Grass* to help get me through my first, and perhaps worst, breakup. Only then was I able to fully understand Deanie and feel understood myself. She and I knew the truth: heartbreak feels like a death sentence.

I thought Jason Kidd and I were a power couple. He was a sophomore at a nearby Catholic high school, quickly becoming a national phenom. But part of the allure for me was that he seemed like such a good guy. He came from a two-parent household and he was Catholic like me. We had this very eighth-grade relationship, despite being in high school. We didn't have sex. I had already lost my virginity, so I was down for it, but it didn't seem like something he had to have in order to be with me.

Two weeks before my junior prom, I went to one of his games. My friends couldn't go and I didn't want to do the thirty-minute drive from Pleasanton by myself, so I asked my dad if he would come along. He loved that I was dating Jason, so that was a no-brainer for him. We sat in the stands, and I saw his parents were in the bleachers across the gym. Next to them was a tall girl with an asymmetrical haircut like Salt's from Salt-N-Pepa, only even shorter on one side and longer on the other. I took her to be a cousin or family friend. She was wearing Jason's #32 wristband, and I thought, *How sweet. He gave his cousin his wristband.*

Then I noticed that he was wearing a #22 wristband. When you as a player wear someone else's jersey number it means one of two things: You are paying tribute to a significant other who plays, or you are honoring a player who died. Now, my number was 21, so I made up this scenario in my head about who #22 could be. My teenage levels of narcissism and drama wrapped in a crazy double helix of denial. I decided Jason had a friend who died. Jason was so sensitive, paying homage to this person via a sweatband. RIP #22, I hardly knew you.

During the game, a few of his friends came over to me, led by a female friend of his with a severe case of a Valley Girl accent. "Soooo, are you and Jason going to prom?" she asked.

"Yeah," I answered, innocently.

"Uhhhhmmmmm, I might, like, hold off on those plans."

I flew right past the obvious dig. Why would Jason be busy? We had talked about prom. He's didn't have a game. Clueless Valley Girl.

Then, a guy friend of his came up to me.

"Hey, you know, whatever happens with you and Jason," he said, pausing for a second, "you know, we're always gonna be friends. *I* think you're really cool."

"Oh," I said. "Okay."

See this is what grown-up love was about. You created connections with his friends. And even though you know you will never, ever break up—because that would be preposterous, right?—you keep those friendships you made. I filed that knowledge away for a time I would never, ever need it.

Jason's team won, and right after the game ended the high school gymnasium ritual of pushing in all the bleachers began. Jason was already doing postgame interviews in high school, so they had left one of the bleachers open for the entire team to sit and wait for him. He was literally surrounded by a ring of reporters. And at six foot four as a sophomore in high school, he was head and shoulders above the crop of people jotting down what he said. I could clearly see his face as I stood standing off to the side with my dad. Across from us, pointedly not saying hello, were Jason's parents and this girl "cousin."

Then his teammates started a chant:

"Just do it, you pussy. Just do it." Over and over, and Jason kept looking at me and then back at the team and then back at me.

My dad smelled what was coming. "We should go, Nickie," he said, as if the idea had just occurred to him. "We should just get out of here."

"Just do it, you pussy," the chant continued. "Just do it."

"We need to talk," Jason yelled to me over the reporters. They all turned to look at me.

The chant stopped, and the gym was silent except for the squeaks of sneakers as his teammates leaned forward in anticipation.

"Let's go, Nickie," Dad said.

"No, Dad," I said, in my most dramatic voice. "I want to know the truth."

But I couldn't let go of hope.

"Um, is it positive?" I said, giving the thumbs-up sign. "Or is it negative?"

Jason gave a thumbs-down sign. The team went "OHHHH-HHH!" in unison.

Condemned to death by heartbreak, I ran from the arena.

He called me that night to officially break up with me, which is exactly what he had done to the girl he dated before me. Karma is a bitch that surfaces quickly. I went into this very quick whirlpool of a downward spiral. I began writing a lot of sad, terrible poetry. I even incorporated my vocabulary words into the verse with lines like "You are the crystal sextant leading me to my fate." Then there was a poem I called "Little Boys."

Little boys like to play
Childish games from night to day.
They think they're grown, but to their dismay
They're years from where manhood and maturity lay.

The fact that I remember this, thirty years later, speaks volumes about where I was at that time. It's just one from a full three-ring binder of musings on my despair. I asked myself if #22 gave Jason more than I did as #21? Just as Deanie tortured herself over Juanita, I wonder if I had been naïve to think he didn't want sex. Was that the deal breaker? 'Cause, jeez, tell a girl.

I also had the terrible realization that I now had two weeks to find a date for fucking prom. I'd just been dumped by Jason Kidd, so it had to be a *good* date.

There was another black kid that had moved to Pleasanton, a guy named Walter. He was a senior when I was a junior, and he was the running back on the football team. He was really cute, and I decided his looks alone made him my best candidate. Even though my heart was still broken, the pictures would tell a different story. As one of my girlfriends said, "The pictures are going to last a lot longer than your memory."

My vanity about the optics was so consuming, I even convinced myself I had a crush on him. It was him all along. To hell with Jason. I just had to actually talk to Walter first. I decided that the best way to not take another hit to my dignity was to ask him in the most casual, devil-may-care way. If I just ran into him and tossed it off . . .

Walter lived in the Val Vista development, right at the entrance to a cul-de-sac. Saturday afternoon I decided to do a drive-by in my mom's Cutlass Ciera. I went by the house and didn't see anybody around. I was relieved and realized that this was a fool's mission. Worse, I realized that the problem with doing a drive-by in a cul-de-sac is that it's actually two drive-bys. I went around the circle, and as I was a few houses down from passing again, his garage door started to open. Shit.

I gunned the engine and saw his dog flying down the driveway. This crazy dog ran right in front of my car! And I panicked: the teen driver in her mom's Cutlass hit the gas instead of the brake. The last thing I saw was his dog jumping for my mom's hood ornament.

I braked again and looked behind me. The dog was running in circles, fine. He had crouched under my car as I ran over him. Stunt dog. I pulled over and had the shakes. I just did a drive-by of my faux crush's house and almost crushed his dog.

Lesson learned, I just called him. I didn't tell him I was only choosing him for the optics. And karma got me. A week before prom, Walter got the goddamned chicken pox. He was no longer contagious on the big night, but he was covered head to toe in chicken pox scabs.

Through *Splendor in the Grass,* I also saw the way out. In the film—spoiler alert!—Deanie tries to kill herself and her parents have her institutionalized. This is the part you need to see, my brokenhearted one: While she's locked up, Bud goes to Yale and completely blows it. His family loses everything when the stock market crashes and he has to come home and work the ranch. Deanie, sprung from the nuthouse, gets a new dude and goes to see Bud. She's got her rich girl gloves on and she's at their filthy farm with chickens everywhere. There's Bud, working with his dirty hands and hanging out with his new girl, who looks like a mess. You see it in Deanie's face: Whew, I dodged a bullet.

So I say to my patients, the friends going through a bad split, "You are Deanie." We waste our nutty on people who don't deserve it. Wait it out. He's gonna end up dirty with chickens and #22, and you're going to come out on top. Trust me on this one.

PRO TIP: WATCH *WAITING TO EXHALE* AND LIVE IN THE SOUNDTRACK

This is for when things get really messy, as they did for me in my early twenties when I couldn't wait for my Greek-Mexican beauty school dropout to break up with me, and then would do anything to get him back.

Alex and I had moved to L.A. together, against the wishes of his parents, who called him a nigger lover. So there was that little hurdle. I was still at UCLA, and I used my own student loan and my Payless settlement money to finance his beauty school tuition. I hated the Payless money and saw it as blood money, payment for being put in an unsafe situation that allowed me to be raped. Alex had no problem with taking that money, and in many ways saw it as something he had a right to because of what, he said, *we* had been through.

That was bad enough, but then he dropped out. This was a habit. He'd gone to junior college to play basketball and then enrolled at California State University, Northridge, but didn't stay.

Now he didn't even want to finish his hours to get his license from beauty school. All he had left was basketball. Every day, he would just play pickup basketball games at a court in Burbank, right around the Disney studios. Not for money, mind you. There was no hustling in the least. It was just one endless loop of pickup games. His ambition didn't match mine, and as I completely supported him, I began to resent the other costs I was paying for being in an interracial relationship. We got snickers and stares everywhere we went, and his parents had wanted nothing to do with me until they saw the depth of his emotion when I was raped. It just wasn't worth it if I couldn't respect him.

I bought the *Waiting to Exhale* soundtrack just before I drove home to Pleasanton for Christmas break. I listened to it all the way there and all the way back. There are five stages of grieving love, and they are all there in that soundtrack: denial, anger, bargaining, depression, and acceptance. I resolved to end things with Alex through listening to those songs, but I didn't know how I was supposed to leave someone who was so absolutely dependent on me.

In Pleasanton I ran into Keith, who had been a senior at a nearby high school back when I was a freshman. Home for Christmas, we met up at a bar in Old Town Pleasanton. He was a star soccer player who got a scholarship to UCSB, and now he was in law school in San Diego. We hit it off and exchanged information. And we kept talking. He was very much like me if I hadn't had those Omaha summers to undo parts of my assimilation. He was so terminally corny.

I fell in Deep Like with Keith and began lying to Alex about reasons to go to San Diego. On the drives, I listened to my angst soundtrack of Whitney Houston, Chaka Khan, and Toni Braxton. As Toni sang "Let It Flow," I liked the idea of Keith even more. There was never an "Oh my God I want to fuck you" moment. But when you are young you start thinking that if you want to be a grown-up, you need a résumé guy. Someone who looks good on paper. Keith could be that guy for me.

My plan was to become brazen enough about Keith that Alex would break up with me. It's a trick I learned from my dad: you create a bad enough situation that the other half of the partnership just wants out. After all, Alex had always said, "If I ever find out that you're cheating, I'm just gonna leave."

One day I was driving down Wilshire in Westwood, just leaving the UCLA campus in my little Miata. My pager went off—call me Grandma and I'll kill you, but this is how we texted in the olden days. It was Alex.

"911," it read, which is how we kids expressed "Call me back now!" Then the numbers "04," which, upside down, spell out "ho."

"Oh," I said when I read "ho." I pulled into a 76 gas station on Wilshire and went to a pay phone.

"Get. Home. Now" was all Alex said.

I am not joking: My heart was dancing. He knew something and had called me a ho. The nuclear option was in play and I didn't have to do a thing. I listened to Whitney's "Exhale (Shoop Shoop)" on repeat the whole drive on the 405, joy filling me as I practiced my sad face. "Oh my God," I rehearsed in a flat, dull voice. "I can't believe this."

Alex was waiting with an envelope in his hand, addressed to me from Keith. I had two realizations. First, Alex had opened my mail, which just seemed rude. Second, corny Keith had sent a fucking love letter to my house. Just call me, dude.

"Here," Alex said, handing me the letter.

I took my time, reader. I took my sweet damn time wading through that boring-ass letter, and on page 2, I finally got to the portion of the program that sparked this scene.

"I've just got to say," Keith wrote, "the fellatio this weekend was very good."

I nodded a double confirmation—one for Alex now knowing I was cheating and one for Keith being corny enough to say "fellatio." I will say, however, that wanting to be caught cheating is different from having the specifics in print. So I just put on my game face.

"What is that?" Alex said, in a dramatic tearing-me-apart voice.

I paused. "It is what it is."

Nailed it! You know when you say shit and you think, Oooh, that was good. I was really impressed with myself.

Alex was just incredulous and looked like he was about to cry. "Did you suck his dick, Nick?"

Look, I don't know if it was the Seussian title of *Did You Suck His Dick, Nick?* or the stress of the situation, but I just fell out into a lean-on-a-chair fit of laugh-crying.

"I did!" More laughter. "I did! What more proof do you need? Yes, 'fellatio.' I did."

This had to be it, right? It was over now.

Nope.

"I can't live without you," he said. "We can work this out."

Record scratch.

"You said you would leave if I cheated," I said, holding back what I wanted to say: "A deal is a fucking deal. Get OUT."

He started singing "Nobody Knows" by the Tony Rich Project. "Why didn't I say the things I needed to say? How could I let my angel get away . . . ?"

"You need your space to heal," I yelled, cutting him off before the chorus. "I don't deserve you. Go!"

Alex left, and then everything went radio silent. I'd gotten what I wanted, shoop shoop. But then I was stuck with Keith. He came to Black Graduation at UCLA, officially called the Afrikan Graduation Ceremony since its start in 1979. In front of all my cool friends, he gave me a crystal vase as a present. He was suddenly Grandpa to them. They were all taking pictures with it, putting the vase on their heads, pretending to drink booze from it. Then he corrected my grammar. Like the time I said "I think it would be funner to just do that."

"Funner? Is that a word?" he said. "Did you just make that up?"

So that ended that, just about the time I found out that Alex had fucked one of my best friends and was also dating a model and a Janet Jackson dancer. I was stuck with Crystal Vase Grammar Cop, and he had upgraded to a backup dancer? Hell, no. What if Alex was the one and I screwed it up because I was chasing a cornball? What if nobody ever loves me again?

So I became obsessed with what he was doing. Everything he was doing. I went back to the grief side of *Exhale,* with only Whitney's halting breathy voice to help. "Yes, why *does* it hurt . . . so bad, Whitney?"

If you're in the crazy-hurt passage of heartbreak, let's go on this ride together, shall we? One night I decided it made perfect sense to put on all-black clothing and a black knit cap and borrow my friend's car. I drove to Alex's apartment, where he now lived with his old college teammate. I closed the car door softly and skulked my skully-hatted ass into his bushes so I could look in his window. I just wanted to see his face. I wanted to know who he was with. This seemed perfectly rational.

There were no lights on, so when I got to the window, I could see myself reflected in the glass. I looked at my eyes, shining brightly at me.

"You are officially the psycho bitch," I said.

I'm not supposed to be in the bushes looking in someone's window. So I slowly, ever so slowly, crept back to the car like a hapless cat burglar coming up empty-handed.

I could have avoided all this if I just watched Angela Bassett in *Waiting to Exhale*. Angela plays Bernadine, who sets her husband's car ablaze, lamenting all the times she put him first, making herself the background to his foreground. She didn't pay for his beauty school, but she did become his secretary. It's the scene that created the term "Angela Bassett moment," an epic declaration of self-worth that I wanted for my mother and for everyone who realizes they got played. As I watch, I start screaming, and I can do every word. "But the worst, oh the fucking worst," she says, ripping his clothes out of his closet, only to later light the cigarette that will set them and his car ablaze. "The worst thing is that he made me move out here where my children are in school with only one other black kid so they won't be improperly influenced. Well, guess what, John? *You're* the motherfucking improper influence! Get your shit, get your shit, and get out!"

It's the moment where you reclaim your sanity by going insane, the burst of clarity that comes with blind rage. So, let Angela have it for you, breathe in the smoke from the car, and move on with her out of the bushes. In retrospect, I can say to myself, "Are you kidding me? Why would you lose it over that freaking loser?" But I know it doesn't ever feel like that in the moment. It feels reasonable to be in all black wearing a skully as you crouch in someone's bushes. Absolutely fucking reasonable.

PRO TIP: GIVE YOURSELF THE FULL TINA TURNER EXPERIENCE

What's Love Got to Do With It is, of course, based on Tina Turner's memoir, *I, Tina*. After my Greek-Mexican beauty school dropout, I went into full Tina immersion. I watched the movie, I read the book, and I had *that* film's soundtrack on repeat. If she'd put out a Tina Crunch cereal, I would have had it every morning.

I prescribe the Tina combo when you just want the pain to be over. You are about done with the nutty, even though it was supposed to be over months ago, and your instinct for independence needs a shot in the arm. Watch Angela Bassett play Tina finding that fire within her to go from her lowest to being Tina freaking Turner. She tells a divorce judge that she doesn't need anything else but freedom and her name. "I'll give up all that other stuff, but only if I get to keep my name," she says defiantly. "I've worked too hard for it, Your Honor."

Cut to me watching it for the fifteenth time, screaming, "Goddammit, give me my name! I just want my name." When I had my divorce, I went back and watched Tina. I still had my name.

I'm making a lot of jokes to cheer you up, but take this seriously: If you are feeling humiliated and broken by the weight of pain over someone trifling, be Tina. Let yourself be forged in this fire. I, for one, started my adolescence wanting to be Molly Ringwald, but I spent my twenties wanting to be Tina Turner.

As for that craziness I felt, one day I woke up and I just didn't feel it anymore. It left. It took time, but it left. It was as if the crazy was a gas bubble. You're just really uncomfortable and the very core of your body, your stomach and chest, hurts. And then you fart or drop a deuce and the pain leaves you. I promise you, it gets better. You will fart your way to healing, I swear.

PRO TIP: CUSHION THE BLOW WITH SOMEONE ELSE'S BODY

It's always beneficial in a breakup to have somebody else lined up. I really like to move right in and have a Plan B, C, D, and E in place before Plan A has expired.

As you go about this, your best game is honesty. Tell Plan B exactly where your head is at. "Do you want to be here? Yea or nay?" I don't even say, "This is a rebound." Don't even put that much weight on it. It's just fun. Tell them it's like hooking up with someone on vacation. Staycation sex.

It's on them if they think they can change the situation between you to create a lasting arrangement. Let them try, but at least you were very clear about your motivation from the start.

As you refocus your energy on someone else's privates, you save yourself the drudgery of going over in your mind what went wrong. Bitch, you know what went wrong. Unless this is your first guy, you're not that clueless. By your early to mid-twenties, you've been through this a few times, so you gotta know there's a common denominator in these equations—and it's *you*. I, like many women, know what the hell is wrong with me. Whether we choose to do something about it remains to be seen.

I know a lot of people talk about closure, "giving yourself time to mourn." Ehhh. Let's not play these games. I think the whole "pussy moratorium" thing is just some puritanical garbage to keep women chaste. I see it all the time in Hollywood. After the end of a relationship, an actress or famous woman has to publicly announce that her legs will be closed until further notice. Like some exorcist has to come in to flush out the demons from her vagina. Potential suitors, please wait until the little old lady from *Poltergeist* comes out and says, "THIS HOUSE IS CLEAN!"

You will hear, "You really need to work on yourself before you jump right into something else." Oh, please, who's got that kind of time? I got shit to do. I'm trying to work, I'm trying to get home to watch *Scandal,* and I'm trying to get it in. I could get hit by a bus tomorrow, and here I am using this time to work on myself.

By the way, you can work on yourself and still have sex with someone at the same time. Or at least *around* the same time. Your pussy and brain don't have to take turns. Besides, there's a bunch of hours in the day. You can actually get to therapy and go on a date on the same day.

Bonus Pro-tip: Booze Pairings to Heal Heartache

I will keep this short in case you are already reading this book at a bar. There are only two options for drinking your pain away after a breakup: red wine or tequila. Never mix, never worry.

Choose red wine if you'd like a warm hug and maybe a nap. A Malbec is that slightly bitter pal who rallies to say, "There, there, we'll get through this." A Cabernet is a model of efficiency, drinkable with a high alcohol content. With all of its varied flavors, Pinot is the one who'll encourage you to keep a sense of mystery.

But if you want to skip all that and just get to the point where you fuck one of his friends? You go tequila all the way. I prescribe straight, no chaser.

Either way, first round is on me.

twelve

ON MEAN WOMEN
AND GOOD DOGS

One morning in early 2012, I got a call from *Essence* magazine. They wanted to give me the Fierce and Fearless award at their pre-Oscar luncheon in February. I had to give a speech, which I figured would last about thirty seconds. "Thank you," I'd say. "Yay, women."

Then they said I would have five minutes.

Whoa, I thought.

"If you give us your speech we can have it printed," they offered. That made it real. My instinct to protect myself shot up, and I immediately went to standard Hollywood cliché bullshit.

I started writing my speech on my laptop, saving the draft as a file titled "Fierce and Fearless." For days I would just look at the words on my computer screen. How was I supposed to be either of those things? I kept asking myself. I was so afraid that if I told the truth I would face judgment and rejection.

"We live in a town that rewards pretending," I typed. "And I had been pretending to be fierce and fearless for a very long time. I was a victim masquerading as a survivor."

I went to delete those lines, but kept going. "I used to revel in gossip and rumors. And I lived for the negativity inflicted upon my sister actresses or anyone I felt whose shine diminished my own. I took joy in people's pain and I tap-danced on their misery."

It was the most honest I'd ever been in my life. When the day came, I put on the armor of a green vintage Versace above-the-knee dress, and I took a deep breath as I approached the podium.

As I spoke, I felt the room become still. The murmur of chatter and ding of forks against plates stopped as I read my truth. People began to put arms around each other's shoulders, drawing them closer and crying. I stammered just slightly at one point, and I felt a wave of love come at me. These incredible, fierce women were all listening, pulling for me. Oprah Winfrey was there, her mouth wide open. Her seatmate Iyanla Vanzant reached over to close her mouth for her. "I had never heard anyone be that honest in public or private," Oprah said, "about the competition and fierce drive to be seen and succeed in Hollywood."

To be seen.

Leave it to Oprah to get to the heart of the matter. I was desperate just to be seen. I was afraid of anybody else getting attention. Because there's only so much to go around. With Oprah's benediction, people started acting like I was the Messiah and I would lead Hollywood's actresses to the promised land of mutual love. I wasn't ready. "I'm still in my own shit," I said.

And I really was. I had only recently found the courage to get up on that dais and be honest. I had been hiding, sometimes literally. I am someone who physically hides when I am feeling, let's say, stressed in a situation. Behind a garbage can, behind a tree. If I am somewhere and get an attack of the feels, I look for the nearest place to stash myself. I am the Where's Waldo? of emotional availability.

There was a particular moment in my life when I found myself hiding under my bed. I was in my early thirties and my life was a disappointment. My divorce was final, and I decided my career was over because a show I had a lot of hopes for was canceled. I slipped off my bed, looked underneath, and thought, Well, that looks cozy. So I scooted myself in, intending to stay there, oh, I don't know, forever.

My dog Bubba Sparxxx came into the bedroom to investigate my disappearance.

Bubba was a huge dog, about 130 pounds of Mastiff–American bulldog mix, but he was determined to do a marine crawl under that bed to get to me. His path to me was precise, like a longtime soldier carrying out a mission. We did have history. We had found each other in the middle of the night while I was shooting *Cradle 2 the Grave* at Los Alamitos Army Base, near Long Beach, California. It was a night shoot, and at 2 A.M., my costar DMX decided he wanted to buy some dogs. He needed a litter of dogs brought to the set right then. People just stood there, dumbfounded. I said, "I think I can help you."

So I called my then-husband Chris, who knew a guy who bred Royal Bandogs, mastiffs bred specifically with American bulldogs. So Chris called the breeder and this man showed up to the set at 3:45 A.M. with laundry baskets full of puppies. There were probably five or six dogs in total, all of them brown except one little white one. They were all so cute, and DMX picked out two, quickly naming them Pebbles and Bam Bam.

"You can take one of the dogs, too," the breeder said to me. "You got me the sale."

They were all adorable, but the little white one with a few brown spots seemed to call to me. I picked him up, round and white like a seal, and looked in his little amber eyes.

"Aw, you have an outie," I said, rubbing his little stomach.

"That's actually a hernia," said the breeder. "He's the runt. The hernia will either retract as he grows or he'll need surgery."

We needed each other.

"He's the one," I said. I named him Bubba Sparxxx after the white country-rapper, and he became my soul mate and best friend. He could tell when I came home frustrated. He'd stay very chill and wait for me to come around, without being pushy or needy. If I had big news, he was hyped about it before I even had a chance to articulate it to him. Whenever I had parties and he had the sense that some plus-one might be the least bit shady, he wouldn't let them walk around the house. Bubba never growled at anyone who wasn't foul.

He was just super intuitive. Which is how he knew to be under the bed. This huge lug of a dog crawled under the bed to look me in the eye. We regarded each other for a long time.

"Is this what we're doing today?" he said with his eyes. "Okay. It's cool, I just want to know. 'Cause I'm under here."

When I didn't respond, he began to lick my face. It was one of those moments where you just realize, Well, this is the most pathetic scene ever.

"Bubba," I said, "I think this is what the lady was talking about."

The lady was a trainer and life coach who had been hounding me at events. I had literally run from her at red carpets. It was like she could see through the façade. "When you're ready, call me," she'd say, pointing at me like a black female Tony Robbins. "You've got my number. You'll know when you're ready."

I reached up to get my cell from the bed. I had put her in my phone as Coach.

"Gabrielle," she answered, like she'd been waiting.

"I think this is what you were talking about when you said I'd know when I was ready."

WE MET IN A GYM ON A RAINY NOVEMBER DAY. SHE IMMEDIATELY PUT BOX-ing gloves on me. I started punching the heavy bag, going strong to impress her.

"What's on your Happy List?" Coach asked.

"My what?"

"You gotta do a Happy List," she said. "Tell me the things that make you happy."

I stalled, hitting harder. She asked me again, pointedly this time. Like a drill sergeant. "What makes you happy?"

I had nothing. I couldn't think of a single thing or single recent time I'd even been happy. Right away, I felt like I was failing a test. I started to cry, and my heart raced as my anxiety kicked in. I couldn't even do this right. My arms started to get numb from punching, so I slowed down.

"Come on," she yelled. "Give me three things and I'll let you stop punching the bag."

I kept punching, finally saying through gritted teeth, "Real butter."

Punch.

"Ground beef."

Punch. What else? Punch.

"Imitation crab," I said.

Punch.

I stopped, exhausted. Coach was looking at me with a mix of disgust and concern.

"Bitch," she said, "did you say imitation crab?"

In my mind, it was the best parts of the crab but so much less expensive.

"You don't even love the real thing?" she asked. "Can we just start there? The fact that they're all food items, we'll get to that later. Let's stop here, because there's so much more that we gotta get to before we can even think about nutrition."

She gave me the homework of writing down ten things that made me happy. We agreed to meet twice a week.

I went home and I couldn't get past the three. Real butter, ground beef, and imitation crab meat. I went back to her with the same three things the following week.

She shook her head at me again, and that session we didn't work out at all. We just sat in the gym and she threw out questions, dissecting the smallest pleasures of life.

"Do you like sunsets?" she asked. "Do you like sunrises?"

Even that made me cry. I didn't know.

"Um, uh," I ugly-cried. "Sunsets."

"Do you like crushed ice?" she asked. "Whole cubes?"

I panicked again, weighing the merits of both. "Um, when there's a bowl of ice . . ." I paused. I had something. "I like really, really cold Coronas."

"That's five," she shouted. She was the Annie Sullivan to my Helen Keller, helping me make sense of my world. I couldn't think of any more.

"You can't even think of ten things that make you happy," she said. "What made you think you were ready for marriage? How is someone else supposed to make you happy if *you* don't even know what makes you happy?"

We started in November, and by January I had finally found my ten things. Bubba was on the list. Before that, I couldn't say he made me happy because he was such a good dog I didn't think I deserved him. Coach and I started examining that kind of thinking, too, and started unraveling my life decisions from there.

One night I took Coach along with me to a party. By then I was less guarded with her and feeling bold. We were in a room at the party and I started holding court, using my well-honed ability to turn a phrase to tear down an actress who wasn't present. It was well honed because I used to feel I had to do it for survival, but now it was like I was killing for sport. As I ripped this absent woman to shreds, I felt like I was being fed as these people laughed and looked at me with faces that said, "More, more."

When I was done, there was nothing left of my target.

"How did that change your life?" Coach asked me after my performance.

"Excuse me?"

"Did you get her guy?" she asked. "Did you get her job? Is your house bigger now?"

I looked down at the ground, completely called out.

"What positive happened in your life because you tore this woman down?" she asked. "And, by the way, you showed exactly how much power she has over you because you spent an hour talking about her to a roomful of people."

I realized what I had been doing. When you're in a place where you don't know what makes you happy, it's really easy to be an asshole. I put other people's pain on my Happy List.

I went home that night, and sure enough, my house was not bigger for tearing that woman down. Bubba came to greet me and we sat in the living room.

"I'm trying, Bubba," I said. "You weren't always perfect, either."

Bubba was in fact a terror until he was two and a half, a whirling dervish of energy. My husband and I were with him in the park when we realized we needed to have him trained. A little boy was calling to him, so Bubba ran down an incline at full speed. His legs got away from him and he rolled into the kid like a bowling ball. The kid's mom thought it was funny, thank God, but then, as the boy was on the ground, Bubba sniffed him and then peed on him.

The first time we worked with a dog trainer, he bit the trainer. Which was a blessing, because that led me to trainers at a ranch that bills itself as the Disneyland of dog parks. They helped Bubba become the best dog in the history of dogs.

He changed. So could I.

AFTER MY *ESSENCE* SPEECH, THE MEDIA LATCHED ON TO THE MEAN-GIRL narrative of what I was saying. They missed the point, because it's not like I was some kid slamming people into lockers or spreading rumors about a sophomore. I was talking about being a woman. It's not like you age out of bullshit. It just sort of shape-shifts.

Because I was a mean woman, I can spot them. Game recognizes game, right? You encounter them every day if you work with other people, period. Whether you're a teacher, a lawyer in a large firm, or a stay-at-home mom. There is an epidemic now of people "being real" when they're being anything but. It's the person who loves being "someone" who notices every little thing wrong with what you say, do, wear, or think, and has to point it out. Those mean women, and mean men, affect people's opportunities and experiences, at work or with their children.

When I see negative comments about me online, if I have time I will go down the rabbit hole of social media to see how great the life of the troll really is. Because you never know, maybe they're right. Maybe they have something to teach me or for me to aspire to. I've done it countless times, Instastalking, Twitter stalking. Never once have I learned something from someone who talked shit. If anything, it's "Baby, you really don't want to put a bull's-eye on your back." But so many people really love the attention they get by trolling. It's a temporary cure for their invisibility.

The problem is, there's always an audience for negativity. There could be someone with a bullhorn screaming, "I've got a beautiful script here that gives a deeper insight into the human experience." And few in a crowd would pause. And then someone says "I've got Jennifer Lawrence's nudes," and a line will form. Negativity and the exploitation of other people's pain drive so much of our culture and conversation.

I know that, but I can still get caught up in my feelings. Recently I had an absolute complete meltdown over something said about me online. It was a castoff of a line, a joke the woman posted to get "oh the shade" likes and eyeballs. But I became fixated on it, imagining what I would say to her if she said it to my face, and knowing she never ever would.

I was with a friend when I saw it and held up my phone for her to see the post. I was full of "get this bitch" bravado, but she took my forearm and gently lowered it. Looking me in the eye, she said: "An empress does not concern herself with the antics of fools."

She smiled, so I smiled. That kindness, one empress to an-other, one woman to another, released me from the bullshit.

BUBBA DESERVES A CODA, BECAUSE HE'S THE ONE WHO GOT ME HERE. HE remained a good judge of character to the end. When Dwyane first came around, Bubba was apprehensive. One day, two full years into our relationship, the three of us were in the park and Bubba jumped up on the table where D was sitting. Bubba looked D in the eye, just like he'd done to me that morning under the bed. Then Bubba leaned in to nuzzle him. He was saying, "I like this guy."

From where I'm writing this, I can see Bubba's giant paw print in plaster. Yes, I really am that dog person. When he was twelve, he was given a year to live. By the grace of modern medicine and my pocketbook, we were able to keep him alive until he was thirteen. At one point we were thinking about getting him a new kidney. You had to agree to adopt the kidney-donor dog and com-mit to flying your sick dog up to UC Davis. Like I said, I'm that dog person. But we decided Bubba was old and it would all be too much to put two dogs through. When he finally passed, my whole circle went into mourning. If you knew Bubba, you loved Bubba.

When I call upon my ancestors and people who've passed to get me through something, I talk to him, too.

He saw me at my worst and my meanest, and he loved me anyway.

thirteen

WARNING: FAMOUS VAGINAS GET ITCHY, TOO

Dwyane and I are alone in the car outside the Walgreens in Miami.

"Just go in there," I say.

"Nope."

"You know what I use," I say. "You're in and out."

"You do it."

The subject is, of course, tampons, which I do not want to buy. Whenever I am in the feminine care section of any pharmacy, no matter how incognito I go, it's like an alert goes out. "Attention customers, Gabrielle Union has her period. Go say hi!"

Because if he goes in, yeah, he gets swarmed, but the response is "What a catch! He buys his wife tampons!" If I go in, whether it's a light day or it seems like I've been shot in my vagina, that intimate knowledge is sought out. Having knowledge about someone tending to her vagina is like sneaking a *Playboy*. "I saw Gabrielle Union buying *tampons!*" I'm a bleeding spectacle.

So you can imagine how unprepared I was when I suspected I had a yeast infection. 'Cause you know how loaded that is. Women aren't allowed to just get yeast infections as, say, part of the body's natural defense mechanism. We have to have caused it in some way—by wearing our underwear too tight, not changing our tampons often enough. Men can have jock itch for days and never once have to explain why.

I felt the first twinge while I was on a late-night flight to visit a guy I was dating before I married D. Let's call him Bachelor 1. B1 was extremely hung, and at the time he was sharing a beach house with his huge penis in Miami. The plan was that I would get to his place Friday night and he would arrive the next morning. This is also a guy who didn't believe women pooped, so a "Hey, shucks, I have a yeast infection" conversation was out of the question.

"Get thee to a CVS," I told myself upon landing.

It was about 1:00 A.M. by the time I stashed my bags at his place and set out for the 24-7 drugstore on Miami Beach. Here's what's great about a pharmacy by the beach in the middle of the night: nothing. It is teeming. Full. You think you are going to find it hopping with horny teens buying condoms, but it's a drunk in every aisle, white boys trying to figure out which cold medicines will make them higher, and, here and there, a crying girl hobbling along on one heel, looking for flip-flops. And in this particular outpost, one Gabrielle Union, trying to score some Monistat under cover of night.

I marched in, determined to be a grown woman seeing to her

over-the-counter vaginal cream needs. I was about three steps in when, I swear, every head in the place turned. My eyes darted to a display by the register.

"Twizzlers!" I said, striding over and picking up that bag like it was just the thing I was after and I couldn't believe my luck.

The guy at the register was a heavyset twenty-something who the managers probably thought looked intimidating enough to work the night shift. "Just these Twizzlers," I said, scanning the candy display in case I had any other last-minute sugar needs.

"Are you . . ." he said.

"Yes," I said. "How are *you?*"

"Do you want a bag?"

"No," I said. "I'm good."

Back in my car, I called a girlfriend on the West Coast. She always had an answer for everything. "Listen, I need to figure out a home remedy for a yeast infection."

"Cranberry juice," she said, not missing a beat. Dr. Quinn, Beverly Hills Medicine Woman. "Like, a boatload."

"On it," I replied. I waltzed right back into that CVS, waving hi to my register friend, as I pointed to the refrigerated section as if I had suddenly become parched. There were fifteen-ounce and sixty-four-ounce bottles of Cran-Apple, which I thought of as Regular and Maximum Strength. "Go big or go home," I said to myself, grabbing the sixty-four with one hand.

"Thirsty," I said to my register friend.

I drove back to B1's house, guzzling the cranberry juice the whole way. I still felt that now familiar and becoming-more-intense-by-the-minute burning, so I called my Dr. Quinn again.

"911, what's your emergency?" she said.

"When will it work?" I asked.

"You got a low-sugar one, right?"

"I got Cran-Apple."

"Gab, that's pure sugar. It will only make it worse!"

"Why didn't you tell me?" I yelled. "I just drank a half gallon of the shit." Malpractice!

"I think we need to try yogurt," she said. "You got to get some yogurt up in there. It will help."

"Stay with me," I said. I ran to B1's fridge and scanned the paltry bachelor contents.

"Okay!" I yelled, grabbing a Dannon vanilla. The flower of the vanilla plant beckoned me back to feminine health. "Doctor, I'll call you back," I said.

I wiggled out of my jeans and laid paper towels on the kitchen floor. Here goes nothing, I thought. I did my best, slathering the cold yogurt all around my vagina, but I couldn't quite get it inside to where the action needed to be.

Still lying on the floor, I reached again for the phone.

"I can't get it in," I nearly screamed. "It's too thick." The irony of saying this in the home of big-dicked B1 was not lost on me.

"You can't, like, spoon it in there?"

"No," I said. "And I can't make a syringe out of a ballpoint pen. I'm not freaking MacGyver."

She paused, as if she were consulting her witchy book of spells. "You need to make a tampon kind of thing," she said. "Suck the yogurt into a straw, insert it in like a tampon, and you can squeeze the yogurt up in there."

I went through every drawer in the kitchen. "What grown-up keeps straws?" I asked.

"I don't know your life," she said.

"You now know more than most."

"Well, go get one," she said. "A big, wide one. Like the ones at McDonald's."

I now took my yogurt-covered vagina to the McDonald's by the Delano that was open all night. Inside, there was a long line of the drunk people who weren't at CVS, the ones who had consumed enough alcohol at 2:30 A.M. to give up on their diets and give in to their cravings for French fries. The Girl Scout in me felt like I had to wait in line and at least buy a drink, but soon enough people started to recognize me.

So I jumped off the line and went right to the straw dispenser. I ripped the paper off and held it to my eye like a pirate with a telescope. "That should do it," I said aloud turning to see an employee stopping the work of sweeping to stare at me.

"Hi," I said, a little too loudly, grabbing a second one to ensure the sterility of this new medical tool. "You have a nice night."

While driving, I tried to calm my frayed nerves by imagining what that woman would tell her friends the next day. "Gabrielle Union was in here high as a kite looking for a coke straw!" Miraculously, this line of thinking did little to calm my frayed nerves.

Back at B1's, I learned that sucking yogurt through a straw is a little tougher than you'd think. But I did it. And once again I lay on the floor to squeeze the yogurt in. Whether it was psychosomatic or just psycho, I immediately felt like it was working. I hit redial.

"Is this the Dannon help line?" I asked.

"Dannon?" she said. "I hope you used plain."

"Shit, he only had vanilla."

"Christ," she said, laughing, "what is wrong with you?"

"That," I said, peering down at my yogurt vagina, "is a very fair question."

The absurdity of the whole night washed over me and I finally laughed. I was so scared of being judged for being a woman with a yeast infection that I was willing to put myself through any number of humiliations. I waltzed into a CVS, twice, and never left with what I needed. I stole a straw from McDonald's in the middle of the night! All to avoid my register friend knowing. I resolved that that would be the last night I found myself lying on some guy's kitchen floor shoving yogurt up my hoohah. I would live a more authentic life.

To a point. B1 rolled up the next morning, and he greeted me with a kiss.

"I ate your yogurt," I blurted out, trying very hard to seem not at all suspicious.

"Okaaaay," he said.

"I ate it," I said. "Just ate it."

He looked at me like I was crazy. Which I was. I mean, what else does one do with yogurt?

fourteen

GROWN-ASS-WOMAN BLUES

We are the ladies who lunch.

I have two girlfriends around my age, Michelle and Gwen, who I meet every few months or so for lunch when I am in Los Angeles. We are grown-ass women, and we are the only ones who understand each other's grown-ass problems.

"I apologize in advance for looking like a robot," I said when I came to the table at our last gathering. "I threw my neck out dancing."

"How?" asked Gwen.

"I tried to whip my hair back."

You see? Grown-ass problems.

"At least you're having fun," Michelle said, with Gwen silently nodding. They are both single, Gwen newly so after a twelve-year marriage. Michelle is awesome, but she never found anyone. That's the word she uses: "Anyone." Not even "the right guy." She is fun, and smart, and pretty, and she told me she feels invisible when she goes out. She sees what happens to the women her age who fight against invisibility to try to stand out. The ones who raid their daughters' closets or the ones who try so hard to lead a boisterous *Real Housewives* camera-ready life with a steady supply of booze. They at least draw attention, if fleeting, but Michelle doesn't want that. She's stuck, because if she does what comes natural to her and keeps it low key, guys won't even notice her. But if she shows she wants a relationship, men will flee.

"I have to act like I don't want it," she told me, "and then act surprised when it doesn't happen."

Meanwhile, Gwen is hot as hell and knows it. She got out of her marriage and went right to the bars. But that doesn't mean the puzzle isn't complicated for her as well.

"The men our age won't look at me," she said. "And I'm this weird science experiment for younger guys, chasing older pussy."

Single or partnered, successful or striving, we grown-ass women of the world share the feeling that we're all in an experiment that no one is particularly interested in watching except us. I see us all grasping at the straws of staying present in our lives and families and careers. Who knows how we will fare? I can only speak to my experience, so that is what I will do. To wit: Can an actress age in Hollywood and continue to work? All previous research has shown the answer to be a hearty NO, but it seems for my peers that so far, we are working way more than then we did in our twenties. But it's the opposite for my nonactor friends as they get older. Their competition for new jobs is younger people who make less and don't have families that they have to take off for. Oh shit, they say, we're those people that *we* pushed out. Women are told to "lean in." Yeah, right. "Lean in so I can push you over."

At lunch, Michelle told us about "the new black" at her company. "She's young and dope," she said. "And she's talking to me about dating. I'm like, 'Fuck you and your dating problems. You're me twenty years ago when I used to get dick.'"

We all nodded, except me, on account of my neck. I kind of moved forward.

"I have no patience for her," she said.

"That's because even though there are all these things that are supposed to be marked against her," said Gwen, "her skin color, the fact that she's a woman—none of that matters next to the fact that you're older. She gets your spot."

"Yeah," I said, swiveling my whole body to look at Michelle, "but who better to help her navigate that than you?"

"I'm not training the competition to do my job," said Michelle. "Would you?"

Um, no. And I thought about my own hypocrisy: Just the night before I had attended a pre-Oscar cocktail party for women in film. There I had met a young actor named Ryan Destiny. She had appeared in the Lee Daniels series *Star*. I had heard that she looked like me. I saw her in person and she looks like I literally gave birth to her. Gab 2.0, only better.

"Oh my God," she said. "I am finally meeting you. This is so amazing."

"What are you, twelve?"

"Twenty-two."

"Shit."

"I admire you so much," she said. "If you could mentor me . . ."

Bitch, fuck you, I thought. You want me to mentor you? The press is literally calling you the next Gabrielle Union . . . "except she can sing and dance!"

I smiled, and the photographers came over. They needed to document this moment of "Look who's old!" And I get it, because I have a reputation for never aging. And God, do I love that rep. But as the flashbulbs went off, I was suddenly terrified that the ruse would be up. Dorian Gray, turning to dust as she is photographed next to someone called the next Gabrielle Union.

Looking at Michelle and Gwen, I remembered not just the fear of suddenly looking decrepit next to this young woman, but the wave of panic that if I imparted my knowledge, I would lose in some kind of way. Would I be aiding and abetting myself into forced retirement and exile by helping this drop-dead gorgeous woman? A better, hotter, more talented version of me twenty-five years ago?

To be the women my friends and I are supposed to be, we are supposed to support the women coming up behind us. It's just hard to do that happily when you're finally at the table, and you feel any moment someone's going to come up, tap your shoulder, and say, "I think you're in my seat." It took me a long time to get that seat, goddammit. I'm not ready to move over just yet.

This fear resonates through every industry. For my friends in corporate America there's a reasonable fear about "mentoring" young women to be their best selves if that means they could take your job. Younger women are literally dangled in front of their older peers as a you-better-act-right stick to keep older, more experienced women in line. Because we've all seen a pal replaced for a younger, cheaper model with lower expectations and more free time for overtime or courting clients. Modern business is set up to squeeze out women who "want it all"—which is mostly just code for demanding equal pay for equal work. But the more empowered women in the workforce, the better. The more that women mentor women, the stronger our answer is to the old-boys' network that we've been left out of. We can't afford to leave any woman behind. We need every woman on the front lines lifting each other up . . . for the good of all of us and the women who come behind us.

It's tough to get past my own fears, so I have to remind myself that this is an experiment, to boldly go where no grown-ass woman has gone before. When we refuse to be exiled to the shadows as we mature, we get to be leaders who choose how we treat other women. If I don't support and mentor someone like Ryan, that's working from a place of fear. And if I put my foot on a rising star, that's perpetuating a cycle that will keep us all weak. The actresses in the generation before mine were well aware of their expiration dates, and they furiously tried to beat the clock before Hollywood had decided their milk had gone bad. Yes, there were some supremely catty women in Hollywood who actively spread rumors about younger stars so that they could stay working longer. But there were also way more amazing women who thought big picture. They trusted that if they uplifted each other, in twenty years, there might just be more work to go around. Women like Regina King, Tichina Arnold, Tisha Campbell-Martin, and Jenifer Lewis went out of their way to mentor and educate the next generation. That empowerment is why we have Taraji P. Henson, Kerry Washington, Viola Davis, Sanaa Lathan, and more starring in TV shows and producing films. That creates yet *more* work for the next woman up. That's what can happen when we mentor and empower. That's what happens when we realize that any joy we find in the next woman's pain or struggle is just a reflection of our own pain: "See how hard this is? Do you appreciate how difficult this is?" Instead, I want to heal her and me.

Christ. First a stiff neck and then I have to have this moral code? Nobody said being a grown-ass woman was easy.

fifteen

GET OUT OF MY PUSSY

I decided to finally go get this persistent pain in my hip checked. And my doctor in Miami, who happens to be a friend's dad and one of the world's leading neurosurgeons, told me to go for an MRI and X-ray at the hospital. Coincidentally, another fake round of "Gab's Knocked Up!" stories was making the rounds at exactly the same time. The photo evidence was that I'd worn a coat. In Toronto. At night. In winter. For sure, knocked up.

So here I am, walking into a hospital—right in the heart of Miami-Dade County—and everyone's clocking me. By the time I get to the imaging center, I've run through a gauntlet of knowing glances and "I see you" smiles. I know exactly what all these strangers are thinking. And there, as I am filling out the forms, is the question: "Are you pregnant?" I check "No."

"Head to room two and wait," says the lady behind the desk.

I go in, disrobe, put on the tissue-paper-thin gown, and sit on the table, tapping my feet on the step.

You know how, when you're in the doctor's office, each time the door opens, you think, This is it! and you raise your head expectantly, with a half smile that says, "I can make pleasantries but I will also take your role seriously"? This happens a couple of times.

The first time, there's a knock on the door and a nurse walks in. "I just want to double-check," she says, studying me. "We ask all women this: Are you pregnant?"

"Nope, it was on the form. I marked no."

"Okay. I just wanted to make sure."

Not a minute goes by before a different woman pops her head in.

"Yeah, okay. So, just want to make *sure*," she says, drawing out "sure" as she looks me up and down. "Um, you've got no hairpins in your hair, no metal on. Your earrings are out?"

"Yes."

"Are you pregnant?"

"Nope. Not pregnant. Put it on the form."

"Well, hey, yeah, just making sure."

Finally, the X-ray tech arrives, and my hip and I are ready for our MRI close-up.

Ah, but my uterus is not done stealing the show. Because two *more* women walk in. How many damn people work here?

"Just want to make sure . . ." says the tall one. "You're not pregnant?"

Now I am just sad.

"No."

The shorter woman pats my leg in a rocking, petting motion.

"I just want to make sure you're not pregnant," she chimes in. "Because we really need to know. Because—"

Then I am angry.

"NOPE. NOT PREGNANT," I say, loudly, my heart beating fast and my arms becoming numb from anger.

"I filled out the form. You're now the fourth person to ask me. I am *not* pregnant. I know what the Web sites say. I'm telling you I'm not pregnant. If I was, I wouldn't fucking be here."

They quickly leave. And I lie there, thinking about how some Internet clickbait affected my medical care, thinking about what they will say about that girl Gabrielle Union, who came into the office today and is actually such a bitch.

When it is over, I do my best not to look at anyone. I keep my head down and put my sunglasses on as protection. I am almost to the door of the waiting room when another patient looks up from her magazine. She smiles and I smile back.

"You and Wade," she says, "would have such pretty babies."

I am out of the office before the tears come.

YES, DWYANE AND I WOULD HAVE SUCH PRETTY BABIES. BUT I HAVE HAD eight or nine miscarriages. In order to tell you the exact number, I would have to get out my medical records. (I am also not sure what the number is where you start to think I must be nuts to keep trying.)

I never wanted children before Dwyane. I was afraid to be attached to a man for life if our relationship didn't work out. After D got custody of the three children we raise, I was bursting with joy at every milestone—every basket scored and tough homework assignment completed. I was fulfilled raising children, a joy I never saw coming. Wanting to have babies with

Dwyane was a natural desire built on that joy. Dwyane wanted children with me for a long time before I was fully on board. For me, it was just a maybe, but one day we were with a friend's daughter and she smiled at me. My ovaries literally hurt. And I knew it was time.

For three years, my body has been a prisoner of trying to get pregnant—either been about to go into an IVF cycle, in the middle of an IVF cycle, or coming out of an IVF cycle. I have endured eight failed IVF cycles, with my body constantly full of hormones, and as you've probably figured out by now, yes, I am constantly bloated from these hormones. (It also means I have forgotten my normal baseline emotional reaction to any given situation, and have no idea whether it would resemble my I'm-going-to-hop-off-the-roof reaction.)

For as long as I can remember now, Dwyane and I have lived in this state of extended expectation. Did it take? Is the embryo normal or abnormal? Will I stay pregnant? We are always in some stage, waiting for some news, some sign that we can move on to the next stage. This child we want to have has been loved even as an idea. Each attempt at IVF is a loving action. So we remain here, bursting with love and ready to do anything to meet the child we've both dreamed of.

Many of our friends have had their marriages end with the stress that comes with fertility issues and the accompanying feelings of insecurity and failure, not to mention the testing and retesting, defining and redefining, of your identity as a woman. And this whole deal has wreaked havoc on my social life. I now hate going to baby showers, but the invitations are *constant*. I find myself making up excuses to avoid them. I hate hanging out with mothers who constantly talk about their kids—and what mother doesn't love to talk about her kids? (Well, actually, I do have some mom friends who can't stand their kids most of the time. Them, I like!)

People who know about my fertility issues often hand their babies to me to hold, or text me pictures of babies ("to keep your hope alive!" they say). Nobody seems to think that's insensitive, or maybe hard for me. So, no, I will not look at your Instagram if it's full of babies. Though D and I did enjoy the video a friend sent of her toddler sitting on the toilet and taking a crap—her face wrinkling with effort, then suddenly melting into surprise and relief. Comic gold! We watched it seventy-six times.

I did force myself to go to one baby shower recently, because I knew the woman had struggled with IVF. I wanted a winner's insight. I wanted to know what had pushed her to the finish line. "I sat my ass down," she said. "I quit my job and I stayed home and sat my ass down. That's all I focused on. That's all I did."

"That's all?" I wanted to say. "You gave up the work that you love?"

That's all.

Unfortunately, I kind of function as a single-income household. I may not support the family I've created with D, but I have several households of various family members I am alone responsible for. People assume I have a rich husband who pays for everything, practically giving me a salary. I don't, and I don't want that. So not working is simply not an option for me. And I know it's not an option for many women who want an opportunity to be a parent. It's awesome if that works in your life, and many people have assumed I can go this route, but the bank is weird about wanting their money. Those mortgages don't pay themselves. Maybe not asking my rich husband to pay all my bills makes me selfish and not mother material. But if I did that, I'd already feel like I failed as a mother.

DURING ANOTHER RECENT PREGNANCY RUMOR, I HAD TO DO A PRESS line, which is what you see when a celebrity is talking to a bunch of reporters at an event. *Ocean Drive,* a Miami-based magazine, was having a big party celebrating my being on their cover. I was happy to do it because I liked the article and the accompanying pictures. At the event, the editor of the magazine comes up.

"Oh my God, I loved #periodwatch," he says. It was the hashtag I created for my bloating.

I laugh. "Thanks."

He looks down. "I see you have a crop-top on tonight."

"This is my 'I swear to you, I am not pregnant' outfit," I joke.

It works. Reporters can tell I am not pregnant. Habeas corpus. Present the body. But it allows for a different question instead, posed by a gaggle of perfectly nice-looking people holding iPhones and tape recorders to my face: "Do you guys want to have kids?"

To avoid getting angry, I pivot toward what I think is a joke. "Have you ever asked my husband that question? Or any man?" Crickets. So I keep going. "'What's happening in your uterus?' 'How do you balance it all?'" hypothetical Reporter Me asks Celebrity Me. I pause, less joking now, my brittle anger just peeking through. "Until you ask my husband those same questions, I just can't answer them anymore."

But I can't stop. I can't help myself.

"Do you know why no one asks men how they balance it all? It's because there is no expectation of that. Bringing home money is enough. We don't expect you to be anything more than a provider, men. But a working woman? Not only do you have to bring home the bacon and fry it up, you gotta be a size double-zero, too. You've got to volunteer at the school, you've got to be a sex kitten, a great friend, a community activist. There are all these expectations that we put on women that we don't put on men. In the same way, we never inquire about what's happening in a man's urethra. 'Low sperm count, huh? That why you don't have kids? Have you tried IVF?'"

I have no takers on my rant. I am off the script and there is no editor alive who will use those lines in a caption or post about "Gabrielle's Baby Dreams." It reminds me of the time I did another press line with an actress who happened to know one of the reporters pretty well.

"How do you stay in such great shape?" asked the reporter.

"You know I don't eat," cracked my actress friend.

"No, I need something I can use," said the reporter.

"Oh." The actress thought for a second. "I eat broiled salmon and chicken with a lot of steamed veggies. After a while, you just really crave healthy food."

There you go: There's a script. You follow it. I mean, can you imagine if I said I didn't want kids? Say I answered "Do you and Dwyane want kids?" with "No." A woman in the public eye who doesn't want kids? She-devil. You probably kick puppies. And if you say, "Yes, I would like to have kids," they ask, "When are you starting? Have you had trouble? Are you facing infertility? What's wrong with your uterus? Do you have vaginal issues?" Wanting and not having opens you to all these rude, insensitive, prying questions that people ask. And if you do a full open kimono and say, "Here's the deal. I am doing IVF," the questions just get more personal, deeper. "Are you pregnant this week? This month? How did this cycle work out?" "Is your estrogen rising?" "How can I watch you on *Being Mary Jane* if I don't know the plans you have for your uterus?"

It's as if the whole world has a form, and they just really, really need to know if I am pregnant.

I want to scream, "Get out of my pussy! Just. Get. The. Fuck. Out."

That's the real story. Gabrielle Union's Baby Hopes: "Everyone Needs to Get Out of My Pussy!"

sixteen

AND GABRIELLE UNION AS . . . THE STEPMOTHER

My husband Dwyane has three sons, and in our home we are raising his two older sons, Zion, nine, and Zaire, fifteen, and also Dwyane's sixteen-year-old nephew, Dahveon, whom we call Dada. I am freakishly devoted to these boys. Zion is a fourth-grade genius and a born entertainer. He's me after a couple of drinks, making smart-ass comments and entertaining people. Dada and Zaire are both freshmen and girl crazy. Dada is Mr. Cool, letting friends seek him out, while Zaire is hyperconscious of the people around him. He is receptive to kindness and he is the one who will call you out if you're dismissive. He is desperate to make us proud, and one of my jobs as a stepmother is to remind him how smart and amazing he is. These boys are totally worthy of all the devotion I can offer.

When I first met the boys, I just wanted to be authentic. "I'm a cool motherfucker," I said to myself, checking my teeth in the mirror in the minutes before the introduction. "People like me." It was like we were all on a blind date. "Where are you from? What are your hobbies? What are your favorite movies?" And on we went.

As our relationship grew, I was determined to never try to be BFFs with the boys. I did my best to be a cool, reasonable, consistent adult. That's my advice to you stepparents out there. Whatever it is that you are, just be consistent. You can't be the cool permissive hippie one day and the disciplinarian the next. And to all current or potential stepmothers: unless the mother is dead or in jail—and even then—it's just a mistake to even try to scoot into her place. No one wants their mother replaced, whether she's Mother Teresa or a serial killer.

The boys were in on it when Dwyane proposed to me in December 2013. We all went to brunch in Miami and then the guys told me they wanted to go on a tour of our new house, which was still under construction. I say under construction, but it was more like a few pieces of wood and some nails.

"Are you gonna do your hair?" Dwyane asked me several times. "Are you gonna put on makeup?"

"To go to a construction site?" I asked. "No."

When we got there, the boys ran ahead of us to stand by what would eventually be our pool. "We want to do a presentation for you," said Zion. I thought they were going to do some kind of skit.

"Turn around," said Zaire.

So Dwyane and I faced away from the boys.

"Okay, we're ready," they said in unison.

The boys were all there with a sign. "Nickie, will you marry us?"

"Oh God, D," I said, thinking the boys were doing this on

their own. They had been after us to get married for two years. "This is awkward," I said, turning to Dwyane.

He was down on one knee with a ring.

"Will you marry us?"

"Oh," I said. "Oh. This is a thing. You guys are serious. Yes. Of course, yes!"

I love that they had agency in asking me to join the family. I never wanted to be the party crasher. The boys would have been especially vulnerable to someone trying to manipulate them because, as kids being raised by a male figure in a world that valorizes mothers as the sole models of nurturing, they all love the idea of "moms." If "traditional" moms had trading cards, they would have all of them. "The Cookie Baker." "The Classroom Volunteer." I don't fit into a traditional role, and I have too much respect for myself and these boys to attempt to fake it. They worship my mom, who they call Grammy, and my dad's wife, Nana to them. These women take being grandmothers very seriously, going to every school play and recital they can. They don't miss many.

But I do. A lot of events happen when I am literally out of state, at work. It doesn't matter why—all kids know is that you're missing it. It's even harder for D. He misses things because it's a game day, or he has practice. Even if he is in town, his work hours are not like anybody else's. He doesn't have the luxury of taking off early or having someone cover his shift. There are periods of time when neither of us is present, and this is not what either of us wants. As much as I try to be consistent, I'm often just absent. It's shockingly easy to parent by text or apps like Marco Polo or WhatsApp. But that feels lazy, and the whole time I'm using any of them I am thinking, I'm failing them. I'm failing them. I'm failing them.

I wish I had a job where the boys could see me leave for work in the morning and come home at night. They could watch me work on my lines and be a producer. I film *Being Mary Jane* in Atlanta, and I do movies wherever the good work is. I'm gone for a week, then swoop in for thirty-six hours of in-your-face time before flying out again. Even when I do get an extended break, they have the real lives of teenagers. They have family to visit and tournaments to play.

As I beat myself up about this, I realize that society does not provide great models of black women as nurturers of black children. Maybe as caregivers to white children, or the sassy, sage, asexual sidekick to a long-suffering white woman. Or maybe the "beat some sense into you" black mother we've seen in viral videos, but never as loving, kind, sensitive, or nurturing to black children. Recently our family was in our living room in our new house in Chicago. I was on the cream couch with my feet up on D's lap. He was just home from practice and telling a story about the ride home. It was a brutally cold day, about five degrees below zero, and his driver stopped at a light. They watched a woman get her toddler out of the car and put him out on the street while getting her stuff out of the trunk. The kid was basically standing in traffic, and without a coat. The light changed, but D's driver wouldn't go until the kid was safely out of the street. D nearly got out to help.

The woman then put on her own coat, finally took the child's hand, and proceeded to walk down the street still holding his coat. Now, I think we've all been with small children, and yes, getting them in and out of cars is a pain in the ass, but still. It was freezing—put the coat on the kid.

Zaire and Dada both said at the exact same time, "She was black, right?"

D paused. "Yeah."

The positive vision of motherhood, of nurturing love, is white. And I worry that my presence, flying in and flying out of their lives, is not offsetting the overriding schism between black womanhood and black motherhood. I can't catch up enough to undo the daily damage, and I hear that familiar mantra resounding in my head: I'm failing them, I'm failing them, I'm failing . . .

My very existence as a stepmother is a sign of failure and loss. Because, frankly, nobody likes the stepmother. The resounding message out there is "Bitch, sit down." I get that the idea of a stepmom is terrifying to a lot of biological moms. It can be hard to take the idea that somebody else is helping to raise your kids. Somebody else is at school on behalf of your kids.

"I didn't think you'd come," a teacher or administrator will always say when I go to the school. "What a surprise!" Part of that is that they see me in movies and on television. But I've also seen them do that to any woman with a job. Some of the other working moms and I formed an alliance at the boys' last school, but out of all the working moms I was the only stepparent. An understudy unfamiliar with the script, showing up and ad-libbing her ass off.

As a stepmother you have to remember your place. You play your position and stay in your lane. You don't overstep, and you're very aware that some people are waiting for that moment when you go too far. In interviews and even here in this book, I consciously refer to "our boys" or "the boys." You're not going to catch me saying, "my boys," and definitely not "my sons." I know how that would sound.

But any parent—step or otherwise—will go hard in the paint for the kids they love.

I am also very conscious that I am helping to raise young black men in a world where they are often in danger. I have watched them grow, and I have watched the world's perception of them change as they do. Zaire is now six foot one and Dada is five foot nine. They are not freakishly tall by the standards of their classmates, but after about nine years old, young black boys are suddenly perceived as young black men, and things start to change.

So, for their safety, I have taken to dropping these terrible Black Bombs on the boys. Black Bombs are what I call the inescapable truths of being a black person in this country, the things you do your children a disservice by not telling them about. I feel it is especially important that our boys, privileged black children in predominantly white, privileged neighborhoods, know these truths. Here they are living in luxury—and here I am to say, "Nuh-uh, homeboy. Plymouth Rock landed on *you*. Things aren't going to be the same for you." I tell them this when I see that they have their privilege blinders on.

The first time Zaire and Dada went to a sleepover, they were in sixth grade and we were still living in Miami. I drove them over to their friends' house, and they were opening the car doors before I even finished parking.

"Hold up!" I said. I turned to face them. They were sitting in the backseat, little duffel bags on their laps. "Do not wander around this house."

They looked at me dumbly.

"Only hang out where the family is."

"What?" asked Zaire.

"Because if something turns up missing, guess whose fault it is?"

Their faces were like cartoons—eyes wide, like, "Whaaaat?"

"They think I would steal?" asked Zaire.

"Yes. People think black people steal," I said. "Only hang out where other people are." Have fun at the sleepover, kids!

When they got older, I changed my script a bit. "Don't ever put yourself alone in a room with a white girl," I told them. "Or, in Miami, a Cuban girl."

They always gave me the same look: "Oh my God. Please stop talking."

"Her family is not happy about your little black dick," I said. "They're not happy about any of this." In the same way that we teach children not to run in the street, I need to teach them things to keep themselves alive. I have to tell them, "You talking back to a person of authority is not viewed in the same way as when your little white friend Eddie does it. People look at Eddie and say, 'Ah, here we have the makings of a leader! A free thinker to buck the system.'

"It doesn't matter who your parents are," I say. "You're going to be looked at as a thug or a problem child. Stand up for yourself? You're the bully."

I say to myself: "And the second you're not identified as Dwyane Wade's children, you are just young niggers."

At one of the boys' old schools, a dean said that Dada was bullying another black child. D was away, so I tagged in for the meeting. We had been through other incidents at this school. A boy playing basketball on the court one morning got frustrated when Zaire beat him. He called Zaire a nigger, and Dada jumped up to have his back. They didn't hit him, but this was still seen as poor behavior. Kids said "nigger" around the boys constantly, then blamed it on song lyrics. When I was in Pleasanton, the word simply wasn't as prevalent in music as it is now. There wasn't that handy excuse of singing it to a beat and saying, "Hey, it's the song." With me, it was a word the other kids had clearly heard at home.

"So I've taken the liberty of printing out spreadsheets for all of us," I said at the start of the meeting. "You can easily follow along on the agenda that we're going to cover today . . ."

This is actually not a joke. When I go to school meetings, I come with my books and articles to support what I'm talking about. Whether it's a Harvard study on implicit bias in academia or research into African American teenagers underperforming because they go to school with the burden of suspicion, I was ready to call them on their shit. That day I brought a copy of Ta-Nehisi Coates's *Between the World and Me.* Written as a letter to Coates's fifteen-year-old son, Samori, the book is a sort of guide to surviving in a black body in America.

"I think you should read it," I said, leaning forward to slide the book at the dean, "if you're interested in better reaching the black children whose parents pay tens of thousands of dollars to attend this school.

"So," I said, "did you label the other kid who started this disagreement a bully, or just our kid?"

"I didn't say bullying."

"Well, actually, you did," I said, passing him another printout. "Here's an e-mail chain where you used this very word in describing the incident to our nanny. You think our nanny from Wisconsin can't forward an e-mail?"

I explained the danger authority figures put black kids in when labeling them bullies. And I noted that they felt comfortable using that term because there was near-zero diversity in their faculty.

"What are you saying about black excellence or Latino excellence," I asked, "when the examples they see here are the crossing guard and the janitors? What message do you think that sends?"

It was just a fact that they disciplined others differently than our black boys. "How many times do our kids need to tell you that their classmates are using the word 'nigger'?" I asked. I had screen grabs of texts and e-mails where classmates used the word "nigger" and our kids told them to stop. "My kids have told you this," I said. "And what did you say?"

That had been dismissed as "typical boy behavior." Zaire was a bully. The administrators told me they hadn't thought of things that way. Cue the Oprah "aha" moment of nodding. It was revelation time. They didn't think of things that way because they'd never had to.

Here's the thing. I had to do all that—armed with spreadsheets and e-mails—to be taken seriously as a stepmother. At the end of the day, I could sign them out to take them to the dentist, but I didn't have the power to switch schools. That's D. That's the work of a *real* parent.

But guess what? We switched schools. The school officials could see it coming, and I could tell a stepmother's delivering the death blow made it especially painful.

OUR FRIEND PHIL BOUGHT A HOME IN OUR MIAMI NEIGHBORHOOD AND converted it into a basketball gym. Not just a court—we are talking Olympic-level training facilities. It's insane. I know this is some rich-people shit. When you see me owning the court on Snapchat? That's where I am. I should say this, too: Phil Collins bought J. Lo's house up the road from us. Different Phil. However, if I could get the drum crash from "In the Air Tonight" playing each time I sink a basket? Yes, please.

The gym is about eleven blocks away from our place and our friend Phil gave us a set of keys. "Anytime you want to stop by," he said, "let yourself in."

It was a Tuesday night in April when Zaire and Dada asked me if they could walk to the gym. It was 9 P.M. I was reading and didn't even look up.

"No, it's dark."

And that was that.

Cut to the next night: D was home from the playoffs, in a good mood, and they pulled the old okey-doke, like, "Let's get this sucker." I wasn't in the room.

This time it was 10 P.M., even later than when I said no. The boys were as sweet as could be. "Can we walk to Phil's gym?"

D said, "Sure. Here are my keys. I'm not sure if they work. I think he changed the locks. But try them." I now picture D in that moment, talking in a Jimmy Stewart voice: "Golly, guys! Try these keys repeatedly and see what happens!"

Then D casually came outside to join me on the dock. It was a beautiful night, a light wind coming off the water. Honeymoon weather.

"Hey, babe," I said.

"I told the boys they could go down to Phil's."

Record scratch.

"They just asked last night and I told them no. It's too dark."

"Well," he said, "I told them they could."

"D, it's too dark. People can't see them if they walk down North Bay."

"Babe, we've gotta cut the cord sometime."

I was already up, heart rate flying. North Bay is dark in some stretches, depending on how illuminated neighbors want their houses to be. You can be on a spotlit sidewalk one minute and "lurking" through trees the next.

"They're old enough," he said. "Think about what we were doing at their age." At their age I knew enough about the world to not trust that everything would be okay just because.

"This is an open-carry state, D," I reminded him, getting agitated. "A stand-your-ground state, and all our neighbors have to do to shoot these children is say they felt threatened. What's more threatening to our neighbors than two black boys 'lurking'? Walking down the street in front of their properties? We don't know half our neighbors. Half of them don't live here *half* the time. Do you trust these people to not kill our kids? Do you trust their security to not see our boys as threatening? If someone sees them, and the keys don't work . . . two black kids, D, two black kids."

D paused a moment, peering at me, turning the thought over in his head. "Let's go get 'em," he said. I had dropped another one of my Black Bombs, this time on him.

We literally hopped in the golf cart like *Mission: Impossible,* taking off down North Bay, D at the wheel, me dialing them on speaker.

Zaire answered on the third ring.

"Where are you?!"

"Um . . ."

"*That's* how I know you're fooling around," I yelled, the panic not quite yet unleashed but slowly working its way up my chest. "WHERE ARE YOU? Tell us specifically where you are."

"I think we're on Fifty-first Street. We're walking back. The keys didn't work."

I periscoped my head straight toward D, like, "I told you so."

As we drove our golf cart down the street, a cop car whooshed silently by. The thing about North Bay Road is that it's the most exclusive street in South Florida. A siren or flash of police lights would denote trouble, and if you're spending thirty million dollars on a mansion, you don't want to know there's trouble. That's why, in this neighborhood, police officers just roll up on you silently, like ninjas.

Then another one magically appeared. The squad car slowed down as it reached us, and the officer rolled down the window. Instinct kicked in. Dwyane and I froze.

"Oh," said the cop, genially. "Dwyane Wade."

"Hi," said D.

"Have a nice night," the cop said.

As he drove off, I stared straight ahead and gritted my teeth into a smile. "If you think these cops were not called on our boys, you are fucking delusional," I said.

These are privileged kids, I thought. Lord knows what they would say when the cops reached them. I would like to think they would be polite, but under duress, who knows. I realized it was completely possible they would say, "I *live* here, motherfucker."

Soon we found them on the side of the road, walking toward us. Before we did, I turned to D. His eyes were on the road.

"What did you tell the kids to say when they're stopped by police?" I asked him.

"Well, I told them what to say in case—"

"WHAT did you tell them?"

"I told them to say their full names and our address."

"Wrong answer," I say. "'I'm Dwyane Wade's kid.' *That's* what they say."

AS WE ZOOMED DOWN THE ROAD IN OUR STUPID GOLF CART LOOKING for the kids, my mind flashed back to March the year before. Zaire was in seventh grade and he'd asked if he could take our Dalmatian–pit bull mix, Pink, out for a walk with Dada. It was a negotiation.

"Okay, walk down to the Boshes'," we said. D's old Heat teammate Chris Bosh lived eleven doors down the road. I figured they could walk out the door and I would have our security call the Boshes' security to warn them.

As they bounded out, I stood at the door, ready to drop a Black Bomb. "Wrap the dog leash around your thumb," I said to them. "That way, your fingers are free to spread." This was an actual conversation I had. But this is what you did three years after Trayvon Martin and five months after Tamir Rice. I didn't want the boys to have their hands in their pockets or for them to look as if they were concealing something dangerous.

Zaire started to open his mouth, and I shut him down.

"You've gotta walk Pink that way," I said. "It's not just the police. It's the neighborhood security officers, too. Anyone who is armed can harm you."

Sure enough, the first time they walked Pink, it was a disaster. That was the night someone swatted Lil Wayne's house over on La Gorce Island, near us. Now, if you are a celebrity, swatting is a nightmare. Someone calls 911 as a prank, announces a hostage situation or shooting at a famous person's house, and watches the news as a SWAT team storms the mansion. It's happened to Justin Bieber, Miley Cyrus, Ashton Kutcher—any bored thirteen-year-old can make a call and then watch the show. It's happened to poor Lil Wayne twice.

So there were two boys walking a huge dog as a dozen police cars flew past them. At our house, our security guards started to go crazy, talking about a shooting. Chris's security then radioed in, practically yelling, "Abort mission!" about walking a dog. It was like an international incident.

As more and more cop cars raced by the kids, they froze on the side of the road. They assumed the cars were for them. "Oh my God," I imagined them saying to each other. "This is what she is always talking about!"

The last cop car stopped and rolled down the window, just like they had done with D and me in the golf cart. He was looking at our two black kids. He didn't say a word—just stared.

And what did Zaire do? That boy dropped the leash and ran. Dada followed. They just took off, with a pit-Dalmatian running after them like *Boyz in the Waterfront Community Hood*.

I had gone over this and over this with them, but when the shit hit the Shinola, they just didn't know what to do.

Zaire and Dada told us all the whole story that night in the kitchen. The boys were laughing now, the edges of the experience dulling into an anecdote. I'd poured a glass of Chardonnay to calm myself down. I swirled the wine in my mouth for a second as they talked excitedly, tasting the notes of pear and white chocolate with hints of vanilla. I was drinking wine and listening to what amounted to a boys' adventure story told in a million-dollar custom-made kitchen. None of it would protect us.

"They could have shot you in the back," I said.

BACK TO THE GOLF CART, SEARCHING FOR ZAIRE AND DADA, WHO WERE probably fumbling with their keys and looking to everyone else in the world like two black boys staging a break-in.

I felt mad at them, I felt mad at D, and I felt mad at how black boys seem to be in constant danger. (And these are not just black boys. These are *big* black boys, especially endangered.) How are we supposed to give them all the knowledge, all the power, and all the pride that we can, and then ask them to be subservient when it comes to dealing with the police? "This is how you have to act in order to come home alive."

They are the boys I adore. And people don't value their very breath. It could be extinguished in one second, without thought, leaving a dog to run, dragging its leash the whole way home. A dog, safer from harm than black boy bodies.

seventeen

MITTENS

When Dwyane moved back to Chicago to play for the Bulls, we began renting a Victorian-style house on the Gold Coast. The boy who grew up hearing shootings on the South Side of Chicago now lives in the most expensive neighborhood in the city. The house was built in 1883, and one of the first owners was successful adman Charles Kingsbury Miller, a Son of the American Revolution who proudly traced his lineage to colonial families. For his postretirement second act, he led the charge for legislation to make it illegal to disrespect the American flag. He was especially upset, he said in an 1898 SAR banquet speech, to see the flag "converted into grotesque coats for Negro minstrels." The home was recently restored to preserve its sense of history, so it is easy to imagine Charles returning to visit and the look on his face when he finds me at the door.

When I am in town, I leave the house every morning to walk to the gym. In the winter it is eight degrees in broad daylight, and everyone and their mother is wearing the uniform of a big black puffy coat with the hood up. You can see two inches of everyone's face. As I walk, I see my Gold Coast neighbors scan the visible slash of my skin. They're looking to see if I belong to one of the houses. Am I the cook? The nanny? Whose girl am I?

The sidewalks are narrow here because a lot of our neighbors have literally gated their shrubs. There's the shrubbery in front of their home, then the sidewalk, and then more fenced-in shrubbery before the street. Why they need to wall off their shrubbery is another topic for conversation, but the result is that if you stop to talk with somebody, you literally block the whole sidewalk.

Yesterday on my walk, two women did just that. One had a dog on a short leash and the other was an older woman I recognized as a close neighbor. As I approached them with their backs turned to me, I rehearsed what to say to avoid scaring them.

"Excuse me, ladies," I said in my sweetest, singsongiest voice. The older woman turned, reacting with a full face of pleasantness. But as she saw my two inches of skin, I watched a wave of terror come over her face as her entire body clenched.

I sidled past, and as I walked away, I heard my neighbor say something I couldn't place, but then heard the last word as clear as could be: "thug."

Was she talking about me? The kids? My sweet husband, who I often call Poopy? Something completely unrelated to me? Whatever the answer, I gave my workout to her. I thought about her saying "thug" the entire time I was on the treadmill, pounding out that run.

The next day, as I layered up to make my walk to the gym, I remembered that I had two new pairs of gloves and mittens, both in black and white stripes. I instinctively reached for the gloves, but I stopped.

"Well," I said aloud, "thugs don't wear mittens."

I put the mittens on and went out into the street. Of course I was fumbling with my phone because, honestly, you can't do shit with mittens on. But I was going to make my neighbors feel comfortable, dammit. Surely they would see my black face and say, "But wait, she's got on mittens! She's an acceptable Negro. She *belongs*. Just look at those darling mittens."

That day, I decided to walk through the park instead of on the sidewalk. To save myself two minutes, I cut from the path to walk across a patch of grass. I was four steps in when I got trapped in a quicksand of icy mud. I looked down, my sneakers getting muddier and muddier, and I wasn't sure where to step next.

Suddenly, a sea of children ran toward me. They were probably on a field trip, racing through the park, with their teachers trying to keep up. "What are the teachers going to think about this black lady," I thought to myself, "in a puffy coat and black hoodie, standing frozen in this swamp of mud?"

I panicked, sticking my hands out at my sides. I've got my mittens on, I thought. Those teachers can tell their children not to be afraid. As the kids ran around me, I tried to skedaddle past them, because that is the only word for the ridiculous "walking" I was doing, slipping and sliding across the icy mud. And I became furious. Had I really reassured myself that I could erase four hundred years of history with these fucking mittens? Yes, the mittens were the thing that was going to separate *me* from the other black people who my neighbors deem threatening or, at very least, have decided don't belong on the Gold Coast.

I had dared to go off the path set for me. But when I got to the gym, I didn't think about my neighbors on the treadmill that day. I thought about my friend Ricky Williams. Ricky is a retired Miami Dolphin who I met while I was doing *Bad Boys II*. He would be the first to tell you that he has social anxiety, so we bonded over that right away. I called him Buddha because he was so cosmic and sweet. Like me, he likes to go for walks, and like me, he doesn't always know where he's headed. When I'm filming in new cities, I walk around and allow myself to get lost. And yes, I have been known to aimlessly follow squirrels.

Ricky was showing just that trait in January 2017, before an award ceremony in Tyler, Texas, when this ex–University of Texas prodigal son left his hotel to kill time with a walk. Ricky was strolling through nearby woods when someone called the police because he looked "suspicious." On the body-cam footage, before the officers even got out of the car, one of them said, "That looks like Ricky Williams." It was actually four cops who arrived on "the scene" to search and question him. He was told to put his hands behind his back, and right after they told him to spread his legs, a starstruck young officer asked if he was Ricky Williams.

"I am."

What followed presents a surreal portrait of fame and the black body. On video, the cops seem to slip in and out of seeing him as Ricky Williams, someone whose fame sets him apart, and seeing a black man in a white space. Ricky stands there as the cop runs his hands all over his body. "I'll explain everything to you in just a second," says the cop, pulling Ricky's hotel key card from his pocket. "People don't know who you are, nothing may have happened that was wrong, but we gotta find out."

When Ricky tells them he is staying at the Marriott next door, the policemen seem to leap on this fact as a reason to let him go. "If you tell me you're staying at this hotel," says one officer, "it makes a little more sense as to why you're walking around this area."

Ricky then shows just the slightest crack in his Buddha cool, and points out that the cop had pulled out his hotel card.

"Isn't that the whole point of searching me?" asks Ricky. "To get information?"

"You're not in handcuffs. We're just talking to you."

"Why would I be in handcuffs? I didn't do anything wrong."

"You're acting really defensive."

And then Ricky tells the truth: "Do you know how many times I've been messed with by the cops because I'm black?"

"Oh, no no no no," says a cop, as the others shake their heads. "Come on now."

Yes, come on now. There was an assumption of guilt because of his very identity, and Ricky had to convince these men that he was innocent. The police stopped him as a reminder of the power structure Ricky is supposed to enforce upon himself: he should know that his skin puts him under constant surveillance and that his very presence outside of sanctioned spaces creates the assumption of wrongdoing. It is, in fact, an inconvenience to the police that they have to be bothered to tell him this. By now, as adults, Ricky and I are supposed to have internalized these rules and regulations that come with our very existence. We put on the mittens, we utter singsong hellos, and we stay where we belong.

I cut through the little field at the park that day. If someone had stopped me and I had to try to explain my moves, why I opted to go through the park, why I came across these children, why I was sliding through the mud . . . if I had tried to explain myself, I might have sounded crazy, but really all I would have been explaining away was the presence of my body in a space where it has been decided that black bodies are violent and threatening.

Worse, I am told that people don't want to hear these stories, but the reality is we experience life in a never-ending loop in which we are told that if we just "make it," we will enjoy the fruits of our labor: assimilation. My father tried so hard, but he was pulled out of his Mercedes at gunpoint in Pleasanton on his way to work in a suit. The police said they were looking for an escaped convict from nearby Santa Rita Jail. My father was a middle-aged man who looked nothing like the convict except for being black. There was no neighborhood outcry or protest. No one came to his defense. It was a necessary "inconvenience" for maintaining the safety of the neighborhood.

But what does that say about aspirational living? Hey, you moved into a big house and you made it . . . except you didn't. There's this idea that you will be safe if you just get famous enough, successful enough, pull yourself up by your bootstraps, move into the right neighborhood, do all these things to fully assimilate into the America people have been sold on. We all bought in, and we keep thinking if we just get over this mountain of assimilation, on the other side is a pot of gold. Or maybe a unicorn, perhaps a leprechaun. Any of those is as plausible as the acceptance of the wholeness of me. But there's just another mountain on the other side. And someone will be ready to tell you, "Don't be breathing hard. You need to make this look easy."

Just as the cops were annoyed when Ricky said he had been repeatedly stopped because he is black, discussion of race is often dismissed or talked over unless it is in a sanctioned space. You can talk about your experience at a roundtable on race, but don't talk about yourself at a "regular" roundtable. It is exactly the same as when I would challenge my friends in Pleasanton near the end of high school. "That again?" they would say. "Get off your soapbox." Only now these are grown-ups who fashion themselves as allies. But these are my stories; this is what I have lived. I know what the boys I raise go through, what my husband goes through, and beyond my family, I can watch a video of it happening to Ricky. Each of us experiences these "same things," but each experience has value and deserves telling. I need to write them and read them aloud to constantly remind myself of my reality. I need to hear these stories. If I think mittens—or the way I talk, or the fame I have—will make my breathing and living on this planet permissible.

I am told no one wants to hear about it. I even hear it from other people of color in Hollywood. Some have climbed the mountain and have been able to assimilate so thoroughly, they think they are in a parallel universe. "You're sabotaging your own success by limiting yourself to being a black woman," they say. They tell us that if we just stripped away these layers of identity, we would be perceived not for our color or gender, but for our inner core. Our "humanness."

My humanness doesn't insulate me from racism or sexism. In fact, I think I can deal effectively with the world precisely because I am a black woman who is so comfortable in my black-womanness. I know what I can accomplish. And anything I have accomplished, I did so not in spite of being a black woman, but *because* I am a black woman.

This is not the message that assimilated people of color in Hollywood want to hear. In exchange for a temporary pass that they think is permanent, these ones who've "made it" then turn and yell back to the others, "No, keep going! Assimilation is the key! Deny your victimhood! Let go of your identity."

Better bring your mittens, that's what I know.

eighteen

BIG BANK TAKE LITTLE BANK

Dwyane and I have a ritual involving our favorite show, *Nashville*. I guess I should say our favorite show that I am not on. No matter what, we have to watch it together, preferably at home in Chicago. We have these twin chaise lounges in our theater room, and in winter, we each have a blanket to curl up in, fuzzy on one side, quilted on the other.

We always assemble our snacks beforehand because we don't want to get up during the show. It's all about being able to barrel through the episode. Lately we've been doing Garrett's popcorn in the tubs, half cheese, half caramel corn. Then I have my alkaline water and he's got the bottled water he likes. And of course we have our phones beside us, too, so we can tweet about *Nashville*, which is almost as good as watching *Nashville*. We even have our own phone chargers ready—go big or go home.

If you don't watch the show, just understand that Deacon and

Rayna were everything. Through all their ups and downs, their love endured and we adored them for it. I'm writing this in a hotel in New York City, and D and I have signed in under the alias Deacon Claybourne. (I also check in stealth as Cha Cha diGregorio from *Grease*—the best dancer at St. Bernadette's with the worst reputation—but that is another story.)

Without giving anything away, one of Deacon and Rayna's issues as a couple in country music is that she is the huge singing star and earner in the relationship. When Deacon told Rayna, "It's your world, I just live in it," that was the most honest description I have heard about the inequity of fame and finances in love. I know it rang true for me. That's how all my relationships were before Dwyane. I paid for everything.

The first time my father ever met Dwyane, it was at Dad's house in Arizona. We successfully navigated the whole awkward first meeting, but at the very last second, just as we were leaving, Dad pulled Dwyane back into the house.

"What do you want with my daughter?" he asked, suddenly gruff. "She's got her own shit. She's got her own house. She's got her own money. What do you want with my daughter?"

He wasn't saying, "What are your intentions for my daughter's heart?" He meant, "We have been down this road before and she's come out poorer."

Dad didn't believe that a professional athlete wasn't hiding some problem that would prove a drain on my savings. "I'm doing all right by myself," D then awkwardly explained. "I'm not going to try to use her."

He doesn't need my money, but sometimes I'm Deacon and it really is Dwyane's world. I often work around his life, because I have more flexibility. Because the basketball schedule is the basketball schedule, amen. And, at the end of September, that schedule is our schedule. On top of that, he has many brand and partnership obligations. Then there are the team obligations, the NBA obligations, and in between that there's our family. And then there's us as a couple. A lot of times I am like, "Whatever, just tell me when I can see you."

We are lucky in that we have homes in many cities now, because we're all over the place for work, and that's where I can plainly see the lines of division. I make it clear to people that there is a house I am financially responsible for in L.A., and there is the Miami home Dwyane built when he played for the Heat. "Don't judge the black actress home that I pay for in Los Angeles," I say when folks visit. "I know you've seen the black athlete home in Miami, but this is what I can afford."

D thinks the disparity is funny, probably because he's loaded. There are times when we go to restaurants and D will purposefully forget his wallet so I have to pay. Once, at the end of a large, boozy gathering, I texted him under the guise of answering a question from my publicist. "I wouldn't have said, 'Let's invite your whole team out!' if I knew this was going on the black actress AmEx that you don't chip in for." He loved that one.

When we were designing the Miami home, my husband kept saying things like "Well, I didn't want to sign off on that until you saw it."

"At the end of the day it's your money," I would answer, "so do whatever you want to do."

"But you're the woman of the house," he'd say. "You're my partner, you're here with me."

That was lovely, but in all negotiations, whether it was about wallpaper or if we *really* needed to get an eight-foot-tall Buddha statue in the Miami house, I have learned this lesson: big bank take little bank.

It's a simple rule dictating that whoever has more money wins. Whatever your income bracket, whoever has the power of the bigger purse in the relationship usually has the final decision. In my first marriage, I made more than my husband, so I was big bank. Now, I was decidedly little bank. The sanctity of this rule was never more apparent than when we worked out the prenup. On paper, it's an adult thing to do. Grown-ups with a certain amount of money who care for each other say, "You know what, just in case we gotta jump ship, let's make clear while we really like each other exactly what we're going in with and what we leave with."

The negotiations went on for months before our August 2014 wedding. We started with the right intentions, mind you. My team and I were adamant that we have a prenup to protect myself, because I got taken to the cleaners in my first marriage. Dwyane's team was all in because he had been to the cleaners with his first wife. We both basically bought our respective cleaners, plus the deli next door, and built a new wing on the library across the street. That's how bad those divorces had been. It wasn't that either of us planned on getting divorced. But we also didn't plan on getting cleaned out again, either. Better safe than losing all your money, you know? My first thought was that I wanted to leave the marriage, should things go that way, with whatever I came in with. I wanted Dwyane to know I didn't need his *anything* if I didn't want to be with him. I will give blow jobs in a leper colony before I take a dime from a man I am no longer in love with. That's who I am. I will cut off my nose, or my lips I guess, to spite my face.

But Dwayne felt differently. His team kept pushing. "No, no.

We want to give you something, throw out some numbers." So finally, I gave in. It was like they said, "You can have whatever salad you want," and I asked for a kale salad.

"Actually," they replied with a note of apology, "it's just iceberg lettuce for you."

"But you said I could have whatever I wanted," I answered. "I want kale. Why would you offer me anything if you only wanted to give me iceberg? Don't you care about my health and wellness?"

This was all coming from Dwyane's team, yes, but the person who had proposed to me was now, in theory, lowballing me. It wasn't even about the money, really. The question for me was "What does this man think I'm worth?" There were literally pages going back and forth, detailing my potential worth as a wife. The money went up if I had a child, and then there were even weirder conversations about my own earning potential. When my attorney eventually had to say, "Fuck you, these are her quotes," meaning what I am paid to do a job, I realized we were negotiating my marriage the same way we would a sitcom deal at NBC. My team had to provide examples of my past worth, then factor in my social media power to come up with a number that I needed to protect as my future earnings. And then Dwyane's team came back with, "No, actually, that's not her value. She is worth less than that."

"Worth less." I tried that on in my actress voices. "I am worth less. Worth less? Worthless. Ah, yes, I am worthless." My number was based off my own work, whereas his angle was just "This is what I want to pay."

Big bank take little bank.

It was hell, especially when you're supposed to be marrying your best friend. Finally, three days before the wedding, he became Dwyane again. You know why? Because I signed. He was like Jon Snow, morphing from "Winter is coming" to "I'm in Miami, bitch!" He became ecstatic, throwing off all the layers of anxiety, and there I was underneath them, the woman he loved. He was freed. But I was resentful. Hell, I am still resentful. Which is why when I make him my #ManCrushMonday on Instagram, I say, "As per the prenup, my forever man crush Monday." Does he regret playing hardball? Not in the least. He played to win.

Thank God our wedding was fun. Honestly, our wedding saved our marriage. I fell in love with him five different times that night. When I say I had the time of my life, I really mean every word. After our reception, all the guests were given candles. And then a gospel choir led us in a march, singing "God Is Trying to Tell You Something" from *The Color Purple*. So we marched with our candles, and people shared wishes for us and wishes for themselves. The choir led us into a supersized 1930s juke joint we created just for the night. Questlove was DJing, and one of my favorite bands, Guy, was on the stage. We had a rocking chair rest area for the older folks, and we were surrounded by all of our favorite people—the people who valued us for our real worth. The best thing was that people danced all night. If you left the dance floor it was just to get more booze and then you went right back. It went on for hours, and Dwyane and I were the very last to leave.

I think about our vows sometimes. "If you've ever wondered if I'll leave you, the answer is never," Dwyane said to me in front of all those people. "And if you've ever wondered what I value, the answer is you."

I needed to hear that, and I needed to tell him what I said

in return. "This day is about the two of us coming together and being the best team possible," I said. "So today, I vow to love you without conditions." And I had to add one very important promise:

"I vow not to watch *Scandal* or *Nashville* without you."

Even under the rules of big bank take little bank, so far, so good.

nineteen

THE ROOM WHERE IT HAPPENS

The text came from a number I didn't know. Prince's invites would always be this way. Last minute and straightforward, with the address of a house he was renting in Los Angeles for awards season, or later, a hotel he was taking over for the night.

My first came in 2005. I grabbed my friend's hand and showed her the text. We were at a Grammy weekend party in L.A. and were having a great time, but this was a much better offer.

"We're going," I said. "Now."

The whole way to the mysterious address, I was sure the invitation was a prank. Maybe, I thought, it would be better that way. I was terrified of showing up at Prince's house and being lame. I was sure there were going to be way cooler people than me there, and I was going to be the idiot who said the wrong thing.

The house was at the end of a steep driveway up Mulholland, and my friend and I made our way to the door. I was still waiting for the "Oh, there must be a mistake." But the security guy gave me a nod. Then he looked at my friend.

"Did you get a text?" the large man asked, as politely as possible.

"No," she said.

"I'm sorry" was all he said.

Now, my friend is dope as hell and also happens to be someone famous. You know her, and if I told you her name you would immediately know that of course she could hang. But Prince planned his invite list like a precision instrument. And I had the golden ticket that night.

"You *have* to go in," she said.

"Okaythecarwilltakeyouhomeloveyou," I said, because there was no way I was *not* going in. And I felt lucky to have a friend who understood what this invitation meant.

The first thing I noticed as I walked through the door was that this was definitely Prince's house. Purple tapestries, music blasting, candles everywhere . . .

"Dearly beloved . . ." I said to myself.

To my right was a huge staircase, and to my left, just beyond the crowd, stood Whitney Houston, Mariah Carey, and Mary J. Blige in a small circle. They were still in their Grammy party gowns, looking like my nineties soulful-pop fantasies come to life.

"Oh my God, Gabrielle," Mary said, waving me over. "That picture we took at Quincy's party, I have it on my mantel. I see you every day."

"Really?" I asked, meaning it. Mary J. Blige had a picture of *me*?

"Come, come," she said, drawing me into their circle. I don't really get starstruck, but as I was doing air kisses with these icons,

I thought, How in the hell is this even happening? These gorgeous, important women were in the middle of having a legit kiki. I think that word gets overused, but this was a kiki of epic proportions. Mariah was sipping champagne and telling a story about some guy trying to come on to her. She is an amazing storyteller—deadpan, but landing the details about this chump perfectly as Whitney let out that amazing roar of a laugh of hers. It was like being invited to sit at the cool table. I had grown up watching all these women, dying to meet them, and here they were, having girl talk like at a slumber party with friends and inviting me in. Just some normal superstars, talking about life. Stars, They're Just Like Us, only not at all, because this was Prince's house.

I spotted our host across the room, sitting on the stairs and talking intently to Anthony Anderson. I later asked Anthony what they talked about.

"Jehovah," said Anthony.

Prince was, as he would say, living "in the truth." As a Jehovah's Witness rooted in his faith, he recognized that there were elements of his beliefs that could touch other people. You didn't have to buy the whole faith, lock, stock, and barrel. But there were aspects that he found comfort and guidance in that he wanted to share. As he talked to Anthony, Prince moved his head ever so slightly. Even his smallest movements were musical.

I was mesmerized watching him, and it took Matthew McConaughey to break the spell, running by with a set of bongos. "Wow," I thought, "that is a thing that guy actually does." Then I saw my friend Sanaa Lathan talking with Hill Harper. I spotted Damon Wayans making Renée Zellweger guffaw, and Salma Hayek dancing with Penélope Cruz.

Suddenly, Prince just appeared in front of me.

"Thank you so much for inviting me," I said. Oh God, I thought, what am I supposed to call him? "Mr. Prince."

He smiled. Stop! I screamed in my head. Shut up! I was petrified of saying something stupid. So I did.

"I feel like I should have brought a tuna casserole," I said. Fuck, you idiot.

He raised one magnificent, exquisitely sculpted eyebrow.

"We're both from the Midwest," I said, unable to stop myself from talking. "That's what we do, right?"

His face broke into a smile. "I love tuna casserole," he said, in his low, deliberate voice. "And I liked you on that episode of *ER*. I really liked it."

"How are you watching *ER*?" I said. "You're Prince."

"I see everything," he said.

And I believed him, looking around the room at a completely random collection of faces from music, television, and film. His parties also included writers, directors, and producers of all types of content. There was always a random athlete or two in the mix as well. It was all over the place, and completely inclusive at the same time. I'd never seen anything like it.

THERE WAS A REASON. HOLLYWOOD IS EXTREMELY SEGREGATED. THE whole idea of Black Hollywood, Latino Hollywood, Asian Hollywood—it's very real. And it all stems from who is with you in the audition rooms as you are coming up. Because you are generally auditioning with people who look like you, over and over again, simply because of how roles are described. When it got down to the wire for the role of "Sassy Friend #1," these were the people I saw. That's how I got to know Zoe Saldana, Kerry Washington, Essence Atkins, Robinne Lee, Sanaa, and all the Reginas. Sassy Friend #1 was a black girl between x and y age, and that meant a very shallow casting pool. When it came time to cast a family, I would meet an array of actors who all looked like me. Sitting in those rooms for hours at a time, multiple times a week, you get to know people.

As you all start to rise, it's the same people, who are now deemed the "it folk," who you sit in better rooms with. And those people become your community; they know the struggle you went through, because they went through it, too. And the rooms pretty much stay that way, no matter how high you rise, because for the most part Hollywood doesn't really subscribe to color-blind casting. What Lin-Manuel Miranda did with *Hamilton* is literally unheard of. We black actors meet in the room into which we are invited, but we are often barred from, to steal from Lin, *the room where it happens*. The spaces where deals get made and ideas get traded. Half the time you get picked to do something in Hollywood, it's because someone cosigned for you. "Oh yeah, she's talented, but more important, she's cool," someone with more pull than you will say. "I hung out with her this one time."

But how do you hang when you're not at the same parties? The biggest award show parties come with very rare invites, and the brown people you see there are the same brown people that have been starring in things forever. Unless you spend at least five grand a month on a power publicist to help land a spot, it's not gonna just "happen." Black actresses are rarely deemed the ingénues, or even the up-and-comers. So your work or even a spark of public interest isn't a guarantee. But let's say you make it into the room, whether through pay-to-play or luck. You're in. You got the golden ticket.

So, let's go in together. First off, the light is amazing, but you're too wired from the red carpet to do anything but rush to find the closest drink. These red-carpet appearances are timed to the second, so that there won't be a big collision of big stars. Performers are scheduled and served up like courses at a meal. If your entrance is set for eight thirty and your car gets there at eight? Circle the block, bitch, because someone more important than you has a better call time. And unfortunately, if you have a late call time, a lot of people will have left the party by the time you cross that threshold. That feeling though, when this wall of cameras fires at you and you hear the machine-gun rat-a-tat of clicks, is exhilarating. Your every move creates a new wave of shots.

Once inside, you're just another beautiful person in this beautifully lit room full of writers, producers, directors, and studio heads. Yes, this is a great chance to network and get to know people, but if you are one of only a sprinkling of black folks in the room, how does that even happen? Just because you're there doesn't mean anyone's gonna talk to you—trust me. No one has vouched for you in the way that Prince had. You feel like an interloper, and you go for the familiar. Because you know who is for sure going to talk with you? The other brown people.

Here's the thing about the #OscarsSoWhite discussion. Hollywood films are so white because their art happens in a vacuum. It is made by white filmmakers, with white actors, for imagined white audiences. No one even thinks of remedying the issue through communal partying. Inviting one black actor to the party isn't enough—sorry, folks. We all know you can create even better art by truly being inclusive, but you're never going to get inclusive in your work if you can't figure out how to get inclusive in your social life. If you're an actor of color and you've never had the chance to hang out with somebody and show them you're talented and fun and enlightened and deeper than what you can submit on a résumé, you never have the opportunities to be included. Prince created those opportunities just by throwing a better party. When he included you, you literally found yourself in the bathroom line with some of the world's biggest names in entertainment. How we gauge what success is supposed to look like is different for white actors than it is for black actors. And I am aware that half my résumé looks like crumbs to many white actors.

The films *Deliver Us from Eva* and *Two Can Play That Game*—these are hood classics, if not cult classics like *Bring It On*. A lot of people appreciate these films, but because there aren't any white people in them, they get marginalized and put on a separate shelf. They are underappreciated, but they never lost money. And I will continue to do these movies—ones I call FUBU, For Us by Us—because I love them and I am grateful for them.

I made lifelong friends on the sets of these films. The black Hollywood community is so small that we all came up together and created opportunities for each other. These movies set the stage for twenty-plus years of careers. It's a testament to the community that we, over the years, have always looked out for each other and pitched each other for jobs. I am incredibly grateful for that love we have for one another and the mutual respect of talent that we bring to the table. None of us benefit from tearing each other down. There aren't enough of us. We need each other to lean on.

Now, a lot of white people have been like, "I have loved you since *Bring It On*." But the ones who made sure I had a career were black people. White people will say, "Oh, Taraji just came on the scene with *Benjamin Button,* and now look at her on *Empire*!" The truth is, Taraji has been working for a thousand years.

White people just met Cookie, but black people have known and supported and *loved* Taraji forever.

I remember when Taraji got her first invite to one of Prince's parties. Prince was renting Cuttino Mobley's place and gave an outdoor concert. Taraji was pure joy, dancing and singing. Every single person at that party looked around and thought, "Why isn't it like this all the time?"

I WAS LUCKY TO GO TO ENOUGH OF PRINCE'S PARTIES THAT WE DEVEL-oped a friendship. By that I mean that I went from saying "Mr. Prince" to, at least, "Heeey, Prince." His gatherings were always held around some event or awards show I was going to, and the invites never came directly. One of the last times I saw him, he invited me to a small dinner party in Las Vegas. He was doing a residency at the Rio, and they had provided him with a palatial suite to use for his stay. In attendance that night were Ludacris, Hill Harper, Shaun Robinson, Dave Chappelle, Toni Braxton, Atlanta DJ Ryan Cameron, and me. I was sitting between Luda and Toni, and we were all starving, waiting for Prince to come in and take his seat at the head of the table.

Finally, he arrived and we were served a squash soup. Before we started, he asked us all to join hands in prayer.

"Dear Lord . . ." he said, pausing dramatically, "Jehovah."

Luda, Toni, and I squeezed each other's hands at that. Honestly, I don't remember any other food because I couldn't shut up about how good that soup was. But I remember the conversation. Again and again, over this epic three-hour dinner, Prince kept looping back to spirituality and social responsibility. Even when I told him how much I loved his parties, he explained there was a religious component.

"I want to understand people," he said, "to see what unites them."

He was also funny, repeating phrases he found comical, like "I'm not sayin', I'm just sayin'." Melodic punch lines, over and over, keeping us all laughing.

Then we went to watch him perform. It was after midnight by then, at a small venue so we could get up close. As his guests, we were closest to him, and it felt like as he improvised his set that night, he chose the songs based on the conversations we'd had at dinner. It was like the music was the soundtrack to *us*.

I OWE MY MARRIAGE TO PRINCE. THAT'S WHAT A CONNECTOR HE WAS. IN January 2007, Prince announced, with just a few hours' notice, that he was hosting a Golden Globes after-party on the rooftop of the Beverly Wilshire hotel. When the text arrived, I knew where I had to be. I was heading up in the elevator with Diddy—always Puff to me—and Nia Long, when Dwyane's brother Donny stepped on.

"Oh my God," said Donny. "My brother is your biggest fan."

"Who's your brother?" I asked.

"Dwyane Wade."

"No shit?" said Puffy.

"That's nice," I said.

"Listen," said Donny, almost at his floor. "We've been trying to get in touch with your people about cohosting a party with him for the Super Bowl in Miami. Would you be interested?"

I was already seeing someone in Miami and was head over heels for that guy, so I thought, Why not? I was not thinking of Dwyane as a love interest at all, and I didn't even meet him before the party. I brought Sanaa and Patti LaBelle. I was taking Miss

Patti to the bathroom and D happened to be standing at the top of the stairs.

"Oh, hey," I said. "I'm throwing this party with you."

"Hey," he said shyly.

"Um, we're gonna be over there if you wanna come join," I said. It was just courtesy. He seemed nice enough, but quiet. For me, there was no chemistry.

I didn't take D seriously until much later. He became a friend, and then he became my best friend. We were talking about something completely unrelated to us, and I looked at him and I just knew: I didn't want to be on this planet without him. I didn't want to not bear witness to him succeeding. I chose him.

When Prince died in 2016, Dwyane took his death hard. He hadn't spent any time with Prince, and frankly I was a little like, "Hey, there is a hierarchy of grief, you know . . ." Shortly after Prince died, someone got hold of an old, little-heard Australian radio interview with one of Prince's protégés, Damaris Lewis. She was ballsy, quite funny, and she bragged during the interview that she could call Prince and get him to talk. She did, and basketball came up.

"Well, Dwyane Wade is my favorite player," Prince had said.

Someone played it for D right before a game, and minutes later he teared up over it during the National Anthem. I know this message from Prince said to him, "I am on the right track." For me, it cosigned every wonderful thing I feel about Dwyane. We were both welcome at the party.

The world mourned an icon, playing "Purple Rain," a song I adore but I know he made thirty years before his passing. As tributes froze him in that amber, I noticed that stories of his parties started popping up on entertainment blogs. Whitewashed accounts of people begging Justin Timberlake to sing, with barely a mention of the black or brown guests at the parties. Either the authors didn't notice them, or they just didn't know our names.

I mourn the icon, too, but I grieve the vital connector who brought so many communities together, long after he recorded those radio hits everyone knows by heart. He gamed the system to provide access for talented people to access each other. Perhaps if he were white, he would be celebrated as a modern Warhol, famous not just for his own art, but for creating a space where interesting people with money and talent, or just one or the other, could meet and create. His own diverse Factory. Instead, the parties are reduced to jam sessions, just as the women he gave opportunities to—artists like Sheila E., Wendy & Lisa, Vanity, Apollonia, Chaka Khan, Susanna Hoffs, Rosie Gaines, Misty Copeland, Janelle Monáe, Damaris—are reduced to haremlike roundups. Prince's women. *I'm not saying, I'm just saying.*

I still wonder who could take up his mantle, and if it's even possible. Who could be cool enough to bring all these different, interesting people together in the name of art and communion?

I also have a selfish thought. In all the times I spent with Prince, I wish I'd just once had the balls to ask him, "What is it you see in me? That maybe I am not seeing in myself?"

twenty

A TALE OF TWO MARTINEZES

"Okay, pass your homework to the front."

I'm not going to say a wave of panic washed over me, but let's say it was a splash. I was five minutes into algebra class, the second day of my freshman year of high school. As the guy behind me tapped my shoulder with his paper, I raised my hand.

"I didn't know there was homework," I said, reaching back without looking. I had missed class the day before because there was a mix-up with my schedule. Besides, who gives homework the first day?

"Then you should have asked a friend, Nickie," Mr. Fuller said. I'd heard Fuller was a hard-ass, a Vietnam vet prone to outbursts.

"I didn't know who was in the class," I said.

"You don't have any friends?" he said. "Well, we need to fix that."

Fuller went to his desk and scrawled something on a sheet of paper before taping it to the wall. The sheet had FONU in huge letters.

"Who wants to join the Friends of Nickie Union club?" he said. "Now she'll know who to call the next time she blows off class."

For a long, long minute there was just a stunned tittering, and no one got up. Finally, the guy behind me walked over to the sheet and wrote his name. Ray Martinez. When he sat down, I turned to him.

He leaned in to whisper.

"Do you like Salt-N-Pepa? Have you heard 'Push It'?"

Cue the music. Ray Martinez was a sophomore who had just transferred with his little sister Kristen from somewhere in New Jersey. She was a year younger than me, and everyone called her Sookie. They were Puerto Rican, which people not so lovingly referred to as "Mexican."

Pretty soon after the FONU incident, Fuller took an extended sabbatical. The big rumor was that he'd had a Vietnam flashback and thought a kid was Vietcong. In any case, we had a slew of substitutes for the rest of the term. None of them were real algebra teachers, so the subs basically just gave everyone a passing grade no matter what. We had it made for the rest of the year.

Ray was on my track team, and he could already drive any car he could get his hands on. We'd hang out all the time, bonding over our love of dance music. He had a yellow Sony Walkman with him at all times, and we would listen to the TDK and Maxell tapes his cousins made for him off the radio in New York City. We didn't have BET, and MTV barely played black music by people whose last name wasn't Jackson, so these tapes were golden. The music of KISS-FM and WBLS, freestyle, house, and hip-hop, exuded so much emotion, and we were there for all of it. We started cutting class together, making a pilgrimage to Rasputin's, a record shop in Berkeley, to find dance singles. We'd return in time for track practice, having car-danced the whole way back.

Ray and Sookie's stepdad, Jim, had an old-fashioned Studebaker, and Ray figured out how to jump-start it without the key. Ray and Sookie would roll over in the Studebaker, playing his cousins' tapes, and we'd joyride around, transported to New York by the master-mixes of black and Latino DJs. One time we decided to write a rap song of our own. I say song, but it was just a bunch of dirty sexual lines with cuss words written on notebook paper. Ray put it in his pocket and Jim found it in the laundry. Jim declared me a bad influence and forbade me from ever seeing Ray and Sookie again. That lasted two hours.

Ray started hanging out with all my other girlfriends right away. In his Z. Cavaricci pants, Ray could blend in with the boys, but he took dance class. That was a tell for a lot of the adults around us, who could detect in him what we kids were oblivious to. When it came to Ray, all of our parents were . . . well, there is no nice way to say "homophobic." Not my mom, but certainly my dad. He and all the dads had nicknames for Ray. Sweet Ray, Sugar Ray, and one even referred to him as Ray-Gay. It's not surprising. These were the dads who drove us kids into San Francisco to go to Pier 39, saying, "You're listening to K-F-A-G San Francisco, rocking you from behind."

When everyone you meet says, "fag," it becomes part of your own language. I would use that word to describe a thousand and one things. Saying "You're a fag" was akin to saying "You're a dick." Like "nigger," it was just a negative word, used widely, and

I absolutely used it widely. Even growing up with my very nonhomophobic, openhearted mom, the pull of assimilation overshot my common sense.

One Christmas Eve, my sisters and I were listening to the cast recording of *Dreamgirls* and acting out all the parts. The doorbell rang, and it was Ray and Sookie. She was crying, and the side of Ray's face was swollen. He could barely open his eye. Their stepdad Jim's family was in town, and an extended family member had punched Ray in the face. My mom tended to Ray with ice in the kitchen, and Sookie just told me that the person had called Ray a bad name. Sookie was a year younger than me, but in that moment we formed a small bond that would flourish. I decided Sookie and I were Ray's protectors, even if I didn't know what I was protecting him from.

Ray and my mom returned to the living room and he just happened to know every word to Deena Jones's songs. Despite all the obvious signs, I still assumed Ray was straight, because that's what I thought he was supposed to be as a teenage boy in Pleasanton. He would also go to great lengths to pretend to have crushes on girls, and he even briefly had a girlfriend. There was also a beautiful girl in our class who was desperate to sleep with Ray— and my crew and I pressured him to fuck her. We just wanted him to get some action. We had this same conversation, over and over:

Me: You better fuck that girl.

Ray: I'm not ready.

Chorus: What the hell?!

Looking back, this is the worst-case scenario of peer pressure for a young gay man, and we just kept right on. At seventeen, we realized you only had to be eighteen to see the live sex shows in the Mission District in San Francisco. We were good bluffers, so we'd head into San Francisco and drag Ray with us, basically forcing him into these clubs. "This is how to be straight. Look, that guy likes it! You will, too."

WHEN I WAS A JUNIOR, RAY'S SISTER SOOKIE BECAME MY CUTTING BUDDY. We'd ditch school and go into Oakland, because we had both developed a deep and abiding love of black boys. Every weekend she and I would go to After Dark, an all-ages club twenty miles away in Walnut Creek. After Dark was like Disneyland for brown girls. Every time we went, we found something that never existed in Pleasanton—a whole room of boys who could like us.

We would be *so* pumped when it came time to go out, and put so much into coordinating our outfits. Our go-to look was slightly cropped long-sleeve sweaters with jean shorts and high-tech boots. My hair I modeled after Janet Jackson in the "Black Cat" video.

On the drive over to After Dark, we would always listen to a tape of L'Trimm singing "Cars That Go Boom" to psyche ourselves up. L'Trimm was a hip-hop duo of girls our age. They'd met in high school, just like us. After Dark was in an industrial park, and I remember the walk up to the door was everything. My heart would be thumping, and I would want so much to be a bad bitch and have every head turn when I went in.

The club felt physically big to me then, but it was just a medium-sized, one-story box. They didn't serve alcohol, but older guys would come with booze in their cars. The guys were in groups, separated by city and car. There were these Suzuki Samurai guys, each with a small towel draped across the shoulder, which I never understood. Then there were the 5.0 Mustang guys and the guys with the gold Dayton rims. Even their hubcaps had a message. And separately, there were the ones who always wore polka dots and had Gumby haircuts.

We collected boys' numbers, talking to them on the phone and then calling each other to deliver instant replays. My relationship with Sookie developed separately from my friendship with Ray. I had two best friends. Ray and I shared a hunger for the culture of music that I only heard when I would go back to Omaha. He represented that slice of heaven. He had bigger aspirations than living in a nice house in Pleasanton and maybe achieving membership in a country club. He wanted to travel the world.

With Sookie, I had a kindred spirit and a partner in crime—someone interested in the same type of guys as me. I never had to explain what I felt to her, she just got it. And like Ray, we shared a love of being anywhere but Pleasanton. Going to clubs with her, we met more and more people, and my world expanded beyond high school.

WHEN RAY GRADUATED, HE WORKED AT A MARIE CALLENDER'S RESTAU-rant the summer before college. My girlfriends and I would go in for discounted meals and talk about where we'd go after. Ray was always talking about going to San Francisco, to this one place where he really loved the food. He said he'd get an omelet.

It just became a joke. "Oh, Ray's going to San Francisco for eggs." It never occurred to us—or it never occurred to me—that he was going to be with his community.

That was also the summer of "Ray's Fake ID." Ray and Sook had an older brother, Sam, who looked exactly like him, so he'd borrow his license. Anyone throwing a party knew to call Ray to get booze. It was always all love at the beginning of the party, but once people started drinking, the fag jokes would start.

"Sweet Ray, Ray-Gay . . ."

One time I was sitting on the curb at a party, wearing overalls and my high-tech boots. I was finishing off a forty of Mickey's big mouth, and some kids started in calling Ray a faggot. He didn't say a word, letting it pass. I began to see red.

I broke my forty on the curb and turned it toward the whole crowd.

"He's not a fucking faggot!" I screamed. "He is not a fucking faggot!"

I was threatening an entire party because I didn't want Ray to be other. I would have cut somebody. My friends grabbed me and drove away with me still screaming.

I wish I could say that I was protecting Ray. I was protecting me. I already felt like an outsider, and I had run a shell game on all these people to fit in. I could not allow people to point out another way in which someone close to me was "other." In trying to control the situation, I was unconsciously trying to control Ray.

I WENT TO THE UNIVERSITY OF NEBRASKA FOR MY FRESHMAN YEAR OF college. While I was home for Christmas break we all had a huge party at a girlfriend's house. We trashed the place, so when we woke up the next morning we set about cleaning up. I was in the living room doing as good a job with a broom as my hangover would allow. I noticed that everyone was acting cagey with me.

"What is going on?" I asked.

"Ray, just tell her," someone finally said. "Just tell her."

Ray sat me down on the couch.

"Nickie, I'm gay," he said.

"Really?" I started crying. "Who knows?"

"Everyone."

"Everyone?" I said. "Ray, *I* am your best friend."

Everyone knew but me. He was taking them to gay clubs and opening them up to new worlds. And nobody could have open conversations about this around me, least of all Ray. People just got sick of it.

He took a deep breath, and his tone became angry.

"Do you know how many times I have listened to you say 'faggot' or 'fag'? Now, think of all the times you've complained to me about people saying 'nigger' or talking shit about black people. You were so fucking comfortable using the same language, and you were too selfish to know you were hurting me. You were breaking my heart *every time*."

"I'm sorry," I said, bawling now.

"Yes, you are my best friend," he said, beginning to cry, too. "And I felt like I couldn't share it with you because you were so committed to being ignorant so you could fit in with these motherfuckers. Was it worth it, Nickie?"

I've never been more disappointed in myself. I'd humiliated myself with my ignorance, and in the process hurt one of the people closest to me. It was devastating.

Again and again, I told him I was sorry, and when he hugged me I melted into him on the couch.

"You know when would have been a good time to tell me you're gay?" I said. "That time when I took on the whole party, asshole."

We both burst out laughing. About the lengths I had gone to to protect my notion of his heterosexuality. I was too busy protecting our spots on a Jenga tower of assimilationist bullshit to be the friend he needed.

RAY STUDIED DANCE IN COLLEGE AND THEN GOT A JOB DOING ENTERTAIN-
ment on cruise ships. He was fully out by then, and he would
send me letters from random places. Dusseldorf, Ibiza, Nicaragua. He was wild, living out the adolescence he didn't have in
Pleasanton. When he talked about guys, my know-it-all controlling voice would kick in, lecturing him about safe sex. He told me
he met a Canadian guy, and pretty soon he wanted to just settle
down in one place with him. He moved to Santa Monica.

Sookie moved to New York to work for Urban Outfitters. My
first-ever trip to New York was to visit her in her little walk-up
in Park Slope, Brooklyn. I was twenty-two and got lost on the
subway. I remember going into a bodega to ask for directions and
thinking I was going to be shot.

Living on different coasts, Sook and I didn't see much of each
other throughout our twenties, but when we did it was as best
friends again. As my career took off, she and Ray would joke about
knowing Nickie Union, not Gabrielle. They were very aware of
the difference between Nickie and Gabrielle. They appreciated
Nickie and went out of their way to say that was who they wanted
to be friends with. They wanted to make sure I didn't get lost.

There was this magic time when Sookie and I literally ran
into each other in Vegas. It was early 2006, and it was like seeing
a mirage. Neither of us knew the other would be there, and we
glommed onto each other for the whole night.

She had a secret. The year before, in July, she had felt a lump
in her breast. She was thirty, had just started a new position at
Urban, and was moving into a new apartment. She didn't want to
admit she had a lump. She made a doctor's appointment for September, but when the doctor canceled it she never rescheduled.
Life, as John Lennon said, is what happens when you're making

other plans. It would be six months before she had a diagnosis: advanced metastatic breast cancer.

She made Ray call me because she couldn't talk about it. He was sobbing.

"Stage four?" I said. "Out of how many?"

"Four."

She was afraid to tell me, the same exact way Ray was afraid to tell me he was gay. And I was angry. "How dare you not prioritize yourself?" I wanted to yell at her. "Because now I am going to be without a friend. How dare you be so selfish?" We always internalize the things that happen to other people in terms of how it will affect us. I had literally just run into Sook in Vegas, and then she goes and gets cancer. I wanted to ask her how she had time to go to Vegas and didn't have time to go get that lump checked out?

As time marches on and you look back, you realize how easily this can happen. Like, "Oh, I've got this weird twinge in my thigh . . . but I gotta go to work." When you are busy, you don't think you have the luxury of taking time off to sit in a doctor's office.

We all do it. Nobody wants to even go to the emergency room with a cut. "Okay, I can't get the bleeding to stop. Fuck. I suppose I have to go." You knew five hours ago you needed stitches, but you were just hoping. In her case, it turned out to be stage IV metastatic cancer.

I didn't have that perspective at the time. I needed to be useful and control the situation I secretly felt she had created by not taking care of things earlier. Initially she didn't have enough insurance to cover everything, so that gave me the way to go into fix-it mode. "If money is the only thing standing between life and death," I told her, "we're gonna get the fucking money."

I desperately thought I could save her life. You want to get into Sloan Kettering? Hold on, let me call my publicist and make sure you get in to see the doctors at Sloan Kettering. The Young Survivor Coalition looked like the best organization connecting young women with resources and a path to life, so we were gonna go all in with the YSC. I would become their best celebrity friend. If we had the right amount of money, the right amount of connections, the right amount of networking, then we could beat it. Why else was I famous?

I threw myself into advocacy, hosting small seminars to promote the importance of prioritizing your own health. I used the analogy that they use when you're getting on the plane. "You've got to put your mask on before you help anybody else," I said countless times. "If you prioritize yourself, you're gonna save yourself."

In interviews, I would bring it up constantly.

"Is Will Smith a good kisser?"

"You bet he is," I'd say, "and you know you can bet your life on early detection. Did you know that eleven thousand women under forty are diagnosed with breast cancer every year?"

Susan G. Komen made me a Circle of Promise Ambassador, then a Global Ambassador. In 2008 they sent me to Kumasi, Ghana, to help dedicate the country's first breast health facility, one of the only ones in West Africa. I wanted to bring to the world the message that breast cancer is treatable and survivable.

One of the speakers that day was Dr. Lisa Newman, an African American surgical oncologist out of the University of Michigan. She was talking about what people can expect as far as prognosis.

When I heard her say the word "metastatic," my ears perked

up. That was Sook's diagnosis. It's funny, I thought, I never really knew what "metastatic" meant.

And then I learned.

"Of course," Dr. Newman said, "there is no cure for metastatic breast cancer."

Everything else was drowned out, and I heard her words as an echo. "There is no cure for metastatic breast cancer." But wait. We've got the money. We are seeing the best doctors. We are doing all this work. What do you mean?

Then it all became very clear to me: Sook was gonna die, no matter what we did. There is no cure for metastatic breast cancer. This was three years into Sookie's journey—a sister should have read up on "metastatic" at this point. I definitely shouldn't have been sitting there in Ghana, on the other side of the world from my dear friend, finding out that she was going to die no matter how much I gamed the system.

It was like that moment in the living room with Ray. I was the last to understand the truth I didn't want to accept. Clueless Nickie, thinking she knew what was best for everyone.

FOR RAY AND ME, LIFE BECAME ABOUT TRYING TO SPEND AS MUCH TIME AS possible with Sook. She was still going full speed ahead, lobbying in D.C. and still trying to get into clinical trials for treatment. She got a great boyfriend and a dog. She had hope, but she was very clear that it was more about buying time than finding a cure. The thing that she was excited about was that while she was getting a few more months from the latest clinical trial, what they were learning from her would help other women.

On one of her better days, I was in New York for some work

event. We met down in SoHo at this restaurant, at a time when we knew it would be empty. We just wanted to be girlfriends.

We held hands, and literally as I was asking her what she wanted her legacy to be, what she wanted me to carry on, I felt someone standing next to our table.

"I never do this . . ." she said.

She was a tall woman, well dressed and looking like she knew better.

I turned. "I am so sorry," I said. "This is not a good time."

"This is just going to take a second," she said.

Sook wouldn't look at her. Finally, I turned to the woman and smiled. I chose to satiate this woman's need, just to make her go away.

It was a minute, maybe a minute and a half with Sook that I wouldn't get back. I returned to Sook and again asked her what she wanted her legacy to be. What message she wanted me to carry on.

"I want you to tell people that fear can kill you," Sook said. "I was afraid, and it killed me."

It was my last lunch with Sook.

RAY CALLED ME NEAR THE END OF THE SECOND WEEK OF JUNE 2010.

"Look, it's coming," he said. "If you want to be able to talk to Sook while she is able to respond, you should come now."

I booked a flight to spend the weekend with her in New York. Then I got a call from one of the execs behind *Jumping the Broom*. They really liked me for one of the starring roles, but they had a concern about a false tabloid report that I had torn apart Dwyane's marriage. One of the producers was megapastor T. D.

Jakes, and if I didn't go to a meeting on Friday, I wasn't going to get the part. I made the decision to go. I delayed my flight to get in Saturday morning.

The meeting boiled down to "Will Christian women go to see a movie starring a supposed home-wrecker?" I so wanted people to like me, to choose me, that I was putting aside a very real situation that demanded my immediate presence.

These people knew the situation with Sookie. My friend was across the country dying, and they were still asking me if I was a good enough Christian to sell tickets. I could have had another day with her or even just a few more hours if I hadn't had to convince people I am a good person. I didn't even get the part, and to this day, I regret nothing more than taking that meeting and trying to explain gossip. Rumors that were easily proven false, but why let a little thing like the truth get in the way of a good lie? But I was so stuck in wanting people to like me that I went to the meeting before I got on the plane. Just to try to plead my case to producers and an executive that I was not this home-wrecker described by people who had absolutely no real information about the situation.

When I finally got to Sookie's apartment, Ray met me outside. He tried to prepare me before I walked in.

"It's bad, Nickie," he said. "We've all been on shifts. She wants to die at home."

When I walked in, you could smell death. Decay. I will never forget it. The nurses had transformed her apartment, once this cute little bachelorette pad, into a home hospice. Sook's boyfriend was there, as was her whole family: her mom, her older brother Sam, and her two sisters. Her dad had driven up from New Jersey. And at the center was Sook, in a hospital bed they'd brought in.

"I'm sorry it smells really bad in here," she said.

"It does, actually."

"I wish some of our relationships gave off this smell," she joked. "We'd have known they were over."

"Catch a whiff," I said, "and 'Whoo, see ya.'"

What I loved most was when she said out of nowhere, "Will *somebody* go and get me some hair removal cream?" A side effect of one of her meds was hair growth, and she was getting a mustache. Her sisters were there painting her nails, trying to make her feel as pretty as possible. I was ready to have deep conversations about life and death, but she wanted nothing to do with that. So I gave up control and allowed Sook to lead me.

"I want to talk about the Kardashians," she said. That was Sook, a girls' girl to the end.

Ray joined us, and Sook and I entertained her sisters with stories of growing up in Pleasanton. We laughed about the guys we loved from After Dark, and I told the girls the tales of Little Screw and my Greek-Mexican beauty school dropout. Ray mimed how to jump-start the family Studebaker, and their mom pretended to be shocked at how often we'd done it.

At the end, we are our stories, some shared and some lived alone. I wanted nothing more than for Sook's story to have a happy ending.

She made it to that Wednesday, five years into her diagnosis. I won't turn her into Susan B. Anthony, but she definitely wanted people to prioritize themselves and their health and not to be afraid of going to the doctor. To always get a few opinions and try to live your best life. She didn't want the conversation or our advocacy work to die with her. It couldn't be that Ray and I became breast health advocates to save Sookie, but if we couldn't help Sook, to hell with everyone else. She didn't want that. To this day, I do what my schedule allows, and I am very active in supporting Planned Parenthood. They offer low- and no-cost breast health care, and for a lot of people, Planned Parenthood is the only time they see a doctor. And I always try to incorporate health and wellness anytime I'm speaking, because now it just comes up naturally.

Ray has the longest-running relationship of anyone that I know. He and his partner have a country home in Connecticut— the whole nine yards. As I was writing this I could always text Ray to make sure I had the details down correctly.

And so, *you,* my sweet, patient, understanding reader: Sookie made me promise to tell you not to act out of fear. I can only add that you can be scared to death, as I've been while sharing these stories with you, and do the thing you need to do anyway.

Take care of yourself.

acknowledgments

I want to thank the people of Dey Street Books and Harper-Collins Publishers. Thanks especially to my editor, Carrie Thornton, for her help in bringing this book to the world.

Also to Sean Newcott, Ploy Siripant, Ben Steinberg, Kendra Newton, Heidi Richter, and Lynn Grady.

Thanks to Albert Lee for encouraging me to write a book. And to Kevin Carr O'Leary, for hearing my words and making them sing.

To my manager and enabler Jeff Morrone, the longest, most productive relationship I've ever had. Thank you for believing in me. I am grateful for your vision, and your tireless efforts to help make my dreams a reality.

I also want to thank Holly Shakoor and Stephanie Durning, Patti Felker, Brad Rose, David Guillod, and Todd Shuster for advocating for me. They are the people you want in your corner.

Thank you to my uncle, James Francis Glass, for being the perfect godfather. One who encouraged shenanigans and wacky inappropriate hijinks. And doing it all unapologetically.

Thank you to the people who acknowledge turn signals and let people in. You are the real MVPs.

To my mom, thank you for your love and respect of words, books, and safe learning spaces. You created distant galaxies in a brain hardwired to stay grounded on Earth. Thank you.

Dad, thank you for showing me that real change is possible at any age, and that it's never too late to evolve and live your best life.

To my sisters, thank you for loving me and supporting me. And always letting me be Deena Jones during Christmas sing-alongs.

To the boys, I know I'm gone a lot but I hope that during my absences I am making you proud. Thank you for always having my back and being my protectors.

To my poopy, D . . . Thank you for waking me up with that smile and positive vibes every morning and making me feel invincible and loved completely.

About the Author

Gabrielle Union is an actress and activist. Currently she stars as the titular character in the critically acclaimed drama *Being Mary Jane* on BET. She is an outspoken activist for women's reproductive health and victims of sexual assault. She lives in Miami, Florida.